Education and Economic Development

"This book is very courageous as it maps out a new world, connecting the level of education with economic growth in Romania, giving an entire new perspective. Decoupling growth from consumption and providing an alternative, foster knowledge via a new framework of understanding, giving insights to new society models. The libertarian touch on the educational perspective, balanced off by institutionalised governmental approach gives a full view about the links between economics and education and invites for further research."
—Researcher Razvan Hoinaru *"Queen Mary" University of London, UK*

"In today's taxing environment of burnt-out teachers, publish-or-perish culture in academia, and widespread cultural transformations, where can educators find the energy to inspire new generations? This book aims to not merely help readers survive the most stressful moments, but builds a panoramic vista of thought and learning. In a situation where more and more students and workers leave Romania to find work abroad, the author's integral approach to education is refreshingly optimistic."
—PhD Sid Lukkassen *"Radboud" University Nijmegen, Netherlands*

Daniela-Mihaela Neamţu

Education and Economic Development

A Social and Statistical Analysis

Daniela-Mihaela Neamțu
Ştefan cel Mare University of Suceava
Suceava, Romania

ISBN 978-3-031-20381-7   ISBN 978-3-031-20382-4   (eBook)
https://doi.org/10.1007/978-3-031-20382-4

This Palgrave Macmillan imprint is published by the registered company Springer Nature Switzerland AG.
The registered company address is: Gewerbestrasse 11, 6330 Cham, Switzerland

To my beloved husband, Ovidiu. To our kids, Albert and Yanis.
Thank you for keeping alive the light at the end of the trail.

FOREWORD

Education and Economic Development: A Social and Statistical Analysis is an important work in the specialized literature as it discusses in a comprehensive manner the economy of education from a theoretical, methodological, and, especially, from a practical and applicative perspective. A way of seeing education is in multiple layers connecting national, European, and international levels. The author argues, in an original way, that education is the foundation of a business environment which will finally lead to economic growth and development.

The book itself is the result of a common-sense approach provided with requirements imposed by the scientific methodology in such a way that it succeeds in providing the readers an accurate database on the education-economic development relationship. The starting point was the assumption that education represents a key vector of economic development for any country. This particular aspect is supported by the references to the main approaches on education as a public good, as well as by economics seen as investment (in education). The common denominator between this economic and educational relationship is the human capital. The work is structured into 14 chapters, based on official documents and author's personal via statistical modelling.

The role of education, and especially higher education, in economy and in the society alike is a controversial issue. The specialized literature abounds with interesting analyses and interpretations. Throughout the book, the author has tried and succeeded in identifying the main theories and models which best suit such an analysis, the specific conceptual educational framework, as well as the indicators which best describe the education–economic development relationship, the government's involvement, or the existence of a free market in this particular field. The way the performance or the efficiency of education can be measured both regionally and nationally provide for new methodologies for rankings.

By presenting the content briefly, I do believe that, as a whole, the work presents topic of great interest for the theorists in the academic process and is addressed to the researchers who have the chance of carrying on with their professional development based on a set of the latest important approaches and studies, especially those practitioners either from the educational field or from the economics discipline given the present societal realities. At the same time, the book is addressed also to the decision-makers in order to accomplish the necessary adjustments of the public policies in the field, in the process of analysing the recommendations for the adoption of the new public policies, for their suggestion and usage. Last but not least, the book is meant for all those who are interested in this particular topic and are intellectually curious.

The work entitled *Education and Economic Development: A Social and Statistical Analysis* represents a valuable, well-documented material. This fact makes it not only complex but also original and attractive to reading it.

"Ștefan celMare" University of Suceava   Gabriela Prelipcean
Suceava, Romania
August, 2022

ACKNOWLEDGMENTS

The work *Education and Economic Development: A Social and Statistical Analysis*, a scientific approach initiated within the Doctoral School of "Ştefan cel Mare" University, Suceava, Romania, under the direct coordination of Prof. Univ. Dr. Cristian-Valentin Hapenciuc is a study that has acquired a special significance due to the contribution that, voluntarily or not, has been made, in particular, by those to whom I would like to thank in a few words.

I deeply thank Prof. Univ. Dr. Cristian-Valentin Hapenciuc. Under his auspices and scientific inclination, the doctoral course took the form of a whole, materializing in the present work. In the last ten years, he was a real guide in my scientific and personal life, strongly marking the beginnings of my didactic path, sometimes sinuous, at the Suceava University.

I also want to thank the other distinguished professors from "Ştefan cel Mare" University of Suceava, Prof. Gabriela Prelipcean and Prof. Ionel Bostan. Many thanks to Prof. Constantin Brătianu, from the Bucharest University of Economic Studies (ASE), and to Prof. Teodora Roman from "Alexandru Ioan Cuza" University of Iaşi. They gave me a strong example of professionalism, efficiency, and fairness as a unitary system, matching all those values together.

I sincerely thank my family and friends, for their truly unconditional support and love; for the peace and security they ensured for me throughout the scientific demarche; and for the stability I always found at home.

I bring thanks to all!

CONTENTS

LIST OF FIGURES

LIST OF TABLES

CHAPTER 1

Introduction – The Temporal Dynamics of Education

The foundation of present-day society is based on human resources as a key element for growth and based on education for economic and social prosperity. It has become a true fact that current development relies heavily on education and culture as a business model, some communities having their own internalized ways, while other cultures provide for a more open society. Consequently, education in modern society has become a field of study as well as an object of study for teachers, economists, sociologists, and many other researchers. The progress of a society, considered from both an economic and a social perspective, is accomplished by acquiring knowledge allowing the human potential to be used in the best possible way in various conditions.

Education stands for the foundation of a free and open society, the cornerstone of a powerful and sound state. From a professional point of view, education represents the key foundation of human resource development worldwide. Globally, society itself heads continuously toward a knowledge-based economy, where education and performance are constantly judged against performance indexes, as well as a comparison index, among countries. Numbers and narratives lead to the transformation and valorization of strategic resources based on innovation, learning, and change.

D.-M. Neamțu, *Education and Economic Development*, https://doi.org/10.1007/978-3-031-20382-4_1

The book has focused on the analysis of education as a vector that contributes to social and economic developments, whereas economic development contributes to human well-being. Consequently, the development of the human capital concept and theory implies the appearance of a new branch related to the economic sciences—economics education—which studies the relationship between education and its economic implications. These variables together or separately impact society at large.

The present topic refers to key and relevant economic issues in the twenty-first century. The suggested research topic originated from the belief that a functional and efficient educational system will ensure proper conditions for the labor market and the business environment to develop and to contribute to the economy's development. The approach of the present study pertains, conceptually and technically, to the economic sciences. The impact of education on social and economic development seems to be, intuitively, a positive one given that science itself guides us in proving the existence of this relationship and its significance.

This study investigates the effects that investments in education have on the quality of education. More precisely, if any positive *output*[1] leads to benefits or positive externalities at the micro or macro level in terms of social and economic development. From this perspective, this study has focused on highlighting the crossmatch between the educational market and the labor market, which may infer the balance between the present and the future of educational economics, given that education has become a key vector of the economic performance of human capital.

The issue of scaling up and connecting education and its relationship with social and economic development has become the most current concern, which has been a research subject since it is a strategic priority for modern society by generating all sorts of externalities involving the individual level and society as a whole. The actions sustaining decision-making when approaching strategies and policies in the field of education have been thoroughly studied by specialized national and international research organizations, such as the Ministry of National Education and Scientific Research (MNESR), the Romanian Agency for Ensuring the Quality in Higher Education (RAEQHE), the Organization for Economic

---

[1] *Output* represents the result of the direct beneficiaries of the educational services (starting with the primary education up to the lifelong education) in a given timeframe. The word itself was borrowed from the English language. In terms of the economic field, it refers to the outcome of a person's activity and of an enterprise or of a fixed asset in a specific period.

Co-operation and Development (OECD), the United Nations Educational, Scientific and Cultural Organization (UNESCO), the World Bank, the European Committee, the National Council for Funding Higher Education (NCFHE), the World Economic Forum (WEF), and the European Higher Education Area (EHEA). From this perspective, the present study is supplementary to the approach to educational issues.

The goal of the present study is to demonstrate that education represents a key vector of economic development for any country based on the understanding of the main trends and tendencies in terms of higher education functionality, as well as its impact on human and intergenerational long-lasting and proper development. By taking into account the educational, cultural, economic, political, and organizational dimensions, the present research is geared toward highlighting the economic aspect of education by focusing on the recent debates on considering higher education a public asset and public good. By analyzing the issue of education starting from the concept itself and moving on to its actual dimension, this research means to estimate any qualitative accomplishments in terms of its economic development and cause-effect relationships.

Education is at the center of building human capital. Education along with human capital generates benefits for individuals, social groups, and society itself. Education drives long-term economic growth, spurs innovation, and in effect reduces poverty. In this regard, the vast majority of the world's poor live in East Asia and the Pacific, South Asia, and sub-Saharan Africa. School enrollment and the educational system in these regions mirror their economic development performances. Many children in poor countries abandon school before graduating. Sadly, but not surprisingly, in most low-income countries, children from poor families are at a higher risk and much less likely to obtain an education than children from more affluent families; also, disparity between sexes adds to this discourse. Nowadays, we can still identify low-income countries, in South Asia and Africa, where boys still have the chance to attend school comparing to girls. Corruption, local customs, and lack of accountability also affect the quality of education as a rolling snowball effect over society, despite international efforts.

The main objective of the present research refers to the study and the emphasis of the main existing coordinates and the links between the economic dimensions of education and socioeconomic development. Some of the specific objectives are as follows:

- the presentation of historical and conceptual context referring to the studied topic;
- the analysis and the extension of the relationships among different concepts such as institutionally and human capital;
- the assessment of the education benefits considering that the level of training has a direct impact on the evolution of an individual's income;
- the emphasis of the main approaches, tendencies, and evolutions based on the analysis of the economic growth models;
- the conjectural evaluation based on the use of the PEST method of Romanian higher education, identifying the factors and the causes influencing the system's performance;
- the design of a brief empirical analysis of higher education at the global, European, and regional levels based on *benchmarking* indexes;
- the design of an analysis regarding the interconnection between higher education graduates and employment related to different interest groups; identifying certain ways of improving this correlation.

Both the specialized literature and the resources served as the basis for calculations and analysis for original research and interpretations as part of a complete, systemic, and interdisciplinary approach. Moreover, both the specialized literature and the official documents of several national or international institutions pertaining to the educational system were consulted. Some relevant studies that have been presented in recent international conferences have been used as reference sources within the research. Certain statistical data provided by several institutions, such as Eurostat, World Bank, The National Statistics and Economic Studies Institute, and United Nations Conference on Trade and Development (UNCTAD), have also been used.

The research methodology in this book is mixed, qualitative, and quantitative and has been used both in designing the theoretical chapters and in collecting, systematizing, processing, analyzing, and interpreting information to achieve research goals. We used statistical methods to measure the main indicators in the field of education to provide a quantitative understanding. Taking into account the type of investigative approach, we have combined the qualitative and quantitative methods, and thus we have obtained mixed intersection methods for those two types of approaches.

Other methods, techniques, and procedures that have been used in our research refer to the extensive analysis of both the relevant literature and the good practices highlighted by several publications, the logical analysis, the synthesis, the observation, and the comparison. We have used the Mincerian Model to prove that the school years represent a viable resource for increasing labor productivity and, consequently, of the profits of the formal education beneficiary. We have also used several other mathematical models that justify the relationship between human capital and economic growth and models based on the research and development of endogenous and exogenous models of economic growth. Throughout the empirical analysis, we used a series of regression and correlation models and econometric tests to highlight the existence of a relationship, the degree of intensity, and the significance of the relationship between higher education and economic growth based on the *Pearson* correlation coefficient. The last part of the scientific approach was devoted to a statistical investigation based on the quantitative data coming from the self-management and online questionnaires whose subjects were higher education graduates, whereas the qualitative data were the result of the in-depth, semistructured interview comprising the employers and the recruiters as an investigative group.

The practical value of the study relies on promoting the findings in the Romanian scientific groups as well as in one of the institutional policies, namely, the MNESR (The Ministry of National Education and Scientific Research) and the advisory bodies and in some other local public administration entities. The study itself underlines the role of the university in evaluating the way that the acquired knowledge, abilities, and skills are sufficient to allow higher education graduates to obtain a job in their field of expertise or to continue their academic studies. Consequently, the present study is geared toward ensuring all the necessary conditions for combining academic with individual independent studies in terms of graduates' employment in the labor market. By using similar tools and methodologies, the final results can be extrapolated and aggregated nationwide. The present study's findings are bound to be used on a daily basis, and they will become theoretical and practical support for decision-makers on a micro and macro level.

PART I

The Emergence of Education and Its Economic Dimension

CHAPTER 2

Education: Conceptual and Methodological Approaches

Education is a vast and generous topic, and it is mostly viewed by society from the results angle. This perspective is justified considering that in all the fields of activity, the main attention is given more to the result than to the process. The society's interest in education varies and reaches its peak during the evaluation periods when certain documents are produced certifying the completion of a specific educational path. Theoretically speaking, diplomas of education provide more chances to obtain a well-paid job. This is a reasonable (though not a desirable) approach from the side of its beneficiaries but not of the education providers, also known as educators.

Currently, we witness an expansion of interest in education in new spheres of the human, social, professional, and economic sectors. From an economic science perspective, we witness the existence of study groups: the need for better-informed employees; the phenomenon of expansion and universalization of education, including higher education; the social and economic implications of education; and its role in economic development.

D.-M. Neamțu, *Education and Economic Development*, https://doi.org/10.1007/978-3-031-20382-4_2

EDUCATION—FOUNDATION OF SOCIAL
AND ECONOMIC DEVELOPMENT

Education represents the core element of humanity according to Kant, as "the human being cannot become a human being but through education" (Kant, 1996). Education has evolved over time. Centuries ago, education focused on the human being's transformation to live an intense Christian life, train individuals to serve in the army, and become scholars and artists. Present-day education (apart from the previously mentioned aspects) focuses on instructing the individual according to the existing political and economic situation.

The importance of education as an act of conscience influencing not only the future well-being of a nation but also its power, influence, and existence as a distinct entity both regionally and worldwide is unanimously acknowledged in all fields of activity.

From an etymological point of view, the term education originates from the Latin noun *educatio*, a noun that derives from two verbs:

- *educo—educare*—to raise, to nourish, to care for a plant, for a human being;
- *educo—educere*—to pull out of, to rise, to uplift, both literally and figuratively.

Throughout historical times, as part of the educational process, these two aspects have come together, have coexisted, and have influenced the education as such in terms of the following:

- educational fatalism—an individual represents the very result of the environment; thus, he/she can be raised and cared for by the educator himself;
- educational optimism—which minimizes, or even ignores, the internal factors by offering education a top priority that is able to shape any type of personality starting from a newly born individual viewed as *tabula rasa*.

There is no unanimously accepted definition for *education*. Several commenters have defined the educational phenomenon based on their own field of expertise, such as philosophy, psychology, sociology, pedagogy, and economics. Thus, the complexity and heterogeneity of the educational system confer the term of *education* transdisciplinary attributes.

Education, as a social phenomenon characterizing humans, differs from one historical stage to another based on society's material and spiritual conditions. It is the result of one's specific requirement, namely, the human development for the workforce and its own social existence. Some scholars believe that the early days of education are linked to the beginnings of religion and, thus, the religious servants initiated those around them in certain religious mysteries. The studies on the historical evolution of education have shown that if in the first stage, namely, the early days of humanity, education was meant to pass on the necessary work and social related knowledge to the young generation to survive, the ancient times revealed another facet of education. This type of education had a guild type of nature and was linked to the material means, namely, funding, because the costs of the educational services were significantly high.

Civilizations developed in Ancient near East, in the countries that were situated in the regions of the large rivers (such as the valleys of the Nile, the Tigris and the Euphrates rivers, Indus and the Ganges), had an impact on the forthcoming Greek and Roman cultures. The experience of the ancient cultures has a great influence in the field of education, although some existed in the BC era. The economic situation of a country is closely related to the level of education of that specific nation and not to the length of its borders, as "the countries whose population is highly educated and well trained are the most productive ones from an economic point of view" (Blaug, 1970).

Education is rooted in social nature and has a diachronic nature, which means it evolves and changes from stage to stage based on the structural transformations taking place in the society itself. The education in schools started later in the ancient civilizations. We can state that the origins of education can be traced back to Egyptian civilization since we can find in it the very first advocacy for the role of education in terms of the success of the individual from a material and a spiritual point of view.

This historical approach in terms of ancient civilizations highlights two key aspects related to the role of education that are still valid today: through education, the individual is focused on becoming spiritually enriched and gaining wealth. The desire and need to be educated is a personal choice; thus, the results of the education are first and foremost individual ones. Education, both as a product inside one's family and in the form of formal educational services, takes place at the moment when a family perceives the benefits of education for a new member. Education contributes to the provision of society's key values. There is no such reference to civilization in the absence of education no matter the form that is provided, as history starts with human reasoning and consciousness recording.

The Athenians were the ones who, through education, designed it and speeded the values of a civilization that served as a milestone, constantly influencing the modern world.

The modern educational system dates back to the nineteenth century, a time when Europe and the United States adopted the first laws on children's mandatory education. Although in the United States there had been public schools since the seventeenth century, the idea of a public educational system was out of question until the very first laws on the mandatory education of children. Until the nineteenth century, public schools were an exception, not the rule.

In general terms, education was regarded both as a family and a church issue. Parents were the decision-makers in terms of their children's education, whereas the church was the one that needed to put education into practice. Schools, both in Europe and in the United States, were patronized by churches, whereas priests were the educators who used the Bible as the basic instruction manual. Since there was no mandatory legislation set in place, most of the time, parents had to opt for home schooling by providing their children an informal education that was adjusted to the family needs. This was the reason why children coming from wealthy families were the majority in schools in those days, whereas the children raised by poor families received a precarious education.

Unfortunately, this aspect can still be noticed in present-day schools. Favorable evolutions of education can be traced both in the United States and in Europe, where a sustained growth of literacy has been taking place. "During 1800–1840, the literacy phenomenon had grown from 75% to 90% of the total of population of the northern American continent, an aspect which is also valid for the southern states with a 60–81% raise" (Pană, 2011a). The issue of educating the children could exclusively be their parents' responsibility since they decided whether they were going to be educated or not. In most of the cases, this aspect had to do with the family budget given that an important part of it was set for the children's education.

Plato and Aristotle were advocates for a public system of education. Plato remains in the history of pedagogical thinking for his formulation of the first theoretical system on education shaping human personality. Worth mentioning is that he was against the foundation of a proper school as the sophists were. He founded a group named Paideia, a kind of legal and spiritual fraternity that functioned in the famous Akademia. At the same time, in a counterintuitive and unlike way, he eventually became the founder of educational etatism. By emphasizing the social and cultural functions of education, this great ancient philosopher pleaded for the state's involvement in organizing and conduct of educational institutions. His hidden purpose was to train the top politicians and philosophers to lead the community wisely. The well-known Greek philosopher failed to include the lower class in the group of actual citizens. Consequently, he claimed that craftsmen and artists did not need to have a formal education, except for some knowledge of mathematics, because they could get their education in an informal environment such as the apprenticeship, like a son would get under the guidance of his father. He claimed that "true citizens (like doctors, teachers, soldiers) needed a different educational system" (Pană, 2011b). Unlike Aristotle, Plato considers the state, namely, governmental institutions, only a means of inoculating good citizens with the virtues of living life. Alternatively, Aristotle focused on the state's involvement in the educational system by stating that it was its responsibility to create a public educational system. In his opinion, education "needs to be checked by the public opinion and not by individuals" (Aristotle, 2009).

After the Second World War, the concept of *continuous education* became an active principle, a key idea of reforming projects. One of the earliest examples emphasizing this idea is related to Japan, which, during a workshop in 1974 organized by The United Nations Educational, Scientific and Cultural Organization (UNESCO), made a public statement by announcing that it would reform the educational system by turning it into a *continuous education system.*

One of the consequences of *continuous education* refers to career multiplication and the rapid evolution and change of modern social life. The focus would be placed especially on professional training of the individual who was expected to adjust to different types of new careers.

The complete analysis of the social and economic society highlights a major change in education. To have a real evolution in education, an economic growth model is needed first and foremost to concentrate on the individual's relationships with his environment as well as with his own self-consciousness.

As far as now, we can state that the emergence of the public educational system and the choice for it as such has made the state be committed to family life and more. Based on this fact as well as given that education is provided free of charge, the parents' involvement in educating their children has no importance whatsoever. Consequently, parents' lack of interest tends to grow in parallel with the state's assistance by becoming an ongoing factor. According to Rothbard, one of the reasons for extending the government's influence in the field of education refers mainly to "the altruism which is badly geared toward the educated middle class, a conscious attempt to make the population be part of the pattern that is desired by the leading class" (Rothbard, 2011). The members of this class felt that workers, or the "lower class," should have the chance of joining the type of education that was highly appreciated by the middle class. On the other hand, the expansion of mandatory education can be regarded as a consequence of favoring state mandatory education by Lutheran and Calvinist followers: "Thus, it does not come as a surprise that the oldest American mandatory educational system was founded by the Calvinist Puritans of Massachusetts Bay who were willing to implement an absolute Calvinist theocracy in the New World" (mises.ro).

The issue of public education (state provided) versus private education is an up-to-date topic in itself. To be considered fair based on using a traditional or even conservative approach, the majority of the government has chosen to keep the vast part of the educational "product" as part of the public sector.

For Simion Mehedinți, education is a state issue because it refers to an entire nation and ethnic group: "The value of a nation is judged not based on the length of its borders, but based on the level of its culture. This aspect was also highlighted by Nietzsche himself when he stated: Time will come when everybody is going to think solely about education" (Neagu & Mehedinți, 2004). In his work *Plea for Education*, the Nobel Laureate A. S. Gyorgyi stated: "What we call education is nothing but programming the brain in an early stage when it is more malleable. The future of mankind depends on education, a programming system that can be changed. Education is one of mankind's most important activities" (Gyorghyi, 1981).

For J.S. Mill, one of the most influential liberal thinkers of the twentieth century, education means everything that we do for ourselves and everything that others do for us to attain the perfection of our own nature.

Education does not start and end in school. Education is an ongoing matter throughout life and represents "the activity of managing the mixture between heredity and environment" (Cucoș, 2006).

Education has a purpose in itself, a theoretical and action plan; it is accomplished in school in the best possible way. The educational environment does not solely have to be associated with school because the development of the human being is the result of the interactions between the internal and the external conditions. The external conditions act based on the internal conditions (i.e., the genes, the spontaneous environmental influence, motivation, emotional experiences). The educational environment is both the school environment and the entire environment in which an individual lives.

The issue of the modern world (a concept that was formulated by Aurelio Peccei) has had an impact both on politics and on culture, on education, on the fight for peace, on saving the environment, on promoting the new economic order, etc. The economic environment cannot be addressed by disregarding this contemporary issue because education has always been connected with the issues of the modern world, such as peace, development, the new global order, democracy, environment, scientific humanism, etc. Thus, terms such as "education for peace," "education for a new global order," "education for contribution and development," "education for liberty and democracy," "education for taking care of the environment," and "education for change" have been coined and applied (Macavei, 2001).

Education in its nonformal and informal environment is closely linked with the formal educational environment. The terms formal education, nonformal education, and informal education derive from here.

The formal educational environment refers to the school environment. The nonformal environment refers to the extracurricular environment, which is a group of extracurricular means of acquiring general knowledge or professional skills or extracurricular education.

The informal educational environment is "the result of informal or diffused education," an ongoing process of acquiring knowledge and concepts that cannot be included in any type of institution.

The nonformal type of environment refers to the extracurricular educational environment, whereas its relationship with the formal educational environment is very disproportional. The nonformal educational environment has specific features, such as large diversity, flexibility, differentiating techniques in terms of contents and working techniques, an optional or nonmandatory nature, and more serious management involvement. All three types of educational environments are the key components of the human personality. Considering the situation of contemporary education as a complex phenomenon molding human characters, although these educational environments are distinct as such, they have a complementary relationship among themselves. By focusing on "what is valuable inside an individual, a strengthening of the soul." education refers to a couple of key trends that need to be analyzed when defining and understanding it, such as:

- The spatial and horizontal trend (or axis) refers to the influence of education on all the areas of existence. This approach has led to disregarding all the interpretative and harmful beliefs that education takes place solely within schools. Modern social studies have highlighted the existence of numerous other educational (school-based) resources, some other two main educational environments—the nonformal educational (which takes place in numerous important educational social institutions such as cultural and scientific institutions, media, and economic agencies) and informal education (which refers to a large series of numerous spontaneous, unsystematic, transitory influences in terms of all sorts of social contacts that an individual is part of during several instances during his private life).
- The temporal or vertical-longitudinal trend (axis). Its fundamental meaning refers to a lifelong influence of education. The latest discoveries in the field of age and learning psychology have shown the ability of individuals to learn and to be trained no matter of age but influenced by the psychosocial peculiarities of different age groups (Macavei, 2001).

The next chapter is devoted to the issue of education as a foundation of human development to evaluate the qualitative results of economic development, as Professor Brăilean stated: "The object of true economic knowledge has nothing to do with wealth, the golden young bull whom mankind had worshipped, but the Miraculous Individual who is so little understood, as well as the Good that he needs to observe as a means of reporting himself to a Living Creature that he can improve through work, through gift, through virtue. A human being is, thus, not only an economic product but also a biological, social and cultural creature. The quality of education, access to the values of democracy, access to information, the need to have dignity and equity, all these and many more, can confer to human evolution a new meaning starting from homo oeconomicus to homo socialis and homo culturalis. It is a fact that the human being—culture—development relationship is a very strong one. A poor culture undermines development in the same manner that development needs to be supported solely by real genuine values" (cse.uaic.ro).

EDUCATION—THE FOUNDATION OF HUMAN DEVELOPMENT

The development itself represents a preamble for the improvement of quality of life and comprises both material elements such as infrastructure, quality of the household, standard of living and spiritual elements such as education, freedom of speech, and cultural expression. People are the tools and the beneficiaries and the victims of all their developing activities. Their active involvement in the development process is the key for success. One of the key features of human development refers to the fact that both economic and social development are put into practice by individuals, and consequently, the human potential needs to be perfected based on investing in human beings as well as in the fields of education and culture, especially as ongoing professional training and improvements in health.

The level of education reflects the individual's ability to acquire knowledge, communicate, and be involved in the social life of the community they are part of. It is crucial to be aware of the key role of investing in education by ensuring the prerequisites of real, durable, and healthy development. Knowledge has become the most important factor in creating human wealth as well as the most efficient tool for ensuring the cross-match between the artificial and natural environments.

"By considering knowledge as a key factor in the creation of the foregoing of the human economy, the actual prerequisites for the clean economic activities are set in place whose cleaning mechanisms are going to function constantly within the economic processes which, based on the fact they are synthetically integrated, will enable the human control by using the mind both upstream and downstream. Companies will develop this technique at the beginning, during the actual production, at the end as well as for the future use of the product itself or of the service" (scritube.com).

The trend in terms of endogenous growth, as shown in Fig. 2.1, is closely related to the analysis of education and research and development (R&D), which are considered to be reproducible factors of the economic current economic growth due to the spreading of their benefit effects and of their ability to generate future economic growth. Investments in human capital, education, research and development are the source for positive externalities. The improvement of investments can generate gradual returns by contributing in a positive way and more successfully to total production.

Ramirez et al. (1998), studying the relationship between economic growth and human development, have identified two trends—one starting from economic growth and moving toward human development and the other moving in reverse, namely, from human development toward economic growth. They have discovered the existence of a powerful positive relationship going both ways. As far as public expenditures for social services and education are concerned, they regard them as important connections that establish the relationship between economic growth and human development, while the rate of investment and income distribution represent important links that have an impact on human development and the economic growth relationship.

Boozer et al. (2003) designed empirical strategies to estimate the power of the double connection between human development and economic growth. They concluded that human development needs to be given top priority from the point of view of both economic growth and future human development.

Chakraborty and Mukherjee (2010) confirmed that additional investigations are needed to trace the influential factors (different from the income per capita) that define a country's human development.

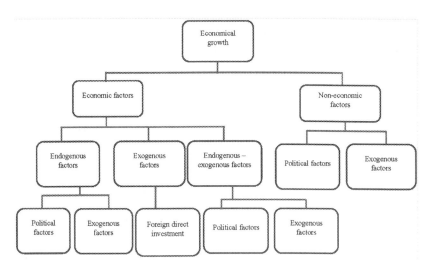

Fig. 2.1   Key factors of economic growth. (Source: Adapted after (Mihuț, 2013), *Economic Growth and the Convergence Criteria for the Emerging Economies from the Central and Eastern Europe.* Doctoral thesis, Cluj-Napoca, p. 19)

According to Ranis et al. (2000), there is a two-way relationship between economic growth and human development. Moreover, the first way refers to economic growth as a result of benefiting from human development based on the gross domestic product (GDP). GDP in particular supports human development through family, governmental, and organizational expenses as well as through those of NGOs. The family and personal expenses will grow in parallel with the economic growth itself, and thus, there will be more expenditures. Consequently, human development will grow as well. Moreover, once there is an increase in consumption, health and education will be enhanced, and this fact will contribute to economic growth.

The fundamental framework of human development is undoubtedly very broad. We claim that human development is not a finished product, as most of the studies have argued, but a means of ensuring future economic growth. From the point of view of human development, people's choices cover three main important areas: life expectancy, the level of education, and access to the necessary economic resources to make a decent living. Human development is thus an important prerequisite for both a society's and an economy's sustainable progress.

The Economic Approach to Education

In the economic literature, education is considered an *industry* in which investments are made (it has a cost of its own); it generates human capital and has an economic impact both on the individual as such and on the community and society. This is the reason why the *educational system* as a whole, and the public one in particular, has become an interesting topic for the development and for putting into practice proper educational policies. An important economic issue refers to the way education, as a key factor of human capital, influences the increase in work productivity, namely, economic growth and consequently a better standard of living.

The current theories on education focus on its role in channeling the individual energies toward producing knowledge by stimulating creativity and innovation. The individual's status in his relationship with education has evolved in economic theory from being a beneficiary and a user of education, as education generates performance in terms of economic growth. Education, as a key social and human study category, has been given several definitions. The most important ones are the anthropocentric (which focuses on the individual) and the sociocentric (which focuses on society) approaches. The anthropocentric approach originates from the Greek philosophy in Plato's works, who mentioned the fact that education was "the art of good habits or the art of developing one's inner skills for their virtue" (Popescu & Brătianu, 2004), (Dunca, 2009).

Aristotle, in his *Politics*, believed that education needed to be an object of public and not private surveillance, as it is meant to train future citizens (Aristotle, 2009).

Plato and Aristotle have essentially contributed to the overall development of the field of economic education. They produced works that were representative of the ancient period. Their works contain both essential elements in terms of teaching practice and important topics for the development of economic science and education. In the pedagogical field, Plato formulated the "concept of the gradual and the progression in education" (Cucoş, 2006). This scholar concluded that the ultimate goal of education was wisdom, which could be attained through two complementary ways—knowledge and learning. Plato's influence on economic education can be seen in the image of the ideal society where the economic activity had an original form of organization focusing on agriculture, the importance of the community itself, the communal living, and the observance of moral values.

Education as a whole and especially economic education took over the dialectic of the relationship between potentiality and reality as well as the principle of intuition and demonstration. The Aristotelian principle stating that "the things that we have to do by learning are the ones that we learn by doing" (Albulescu, 2011) refers to the actual economics lesson based on simulation. Regarding the approach to education from a sociocentric point of view, Aristotle referred to access to education by concluding that all citizens needed to have the chance of being trained, thus achieving absolute virtue.

Having in view of the analysis of human behavior in terms of the allotment of scarce resources, economists have not only foreseen the beneficial role of education for an individual but also have emphasized the advantages of education, which tend to exceed individual education. Thus, the pursuits of the neoclassical economists focused especially on the external consequences of education, which was considered to be more of a social than an individual necessity.

The issue of economic education has gained more importance in the works of classical economists. Thus, it was regarded as a result of the government's action in society together with several other controversial aspects of its intervention, such as public health.

The classical economists were more interested in promoting the pros and cons in terms of state interference than providing certain potential advantages of education for the individual. In political philosophy, the French philosopher Rousseau believed that the government was the result of the people's will in the form of a social contract, "the sovereign who is but a group creature who can be represented but by himself" (Rousseau, 1957).

Rousseau claimed to be a supporter of individual freedom as he did not make use of education as a means for instilling a sense of freedom in people, yet he used it as a means of making them become servants of the state itself. He stated that dignity could exist only for the free people. Rousseau promoted a "social engineering" that was geared toward molding "free" individuals who could contribute to the increase of the state's power. He believed that the role of education was to teach individuals about how to be able to feel as being the citizens of their own country and thus identifying themselves with that large family (i.e., the state) as such. "A free nation is submissive but does not serve; it has superiors, but no masters; it obeys the laws and the laws only and based on the laws it is not submissive to people" (Rousseau, 1958). This is one of the famous pleas for education provided by the state itself and for the state. The French philosopher Rousseau is the founder of the statutory ideology of education geared toward the creation of a type of individual who is obedient to the state and is characterized by consummate patriotism. He disregarded the issue of the possible effects of this type of educational system on the individual.

The economics works of the end of the eighteenth century and the beginning of the nineteenth century approached the issue of the government's involvement in education. Despite the fact that they did not entirely share Rousseau's opinion on statutory education, there was still the question of how education contributed to society's development and to what extent the state contributed to the well-being of society as such based on its actions without infringing on individual freedom. From this point of view, we have to take into account the opinions on education of the most representative classical economists Adam Smith and John Stuart Mill.

Following his success in the field of moral philosophy, Adam Smith began focusing on topics of political economics. He was one of the first economists who stated that the development of a nation did not depend on its quantities of gold and silver but on its people's ability to work (Mistreanu, 2013). In his famous work entitled *Nations' Wealth. A Research on Its Nature and Causes* (1776), Smith emphasized the fact that an educational system could face an inherent lack of incentives (for the refinement of education) and, at the same time, he pleaded for competitiveness in the field of education. Smith rejected the idea that schools should be funded based on taxes and fees and highlighted the fact that in most parts of Europe, the public funds had a low percentage in terms of the schools' financial resources. The founder of economics science formulated the image of a system based on the choice of universities and the competition among them by focusing on the positive effects that such a system could provide both in terms of the quality of services and the universities' reputation. Taking into account the abovementioned facts, Smith emphasized the fact that teachers in public schools were not sufficiently encouraged to increase the quality of teaching and, at the same time, private teachers had more chances of becoming better at their job, as "rivalry and competition encourage getting better even in menial jobs" (Smith, 2005).

It is worth mentioning that contrary to his opinion on higher education as one enabling competition and devoid of an authoritative monitoring body, his approach was totally changed in terms of primary education. Smith declared himself in favor of a mixture of semipublic educational systems whose teachers were to be paid from the public funds. In his opinion, the issue of education could be approached from two different angles: on the one hand, it enabled competition, the choice and the autonomy of the educational organizations as far as higher education was concerned, and, on the other hand, he made use of an elitist approach in terms of primary education. "An intelligent and educated population is always more respectful and tidier than the one that is ignorant and stupid" (Smith, 2005).

John Stuart Mill, a classical economist and the most hailed champion from a liberal point of view, continued to develop the very type of approach illustrated in his famous works entitled *Principles of Political Economics* and *On Freedom*. Mill believed that to eradicate poverty, universal education and maintaining the population's growth in certain limits are of utmost importance. This was why he opted for an educational system that focused on the children of unskilled workers. He stated that "it is impossible to train a poor nation and it is difficult to make those who have lived carelessly be aware of the values of the comfort that they have never experienced or to be conscious of the disaster of a poor existence" (Mistreanu, 2013). He had the same idea as Roebuck that the authority of the parent on his child should be delegated by the state, whereas the state may easily intervene in the moment there is a suspicion that parents abuse the power by having a negative influence on their children's education. Mill extends the idea of harmful action in the form of neglecting a child's mindedness.

This meant that each and every individual had the right to have a minimum standard of education. At the same time, education should not be something that parents or siblings hindered from jealousy or stinginess. Mill concluded that children's education needed to be parents' duty who had to use their own finances to carry it out accordingly. In the event they were not to fulfill this duty, education had to be supported by other sources. Taking into account that the income of the unskilled workers was insufficient, he considered as an alternative to education the merger between the state's involvement and the private initiatives (i.e., charities). "He criticizes the representatives of the laissez-faire orientation who, while supporting the state's minimum help, refused to carry out one of the government's fundamental duties" (Mistreanu, 2013). Because charities were not enough to cover the necessary education, Mill was in favor of the state's involvement in funding elementary schools to make them more accessible for all the children coming from poor families.

In his opinion, education represents the most valuable asset that was desired by that social category who needed it the most. This aspect was due to the ignorance shown by these individuals, and there was the possibility that it could not be provided in sufficient quantities on the market as well as the inability of certain individuals to make a spontaneous choice in terms of the right education. That was the reason why the government's involvement was desired to provide the population with a quality education and training no matter the spontaneous idea that was made known on the market.

In his work entitled *Principles of Political Economics*, he claimed that an individual who has the right to decide for himself was able to think and act for himself. "Each and every one of us is the best decision-maker for his own interest" (Mill, 1915). This proposal, which was strongly supported by his peers and classical economists, was an independent argument that differed from the idea of liberty because there was no way that liberty was disregarded if people had a bad judgment. From that moment on, "Mill's approach on education placed him in a real dilemma" (West, 1965).

Mill slightly changed his opinions in the essay entitled *On Freedom* by shortly repeating the favorable arguments on public education supporting the freedom of the individual and criticized the power abuse of certain persons when they spoke on behalf of others while arguing the use of the government's cohabitation in regard to education by disregarding the laissez-faire principles. In his work entitled *Principles of Political Economics*, he substituted his elitist tone with a paternalistic and careful tone when talking about the people's ability to take care of education based on spontaneous actions. His opinions will contribute to the enforcement of mandatory education in England, one of the few countries in Europe that relied primarily on private education during the second half of the nineteenth century.

In regard to education, he completely disregarded the statement underlying liberty, according to which each and every one of us is the best judge of his own interests. It seemed that ultimately his biggest fear had to do more with the fact that adults were not capable of doing that and that they had to be deprived of their liberty in this matter.

The issue of education became a central focus point during the second half of the twentieth century in the approaches of several economists, such as Milton Friedman, Friedrich A. Von Hayek, and Murray Rothbard. They became famous based on resuming the controversies on the state's involvement in education by stressing out the limitation of the government's involvement in education issues. "Friedman, also known as Adam Smith of our century, made significant contributions in certain fields, such as the methodology of economic research, the defense of the modern market economy as a support of the freedom of choice and of the sovereignty of the consumer, theoretical and practical monetary issues, education" (West, 1965).

Milton Friedman was undoubtedly the one who had a major influence in favor of the freedom of choice and of the competition in the field of education. His pleas generated not only major controversies but also initiated certain actions in this respect. In his works entitled *The Role of the Government in Education* (1955), *Capitalism and Freedom* (1962), *Free to Choose* (1979), his theory on education was discussed by completing the ones that had been formulated by his classical predecessors Smith and Mill. In Friedman's opinion, the government's role was to protect the rules of the game based on imposing the need to obey the contracts by ensuring market freedom.

In his opinion, the belief in liberty characterized the responsible people and not the children or the mentally ill persons. The government's support for each child to benefit from a level of education was justified in the same way that the safety of the buildings and of the vehicles had been approached as a beneficial element for the rest of the members of the community. The couple of situations are also about the differences that manifested as a result of the situation when the owners of buildings or vehicles could decide on selling them in the event they could not afford the costs without subsidies. The separation of the child from his parent who could not afford paying for the needed minimum education would undermine the key significance of the family itself.

Friedman did great service by separating the sums of money coming from different government subsidies for education as from any other field of activity. He accepted the point of view according to which taxpayers had to financially support the education of each and every child, yet he argued that it did not encourage public education. "It is highly likely that each and every taxpayer supports financially the education of each and a very child in any public school" (Friedman & Friedman, 1998). The government's involvement in education requires the enforcement of certain minimal standards on the private schools as well as the foundation of the schools managed by the government and the obligation to attend them.

From this point of view, Friedman claimed that this progress can be achieved in certain situations, such as the following: there were public schools of no interest to the public, while private schools were disadvantaged due to their lack of finance/public funding. Consequently, there was a whole debate in favor of using the voucher system for funding education, which is still a controversial aspect even today. Despite the fact that Friedman's action plan could represent a big step ahead because it could provide parents with a large variety of options based on the fact that it was not just a partial solution that could influence the funding of the education, the issue of the vouchers was criticized. The wrong mentality of the government officials who were responsible for education referred to the fact that they considered themselves the only ones who were capable of understanding and of taking care of the issue of the children, namely, to opt for the best solutions for educating them.

This brief presentation of the ideas of the economists referring to the issue of education cannot be finished without mentioning the contributions of Murray Rothbard and of Friedrich A. von Hayek. They are the most illustrative pleas against mandatory public education and its effects. F.A. Hayek focused on the principles and rationale of a civilization of liberty. His motto seemed to be "humanity's crucial experience" (Pohoață, 1996).

Man is the synthesis of a culture only if he is entirely free and has his own morality. As a follower of individualism, Hayek believed that the researchers of society had to focus on the active individual who, while being centered on his own goals, was forced to choose those efficient ways and means to accomplish them, whereas the actual results depended not only on his taste, wish, and will but also on unpredictable circumstances.

In F.A. Hayek's opinion, liberty was the supreme value in a modern and wealthy society. Based on its freedom, mankind evolved from its primitive stage based on relationships that had been governed by archaic and religious principles toward an "open society" founded on freedom and law, thus enabling the deepening of the social division of labor, the increase in labor productivity, and economic progress as a whole. "Liberty means the absence of constraint, the ability of individuals to pursue their goals. However, liberty does not mean power, which means the ability to do everything and thus impede the liberty of other individuals. Liberty is even more important than economic well-being by being one of its requirements" (Selejean-Sută, 1996).

F.A. Hayek studied and explained the close relationship among liberty, the social order and the rule of law, namely, the legal order. He emphasized the fact that individuals were free to pursue their goals and to use their knowledge for this purpose. Gradually, behavior came into being, and then they were followed by common values or norms that were essential for a peaceful cohabitation. From this perspective, he criticized the elitism of the classical liberals who believed that the education of the ignorant people would solve society's major issues. In Hayek's opinion, there was a genuine match between liberty and the rule of law based on the governance of law provided the laws were nondiscriminatory, worked for all the citizens without any exception whatsoever. For Hayek, the issue of creating an economic or social order originated from "the fact that the knowledge of the circumstances does not come in a concentrated or integrated form, but as scattered fragments of incomplete and sometimes contradictory knowledge of the individuals as distinct human beings" (ecol.ro).

An important contribution referred to the criticism of the principle of equal chances. From this point of view, the type of education based on the equal chances principle was adverse in terms of the development of the society as such given the gene standardized results they generate. A single example quoted by Hayek as the motto for one of the chapters of his book entitled *The Path to Servitude* is sufficient to demonstrate the ugliness of the totalitarian ideology: "The society as a whole will become a single and huge office and a single and vast plant which are managed by the equality in labor and the equality in retribution" (Hayek, 1985).

In his book entitled *Education: Free & Compulsory*, Rothbard offered solid grounds for taking education out of the reign of the state organization. The first chapter focuses on the pedagogical reasons according to which public education should not be mandatory from both an individual and social point of view. Each and every child has his own intellectual capabilities and his own interests. Consequently, the best choice of the teaching method of the period of time devoted to the subjects requires a different approach. The development of civilization and the amplification of the individual diversity led to a decreased interest in uniformity and equalization. It is a well-known fact that state education is totally different from these goals. It is in its nature to focus on the normalization and the flattening of the differences. "Whatever standards the government may impose on the educational system, the iniquity/injustice will govern them because any kind of standardization—in fact, the only viable solution for the government to have control on this field of activity- will have an impact on those who are above or below that standard" (Rothbard, 1999). In his opinion, education was closely connected to the individual who was "trained" throughout his whole life in each and every circumstance (i.e., the formal education).

Thus, Rothbard was in favor of a genuine liberal education which enabled the development of an individual both formally and informally based on his goals or on his family's and not on the bureaucratic bodies'. According to Lew Rockwell, Rothbard was considered the dean of the *Austrian Economics School*, "the founder of the modern liberalism" standing a clear ground in education policy among other fields (LewRockwell.com).

THEORIES ON HUMAN CAPITAL: ASSUMPTIONS, LIMITATIONS, AND ALTERNATIVES

When Adam Smith discussed human factor as a capital generator in his work entitled *Nations' Wealth*, we also compared the individual with a machine generating costs and profits. As a representative of a modern school, within the human capital-economic growth relationship, there were two significant moments in the foundation of the theory of human capital, namely, the A. Smith moment and the K. Marx moment. In Smith's view, technical capital was the expression of human capital, which was tangible and measurable. In exchange, Karl Marx "placed the value analysis and the labour value generating analysis apart from the qualitative benchmarks" (Pohoață & Popescu, 2007).

In his opinion, an individual was considered "a human being who required a lot of time and instruction, who had to prove to have high skills and dexterity being, thus, compared with any type of expensive yet performing machinery" (actrus.ro). According to Smith, the expenditures for educating a person were the essence of the investment in future profit, and they had to be recovered throughout the lifetime of an individual.

Starting from the statement according to which "a human being's main asset are his knowledge," List made a connection between a nation's well-being and "the mankind's spiritual capital,", stating that "the current situation of a nation is the result of the accumulation of all the discoveries, inventions, improvements, and the efforts of all the generations who lived before us. They are the spiritual capital of the actual mankind. Each and every nation is productive as a result of its ability to acquire the accomplishments of all past generations and the way they choose to enhance their own value and produce new ones" (List, 1973).

Like Friedrich List, Alfred Marshall, who is the representative of the neoclassical school, in his work entitled *Principles of Political Economics*, drew attention to investing in education and professional training as a development factor by considering them "national investments," "the most valuable one of the capital is the one invested in the human being" (Lixandrioaia, 2013). In his opinion, education became the key element for the adjustment and professional mobility of the workforce. A. Marshall considered the knowledge as "the most important production sources" and believed that "the organizations develop the knowledge" (Marshall, 1907); thus, he believed that the theory of the human capital was "surreal." Karl Marx, in his work entitled *Human Capital, the Critics of Political Economics*, formulated the idea that an individual's training and not his inner ability is important in understanding the pay gap. He believed that "the workforce is a merchandise and not a capital. As a circulating capital, it operational for the capitalist after it was sold during the manufacturing process" (Marx & Friedrich, 1966).

The concept of human capital was made known by the *University of Chicago* group, which was led by T. Schultz, who, together with his collaborators Jacob Mincer, Gary Becker, and George Stigler, focused on economic growth based on the increase in productivity as a result of investment in education and in the health sector. In their opinion, "the valuable features which can be developed based on adequate investments are known as human capital. By investing in themselves, individuals have more options." Schultz was the one who demonstrated that investments in human capital through education and training are much more efficient than those in physical capital by stating that "the knowledge and the skills are a form of capital and this kind of capital is a key part of the output of an intentional investment" (Schultz, 1962).

Such an approach was formulated in a specific economic context of the destroyed countries during the Second World War and a genuine need for rapid reconstruction. From this perspective, Schultz argued that economists had expected a much longer recovery period of time due to the undermining of the importance of human capital. He stated that "I believe that we made this mistake because we failed to use one capital concept and, consequently, we overlooked its key role in the modern economy" (Schultz, 1961). Jacob Mincer studied the relationship between an extra school year and the foreseen increase of the lifelong returns as shown by the *salary's standard equation* in the *Mincer model,* which estimates the relationship between the salary and its determining factors. He claimed that the sole cost of an extra school year represents the anticipated revenue by overlooking direct costs such as tuition fees (Bedrule-Grigoruță, 2006). Mincer took the credit for establishing the relationship among the training onsite, education, and income and suggested that the total investment in the on-the-job training was almost as large as the investment in education.

According to Mincer, human capital has a dual role in the process of economic growth:

- a supply of skills—as a result of the combination between education and training the human capital represented a production factor together with the physical capital and the manual labor in generating the output;
- a supply of knowledge—it is an innovative source and an important cause of economic growth.

In the work entitled *Investment in Human Being,* Gary Becker, Larry Sjaasted (on migration), George Stigler (on the labor market and job search), Edward Denison (on education and economic growth) focused on many aspects of human capital.

The main ideas in terms of the development of the theory of human capital were formulated by Becker in particular. One needs to highlight the fact that *Becker's theoretical model* on human capital was geared mainly toward higher education (i.e., an individual had the legal age to be eligible to work, and consequently, one could state that he gave up the profits from the business activities by investing in education). The main credit of the theory on human capital was that it formalized the relationship between education and the revenue of the labor market, although "the economic approach on human behavior is not a new one" (Becker, 1994).

According to Lucas (1988), human capital focused on the way an individual took time to perform several activities during a reference current period of time, which had an impact on his future output, whereas the accumulation of human capital represented "a social activity which referred to the interrelationship of the groups of people in a unique manner with no correspondent in the process of the accumulation of the physical capital."

For Cohen and Soto (2007), the role of human capital in economic growth was a highly debated topic in the specialty literature, which has suffered certain changes in recent decades.

Some of the most recent researchers on the theory of human capital are W.A. Lewis, S. Kuznets, D. North, and others. One of the renowned English economists in the field of economic development, W.A. Lewis mentioned that one of the main causes of economic growth was "scientific progress." He identified, apart from education, two more causes of the increase in the output of human factor, such as healthcare and diet.

Kuznets was another famous researcher who approached the topic of human capital. In his effort to identify the causes of economic growth, he concluded that the source of economic development was both the quality and the quantity of the workforce. In other words, it was represented by the skilled individuals who were capable of acquiring the latest technologies. D. North, the third economist who had been awarded the Nobel Prize for his efforts, studied the relationship between economic growth and education, namely, innovation.

Marta Christina Suciu, in her work entitled *Knowledge Economics and the Global Civilization, the Investment and Hope in Man* in 2002 and George Văideanu in *Education at the Crossroads of the Millennia*, which was published in 1988, focused on the importance of education and of the continuation of the learning process even after the graduation of the formal type of education.

Bogdan Voicu was another Romanian researcher who was interested in the theory of human capital. In his study from 2005 entitled *Human Capital: Components, Levels, Structures. Romania in the European* context analyzed the relationship among education, healthcare, and Romania's economic development. His analysis confirmed the lack of access to education and healthcare services, which has a negative impact on the country's economic situation. We can also make reference to the four researchers from *"Alexandru Ioan Cuza" University* of Iași who wrote studies on the topic of human capital. They are C. Popescu, I. Pohoață, G. Mursa (who is also the president of *Friedrich von Hayek Institute* of Romania) and I. Ignat.

On a different stance, Hoinaru et al. (2021) look at the economy of burnout, which is estimated by the World Health Organization to be approximately $300 bn globally. Rather than looking at traditional costs and risks, the authors indicate the novelty of nonfinancial reporting and human resource accounting. This implies awareness of one's own value of a (human) capital inside a work environment and provides incentives for getting higher education and additional trainings within a life-work balance.

The theory of human capital characterizes the microeconomic analysis according to which the growth of human capital ensures a proportionate increase in revenues. Resourceful, talented individuals who have contributed to cultural development have not always evaluated correctly.

That is why human capital can also wear off if individuals make use of it at the right time, and then it will be able to generate productivity and economic growth. The individual scale of human capital is a source of prosperity by improving the standard of living, accumulating profits or stimulating innovation. This can be achieved based on formal education. The creation of human capital is influenced by a series of factors that have a significant and contextual impact on individuals. The main determining factors of human capital can be grouped into four categories: formal education, professional experience in the workplace, the informal life context, and the peculiarities of the country itself.

Formal education molds the social interaction ability and enables the accumulation of knowledge. Vocational education can stimulate native talent, as future university courses and adult training will prepare future employees by specializing them in specific fields of activity.

Work experience represents another factor that brings research skills into attention as well as the individual's work commitment. The third category of factors influencing the training of human capital refers to the informal life framework. The family and the community that an individual is part of will make him acquire a particular learning habit and personal development, certain aspects that will have an impact on his professional development. The latter factor refers to the country of origin specificity, which generally outlines the conditions for creating and accumulating social capital.

For centuries, the theory of human capital has *defined and enacts* issues (Voicu, 2004). However, the majority of analysts have included both educational and biological capital. The educational capital comprises acquired skills as a result of taking part in the formal educational systems, as a result of acquiring the knowledge certified by diplomas, the lifelong skills based on their own efforts, or on the interaction with experts from different fields of activity. In the specialty literature, we have identified three main approaches for the estimation of the educational capital stock:

- the use of the acquired educational level as an approximation of human capital;
- the use of direct tests for the adults to identify the relevant attributes of the business activity;
- the identification of the differences in terms of the adults' income to estimate the market value of these attributes and, consequently, the aggregated amount of the human capital stock.

By generalizing the main approaches to the theory of human capital as shown in Table 2.1, we can state the following: human capital is an expression of an individual's skills and qualities as a result of investments that, provided they are used wisely, will lead to an increase in labor productivity and revenue. Table 2.1 shows the economists' opinions on the definitions of human capital throughout the evolution of economic theory.

Regarding the role of education in the process of economic growth, several authors in the economics literature have conducted both conceptual and empirical research. Some of the remarkable figures are Barro (2001), Barro and Sala-i-Martin (1992), Jorgenson and Fraumeni (1992), Ding and Min (1999), Becker and Lewis (1992), Bils and Klenow (2000), and Duflo (2001).

Education can contribute in several ways to economic growth. This is why the opinions of those who have approached this topic sometimes differ in many aspects. In his book entitled *Human Capital, Social Capital & Economic Growth*, Professor C. Popescu has highlighted three opinions of Meier and Rauch. They believed that two graduates of primary education equal a worker who is a graduate of the secondary education. By estimating efficiency and keeping the number of actual workers the same, the growth of the level of education of the labor force will enhance performance. Thus, the growth of the average number of school years per worker has been associated with an increase in the production per capita. "The educated and uneducated workers represent the *inputs*[1] which are the imperfect

---

[1] *Input*, the word was borrowed from the English language (it consists of *in*—in and *put*—to put, to introduce) and represents the educated labor force based on the production function.

Table 2.1   The evolution of the definitions of human capital

No.	Definition	Author
1.	"the knowledge and skills form the capital and this capital is the result of an intentional investment"	Th. Schultz (1961)
2.	"it comprises the educational capital, the biological capital, the migration capital"	G. Becker (1964)
3.	"the skills and knowledge of an individual which enables him the change of action and an economic growth"	J. Coleman (1988)
4.	"[…] the individual's entire group of productive capabilities including his operational skills in a broader sense: general or specific knowledge, skills, experience…"	B. Gazier (1992)
5.	"the value of the knowledge, skills and experience of a company's employees"	L. Edvinsson and Malone (1997)
6.	"[…] it comprises the age of the individual and the family's income"	L. Edvinsson and Malone (1997)
7.	"a hidden concept, a valorisation of the individuals' skills. A simple definition describes it as the value of the productive skills which are sold by a person"	J. Hartog (2000)
8.	"all the intangible assets brought at their place of work by the individuals"	T. Davenport and Grover (2001)

Source: Adapted after Badea and Rogojanu (2012)

substitutes for the production function because 3 or 30 workers who have a primary education cannot replace an engineer" (Meier & Rauch, 2005). The role of the educated labor force during the manufacturing process is to learn and design technology that will generate more *output* by maintaining constant input levels. Moreover, education allows developing countries to absorb technology. According to these two authors, the economic impact of education needs to be considered based on both a micro and a macroeconomic perspective. The relationship between education and economic growth is visible since a major effect of higher education is that "a better workforce has a higher ability to produce" (The World Bank, 2008). Many of the models of the 1990s have started from the results of P. Barro (1991), who used secondary education as a variable in the economic growth equation both for developed and developing countries. Moreover, the empirical analyses of the relationship between higher education and economic growth have been used, especially by the following economists Stephan (1997), Chatterji (1998), Kwabena et al. (2006), Richard (2006), who have demonstrated that there is economic development where the higher education system is a competitive one. Numerous studies in the specialty literature of the authors Murphy et al. (1991), Tiago (2007), Colombo and Grilli (2005), Tsai and Wu Wang (2010), and Kaili et al. (2019) have demonstrated that by using specializations in higher education as variables, there is a close connection between enrollment in informatics, engineering and science specializations, and economic growth.

The importance of education for economic growth and its contribution to the increase in productivity are unknown aspects in the specialty literature. Moreover, the opinions on the way the level of education makes the highest contribution to economic growth as well as to general tuition, formal training or on-the-job training and primary, secondary or higher education are still unknown.

The Signaling Theory on the Labor Market

The pragmatic criteria refer to the fact that a school's social structure can be difficult as a result of the individual's choice in terms of the training as such because they are the ones who anticipate those choices that can be made, whereas the scientific criticism emphasizes the fact that education and training cannot be directly influenced by the productivity, yet they play the role of the potential productivity indicator for certain employers by acting as a filter that indicates the individual's future possibilities. One of the oldest discussions in the economics of education refers to the controversy between the theory of human capital and signaling or the selection theory (Berg, 1970), (Blaug, 1985), (Dore, 1976), (Spence, 1973), and (Stiglitz, 1975), which is focused on two main ideas:

- although they are both in favor of the assumption that a better education is linked to a higher pay, it disagrees with the relationship between the individual's education and performance. In their opinion, *hands-on learning* (or learning by doing) has a key role because the acquired general knowledge and competences are often not used in the individual's future career, whereas his special skills that are required in his job are formed in his workplace;
- *the selection* or *the screening* when employers do not know the profile of the employee beforehand, they find it difficult to foresee the future skills of those who apply for a job. In that particular instance, they make use of the qualifications and diplomas as a selection system of the skills, of the motivation, of the social setting as well as of the personal desire to be trained, of his knowledge as a starting point of his job.

The signals coming from potential employers might not be trustworthy. That is the reason why many companies will choose their own methods of testing their own applicants. Stiglitz considered the level of education as a selection mechanism of the potential employees grouped in categories reflecting the productivity (Stiglitz, 1975) and stated that the selection process could be beneficial for the entire society as such because the individuals could be directed to the right groups and jobs that fit their level and this fact could benefit the society, too.

We believe that the human capital stock that an individual possesses is established based on his inner abilities and the social environment he comes from. Consequently, education is meant to enhance an individual's native skills by placing him both on the labor market and within society at large. Moreover, according to the theory of human capital, education ensures an increase in the productivity of the human factor, which, in turn, will establish an increase in economic effectiveness as education represents a *vector of the social and economic development* of a national economy.

THE MARKET FOR EDUCATIONAL SERVICES AND ITS PECULIARITIES

The idea having a direct impact on the economic development that education influences the attitude of the members of a society has been highlighted since the 1970s. It served as a basis for the arguments of D. C. McClelland and D. G. Winter (1969) and A. Inkeles and D. B. Holsinger (1974), who believed that *the modernization of society* could be possible without having an adequate attitude, which was the expression of the education itself. This notion represented the human being as an important factor of economic growth. According to E. Durkeim, "the individual who needs to instil education in us is not the man as created by nature, but the man needed by the society and it wants it in the exact way its inside structure requires him to be. To sum up, education is first and foremost the means through which society constantly renews the conditions of its own existence" (Durkeim, 1980).

According to the United Nations Organization, education as a market service has been included in the classification of services as follows: utilities and construction, wholesale trade and retail, restaurants and hotels, tourist facilities and camps, transportation (trips), data storage and communications, financial brokerage, defense and social coercive services, education and healthcare. The educational services market is a consistent and coherent group of educational components that refer to a national system or network. If it offers the members of the society the resolution and/or they meet the needs, interests, demands, individual or collective wishes.

We had to provide an analysis as part of our study given that the transactions of educational services can bring about profits by significantly contributing to a country's social and economic development and to its business performance. The foundation of the educational services market or the "marketing" of education started at the end of the 1970s in several Anglophone countries, such as the United Kingdom, New Zealand, the United States, and Canada, and it is part of the reform policies of those states. They are proof of the fact that the educational market is not a real market but is regulated by the state to a large extent.

However, the modern commercial perception in terms of educational services is a recent one, dating back to the twentieth century. To provide an accurate analysis of the educational market, one needs to respond to the following questions: What is the product that is traded in this market? and Who are the potential clients of that particular product? In terms of the first question, we can state that any kind of "educational product" that exists in the formal educational services market comprises the following elements:

- the educational services as such: the teaching activity of the staff and the evaluation/examination activity of the acquired skills by those who have been trained;
- supporting services: the total amount of management activities of the educational process and of the administration of the assets that are used for actual teaching;
- educational human capital: the amount of knowledge and abilities that have been acquired by the consumers of educational services.

The approach to the educational market also takes into account the actors involved in this market. There are three categories of beneficiaries/clients

- primary clients: the learners, the main and direct beneficiaries of the educational product;
- secondary clients: parents, companies, or other sponsors who are directly involved in the funding of the educational product;

- tertiary clients: future users, the beneficiaries of the workforce represented by the graduates who are not directly involved in the learning process (i.e., the society as a whole). They have acquired this status in relation with the owners of the educational human capital (i.e., graduates) with whom they interact on the labour market. The notion of "client" characterizes the marketing field and can be defined as "an individual, a company or an organization that pays for the professional services of a company or of an organization."

In the market economy, the client is the focal point of a business activity, and the effort is geared toward completely satisfying his needs and wants.

According to Negrilă, education is a system of educational assets referring to values that have to do with human needs. The demand for assets and services in this particular field depends on the intensity of the consumers' motivation. Starting with the individual spiritual needs that stir up the motivation of educational consumers, there will be global social and economic pressure for the manifestation of the educational process. By regarding educational assets as any other type of consumer good, there will be room for the usage of certain indicators such as cost/price and profit.

The market for educational services is a key component of an institution's marketing environment. Market relationships are those that take place between the institution and the outside agents. First and foremost, they are competitive relations with similar entities having exactly the same categories of service beneficiaries. Educational services are not short-term services. The student is indeed a client and he needs to be dealt with accordingly, yet the goal of the entire educational process is to provide him *the working tools* for defining his needs. Culture and the level of civilization are measured based on the type of needs that people verbalize.

In other words, the educational institution is required to create needs rather than answer the existing ones that have been expressed by the clients. The educational institution formulates its offer by taking into account all the outside factors, yet its mission is not to respond to a readily identified need on the market but to a long-term and a broad one instead. Specialization is bound to be set in place later on and will have a major impact on the lives of graduates. The effectiveness of higher education institutions depends on their employability and social inclusion. Competition represents an important characteristic of the educational market. Specialists believe that the encouragement of competition and competitiveness will bring about progress. Worldwide studies, especially those in the United States, England, France, and in other countries where the educational market is very developed and competitive, have shown that the amplification of competition in the training market has increased in parallel with interest in educational marketing.

The Synergistic Model of Educational Marketing was designed based on the main principles of educational marketing by focusing on the consumer and the systemic and synergistic approaches. The role of marketing is to become a bond between those systems interacting synergistically and the systems ensuring not only their own development but also the social and economic development that they act for. In the *Synergistic Model of Educational Marketing*, as shown in Fig. 2.2, there are, on different levels, educational institutions, educational consumers, the workforce, employers, the state, the media, and communication systems.

The SMEM levels delineate in a conventional manner the action areas of its constituents, which, at the same time, are closely connected among themselves, cooperate to obtain the advantages and benefits, and produce synergistic effects at the micro, macro, and mezzo levels.

The 1st level refers to the way educational institutions choose to communicate as education providers and the pupils/students as consumers. The 1st level is, in fact, the educational market comprising the request and offer for education. The key principle governing this level of SMEM is a classical principle, namely, the focus on the consumer.

The 2nd level refers to marketing activities. At this level, the SMEM focuses on the successful transition from education to the workplace and onward. At this level, the request and the offer interact with one another both on the educational market and on the labor market. The "product" is provided on the labor market in exchange for the financial resources coming into the educational market under the form of the funding of the economic environment for the training of the qualified and unqualified workforce as a result of the needs of the labor market.

The 3rd level refers to the relationships between the educational subsystems and the workforce with the society itself, which is represented by the state. Society is represented by the state bodies that set educational and professional standards, and it controls and regulates educational services and their adjustment to the demands of the market. The state ensures

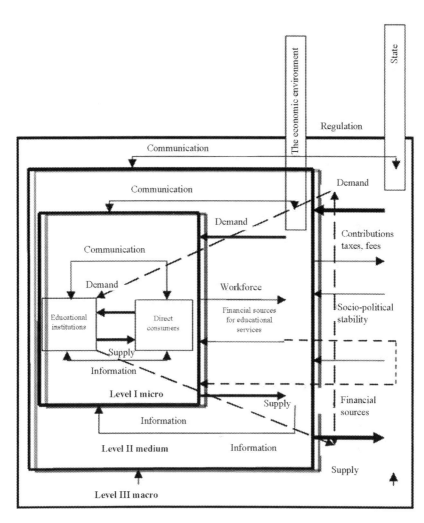

Fig. 2.2   Synergistic model of educational marketing (SMEM). (Source: Adapted after Bulat, 2012)

that markets have social and political stability to function properly based on the overall framework of interdependent development. The reliability of the markets was justified when a society was less complicated; however, once the economic and social relationships have increased immensely, the government needs to guide the actions of numerous people.

The defining elements of the SMEM are the request that is geared in all those instances toward the educational institution providing educational services and the offer of the provider itself, whose mission is to satisfy the needs of its clients from all three levels. Consequently, the educational institution is fully responsible for satisfying the request in the desired quantity and quality in the form of a qualitative educational offer that is able to meet the expectations of direct consumers, employers, and the state. Consequently, as seen, the key central player and the entire focus are on the state and its institutions.

One of the international development goals of all the states that are members of the United Nations Organization and of several other international organizations that is supposed to be fulfilled until 2015 refers to universal access to primary education. We can state that as far as this objective is concerned, the results are satisfactory, and the degree of primary education attendance is rising in all regions of developed countries. To fully ensure basic education, it is necessary to implement certain institutional rules and financial investments in terms of the right of the children to benefit from education worldwide. In conclusion, it is necessary to set in place an institutional analysis in light of the contribution of education to a nation's economic development.

INSTITUTIONALISM IN EDUCATION

Starting with Adam Smith, education was considered an element that contributed to social and economic equality. William Petty was one of the first scholars to support the accurate distribution of education. Some mercantilists supported education as an essential orientation for the improvement of productivity in agriculture and in terms of society's progress in general. During the eighteenth and nineteenth centuries, the school's reformers in the United States enabled the dissemination of education among the poor. Simon Kuznetz predicted that the distribution of income in capitalist states was fairer as workers became more educated.

An economy can be characterized by numerous demographic, economic, institutional, and technological statistics; however, we need to be aware of the way they interact with one another. What is the reason why we refer to all these things related to education? Simply because the key of the present interaction is society's supply of expertise. The national average, if the IQ may be regarded as an indicator of a nation's work quality, has an impact on the standard of living. The increase with a single unit of the IQ of a nation implies a bonus of approximately 0.11% per year of economic growth. Another important variable that influences behavior is the institutional framework.

The institutional framework is the one that establishes a set of sustainable rules that lead to habits and that enable social cooperation based on mutual recognition and acceptance by all the participants involved in the interaction. On the other hand, demography describes the quality and quantity of human beings. This knowledge stock establishes the superior potential that has to do with society's well-being, whereas the institutional framework establishes the stimulating structure of society. In light of these vectors, education demonstrated the dependence on the decisive factors or on the behavior of the individuals in the community.

The Centre for Economic Performance undoubtedly represents the efforts of the human being to monitor the interaction among these three aspects. *The institution* is the term that evolutionist (institutionalist) economists use to describe normal behavior and common behaviors in the community and to describe the ideas and values that are associated with these habits.

There are numerous expressions that define *the institutions* or an *institution*, such as the following: a habit becomes axiomatic based on a repeated usage; a group activity that monitors an individual action; the outlining or certain social behaviors at a higher standard; a way of thinking or acting in a group setting or in people's traditions; and predetermined regular aspects of a related behavior. However, none of the abovementioned definitions fail to offer the terms an equivalent meaning as it was used by the evolutionist economists.

The main goal of the institutional analysis in connection with education is to examine several institutional frameworks that can be associated with economic development. It does not come as a surprise that the institutional analysis on education has been present as a part of the social sciences for more than a century. Starting from the initial studies of sociologists such as Durkeim (1956) and Weber (1947), Veblen (1918) and Waller (1932) and finishing with modern sociologists such as Archer (1979) and Collins (1979), sociology specialists have acknowledged the importance

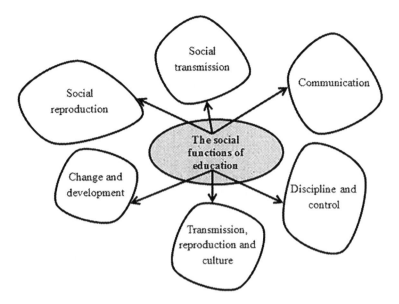

Fig. 2.3 Functions of education in terms of the reported sociological studies. (Source: Author's interpretation after Palicica and Albert (2002). *Sociology and Education* (p. 94). EUROBIT Publishing-house)

of education and its institutional implications. Education, according to Fig. 2.3, contributes to the preservation of the social order through the passing on of the values, standards, attitudes, and knowledge to the succeeding generations and, at the same time, it enables change based on the development and the training of the human capital (Hoinaru et al., 2021).

The organizations and the institutions are in close interconnection where the educational organizations together with the political and the social ones act as agents of the institutional mutations or as factors of fruition of the possibilities created by the institutions themselves. The question of "Why are there richer countries than others?" is crucial for economic theory.

Myrdal believed that as far as economic development is concerned, informal change outside the new institutions is mandatory. There will be positive results only if the technical and scientific modernization takes place at the same time, if the economic reform will take place in terms of the measures that need to be taken so that the role of the informal archaic institutions is diminished. In his opinion, the change within the informal institutions needs to take place with the help of demographic control, with the help of the educational system itself, and through the reform of the agricultural sector.

By criticizing the Western way of approaching the issues of *the third world*, especially by attempting to use the functioning mechanisms of the developed countries within certain environments that were not ready for them, G. Myrdal stated that, as a consequence, new enclave economies appeared—an efficient, yet narrow, industrial sector geared mainly toward the external and not the internal market, as well as a broad but efficient agricultural sector. These measures led only to the disintegration of the economic system, dependency on technology, and the increase in corruption and bureaucracy among office workers. Myrdal's arguments, rather old fashioned, observed the success or failure of national economies from the point of view of the concepts of economic culture or *economic mentality*, namely, from the point of view of a set of stereotypes and values influencing economic behavior and characterizing a large social group.

Another scholar, Samuel P. Huntington, was an American political scientist who was known for his thesis on *the clash of civilizations*. He became famous worldwide when he published his work entitled *The Clash of Civilizations and the Remaking of the Global Order* in 1993. Huntington defined civilization as being "the largest level of recognition an individual can identify with, the one that refers to the values, the social norms and the institutions governing the society as such. 'The components of the order in the complex and more heterogeneous modern world could be found inside the civilizations and among them. The entire world was about to be organized according to the civilizations or was not going to be organized at all'" (Huntington, 1997). He analyzed the national economies from the point of view of dominated—prevailing institutional relationships, especially in the case of those nations facing the option of economic development based on Western mechanisms and the preservation of national identity. "A world where the nucleus states have a leading role or are prevailing is a world of the spheres of influence. A nucleus state can infer order because the member states perceive it as a cultural relative. In the absence of this kinship, a stronger state's capacity to solve conflicts and to impose the order in the region is much more limited" (Huntington, 1997).

First and foremost, he claimed that culture was the clear match of an individual, an identity transcending several other possible identifying dimensions, such as ideologies or occupations. To reach cultural cohesion, Huntington claimed that economic, military, and political successes were essential for any civilization to develop its values, institutions, and culture. Thus, for Huntington, local policy referred to ethnical politics, whereas global politics was the politics of civilizations. "The Western values and institutions had attracted the people from other cultures because they were considered as the source of the Western power and well-being" (Huntington, 1997). The institutional and value systems require a special attention in order to be able to explain to us the reason why people make savings, invest, learn, and seek for useful knowledge. The abovementioned specialty literature demonstrates that institutional factors are mainly responsible for the development disparities among countries. Thus, Friedrich von Hayek argued that a nation's existence and operation were subject to certain rules that made people behave in a certain way that would enable their cohabitation. The human being himself is a creature guided by behavior norms, including the fact that he has certain habits and routines that support him in organizing his activity given the multitude of conditions he lives in.

REFERENCES

Albulescu, I. (2011). *Educational Institutions and Pedagogical Doctrines* (p. 20). Retrieved August 31, 2015, from https://beyondreamz.files.wordpress.com/2010/01/doctrine_pedagogice.pdf
Archer, B. (1979). *Design Studies, 1*(1), 17–20.
Aristotle. (2009). *Politics* (p. 117). Antet XX Press Publishing-House.
Badea, L., & Rogojanu, A. (2012). Controversies on the Higher Education-Human Capital- Competition Relationship. *Theoretical and Applied Economics, XIX, 12*(577), 124.
Barro, R. J. (1991). Economic Growth in a Cross-section of Countries. *Quarterly Journal of Economics, 106*(2), 407–443.
Barro, R. J. (2001). Human Capital and Growth. *American Economic Review, 91*(2).
Barro, R. J., & Sala-i-Martin, X. (1992). Convergence. *Journal of Political Economy, 100*(2), 223–251.
Becker, G. S. (1964). *Human Capital: A Theoretical and Empirical Analysis with Special Reference to Education*, First Edition.
Becker, G. (1994). *Human Capital—A Theoretical and Empirical Analysis of the Education in Particular* (pp. 109–119). ALL Publishing-house.
Becker, G., & Lewis, H. G. (1992). *On the Interaction between the Quantity and Quality of Children*. University of Chicago.

Bedrule-Grigoruţă, M. (2006). *Human Capital and the Investment in Education*. Scientific Annals of 'A.I. Cuza' University, No. 1(52–53) Iaşi, pp. 136–144.

Berg, I. (1970). *Education for Jobs; The Great Training Robbery*. ERIC.

Bils, M., & Klenow, J. (2000). Does Schooling Cause Growth? *The American Economic Review, 90*, Nr.5.

Blaug, M. (1970). *Economics of Education* (p. 56). Penguin Books Ltd.

Blaug, M. (1985). *Where are we now in the economics of education?* 4(1), 17–28.

Boozer, A. M., Ranis, G., Stewart, F., & Suri, T. (2003). *Paths to Success: The Relationship Between Human Development and Economic Growth*. Economic Growth Center, Yale University.

Bulat G. (2012). *Educational Marketing from the Point of View of the Quality and the Labor Market*. Doctoral thesis, The Institute of the Sciences of Education, pp. 17–18.

Chakraborty, D., & Mukherjee, S. (2010). The Relationship Between Trade, Investment and Environment: Same Empirical Findings. *SAGE Journals, 45*(2).

Chatterji, B. (1998). On Education. *JSTOR, 50*(34), Published By: Economic and Political Weekly, pp. 39–43.

Cohen, D., & Soto, M. (2007). Growth and Human Capital Good Data, Good Results. *Journal of Economic Growth, 12*(1), 51–76.

Coleman, J. S., (1988). Social Capital in the Creation of Human Capital. *American Journal of Sociology, 94*, Published By: The University of Chicago Press.

Collins, R. (1979). *The Credential Society: An Historical Sociology of Education and Stratification*. New York: Academic Press.

Colombo, M. G., & Grilli, L. (2005). Founders' human capital and the growth of new technology-based firms: A competence-based view. *Research Policy, 34*(6), 795–816.

Cucoş, C. (2006). *Introduction in pedagogy and the theory of the curriculum*. The Publishing-house of Al. I. Cuza University, pp. 5–7; pp. 45–46.

Davenport, T. H., & Grover, V. (2001). General Perspectives on Knowledge Management: Fostering a Research Agenda. *Journal of Management Information Systems, 18*, 5–23.

Ding, Z., & Min Z. Y. (1999). *Comparative Education Society of Hong Kong*. IJCED, Emerald Publishing.

Dore, R. (1976). *The Diploma Disease: Education, Qualification and Development*. George Allen & Unwin, London.

Duflo, E. (2001). Schooling and Labor Market Consequences of School Construction in Indonesia: Evidence from an Unusual Policy Experiment. *The American Economic Review, 91*(4), Published By: American Economic Associatio.

Dunca, I. I. (2009). *Plato's Politics and Metapolitics*. Lumen Publishing-House, p. 39 *cited in* Popescu, Al. (2004, p. 133).

Durkeim, E. (1980). *Education and Psychology. Didactic and Pedagogical.* Publishing-House.

Durkheim, E. (1956). *Education and Sociology.* New York: Free Press.

Edvinsson, L., & Malone, M. (1997). *Intellectual Capital.* Harper Business, New York.

Friedman, M., & Friedman, R. (1998). *Free to Choose: A Personal Point of View* (p. 130). All Publishing-house.

Gazier, B. (1992). *Economie du travail et de l'emploi.* Paris, Dalloz.

Gyorghyi, A. S. (1981). *Plea for Life. Politică Publishing-House,* 163–164.

Hartog, J. (2000). Over-Education and Earnings: Where Are We, Where Should We Go? *Economics of Education Review, 19,* 131–147. https://doi.org/10.1016/S0272-7757(99)00050-3

Hayek, F. A. (1985). *La route de la servitude* (p. 89).

Hoinaru, R., Robe, A. D., Manea, S. A., Damasaru, C., & Niță, S. (2021). Human Resources Accounting and Accountability: Medical Aspects, Regulation and Economics of Burn Out in Nonfinancial Reporting. *Proceedings of the International Conference on Business Excellence, 15*(1), 695–704.

Huntington, S. P. (1997). *The Clash of Civilizations and the Recovery of the Global Order* (pp. 228–229). Antet Publishing-House, Collection of Political Sciences.

Inkeles, A., & Holsinger, D. B. (1974). *Education and Individual Modernity in Developing Countries.* Leiden.

Jorgenson, D. W., & Fraumeni, B. M. (1992). Investment in Education and U.S. Economic Growth. *The Scandinavian Journal of Economics, 94.* Harvard University and Cambridge, MA, USA.

Kaili, E., Psarrakis, D., & Van Hoinaru, R. (Eds.). (2019). *New Models of Financing and Financial Reporting for European SMEs: A Practitioner's View.* Springer International Publishing.

Kant, I. (1996). *Treatise on School Pedagogy.* P. R. A. Publishing—house.

Kwabena, G. B., Padisson, O., & Mitiku, W. (2006). Higher Education and Economic Growth in Africa. *Journal of Development Studies, 42*(3), 509–529.

List, F. (1973). *National System of Political Economy. Academy of The Social Republic of Romania Publishing-house,* 121–129.

Lixandrioaia, M. (2013). *An Overall Theoretical Framework: the Concept of Human Capital.* Economic Court no. 8/2012 http://tribunaeconomica.ro/blog/?p=602

Lucas, R. (1988). On the Mechanics of Economic Development. *Journal of Monetary Economics, 22*(1), 13–42.

Macavei, E. (2001). *Pedagogy—Theory of Education.* Aramis Publishing—house.

Marshall, A. (1907). *Principles of Economics* (5th ed.). Macmillan.

Marx, K., & Friedrich, E. (1966). *The Capital-Review on the Political Economics, Works* (Vol. 23). Politics Publishing-House.

McClelland, D. C., & Winter, D. G. (1969). *Motivating Economic Achievement.* Free Press.
Meier, G. M., & Rauch, J. E. (2005). *Leading Issues in Economic Development.* New York, Oxford: Oxford University Press.
Mill, J. S. (1915). *Principles of Political Economy,* Ashley Edition, p. 950 http://www.econlib.org/library/Mill/mlP.htm
Mistreanu, L. M. (2013). *Education and Economic Performance.* Doctoral thesis, 'Al. I. Cuza; University, Iași, p. 25.
Murphy, K. M., Shleifer, A., & Vishny R. V. (1991). The Allocation of Talent: Implications for Growth. *Quarterly Journal of Economics, 106*(2), 503–530.
Neagu, C., & Mehedinți, S. (2004). *Vocational Teacher* (p. 156). Terra Publishing-house.
Pană, M. C. (2011a). *Education and Liberty* (p. 33). The Academy of Economic Studies Publishing-House.
Pană, M. C. (2011b). *Education From the Family Institutions to Etatization.* The Academy of Economic Studies Publishing-house. http://www.ecol.ro/content/educatia-dela-institutiile-familiei-la-etatizare
Pohoață, I. (1996). *Universal Economic Doctrines* (p. 108). Gherghe Zane Academic Foundation Publishing-house.
Pohoață, I., & Popescu, C. (2007). *Human Capital, Social Capital and Economic Growth* (p. 2). Al.I. Cuza University Publishing-House.
Popescu, S., & Brătianu, C. (2004). *Quality Guide in Higher Education.* University of Bucharest Publishing—house.
Ramirez, A., Ranis, G., & Stewart, F. (1998). Economic Growth and Human Development. *Working Paper No. 18.* Yale University.
Ranis, G., Stewart, F., & Ramirez, A. (2000). Economic Growth and Human Development. *World Development, 28*(2), 197–219.
Richard, J. C. (2006). *Communicative Language Teaching Today.* Cambridge University Press.
Rothbard, M. (1999). *Education: Free & Compulsory* (p. 7). Ludwig von Mises Institute Auburn.
Rothbard, M. (2011). *Liberal Manifesto: Against the Educational Socialism.* Ludwing von Mises Institute Romania. www.misesRomânia.org
Rousseau, J. J. (1957). *Social Contract.* Scientific Publishing-House.
Rousseau, J. J. (1958). *Speech on the Disparity Among People.* Scientific Publishing-House.
Schultz, T. (1961). Investing in Human Capital. *The American Economic Review (LI),* Nr.1, p. 10.
Schultz, T. (1962). *Reflection on Investment in Man the Journal of Political Economics,* Vol. 70, no. 5, part. 2, Investment in Human Beings, Oct., p. 18. http://www.jstor.org/stable/pdfplus/1818907.pdf

Selejean-Sută, S. (1996). *Economic Doctrines. An Overall View* (p. 171). Efficient Publishing-House.

Smith, A. (2005). *An Inquiry into the Nature and Causes of the Wealth of Nations* (p. 621). A Penn State Electronic Classics Series Publication, Pennsylvania State University. www2.hn.psu.edu

Spence, M. (1973). Job Market Signaling. *The Quarterly Journal of Economics, 87*(3), Published By: Oxford University Press, 355–374.

Stephan, P. E. (1997). Educational Implications of University–Industry Technology Transfer. *The Journal of Technology Transfer, 26,* 199–205.

Stiglitz, J. (1975). The Theory of Screening. Education and Distribution of Income. *The American Economic Review, 25,* 498–509.

The World Bank. (2008). *MENA Development Report,* p. 40.

Tiago, N. S. (2007). Human Capital Composition, Growth and Development: An R&D Growth Model Versus Data. *Empirical Economics, 32,* 41–65.

Tsai, Y., & Wu Wang, S. (2010). The Relationships Between Organisational Citizenship Behaviour. *Job Satisfaction and Turnover Intention, JCN, 19*(23–24).

Veblen, T. (1918). The Higher Learning In America: A Memorandum On the Conduct of Universities By Business Men, http://www.ditext.com/veblen/veblen.html

Voicu, B. (2004). Human Capital: Components, Levels, Structures. Romania in a European Context. *Standard of Living, XV*(1–2), 137–157.

Waller, W. (1932). *The sociology of teaching.* John Wiley & Sons, Inc. https://doi.org/10.1037/11443-000

Weber, M. (1947). *The Theory of Social and Economic Organizations.* New York: Free Press.

West, E. G. (1965, April). Liberty and Education: John Stuart Mill's Dilemma. *Philosophy,* pp. 1–18.

Retrieved June 19, 2014., from http://mises.ro/278/

Retrieved November 28, 2015., from http://www.actrus.ro/buletin/2_2000/articol15.html

http://www.cse.uaic.ro/_fisiere/Documentare/Suporturi_curs/II_Strategii_si_politici_europene_de_dezvoltare_durabila.pdf

Retrieved May 1, 2013., from http://www.ecol.ro/content/liberalismulintraditiaordiniispontane

Retrieved July 22, 2013., from http://www.scritube.com/management/managementuldezvoltariiumane34132.php

Theories and Models on the Relationship Between Education and Economic Development

Economic development is a manifestation of macroeconomic dynamics, which, in terms of the economy's mechanisms and organizational structures, refers to a group of quantitative, qualitative, and structural changes. Considering that the educational institution's main responsibility is to recruit and assign an individual or a group of individuals to several economic positions within a social structure, education has become a variable that significantly influences human society's progress by enabling and hindering its economic development.

Any human being is born and develops in a society, the reason for which education is essential for oneself. The analysis of the *education-social-economic development* dichotomy took shape later, after the Second World War, when education was seen as a central element and one of man's fundamental rights. In this regard, economists are interested in the most accurate evaluation of the possible means of estimating education's efficiency as a modern vector of economic, social, and human development.

Economic growth seems to be synonymous with economic and social progress itself and with *economic development*. However, most economists believe that the notions of *economic growth and development* should not contradict or overlap each other.

The two terms have certain common features as follows: they are both evolving processes that are based on support and use of the same factors. The social goal of both is to improve the standard of living. Regardless of

D.-M. Neamțu, *Education and Economic Development*, https://doi.org/10.1007/978-3-031-20382-4_3

the approach itself, there is unanimous consensus on the fact that development represents a multidimensional concept. Apart from its economic aspect, which is associated with economic growth and progress, social, political, cultural, environmental, scientific, and human issues have equal importance, with sustainability being the new framework for a new paradigm (Hoinaru, 2018).

Economic development refers to several qualitative changes that are related to life in general so that it means that "people will eat healthier, will take care of themselves better and they will know many more things." To be more efficient, it needs to be designed in the form of "the complex of exchanges of the mental structures and the social behaviors allowing the global real product by turning the specific advances into an overall social progress" (bpsoroca.md).

Having in view P. Guillaumont's key definition, we believe that general social progress refers to the supreme development goal. General social progress means achieving certain goals such as:

- fostering the economic development based on removing the intolerable discrepancies related to wealth and social status;
- abolishing poverty and ensuring a decent living for all individuals;
- improving the standard of living by increasing income, ensuring better employability, better education, and easy access to cultural and human values;
- improving the performance of the production factors and of the production itself.

The experience of the economies belonging to the Northern model in implementing these reforms has led to the formulation of the following conclusions:

- the investment in education is a top priority;
- the increase of output contributes to the reduction of the disparity of the revenues;
- the active policies on the job market have led to the reduction of job search and, therefore, the reduction of unemployment rate in the long run;
- the flexibility of the job market and social security are not contradictory goals;

- the ongoing training and the development of the employees' skills are the basic conditions that are necessary for the existence of an elevated adjustment of the workforce;
- Increased employability in the job market is a way of diminishing the pressure that is generated by demographic changes.

The Impact of Higher Education on Social and Economic Development

Considering that education is a national priority in shaping human potential, we are focused on identifying the importance of education for social and economic development based on the human component. The case studies have been based on the examination of the interference areas of the educational, social, and economic environments. Both the quantitative and the qualitative features of the system of economic resources are expressions of the diversity of the components, such as political institutions, legislation, education, cultural environment, market structures, and technological environment.

According to Fig. 3.1, education makes a major contribution to economic development based on the individual who is involved in the educational process. Interference research studies have emphasized the dichotomy of the impact of education on social and economic development as follows:

- by forming productive skills as a result of the relationship between education and economic development;
- by setting up the conditions for the capitalization of economic development by supporting different types of institutions and social behaviors resulting from the education-social institutions-economic development relationship.

To quantify education's economic impact, for the following analysis, we use a series of variable categories that will help us measure the results of the performance of the educational system:

1. The value of personal earnings

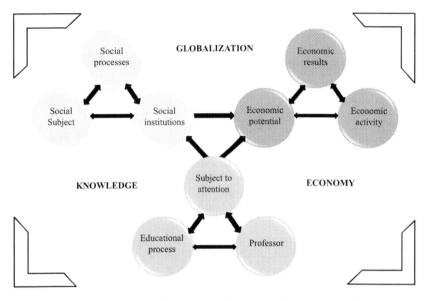

Fig. 3.1 The impact of education on the national economic development. (Source: Adapted after Bucoș, 2014)

Personal earnings are closely related to the level of education. During the recession, according to the OECD entitled *Education at a Glance 2012*, the pay gaps between highly educated individuals and high-school graduates have become more visible. In terms of OECD countries, in 2008, a highly educated male earned 58% more than his high-school graduated counterpart. Earnings vary significantly based on the level of education. Consequently, the findings of a study have shown that the annual average earnings of highly educated individuals have been from 74% to 87% higher (agewise) than the earnings of high-school graduates. Brazil is the country that has the highest discrepancies in terms of university graduates' earnings and those of high-school graduates, which is approximately three times higher than the average in OECD countries.

The cost–benefit analysis of an individual's work period has revealed that the expected net output of the payment of the scholarship, of the taxes and of the anticipated revenue during the academic years is over 11%, a ratio that is compared favorably with the actual returns of the majority of the financial assets (Badea & Rogojanu, 2012). The disparities in earnings as a result of a certain level of education have been accentuated over time. For example, for full-time male workers aged 35–44 years old, the differential earnings between university graduates and high-school graduates increased from 38% during 1980–1984 to 94% during 2003–2007. The pay differences represent the main proof in terms of the *knowledge-based emergent economy*.

The opinions on such pay differences are not always convergent. Some authors, such as A. Weiss, considered the explanation of the pay variations of the graduates of different forms of education who have different years of professional experience unrealistic based only on education itself (Weiss, 1995). He believed that employees with different levels of education have different behaviors that impact their job performance.

2. Finding a job and keeping it

Higher education influences well-being because it provides a signal on the job market, which means an increase in the employment chances of highly qualified individuals, increased mobility in terms of retraining, and an increase in earnings. Recent studies have shown that high salaries are present in regions with higher percentages of university graduates. A detailed econometric analysis indicated that a 1% increase in the workforce as university graduates in a metropolitan area will determine a 1.9% increase in high-school dropouts and a 1.6% increase in the salaries of high-school graduates. The reason for the existence of these high salaries in the areas with an elevated percentage of a highly educated population is the increase in work productivity due to the active involvement of highly educated employees. Additionally, from this point of view, we have emphasized the fact that in the European context unemployment has fairly high values among middle-educated people (i.e.), ranging from 8.8% to 12.5%, whereas for people with higher education, it ranged from 4.9% to 7.6% between 2008 and 2010. In the European Union in 2014, the employment percentage of the highly educated population aged 25–64 was 83.7%, yet we need to consider the reverse and look also at the unemployment rates in a consolidated manner (Trasca et al., 2019).

3. The individuals' health status

The relationship between education and health status has been frequently studied in terms of educational economics, yet the majority of studies have focused on the benefits of higher education for university graduates or for the members of their families. We can state that education has two distinct roles in determining the health status as such. First, the level of education in a household will improve the lifespan of its members because "education influences the crucial factors such as the understanding of the medical treatments, of the risks they face when they chose to have an unhealthy living and ensuring a healthy diet for the children" (Ricci & Zachariadis, 2008). Second, the aggregate level of education in an economy will improve the quality of the medical services offered by that country. This entails a better choice of adopting new ideas and technologies and a better understanding of medical scientific progress.

4. The perception of free time

By having an impact on the salary and, thus, on the income, education changes the way individuals choose to value their own free time and, consequently, the amount of time they spend. "The salary increase for an extra school year leads to both a marginal and unitary increase of the free time which means that the economic well-being generated by this source will tend to increase accordingly" (Haveman & Wolfe, 1984). The way individuals value their free time counts when estimating the total profitability of education because the level of education establishes the number of hours worked, which, in turn, will influence earnings, whereas the differences in terms of earnings represent the key factor for estimating the benefits of higher education.

5. Democratization

The importance of democracy for social and economic development has been highlighted by the sociologist Dewey in his approach to education. He stated that the mission of education was to stimulate individuals in defining their own interests in relationship with the community's interests. According to Lipset, education referred to one of the defining prerequisites of democracy in terms of contributing to the expansion of the individuals' political views, to the identification of their need to comply with the tolerance norms, of refraining from any kind of extremist movements and the increase of the likelihood of rational election decisions. Certain empirical claims of the impact of education on the installation of democratic values were formulated by Bucoș Tatiana in her doctorate thesis entitled *Education—A Key Factor in the Valorisation of the National Economic Prospective*, as a result of the correlation of the Democracy Index, which was calculated by the *Economist Intelligence Unit Organization* by using six groups of indicators, with the Hope for School Life Index, which was calculated by *The United Nations Statistic Division* (UNSD). She suggested the existence of an increased flexibility of democracy in terms of education, which was a characteristic of all countries worldwide. The countries occupying a position in the ranking of fully democratic countries are characterized by high educational levels. Hence, we observe that there is a strong correlation between the level of education and democratic development, derived from the ability of democratic regimes to create favorable conditions for the long-term stability effecting further in social and economic developments. Interesting enough is that proportions are also kept for countries in transitions.

6. Crime

A higher level of education will bring about pay increases, which, in turn, will increase the opportunity cost of illegal activities. Highly educated individuals will benefit, apart from a potential high salary, from many more opportunities to obtain a job and a low risk of unemployment and thus more benefits throughout their life. This will keep them away from getting involved in criminal activities.

7. The decisions of an individual as a consumer on the market

There is the assumption that, through education, an individual has access to database, information, and ideas that might help him in his more efficient consumer decision. The study carried out by R.T. Michael on the relationship between education and consumption suggested that an increase in the number of school years changed the consumers' budget allocation in the same way as the income; thus, their contribution to their family well-being was similar to an increase in their family budget (Michael, 1975).

8. Level of pollution

Generally, education, no matter its level, creates the conditions for taking care of the environment. The influence of higher education on the environment is a much debated issue because a high level of education is the foundation for technical progress and the intense exploitation of resources. Some authors believe that this aspect could lead to a higher level of pollution. In their study, Appia and McMahon highlighted the fact that a 2% increase in the sums that were invested in education caused a 0.3% reduction in the ratio of forest destruction in Africa.

9. Technological progress

The set of competences as part of the educational system focuses both on the shaping of the productive and the consumption prospective, which are responsible for a country's micro- and macroeconomic performances. Informational and media skills/competences will ensure the productivity of the human factor, which is becoming more and more efficient, competitive and which will find favorable solutions and conditions for the marketing of products and services of large consume (those products and services, in turn, are associated with new technologies). In turn, career and life skills ensure optimal employability of the individual on the job market and the establishment of a favorable environment for social existence. The innovative skill and the learning skill have a key role for the given model. They will provide the development vector of the national economies and the design and distribution of the innovations by establishing the rhythm of social and economic development in the knowledge-based economy. Education represents the human potential that is capable of ensuring both the development and the distribution of the latest technologies and the effectiveness of the management of the material, financial resources and time resources. Education, as part of the shaping of the set of competences, ensures favorable conditions for the efficient inclusion of the human component in the system of economic resources and the enhancement of the potential of the entire system of economic resources thanks to the development of technological environment.

10. Migration

A controversial aspect refers to the *brain drain* phenomenon because individuals possessing an elevated level of human capital choose to leave the country of origin where they have no financial resources according to their skills and migrate to developed countries. In this situation, the beneficiary of a high level of education is the host country, while the country of origin, which spent money on the training of the individuals, cannot recover it.

11. The increase in the level of culture and the multiplication of human capital

Based on the empirical analyses on the relationship between education and the complex feature of human capital, the multidimensional impact of education on a country's economic development has been highlighted. An individual's yield in producing human capital rises proportionately to his level of education. Educated persons will be more inclined to learn even after graduation by taking part in *workshops*, training courses in the field, or personal development courses. Education needs to promote common cultural values that are meant to diminish the social gap among individuals. This is a key function in heterogeneous societies.

12. Social cohesion

Education supports the change in behaviors and a more open attitude toward disadvantaged groups by facilitating their inclusion and social cohesion. The role of investing in education can be approached both from the point of view of the potential future generation of high future revenues for an individual, of the personal satisfaction, of the flexibility in choosing a job, of the high social status, and from the point of view of contribution to the social and economic development of the investments in education that are accomplished through a macroeconomic approach. We believe that education, as part of the social cohesion, contributes to the shaping up of the favorable conditions for the harnessing of the economic prospective for the individual himself or herself and for the national economy.

Education and Economy—In the Vision of the Economic Growth Models

The literature, focusing on economic growth, approaches education from the point of view of human capital. Education is regarded as the main important *input* in producing this type of capital, which, in turn, refers to "the stock of the competences and experiences contributing to the increase of the productivity of the human factor" (Stiglitz & Boadway, 1994). The impact of education on economic growth has been demonstrated by a series of empirical studies. T. Schultz emphasized the fact that approximately 60% of the GDP of the United States during 1929–1956 could not be justified based on the use of the existing models of economic growth because between 36 and 50% of this income was the result of the increase in the level of education of the workforce (Schultz, 1961). By undertaking a comparative analysis of the national income per capita, the existence of natural resources and the level of education for different countries, J.K. Norton observed a positive correlation between the level of education and the national income per capita irrespective of that particular country's natural resources (1958).

We have noticed that the trend in the perception of the role of human capital in economic growth is sinuous; thus, the approach was not unanimously accepted by economists. This fact has required the necessity of focusing on the critical analysis of its constituent factors, namely, on education in our particular case. The analysis of the correlation between *education and economic growth* has a long history as such. A. Smoth, A. Marshall, and T. Schultz regarded expenditures for education as an investment. Starting with *Nations' Wealth* by A. Smith, human capital has been considered a stock that is part of goods and is involved in shaping a nation's wealth. This topic was extensively debated in the works of Ricardo, Malthus, Marx, Harrod, and Domar, and served as a foundation for the future drafting of human capital in actual theories on economic growth. The present theories on economic growth refer to the use of econometric models that are capable of quantifying the effects of different variables on macroeconomic results.

The approach to the impact of human capital on economic growth is expressed either in the form of enlarging the neoclassical Solow type of model or in the form of *endogenous models* of economic growth supported by Romer and Lucas.

The exogenous models according to Table 3.1 on economic growth during the 1960s can be considered as an attempt to shape the role of education in economic growth. The common feature of these two models is that economic growth results from the improvement of work productivity, which, in turn, is the result of investments in education (Bucoș, 2014).

One of the first models in this sense is the Uzawa model, which relies on two assumptions:

Table 3.1   Exogenous models of economic growth

Model's author	Name of the study	Role of education in ensuring the economic growth
Arrow K. J.	"The Economic Implications of Learning by Doing," 1962	Designing new technologies that are used in the production through human capital. Learning by doing ensures increase in work productivity.
Uzawa H.	"Optimum Technical Change in an Aggregative Model of Economic Growth," 1965	The productivity of the work factor derives from using the latest technologies. The variation of the technological level is established based on the rate of the workforce employed in the educational sector. Education ensures the increase of the workforce that grows proportionally with the rate of the workforce that is employed in the educational field.
Nelson R., Phelps E.	"Investment in Humans, Technological Diffusion and Economy in Which There Is Exogenous Technical Change," 1967	A company's technological level depends on the acquired stock of human capital. The society's educational level is in a functional dependence of the share of the workforce that is employed in the educational sector out of the total number of employees.

Source: Adapted after Holland et al. (2013)

1. The workforce is divided into two categories: laborers and educational or teaching assistants or teachers;
2. There is rising, nonlinear dependency between the output of the work factor and the number of educators corresponding to a laborer.

It is believed that the efficiency of the workforce will increase in parallel with the rise of the employment rate in the educational sector. Consequently, work productivity will increase in the same proportion as the percentage of the population working in the educational field but slower than the relationship between the workforce in the educational field and the total labor force.

In the model designed by R. Nelson and E. Phelps, education has the role of enabling the flow of technological information. In this particular model, education is considered as the process of training the productive actors to attract and transmit technological information to the sectors of the economy.

Based on Schumpeter's assumption that the inventions do not depend on other economic variables, namely, they are an exogenous variable, the result is that they have a constant pace of development.

The model designed by K. Shell refers to educational planning, which requires limited resources for the educational sector to stimulate the level of education. This particular model can be considered a synthesis of the Nelson-Phelps and Uzawa models. In this approach, society's educational level is a variable that is functionally dependent on the rate of the workforce that is employed in the educational sector out of the total number of the workforce. The function of education is characterized by a decreasing efficiency in relationship with the actual efforts. This means that rapid economic growth can be achieved based on the improvement of the educational level of the workforce. At the same time, similar to the production sector, the educational effort complies with the rule of decreasing yields.

In the 1990s, there were a series of attempts to rehabilitate the Solow model by modifying the key equation of this model. There was an extension of the exogenous Solow model through the inclusion of human capital *inputs*. An important model in the group was suggested by the economists Mankiw, Romer, and Weil (MRW for short) in their work entitled *A Contribution to the Empirics of Economic Growth* (1992). In this model, education appeared as a private *input* that was remunerated according to marginal productivity. By analyzing the GDP per capita (of active age in 1985) in 98 countries, nonproducers of petrol, Mankiw, Romer, and Weild drew the following conclusions: the coefficient of accumulating human capital was an important one, which means that, together with the accumulation of physical capital, the accumulation of human capital would lead to an increase in GDP per capita. It was assumed that in the MRW model, there were two types of work—qualified and unqualified. The rate of trained individuals was established by the rate of labor force with a high-school diploma. Thus, based on their analyses, they changed the Solow function of production as follows:

$$Y = K^\alpha H^\beta \left(AL \right)^{1-\alpha-\beta}, \tag{3.1}$$

where H represents the stock of human capital, K is the physical capital, L is the labor force stock, and A is the level of the technologies (Bucoș, 2014).

In the MRW model, human capital is an independent variable of economic growth, whereas the empirical analyses made the authors conclude that "education is a major factor of economic growth" (Mankiw et al., 1992). Mankiw, Romer, and Weil took into consideration the depreciation of human capital. They believed that human capital depreciated in the same proportion as physical capital, whereas the growth ratio of human capital was estimated by using the same accumulation function.

According to the MRW model, human capital was not a constant value, as its variation depended on the difference between the created human capital and the depreciated human capital during the analyzed period.

The studies in this field have shown the depreciation of human capital given technological progress, and the depreciation level of human capital corresponds to the obsolescence of human capital. In the event that technical progress generates the obsolescence of knowledge and skills acquired during the school years, the high ratios of technological innovation will produce high ratios of the obsolescence of human capital. Consequently, economic growth can be ensured only based on maintaining the output of the human factor. This can be achieved by investments in continuous education. In the exogenous approach, human capital as a product of education is characterized by a nonproportional marginal yield. A series of investigations have revealed increased marginal yields of investments in human capital for the lower levels of education as well as decreased marginal yields for the superior levels.

In the 1980s, starting with the works of Romer (1986) and Lucas (1988), there was a massive increase in the number of studies on endogenous economic growth. The new models of economic growth tried to get rid of the postulates of the neoclassical approaches according to which economic growth was related to the exogenous ratio of technical progress. The promoters of these models explained economic growth in light of the endogenous factors by sometimes turning the exogenous factor of technical and scientific progress into an endogenous one.

Endogenous models are based on the assumption of the nondecrease in the efficiency of human capital. The endogenous approach to economic growth includes growth model technologies and specifies that technological changes result from the decisions of businesspeople regarding investment in education. Endogenous economic growth means that it is in a close relationship with the market forces and is opposed, from this point of view, to the classical theory of exogenous growth, which claims that the phenomenon does not depend on these forces. Endogenous methods have been extremely helpful for understanding the impact of growth on public, commercial, fiscal, and educational policies.

The main models representing the latest approaches to economic development for which investments in education have the role of generating economic growth are the following:

- the AK model;
- the models based on research and development (R&D);
- the model of the accumulation of human capital.

Robert Lucas (1988) was a promoter of the model of the accumulation of human capital. The model focused on the following ideas:

- economic growth depends on the quality of human capital;
- human capital is both an additional and a substitute factor of technical progress;
- the stock of human capital depends on the individuals' decision to invest in education;
- the investments in human capital have a nondegressive marginal yield that will ensure limitless economic growth;
- the interest in investing in human capital is a nondegressive one.

There are two sectors coexisting in the Lucas model, namely, the productive sector and the educational sector. The first produces physical capital assets that, according to Lucas, can be acquired and are nondegressive or have constant marginal productivity. In the second sector, human capital is formed and acquired based on that particular piece of human capital that is not used in the production sector.

The AK type of endogenous models was introduced by the economist Rebelo and King (1990). In his models, production was described in the function $Y_t = A_t K_t$, where A_t was a constant with a positive value reflecting the level of the applied technology in the production during the t period of time, whereas K represented the aggregated capital used in the production during the same t period of time. I comprised the physical, financial capital as well as the human capital and other forms of capital. In this particular model, economic growth is endogenous and has a long-standing nature due to the capital factor, which requires time to be productive. In the specialty literature, this assumption was named *time to build*. Jevons (1871) was one of the first economists who underlined the need to associate capital with the time factor. Unlike the Solow model, which presents two variables determining economic growth, the AK models have a single

K variable, namely, the work factor, which is used during production and is represented by the stock of human capital as a component of the aggregated capital. At the same time, the physical capital associated with a certain technology can generate goods only in association with the human capital that corresponds to the requirements of the applied technologies.

The qualities of human capital and its correspondence as well as technological exigencies are "designed" based on the educational process.

Economic growth is the result of the enhancement of human or physical capital, as they are both accompanying each other. The changes occurring in one of them will bring about changes in the others. The need for change was regarded differently by the authors of the models. Thus, Rebelo and King (1990) considered the accumulation of human capital as an incentive, Barro (1990) focused on the technologies as a result of the government's investments in the research and development sectors, whereas Romer (1986) was more interested in the accumulation of physical capital leading to the improvement of human capital due to the *learning-by-doing* phenomenon. For each and every AF model, education has an important role. Consequently, the human capital referring to the knowledge, the skills acquired during the educational process, and the findings of the research and development sectors are the result of the cognitive skills of the individuals working in this field, whereas the *learning-by-doing* phenomenon is related to t, the period of time.

Research and development models (R&D) provide an explanation of economic growth over a long period of time in light of technical and scientific progress as a result of research and development activities (R&D). The promoters of the model were Romer (1990), Aghion and Howitt (1992), Grossman and Helpman (1991). Romer (1990), for example, claimed that, provided the ideas and knowledge were regarded as public assets characterized by nonrivalry and nonexclusivity, the technical progress was going to be slow and that would make the endogenous economic growth difficult to achieve. The investments in research were to be made solely during the existence of imperfect competition when companies obtained an economic profit. The existence of monopolistic income was to mobilize private commercial agents toward investing in research, which would lead to the design of new products and technologies.

Endogenous economic growth can be ensured only when externalizing the previous results of C&D activities that are capable of sustaining the output of the production factors. The authors of the model assumed that during period t, the (Y_t) GDP was produced by using the (H_t) human capital and the (K_t) physical capital according to the Cobb–Douglass function:

$$Y_t = A_t^\delta H_t^{1-\alpha} K_t^\alpha, \qquad (3.2)$$

where A_1 is the technological standard used in the economy, δ is the elasticity of the technology, and α is the capital ratio. The model reflects the relationship between technology and human capital, namely, a higher level of human capital allows workers to use existing ideas more efficiently, and consequently, there will be an increase in the absorption of technologies.

The accumulation of human capital is achieved through formal education, which plays a key role in this model. Starting from the idea that education and technology mutually reinforce each other, the lack of an educated workforce will not impede the adoption of external technologies; instead, it will decrease both its efficiency and its absorption rate. At the same time, the inefficiency of the educational system will hinder the development of their technologies. Based on the given model, we can conclude that education influences the ability of a company to develop or adopt new technologies, whereas the tendency of companies to invest in C&D depends on the level of education of a country's population.

We believe that an inefficient educational system will drive the national economy toward development supported by external technologies, which, when used with a low degree of efficiency, will considerably decrease the competitiveness of the national economy. These situations are interesting not so much in terms of the level of education referring to ratio and school years but in terms of the results of the educational process expressed by the cognitive and the creative skills.

The analyzed endogenous models demonstrate the ability of the economic system to maintain the tendency of long-term economic growth as a result of investments in education. These approaches represent the methodological foundation of our study.

The reporting of the results of the educational phenomenon on the economic sector is related to the existence of certain channels that allow the valorization of different scales of the human factor, which boosts the positive evolution of the macroeconomic indicators, as shown in Fig. 3.2.

There is a series of diverging criteria in terms of the endogenous and exogenous criteria of economic development (Table 3.2). Therefore, there are economic models that consider education as a factor of economic

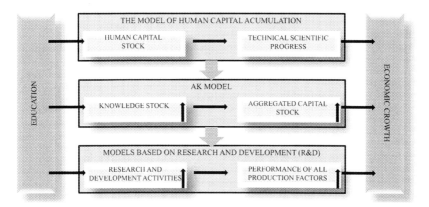

Fig. 3.2 Education-human capital-economic growth in the endogenous models. (Source: Adapted after Holland et al., 2013)

Table 3.2 Comparisons regarding the endogenous and exogenous models

Exogenous models	*Endogenous models*
The investments in education ensure short-term economic growth	Investments in education ensure long-term economic growth
The human capital is a result of education and is characterized by a nonproportional marginal efficiency	The human capital is a result of education and is characterized by a nondescending marginal efficiency
The technological changes are an exogenous factor ensuring economic growth	The technological changes are an endogenous factor of the economic growth which result from the decisions of the businesspeople in relationship to the investments in education
The technological changes will have an impact on the depreciation of the human capital in the educational process	The technological changes contribute to the increase of the stocks of human capital
The investments' nonproportional efficiency will ensure higher ratios of economic growth in the less developed countries by enabling the leveling of the level of income per capita between the rich and the poor countries	The nondecreasing efficiency of the investments in education will enable the rich countries to maintain their position while increasing the gap between them and the rest of the world

Source: Author's contribution based on the information of Holland et al. (2013)

growth emphasizing the dispersion of education's role in the economy during the second half of the twentieth century, whereas there are economic models emphasizing the difficulty on quantifying the economic effects of education.

The models of economic growth highlight the existing relationships between education and macroeconomic performance. Because the macroeconomic indicators are, in fact, the result of the valorization of the available economic resources, we intend to accomplish a separation of the research methods that were used by the promoters of several models of economic growth to identify the methodology that will be used in our study. Regardless of the recognition of the means of education's influence on macroeconomic performance, the relationships between macroeconomic performance and the measurement indicators of education are well documented in the form of mathematical models. The multitude of econometric models that focus on the impact of education on economic growth can be explained by the lack of a common indicator for the measurement of the level of education, as the econometric models identify the relationships that exist among several parameters for the measurement of educational level and GDP evolution (i.e., Appendix 3).

According to the table from *Annex 3*, we can conclude that:

1. the education's efficiencies in the models of economic growth are rendered by the changes within the type GDP per capita indicators or the GDP corresponding to a person who is economically active;
2. The quantification of the impact of human capital on the dynamics of the macroeconomic variables takes place based on the stock indicators or the capital flow that has been identified by the researchers through the tuition rates, in general, or divided by gender, sometimes by grouping the population based on the level of education, the school years (primary, secondary, university/tertiary), and the average enrollment in the educational system expressed by the average number of years in general or divided by the educational levels. The measurement indicators of the acquired volume of human capital can be quantified in relation to the total number of persons who are economically active.

We consider as a priority in analyzing the indicators of education referring to the total number of the population, the studies focusing on the education acquired by the persons that are active economically by overseeing the idea of the existence of some externalities which, as the future chapters show, have significant effects on the macroeconomic results.

In our research, we consider as important the following conclusions based on the economic growth models as a result of using econometric methods, namely, the contribution of several educational levels is related to the stage of development of a country (i.e., the impact of secondary education is higher in developing countries than in OCDE countries, while higher education is bound to have a larger impact in OCDE countries than in developing countries); education generates indirect benefits for economic growth (i.e., by stimulating investments in physical capital, by enhancing the development process and the adjustment of technologies), the quality of education and the efficiency of allocating resources for different levels of the educational system, which are very important for countries' future development. The design of the models of economic growth based on the econometric methodologies has enabled the outlining of the close relationship between the level of education and macroeconomic performance. At the same time, in terms of several models, the elasticity level of the macroeconomic indicators referring to the improvement of the population's level of education is different; thus, in the Barro model (1990), an increase of 1% in enrollment in primary and secondary education ensures an increase in GDP per capita of 2.5–3 percentage points. The same increase in the enrollment rate will have a 0.3% effect on the GDP for the MRW model (see Appendix 3). We believe that the difference between the results of these models is a consequence of certain methodological issues, such as the correlation of the GDP variable with several variables from the regressions of these two models.

The disadvantages of the research econometric methods that are used for the economic growth models are the result of their use, which refer to the analysis of long-term data, statistical data, and a broad sample of countries. When referring to the abovementioned data, we can observe that the statistical data during a 20–30-year period of time are involved, and the number of the analyzed countries is close to 100. Only under these conditions will the results of the analysis be relevant from an econometric point of view. In our opinion, the findings of these studies will allow identification of the laws that are important from the point of view of theoretical science, yet they have a low practical importance for the following reasons:

1. the long-term analysis of the statistical data has an ex-post feature, the results being less important for the government's educational policies given the dynamic peculiarity of the social and economic life;
2. The analysis of a sample of 70–90 countries allows the emphasis of the general laws on the economic impact of education by disregarding the impact of education nationwide.

The econometric studies based on a broad sample of countries have the tendency to include certain countries with different levels of development to expand the sample. Consequently, the findings represent an average based on the data characterizing a large number of very heterogeneous countries whose educational systems vary considerably from the point of view of the content, succession, and quality.

There is considerable proof regarding the existence of a high degree of heterogeneity of the parameters that are used in the economic growth regressions characterizing different countries. We believe as unjustified the extrapolation of the results of this kind of analysis of the national economies to formulate the recommendations in terms of the educational policy. The partition of the sample into countries based on their level of development clearly indicates the different impacts of education on those countries that are part of the subsamples. At the same time, when the estimation is done based on a homogenous group of countries (e.g., OCDE), the results need to be carefully interpreted due to the small size of the sample.

Another drawback in using the econometric regression method of economic growth refers to the fact that the given method fails to differentiate the educational systems of the countries under analysis. The evaluation of the impact of an extra school year on economic performance means that an extra year of secondary education in the United States equals a year of secondary education in Mexico. We believe that this approach to education is partially accurate, as the organization of education nationwide has its peculiarities. Therefore, the achievements of the national economy will differ from country to country due to the dynamics of educated population. Thus, the abstraction of several differences characterizing the educational systems is unjustified and will lead to an erroneous interpretation of the education's economic impact in different countries, whereas the recommendations of the educational policies that have been formulated based on these conclusions will be inefficient.

An attempt to restore the given research methodology was made by Hanusek and Kim (1995), who tried to avoid estimating the impact of education by exclusively using quantitative methods. Given that educational systems of different countries differ in terms of the resources, organization, duration, and results, they tried to quantify education's qualitative differences by including in the model the cognitive skills as a result of the educational process, as their interpretation is done based on the results of the school evaluation tests. The model suggested by Hanusek and Kim referred to the correlation of the educational results with the countries' macroeconomic performances. The educational results were focused mainly on the skills that were acquired during the science subjects.

Regarding education's multidimensional character, we consider it necessary to mix the quantitative methods of econometric research with qualitative methods in analyzing the object of research. At the same time, we consider it necessary to include in the research certain elements that were traditionally associated with the object of the pedagogical research (i.e., the capacity of education to generate values, skills, competencies), resulting in the understanding of the correlation between the educational phenomenon and the economic performance of the national economy. In our inquiry, this type of correlation will be achieved through the involvement of education in the shaping of the elements of national economic prospects.

REFERENCES

Aghion, P., & Howitt, P. (1992). A Model of Growth Through Creative Destruction. *Econometrica, 60*(2), 322–351.

Badea, L., & Rogojanu, A. (2012). Controversies Regarding the Higher Education-Human Capital-Competitiveness Relationship. *Theoretical and Applied. Economics, XIX*(12(577)), 131.

Barro, R. (1990). Government Spending in a Simple Model of Endogenous Growth. *Journal of Political Economy 98*, October, 103–125.

Bucoş, T. (2014). *Education—An Important Factor for the Valorisation of the National Economic Potential.* Doctoral thesis, The Academy of Economic Sciences of Moldova, Chişinău, pp. 40–48.

Grossman, G. M., & Helpman, E. (1991). Trade, Innovation, and Growth. *The American Economic Review, 80*(2), 86–91.

Hanusek, E. A., & Kim, D. (1995). *Schooling, Labour Force Quality and Economic Growth.* National Bureau of Economic Research, Massachusetts Avenue Cambridge.

Haveman, R., & Wolfe, B. (1984). Schooling and Economic Well-Being: The Role of Nonmarket Effects. *Journal of Human Resources, 19*(3), 377–407.

Hoinaru, R. (2018). What Are the Objectives of Corporate Reporting? Sustainable Value for Who?. In *Proceedings of the International Conference on Business Excellence* (Vol. 12, No. 1, pp. 436–445). Sciendo.

Holland, D. et al. (2013) *The Relationship Between Graduates and Economic Growth Across Countries.* Department for Business Innovations & Skills (BIS) Research Paper No. 110, p. 19.

Jevons, W. S. (1871). The Theory of Political Economy, History of Economic Thought Books from McMaster University Archive for the History of Economic Thought.

Lucas, R. Jr., (1988). On the Mechanics of Economic Development. *Journal of Monetary Economics, 22*(1), 3–42.

Mankiw, N. G., Romer, D., & Weil, D. A. (1992). Contribution to the Empirics of Economic Growth. *The Quarterly Journal of Economics, 107*(2), 433.

Michael, R. T. (1975). Education and Consuption. *National Bureau of Economic Research,* 233–252.

Norton, J. K. (1958). Education Pays Compound Interest. *National Education Association Journal, 47,* 57.

Rebelo, S., & King, R. (1990). Public Policy and Economic Growth: Developing Neoclassical Implications. *Journal of Political Economy, 98*(5).

Ricci, F., & Zachariadis, M. (2008). Longevity and Education Externalities: A Macroeconomic Perspective. *Working papers 09.02.278,* University of Toulouse, p. 2.

Romer, P. M. (1986). Increasing Returns and Long-Run Growth. *Journal of Political Economy, 94*(5).

Schultz, T. (1961). Investment in Human Capital. *The American Economic Review, 51*(1), 119–136.

Stiglitz, J., & Boadway, R. (1994). *Economics and The Canadian Economy* (p. 116). W.W. Norton & Company.

Trasca, D. L., Stefan, G. M., Aceleanu, M. I., Sahlian, D. N., Stanila, G. O., & Hoinaru, R. (2019). Unique Unemployment Insurance Scheme in Euro Zone. Terms and Conditions. Impact. *Economic Computation and Economic Cybernetics Studies and Research, 53*(2), 241–256.

Weiss, A. (1995). Human Capital vs. Signalling Explanation of Wages. *Journal of Economic Perspective, 9*(4), 133–154.

CHAPTER 4

Economic Scale of Education

In H. Simon's opinion, a laureate of the Nobel Prize, in his effort to explain the complexity of global dynamics based on knowledge, education was "the number one component of economic development." Thus, it was obvious that by accelerating the dissemination of knowledge in the worldwide economy, the main competitive force worldwide is the quality of human resources. Moreover, the quality of human resources and individual skills are related to the quality of the knowledge acquired during the school years. Access to education, especially higher education, is sometimes hindered by high costs. Educational consumers do efficiency cost calculus before making a decision on investing in their own training because any person when he or she needs to decide on anything for his or her own benefit focuses on satisfying certain needs or wishes to improve their condition to evolve and reach a landmark in their personal development (Symanski & Henard, 2001).

EDUCATION BETWEEN COSTS AND BENEFITS

The empirical studies in the specialty literature on education as part of the economic development equation have been divided into two categories: those studying the actual causal relationship between the level of education and the personal income, on the one hand, and, on the other hand,

© The Author(s), under exclusive license to Springer Nature Switzerland AG 2023
D.-M. Neamțu, *Education and Economic Development*,
https://doi.org/10.1007/978-3-031-20382-4_4

those studying the existing correlation between education and productivity. The findings of these studies vary and demonstrate that, basically, there is a positive relationship among the level of education, the individual's performance, and his income.

The Beckerian theory model starts from the following assumptions referring to higher education:

a) during their school years, students do not get paid except for the event when they are involved in gainful activities that take place before/after classes or during their holidays;
b) the earnings that are associated with these possible activities that they are part of are less than those that they could get if they were not enrolled in higher education because that would mean a higher job commitment;
c) the difference between what they might earn and what they actually earn is an indirect schooling cost based on the opportunity cost itself;
d) the tuition fees, the study materials, and the transportation and renting costs associated with the education represent the direct costs;
e) the net gains are the result of the difference between the potential gains and the total costs. The net gains obtained throughout the educational process are expressed by the identity (Zgreabăn, 2011):

$$W = MP_0 \left(MP_0 - MP + k \right) = MP_0 - C$$
$$C = \sum \left(MP_0 - MP + k \right) \tag{4.1}$$

where MP_0—the marginal production that could have been acquired;
MP—the marginal production itself, which is equal to the costs;
k—direct costs;
C—the sum of the direct and indirect costs.

By using the abovementioned relationship, which renders the cost of tuition, Becker estimated the cost of education, and later on, he estimated the rate of return of the investment in education by inserting into the equation the actual values of the net gains.[1]

$$d = V(Y) - V(X) = \sum_{i=0}^{n} \frac{Y_i - X_i}{(1+i)^{i+1}} \qquad (4.2)$$

By doing so, the cost of investing in human capital equals the foreseen net gains when making an investment is much preferred instead of doing an activity with no investments required whatsoever. If the Y activity requires an investment to be made only during its initial stage and if X does not need any of it, the cost of choosing the Y activity instead of the X refers only to the difference between the net gains during the initial stage, whereas the total profit would have been the expression of the actual value of the difference of the net gains during the last period of time.

Based on this reasoning, Becker enriches the model of investment in human capital and applies this approach to other variables, such as vocational training, information on the favorable chances of obtaining a job, medical assistance, or moral support, considering that "the analysis of on-the-job training leads to general results and can be applied to other types of investments in human capital" (Becker, 1994).

Based on this study, a series of key factors can be identified:

a) The investment in human capital is considered insecure due to certain factors, such as the life span and unpredictable events.

b) Only those families with high income will be the ones with access to education. A preference is given to the funding of the investments in personalized type of training which is detrimental to the general courses because the specialty knowledge rather than the general ones is much more important for companies.

---

[1] According to Becker, if Y_0 is considered to be an activity which enables a person to get a series of Y_0 net gains during 1 to Y_n last analyzed period of time, the actual value of the series of Y net gains will be expressed by the equation:

$$V(Y) = \sum_{i=0}^{n} \frac{Y_i}{(1+i)^{i-1}}$$

where i is the discount rate which is supposed to be identical in the beginning for the sake of simplification. If X represents another type of activity with a series of net gains $X_0 - X_n$ and with an actual value, then the actual value of the profit as a result of choosing the Y activity would be expressed by Equation (2.4).

c) Unlike the material investment, the investor in the human capital faces the pressure of not being late when investing as such due to the delay cost, which is defined as the reduction of the profit period based on the very moment of investing in education.

d) The investment in human capital is a form of accumulating *inputs*. The individuals will give up on actual consumption to increase their future profits. The domain of investing in people is characterized by the existence of a value of one hour of work for each and every employee. This difference results from the fact that individuals invest in themselves in terms of different levels of education.

The Beckerian model relies on the increase in the marginal productivity of trained individuals, which, together with the increase in incomes, is the main factor leading to the demand for education. His research is also important in terms of the theory of distribution, as Becker mainly focuses on the intergenerational distribution of income. From this point of view, the theory of human capital can be considered a distributional theory in itself because it explains the distribution of earnings among the members of society based on productivity differences that depend, in turn, on education. Moreover, the estimation of the internal rate of profitability of investing in education was originally formulated in Becker's studies on human capital, for which the level of taking part in education represents a decision to improve investment in education. It is assumed that individuals will train themselves up to the point when the actual value of the expected benefits will equal the direct and indirect costs of education costs. The educational mechanism is expected to improve individuals' productivity. Consequently, they will be entitled to expect to have a better income on the labor market.

According to Cojocaru and Făuraș (2006) in their work titled "Education in the Economic Approach," the decision to invest in one's own education is based on individual well-being, which, in fact, refers to a unique set of goals that can be reached through the assets provided by the economic and social system (Neamtu & Scurtu, 2013).

The fundamental hypothesis on investing in education relies on the following reasons (Cojocaru & Făuraș, 2006):

1. It is assumed that the individual is a rational human being, maximizes his well-being throughout his entire life, and displays a constant behavior in time;

2. The improvement of the level of education leads to an increase in the productivity level, which, in turn, will be represented by an income rise;
3. The effects of education are especially of a private nature.

The present analysis will focus on an actual example, which is illustrated in Fig. 4.1.

Continuous education implies certain costs both for students and for their parents. The cost of this particular action measures "the gain made" by "losing" the best alternative (sacrifice choice) and represents a kind of decision based on the *cost–benefit method*, namely, the evaluation and the comparison[2] which are considered in terms of the opportunity costs. The latter refers to the profits that an individual would have expected to have got if he or she had opted for acting on the job market instead of continuing his or her education. The graphic comparison of these variables can be

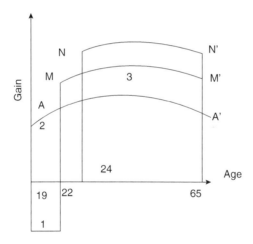

Fig. 4.1   Cost–benefit analysis in terms of deciding to invest in education. Source: Avram, E. (2012). *University Marketing—An Approach from the Point of View of the Higher Education Consumer*, doctoral thesis, The Academy of Economic Sciences, Bucharest, pp. 19–20 *cited in* Suciu, M. C. (2000, pp. 66–69)

[2] It takes into account the direct costs (i.e., the tuition fee, administrative expenditures, etc.), the alternative costs (i.e., giving up to the immediate gains in favor of the future ones), and the anticipated nonmonetary benefits.

illustrated by the size of the profits of the higher education graduates who are hired at the age of 19 (i.e., the AA's curb) and of the costs and salaries of the higher education graduates who are hired at the age of 22 (i.e., the MM's curb), namely, immediately after they graduated from the university.

The AA' curve represents "the profile of the earnings corresponding to the decision to enter the labor market immediately after finishing high school, at the age of 19" (Suciu, 2000). The MM's curb stands for the value of the profit corresponding to the decision of looking for a job right after graduating from a bachelor's degree, namely, at the age of 22.

Area 1 of the scheme illustrates the *direct costs* that are generated by the continuation of the studies, whereas area 2 reflects the *indirect costs*, namely, the income that is given up for taking part in the academic training. Both areas 1 and 2 represent the total cost, namely, the sums that were spent on the university courses. Area 3 represents the gross increase of the income when having a university diploma, whereas area 4 reflects the income as a result of a master's degree (i.e., around the age of 24). Areas 3 and 4 represent the additional income that is possible to get throughout an active life on the job market between the ages of 22 and 65 for a bachelor's and a master's diploma compared to the income related to the high-school diploma.

Vadim Cojocaru claimed that a rational decision in terms of the efficiency of investing in higher education needs to take into account the fact that higher education studies vary from 3 to 5 years, while additional gains will be present for the entire active life. Consequently, the method of updating the future benefits in terms of the continuation of the studies can be used by Suciu (2000).

Vadim Cojocaru and Călin Făuraş also claim that the sum obtained in year 1 (V_1) can be calculated based on the following equation:

$$V_1 = V_p(1+i), \tag{4.3}$$

where V_p is the actual value and i represents the interest rate. This equation will help us calculate the present value of a future income (i.e., in the following year):

$$V_p = \frac{V_1}{1+i} \tag{4.4}$$

To obtain an overall image of the costs and benefits of education in a given period of time (i.e., 5–6 years for certain specializations such as medicine and architecture), we will resort to extending the previous formula (Suciu, 2000):

$$V_p = \frac{E_1}{1+r} + \frac{E_2}{(1+r)^2} + \ldots + \frac{E_n}{(1+r)^n} = 0 \qquad (4.5)$$

where E_1, E_2 ... E_n represent the increase in expected profit for each and every year of study, n is the individual's hope for an active life, and i is the interest rate.

In this particular case, the income corresponding to the five years of academic studies (E_1, E_2, E_3, E_4, E_5) will represent the direct and indirect costs corresponding to each academic year.

In the event that we would like to determine whether the investments in an individual are justified by his education, we will make use of the internal rate of recovering the investment (r), also known as the private output of investing in human capital. It is the discount rate for which the net discounted value of the investments in the human capital is zero:

$$V_p = \frac{E_1}{1+r} + \frac{E_2}{(1+r)^2} + \frac{E_3}{(1+r)^3} + \frac{E_4}{(1+r)^4} + \frac{E_5}{(1+r)^5} = 0 \qquad (4.6)$$

where E_1, E_2, E_3, E_4, and E_5 represent the direct and indirect costs corresponding to the five academic years, respectively, and r is the highest rate that can be paid by somebody for financing the investment in educational capital.

The adoption of an adequate decision means making a comparison between *i* and *r*. Thus, if r > i, then the investment is profitable. When r < i, the investment in education is no longer profitable. Consequently, it will be profitable to invest only up to the limit where r = i.

The analysis, which was done on the version of the 1st cycle of academic studies (three years), has shown that r > i, which means that the investment is a profitable one.

The rate of recovering the investment in educational capital varies based on the cycles of education. For master's and doctoral studies, the alternative costs are high, and the rate of recovery of investment in educational capital is lower than that for mandatory secondary education, whereas alternative costs for this level are nonexistent (i.e., the highest recovery rate). As a result of the abovementioned issues, we have reached the conclusion that once the level of education or the number of years of study increases, the evolution of the recovery rate of investment in this field will decrease.

Each and every training year in an institution of higher education according to the predictions in the USA brought a 5–15% "formational addition" to the annual income, while the average rate of the profit of the actual capital was only 4%. Based on this fact, the decision was made for education to occupy the top position in the social needs system of the Americans. For different levels of education, the recovery rate of investing in human capital is different. We would like to specify the fact that the highest recovery rate refers to secondary education because the alternative costs for this level are nonexistent, as it is mandatory, whereas the lowest recovery rate corresponds to the master's degree and to Ph.D., as the alternative costs are high.

Psacharopoulos (1973, 1985, 1994, 2004) designed a rate of return for the educational field. The conventional rate of return presents higher education from a less favorable perspective than the primary and secondary rates as can be seen in Fig. 4.2.

Psacharopoulos and Patrinos analyzed the studies on 98 countries and concluded that the social rates of return of the investments in primary education are the highest of all (i.e., 18.9%), followed by secondary education (i.e., 13.1%). Higher education has the lowest rates (i.e., 10.8%) as shown in Table 4.1. This model of the private rates of return is more or less true. These findings are used on a large scale to discourage public investments in higher education and to focus on primary education.

The rate of return for higher education is less than that for primary education; however, higher education has an attractive rate for society (over 10%) as well as for individuals (19%) (Psacharopoulos & Patrinos, 2004). The lowest profits can be seen in the countries with low and average incomes.

Table 4.2 shows the rate of return corresponding to higher education based on the regional average (%). There are major variations in the rate of return among countries. In general, they indicate the fact that investments in higher education have positive effects both for individuals and for society itself. The declining rates of return throughout time are not the same for all countries. For example, in some Asian countries, the rate of return

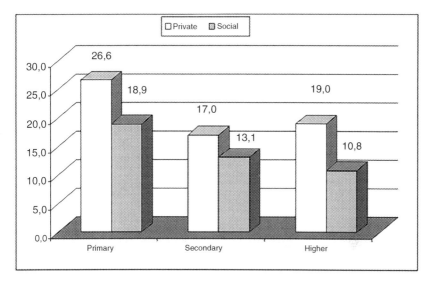

Fig. 4.2 The profit of the investments based on levels of education. Source: adapted after Psacharopoulos and Patrinos (2004). *Returns to Investment in Education: A Further Update Education Economics,* Vol. 12, No. 2, p. 15. http:// elibrary.worldbank.org/doi/pdf/10.1596/1813-9450-2881

is rising. This could be the result of the rapid growth of the demand for the educated workforce.

From a statistical point of view, the rates of return represent the relationship between lifetime earnings and educational costs (Tilak, 2003). After the adjustment of the direct costs associated with the corresponding levels of education (e.g., tuition) and taking into account that the value of a certain amount of money varies the moment it is spent or received, the remaining difference can be expressed by the reported costs. The rates of return are considered to be private when they depend on the differences between the money from home and the tuition fees coming from the students and their families.

After the social and private rates of return are calculated, it becomes easy to take notice of the difference between these tariffs and the way society at large benefits from them. This particular difference offers an economic justification for the government's actions. In the event the social return exceeds the private beneficiary, there is a clear indication that the

Table 4.1 Profits from investing in education based on the level of education during 2004 on average per capita (%)

Incomes per capita	Average per capita (USD)	Social			Private		
		Primary	Secondary	Higher education	Primary	Secondary	Higher education
High ($9266 >)	22,530	13.4	10.3	9.5	25.6	12.2	12.4
Low ($755 or <)	363	21.3	15.7	11.2	25.8	19.9	26.0
Average (up to 9265)	2996	18.8	12.9	11.3	27.4	18.0	19.3
Global	7669	18.9	13.1	10.8	26.6	17.0	19.0

Source: adapted after Psacharopoulos and Patrinos, *Returns to Investment in Education: A Further Update Education Economics,* Vol. 12, No. 2, (August 2004), p. 15. http://elibrary.worldbank.org/doi/pdf/10.1596/1813-9450-2881

Table 4.2 The comeback rate of higher education

	Social	Private
Asia*	11.0	18.2
Europe/Middle East/North Africa	9.9	18.8
Latin America/Caribbean	12.3	19.5
OECD	8.5	11.6
Sub-Saharan Africa	11.3	27.8
World average	10.3	19.0
* Non-OECD		

Source: adapted after Psacharopoulos and Patrinos (2004). *Returns to Investment in Education,* Vol. 12, No. 2, p. 15

http://elibrary.worldbank.org/doi/pdf/10.1596/1813-9450-2881

unhindered functioning on the private markets (the so-called laissez-faire) will make education less popular from the society's point of view (this fact is because private markets are based on making a profit, whereas society is based on decisions regarding social data). Moreover, in the situation when the social rate of returning to primary school would exceed that of higher education, it is obvious that primary school represents a more profitable investment than higher education. These analyses have concluded that there was a larger difference in terms of primary education than in terms of higher education, and consequently, government action was more justified for the first level than for the latter. The benefits of higher education are larger and are separate from the extra profits of the individuals (Annex no. 3a).

The Impact of Education on the Economy

The investment in education has a specific impact on the process of economic development. The educational factor is holistically integrated into the conduct of the economic process. One cannot specify that a certain level of education—from the point of view of the number of years or the tuition paid for the instruction of the individuals taking part in an active process—is necessary for ensuring the carrying out of an economic activity.

The same level of education manifests differently from individual to individual, from one economic process to another. Part of the benefits of this type of investment can be measured; some cannot, which means that they are not less important. The institutional or individual decisions of investing in education generate both private and social benefits. The investments in education will generate profits not only for the human capital carrier but also for the entire society, which will benefit from the increase in the workforce offer and the number of higher-educated individuals (they are called externalities). From this perspective, we refer to Friedman's conclusions: "[I]t is impossible to talk about a stable and democratic society without fully accepting a set of common values and a minimum literacy level and knowledge of the citizens. Both that child as well as his family will profit from this education and other members of the society at large by promoting a stable and democratic society" (Friedman, 1955).

According to the Organization for Economic Cooperation and Development (OECD)'s study, titled *Highlights from Education at a Glance 2009*, the particular studies on the individuals' earnings in terms of the level of education are as follows (OECD, 2012):

- the gains tend to grow proportionally with the individuals' level of education;
- the premium of gains corresponding to the higher education level is a consistent one and exceeds 50% in more than half of the studied countries;

- the advantage in terms of the gains of those with higher education increases as they age; however, it decreases in terms of those having a lower level of education.

It should be noted that there is a strong and positive relationship between the levels of education and the average gains. The university graduates earned more per total in comparison with the high-school graduates in all the countries that were part of the OECD study. Moreover, the rate of employment, as a whole, increases in parallel with the rise of the individuals' level of education. More than 40% of the less-educated individuals than the secondary level are unemployed.

The studies have emphasized that the individual choices of investing in education of the OECD countries are influenced by the following premises:

- the incentives for the university graduates are usually bigger than for those who graduated lower forms of education;
- higher education provides significant incentives in most countries by generating net profits of over US $100,000 throughout an active life on the labor market in the Czech Republic, Hungary, Ireland, Italy, Poland, Portugal, and the USA;
- Except for Australia, Denmark, Korea, Norway, Spain, and Turkey, as far as women are concerned, the incentives in terms of personal investment in higher education are usually lower.

According to the OECD (2009) report, the benefits of investing in acquiring higher levels of education are not limited to the individual, but they refer to the society itself, which is why in conclusion (OECD, 2012):

- on average for the OECD state members, the actual total value of the public investment that is necessary for a person to acquire higher education is US $28,000;
- the public net benefit for this type of public investment exceeds US $50,000;
- similar to the individual benefits, the benefits of society are larger when the individuals are university graduates in comparison with those who are high-school graduates.

The framework shown in Fig. 4.3 suggests several possible ways in which higher education can contribute to economic growth both in

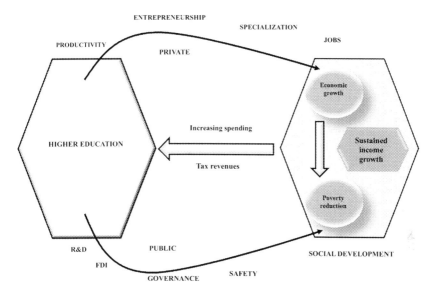

Fig. 4.3 The impact aspects of higher education on economic growth. Source: adapted after Ozsoy Ceyda (2008) *The Contribution of Higher Education to Economic Development,* Publishing Global Conference on Business & Economics, Italy *cited in* Bloom et al. (2006, pp. 15–16)

private and in public systems. The benefits of individuals refer to better employment opportunities, higher salaries, and better means of saving and investing. These benefits lead to the improvement of the quality of life by enabling individuals to work more efficiently for a longer period of time, thus consolidating their incomes throughout their lives.

The public benefits are less known on a large scale. This is the explanation for the governments' lack of interest in terms of higher education as a means for making public investments. The large earnings of university graduates may contribute to the increase in profits from taxes and thus financing the state. This means a higher consumption from which the individuals from the educational field benefit.

Ake (2009) claimed that the investment in education costs a lot; it meant significant financial efforts, whereas its benefits could not be noticed right away. However, he embraced the idea that this type of investment would lead to a significant rise in income as such. In the model suggested by the author in terms of the investment in education, its utility function was supposed to be concave and differentiable at least two times. According to the author, the income that could be earned when hired would be diminished or would disappear once another form of education was to be chosen (Andersson, 2009).

A causal relationship between education and earnings was also identified in the empirical studies of Card (2001). Thus, the increase in the number of studies as a result of a form of higher education would lead to an increase in earnings. For many individuals, it is a well-known fact that education is a steppingstone in life, an opportunity to find a better job and obtain a higher income. Considering the abovementioned facts, one can sometimes wonder whether investing in education would be a good option.

In terms of education, there have been two different approaches: *non-pecuniary externalities* and *pecuniary externalities*. As far as *nonpecuniary externalities* are concerned, Jacobs (1986) and Lucas (1988) demonstrated that education's outside effects would act in the form of the exchange of ideas, imitation, and *learning by doing* and not based on prices. Another point of view was that in a region where the average level of the population's education is high, the rhythm of technological progress is continuous. In Lucas' model, the externalities generated by human capital and the company's and community's knowledge are capable of ensuring an increase in productivity and, consequently, an increase in income due to the workforce's ability to use the existing technology. The social feature of the accumulation of human capital derives from education's externalities.

Similar to Lucas, Romer highlighted the dependency of GDP per capita on human capital. This is based on the stock of human capital from the research and development (R&D) sector enabling innovations. In this model, the technological level is not constant; however, it is a variable that depends on the level of education of a country's population. Romer's conclusions are relevant for the OECD countries, which are technological leaders (as stated by Griliches). Nonetheless, the theory does not apply to developing countries. For these countries, Lucas focused on the population's average level of education, which enables the dissemination of the technology.

The pecuniary externalities were initially described by A. Marshall, who demonstrated that an increase in the internment of the specialized factors in a certain region would ensure the demographic internment of the industries in that region. This type of externality was rediscovered by P. Krugman in his work titled *History and Industry Location: The Case of the Manufacturing Belt* (1991). In his opinion, there is a direct relationship between the average level of education and the location of the economic activity. The higher the level of education of the workforce in a region, the more companies' investments in the physical capital, as education generates pecuniary externalities in the form of the extension of the research processes.

The studies focusing on the education's economic impact bring about education's monetary or nonmonetary *private effects* (i.e., the theory of human capital) or its *external effects* from the point of view of its impact on GDP, as they also have a monetary effect. In Fig. 4.4, we present education's externalities on the rise of GDP and the externalities influencing economic development in several ways.

The private noneconomic benefits comprise a variety of education's potential effects influencing individual well-being. Highly educated individuals can adjust much better to various life conditions, and moreover, they are able to adapt to these conditions to satisfy their individual

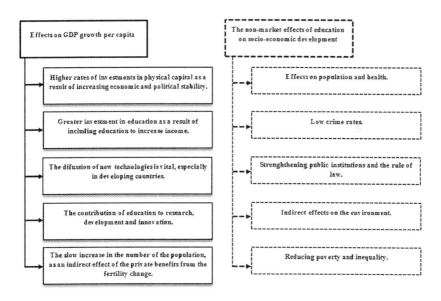

Fig. 4.4 Education's externalities as a public asset. Source: adapted after Huru (2007). *Investments, Capital-Development,* Economics Publishing-house, Bucharest, pp. 116–118

preferences. As far as the individual is concerned, additional education seems to be related to an improved state of health and to an increased life expectancy. An extra benefit for higher-educated individuals refers to superior knowledge and skills in terms of market operations and transactions. This benefit is also known as *the consumer's efficiency*. Hanusek highlighted the following fact: an individual who had attended an extra school year was more efficient as a consumer due to his extra income. This particular form of efficiency originates, on the one hand, from the consumption of ordinary goods based on a high income and, on the other hand, from the level of information during the individual's consumption. The ability to make efficient connections on the labor market combined with the reduction of the period of time spent for the actual job search is also the key component of this kind of benefit. Moreover, employers are able to obtain advantages by hiring better trained individuals. The efficient match of the employees with the corresponding job will lead to the cutting down of a variety of costs that the employee has to pay (i.e., training costs, recruiting costs), as well as the decrease in productivity during the employees' transition (Annex 6).

Meulemeester J. L. and Rochat D. highlighted the fact that a certain type of education would continue to dominate the investment needs and requirements to ensure more rapid economic growth. The investment in higher education is as important as any other kind of investment because it offers its beneficiaries numerous long-term and short-term advantages individually, socially, and from an organizational point of view, as shown in Fig. 4.5.

A high social status, a higher employment rate, and a broader set of cultural benefits are some of the advantages that university graduates have. A proof that lays at the foundation of *the beneficiary needs to pay the* type of argument pleads for the private financing of higher education.

Consequently, most of the time, free-of-charge things bring about irrational consumption and waste, which would be the second reason for personal investment in higher education. Excessive demand in higher education refers to the economic optimum. If we reference the findings of the specialty literature in terms of the advantages of personal investment in higher education, we believe that they all enable higher education institutions to attract more valuable students in universities by opting for quality services to ensure long-term success and efficient collaboration in the labor market based on training specialists for all fields of activity.

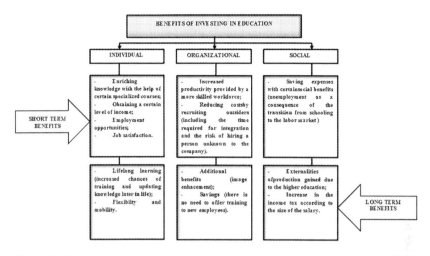

Fig. 4.5   Benefits of investing in education. Source: adapted after Avram (2012), *University Marketing—An Approach from the Point of View of the Higher Educated Consumer*, doctoral thesis, Academy of Economics Studies, Bucharest

THE MINCERIAN EQUATION

The relationship between the level of education and the evolution of the individual earnings can be found in the microeconomic studies of the economics literature. This is the reason why most of the economic literature devoted to this topic is basically a technical one and dominated by the econometric models that help in testing different hypotheses by using the empirical data. Jacob Mincer is considered to be the pioneer of the estimations associating the achieved level of education and the salary at the individual level in his famous Mincerian equation.

The emphasis on this relationship is based on the belief that the school years represent a viable source of increasing productivity and, consequently, of the earnings of the beneficiary of a formal education, namely, the easy way of accessing the necessary data for testing this kind of correlation. Basically, *it makes use of several assumptions* (Mincer, 1970), such as

1. the graduation of an extra study year generates solely the opportunity cost of the needed time for this purpose;
2. the proportional growth of the earnings due to an extra school year is preserved in time. Based on these assumptions, Mincer concluded

that there was a positive relationship between the increase in individual earnings and the number of school years. A characteristic of this model is the fact that the time spent in school is considered to be the determining cause of earnings, as the following statements will reveal.

The Mincerian salary equation is a well-known model for analyzing the way an individual's education and experience have an impact on his salary.

$$W_i = \beta_0 + \beta_1 S_i + \beta_2 X_i + \beta_a X_i^2 + \varepsilon_i \qquad (4.7)$$

where W_i represents the logarithm of the salary for individual "i"
S_i—schooling years
ε_i—residual value
X_1–X_i—other factors influencing the income, different schooling years.
The reason why the β_1 coefficient of schooling is considered to be the settlement rate is proof of the fact that the schooling decisions are made based on leveling of the two updated values. One of them is calculated for a higher level of education, whereas the other is calculated for an inferior level.

Considering that this model refers to education as an investment in individual human capital, people opt for a certain number of years of study by focusing on maximizing the present value of lifetime earnings. In this context, the question is as follows: How can education help in getting higher salaries detrimental to others?

According to Jrajda (2003), as a result of the analysis based on the data available for the Czech Republic in 2002, the benefits of a school year were almost 10% for the young adults aged between 24 and 44 years old and 8.7% for the older generation aged 45 and 61 years old.

Based on the data of the international research program (International Social Survey Program—ISSP, 1995), Harmon (2003) tried to establish a relationship between the time spent in school and the income itself. For Bulgaria, the authors noticed a difference in terms of the annual incomes of approximately 4.96% for men and 6.24% for women.

These estimations indicate that there is a limited level of direct financial benefits for those leaving school at an early stage and graduating from secondary education. On the other hand, this analysis does not take into account other key variables, such as unemployment, social assistance, and taxes.

Based on Annex no. 5, in all OECD countries, higher-educated individuals earn more in comparison with those with a high-school diploma who, in turn, have a much higher income than those who are not part of this category.

In many countries, high-school education represents the starting point for future studies and *trainings* in terms of relatively short-term earnings. In other words, they represent the milestone of how earnings linked with the level of education can be estimated. Once the costs of private investment in high-school education increase in the majority of countries, earnings will also increase, and they are an important incentive for people to invest time and money in education. The income differences between the higher-educated individuals and the high-school graduates are more visible than between the high-school graduates and the other levels of education. The type A higher-educated individuals (i.e., academic research) or those that are involved in an advance research program earn approximately 70% more than high-school graduates and have employment benefits. In contrast, there are those without this type of education earning 20% less than the high-school graduates. Chile, Brazil, Hungary, Turkey, and the USA have the highest difference in terms of income based on the level of education. In Brazil, Turkey, and the USA, undergraduates are the most penalized and earn at least 35% less than graduates. This fact is illustrated in Fig. 4.6.

In Chile, Brazil, and Hungary, the individuals with higher education are most stimulated in comparison with those who are less educated, as they earn more than double the income of a high-school graduate.

For OECD countries, earnings depend on the level of education in different educational stages. Figure 4.7 indicates that in the OECD countries, there are no major differences in terms of the earnings-based level of education genderwise. There is a different situation in terms of the level of education because a man or a woman earns approximately 70% more than a person of the same gender who is a high-school graduate. However, there are major differences among countries. In Chile and Brazil (both for women and for men); Greece, Hungary, and Slovenia (for men); and Ireland (for women), higher education graduates earn double the number of high-school graduates.

In Australia, Estonia, Ireland, Israel, Japan, Korea, Spain, Switzerland, and the UK, women's relative income is 10% more than men's, while in

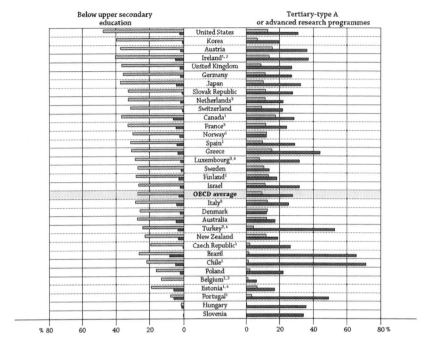

Fig. 4.6 Individuals' relative incomes based on the level of education and age groups. Source: OECD (2014). *Education at a Glance 2014: OECD Indicators,* OECD Publishing, pp. 134–136. https://doi.org/10.1787/eag-2014-en

Chile, The Czech Republic, Denmark, Finland, France, Greece, Hungary, Italy, Luxembourg, Poland, Slovakia, Slovenia, and Sweden, men's income is 10% more than women's. In both cases, the differences are linked to the earnings of the members of the same gender who are high-school graduates and who have a stable job. When the comparison is done based on gender, one can see a tendency to approximate the fact that there is a higher difference related to earnings.

Another complex analysis confirming the findings of the OECD report was done by the statistics labor office in the USA (BLS Reports, 2014—*Highlights of Women's Earnings in 2013*), which presents the actual earnings of the employed population as the result of using a national, monthly questionnaire on approximately 60,000 households. The questionnaire obtained accurate results and indicated that the average weekly

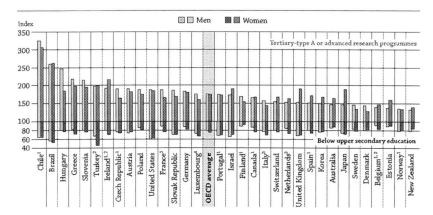

Fig. 4.7 Employees' relative incomes based on the level of education and gender. Source: OECD (2014). *Education at a Glance 2014: OECD Indicators*, *OECD Publishing*, *pp. 134–136*. https://doi.org/10.1787/eag-2014-en

earnings vary significantly based on the level of education. As far as the employees over 25 years old are concerned, the weekly earnings of those without a high-school diploma were $472, as a percentage it represented two-fifths of the earnings of the university graduates, the latter ones earning $1194 in 2013. As far as the high-school employees who are not graduates of a nontertiary (colleges) form of education, the average income was $651, which is less than a half in comparison with the earnings of the university graduates, whereas for the nontertiary higher education graduates with a college diploma or an associate degree the income was 74%, which represents an approximate of two-thirds of the total income of the university graduates.

In terms of each and every level of education, women are in a better position in terms of the increase in income. Both women and men without a high-school diploma experienced a decrease in their income as a result of inflation starting from 1979. As a result of the inflation adjustment, the incomes of the women who are high-school graduates had a 32% increase in 1979, while the men's decreased by only 18% during the same period of time.

Patrenostru (1999), using the data of the *Integrated Enquiry in the Households 1914* in Romania, observed that an increase in the benefits of education and of the experience was very important both for women and for men both in rural and in urban areas. Moreover, in rural areas, especially for women, the benefits of education are higher than those in urban areas. To analyze the determining factors of the salary incomes that are earned both by men and by women in the public and private sectors, Skoufias' (2003) empirical study used specific data taken from the same transversal structures, namely, from *Integrated Enquiry for Households 1994*. As far as the public sector is concerned, the association between the levels of education and the marginal ratio of the education's benefits must be taken into account. It has a lower value for women than for men. In terms of the private sector, which was developing at the moment when the analysis was conducted, high-school education generated a higher marginal ratio for women than for men. The pay gap between men and women is higher for the private sector than for the public sector (i.e., 24.9% and 15.4%). The specialized studies in which Romania appears, Ion (2013), Voinea (2011), Andrén (2005) estimate the impact of the years of study on the monthly incomes in the period 1950–2000, at an almost constant value of 3–4% in the years of socialist education, the coefficient of the years of study in the equation of regression of earnings increased continuously throughout the '90s, reaching 8.5% in 2000. This aspect is linked with the forecasts based on the macroeconomic data for southeastern Europe, according to which an extra school year will lead to an increase of 8.5% of the salary.

Despite the abovementioned facts, recent studies have increasingly insisted on the necessity of considering the relationship between the level of education and the evolution of earnings as one with rather qualitative implications than one based on *quantitative inputs*. Despite the fact that the relationship between education and individual performance seems to be clear, there is still ambiguity regarding the way education has an impact on the increase in incomes. The challenge for economists refers to the following aspects: the way the resources allocated for education turn into certain effects of a certain quality. The most difficult task is undoubtedly to measure the quality of the educational *inputs*, which refer to the acquired skills of the individuals as a result of being educated in a formal educational system. However, some authors suggest the use of the students' evaluation tests as a possible useful tool in this respect (Hanushek 2010).

Figure 4.8 highlights the estimations regarding the evolution of earnings based on the Mincerian equation (i.e., the columns of the graph), namely, the way those estimations are adjusted as a result of the calculation and the IALS (i.e., International Adult Literacy Survey) test results. For

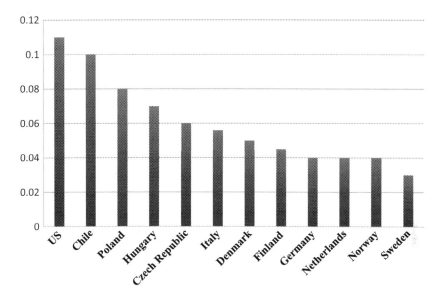

Fig. 4.8   Rates of earnings based on the school years. Source: Hanushek and Wossmann (2007). *The Role of Education Quality in Economic Growth,* World Bank Policy Research Working Paper 4122, p. 15

example, Finland performs the best in terms of the quality of mathematical and science types of education. This fact confirms the PISA (i.e., Programme for International Student Assessment) test results.

According to the PISA study (hotnews.ro), which was designed by the Organization for Economic Cooperation and Development (OECD) and conducted in 2012, which evaluated over 510,000 students from 65 countries in the fields of mathematics, literacy, and science, in the mathematics field, Romania scored 445 points (with 4.9% over the last score in 2009) in comparison with 494 representing the average score of the OECD countries and 613 the best score in the reference year, which was registered in Shanghai, China. The top position in the mathematics field with the best results is occupied by students from Shanghai, China, and Singapore. The countries that come right after are as follows: Hong Kong, Taiwan, South Korea, Macao, Japan, Liechtenstein, Switzerland, and Netherlands. Some countries, such as Cyprus and Bulgaria, scored lower, whereas Romania is part of the group of countries with results that are "statistically significantly lower than the average of the OECD." Mathematics has been the reference point, according to OECD, because it is considered that these competences from the *hard* zone are the key elements for the future results of the young adults. These results will have a long-term impact on their ability to continue their university studies and on their future income (Caraiani et al., 2020).

If we make reference to the position of Romania in the field of literacy, we have discovered that it occupies the 50th position out of 65, scoring 438 points compared to the average 496 points of the OECD countries, the top position being occupied by Shanghai, China. In descending order, the ranking continues with much lower scores for Bulgaria, Kazakhstan, Malaysia, Mexico, Montenegro, Uruguay, Albania, Brazil, Argentine, Tunis, Jordan, Colombia, Qatar, Indonesia, and Peru. In the field of science, Romania occupies the 49th position with 439 points in comparison with 501 points as the average of the OECD countries. These educational results have been influenced, on the one hand, by the students' social and economic situation affecting the level of performance, and consequently, it is highly likely that those coming from families with low income or from immigrant families have poor scores in literacy, mathematics, and science.

This type of evaluation is an obvious progress in terms of identifying the means of obtaining a better understanding of the way education is related to an increase in income. However, we believe that this type of evaluation has some drawbacks. As we tend to focus on the quality of education, we believe that its evaluation based on certain simplified and general tests fails to explain both the evolution and the distinction of earnings on the labor market. The fact that certain activities require specific skills that cannot be evaluated based on the abovementioned test is a solid reason in this respect. Moreover, certain activities generate higher incomes as a result of work experience and are proven based on the existing competition in the market.

The trajectory of education–income–productivity has been frequently studied in the economics specialty literature due to its role in ensuring a nation's economic prosperity. The nation's standard of living is given by the economy's productivity, which is measured as a value of the production of goods and services that have been achieved per resource unit (knowledge, capital, human resources, natural resources). We can thus state that productivity is responsible for the standard of living for a region or for a country based on incomes, capital gains, or other resources. Any modern society's goal is accomplished through the creation of an advanced economy as a result of the effort and the training of the human factor in using as efficiently as possible each and every natural, human, and financial resource. Efficiency represents the key word when implementing best practices in the field. It depends to a great extent on the quality of the workforce and the human factor. Consequently, the continuous updating of higher training and education represents the essential factor in using human resources efficiently. Recent studies have highlighted the existence of a tight relationship between education and work productivity. The concept of the quality of work as a component of a competitive economy has several facets that refer to the level of education, the quality of the workplace, life-long learning, health, gender equality, inclusion and access to the labor market, social cohesion, and performance. People with their skills and abilities, with their experience and acquired knowledge, are the manufacturers of all the economic goods (Pupăzan Mungiu & Vasilescu, 2011).

Nelson and Phelps stated that an educated workforce eliminated the actual technological barriers and facilitated increases in productivity. As far as the developed economies are concerned, there are strong relationships between education and productivity, education and salaries, salaries and productivity, and, consequently, productivity and economic growth. Education, in this relationship, provides the reason why more educated individuals earn more. This statement is supported from two points of view: on the one hand, university graduates tend to be compensated for their studies, whereas, on the other hand, educated individuals demonstrate their ability to more efficiently use the resources of the economy to produce a profit (Fig. 4.9).

In a study designed by the American Organization, "Partnership for 21st Century Skills," which is made up of educational institutions, foundations, and American business people, the profile of the university graduate was compiled according to the exigencies of the twenty-first-century economy. Based on this model, the key position for the individual's economic success refers to the set of knowledge and skills related to standards, the curriculum, the goals of his professional development, and the quality of the educational environment.

According to the model shown in Fig. 4.10, the set of competences as a result of the educational system focused both on establishing the production and on the consumption potentials, which, in turn, will influence a country's micro- and macroeconomic performances. By being part of the establishment of a set of competences, education will ensure the

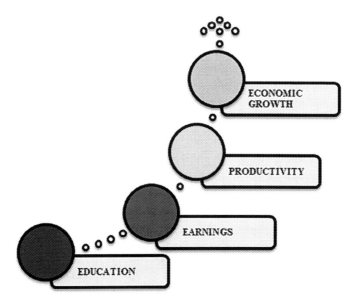

Fig. 4.9 Education, income, productivity. Source: adapted after Nelson and Phelps (1966) *Investment in Humans, Technological Diffusion and Economic Growth*, The American Economic Review, Vol. 56, No. 1/2, pp. 69–75

conditions that will enable both the efficient involvement of the human component within the economic resources system and their expansion on the productivity of the entire economic system based on technological development.

The empirical studies have demonstrated the statistical relationship between work productivity and the average results of the PISA (2000–2009) testing on a sample of eighteen countries that were grouped into three blocks according to their social and economic development. Consequently, the increase in GDP given the high PISA results is the consequence of the increase in the workforce's productivity resulting from the skills acquired through the educational system, which, in turn, is expressed by the statistical data. The positive dependence that manifests among these factors suggests the existence of certain channels of conveying cognitive skills as a result of a certain level of education influencing work productivity, although the correlation ratio is placed in the area of the average correlations (r=0.41) as one transmission channel crosses innovation activity. The

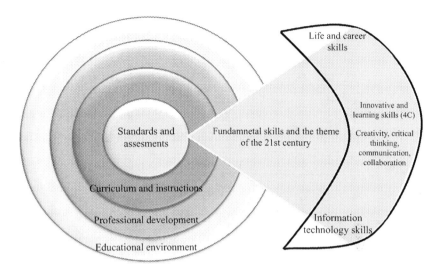

Fig. 4.10 Adjustment after the *output* model of the educational system in the USA. Source: adapted after *21st Century Skills, Education & Competitiveness, A Resource and Policy Guide*, (2008), www.21stcenturyskills.org. p. 13, accessed on 10.08.2015

statistical data shown in appendix no. 7 demonstrate the existence of a positive correlation between PISA testing and the innovative performance of Bucoş (2014).

Moreover, the cross-referencing of the PISA results with the investments in the research and development has shown that the excellent results of the PISA testing have been associated with high investment ratios in research and development, which is a clear indication of the tendency of decreasing yield along with decreasing cognitive skills acquired within national educational systems.

Last but not least, the high scores of the PISA tests have also been associated with a high number of patenting requests per million persons. This will have an impact on national work productivity.

To highlight the abovementioned dependencies (Fig. 4.11), a correlation has been made between these results and work productivity based on the number of applications for the patent of the inventions in cutting-edge technologies (Bucoş, 2014).

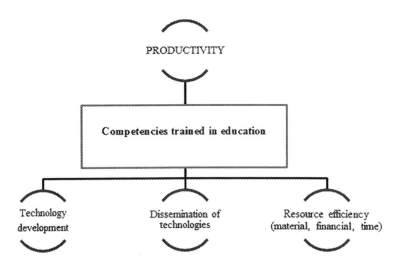

Fig. 4.11   Skills resulting from the educational system and productivity. Source: author's contribution

The analysis itself has emphasized the existence of an excessive sensitivity of the patent applications for the ability of the educational system to create cognitive skills, as the flexibility ratio within the linear regression accounts for 57%. Playing its part, the high ratio of patent applications of innovations in cutting-edge technologies will ensure an increase in labor productivity nationally with an estimated sensitivity of 22.5% (Bucoş, 2014). Moreover, there is a close and stable relationship between the quality of the workforce and economic growth. Hanusek believed that the estimated value of the ratio of cognitive abilities suggests that an increase with a standard deviation from the test results (or with 100 points on the PISA scale) will generate an annual rate of economic growth of 1.74 percentage points. The explanation in terms of a better performance of 100 PISA points results from the estimation done by the OCDE, according to which 39 points equal one school year. The estimations show that if Romania were to reach the OECD average (i.e., 500 points), the GDP could have a 0.95% increase.

We believe that the main self-expansion and development of the human factor, of a superior capitalization of the creative and proactive potentialities of the human being, represent the training and refinement process, which can be cumulated and expanded on a long-term basis and on several levels. As a priority, we would like to mention the improvement of the level of education, culture, and knowledge of technical and professional training according to the employability demands of the economic sector and the skills of society's human resources. By analyzing these aspects from a different angle, some countries are focused on producing highly qualified individuals, a high percentage of university graduates who fail to actually respond to the market's demands due to erroneous policies. All the skills and knowledge that are acquired by the educated individuals fail to target the right places: engineers work as bus drivers or migrate to rich countries, the accountants work as salespersons in stores, and the list goes on. This aspect implies many more issues related to the recruitment of the candidates based on their experience detrimental to their education and the small differences between the incomes of a university graduate and a high-school graduate. This is the reason why we have left plenty of room for future addendums in the following chapters.

REFERENCES

Andersson, A. E. (2009). *Returns to Higher Education*, CESIS Electronic Working Paper Series, Paper No. 163, The Royal Institute of Technology Centre of Excellence for Science and Innovation Studies.

Becker, G. (1994). *Human Capital – A Theoretical and Empiric Analysis with Special Attention Given to Education* (p. 59). ALL Publishing-house, Bucharest.

Bucoş, T. (2014). *Education - Key Factor in the Capitalization of the National Economic Prospective*, doctoral thesis, Chişinău, pp. 81-82.

Caraiani, P., Dutescu, A., Hoinaru, R., & Stănilă, G. O. (2020). Production Network Structure and the Impact of the Monetary Policy Shocks: Evidence from the OECD. *Economics Letters, 193*, 109271.

Cojocaru, V., & Făuraş, C. (2006). *Education as Part of an Economic Approach* (p. 10). Academy of Economic Studies of Moldova Publishing-house.

Costache, L. coord. UNICEF (2014). *The Cost of the Poor Investment in Education in Romania*, Alpha MDN Publishing-house, Bucharest, p.54.

Friedman, M. (1955). *The Role of Government in Education. From Economics and the Public Interest*, ed. Robert A. Solo, by the Trustees of Rutgers College in New Jersey. Reprinted by permission of Rutgers University Press, p.22.

Lucas, R. (1988). On the Mechanics Development. *Journal of Monetary Economics, 22*(1), 3–42.

Mincer, J. (1970). The Distribution of Labor Incomes: A Survey With Special Reference to the Approach on the Human Capital. *Economics Journal, 8*(1), 8. electronic format on *www.kumlai.free.fr*

Neamtu, D., & Scurtu, L. (2013). *Education, Welfare and Economic Growth, Post Crisis Economy: Challenges and Opportunities, "Lucian Blaga"* (pp. 161–168). University of Sibiu Publishing-House.

Nelson, R. R., & Phelps, E. S. (1966). Investment in Humans, Technological Diffusion and Economic Growth. *The American Economic Review, 56*(1/2), 69–75.

OECD. (2012). *Highlights from Education at a Glance* (pp. 38–40). OECD Publishing. http://www.oecd.org/edu/highlights.pdf.

Psacharopoulos, G., & Patrinos, H. A. (2004). Returns to Investment in Education: A Further Update. *Education Economics, 12*(2), 16.

Pupăzan Mungiu, M. C., & Vasilescu, M. (2011). *Productivity – A Means of Expressing the Economic Performance and Efficiency*, Annals of "Constantin Brâncuşi" University, No.3, Series of Economics, Târgu Jiu, p. 126.

Suciu, M. C. (2000). *Investing in Education* (pp. 68–70). The Economics Publishing-House.

Symanski, D. M., & Henard, D. H. (2001). Customer Satisfaction: A Meta-Analysis of the Empirical Evidence. *Journal of Academy of Marketing Science, 29*(1), 16–35.

Tilak, J. (2003). *Higher Education and Development* (p. 3). International Seminar: University XXI, Brazil.

Zgreabăn, I. E. (2011). *Education from an Economic Point of View, Case Studies: Romania*, doctoral thesis, The Academy of Economic Sciences of Bucharest, pp. 35-36

CHAPTER 5

Higher Education for the Social and Economic Development

Higher education is the educational level facilitated by the successful completion of a university study program. Given the confusion that may result from the use and translation of terms from one system to another, depending on the country, we use as an explanation the fact that higher education complements secondary education, providing learning activities in specialized fields of education and aiming at learning at a high level of complexity and specialization. An immediate delimitation is necessary in the sense of understanding what is predominantly interpreted in practice, namely the distinction between tertiary[1] education and higher (university) education. The latter is part of the first one, taking place mainly in universities and other institutes of this type, not including advanced vocational education and professional education.

A clear classification of higher education worldwide is given by the OECD through *The International Standard Classification of Education* (ISCED) system (UNESCO, 2011, applied since 1970, in the idea of ensuring a standardized basis of statistical reporting in education, through which a clear comparison between states can be made. Over time, it has been operated with several versions of the methodology, the last being

---

[1] At national level, according to the stipulations of the National Education Law no. 1/2011 with subsequent amendments, "tertiary education" is defined as that educational sector which includes higher education and nonuniversity tertiary education (post-high schools).

D.-M. Neamțu, *Education and Economic Development*, https://doi.org/10.1007/978-3-031-20382-4_5

ISCED 2011, which facilitates the transformation of national education data into internationally agreed categories because education systems vary in terms of content from one country to another and need a common reference denominator. In this respect, higher education comprises ISCED levels 5, 6, 7, and 8, generally referred to as "short-term higher education," "bachelor's education or its equivalent," and "doctoral education or its equivalent." Higher education in Romania includes not only academic education (ISCED 5, 6, 7, 8) but also advanced vocational education (ISCED 5), the programs of this level being offered by educational institutions, different from those at level ISCED 6, 7, 8.

Higher education levels, starting predominantly with ISCED 5, are the main steps at which young people choose to enter the labor market, which is also due to reaching the minimum legal working ages. Once with higher education, specializations begin to develop, many necessary for better insertion into the labor market and a match with their workforce needs. The main institutions that provide higher education are universities and polytechnics (technical and technological academic institutions), regardless of whether they are public or private. At the global level, higher education is often confused with tertiary education; in some cases, the two terms are similar, or their differentiation is insignificant. In others, some clarifications are necessary, as shown in Fig. 5.1. The international definition of tertiary education (postsecondary education) is divided into two parts, namely type A higher education and type B supplementary education. A qualification in higher education at grade level needs a minimum term of three years to be obtained, or in some cases four, even five. It will have a theoretical basis, will be at a level that would qualify someone to work in a professional field, and will usually be taught in an environment that also includes advanced research activity. In short, higher education means, mainly and in general, university-level education.

In the area of higher education, university education does not encompass vocational education and *training*, known as further education in the United Kingdom or *continuing education* in the United States (Şerbu, 2012). University education involves obtaining a university degree (bachelor's, master's, doctor's) in addition to the certificates or diplomas specific to vocational education or *training*. They are recognized around the world as specialized expertise supported by a wide range of skills that employers find very useful. For example, the World Bank, in numerous studies, equates the two terms "tertiary – superior." In this scientific

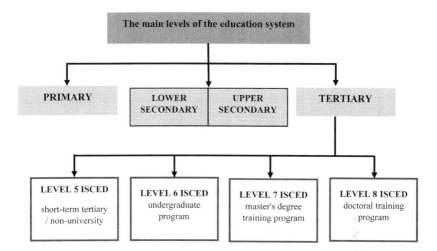

Fig. 5.1 The classification and the importance of the main levels of higher education according to ISCED 2011. Source: author contributions based on UNESCO data, Institute for Statistics (2011) *International Standard Classification of Education*, ISCED

approach, we use the concept of higher education with special reference to university level education (ISCED 6,7,8—as referred previously within Fig. 5.1).

The contribution of higher education to economic growth presupposes the dynamic interaction of several factors. First, it is increasingly obvious that higher education contributes to economic growth through the "production of knowledge, research," which takes place within leading universities through activities in the field. Second, it is recognized that universities and colleges contribute to national economic growth through "knowledge dissemination," resulting from positive feedback. Last but not least, it is known that higher education contributes to the "transmission of knowledge" through extensive and varied teaching activities. Economists have focused on these activities, which can be quantified by enrollment, by the number of graduates who complete postsecondary education, by the degree of graduation of university education, and by the expenses and incomes of students (Becker and Lewis 2003).

In the current transformation of nations, in which all the pillars of economic, social, political, and civic order have known a new dynamic, in an attempt to adapt to the present conditions, the contribution of higher education becomes increasingly evident in Romanian society. Universities have frequently been perceived as key institutions in the processes of social change and development. The most explicit role assigned to them was highly skilled labor productivity and the conduct of research processes to meet the economic needs perceived by society. Higher education contributes not only to the training of competent workers but also to the creation of a workforce eager to acquire new knowledge, which contributes to social and economic growth and development. Higher education creates new attitudes and produces vision changes necessary for the socialization of individuals and for the modernization and transformation of societies. Finally, higher education helps to form a strong nation-state not only through teaching and research but also through the absorption and dissemination of knowledge.

The need to draw attention to the importance of the human element brings to the fore the need for the development of human resources from the perspective of learning and self-improvement throughout life.

We live in a time when knowledge is increasingly important for the development of contemporary societies and economies in a world of rapidly circulating capital with revolutionary people and communication technologies. In this context, knowledge is becoming the main engine of economic growth, and education has become increasingly the foundation for individual prosperity and social mobility. The research undertaken on the link between higher education and well-being is not new but is still up to date. Several empirical studies in the literature have focused on the effects that different levels of education have on economic growth. From this perspective, the results obtained converge on the fact that higher education has a greater influence on economic growth in developed countries, while in the case of developing countries, basic and secondary education are priorities. Examples of this are the studies of Psacharopoulos and Patrinos (2002), Petrakis and Stamatakis (2002), Papageorgiou (2003), Teles and Andrade (2008), Vandenbussche, Aghion and Meghir (2006), according to which higher education has a strong effect on economic growth. "Higher education is necessary to satisfy some of the high aspirations of a society. Historians, archaeologists and men of letters have reviewed the past and present in a way that shapes the future and nourishes the roots that bind communities together. Universities, both students and professors everywhere, are uniquely motivated to keep alive the values of freedom and universality – of individual dignity, as well as the brotherhood of people. Additionally, universities are generally the biggest source of change, not just technological changes but also social and cultural changes." Patel, 2003

In Romania, during the nineteenth century, authors of economic studies such as I. Ghica and P. S. Aurelian saw in education the step toward modernity and civilization. In his work *Economic Works*, D. Xenopol emphasized a reality that was not given the necessary attention: "always the intellectual brilliance of a people has been like a flowering of the material welfare" and between "the material and the intellectual state of a people," there is an indestructible relationship in which "the material is the means and the essential condition of the intellectual's development" (Xenopol 1967).

In recent decades, more than ever, politicians in different states have turned their attention to higher education. Everywhere, higher education was considered to be *the key to the growth and development of national economies* (George, 2006. The role of higher education is not limited only to promoting the economic development of states and providing various opportunities for individuals but also extends to supporting cultural diversity and political and commercial democracy (Marginson, 2010). Higher education and its products generate significant effects at the local, regional, and global levels, making in this context a priority both for individuals and for society.

In the US, a recent study highlighted that the proportion of individuals who believe that higher education is *absolutely necessary for success* increased from 31% in 2005 to 55% in 2009. There are countless data that support these perceptions: the U.S. statistics office has found that an *American student educated* in a college earns, over the course of his life, twice as much as an individual with a *high school degree*. Higher education generates both broad economic growth and individual success. For example, a recent study found that the academic environment contributed almost 60 billion to the UK economy between 2007 and 2008. This impact, of course, is visible not only at the national level but also globally.

A multitude of ideas and innovations accompany the proliferation of exchange between universities, faculty, and students. For the past decade alone, UNESCO reports a 57% increase in those studying outside their home country. Examples of this trend of growth, exchange, and collaboration include the following:

- the recently expanded ERASMUS study program of the European Union sends hundreds of thousands of students to 4000 institutions in 33 countries each year;
- Persian Gulf states have recruited *international branches* with investments of hundreds of millions of dollars—*Education City* in Doha involves six American universities on 14 square kilometers of land. The new campus of the university in New York in *Abu Dhabi* opened in the fall of 2010, preparing for the enrollment of students from over 39 countries. We can count over 162 branch campuses of Western universities in Asia and the Middle East—which means a 43% increase in just three years; Singapore hosts 90,000 international students, as well as a campus of INSEAD—the *European Institute of Business Administration* and cooperation programs with at least four American universities;
- China has projected an explosion in higher education, the most dramatic in human history. Between 1999 and 2005, the number of people *who had a diploma* increased four times—more than 3 million euros. By the end of calendar year 2014, China is expected to become the largest producer of doctorates (PhDs), scientists, and engineers;
- In India, the number of participating universities doubled in the 1990s, and demand continues to grow. India's Ministry of Human Resources Development stated that India needs more than 800 new higher education institutions by 2020, with the aim of increasing *the participation rate* from 12.4% to 30%;
- In Ireland, the *age rate of participation* increased from 11% in 1965 to 57% in 2003 and from 2013 to 68%.

It is noticed that these partnerships have blossomed boundlessly, in a way that truly matters—improving life in various aspects. Among other studies, documents, and data, the contribution of higher education to economic development has been demonstrated in a context with data collected from 49 countries in the Asia-Pacific region (Tilak, 2003. Using the gross registration rate and the higher education graduation rate as indicators, the results of the research showed that both can have positive effects at the level of economic development, with the measurement being made at the level of gross domestic product (GDP) per capita. It has also been demonstrated through this research that the prospects for economic development increase with the number of the population with higher education. Krueger and Lindahl (2001) believe that the education system is the key to a nation's economic growth. In this respect, the differences between the developed and the less developed countries are largely due to the education of the members of these nations, and Mankiw, Romer, and Weil (1992) reinforce this point of view, considering that education is the key element in explaining the economic growth of different states.

National agendas place increasing emphasis on higher education policies. A widespread of these ideas in a global knowledge-based economy is also because higher education is a major contribution to economic competitiveness, which has made quality tertiary education a more important objective than ever, both in developing and industrialized countries.

Higher education contributes to economic and social development through four main missions, according to a study by the Organization for Economic Co-operation and Development (OECD, 2008):

- human capital formation (through teaching);
- building the foundations of knowledge (through research and knowledge development);
- dissemination and use of knowledge (through interaction between researchers);
- maintenance and preservation of knowledge (through their transmission between generations);

Currently, higher education has diversified greatly for a number of reasons such as creating a closer link that reflects the reality between higher education and the world in which we live, with a more careful focus on the needs of the labor market, ensuring geographical and social access to university education, and providing professional training based more on practice than on theory. To be able to correlate the increasing diversity of qualifications with the expectations of graduates, in the context of a constantly changing world, from a technological point of view, higher education plays an important role in the economic development of nations.

Some countries, such as the Philippines or Thailand, which have a medium or high level of registration index, are classified as "dynamic leaders." The other countries, which do not place so much emphasis on the development of the higher education system, tend to be "marginalised." There is no country that reaches a medium or high level of technology index among those that have a low level (below 10%) of the registration index in higher education.

The idea that higher education and economic growth are pillars in a relationship of dependency is not supported by all researchers in the field. Important research has shown that often the direct or indirect economic impact of universities on the regions or local communities, of which they are a part, is overestimated. Research has been conducted in the US to examine whether large investments in higher education indeed have the expected effect and offer increased returns for the local economy.

Research by Vedder in the U.S. has shown that states that allocate more funds to universities or colleges do not have rapid economic growth compared to those that allocate low funds. This study, having no intention of doubting that higher education is an important factor in promoting economic growth, suggested that the return on public investment in university education is limited. Bloom and others have put to the test the old international claim that tertiary education has a minor role in promoting economic growth, and reviews of their studies have highlighted the impact that higher education can have on poverty reduction and economic growth in Sub-Saharan Africa, where the registration rate is the lowest in the world (approximately 5%). The bloom authors and others confirm Tilak's findings, listed earlier, according to which one of the possible ways in which developing countries can strengthen their economic growth with the help of higher education is technological development. In an economy of knowledge, higher education can help nations gain ground in what technologically advanced societies mean through graduates of university studies, who are more aware of the importance of new technologies and who are able to use it.

Recent evidence suggests that higher education has a double nature and is both the result and a determinant of revenue, which can produce public and private benefits. Higher education can increase tax revenues, increase savings and investments, and lead to a society with a civic and entrepreneurial spirit. It can also contribute to improving a nation's health, developing technology, and strengthening governance.

The public benefits are less recognized, which explains the disinterest of most governments in using higher education as an engine of public investment. This does not prevent society as a whole from benefiting from the footsteps of individual earnings. The financial needs of states and taxes collected by governments are strengthened by the high incomes of highly educated people. These incomes also bring increases in market consumption, from which producers benefit, regardless of the education they have.

The World Bank's strategy takes into account the fact that to make higher education an engine of economic development, it is necessary to adopt a number of policies of good practice. Among them, we mention:

- development of a national strategy for human resources development;
- granting institutional autonomy associated with appropriate accounting mechanisms that allow the development of opportunities for system differentiation and institutional innovation;
- reforming the financing arrangements to provide incentives to achieve policy objectives while providing the necessary stability to institutions in strategic planning;
- encouraging diversity in teaching and assimilating approaches to facilitate the specialization of institutions;
- promoting the development of regional and national postgraduate programs—the best way to strengthen the academic staff and the research capacity;
- looking for alternatives for low costs of accessing tertiary education.

As J. D. Wolfensohn stated in 2000: "It is impossible to have a complete education system without an adequate and strong system of higher education. ... I am not suggesting for a moment that primary and secondary education are not at the heart of development ... [but these two forms] are not enough. We need to have centers of excellence, learning and training, if we are going to eradicate the problem of poverty in developing countries ... the key is higher education, not just in terms of technology, but in creating people who are smart enough to be able to design and use it."

References

George, St. E. (2006). *Positioning Higher Education for the Knowledge Based Economy*, Higher Education. http://www.anc.edu.ro/uploads/images/Legislatie/ISCED_2011_UNESCO_RO_final.pdf, accessed on 9.08.2015, p.45.

Marginson, S. (2010). *Higher Education in the Global Knowledge Economy*, Procedia Social and Behavioral Science, p. 696.

Patel, I. G. (2003). *Higher education and economic development* (p. 668). Publishing Corporation New Delhi: National Institute of Educational Planning and Administration.

Șerbu, M. V. (2012). *The Interdependence Between Higher Education and Economic Development with Reference to the Requirements of the Labor Market*, PhD thesis, The Academy of Economics Studies of Bucharest, pp. 25–26.

Tilak, J. B. T. (2003). *Higher education and development.* Int Seminar, University XXI, Brazil.

UNESCO, Institute for Statistics. (2011). *International standard classification of education.* ISCED.

PART II

Practice Beats Theory

CHAPTER 6

Case Studies of Best Practices in Higher Education

Globalization is the most important phenomenon in the contemporary world. It comes with a network structure of societies creating the world's virtual space, which will complement the physical space. Becoming immediately a slogan, a magical incantation for unraveling all the mysteries of present and future, the word "globalization" sits on everyone's lips, characterized more by ubiquity than by precision.

Bringing up the importance of economic growth, we reiterate the idea that education is a component of economic policies, which contributes to the improvement of the living standards of individuals to aspiration, to a higher condition, regardless of the present. The less skillful subsequently take over the successful experiences of the former, who set the tone for new trends and try to adapt them to their own requirements.

This new and complex reality of today's world, whether we know it or not, whether we like it or not, and whether we support or reject it, is moving forward increasingly, encompassing ever-increasing social spaces and human destinies. At the same time, globalization facilitates the process of cultural transmission, namely, of preferences, values, and norms of behavior, through intercultural dialog as a result of social interactions on a global scale. In this context, descending from the ivory tower of abstract constructions, in this chapter, we have proposed highlighting some examples of good practices in the field of education and investment in education, which have proven to be real successes and socioeconomic progress.

© The Author(s), under exclusive license to Springer Nature Switzerland AG 2023
D.-M. Neamțu, *Education and Economic Development*,
https://doi.org/10.1007/978-3-031-20382-4_6

The eloquent examples were chosen based on the research and benchmarking indicators, which we will expose in depth in the ninth chapter and can constitute a veritable collection of *best practices*,[1] together with the other constituent elements.

THE UNITED KINGDOM

With a well-deserved reputation as Europe's "science engine", the United Kingdom attracts the most renowned academics and private sector specialists, providing a friendly space for students from all over the world. Statistics explain that approximately 2 million students study in universities and university colleges in the United Kingdom, 5% come from member states of the European Union and 6% come from other countries. Higher education in the United Kingdom is characterized by diversity and wealth in all its spheres: financial, curricular, managerial, educational, and research offers. Being known for steadfastness, it constantly cultivates a very own education system, capitalizing on the principles of social democracy on the basis of British tradition. This classical stability and tendency of British education is because it preserves through traditions and customs a stable education through its best and best, operating with great caution in the field of changes in educational doctrine and in the policy that determines it essentially.

The fundamental objectives of higher education in this country can be formulated as follows:

- gives people the opportunity to develop their skills and to capitalize on their intellectual potential both personally and for working in an organized environment;
- contributes to the economic and cultural success of a diverse nation;
- contributes to the advancement of understanding and knowledge through learning and research.

[1] *Best practices*, an expression derived from English made up of (*best*-optimal and *practice*-clientele, skill, habit, exercise) and represents, in this endeavor, successful experiences, and examples of good practices.

The most important universities in the United Kingdom have become famous, especially due to the offer of postgraduate master's and doctoral programs, four of the top six universities in the world being in the United Kingdom. The duration of postgraduate programs can be one year through intensive courses and two or three years for research courses. We must emphasize the special importance of university scientific research in UK, in particular, in that there is a very strong tradition of this.

The contribution of scientific research in the United Kingdom is estimated at 5.5% of the world, and 8% of all scientific journals are published in this country. It is indeed a record that impresses and stresses, once again, that performance means tradition, proper funding, and quality (Brătianu and Atanasiu 2002).

The tuition costs for undergraduate studies vary between £6000 and £9000/year for state universities, and students can opt for other funding opportunities such as university scholarships (£500–2000/year), *part-time jobs*[2] (£400/month—minimum), and *Tuition Fee Loan*.[3] Almost three-quarters of the United Kingdom's higher education funds come from the private system, which has doubled in the last ten years.

- Population with higher education: 39.4%
- Average annual growth level: 4%
- Share of expenditure on education in GDP: 6.5%

According to Organization for Economic Co-operation and Development (OECD) analysts, investments in the education system are

[2] *Job part-time*, a word borrowed from the English language consisting of (*part*—part; and *time*—time) which represents a part-time job, incomplete norm.

[3] *Tuition Fee Loan* is a government loan that fully covers the tuition fee for students admitted to a bachelor's degree program in the United Kingdom at a state university. All students in the European Union can apply for this loan, which is automatically granted without selection. Being a loan, it will have to be repaid only after completing studies, provided that the annual income exceeds a certain threshold depending on the country where one chooses to stay after completing studies. For example, if a student chooses to stay in the United Kingdom after completing his or her studies, he or she will not start repaying the loan until his or her annual income is over £21,000/year. Once it has reached this threshold, he/she will start to repay gradually, through the national tax system, a percentage of the amount exceeding this threshold. If he/she earns £21,100/year, in the following year he/she will repay 9% of £100 (£9), leaving his/her income very little affected. This loan has no bank interest, but it is adjusted annually to the inflation rate. http://adevarul.ro/educatie/studii-in-strainatate/sistemul-universitar-marea-britanie 1_50a51a867c42d5a66368effe/index.html

bearing fruit, given the number and training of graduates. Over the past decade, the United Kingdom has become one of the most attractive destinations for students around the world, surpassed only by the United States.

SWEDEN

Sweden, an open multicultural society, seems to have the role of promoter of a new model, not only in family behaviors but also in the evolution of the relationship between education and work. Higher education in Sweden complies with the rules of the Bologna system and is therefore similar to that in Romania and other European Union countries. Sweden is an egalitarian society with a single education system, so the Education Act provides equal rights to education for all young people regardless of gender, nationality, or social status. The emphasis is also on values, on learning by doing, and most importantly on innovative thinking, which is indispensable for a sustainable, modern society. The academic path is quite open, the student not being obliged only to a common core, having for the rest access to a free of choice curriculum: "it seems that there is a great freedom that comes with a great responsibility." Being a country with an interesting, creative, and tolerant culture, with horizons open to democratic dialog and inclusion, all this argues Sweden's long tradition in the education of international students.

Public education in Sweden is free of charge, subsidized by the Swedish state. There are 61 higher education institutions in Sweden. Of these, 14 are public universities, 22 are public university colleges, 3 are private universities, 9 are private university colleges, and 13 are private organizations that have the right to give ratings in the field of psychotherapy. The oldest is the University of Uppsala, founded in 1477, and 9 of the 61 institutions of higher education are among the top 500 best universities in the world. The Swedish are very attached to the idea that the state is a kind of "house of the people." Everyone in Swedish society is under the same roof, and everyone will be protected. The country is sixth in the Human Development Index of the United Nations (UN) Development Programme, and UNICEF ranks second in terms of the well-being of children's lives. Sweden is part of the group of Scandinavian countries, which is clearly distinguished by the education policy pursued.

The government stresses the importance of strong education through grants. The granting of subsidies in Sweden and, in general, in education in the Scandinavian countries can only be justified on two grounds: efficiency and equity. Moreover, subsidies to education are considered necessary to facilitate access to all types of education, regardless of parents' income. Subsidies to education in Sweden and Finland for tertiary education are particularly high. They do not correct market failures, nor do they generate equality to a greater extent.

It is worth pointing out that Sweden is spending considerable sums to make an important contribution to a more dynamic and flexible economy, in which unemployed people engage more quickly with the help of retraining.

- Highly educated population: 30.4%
- Average annual growth rate: 3.6%
- Share of expenditures on education from GDP: 7%

POLAND

Poland managed to develop a high-performance education system, a quarter of a century after 1989, when it came out from the communist regime, occupying the top PISA tests (Programme for International Student Assessment) and having the fastest growth among the developed states of the world. An essential element of Poland's success was the ability of decision-makers to rethink the education system through the reforms implemented in the late 1990s and early 2000s. To be able to observe the evolution of Polish education, we also consider the context of the functioning of Poland as a state.

Since joining the European Union in 2004, Poland has made considerable and continuous progress, above all, from an economic point of view: it is one of the fastest growing countries in the EU economy, with a GDP per capita of $12,700, in 2013. It ranks first in the top beneficiaries of European funds, considered vectors, in terms of education development. A key principle of reform in the education system was the examination system at the end of each educational cycle. In this way, the aim was to lower the school dropout rate and improve the quality of education.

A series of reforms have also been implemented in the functioning of teaching staff. In short, the promotion and motivation of teachers with good salaries and bonuses is based on the degree of training and performance of teachers. The average salary in Poland is 750 euros per month, which is higher than in neighboring countries but still very low according to Western standards. All these factors have led to a spectacular increase in the quality of Polish education, which was visible in the PISA-type OECD test results.

Poland, traditionally imitating the German model, has a highly valued system of higher education and an impressive number of universities, some of which are of international repute. Jagiellonian University of Kraków was created in 1364, the second oldest in Central Europe after the University of Prague, Karolinum, dating from 1348. University studies last three years in the case of the bachelor's degree cycle and two years for the master's degree, according to the Bologna Process, except for the Law that lasts five years.

The Organization for Economic Co-operation and Development (OECD) recently criticized Poland, in a study on Polish education (Dziewulak 2013)—Poland being considered to be part of countries with a modern and efficient education—for the fact that the strategies used do not take into account, in a real way, the activity of students after completing higher education. Even though Poland has undeniably succeeded in ensuring broad autonomy for universities, higher education is not anchored to the needs of the market. In this respect, the OECD recommends Poland to improve the system of granting scholarships while drawing attention to the high tuition costs.

- Highly educated population: 20%
- Average annual level of growth: 2.5%
- Share of education expenditure on GDP: 5%

The revised education system meant the application by educational institutions of the best universal practices, the support of teachers in the process of permanently improving their teaching strategies, and, last but not least, the adoption of innovative and proactive visions in relation to all the aspects that the educational process involves.

SOUTH KOREA: THE MIRACLE ON THE HAN RIVER

Additionally, called the "Land of Quiet Mornings", South Korea is one of the most beautiful settlements, positioned in the south of the Korean Peninsula, with the greatest geostrategic importance in the area between the colossi of the East Asian continent, China and Japan. Being at the forefront of cutting-edge technology, it experienced rapid economic development, becoming the *Miracle on the Han River* within 50 years, with the end of the Korean War (1953). Known by the pseudonym of the Asian tiger, along with other Asian tigers, South Korea still has the spirit of a state with a long history, a country where ancestral traditions, such as Confucian heritage, continue to thrive and cohabit with ultramodern society.

Over the past four decades, South Korea has demonstrated incredible development, becoming a high-tech industrialized economy. If in the 1960s GDP per capita was comparable to that of the poorer countries of Africa and Asia, where only a third of the adult population had graduated from secondary education, today 97% of Korean individuals, aged between 25 and 34, have completed high school education, thus registering the highest rate in this respect among the main developed countries globally. South Korea currently has the best education system in the world, according to a ranking made annually by the British company Pearson, which operates in the educational field. The first premise, since the economic reconstruction began, started from the suggestive phrase "Education first!" The Asian country advanced with a position in 2014, downgrading Finland, which won the title in 2013.

The ranking was drawn up by Pearson, a British company active in the field of education, which takes into account not only the estimated annual graduation rates (including from higher education) and the share of college enrollment but also the results obtained by students on a series of universal tests held every three or four years in areas such as mathematics, exact sciences and language skills. Students in South Korea are considered the best in the world in mathematics and other exact sciences, which denotes great seriousness in preparing them for exams, which are considered very important events in society.

Another strategy of the Korean education system is the "shadow education" system (Bloom et al. 2006). It consists of engaging young students in tutoring activities, and they are prepared after class by tutoring teachers. The model of this education dates back to the seventh century, when the richest families hired tutoring teachers for their school children. South Koreans took over this model to the extreme, and created a competitive education system so that in 2013, over 74% of students attended this form of training.

South Koreans have taken this to the extreme and created such a competitive education system that in 2013, over 74% of students were undergoing this form of training. In South Korea, there are more teachers who offer tutoring than teachers in Korean schools, and this activity brings hundreds of millions of dollars to the Korean state in the first phase, after which the effects of training bring even more economic advantages. In general, the cost is $2600 per year for a child who attends this form of training daily.

Korean civilization impresses the intensity and dynamism of the Asian pace of work and the work well done. Tens of thousands of students who missed out on entry to top universities spend the next year studying in private institutes to achieve success in top Korean universities.

The probability of being admitted after the daily meditations in which they participate, *hagwons*,[4] is over 70% of the number of those rejected. Almost 100% of students enter high school, and over 80% of them complete high school, continuing their studies in universities. The growing demand for education was not inhibited in any way, but on the contrary, when needed, it was met and supported by the addition of the places available for enrollment at high schools and universities, as well as by the hours for study. Parents have helped complement public investment in education with high levels of their private investment.

The harmonization of the qualifications and skills taught with the real needs of the labor market has given a high degree of social mobility to those taught and trained, which has also allowed individuals to benefit both the economy and society as a whole from the investment in education. The education system offers Koreans great chances of employment: only 2.6% of adults holding at least a baccalaureate degree are unemployed, less than in any other country assessed by the OECD, with the exception of Norway. Additionally, investments in the higher education system or in research programs represent the highest percentage of GDP, although most of them do not come from the state budget (over 72% of the funds come from the private sector). With a troubled history but also

---

[4] *Hagwons*, a word borrowed from Korean (*hakwon* or *hagweon*), denotes the private institute that offers different forms of education: additional education; remedial education (for children who are lagging behind with training); training in areas not covered by schools; to prepare pupils for improving the results of school tests and to prepare students for the entrance exam in universities.

a quality education, South Korea can boast three universities in the top 500 of the best institutions of higher education in the world.

• Percentage of the population with higher education: 40.4%
• Average annual growth level: 4.9%
• Share of expenditure on education in GDP: 7.6%

The top of the most effective education systems in the world was compiled by Pearson research (ziare.com) (Table 6.1). John Fallon drew attention to the economic importance of improving education systems and praised the success of curricula in Asian countries, which occupy the top positions. The ranking was drawn up on the basis of international tests, and higher education was also taken into account. South Korea is at the top of the ranking, with the next three positions being occupied by Asian countries, namely, Japan, Singapore, and Hong Kong. The success achieved by Asian countries, according to Pearson representatives, is due to the culture that schools and teachers in general enjoy a great deal of respect, taking responsibility for a better life. In fifth place is another country in Europe, namely, Finland, followed by the United Kingdom, Canada, and the Netherlands. In addition, Russia, in 13th place, is one position away from the United States, which ranks 14th in the ranking. At the European level, the most effective education system is in Finland, followed by the United Kingdom, which stands ahead of the Netherlands, Ireland, Poland, Germany, and France. Finland has thus far occupied the first position in this world ranking, but it was reached at the level of 2014 by four

Table 6.1 The chart of the educational system

1. South Korea	11. Denmark
2. Japan	12. Germany
3. Singapore	13. Russia
4. Hong Kong	14. United States
5. Finland	15. Australia
6. United Kingdom	16. New Zealand
7. Canada	17. Israel
8. The Netherlands	18. Belgium
9. Ireland	19. Czech Republic
10. Poland	20. Switzerland

Source: Author's contribution based on data processed by Pearson studies

Asian countries. Its drop is obvious and is part of a trend in the degradation of the education system in the Scandinavian countries. The rise of Poland, which managed to reform its postcommunist educational programs and reach directly to 10th place, is remarkable. In 2014, Romania ranked 31st, being also among the analyzed countries, climbing one position compared to 2013. Brazil ranked 38th, Mexico 39th, and Indonesia 40th.

Statistics provided by Eurostat, the Statistical Office of the European Union as can be seen in Table 6.2, show that in countries such as the United Kingdom, Sweden, or Belgium, more than 30% of the population has higher education, and this is also reflected in the world's economic development, while the percentage in Romania is only 13.1%, positioning it in the last place in the EU (Fig. 6.1).

What is spectacular is that a number of developing countries can also be of reference through their intervention actions and policies aimed at increasing the quality of their education systems, which have managed to take important steps in this direction: India, Brazil, and Chile. These countries have opted to reform the top-down education system, aiming, first of all, at improving management, decentralization, and legislative changes and rethinking funding by supporting innovations. The World Bank study (2007) on economic growth showed that these countries combined three important factors: capital accumulation, the efficient allocation of resources, and technological development.

With the caveat that our scientific approach is centered on the approach of higher education from the perspective of the contribution made to socioeconomic development, the presentation of the results of such analyses specific to society has highlighted the fact that the most developed and competitive economies at the global level are those that invest heavily in knowledge.

The selection of states for which we carried out this analysis was based on eligibility criteria, given the specificity of each of them, both as a geographical position and in terms of culture and rankings. At the same time, they enjoy successful educational systems and outstanding performance in the field of education.

In our opinion, at the moment, Romania needs a public education system that suits its real needs. There is no ideal system, and we do not opt for the idea of encouraging the copying of models throughout the public education system because it is not natural, as every education system must meet the needs of every society it develops. Beyond the comments that

Table 6.2 The structure of the population based on the level of education in 2013 as the weighted average of the total population aged between 15 and 74 years old (% of the total)

Country	Population with education			Country	Population with education		
	From the preschool, primary, and gymnasium cycles	Professional, high school, and postsecondary	University		From the preschool, primary, and gymnasium cycles	Professional, high school, and postsecondary	University
United Kingdom	23.0	42.2	34.8	Germany	18.4	56.8	24.8
Ireland	30.4	35.1	34.5	Slovenia	20.3	56.1	23.6
Luxembourg	27.1	39.0	33.9	Greece	39.2	38.4	22.4
Cyprus	29.0	37.6	33.4	Poland	18.1	60.3	21.6
Estonia	16.8	50.3	32.9	Bulgaria	24.7	53.8	21.5
Finland	23.6	43.8	32.6	Hungary	25.4	55.6	19.0
Sweden	24.9	44.6	30.4	Czech Republic	13.5	69.2	17.3
Belgium	33.4	36.6	30.0	Austria	23.4	59.4	17.2
Spain	49.7	21.9	28.5	Slovakia	16.1	66.8	17.1
Lithuania	16.7	54.9	28.4	Portugal	62.8	20.9	16.4
The Netherlands	31.3	40.6	28.1	Croatia	27.6	56.2	16.2
Denmark	31	41	28	Malta	58.6	25.9	15.6
France	30.5	42.1	27.4	Italy	47.6	39.0	13.4
Latvia	17.9	56.1	26.0	Romania	31.8	55.1	13.1
				EU average (28 countries)	30.3	45.5	24.2

Source: Author's contribution based on Eurostat, updated in May 2014

Note: The data in the table were ordered in decreasing order according to the share of the population with higher education in the total population aged between 15 and 74 years

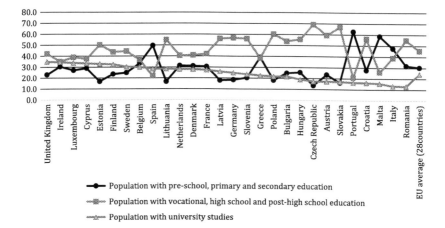

Population with vocational, high school and post-high school education
Population with university studies

Fig. 6.1 The structure of the population based on the level of education in 2013 as a percentage of the total number of the population aged between 15 and 74 years old (% out of the total). (Source: Author's contribution)

can be made about the examples offered, they communicate the fact that *education has the difficult mission to convey a culture accumulated for centuries but also a preparation for the future in a largely unpredictable measure.*

References

Bloom, D., Canning, D., & Chan, K. (2006). *Higher Education and Economic Development in Africa* (p. 83). Harvard University.

Brătianu, C., & Atanasiu, M. G. (2002). *Quality Assurance in Higher Education in the UK* (p. 14). Economic Publishing House.

Dziewulak, D. (2013). *Szkolnictwo wyzsze w swietle raportow edukacyjnych*, Studia BAS, Nr.3(35), pp. 149–174.

http://www.ziare.com/scoala/educatie/topul-surprinzator-al-celor-mai-bunesistemede-educatie-tari-din-asia-pe-primele-locuri-1297731

CHAPTER 7

Empirical Analysis of the Relationship Between Higher Education and Economic Development

The relationship between higher-level education and economic growth was based on an analysis of their linkage for the period 1971–2013 for the following countries: United Kingdom, Poland, Sweden, South Korea, and Romania. We used the participation rate in higher education (or as defined in the world-recognized databases of the World Bank—School enrollment ratio/gross enrolment ratio) as an indicator for evaluating the changes in higher education, that is, gross domestic product per inhabitant (expressed in USD per inhabitant) as an indicator of economic growth. The choice of the five countries included in the research is justified by the investments made in education, correlated with the economic growth of these countries.

This study investigates the econometric dimension of links between the two economic and social variables to justify the proposed goal, namely, to prove the existence or nonexistence of direct statistical relations between higher education and the economic growth of their meaning and significance.

The analysis was carried out on the basis of data existing at the level of five countries, United Kingdom, South Korea, Poland, Romania, and Sweden, according to the information provided by the World Bank and United Nations Conference on Trade and Development (UNCTAD). The variables taken into account are the *gross domestic product per inhabitant* and the rate of participation in tertiary education for the countries mentioned for a period of more than 40 years. The data were processed with the help of the Statistical Package for the Social Sciences (SPSS) program using a series of methods, such as the graphical method, regression and correlation analysis, specific econometric tests to identify the existence of the link, establishing the meaning and shape of the link, and determining the degree of intensity of the link.

Our empirical approach presents a series of similarities to but also differentiations from the line of thought and empirical approach made by de Meulemeester and Rochat (1995) in their work *A Causality Analysis of the Link Between Higher Education and Economic Development*, of the one made by Avram (2012) *Investment in education and socioeconomic development in the new knowledge-based economy and society*, doctoral thesis, respectively the study conducted by Șerbu (2013) *The interdependence between higher education and economic development by reference to the requirements of the labor market*.

Regarding the similarities between the analysis carried out through our research and the aforementioned studies, they consist of a similar methodology and the use of the variable gross domestic product per inhabitant. The main differentiations concern, in particular, the distinct countries over which we have carried out the analysis and the related time periods, as well as the method of analyzing the data. The countries that have already been analyzed are Japan (1885–1975), France (1899–1986), Italy (1885–1986), England (1919–1987), and Australia (1906–1986)—the study by de Meulemeester and Rochat (1995); Norway, Switzerland, and the United States (1987–2008)—the study by Avram (2012); and Finland, Norway, Switzerland, Ireland, and Austria (1980–2009)—the study by Șerbu (2013). Ultimately, the results we obtained for the case study of Romania differ, and implicitly the conclusions that follow. Consequently, our research contains data/analyses regarding the case of the Romanian higher education system and, especially, that of South Korea, which complement the analyses already carried out, by providing important clues related to the trend of economic growth from the perspective of higher education.

EVOLUTION OF THE PARTICIPATION RATE IN TERTIARY EDUCATION (%) IN THE PERIOD 1971–2012

The data on the population participation rate in tertiary education in the five countries that are the subject of our research, South Korea, Poland, Romania, Sweden, and the United Kingdom, for the period 1971–2012, are centralized in the table in Annex 8.

The data available on the World Bank's website for the period 1971–2012 highlight an upward evolution of *the population's participation rate in tertiary education* in the case of the five countries covered by the research. The participation rate in tertiary education represents the total number of students enrolled in higher education, regardless of age, as a percentage of the total population, from the official age group corresponding to higher education. The purpose of using this indicator is to highlight the general level of participation in tertiary education in a certain period of time.

The method of calculating this indicator consists of dividing the total number of students enrolled in tertiary education, regardless of age, by the total population in the official age group corresponding to tertiary education, multiplied by 100 (Ghioarcă 2015).

$$RP\hat{I}T^{t} = \left(E^{t} / P^{t}_{a}\right) \times 100, \qquad (7.1)$$

where:

$RP\hat{I}T^{t}$—participation rate in tertiary education in school year **t**

E^{t}—the total number of pupils enrolled in tertiary education in school year **t**

P^{t}_{v}—population in age group **v**, the official age group corresponding to tertiary education in school year **t**

This indicator reflects, based on the necessary data presented, the capacity of the education system to allow the access of students from the respective group, both in public and private education.

The chronogram describing the evolution of the participation rate of the Romanian population in tertiary education in the period 1971–2012 is below the values corresponding to the other four countries included in the analysis, as can be seen in Fig. 7.1. We can see that although South Korea had a participation rate in tertiary education of 7.25% in 1971, much lower compared to Romania (9.29%), it registered a very rapid

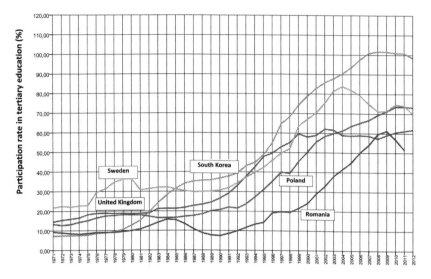

Fig. 7.1 Rate of the involvement of the population in tertiary education between 1971 and 2012 (%). (Source: author's contribution)

growth after 1979, surpassing after 1982 all the other four countries under analysis. In 2006, the participation rate in South Korea exceeded 100%, reaching a maximum share of 101.57% in 2007.

EVOLUTION OF GROSS DOMESTIC PRODUCT PER INHABITANT FOR THE PERIOD 1971–2013

The data on the gross domestic product per inhabitant available on the website of the United Nations Conference on Trade and Development (UNCTAD) for the period 1971–2013 were centralized and are presented in the table in Annex 9.

The chronograms corresponding to the evolution of the *gross domestic product per inhabitant* in the five countries included in the research show an upward trend.

Based on the data represented in the graph in Fig. 7.2, we can see that Sweden has the highest gross domestic product per inhabitant, followed by the United Kingdom and South Korea, Poland, and Romania. In 2013, Romania was in the last place among the five countries analyzed, with a

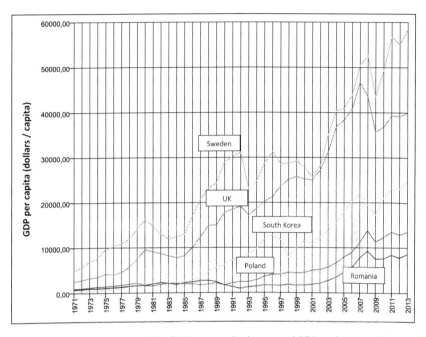

Fig. 7.2 The evolution of the GDP per capita between 1971 and 2013. (Source: author's contribution)

gross domestic product of $8592.20 per inhabitant. The gross domestic product per inhabitant in Poland has experienced a similar evolution to that of Romania, but at a higher level.

CORRELATION BETWEEN THE PARTICIPATION RATE IN TERTIARY EDUCATION (%) AND THE GROSS DOMESTIC PRODUCT PER INHABITANT ($)

The study of the connection between the two variables can be achieved by using regression and correlation analysis, which offers the possibility of identifying the existence of the connection, establishing the meaning and shape of the connection, and determining the degree of its intensity. An elementary method that allows us to establish the existence, meaning, shape, and intensity of the connection between variables is the graphical method. This method consists of the graphical representation in a system of coordinate axes of the pairs of values corresponding to the two analyzed variables, the graph being called the correlogram or the diagram of the point cloud. To measure the intensity of the link between the analyzed variables, we used the correlation ratio, which is calculated thus (Jaba 2002):

$$R = \sqrt{1 - \frac{\Sigma(y_i - y_x)^2}{\Sigma(y_i - \bar{y})^2}}. \tag{7.2}$$

In the economic and social field, stochastic (Druică 2011) links are the most frequent, and the specific character of these links lies in the fact that they cannot be verified for each case separately, but only at the level of the whole. They can be classified by the form of the link:

- linear links—which are expressed by the linear regression equation:

$$y = a_0 + a_1 x \quad \text{simple} \tag{7.3}$$

$$y = a_0 + a_1 x_1 + a_2 x_2 \quad \text{multiple} \tag{7.4}$$

- nonlinear links—are expressed by the equation of a curve (parable, hyperbole, exponential function):

$$y = a_0 + a_1 x + a_2 x^2 \quad \text{parabolic link} \tag{7.5}$$

$$y = a_0 a_1^x \quad \text{exponential link} \tag{7.6}$$

$$y = a_0 + \frac{1}{a_1} x_1 \quad \text{hyperbolic link} \tag{7.7}$$

The determination of the curve is made using the graphic method (correlogram or the point cloud diagram). Additionally, there are several types of models for determining the general trend of the numerical series. The main models used in economic calculations are as follows:

$$y = a + bx \quad \text{linear model (simple regression)} \tag{7.8}$$

$$y = a_0 + a_1 x^1 + a_2 x^2 + \ldots + a_k x^k \quad \text{polynomial model of order } 2, 3, 4, 5 \tag{7.9}$$

$$y = a + b^* \ln x \quad \text{logarithmic model} \tag{7.10}$$

$$y = a^* e^{bx} \quad \text{the exponential model} \tag{7.11}$$

$$y = a * x^b \quad \text{power model} \tag{7.12}$$

The graphical representation of the data series for all five countries highlights the fact that the evolution of the analyzed phenomenon can be approximated by a *regression model of linear, cubic, exponential, or power type*, based on *the ratio of determination* (maximum principle) and *the square of the modeling errors* (minimum principle) (Druică 2011). The choice of the best regression model was made based on the *coefficient of determination*, which shows in what proportion the dependent variable is explained by the regression model. This indicator is calculated by squaring the correlation ratio. In this context, a Pearson analysis was chosen, and the value of the Pearson correlation ratio was calculated using the SPSS program.

To verify the significance of the correlation report, we used the F test, defined by the following relation (Druică 2011):

$$F = \frac{n-k}{k-1} \cdot \frac{R^2}{1-R^2} \tag{7.13}$$

in which n represents the number of observed values; k is the number of groups constituted in relation to the independent variable; R^2 is the coefficient of determination.

If the value of the F test is greater than the tabular value, and the corresponding Sig.[1] value is less than 0.05, we can say that the linear link between the two analyzed variables is significant. The modeling of the analyzed variables is preceded by the realization of a descriptive analysis of each variable to study the characteristics of the distributions of the model variables. As a result of the processing of data on the values of the variables of *gross domestic product per inhabitant* and the *rate of participation in tertiary education*, the results are presented in Annex 10.

---

[1] The value of 'p' or the indicator 'Significance' (level of significance, Sig.) indicates the representativeness of the results of the statistical test. The value of this indicator is compared with the value of 0.5; if the value of Sig. is less than this threshold, then the result is statistically significant, otherwise the result of the test becomes insignificant, implicitly accepting the null hypothesis.

ANALYSIS OF THE LINK BETWEEN THE PARTICIPATION RATE
IN TERTIARY EDUCATION AND GDP PER CAPITA
IN THE UNITED KINGDOM

The graphical representation in the same axis system of the link between the two variables for the period 1971–2012 in the United Kingdom is shown in Fig. 7.3.

The graph in Fig. 7.3 highlights the existence of a direct link between the *participation rate in tertiary education* and *the GDP per inhabitant* in the United Kingdom for the period from 1971 to 2012. For this purpose, the *power model* has been chosen to shape the link between *the participation rate in tertiary education* and *the gross domestic product* per capita in the United Kingdom. The values obtained for the *Pearson correlation*

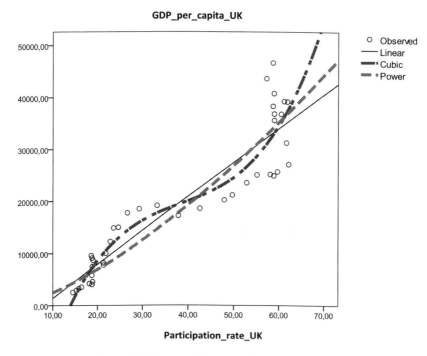

Fig. 7.3 The relationship between the ratio of involvement in tertiary education and GDP per capita in the United Kingdom between 1971 and 2012. (Source: author's contribution based on the analysis in the SPSS 22 program)

ratio, the coefficient of determination, and *the estimated standard error* are centralized in Table 7.1.

The value of the Pearson correlation ratio highlights the fact that there is a very strong link between the *participation rate in tertiary education* and *the gross domestic product* per capita in the United Kingdom between 1971 and 2012. *The correlation ratio* is equal to 0.934 for the *power model. The coefficient of determination* in Table 7.1, expressed in percentages, shows that the change in the variable *gross domestic product per inhabitant* is determined in a proportion of 87.2% by the variable *participation rate in tertiary education*; the rest up to 100% is due to random factors.

The general shape of the *power model* is given by the relationship (7.14):

$$Y = a^* x^b \tag{7.14}$$

The estimation of the parameters of the *power model* is represented in Table 7.2

Based on the data in Table 7.2, we can write the estimated equation of the model *gross domestic product per inhabitant* in the United Kingdom for the period from 1971 to 2012, as follows:

$$\frac{PIB}{loc} = 81,284^* R_p^{1483} \tag{7.15}$$

Table 7.3 presents the estimates of the two components of the variation, the corresponding degrees of freedom, the estimates of the explained

Table 7.1 Pearson correlation link, the determination coefficient, and the estimated standard error

Pattern	Pearson Correlation Report (R)	Coefficient of determination (R^2)	Adjusted coefficient of determination	Estimated standard error
Linear	0.924	0.854	0.850	7232
Cubic	0.932	0.868	0.858	4982.841
Power	0.934	0.872	0.869	0.308

Source: author's contribution based on analysis in the SPSS 22 program

Note: The independent variable is participation rate in tertiary education in the United Kingdom

Table 7.2   The rates of the GDP model

	Nonstandard coefficients		Standard coefficients	t	Sig.
	B	SE	Beta		
Ln (UK participation rate)	1483	0.090	0.934	16.531	0.000
(Constant)	81.284	25.763		3155	0.003

Source: author's contribution based on analysis in the SPSS 22 program

Note: The independent variable is participation rate in tertiary education in the UK

Table 7.3   ANOVA

	The sum of the deviations	Df	Average deviation	Test F	Sig.
Regression	25.916	1	25.916	273.262	0.000
Residual	3794	40	0.095		
Total	29.710	41			

Note: The independent variable is participation rate in tertiary education in the United Kingdom

Source: author's contribution based on analysis in the SPSS 22 program

and residual variances, the calculated value of the Fisher ratio, and the significance of the test.

To verify the significance of the correlation ratio, the F test was used. The Sig. value corresponding to the F test is less than 0.05. Under these circumstances, we can say that the built-up model explains the dependence between variables through a *nonlinear power-type bond*, which is considered significant.

LINK BETWEEN *PARTICIPATION RATE IN TERTIARY EDUCATION* AND *GROSS DOMESTIC PRODUCT PER INHABITANT* IN SOUTH KOREA

The graphic representation of the link between the two variables for the period 1971–2012 in South Korea is shown in Fig. 7.4.

From Fig. 7.4, it is noted that there is a direct link between the *participation rate in tertiary education* and the *gross domestic product per inhabitant* in South Korea for the period under review. The graphic representation of the data series made in Fig. 7.4 highlights that the evolution of the

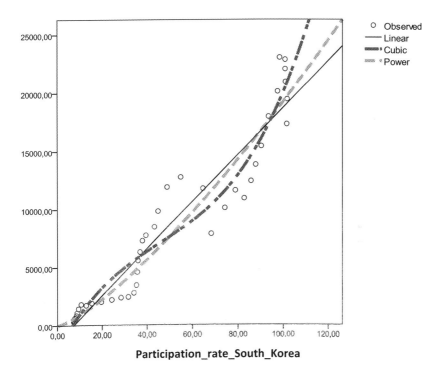

Fig. 7.4 The relationship between the ratio of involvement in tertiary education and GDP per capita in South Korea between 1971 and 2012. (Source: author's contribution based on the analysis in the SPSS 22 program)

analyzed phenomenon can be approximated by a *power model* to shape the link between the *participation rate in tertiary education* and *the gross domestic product* per capita in South Korea.

The value obtained for the *Pearson correlation ratio* shows that there is a very strong link between the *participation rate in tertiary education* and *the gross domestic product* per capita in South Korea for the period under review. *The coefficient of determination* in Table 7.4, expressed in percentages, shows that the change in the variable *gross domestic Product per inhabitant* is determined in a proportion of 93.9% by the variable *participation rate in tertiary education*, the rest up to 100% being due to random factors.

Table 7.4   Pearson correlation link, the determination coefficient, and the estimated standard error

Pattern	Pearson Correlation Report (R)	Coefficient of determination (R^2)	Adjusted coefficient of determination	Estimated standard error
Linear	0.954	0.911	0.908	2217.812
Power	0.969	0.939	0.937	0.324
Cubic	0.964	0.929	0.924	2022.954

Source: author's contribution based on the analysis in the SPSS 22 program

Note: The independent variable is the participation rate in tertiary education in South Korea

Table 7.5   The rates of the GDP model

	Nonstandard coefficients		Standard coefficients	T	Sig.
	B	SE	Beta		
Ln (participation rate in tertiary education)	1338	0.054	0.969	24.716	0.000
(Constant)	40.598	8083		5022	0.000

Source: author's contribution based on the analysis in the SPSS 22 program

Note: The dependent variable is ln (gross domestic product per inhabitant)

The estimation of the parameters of *the power model* is presented in Table 7.5.

Based on the data in Table 7.5, we can write the estimated equation of the *power model* for *gross domestic product per inhabitant* as follows:

$$\frac{PIB}{loc} = 40,598^* R_p^{1338} \qquad (7.16)$$

Table 7.6 centralizes the estimates of the two components of the variation, the corresponding degrees of freedom, the estimates of the explained and residual variances, the calculated value of the Fisher ratio, and the significance of the test.

The Sig. value corresponding to the F test is less than 0.05, which allows us to state that the built-in model explains the dependence between variables by a *nonlinear power-type bond*, which is considered significant.

Table 7.6 ANOVA

	The sum of the deviations	Df	Average deviation	Test F	Sig.
Regression	63.990	1	63.990	610.875	0.000
Residual	4190	40	0.105		
Total	68.180	41			

Source: author's contribution based on the analysis in the SPSS 22 program

Note: The independent variable is the participation rate in tertiary education in South Korea

LINK BETWEEN PARTICIPATION RATE IN TERTIARY EDUCATION AND GROSS DOMESTIC PRODUCT PER INHABITANT IN POLAND

The graphic representation of the link between the two variables for the period 1971–2012 in Poland is shown in Fig. 7.5.

From Fig. 7.5, we consider that there is a direct link between the *participation rate in tertiary education* and *gross domestic product per inhabitant* in Poland, which can be approximated by an *exponential model* to shape the link between the *participation rate in tertiary education* and *the gross domestic product per inhabitant* in Poland.

The values obtained for the *Pearson correlation ratio, the coefficient of determination*, and *the estimated standard error* are centralized in Table 7.7.

The general form of the *exponential regression model* is given by relation (7.17):

$$Y = a^* b^x \tag{7.17}$$

The value obtained for the *Pearson correlation ratio* shows a very strong link between the *participation rate in tertiary education* and the *gross domestic product per inhabitant* in Poland. The *coefficient of determination* in Table 7.7, expressed in percentages, shows that the change in the variable *gross domestic product per inhabitant* is determined in a proportion of 94.4% by the variable *participation rate in tertiary education*, the rest up to 100% being due to random factors. The estimation of the parameters of the *exponential model* is made in Table 7.8.

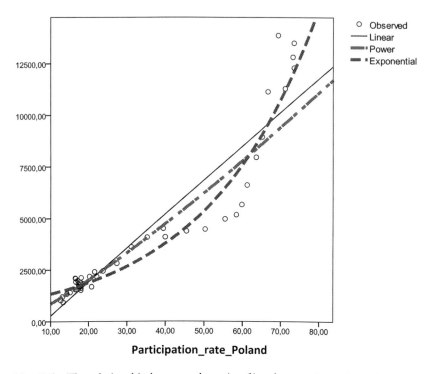

Fig. 7.5 The relationship between the ratio of involvement in tertiary education and GDP per capita in Poland between 1971 and 2012. (Source: author's contribution based on the analysis in the SPSS 22 program)

Table 7.7 Pearson correlation link, the determination coefficient, and the estimated standard error

Pattern	Pearson Correlation Report (R)	Coefficient of determination (R^2)	Adjusted coefficient of determination	Estimated standard error
Linear	0.934	0.872	0.869	1391.420
Exponential	0.972	0.944	0.943	0.187
Power	0.970	0.941	0.940	0.192

Source: author's contribution based on the analysis in the SPSS 22 program

Note: The independent variable is the participation rate in tertiary education in Poland

Table 7.8 The rates of the GDP model

	Nonstandard coefficients		Standard coefficients	T	Sig.
	B	SE	Beta		
Participation rate in tertiary education	0.035	0.001	0.972	26.050	0.000
(Constant)	942.996	51.535		18.298	0.000

Source: author's contribution based on analyses in SPSS 22 program

Note: The dependent variable is ln (gross domestic product per inhabitant)

Table 7.9 ANOVA

	The sum of the deviations	Df	The sum of the deviations	Test F	Sig.
Regression	23.630	1	23.630	678.627	0.000
Residual	1393	40	0.035		
Total	25.023	41			

Source: author's contribution based on analyses in SPSS 22

Note: The independent variable is the participation rate in tertiary education in Poland

Based on the data in Table 7.8, we can write the estimated equation of the *exponential model* for the *gross domestic product per inhabitant* as follows:

$$\frac{PIB}{loc} = 942,996^*0035^{Rc} \tag{7.18}$$

In Table 7.9, we centralized the estimates of the two components of the variation, the corresponding degrees of freedom, the estimates of the explained and residual variances, the calculated value of the Fisher ratio, and the significance of the test.

The Sig. value corresponding to the F test is less than 0.05, which allows us to state that the built model explains the dependence between variables by a *nonlinear link of exponential type*, which is considered significant.

THE LINK BETWEEN THE *PARTICIPATION RATE IN TERTIARY EDUCATION* AND THE *GROSS DOMESTIC PRODUCT PER INHABITANT* IN ROMANIA

The graphic representation of the link between the two variables in Romania is shown in Fig. 7.6.

Based on the graph in Fig. 7.6, we can appreciate that between the *participation rate in tertiary education* and *the gross domestic product per inhabitant,* in Romania, there is a direct link, which can be approximated by an exponential model to shape the link between the *participation rate in tertiary education* and *the gross domestic product per inhabitant* in Romania.

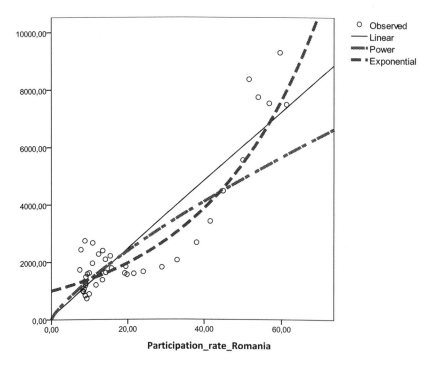

Fig. 7.6 The relationship between the ratio of involvement in tertiary education and GDP per capita in Romania. (Source: author's contribution based on analyses in SPSS 22)

The values obtained for *the Pearson correlation ratio, the coefficient of determination*, and *the estimated standard error* are centralized in Table 7.10.

The value obtained for the *Pearson correlation ratio* shows a very strong link between the *participation rate in tertiary education* and the *gross domestic product per inhabitant* in Romania. *The coefficient of determination* expressed in percentages shows that the change in the variable *gross domestic product per inhabitant* is determined in a proportion of 76.7% by the variable *participation rate in tertiary education*, the rest up to 100% being due to random factors. The estimation of the parameters of the exponential model is made in Table 7.11.

Based on the estimated coefficients in Table 7.11, we can write the estimated equation of the *exponential model* for *Gross Domestic Product per inhabitant* as follows:

$$\frac{PIB}{loc} = 998,882^{*}0034^{Rc} \tag{7.19}$$

ANALYSIS OF THE LINK BETWEEN *PARTICIPATION RATES* IN *TERTIARY EDUCATION* AND *GDP* PER CAPITA IN SWEDEN

The graphical representation of the link between the two variables for the period 1971–2012 in Sweden is shown in Fig. 7.7.

From Fig. 7.7, it is noted that between the *participation rate in tertiary education* and the *gross domestic product per inhabitant* in Sweden, for the period under review, there is a direct link, which can be approximated by

Table 7.10 Pearson correlation link, the determination coefficient, and the estimated standard error

Pattern	Pearson Correlation Report ®	Coefficient of determination (R²)	Adjusted coefficient of determination	Estimated standard error
Linear	0.898	0.807	0.802	1004.054
Exponential	0.876	0.767	0.761	0.322
Power	0.823	0.678	0.669	0.379

Source: author's contribution based on the analyses in SPSS 22

Note: The independent variable is the participation rate in tertiary education in Romania

Table 7.11 The rates of the GDP model

	Nonstandard coefficients		Standard coefficients	T	Sig.
	B	SE	Beta		
Participation rate in tertiary education	0.034	0.003	0.876	11.336	0.000
(Constant)	998.882	81.978		12.185	0.000

Source: author's contribution based on analyses in SPSS 22 program

Note: The dependent variable is ln (Gross Domestic Product per inhabitant)

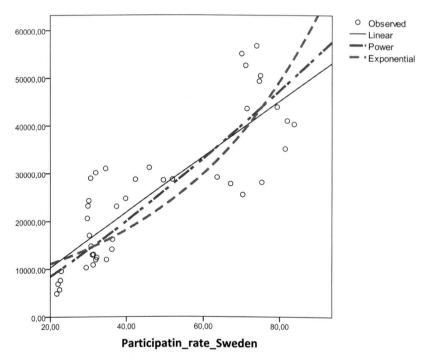

Fig. 7.7 The relationship between the ratio of involvement in tertiary education and GDP per capita in Sweden. (Source: author's contribution based on analyses in SPSS 22 program)

Table 7.12 Pearson correlation link, the determination coefficient, and the estimated standard error

Pattern	Pearson Correlation Report (R)	Coefficient of determination (R²)	Adjusted coefficient of determination	Estimated standard error
Linear	0.838	0.703	0.695	8000.464
Power	0.850	0.722	0.715	0.344
Exponential	0.806	0.650	0.642	0.386

Source: author's contribution based on the analyses in SPSS 22

Note: The independent variable is the participation rate in tertiary education in Sweden

a *power model* to shape the link between the *participation rate in tertiary education* and the *gross domestic product per inhabitant* in Sweden. The values obtained for *the Pearson correlation ratio, the coefficient of determination*, and *the estimated standard error* are centralized in Table 7.12.

The Pearson correlation report indicates that there is a strong link between the *participation rate in tertiary education* and *the gross domestic product per inhabitant* in Sweden for the period under review. *The coefficient of determination* expressed in percentages shows that the change in the variable *gross domestic product per inhabitant* is determined in a proportion of 72.2% by the variable *participation rate in tertiary education*, the rest up to 100% being due to random factors.

The estimation of the parameters of the *power model* is carried out in Table 7.13.

Based on the values obtained for the coefficients, according to Table 7.13, we can write the estimated equation of the *power model* for the *gross domestic product per inhabitant* as follows:

$$\frac{PIB}{loc} = 206,339^* R_p^{1240} \qquad (7.20)$$

The Sig. value corresponding to the F test is less than 0.05, which allows us to state that the built-in model explains the dependence between variables by a *nonlinear power-type bond,* which is considered significant.

Table 7.13   The rates of the GDP model

	Nonstandard coefficients		Standard coefficients	T	Sig.
	B	SE	Beta		
Ln (participation rate in tertiary education)	1240	0.122	0.850	10.195	0.000
(Constant)	206.339	94.714		2179	0.035

Source: author's contribution based on analyses in SPSS 22 program
Note: The dependent variable is ln (Gross Domestic Product per inhabitant)

REFERENCES

Druică, E. (2011). *Econometrics,* course support.
Ghioarcă, I. R. (2015). *South Korea—The Best Education System in the World* http://powerpolitics.ro/coreea-desud-cel-mai-bun-sistem-educational-din-lume/
Jaba, E. (2002). *Statistics* (3rd ed.). Economic Publishing House.

PART III

Understanding the Numbers and Narratives. Good and Bad News

CHAPTER 8

Trends and Evolutions of Higher Education Related to the European Integration and Membership

Currently, the European Union is an economic, social, and political entity under continuous construction, the result of a process that began more than five decades ago. In his historic declaration of May 9, 1950, R. Schuman stated that "Europe will not be built all at once or on the basis of a single plan, but will develop on the basis of accumulations based on the de facto solidarity of European states that regained their national sovereignty after the Second World War.". The basis of the creation of the integrative structure in the European area was obtaining and maintaining military and political stability through economic means and the need for economic growth and development in a different plan than the national one.

The fifth wave of EU enlargement in May 2004 covered the largest number of countries, that is, eight Central and Eastern European countries: Poland, Hungary, the Czech Republic, Slovakia, Estonia, Latvia, Lithuania, and two Mediterranean countries: Cyprus and Malta. They represent 34% of the EU's area with 15 Member States, 29% of the population and 5% of GDP. In 2007, two new states joined the EU integrative construction, namely, Romania and Bulgaria. Croatia became a Member State of the European Union on July 1, 2013. To ensure sustainable economic growth, it is necessary to orient the economic growth strategy toward the level of innovation and competitiveness, the benefits of which will be better assessed.

© The Author(s), under exclusive license to Springer Nature Switzerland AG 2023
D.-M. Neamțu, *Education and Economic Development*,
https://doi.org/10.1007/978-3-031-20382-4_8

In this chapter, one of the central objectives is to analyze and evaluate trends in education in the context of the European Union in the 2004, 2007, and 2020 accession waves. The main working coordinates were the following: the new Member States at the European Union level converge toward each other in terms of growth rates of GDP per capita, of inclusion rates in higher education, of the evolution of the percentage of GDP allocated to education, of financing of research and development activities, of the participation rates of the population aged 25–65, in lifelong learning, of investment in education, and of the fields of study preferred by students. The degree of synchronization of indicators on the education component has intensified with integration into the European Union.

This section analyzes the synchronization of fluctuations in European education, as well as the factors that could encourage this phenomenon based on the economic, political, and trans-cultural context. The European dimension of education and experience in EU education programs contributes to the standardization and synchronization of European education systems, bringing it up at the beginning of the new millennium.

The most recent literature includes comparative analyses on the synchronization of economic fluctuations of the countries of Central and Eastern Europe. The results of these empirical studies reveal that they largely depend on the level of homogeneity of the analyzed group. The studies, carried out on countries with a similar level of economic growth, confirm the appearance of the phenomenon of equalization of the income level, while those carried out at the world level deny the existence of such a trend (Matkovski and Prochniak 2004). The more different the cultural, institutional, and socioeconomic relations between countries, the less one can estimate the degree of synchronization under the influence of the Bologna Process. However, the trend in education is complex, and the systems, although they are moving toward the same general direction, start from different points and advance at different speeds.

Indeed, the retrograde character does not in itself guarantee that one nation will catch up with the others. In our opinion, we admit that there are several factors that influence the process of catching up. Among them, we take into consideration the educated and well-trained workforce (expenditures per student, investments in education as a percentage of GDP, enrollment rate in higher education, higher education graduates, school dropout rate, participation rate in lifelong learning), financing of research and development activities, and evolution of GDP per capita over a period of 15 years between 2000 and 2014. Abramovitz synthesizes this group of characteristics as *social ability* (Abramovitz 1986).

PUBLIC SPENDING FOR HIGHER EDUCATION DURING 2000–2018

Since March 2001, the European Council has decided that one of European Union's goals for higher education must become knowledge-based economy, the most competitive and dynamic in the world, capable of supporting economic growth with better jobs and greater social cohesion. Education is certainly the main driver for achieving this ambitious position, and as a result, each Member State must increase investment in education to a greater extent in higher education institutions.

In this respect, the result pursued by educational policies, whether at the national or international level, is to increase the proportion of private funds to reduce the impact of the cost of education on government resources. The state budget is the main source of funding for higher education, providing up to 90% of total expenditure in countries such as Finland and Sweden. A fairly good score of 81% is noted in Slovenia, a country that is part of the 2004 wave of accession to the European Union, the others staying in the range of 68–79%. There are also countries where government spending is increasingly low, for example, the United Kingdom (50%), Slovakia (65%), Italy (68%), and Poland (69%). We must bear in mind that a small contribution by the government must be offset by a greater investment from private institutions and households and, in most cases, the responsibility for funding lies with students and their families and less, to no means, private companies. The financial figures indicate, in Table 8.1, that although the state is the main engine of higher education funding and has the upper hand on both legal and financial mechanisms to create a competitive environment for higher education institutions, it does not allocate enough funds compared to the policies and recommendations at the European level. There is a tendency to increase public spending on higher education (or to return to the previous level of funding). For example, if in 2013–2014 the largest increase in funding for the university system occurred in Portugal, one of the states that opted for a tough austerity program after the onset of the crisis, for 2017–2018 (where data for most countries were available in May 2022), the highest increase was recorded in the Czech Republic (with more than 40%), followed—in both terms, of

Table 8.1   The funding of higher education—annual expenditure on educational institutions per pupil/student in public institutions

	2018 vs. 2017		2019 vs. 2018*	
	Evolution (calculated in PPS)	Nominal evolution (calculated in euro)	Evolution (calculated in PPS)	Nominal evolution (calculated in euro)
Increase over 10%	Czech Republic, Estonia, Latvia, Lithuania, Poland, Romania	Czech Republic, Estonia, Latvia, Lithuania, Malta, Poland, Romania	Denmark, Greece, Croatia, Lithuania, Malta, Poland, Romania, Slovenia	Denmark, Greece, Croatia, Lithuania, Malta, Poland, Romania, Slovenia
5%–10% increase	Malta, Hungary, Austria, Greece	Hungary, Austria, Slovakia	–	Germany, Cyprus
1% to 5% increase	Belgium, Bulgaria, Germany, Spain, France, Croatia, Portugal, Slovenia, Slovakia, Sweden	Belgium, Bulgaria, Germany, Greece, Spain, France, Croatia, Portugal, Slovenia	Germany, Spain, France, Cyprus, Netherlands, Austria, Sweden	Belgium, Spain, France, Netherlands, Austria
Stable	Denmark, Ireland, Italy, Netherlands, Finland	Denmark, Ireland, Italy, Netherlands, Finland	Italy, Norway	Ireland, Italy, Finland, Sweden, Norway
Decrease 1% to 5%	–	–	Estonia, Ireland, Finland	Estonia
5% decrease to 10%	Cyprus, Luxembourg	Cyprus, Luxembourg	–	–
Decrease over 10%	–	–	Latvia	–

Source: Author contributions based on data from https://ec.europa.eu/eurostat/databrowser/view/educ_uoe_fini04/default/table?lang=en, accessed on 31.05.2022

* For 2019 data are not available (as for May 2022) for: Bulgaria, Czech Republic, Luxembourg, Portugal, Slovakia

** United Kingdom is no longer included in Eurostat data

total spending and spending on public institutions—by Baltic countries (Estonia, Latvia, and Lithuania). Somewhat surprisingly, from a large decrease in higher education funding in Romania for the 2012–2013 period, data for 2017–2018 show a significant increase of over 13% and an even larger increase in funding per student in 2019 compared to 2018, with more than 22%.

Most other countries have kept the level of funding stable in 2018 compared to 2017 or increased the amounts invested in higher education, with only two EU countries registering decreases of more than 5% in public funding, according to Table 8.1.

A special remark must be made for Denmark, whose funding per student recorded a steady evolution in 2018 compared to 2017 but recorded a significant 15.8% increase (in PPS) in funding per student in public institutions in 2019 compared to 2018.

The evolution of public expenditures, regarded as a percentage of GDP, is shown in Annex no. 11, which marks a fairly safe migration to the range of 1–2% of GDP, where most countries were in 2011. Countries that invested more than 1.8% of GDP in 2009–2013—Denmark, Sweden, and Finland—introduced policy changes that led to a reduction in public contributions below the 2% line, with the exception of Denmark, which remained at 2.2% in 2018 because it started in 2009 with the highest percentage of GDP, that is 2.34%. Countries below the 1% limit in 2001 generally tended to remain within the same in 2018, with the exception of Cyprus, which started from 0.64% of GDP in 2000 and managed to almost double the percentage by 2017. As a result of this development, the countries that joined the EU in 2004 registered in 2018 less than 1% investment of GDP, with the exception of Estonia (1.18%), Poland (1.06%), and Slovenia (1.01%), compared to Romania and Bulgaria, which keep the same trend of 0.75% and 0.81% (for Bulgaria, the data are available only for 2017) investment of GDP, respectively. Romania registered an increase in public expenditure for higher education as a percentage of GDP in the period 2007–2009 (with values of 1.09% and 1.13%, respectively).

Expenses Per Student in Euro PPS,[1] at Higher Education Level (ISCED 5–6)

It is well known that to have high-performing educational institutions, a country has to invest a generous proportion of GDP in the higher education sector. Another way to estimate the level of spending on higher education is to measure annual expenditure per pupil not in nominal terms but, by reference to purchasing power standards (PPS = purchasing power standard), a method that usually helps to eliminate from international comparisons the distortions introduced by the high discrepancies between price levels in different countries.

The annual costs per student, as shown in Table 8.2, have increased at the level of all the countries analyzed, which is explained by the expenditure on equipment and libraries caused by the general inflation of prices. The increase in spending does not seem to reflect a change in education policy or a greater interest in funding higher education but only an increase motivated by inflationary prices in each EU member country. This is based on the fact that there are no sudden year-on-year increases, with the exception of countries that joined the EU after 2004, with larger year-on-year increases for 2017, 2018, and 2019.

The stability of annual expenditure per student allows us to group countries into four large groups based on this financial indicator and 2018 data—available for all countries except for the United Kingdom. The first group contains member countries whose expenditure per student is approximately 4732.7 Euro PPS. In this case, the basic countries were made up of Greece, Romania, and Bulgaria, with a much lower than average value for Greece throughout the entire 2012–2018 interval. The hierarchy and gap have not changed significantly, with the overall level of expenditure per student in Bulgaria and Romania being approximately 53% of that of the overall European Union.

The second group, in addition to the countries that joined 2004, namely, Lithuania, Latvia, Slovakia, Hungary, and Poland, includes the Latin

---

[1] PPS—*Purchasing Power Standard*, the standard of purchasing power, is an artificial form of monetary unit. Theoretically 1 PPS can buy the same amount of goods or services in all countries included in the analysis. For further details see:
http://epp.eurostat.ec.europa.eu/statistics_explained/index.php/Glossary:Purchasing_power_standard_(PPS)

Table 8.2 The yearly expenditures per student for higher education (ISCED 5–8 (Methodology after 2012 includes all ISCED 5–8 levels))

-Euro-PPS-

Country	2012	2013	2014	2015	2016	2017	2018	2019
1. Poland	7557.9	:	8176.9	8895.3	8105.4	8382.1	9406.4	10,714.8
2. Hungary	6095.9	7346.0	6222.9	6374.9	7026.8	8519.7	9164.6	8452.8
3. Czechia	8715.5	8338.3	8488.5	8970.7	7810.5	8600.3	12,114.0	:
4. Slovakia	:	7678.6	8297.2	12,713.4	8561.4	8427.3	8662.6	:
5. Slovenia	8664.5	9012.5	9079.6	9213.6	9112.0	9811.2	10,055.3	11,151.2
6. Estonia	5728.5	7770.0	7842.4	11,412.7	13,313.6	10,812.4	12,684.1	12,345.5
7. Latvia	5293.8	4225.8	4555.8	5493.3	4589.1	6122.4	6888.5	6016.2
8. Lithuania	6772.8	6689.5	7644.8	7751.2	5494.0	5664.0	6497.3	7474.6
9. Cyprus	15,674.0	15,855.1	13,993.8	15,102.4	14,940.7	18,072.3	16,609.5	17,415.8
10. Malta	12,627.1	13,925.0	14,065.1	13,866.9	14,858.6	14,275.8	15,673.9	17,997.8
11. Romania	4931.8	4249.7	4352.9	5427.3	5056.4	5335.1	5873.5	7231.0
12. Bulgaria	3632.1	3802.5	4433.6	4515.8	4519.1	5736.6	5904.5	:
13. Croatia	:	:	8448.8	:	6452.7	6468.1	6589.2	7324.3
14. Austria	13,083.3	12,991.8	13,140.3	14,018.1	14,145.6	14,253.3	15,046.6	15,584.3
15. Finland	16,065.8	15,889.5	16,159.8	18,634.3	19,323.6	18,779.9	18,911.4	18,701.4
16. Sweden	17,744.4	17,795.3	18,129.8	18,749.7	18,115.9	18,142.5	18,620.8	18,983.3
17. Spain	9203.7	9576.2	9492.4	9684.1	9452.1	9710.2	9938.7	10,374.0
18. Portugal	6807.0	7608.7	8126.5	8340.5	7993.7	8070.3	8204.2	:
19. Greece	2639.1	2447.9	2582.7	2675.5	2394.3	2294.0	2420.2	2911.7
20. Denmark	:	12,450.3	12,165.1	:	13,449.1	12,839.9	12,929.0	14,972.1
21. Ireland	11,579.2	10,844.0	10,627.9	18,125.9	18,003.8	16,549.2	16,511.0	15,982.5
22. United Kingdom	:	:	:	:	:	:	:	:
23. Netherlands	14,308.8	13,647.3	13,636.0	14,161.7	13,887.1	13,920.9	13,936.8	14,206.8

(continued)

Table 8.2 (continued)

Country	2012	2013	2014	2015	2016	2017	2018	2019
24. Belgium	12,857.4	13,282.9	13,444.4	13,734.6	14,478.4	15,136.2	15,814.9	16,299.5
25. Germany	13,344.7	12,862.2	13,099.2	13,342.1	13,242.1	13,444.9	14,030.5	14,653.6
26. France	12,194.1	12,555.3	12,469.5	12,879.4	12,138.1	12,257.7	12,575.9	13,124.6
27. Italy	7654.5	8256.6	8326.4	8494.5	8414.0	8581.5	8636.1	8711.3
28. Luxembourg	*	*	*	*	*	*		

-Euro-PPS-

Source: https://ec.europa.eu/eurostat/databrowser/product/page/EDUC_UOE_FINI04

* data not available on 31.05.2022

countries (Portugal, Italy, and Spain), as well as Croatia (from the 2013 wave of EU accession). The average annual expenditure per student is 8220.8 Euro PPS, with the top ranked (Spain) registering a value greater by 52% than the bottom ranked (Lithuania). The third group contains those countries whose average is approximately 12,617 Euro PPS. This category includes Slovenia, Czech Republic, and Estonia (all from the 2004 wave), as well as France, Denmark, Netherlands, and Germany (with the highest value from its group in 2018—14,030.5 Euro PPS. This is a transition group for countries heading to group 4, the one centered around the figure of 16,741.2 Euro PPS. Seven countries are the basis of this group, in this order from lowest to highest value: Austria, Malta, Belgium, Ireland, Cyprus, Sweden, and Finland. The highest (by far) recorded annual expenditure by students in public institutions in 2018 and in Euro PPS is registered by the United Kingdom, with a value of 33,513.6 Euro PPS.

The answer is found in Jongbloed's words "there is no uniform production technology in higher education," and the major differences between groups of countries may not hide massive discrepancies in the quality of higher education; more explicitly, students in group 1 countries are as prepared as those in group 4 countries, who invest three times as much in education.

Gross Domestic Product (GDP) Rate in the Period 2000–2020

This indicator is the most important reference point of the economic situation within a country. If the gross domestic product rate is increasing, then wealth will be felt at a higher level. On the other hand, if GDP falls, then the level of economic life will decrease. Higher education may depend on this indicator because a causal relationship can be observed between these two components. The more economically developed countries, especially in Western Europe with a high GDP, also have a much better education system, with major investments in education, compared to countries that have a lower GDP. Higher education can also influence the GDP trend. The more educated and innovative citizens a country has, the more GDP will be displayed on a growing trend. In this context, the quality of higher education is an indispensable factor in the well-being of a nation.

The relationship between the standard of living measured by GDP and education has always been a topic of discussion and is still very interesting.

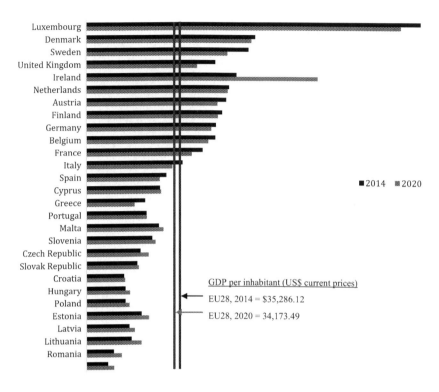

Fig. 8.1 Comparison of the GDP per capita in the EU countries in 2014 and 2020. (Source: Author's data-based development http://databank.worldbank. org/data/reports.aspx?source=2&country=&series=NY.GDP.PCAP. CD&period= accessed on 31.05.2022)

In the work of the authors Olaniyan, D.A., Okemakine, T., it is argued that education is necessary to improve the productive capacity of a country and argues the reasoning behind the investment in human capital. An educated population is a productive population that maximizes the level of knowledge and efficiency, which contributes to a much more productive economy.

In this context, we have used GDP per capita in USD current prices as an indicator to measure the standard of living within a nation. Figure 8.1 shows that Western European countries offer the population a higher standard.

At the level of 2000 (USD current prices), Luxembourg ($48,659.60), Denmark ($30,743.55), Sweden ($29,624.91), and the United Kingdom ($28,223.07) are the top places in the country rankings. If we look at the countries from the 2004 accession wave, we see that with the accession to the European Union, the GDP increased in 2005 almost double compared to 2000, for states such as Cyprus (73.5% increase), Slovenia (77.4% increase), and Poland (78.2%), with the lowest growth rate in Malta (52.3%). At the same time, the GDP per capita of the other six countries from the 2004 accession wave more than doubled for the same period of analysis. The same upward trend was registered in the countries that joined the EU in 2007, with GDP per capita in Romania being $2836.04 higher in 2020 than in Bulgaria. At the level of 2020, the EU countries (United Kingdom included, before Brexit) keep more or less the same rankings, namely, Luxembourg ($116,356.16) in first place, Ireland ($85,422.54) ranking second with a significant increase in GDP per capita between 2014 and 2020, Denmark ($61,063.22), Netherlands ($52,396.03), and Sweden ($52,274.41). Croatia, although it joined the European Union in 2013, has a higher GDP than the countries that are part of the 2007 accession wave, Bulgaria and Romania, but on a downward trend of the GDP per capita gap between them (from $3718.7 in 2004 to $1217.4 in 2020 compared to Romania). We see that countries such as Romania, Bulgaria, and Latvia have a growing tendency from this point of view, showing certain developments.

THE EVOLUTION OF THE PERCENTAGE OF GDP FOR EDUCATION DURING 2000–2020 PERIOD

According to Table 8.3, there is an increase in the total value of investment in education in the 28 countries of the European Union (EU28) in the period 2000–2009. The average value of investments in the EU 28 total is on a positive trend, the trend being generally upward in these countries. According to the *Eurydice Report—Financing Education in Europe—The Impact of the Economic Crisis* carried out by the European Commission, which has analyzed the evolution of investments in education, highlights several distinct trends. In the period 2000–2007, Denmark, France, Italy, Portugal, Finland, Croatia, Austria, and Sweden kept the value of investments at a similar level because these countries allocate some of the highest investment amounts per human capital since 2000. Denmark, France, and

Table 8.3   The trend of investment in education, as a percentage of GDP in the EU 28, in the period 2000–2018

Country	2000	2002	2005	2008	2010	2013	2014	2015	2016	2017	2018
1. Poland	5	5.4	5.5	5.1	5.2	4.9	4.9	4.8	4.6	4.6	4.6
2. Hungary	4.9	5.4	5.5	5.1	4.9	4.0	:	4.3	4.5	4.2	4.1
3. Czechia	3.7	4.2	4.1	3.9	4.3	4.0	3.8	3.8	3.6	3.8	4.2
4. Slovakia	5.8	4.3	3.9	3.6	4.2	4.0	4.1	4.6	3.9	3.9	4.0
5. Slovenia	3.9	5.8	5.7	5.2	5.7	5.1	5.0	4.6	4.5	4.5	4.6
6. Estonia	5.3	5.5	4.9	5.6	5.7	4.9	*	*	*	*	*
7. Latvia	5.4	6.6	5.1	5.7	5.0	4.9	5.3	5.3	4.7	4.4	4.3
8. Lithuania	5.9	5.8	4.9	4.9	5.4	*	4.4	4.1	3.9	3.7	3.7
9. Cyprus	5.3	6.6	7.0	7.5	7.9	6.1	6.1	6.2	6.0	5.8	5.5
10. Malta	4.3	4.2	6.6	5.7	6.7	5.6	5.1	4.9	4.8	4.3	4.6
11. Romania	2.9	3.5	3.5	*	3.5	2.7	2.8	2.7	2.6	2.7	2.8
12. Bulgaria	3.4	3.9	4.3	4.4	4.1	4.1	4.2	3.9	3.9	4.1	4.1
13. Croatia	*	3.7	4.0	4.3	4.3	*	*	*	3.8	*	*
14. Austria	5.6	5.7	5.4	5.5	5.9	5.5	5.4	5.4	5.4	5.3	5.1
15. Finland	5.7	6.2	6.3	6.1	6.9	:	6.8	6.8	6.6	6.1	5.9
16. Sweden	6.8	7.4	6.9	6.8	7.0	7.2	7.1	7.1	7.1	7.1	7.2
17. Spain	4.2	4.3	4.2	4.6	5.0	4.2	4.2	4.2	4.1	4.1	4.0
18. Portugal	5.2	5.3	5.2	4.9	5.6	5.2	5.0	4.8	4.7	4.9	4.6
19. Greece	3.2	3.6	4.1	*	*	3.6	3.6	3.7	*	3.4	3.6
20. Denmark	8.1	8.4	8.3	7.7	8.8	*	*	*	6.8	6.5	6.2
21. Ireland	4.2	4.3	4.7	5.7	6.4	5.3	4.9	3.8	*	*	*
22. United Kingdom	5.5	5.1	5.3	5.3	6.2	5.9	5.9	5.7	5.4	5.4	5.2
23. Netherlands	4.6	5.2	5.5	5.5	6.0	5.6	5.5	5.4	5.5	5.2	5.4
24. Belgium	5.9	6.1	5.9	6.4	6.6	6.6	6.5	6.4	6.3	6.3	6.3
25. Germany	*	4.7	4.6	4.6	5.1	4.6	4.6	4.5	4.5	4.5	4.6
26. France	5.5	5.9	5.7	5.6	5.9	5.5	5.5	5.5	5.4	5.5	5.4
27. Italy	4.3	4.6	4.4	4.6	4.5	4.2	4.1	4.1	3.8	4.0	4.3
28. Luxembourg	3.6	3.8	3.8	*	*	8	4.0	3.9	3.6	3.6	3.7

Source: Author contributions based on Eurostat data https://ec.europa.eu/eurostat/databrowser/view/EDUC_UOE_FINE06__custom_2743089/default/table
*No data registered on 01.06.2022

Sweden significantly increased investment in education in response to the global financial crisis between 2009 and 2012. Finland has also kept it stable, while Portugal had a cut in 2008, followed by a return to its usual value in 2009.

The global economic crisis, which started in early 2009 in the EU, has turned into the most known European trend, with an average spending for

EU 28 on a downward trend. Italy again increased investment in education after 2016, and the same trend was noted for Romania and Bulgaria. Overall, 13 out of 28 EU countries increased their funding in education as a percentage of GDP in 2018.

Another trend is characterized by slow but steady growth in the case of countries like Belgium, Germany, Poland, Slovenia, and the Netherlands, alternating with short periods of decline within a year or two, as is the case with Malta and the Netherlands. Bulgaria, the Czech Republic, Estonia, Ireland, the United Kingdom, Spain, Latvia, Lithuania, Romania, and Hungary are part of the group in which investment in education had an upward trend in the period 2000–2008, which cannot be confirmed in the case of the next period, namely, 2009–2012. The countries that continued to increase investment in education after this period were the Czech Republic, Austria, Ireland, Malta, and the United Kingdom. In contrast, Romania and Bulgaria stand out. We note that Romania, although it occupies the last place at the EU level, with the lowest percentage of GDP allocated to education, has not only decreased the actual value of the money allocated to education but also the percentage of GDP that it has decided to redirect in this respect. Considering the statement according to which education is a national priority and from the way in which the state chooses to invest in it, there is a total discrepancy, taking into account the aforementioned aspects.

The Percentage of GDP of Spending on Research and Development in Countries of the European Union

A growing interest has been felt in recent decades to identify the determinants of economic growth. Regarding the major role of research and development in economic and social progress, a consensus is reached both in the specialized literature and in the economic environment. This indicator is very useful in analyzing the higher education trend because it provides information about the support that the EU countries give to the design of innovative ideas. Our approach also supports the "Research & Development" component as being intrinsically linked to the entire issue of educational quality that is specific to any nation in the world. The line

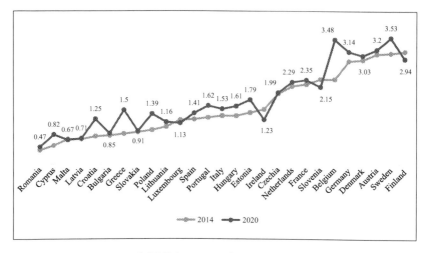

Fig. 8.2 Percentages of GDP in terms of expenditures based on research and development services in EU countries in 2014 and 2020. (Source: Author contributions based on Eurostat data, 2020. *Most of the data available for 2020 are provisional)

of reasoning is reiterated in several studies, suggesting that there are interactive effects between the level of education of the workforce and technological activity, such as the intensity of research and development within a country.

The field of research and development is supported by financial and human efforts by all the countries of the world because they represent the road to competitiveness, growth, and economic prosperity. According to Fig. 8.2, the developed countries are particularly noteworthy, for which this area is a priority, as it benefits from important financial resources. Beyond the methodological aspects, the fact is that the evolution of this strategic sector of activity has been decreasing compared between 2009 and 2014 and slightly regained momentum until 2020 but without reaching the 2011 value, which is likely to compromise our chances to advance toward production with a pronounced innovative character and higher added value.

As a yardstick, it would be useful to present the European ranking in the field at the level of 2014 and 2020. The 2014 top position was dominated by the Northern countries, by reference to several countries in the south of the continent. Finland (3.15%), followed by Sweden (3.10%), Austria (3.08%), Denmark (2.91%), and Germany (2.88%). By comparison, in 2020, the data show a change in the hierarchy, with Finland only ranking sixth and Belgium advancing to second place, with 3.48%. Sweden took over first place with 3.53%. The maximum point is represented by the year 2009, the trend in the period 2000–2009 being an upward one, the period 2009–2014 being downward (except for countries such as Lithuania, Czechia, and Cyprus), and the period 2016–2020 reversing again toward a positive trend for most EU countries. The 2020 level in most European countries from the 2004 wave was higher than in 2014, apart from Malta, and with significant improvement in 2020 compared to 2014 for Poland (from 0.94 to 1.39). Here, we note the presence of Hungary, which in terms of gross expenditure is the best in 2020 (1.61%), along with Estonia and the Czech Republic, but the ranking culminates with Slovenia (2.15%). Romania occupies the last place both in 2014 and 2020 (with 0.38% and 0.47%, respectively), being overtaken by Bulgaria and Croatia. The level of these expenses oscillated between 2007 and 2020, with a decreasing trend. Even if before 2009, Romania was in the "trend," a short distance from Poland, it later neglected this key area and lost significant ground. The maximum level of this indicator was reached in 2007–2008, when it approached 0.6% of GDP. After four years, in which it seemed to have fallen just below the threshold of 0.5% of GDP, the amounts allocated to research and development fell below 0.4% of GDP (0.38% in 2014) and regained toward the end of the analysis period, with 0.47% in 2020.

THE RATIO OF THE POPULATION AGED BETWEEN 25–64 YEARS IN LIFELONG LEARNING (LLL)

The concept of lifelong learning has become a necessity for anyone who wants to be competitive in the long run, given the new paradigm of knowledge economy when you have to successfully face the challenges of global competition and cutting-edge technologies. The demographic changes in Europe and the aging of the population require a readjustment to new technologies and a refreshment of knowledge previously acquired through participation in lifelong learning programs. Although the elements relating to lifelong learning can be found in isolation in different countries, a systematic effort is needed to more deeply understand the basic principles of

Table 8.4 Ratio of the involvement of the population aged between 25 and 64 years old in ongoing training

Country	2000	2005	2010	2012	2014	2020	2021
1. Poland	*	4.9	5.2	4.5	4.0	3.7	5.4
2. Hungary	2.9	3.9	2.7	2.9	3.3	5.1	5.9
3. Czechia	*	5.6	7.5	11.1	9.6	5.5	5.8
4. Slovakia	*	15.3	16.2	3.2	3.1	2.8	4.8
5. Slovenia	*	4.6	2.8	13.8	12.1	8.4	18.9
6. Estonia	6.6	6	10.9	12.8	11.6	16.6	18.4
7. Latvia	*	7.8	5.1	7.2	5.6	6.6	8.6
8. Lithuania	2.8	6.1	3.9	5.4	5.1	7.2	8.5
9. Cyprus	3.1	5.9	7.7	7.7	7.1	4.7	9.7
10. Malta	4.5	5.2	6	7.2	7.7	11.0	13.8
11. Romania	0.9	1.6	1.2	1.4	1.5	1.0	4.9
12. Bulgaria	*	1.3	1.2	1.7	2.1	1.6	1.8
13. Croatia	*	2.1	2.5	3.3	2.8	3.2	5.1
14. Austria	8.3	12.9	13.8	14.2	14.3	11.7	14.6
15. Finland	17.5	22.5	23	24.5	25.1	27.3	30.5
16. Sweden	21.6	17.4	24.4	27.0	29.2	28.6	34.7
17. Spain	4.5	10.8	11	11.2	10.1	11.0	14.4
18. Portugal	3.4	4.1	5.7	10.5	9.6	10.0	12.9
19. Greece	1	1.9	3.1	3.3	3.2	4.1	3.5
20. Denmark	19.4	27.4	32.5	31.6	31.9	20.0	22.4
21. Ireland	*	7.4	6.8	7.5	7.0	11.0	13.6
22. United Kingdom	20.5	27.6	19.5	16.3	16.3	:	:
23. Netherlands	15.5	15.9	16.6	16.9	18.3	18.8	26.6
24. Belgium	6.2	8.3	7.2	6.9	7.4	7.4	10.2
25. Germany	5.2	7.7	7.7	7.9	8.0	7.7	7.7
26. France	2.8	5.9	5	5.7	18.4	13.0	11.0
27. Italy	4.8	5.8	6.2	6.6	8.1	7.2	9.9
28. Luxembourg	4.8	8.5	13.4	14.2	14.5	16.3	17.9

Source: Author contributions based on Eurostat data, accessed on 20.05.2022. http://ec.europa.eu/eurostat/tgm/table.do?tab=table&init=1&language=en&pcode=tsdsc440&plugin=1
*No data available on 01.06.2022

lifelong learning and to change people's mentality in this regard. The situation in Europe is presented in Table 8.4.

At the 2020 level, the Nordic countries are in first place, where the percentage of lifelong learning is very high.

The top ranked countries are followed by Luxembourg, France, and Austria, among others, but the lowest values are recorded for the countries in Central and Eastern Europe, namely, Bulgaria, Slovakia, and Romania, in both 2020 and 2021, with a significant decrease in rank and value for

Greece (from 4.1% to 3.5%). Noteworthy would be the success of Slovenia, which is positioned at a high level close to the European Union average and whose ratio increased from 8.4% in 2020 to 18.9% in 2021. The result achieved by Slovenia is explained by the investments made in education after 1999. The vector of success was the identification of the values in education and their promotion.

Number of Students in Higher Education (1000) (ISCED 5–6)

An important message of this analysis is that the scarcity of recent statistics on the number of actual students in higher education makes it difficult to manage this indicator. There are data on the number of students (in a certain age range) who enrolled in studies and the number of graduates until 2012. Between 2000 and 2008, according to statistics, the higher education sector experienced impressive development. The total number of enrollments in higher education increased by 133% in Romania—a higher growth rate compared to the EU average. In fact, at a time when the country's population was in decline, the university education sector in Romania covered one-fifth of the increase in the higher level at the EU level. The sharpest increase in the number of students in Romanian universities occurred between 2004 and 2009, while the number of students enrolled in the EU, as a whole, remained constant. Five Member States reported more than 2 million students at this stage, namely, the United Kingdom, Germany, France, Poland, and Italy; together with Spain, these six countries made up just over two-thirds of the EU's higher education. In the period 2009–2020, a downward trend followed for Romania. Among the possible factors that contributed to this decline are the demographic decrease, the decrease in the percentage of possibility of the baccalaureate exam, and the financial component.

THE RATIO OF OPTING FOR HIGHER EDUCATION IN THE EU—POPULATION AGED 30–34 YEARS OLD

Regarding the evolution of attendance of higher education courses—people aged between 30–34 years, as evidenced by Table 8.5, this indicator increased for the EU-28 area by 5.1 points, from 36.5 in 2014 to 41.6 in 2021. The best performance in the EU was recorded in 2021 by Luxembourg (62.5%), Ireland (62%), Cyprus (61.5%), and Lithuania

Table 8.5 Ratio of participation in higher education in the EU population aged between 30 and 34 years old during 2000–2021

Country	2000	2010	2014	2015	2016	2017	2018	2019	2020	2021
1. Poland	12.5	35.3	42.1	43.4	44.6	45.7	45.7	46.6	47.0	45.9
2. Hungary	14.8	25.7	34.1	34.3	33.0	32.1	33.7	33.4	33.2	35.5
3. Czechia	13.7	20.4	28.2	30.1	32.8	34.2	33.7	35.1	35.0	36.5
4. Slovakia	10.6	22.1	26.9	28.4	31.5	34.3	37.7	40.1	39.7	40.2
5. Slovenia	18.5	34.8	41	43.4	44.2	46.4	42.7	44.9	46.9	49.2
6. Estonia	30.8	40	46.6	42.7	43.3	45.6	44.6	44.0	41.5	43.1
7. Latvia	18.6	32.3	39.9	41.3	42.8	43.8	42.7	45.7	49.2	47.7
8. Lithuania	42.6	43.8	53.3	57.6	58.7	58.0	57.6	57.8	59.6	60.2
9. Cyprus	31.1	45.3	52.5	54.5	53.4	55.9	57.1	58.8	59.8	61.5
10. Malta	7.4	21.5	26.6	29.1	32.0	33.5	34.8	38.9	39.8	43.6
11. Romania	8.9	18.1	25	25.6	25.6	26.3	24.6	25.8	26.4	24.8
12. Bulgaria	19.5	27.7	30.9	32.1	33.8	32.8	33.7	32.5	33.3	32.7
13. Croatia	16.2	24.3	32.2	30.8	29.3	28.7	34.1	33.1	34.7	33.7
14. Austria	.	23.5	40	38.7	40.1	40.8	40.7	42.4	41.6	43.0
15. Finland	40.3	45.7	45.3	45.5	46.1	44.6	44.2	47.3	49.6	44.9
16. Sweden	31.8	45.3	49.9	50.2	51.0	51.3	51.8	52.5	52.2	51.9
17. Spain	29.2	40.6	42.3	40.9	40.1	41.2	42.4	44.7	44.8	46.7
18. Portugal	11.3	23.5	31.3	31.9	34.6	33.5	33.5	36.2	39.6	43.7
19. Greece	25.4	28.4	52.2	40.4	42.7	43.7	44.3	43.1	43.9	44.3
20. Denmark	32.1	41.2	44.1	45.7	46.7	48.4	48.7	49.4	49.8	52.5
21. Ireland	27.5	50.1	52.2	53.8	54.6	54.5	56.3	55.4	58.1	62.0
22. United Kingdom	29	43	47.7	47.8	48.1	48.2	48.8	50.0	:	:
23. Netherlands	26.5	41.4	44.6	46.3	45.7	47.9	49.4	51.4	54.0	53.4
24. Belgium	35.2	44.4	43.8	42.7	45.6	45.9	47.6	47.5	47.8	49.9
25. Germany	25.7	29.8	31.4	32.3	33.2	34.0	34.9	35.5	36.6	37.8
26. France	27.4	43.5	44.1	45.1	43.7	44.4	46.2	47.5	48.8	49.5
27. Italy	11.6	19.8	23.9	25.3	26.2	26.9	27.8	27.6	27.8	26.8
28. Luxembourg	21.2	46.1	52.7	52.3	54.6	52.7	56.2	56.2	62.2	62.5

Source: Author's contribution based on http://ec.europa.eu/europe2020/pdf/themes/28_tertiary_education.pdf; http://ec.europa.eu/eurostat/tgm/table.do?tab=table&init=1&plugin=1&language=en&pcode=t2020_41, accessed on 20.05.2022

(60.2%), while the worst was recorded in Croatia, Bulgaria, Italy, and Romania (last position in 2021, with 24.8%, even lower than the 25% which placed her also last in 2014).

Total Number of Higher Education Graduates in the Period 2000–2021

As a result of the expansion of access to higher education, the annual number produced by Romanian universities has quadrupled since 2000 and at the EU level by 35%, which means an increase of 4.3% per year. The overall increase in the number of higher education graduates has been particularly strong, more than 10% per year, in Romania, the Czech Republic, and Slovakia, where the number of students has increased significantly since 2000. Between 2000 and 2009, the number of higher education graduates increased in the EU by approximately 57%; after this period it was registered a decrease in the number of higher education graduates. Though, the countries producing the largest number of graduates are: United Kingdom, Germany, Poland, and Slovenia, Malta, Cyprus, Estonia.

SCHOOL DROPOUT

At the EU level, the average early school leaving ratio has steadily improved since 2014, with approximately 9.9% in 2020 and 9.7% in 2021*, compared to the 11.8% (EU-27 from 2020) and 11.2% (EU-28 2013-2020) recorded for the same indicator in 2014. The lowest performers are the Spaniards and the Romanians, with rates of over 16% and 15.6%, respectively, in 2020 (significantly improving only for Spain—13.3% in 2021), while early leavers from Slovakia and Slovenia are twice as few as the Romanians, and in Poland, the dropout rate is three times lower than in Romania, according to the latest data, as shown in Table 8.6.

Romania ranked 27th out of the 28 countries analyzed at the EU level in 2020, being outranked in this negative top only by Spain (the same situation as in 2014) in terms of early leaving the education system, still having one of the highest school dropout rates. In 2014 and 2020, over 18% and 15.6%, respectively of Romanians aged between 18 and 24 who graduated from the gymnasium at most did not express in any way their desire to continue their studies in 2011. After the 2010–2013 period, when Romanians began to be more concerned with continuing their studies, the early leaver percentage for the population aged 18–24 years abruptly increased again until 2015, when the tendency was reversed, toward less dropout ratios. The best, from this point of view, are positioned in 2020: Croatia (2.2%), Greece (3.8%), Slovenia (4.1%), Ireland (5.0%), Poland (5.4%), and Lithuania (5.6%), while in Bulgaria, the dropout ratio in 2020

Table 8.6 Dropout ratio (early leavers) of 18- to 24-year-old population in the EU

Country	2010	2012	2013	2014	2015	2016	2017	2018	2019	2020	2021*
1. Poland	5.4	5.7	5.6	5.4	5.3	5.2	5.0	4.8	5.2	5.4	5.9
2. Hungary	10.8	11.8	11.9	11.4	11.6	12.4	12.5	12.5	11.8	12.1	12.0
3. Czechia	4.9	5.5	5.4	5.5	6.2	6.6	6.7	6.2	6.7	7.6	6.4
4. Slovakia	4.7	5.3	6.4	6.7	6.9	7.4	9.3	8.6	8.3	7.6	7.8
5. Slovenia	5.0	4.4	3.9	4.4	5.0	4.9	4.3	4.2	4.6	4.1	3.1
6. Estonia	11.0	10.3	9.7	12.0	13.7	11.4	11.8	12.0	11.2	8.5	9.8
7. Latvia	12.9	10.6	9.8	8.5	9.9	10.0	8.6	8.3	8.7	7.2	7.3
8. Lithuania	7.9	6.5	6.3	5.9	5.5	4.8	5.4	4.6	4.0	5.6	5.3
9. Cyprus	12.7	11.4	9.1	6.8	5.2	7.6	8.5	7.8	9.2	11.5	10.2
10. Malta	21.4	18.1	17.1	17.0	16.3	15.6	14.0	14.0	13.9	12.6	11.0
11. Romania	19.3	17.8	17.3	18.1	19.1	18.5	18.1	16.4	15.3	15.6	15.3
12. Bulgaria	12.6	12.5	12.5	12.9	13.4	13.8	12.7	12.7	13.9	12.8	12.2
13. Croatia	5.2	5.1	4.5	2.8	2.8	2.8	3.1	3.3	3.0	2.2	2.4
14. Austria	8.3	7.8	7.5	7.0	7.3	6.9	7.4	7.3	7.8	8.1	8.0
15. Finland	10.3	8.9	9.3	9.5	9.2	7.9	8.2	8.3	7.3	8.2	8.2
16. Sweden	6.5	7.5	7.1	6.7	7.0	7.4	7.7	7.5	6.5	7.7	8.4
17. Spain	28.2	24.7	23.6	21.9	20.0	19.0	18.3	17.9	17.3	16.0	13.3
18. Portugal	28.3	20.5	18.9	17.4	13.7	14.0	12.6	11.8	10.6	8.9	5.9
19. Greece	13.5	11.3	10.1	9.0	7.9	6.2	6.0	4.7	4.1	3.8	3.2
20. Denmark	11.5	9.6	8.2	8.1	8.1	7.5	8.8	10.4	9.9	9.3	9.8
21. Ireland	11.9	9.9	8.7	6.7	6.8	6.0	5.0	5.0	5.1	5.0	3.3
22. United Kingdom	14.8	13.4	12.4	11.8	10.8	11.2	10.6	10.7	10.9	:	:
23. Netherlands	10.1	8.9	9.3	8.7	8.2	8.0	7.1	7.3	7.5	7.0	5.3
24. Belgium	11.9	12.0	11.0	9.8	10.1	8.8	8.9	8.6	8.4	8.1	6.7
25. Germany	11.8	10.5	9.8	9.5	10.1	10.3	10.1	10.3	10.3	10.1	11.8
26. France	12.7	11.8	9.7	8.8	9.2	8.8	8.8	8.7	8.2	8.0	7.8
27. Italy	18.6	17.3	16.8	15.0	14.7	13.8	14.0	14.5	13.5	13.1	12.7
28. Luxembourg	7.1	8.1	6.1	6.1	9.3	5.5	7.3	6.3	7.2	8.2	9.3

Source: Author's contribution based on the data available on 20.05.2022 https://ec.europa.eu/eurostat/databrowser/product/page/SDG_04_10

* Break in time series; 2020 data accounted for below analysis

was 12.8%, and in Hungary, it was 12.1% (higher than the 11.4% recorded in 2014). On average, the share of young people who drop out of education prematurely in the EU is 9.9% at the level of 2020, better than the 11.8% recorded in 2014.

HIGHER EDUCATION GRADUATES IN FIELDS OF STUDY IN THE EU

According to the data in Annex no. 12 (a) and (b), it is noted that, at the level of the European Union, most higher education graduates between 2000 and 2012 preferred the fields of social sciences, business administration, and law (32.85%), followed the fields of production engineering and construction (15.01%), health and well-being (14.35%), humanities and arts (12.23%), and sciences of education and continuous training (8.04%).

Based on the 11 ISCED fields of studies and with only slightly different large groups of educational fields, the 2019 data show the same

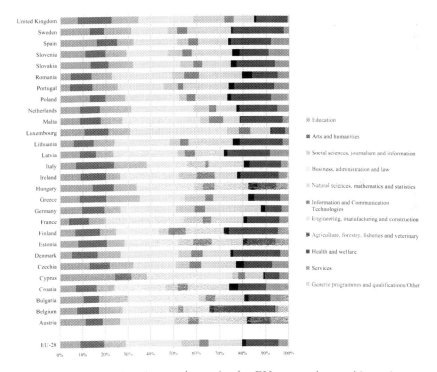

Fig. 8.3 Higher education graduates in the EU grouped on subjects during 2019. (Source: Author's contribution based on Eurostat data, 06.06.2022)

tendencies, with 24.66% for business, administration, and law alone (plus the 9.59% who prefer social sciences, journalism, and information), followed by engineering, manufacturing, and construction (14.58%), and by the health and welfare field (14.12%). The fourth place in the preferences of EU students is occupied in 2019 (as it was in 2012) by the arts and humanities field, with 10.57% graduates of higher education in the European Union. From the graph shown in Fig. 8.3, we also note that EU students' preferences for certain fields of study are similar to the tendencies registered in Romania. Most of them chose as fields of study business administration and law (26.72%), engineering, manufacturing, and construction (18.64%), and health and welfare (11.24%), followed by social sciences, journalism, and information (9.17%).

REFERENCES

Abramovitz, M. (1986). Catching-up, Forging Ahead and Falling Behind. *Journal Economic History, 46,* 385–406.
Dima, A. M. coord. (2013). *Multivariate Critical Analysis of Convergence in European Higher Education* (p. 5). Research project, The Academy of Economics Studies. *cited in* Matkovski, Z., Prochniak, M. (2004, p. 7).

CHAPTER 9

Systems of Benchmarking Indicator Characterizing Modern Economy

Benchmarking consists of a system of procedures for the discovery, adaptation, and implementation of best practices. This concept comes from the English term *benchmark* (milestone, reference) and is widely used in the United States to transpose the fact that the world is in a continuous evolution, and in this framework, one can use the comparison of one's own organization with other organizations accepted as being of reference in various fields. "*Benchmarking* is the search for industrial practices that lead to superior performance" (Robert Camp, North American Benchmarking School, 1990).

Two historical facts convincingly illustrate why *benchmarking* is so necessary. The first historical fact originated in China and is over 2500 years old. The second truth comes from Japan, a country where it is practiced with great success, and it is not known when it dates. In 500 BC, Sun Tzu, a Chinese military strategist, wrote: "if you know the enemy and you know yourself, you should not fear the outcome of a hundred battles." These words of Sun Tzu are in fact the way to success in all situations created by business entities. Survival in the market and conducting management battles, solving current business problems, are all forms of war, which can be conducted according to the same rules as those of General Sun Tzu. The second historical fact is contained in the Japanese word "dantotsu," which means to be "the best of the best." This is the quintessence of benchmarking. *Benchmarking* has been practiced since the 1950s

D.-M. Neamţu, *Education and Economic Development*, https://doi.org/10.1007/978-3-031-20382-4_9

by certain international companies. The term refers to a fairly simple idea, namely, the continuous measurement of the services and practices of a company with the strongest competitors or those companies considered to be leaders in a certain field, to bring closer to excellence, according to the definition of T. Kearns, from the company Xerox. A method initiated by Rank Xerox in the 1980s, *benchmarking* began to be increasingly used to evaluate organizations.

A relatively recent practice, especially common in the Anglo-Saxon space, is that of also using *benchmarking* within higher education institutions. Multiple *benchmarking* systems, covering various aspects of the activities of university centers, from the conduct of research and academic processes to administration, structured on different levels of analysis, are currently used by the United States and the United Kingdom.

The desire of higher education institutions to provide examples of good practice, learning from experience, has existed since the foundation of the institutions themselves. With the emphasis on the recognition of the international role of the university, this desire has taken various forms, such as delegations for observing the functionality of a higher system, collaborations between professional institutions and organizations to support academic activities and mediation of standards, and sharing common interests by meeting professional associations that are both academic and nonacademic (CHEMS 1998), according to *Benchmarking in Higher Education: An International Review*, a 1998 document by the *Commonwealth Education Management Service*.

The creation of a formal framework for comparison between institutions is the novelty generated by *benchmarking*. "The progress of information technology, which simplifies the collection and administration of data, the cultivation of the competitive spirit at international level and the increase of interest in increasing quality" (ARACIS 2009) were some of the reasons that led to the recent development of *benchmarking* among higher education institutions.

Organizations such as the OECD, the World Bank, or the World Economic Forum, but we are not limited to, together with the Lisbon Agenda at the level of the states mentioned, and a series of studies are contributing to the development and offering strategies for quantifying the progress that countries are making in the process of convergence toward the new economy.

THE GLOBAL COMPETITIVENESS INDEX

To analyze the impact that education has on the economic competitiveness of a country, we will focus on the following important indicators: Global Competitiveness Index (GCI), European Human Capital Index (HCI), European Lifelong Learning Index (ELLI), Knowledge Economy Index (KEI), and Human Development Index (HDI).

The Global Competitiveness Index (GCI) is an indicator developed by X. Sala-i-Martin and E. Artadi, and the CGI 4.0. introduced it in 2018, with some differences in the calculation methodology compared to its previous version. This indicator includes both microeconomic and macroeconomic aspects, bringing together information about the competitiveness of enterprises. This new index is composed of a set of 12 pillars (with a structure and calculation methodology changed from the previous version) divided into four main domains: Enabling Environment (pillars 1–4: institutions, infrastructure, ICT adoption, macroeconomic stability), Human Capital (pillars 5–6: health, skills), Markets (pillars 7–10: product market, labor market, financial system, market size), and Innovation Ecosystem (pillars 11–12: business dynamism, innovation capability).

The last edition of the *Global Competitiveness Report* was issued in 2019 and not in 2020 due to the pandemic, and it was calculated for 141 economies of the world, accounting for 99% of the world's GDP, and is based on a complex of factors, aggregating 103 individual indicators, such as gross domestic product and inflation rate, the quality of infrastructure, education and health systems, the characteristics of the market of that state and the legislative provisions of a country, some of them on a scale from 1—the weakest to 7—the best, similar to the calculation of the former version of the Global Competitiveness Index, while the overall GCI 4.0 is reported as a "progress score" on a 0-to-100 scale.

According to the *Global Competitiveness Report*, 2019 (Fig. 9.1), published by the World Economic Forum, the most competitive economy in the world at the level of 2019 is Singapore, followed by the United States, Hong Kong, the Netherlands, Switzerland, Japan, Germany, Sweden, the United Kingdom and Denmark, in this order.

Our research focuses on the selection and analysis of five countries in Europe and Asia: Romania, the United Kingdom, Sweden, Poland in the context of the European Union, and South Korea in the context of Asia.

The criteria behind this selection were the following: the different socioeconomic, cultural, and political contexts that support the

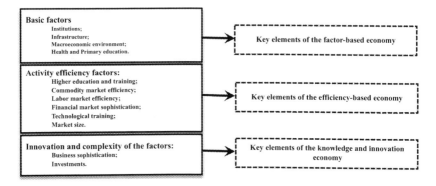

Fig. 9.1 Global Competitiveness Index (Source: World Economic Forum, WEF, 2014)

educational system, strategic geographical positions, policies, and strategies for the development of the most competitive economies of the world. We also considered the specific indicators of the economic system, captured in Table 9.1: innovation, level of development, GDP/inhabitant, and population of countries. The United Kingdom ranks first in Romanians' preferences for studying abroad due to the quality of British education and the funding possibilities offered by the British state. British universities are investing heavily in research, with the United Kingdom recognized as a world leader in this field.

Another example, which I considered suggestive, is Sweden because it is part of the group of Nordic countries, where economic competitiveness and education are relevant. Sweden is currently one of the few examples of success at the European level through political stability, economic performance and a good state of public finances. In this sense, there is also a well-established Swedish model.

In addition to these states, which, due to relative stability, have experienced specific developments in terms of economic, political, and administrative systems, another state under analysis is Poland. It is, obviously, about how a former socialist country, such as Romania, managed to escape from the shadows of its communist past and even become an economic model for the European Community. This state, which has also known the developments under a democratic regime in the last two decades, provides an example of an educational framework, which, similar to the French

Table 9.1   Comparison indexes for the selection of the analyzed countries

Comparison indicators	Romania	Poland	The United Kingdom	Sweden	South Korea
Population (millions)	19.5 (worldwide) 60	38 (worldwide) 38	66.5 (worldwide) 22	10.2 (worldwide) 88	51.7 (worldwide) 28
GDP per capita US$	12,285.2 worldwide) 76	15,430.9 worldwide) 71	42,558 worldwide) 30	53,873.4 worldwide) 21	31,345.6 worldwide) 44
Share of GDP (in PPP) to global GDP (%)	0.71	0.90	2.25	0.4	1.58
Position in the GCI 4.0 top 2019	Rank 51	Rank 37	Rank 9	Rank 8	Rank 13
Innovation capability	Rank 55	Rank 39	Rank 8	Rank 5	Rank 6

Source: Author's contribution based on the data available on the World Economic Forum, WEF, 2019 and data available on data.worldbank.org, accessed on June 6, 2022

framework, also presents a series of peculiarities that can influence the rise of Romania.

From the Asian area, we selected South Korea, which is among the most advanced countries in the world, with the highest degree of digital interconnectivity and a global leader in the economic field. Success has focused on the human resources involved consciously and dedicated to the projection of the nation's goals.

An overall analysis of the scores obtained by the countries of the European Union, as well as South Korea, is highlighted by means of Fig. 9.2.

Among the European Union countries, Croatia obtained the lowest score (61.94) in the Global Competitiveness Index, a somewhat surprising result, with the previous lowest-performer in the European Union, at the level of 2014 being Greece—the expected result, due to the difficult situation in which this country has been found in recent times. In the economic competitiveness ranking, Romania obtained a score of 64.36, occupying 51st place in 2019, with an improved score by 1.4% compared to 2018 (the first year the GCI 4.0 was introduced) and one position up. In this situation, at the level of the European Union, Romania is only ahead of Croatia and Greece, which are ranked 63rd and 59th

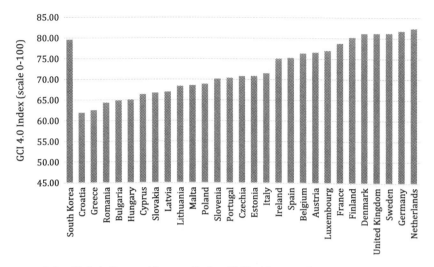

Fig. 9.2 Global Competitiveness Index 2019. (Source: Author's contributions based on data from https://countryeconomy.com/government/global-competit iveness-index)

respectively. Germany, although it represents a fairly stable competitiveness profile in all areas, was down four positions in 2019, ranking 7th. The United Kingdom lost just one position in 2019, ranking 9th. The Czech Republic also decreased by three places compared to 2019, from 29th to 32nd, according to the data presented in Annex no. 13.

Referring to the situation of the indicators related to education from pillar 6 (Skills) in CGI 4.0, the top average score in the ranking was attributed to Switzerland (86.72), followed by Finland, with a score of 85.69, Denmark (with 85.69), the Netherlands (84.62), and Germany on the 6th place, with a score of 84.18. For the indicator years of schooling, the top performer is Germany (with an average of 14.13 years), followed by Switzerland, Canada, Estonia, and Slovakia (all with more than 13.64 mean years of schooling).

For the subindicator Skillset of university graduates (series unit 1–7), Switzerland is again placed in the first place, with a score of 6.01, followed by Singapore (5.72), Finland (5.69), the Netherlands (5.61) and Belgium in 5th place, with 5.50, a ranking similar to the former Higher Education and Training indicator from CGI 2014.

A comparison of the scores obtained, on the pillars taken into account when calculating the Global Competitiveness Index, by five countries, including Romania, was made using the polar chart in Fig. 9.3.

Analyzing Fig. 9.3, in terms of pillar 6 (skills), Sweden holds the highest score (83.73) among the five countries analyzed, occupying the 7th position in the world ranking, followed by the United Kingdom, which ranks 11th, with a score of 81.91. We note that Romania has the lowest score (62.49) among the analyzed countries, occupying only 72nd place in the world and with a slightly improved score compared to 2018 (61.84). Poland descended five positions since 2017, occupying in 2018 the 34th position, with a score of 72.11.

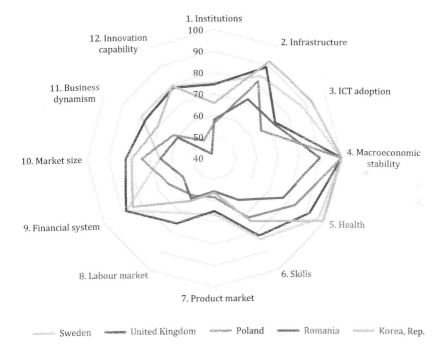

Fig. 9.3 Global Competitiveness Index based on influencing factors in 2019. (Source: Author's contribution based on the World Economic Forum data (http://www.weforum.org/))

In the case of the indicator "Skillset of university graduates" from the same pillar, Sweden also holds the main position, by a 0.45 difference to the United Kingdom, both managing to create a high-performance tertiary education system. More specifically, the Swedish education and training system is of high quality, recording very high scores in many of the dimensions, which are essential for the creation of a knowledge-based society. Although Poland is a country that has managed to develop an education system, which has taken the country to the top of the PISA tests, and with the fastest economic growth among the developed countries of the world, its ranking is very low (only 103rd in the world) and just ahead of Romania (ranked 110th for the same indicator).

The evolution of the scores recorded by Romania for the period 2017–2019 on pillars of the Global Competitiveness Index is shown in the polar diagram in Fig. 9.4.

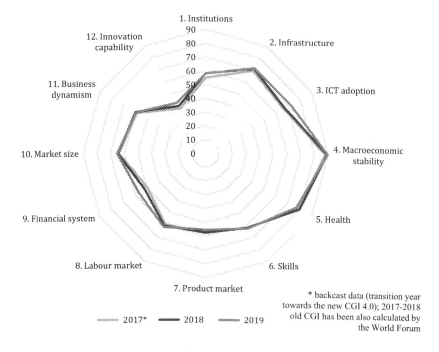

Fig. 9.4 Global Competitiveness Index 4.0 based on influencing factors in Romania between 2017 and 2019. (Source: Author's contribution based on the World Economic Forum data: http://www.weforum.org/)

From the perspective of the old Global Competitiveness Index, in the period 2008–2014, Romania, although it obtained high scores in the health and primary education pillar, experienced very few visible increases in the period 2008–2014. We cannot speak of an upward trend in terms of factors supporting innovation and business sophistication, the scores being insignificant (3.2 points out of 7). The same is valid for the 2017–2019 period on the new pillars, with a small positive change in terms of innovation capability (42.33 in 2019, 37.58 in 2017) and insignificant improvement for the 6th pillar (Skills)—62.49 in 2019 and 62 in 2017. From the perspective of the GCI 4.0 and on the new unitary scale 0-to-100, at the level of 2019, Romania ranks 51st out of 141 countries analyzed, with a score (64.36) just above the upper-middle-income group average GCR (2019), and with a score for the 6th pillar placing Romania on the 72nd place out of the 141 analyzed countries.

Beyond all the comments that may occur in relation to these issues, it is important for Romania to encourage access to basic education, which is an essential requirement for ensuring a future educated population, meant to provide the premises for long-term sustainable socioeconomic development.

The results reveal that the level of socioeconomic development and the competitiveness of an economy are correlated with the overall performance of the respective country in terms of primary education, higher education and training, with emphasis on the quality of education, management of educational institutions and investments in research and training.

Given the general information provided and, in this case, of those revealed by the Global Competitiveness Index, we consider useful for this research approach the *Global Competitiveness Report* of the World Economic Forum because it also incorporates education variables, which determine the selection of these countries in our empirical approach, as well as the revealing of trends and good practices manifested by these states.

THE KAM METHOD

The interdependence of the "knowledge—competitiveness economy" can also be seen from the ranking of the world's states, elaborated annually by the World Bank, within the *Knowledge for Development Program*, depending on the value of two indicators, which reflect their path toward a knowledge economy (Knowledge for Development– *www. worldbank.org*).

The Global Knowledge Economy Index (KEI—Knowledge Economy Index) appreciates the extent to which the environment of a state is favorable to the efficient use of knowledge for economic development based on four pillars of the knowledge economy:

1. Institutional regime and economic incentives (tariff and nontariff barriers, legal norms, quality of economic regulations)
2. Education (adult education rate, secondary and tertiary schooling rate)
3. Innovation (copyright protection, patents registered by the US Patent and Trademark Office, number of published scientific and technical articles)
4. Information and Communication Technologies (number of phones and computers that return to 1000 inhabitants, internet access). This KEI indicator includes the KI—Knowledge Index (education, innovation, and ICT—Information and Communication Technology) and, in addition, includes an assessment of some government policies aimed at establishing the rule of law and liberalizing economic life for citizens and business organizations (this fourth pillar we will call the indicator "economic liberalization")

The Knowledge Index (KI), which measures the ability of states to generate, assimilate, and disseminate knowledge, is based on three of the four pillars of the knowledge economy indicated above: education, innovation, and ICT.

The Global Knowledge Index (GKI) is a joint initiative between the United Nations Development Programme (UNDP) and the Mohammed Bin Rashid Al Maktoum Knowledge Foundation (MBRF); it has been produced annually since 2017 as a summary measure for tracking the knowledge performance of countries and replaces the former Knowledge Economy Index (KEI), which was formerly elaborated annually by the World Bank.

According to details from the Global Knowledge Index, 2020 UNDP and MBRF (2020), the new index aims to measure the "multifaceted concept of knowledge" and tracks down the knowledge performance of countries in seven areas:

1. Preuniversity education
2. Technical and vocational education and training
3. Higher education

4. Research, development, and innovation
5. Information and communications technology
6. economy
7. General enabling environment

The calculation of the Global Knowledge Index was made for 138 economies of the world and is based on a complex set of factors, summing up to 199 indicators, such as gross domestic product and inflation rate, the quality of infrastructure, education and health systems, the characteristics of the market of that state and the legislative provisions of a country, on a scale of 0—the weakest to 100—the best.

If we were to make a list of the top ten most competitive countries in the world and the top ten countries with the most developed knowledge economy, according to the Global Competitiveness Index 2019 and the Global Knowledge Index 2019, we can see that eight out of ten countries are present in both lists.

Those presented in Table 9.2 demonstrate once again the link between the competitiveness of a state and its capacity to produce, disseminate, and assimilate knowledge for economic development. According to the value held by the aggregated GKI, it follows that Switzerland retains its leading

Table 9.2 Countries with the highest competitiveness and the most developed knowledge-based economy (2019–2021)

Ranking	GCI 4.02019*	GKI 2019	GKI 2020	GKI 2021
1	Singapore	Switzerland	Switzerland	Switzerland
2	United States	Finland	United States	Sweden
3	Hong Kong	United States	Finland	United States
4	Netherlands	Singapore	Sweden	Finland
5	Switzerland	Luxembourg	Netherlands	Netherlands
6	Japan	Sweden	Luxembourg	Singapore
7	Germany	Netherlands	Singapore	Denmark
8	Sweden	Denmark	Denmark	United Kingdom
9	United Kingdom	United Kingdom	United Kingdom	Norway
10	Denmark	Hong Kong	Hong Kong	Iceland

Source: Author's contribution based on the Global Knowledge Index 2019 and 2020, UNDP and MBRF, the *Global Competitiveness Report*, 2019, WEF, and infographics from https://knoema.com/infographics/

* The Global Competitiveness Index has not been calculated for 2020 due to the COVID-19 pandemic and was not yet issued; the last check was made in May 2022 (GCR 2020)

position (registering a KGI value of 73.2 and 73.6 in 2019 and 2020, respectively, and a lower value of 71.5 in 2021) as the most advanced knowledge economy in the world, ranking first in 2011 on the higher education (71.3) R&D and innovation pillar (with a score of 57.2) and on the 13th place on the ICT pillar (67.8), down by three positions from 2020 to 2021. The top position of the innovation pillar is due to the increase in royalty and receipt payments, Science and Technical articles and patents; Sweden's competitiveness in the ICT pillar is largely reflected in the increase in the number of Internet users. In the same context, we note that, for the higher education pillar, Switzerland also places 1st place in 2019.

An overview of the scores obtained by the countries of the European Union and South Korea is highlighted in Fig. 9.5.

Out of the countries of the European Union, Greece scored the lowest (46.8) for *The* Global Knowledge Index 2020, *2021.* Romania scored 48.5 (2020) and 54.3 (2021), just ahead of Bulgaria in 2020 (with 48.3) and one place down in 2021. Finland occupies the top position in 2020, scoring 70.8, and it is closely followed by Sweden, with 70.6. They changed places in 2021, with Sweden ranking first (a score of 70). The data in Fig. 9.5 show that the northern countries score the highest in the GKI

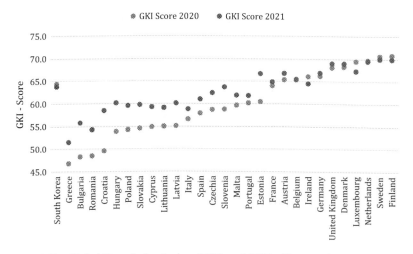

Fig. 9.5 Global Knowledge Index, 2020 and 2021. (Source: Author's contribution based on the Global Knowledge Index, 2020 and 2021)

indicator (they entered the top ten rankings worldwide in both 2019 and 2020). All seven GKI areas (i.e., the knowledge-based economy) are well developed and well balanced. The data also show that while countries from Central and Eastern Europe had higher increases between 2020 and 2021, the top ten performers in the European Union recorded very similar scores for the same comparison period, with the exception of Luxembourg, who also exited the top ten worldwide in 2021.

The changes during 2000–2012 in terms of the place occupied by the countries of the European Union and South Korea in the classification of the World Bank based on the former Index of Knowledge Economics are shown in Fig. 9.6.

From Fig. 9.6, it can be seen that there are a number of countries that have made progress, while others have made a setback in the period

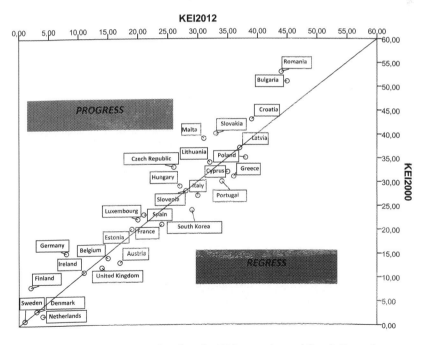

Fig. 9.6 Ranking changes related to the EU countries and South Korea between 2000 and 2012. (Source: Author's contribution based on www.worldbank.org data)

2000–2012. The countries that are above the line, such as Romania, Bulgaria, Hungary, and so on, have climbed to the top made by the World Bank. Poland, South Korea, and the United Kingdom are below the line, marking a setback for the period under review.

The comparison between the 2017 and 2021 Global Knowledge Index shows that all EU countries and South Korea recorded overall progress. Sweden, for example, has maintained leading positions in both the World Bank rankings and the new UNDP's Global Knowledge Index. It is clear that to be competitive, the economy must be based on an educated and qualitative population and on an innovative and efficient economic and institutional system that supports this approach.

Of course, the knowledge-based economy also requires a greater role for universities in society. First, universities need to rethink their missions, in which, in addition to learning and providing frameworks, they anticipate the activation of the fields of research and marketing of research products, respectively, to be more actively involved in the transfer of knowledge and technologies.

THE HUMAN CAPITAL INDEX [1]

In the literature, there are different opinions related to the accurate measurement of the Human Capital Index of persons, which is very difficult and even impossible, in a quantitative form. As a concept with several valences, there are various indicators that try to approximate this level of human capital, for example, the Human Capital Index, drawn up by the Council of Lisbon in 2012, and the Human Capital Index elaborated by the World Bank.

The Human Capital Index is an indicator that summarizes various aspects of the workforce available within a country. The indicator includes both quantitative aspects (related to volume and territorial distribution) and qualitative aspects (related to education and productivity). The 2020 updated edition of the *Human Capital Report* incorporates most recent available data for 174 economies and is not designed as a ranking but with the index ranging from 0 to 1, so an HCI value of, for instance, 0.5 implies that a child born today will be only half as productive as a future worker *Human Capital Report* (2020a, b), for example. The new HCI was

---

[1]**The Human Capital Index has not been calculated recently/the methodology or its structure has been changed. For the last years there are no data available.

introduced in 2018 with a new methodology and structured on three main components Kraay (2018) and subsequent indicators for each: survival (probability of survival to age 5), school (expected years of school, harmonized test scores) and health (survival rate age 15–60, fraction of children under five not stunted). The Human Capital Index 2020 basically measures the human capital that a child born today can expect to attain by his 18th birthday, given the risks of poor health and poor education prevailing in his country, and the index score ranges from 0 to 1, where a value of N indicates that a child born today can expect to be HCI × 100 percent as productive as a future worker as she would be if she enjoyed complete education and full health.

In an ad hoc top of the states, by the Human Capital Index score, most of the EU countries have among the top ten scores in the world (many with the same score), the highest ranked being Finland, Sweden, Ireland, the Netherlands, United Kingdom, Estonia, Slovenia, and Portugal. Finland's exemplary education and environmental systems place it in the top, ahead of the highest-ranked Nordic countries, way back from 2010, according to Annex nos. 14 and 15. On the other side of the spectrum are (largest to smallest score) Slovakia, Bulgaria, and Romania. The graphic representation of the scores obtained by the countries of the European Union and by an Asian country, South Korea, is shown in Fig. 9.7.

The latest data available as of May 2022 on the Human Capital Index use the newest data as of March 2020 *Human Capital Report* (2020a, b), with *The Human Capital 2020 Update. Human Capital in the time of Covid-19* report issued by the World Bank Group. According to these results, Romania and Bulgaria have the lowest scores, while Greece has significantly improved its score since 2012, advancing several positions in this EU and South Korea top, albeit with a lower score than in 2012. Based on the score obtained, Romania has a score of 0.584, ranking last in the EU, and South Korea top, with other EU countries scoring much higher (i.e., Poland—0.753, the United Kingdom—0.783, Sweden—0.795 and Finland—0.796), while South Korea recorded a score of 0.799.

The countries occupying the top ten positions in the world in the rankings rely mainly on *harmonized test scores*, as components of the Human Capital Index, the case of Estonia, Finland, and Poland, or on the *expected years of school*, in the case of Ireland, the Netherlands, and the United Kingdom. Poland scores relatively well, with the 8th out of 48 recorded scores (same ranking for the same score) relying on the HCI components *expected years of school (6th score from the EU countries)*, as well as on the

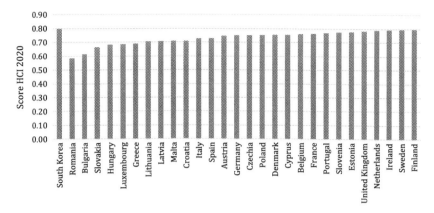

Fig. 9.7   Human Capital Index for the countries of the EU and for South Korea in 2020. (Source: Author's contribution based on the *Human Capital Report* data, 2020: http://www.weforum.org/. The Human Capital Index has not been calculated recently/the methodology or its structure has been changed. For the last few years, there are no data available)

harmonized test scores (with the 8th largest score in the world). A comparison of the scores obtained on the main components of the Human Capital Index by Sweden, the United Kingdom, Poland, Romania and South Korea is shown in Fig. 9.8.

Analyzing the component of the education index, we find that Romania scores a value close to zero (0.077), while the United Kingdom is the leader with a score of 1.031, Sweden obtained a score of 0.977, and Poland 0.376 and South Korea 0.899 with real reasons for these discrepancies.

At the national level, the levers through which we can become more competitive must be identified, choosing a strategic direction of development, which will ensure the expected changes by developing tactics, leading to the achievement of results of immediate improvement. Romania ranks 69th in the world, based on the human capital indicator, calculated as an index of four pillars:

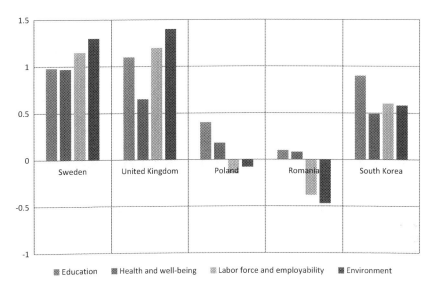

Fig. 9.8 Human Capital Index based on the components during 2012. (Source: Author's contribution based on the *Human Capital Report*: http://www.weforum.org/)

- *Health and well-being*—from childhood to adulthood, Romania ranks 61st.
- *Education*—in its quantitative and qualitative aspects, in the initial, primary, secondary, and higher sector (tertiary), it occupies 57th place.
- *Labor force and employability* (the level of absorption of labor by the labor market) measure the experience, talent, knowledge, and continuous vocational training received by the working population of a country. *The labor and employability* pillar is the strongest in the Scandinavian area, while Romania registers negative values.
- *Stimulating environment*—captures the influences of the legislative system of infrastructure and other factors that highlight human capital. The physical and socioeconomic context critically determines the value of human capital because it determines how personal attributes are rewarded. An environment recognized as more stimulating in relation to another will be even more attractive, according to the policies of the countries ranked in the top ten.

Before presenting the scores recorded by the countries under analysis regarding the Human Capital Index, the second edition of 2015, we discussed some of its characteristics compared to the first edition, 2013, of the *Human Capital Report*. Following the positive reactions received since the publication in 2013 of the Human Capital Index, the basic model has been revised in detail, and a series of methodological clarifications have been added to deepen the analysis in the second edition in 2015. The main changes in relation to the first edition were the following:

- The four original pillars of the first edition, *education, employment, health, and the stimulating environment*, were replaced by five columns for age groups, selected to capture the most important phases of the development of individual human capital as well as the demographic structure of the country: *under 15 years, 15–25 years, 25–54 years, 55–64 years* and *65 years and over*. The population charts that appear on country profiles have been fundamentally redesigned to align with these age groups and to provide real, additional information on the basic index.

- Countries are assessed on the basis of a concise set of indicators on horizontal themes on *learning and* employment. To avoid duplication of the initial variables and those results, measures that were previously included in the *Incentive Environment* category are no longer included in the Index and have been partially moved to the section containing additional information of the Basic Index. The *health* category was absorbed by the unique, highly analytical concept of *life expectancy according to health* (HALE) (World Economic Forum 2015).

- For data standardization, a *z score* transformation was used in the first edition. While this allowed for the relative distribution of the data to be retained, measuring the country's performance according to the significance of the data set has resulted in different countries' scores from year to year. Another reason was that many were not familiar with the *z scores*. In an attempt to solve some of these problems, the data in the revised edition were standardized using the *ideal reference points*.

- To obtain the score and the ranking position of a country, the first edition was awarded the equivalent of a value equal to 25% for each of the four thematic pillars. In accordance with the careful demographic approach of the second edition, as well as with the aim of taking into account the contribution of each individual to the perfor-mance of a country's human capital, the total score and position in the index ranking of a country are obtained by appreciating the aver-age performance of the country for each age group by percentage values of that age group within the distribution of the population worldwide.

There are three key indicative concepts underlying this 2015 edition of the Human Capital Index. *The first concept* is to focus on *training and employment outcomes*, more than on input data or environmental variables. *The second concept* is focused on *demographic statistics*. Where possible, the Human Capital Index provides a generational perspective and divides indicators according to five distinct age groups, highlighting aspects that are particularly essential to the development of the human capital of each cohort. *The third concept* is represented by standardization; that is, the Human Capital Index holds for all countries the same standard for mea-suring the *distance of countries to the ideal state*. By establishing an abso-lute measure of the countries' performance, the 2015 revised edition of the Human Capital Index allows comparisons both within and between countries, from year to year. Future annual editions of the report will allow countries to track progress and changes in human capital investment and implementation gaps over time.

The Human Capital Index contains two horizontal themes—*learning/ education* and *labor force*—which are analyzed in five columns, represent-ing the age groups *under 15 years, 15–24 years, 25–54 years, 55–64 years,* and *65 years and older.* These two intersecting themes assess the success of countries in developing people's skills and abilities through learning and implementing this necessary knowledge by providing a productive workforce.

The first horizontal theme, according to Fig. 9.9, *learning/education*, contains several subpages related to education: enrollment in educational institutions and the quality of education that influences the future work-force; the level of education of those already in the workforce; on-the-job training both through formal on-the-job training and through experience learning, tacit knowledge and learning from colleagues. These subparts are distributed over the five columns of the age groups.

The second theme arranged horizontally can be seen in Fig. 9.10, where *employment* identifies several areas of activity, such as the economic partici-pation submedia measuring the level of labor market participation in the

Age group under 15 years	Age group 15-24 years	Age group 25-54 years	Age group 55-64 years	Age group 65 and over
School enrollment	School enrollment	Educational level	Educational level	Educational level
Primary school enrollment rate	Enrollment rate in tertiary education	Rate of educational level – primary education	Rate of educational level – primary education	Rate of educational level – primary education
Enrollment rate in secondary education	Enrollment rate in vocational education	Rate of educational level – secondary education	Rate of educational level – secondary education	Rate of educational level – secondary education
Rate of duration of basic education	Educational level	Rate of educational level – tertiary education	Rate of educational level – tertiary education	Rate of educational level – tertiary education
Gender difference in secondary school enrollment, girls versus boys	Rate of educational level – primary education			
	Rate of educational level – secondary education			
Quality of education	Quality of education	Learning at work		
The quality of primary schools	The quality of the educational system	Staff training services		
	Youth literacy index	Economic complexity		

Fig. 9.9   The structure of the Human Capital Index related to the topic of education. (Source: World Economic Forum (2015), *The Human Capital Report. Employment, Skills and Human Capital Global Challenge Insight Report*, p. 4)

Age group under 15 years	Age group 15-24 years	Age group 25-54 years	Age group 55-64 years	Age group 65 and over
Vulnerability	Economic participation	Economic participation	Economic participation	Economic participation
	Labor force participation rate	Labor force participation rate	Labor force participation rate	Labor force participation rate
	Unemployment rate	Unemployment rate	Unemployment rate	Unemployment rate
	Unemployment rate	Unemployment rate	Unemployment rate	Unemployment rate
Incidence of child labor	Absence rate in employment, education or training	Gender gap in employment, proportion of women versus men	Healthy life expectancy at birth	Healthy life after 65 years
	Long-term unemployment rate			
	Qualification	Qualification		
	The incidence of above average education	The share of highly qualified employment		
	The incidence of under education	Share of medium-skilled employment		
	Diversity of qualifications	Ease of finding qualified employees		

Fig. 9.10   The structure of the Human Capital Index related to the topic of employment. (Source: World Economic Forum (2015), *The Human Capital Report. Employment, Skills and Human Capital Global Challenge Insight Report*, p. 4)

respective country of people of all ages and from all origins; the skills dimension assesses whether people's education and knowledge are in line with the economic profile of the country concerned; and vulnerability measures the incidence of exploitation-based employment relationships, which reduces the potential of individuals in the long run.

Ranking of the *top ten* of the 2015 edition of the Human Capital Index, Annex no. 14 is dominated by European countries, especially the Nordic countries and Benelux states, including two countries from Asia and the Pacific region and one country from the North American region. The leaders of the index are high-income economies, which have attached great importance to the high level of education and to high-skilled jobs. Finland, with a score of 85.78, is the best performing country in the world when we consider building and mobilizing the potential of human capital, occupying the top place in the pillars of the age groups *under 15 years* and *25–54 years*, for the other age groups being in the *top ten* ranking. Norway, in second place (83.84), and Switzerland, in third place (83.58), follow it closely, with a notable performance for all age groups, although they are not in the *top ten* ranking for the pillar of the *under 15 years* age group. Canada, with a score of 82.88, is the only North American country in the *top ten*, occupying the fourth position, being the global leader for the pillar of the *15–24 years* age group. Japan (82.74) stands out for its pillars in the age groups *55–64 years* and *over 65 years*, which is amplified by the longevity and education of its older population but hindered by the relatively low participation of the workforce in the prime age group, fit for work, mainly because of the difference between women and men. Sweden, which ranks sixth (82.75), slightly outperforms Denmark, which is in seventh position (82.47), although both have strong results for all age groups. New Zealand, with an index score of 81.84, is the only country in Asia and the Pacific region and ranks ninth in the *top ten* rankings and leading places for all pillars of the age groups, except for the pillar of the age group *25–54 years*, mainly due to a comparatively lower economic complexity and low participation rate in employment. The Netherlands (8), with an index value of 82.30 and 81.12 for Belgium (10), have strong scores on the pillars of the younger age groups but are penalized by the relatively low participation of the population in the labor market and a fairly high unemployment rate among the groups *55–64 years* and *over 65 years*, despite strong health and educational outcomes.

As seen in Fig. 9.11, at the European level, Romania ranks 25th out of the 28 member countries analyzed, downgrading Greece—26th place, with a score of 73.70, Spain—27th place, with a score of 73.30, and Bulgaria, which finishes the European ranking with a value of 72.81. Greece obtains this score because it is affected by a youth unemployment rate in the *25–54 years* age group and a low quality of the education system. On the side of the positives, it has a well-educated population, with

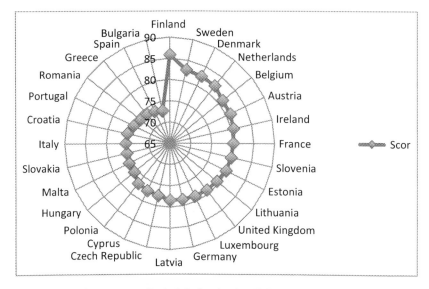

Fig. 9.11   The Human Capital Index in the EU countries. (Source: Author's contribution based on the data of the *Human Capital Report*, 2015)

a higher level of education among the age group *55–64 years* and with a high hope of healthy life. Spain and Bulgaria share the overall profile of Italy and Greece, with high rates of unemployment in the *15–24 years* age group, despite the very high level of diversity of skills acquired and the participation of the population in the *15–24 years* age group in higher education and training.

At the level of the countries under analysis, South Korea, the United Kingdom, Sweden, Poland, and Romania, the ranking is led by Sweden, followed by the United Kingdom with a score of 79.07, which ranks it 19th in the world, then South Korea, with a value of the Human Capital Index of 76.84 and the world 30th position, Poland with a score of 77.06, the 28th place in the world and Romania with a score of 73.94, which gives it the 39th position in the world ranking. On the pillars of the age groups, according to Fig. 9.12, Sweden, the United Kingdom and South Korea are best positioned, especially in the *under 15 years* age group, with equal scores, followed by Poland at a fairly small margin and Romania.

Romania scores low in terms of the pillars of the *15–24 years old* and *25–54 years old*, the population's participation rate on the labor market,

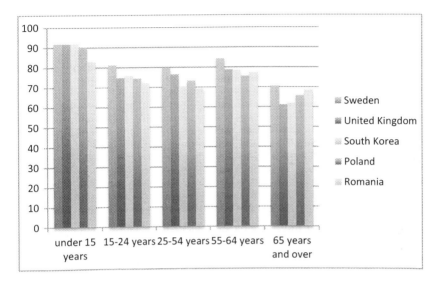

Fig. 9.12   The Human Capital Index related to age groups. (*Source*: Author's contribution based on the data of the *Human Capital Report*, 2015)

the unemployment rate, the participation rate in higher education and continuing education. Romania scores higher in the enrollment rate in secondary education and the graduation rate of basic education of the age group *under 15 years*, as well as on the pillars of the age group *55–64 years*, especially in terms of longevity and employment.

This country stands out, according to the *Human Capital Report* (World Economic Forum 2015), with a labor market participation rate of 56.5% of the total working population, a 52.4% employability rate and an unemployment rate of 7.3%.

Poland shows low scores on the pillars of the unemployment rate for the age group *15–24 years* and the quality of professional training of employees in the workplace for the age group *25–54 years*. It is positioned very well on the pillars of the age group *under 15 years* due to the quality of the initial educational system.

The United Kingdom has a high participation rate in tertiary education, so there is a high qualification for the age group *25–54 years*. On the pillar of continuing education and training would score lower, indicating that there could be room for improvement. A fairly high score is also recorded on the pillars of the *55–64 years* age group, with a high value on the participation rate in the labor force and longevity.

South Korea is part of the *top* five countries, occupying 5th place in the world on the pillar of the enrollment rate in tertiary education. Unlike other countries, perceptions of the quality of its education system are relatively different. It is a rather serious problem that there is much pressure and competition in the Korean education system. The diversity of areas for the preparation of students must be one of the government's priorities, as all students opt for law schools. As a result of this situation, the country has a low position in the ease of finding qualified employees and in the participation in the labor market for the age group *25–54 years*.

The results obtained on where countries are positioned at every stage of a life cycle of human capital development offer the possibility of better-purpose political intervention and human resources planning.

THE EUROPEAN LIFELONG LEARNING INDEX[2]

The European Lifelong Learning Index (ELLI) is an initiative of the Bertelsmann Stiftung organization (www.elli.org), which aims to assess the process of lifelong learning. The European Lifelong Learning Indicator includes information on the scale and quality of courses (such as lifelong learning) in various countries of the European Union. The Lifelong Learning Index, calculated in 2010, measures learning performance in four areas: learning to know in an educational system (Learning to know), learning to do—vocational, professional education (Learning to do), learning to be—for personal development (Learning to be), and learning for social cohesion (Learning to live together).

In relation to Fig. 9.13, "The European Lifelong Learning Index exclusively measures how the learning conditions present in a country facilitate economic and social well-being" Stiftung (2010). The study shows that Nordic countries such as Denmark, Sweden and Finland, plus the Netherlands, come first. Denmark and Sweden are the European countries that have implemented the idea of lifelong learning with the greatest success.

---

[2] **The European Lifelong Learning Index has not been calculated recently/the methodology or its structure has been changed. For the last years there are not data available.

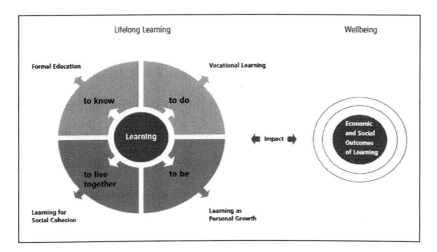

Fig. 9.13 The European Lifelong Learning Index. (Source: Adapted from the *ELLI Report*, 2010)

As seen in Fig. 9.14, the economies of the world are increasingly focused on knowledge and skills, with education being one of the dominant forces for the success of people and states.

The most recent data on the European Lifelong Learning Index are from 2010, a year that coincided with a period of global economic crisis, the strongest effects of which have been felt in Europe.

According to Fig. 9.15, there is a group of four states (Denmark, Sweden, the Netherlands, and Finland) that achieved high performance, followed by another group comprising most of the central European countries and the Anglo-Saxon countries. Below the EU average, according to the *ELLI Report*, are the southern and eastern European states, the Czech Republic and Poland. The lowest level is recorded in countries such as Hungary, Greece, Bulgaria, and Romania.

It is worth mentioning the success of Slovenia, which is positioned at a high level close to the European Union average. The result achieved by Slovenia is explained by the investments made in education after 1999. The vector of success was the identification of the values in education and their promotion.

From Fig. 9.15, we note that Romania has an index of 17.31, this country occupying the last place in the EU in terms of lifelong learning,

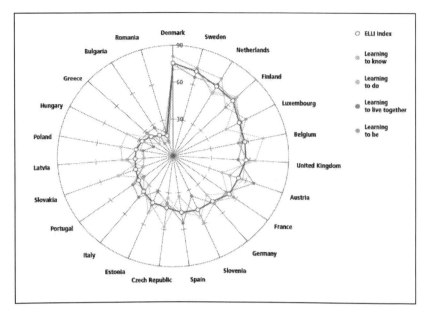

Fig. 9.14 European lifelong learning in the European context. (Source: Author's contribution based on the *ELLI Report*, 2010)

because the percentage of the population aged between 25 and 64 participating in education and training in Romania is much lower than the average of the member states.

The global education system in Sweden and, in general, in the Nordic countries supports performance, as demonstrated by the high PISA test results. In addition, in Sweden, participation in higher education is free of charge, and the allocation of expenditure on education is generous, encouraging overall and large-scale participation of adults in formal education.

The United Kingdom is in line with this trend, since almost three quarters of funds allocated to higher education come from the private system, amounts that have doubled in the last ten years. Nor is it overlooked over Poland, which has managed to develop an education system, which has led the country to the top of the PISA test results, with the fastest economic growth among the developed countries of the world.

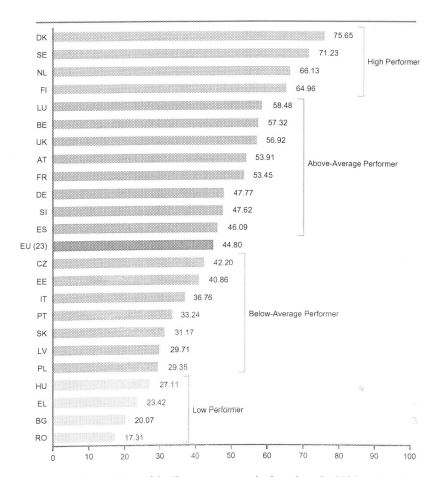

Fig. 9.15 The ranking of the European countries based on the Lifelong Learning Index in 2010. (Source: Adapted from the *ELLI Report*, 2010)

Consequently, education must become the number 1 project in Romania for the next ten years because through education, society can change, first of all, its mental infrastructure and its economic development. Adaptive change in education is an exercise in collective, deep learning of the whole of society, based on trust, honesty, competence, performance, competition, and courage that can generate irreversible benefits—in the short, medium, and long term, for all individual and institutional actors of a nation.

The Human Development Indicator

In this regard, we will mention as relevant the Human Development Index (HDI), the Human Development Index (HDI) invented by the Pakistani economist Mahbub ul Haq for most UN member states, which is updated every year by the United Nations Development Programme (UNDP) and published in the Human Development Report. The HDI is a quantitative measure of the degree of a country's success in developing its human capital. The introduction of this index in the early 1990s was caused by the need to measure human progress. The HDI also accurately reveals the structure and direction of the progress (or regression) of human capital in the course of a country's economic growth, as well as the problems that accompany this progress in approximately 189 countries (for the last 2020 edition). The HDI is considered useful because it is more complex because it measures other human possibilities alongside income. It is a stable indicator due to its components, which is one of its main qualities.

The Human Development Report, 2020 is the 30th anniversary edition and is divided into three main chapters, namely, renewing human development in the Anthropocene, the mechanism of change to catalyze action, and exploring new metrics. Furthermore, the Report proposes the Planetary pressures-adjusted Human Development Index (PHDI) and a new generation of dashboards (Human Development Report 2020). The PHDI is created by multiplying the HDI by an adjustment factor (arithmetic mean between CO_2 emissions per capita index—production based, and the material footprint per capita index). The higher the planetary pressure is, the lower the value of PHDI, while the lowest planetary pressures, in ideal conditions, make PHDI (HDI Human Development Report 2020).

According to definitions included in the Human Development Report 2020, which present data for 2019, the HDI revised calculation takes into account four basic indicators:

- life expectancy at birth—measures longevity, which is directly influenced by the level of development of the country;
- expected years of schooling—represents the number of years of schooling that a child of school entrance age can expect to receive if prevailing patterns of age-specific enrollment rates persist throughout the child's life;

- mean years of schooling—average number of years of education received by people aged 25 and older, converted from education attainment levels using official durations of each level; and
- standard of living ($I_{GNI/capita}$)—as a measure of the standard of living, gross national income (GNI) per capita is used, calculated at purchasing power parity (with 2020 Report data being calculated in 2017 PPP$).

Depending on the level of development of the world's countries, the VALUES of the HDI can have a very high VALUE of the HDI, greater than or equal to 0.8; a high HDI value, greater than or equal to 0.7 but less than 0.8; an average ID value, greater than or equal to 0.55 but less than 0.7; and a low HDI, less than 0.55. HDI and other synthetic indicators can only provide a broad proxy for some of the key aspects of human development:

- the value of GNI/per capita at purchasing power parity (PPP) expressed in dollars;
- life expectancy at birth (years);
- the average number of adult education years over 25 years; and
- school years, which are expected to be followed by children.

The level of the HDI varies on a scale between 0 and 1; the level of human development being higher the closer it is to the value 1, which implies a life expectancy of 85 years, 20 years of literacy and inclusion in universal education and a per capita income of more than US$65,000 (2017 PPP$).

Figure 9.16 provides a complete radiography of the level of human development in the countries of the world, a global appreciation of the progress and the different strategies that have been followed by states to achieve human well-being, with the education component occupying an important place.

With a life expectancy at birth of 76.1 years (73.8 in 2013), 14.3 expected years of schooling, an average number of 11.1 years of schooling of the population over 25 years (10.7 in 2013) and with a GNI per capita of approximately $29,497 (at 2017 PPP$), Romania ranked at the level of 2020 in 49th place in the world in terms of the value of the HDI (Annex 17), up by just a few positions since 2013 (54th place in 2013). This value of the indicator highlights, in essence, the correspondence between it and

Human Development Index (HDI) - 2019

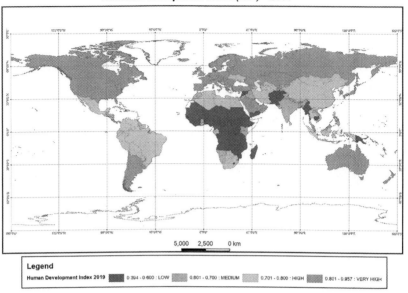

Legend

Human Development Index 2019 ▓ 0.394 - 0.600 : LOW ▓ 0.601 - 0.700 : MEDIUM ▓ 0.701 - 0.800 : HIGH ▓ 0.801 - 0.957 : VERY HIGH

Fig. 9.16 The world map of the Human Development Index (HDI) in 2019. (Source: Author's own elaboration in Power BI, based on primary data from technical annexes to the *Human Development Report* (2020), *The Next Frontier: Human Development and the Anthropocene,* published by UNDP)

the real performances of Romanian society, not only in terms of the successful evolution of the gross national income but also by highlighting the progress made on the scale of the level of human development. Romania's most favorable situation, given the components of the index, for 2019 refers to the gross national income per capita, which places Romania in the 48th position out of the 189 countries analyzed (one rank higher than its overall position) and the mean years of schooling. According to Fig. 9.17, Romania registers a very good value of 11.1 years, the average of the school years. As an order of magnitude worldwide, the value of the indicator is on the 24th position (18th in 2013). The highest value is recorded by Germany, with 14.2 years, followed by the United States, Switzerland, and Canada, each with approximately 13.4 years. The United Kingdom registered a value of 13.2 years, while Norway has a value of 12.9, followed by Australia (12.7 years) and Denmark (12.6 years). Sweden and

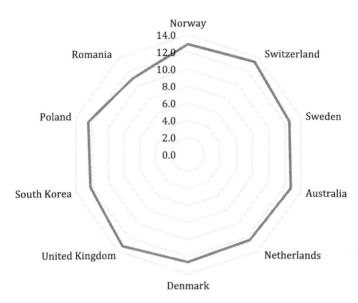

Fig. 9.17 Mean years of schooling worldwide for 2019. (Source: Author's contribution based on the *Human Development Report* (2020), *The Next Frontier: Human Development and the Anthropocene* published by UNDP)

Poland each have 12.5 years, the Netherlands has a value of 12.4 years, and South Korea registered a value of 12.2 for the component *mean years of schooling*, according to Annex no. 17.

The difference between the world maximum and the value of Romania is 3.1, which is quite a large spread and even larger than the 2.1 gap recorded in 2013.

The second indicator with good value is the expected years of schooling. In no other classification in the field of human development, Romania has had a better position than in the case of this indicator. The size of this indicator in 2011 was 14.9 years, the 20th value worldwide (together with Slovakia), preceded by 37 countries. In 2019, however, the value of the indicator was significantly lower (14.3 years). In this respect, Romania's classification is much worse than in 2011, registering only the 39th highest score (rounded to.0), being out passed by countries such as Peru, Ecuador, or Tunisia, which ranks much lower in the overall HDI index. This time, the first place in the world hierarchy is held by Australia 22.0, Belgium 19.8, Sweden 19.5, Finland 19.4, and Iceland 19.1. In

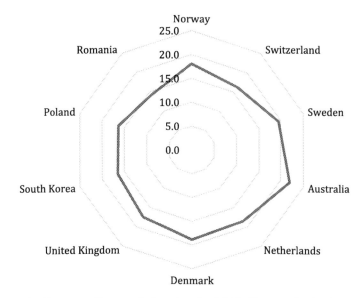

Fig. 9.18 Forecast of years of education for 2019. (Source: Author's contribution based on the *Human Development Report* (2020), *The Next Frontier: Human Development and the Anthropocene* published by UNDP)

descending order of values, according to Fig. 9.18, we note Sweden (19.5), Denmark (18.9), the Netherlands (18.5), Norway (18.1) and the United Kingdom (17.5). In the second category range, we see South Korea (16.5), Switzerland and Poland (each with 16.3), while Romania occupies the last position out of the ten analyzed countries, with an expected 14.2 years of schooling.

The indicator at which Romania registers the third position out of the four indicators analyzed is life expectancy at birth, with a much lower performance worldwide, in 2019 of 76.1 years, which is better than the 73.2 years registered in 2010 and 73.8 years registered in 2013. Hong Kong ranks first, with 84.9 years, followed by Japan (84.6), Switzerland (83.8 years) and Singapore (83.6 years), all with at least one year more than the values recorded in 2013. According to Fig. 9.19, at the level of the analyzed countries, all countries except Poland and Romania have life expectancy at birth above 80.9 years.

The last place in terms of the country's performance is the gross national income. With 17,433 $ GNI/inhabitant Romania ranked 70th in 2013,

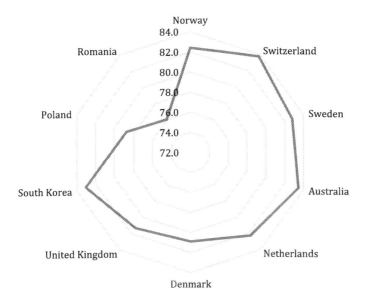

Fig. 9.19 Life expectancy at birth for 2019. (Source: Author's contribution based on the *Human Development Report* (2020), *The Next Frontier: Human Development and the Anthropocene* published by UNDP)

compared to 2010, $12,844, and in 2009 with $14,460, 8% below the level of 2008 (World Bank, 2011). The 2019 data show a great improvement to this extent, with a GNI value of 29,497 (2017 PPP$) The maximum size of GNI per capita at purchasing power parity (PPC) is an exception, of Liechtenstein ($131,032), Qatar ($92,418), which switched places on the top of the hierarchy since 2013, followed by Singapore ($88,155) and Luxembourg ($72,712), while United Arab Emirates lost a few places since its third position in 2013, ranking only 7th in the 2019 top, below Switzerland and Ireland. In other words, at the top of the world hierarchy, we find countries with large oil and gas resources, as well as highly developed economies. As a curiosity, we point to the 27% increase in GDP in the case of Qatar in 2011 compared to 2010, when it had $79,426 and was the second place after Liechtenstein ($81,011) Mărginean (2012). Australia occupies the 5th position in the world in terms of the value of the Human Development Index, according to Fig. 9.20, in relation to the analyzed countries and the sixth position in

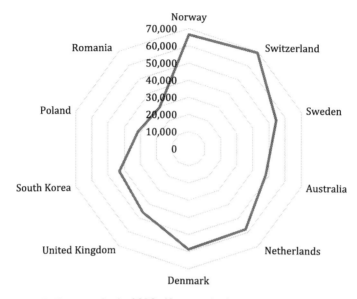

Fig. 9.20 GNI per capita in 2019. (Source: Author's contribution based on the *Human Development Report* (2020), *The Next Frontier: Human Development and the Anthropocene* published by UNDP)

terms of GNI per capita, with 48,085 (2017 PPP$). Just below Switzerland (with $69,394), the top for the analyzed countries is occupied Norway ($66,494), followed in descending order by the Northern European countries (Denmark, the Netherlands, and Sweden), all with GNI per capita between $54,000 and almost $57,700. The next group (GNI per capita between $43,000 and $48,000) is formed by Australia, the United Kingdom and South Korea, while Poland and Romania close the top with much lower values ($31,623 and $29,497, respectively).

Montenegro, which has a GNI per capita lower than Romania's (of $21,399 per capita—in 2017 purchasing power parity), is ranked 48th in the ranking by HDI, one place above Romania, while Croatia (also with a slightly lower GNI per capita of $28,070), ranks in 2019 six places higher than Romania in the overall Human Development Index 2019.

The quality of the medical act and of the medical education of the population materialized in life expectancy determines the situation in Romania (Mereuţă, 2014). Bulgaria, which ranks 56th in the world according to the level of human development 2019, has a life expectancy of 75.1 years, an average number of 11.4 years of schooling for the population over 25 years (placing her ahead of Romania), and a GDP per capita lower than that of Romania, of approximately $23,525/inhabitant, calculated at the 2017 year-level purchasing power parity. Oman in the Middle East, an oil exporter, had in 2013 a GDP per capita at purchasing power of over $42,000, more than double that of Romania, but ranks below in 2019 (approximately $25,944). In this context, it is situated after this country in the HDI ranking, being in 60th place (as it was in 2013) because the population of Oman has, on average, 9.7 years of schooling (improved by 2.1 years since 2013). This index shows that it is useless to have a fairly high GDP per capita if it is distributed unequally, and the money goes in other directions, while the majority of the population has six to nine classes. Turkey, a state that has a GDP per capita behind Romania's in 2019 (but bigger in 2013, with almost $18,400/inhabitant of PPP), pays tribute to the low level of education and is ranked 54th in the HDI ranking. On average, Turkey's residents over the age of 25 have 8.1 years of school (improvement from the 7.6 years of school recorded in 2013).

Regarding the size of the HDI, Romania held the 54th position in the ranking of countries in 2013, with a value of 0.791 (84% of the maximum for Norway of 0.944) at a distance of 0.153. For 2014, according to the Human Development Report 2015, Romania is ranked 52nd with a value of 0.793. In the world top of the countries, according to Jahan (2015), in terms of human well-being, the first position is occupied by Norway in 2014 with a score of 0.944, maintaining its position in 2013, and the second position is occupied by Australia with a score of 0.935, followed by Switzerland with a score of 0.930. In fourth place is Denmark, with a score of 0.923, and the Netherlands was downgraded to the level of 2014, occupying the fifth position in the world, with a score of 0.922.

In the 2019 ranking, Romania improved her position, ranking 49th, 86.5% of Norway's score, and at a distance of 0.129 points. In the ranking of the analyzed countries, Sweden, the United Kingdom, South Korea, Poland, and Romania are ranked first (apart from the world leader, Norway). Worldwide, the ranking is led by Norway—0.957, Switzerland and Ireland—each with 0.955, Hong Kong and Iceland—each with 0.949, Germany—0.947, Sweden—0.945, the Netherlands and Australia—each with 0.944, and on the 10th position is Denmark, with 0.940. The United States lost several positions since 2013 and barely ranks in the top 17th position in 2019, with a score of 0.926.

As shown in Fig. 9.21, this represents an overall radiography of progress based on the scores recorded at the level of the four pillars. Romania, with a life expectancy at birth, at the level of 2019, of 76.1 years, with a mean years of schooling of 11.1 years, with a score for the expected school years of 14.3 years, and with a GDP per capita of $24,497, earned two positions compared to 2014, being now part of the category of countries with a very high level of human development, leaving behind Bulgaria (56th place in 2019, losing also two positions since 2014) this year as well.

One aspect of interest concerns the evolution of the HDI for Romania during 1980–2020.

From Fig. 9.22, we note that Romania, although it started from a value approximately equal to that of Poland, stagnated at the level of 1980, noting a gap in the period 1990–2014 in favor of Poland that was maintained during 2015–2019. South Korea recorded an upward trend from 0.628 in 1980 to 0.904 in 2014, and the gap between South Korea and the United

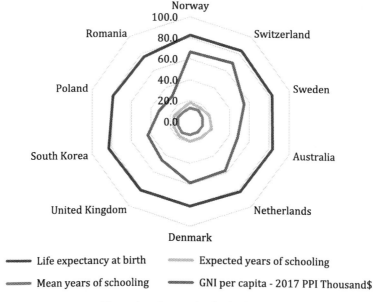

Fig. 9.21 Overview of the analyzed countries for the four pillars of the HDI. (Source: Author's contribution based on the *Human Development Report* (2020), *The Next Frontier: Human Development and the Anthropocene* published by UNDP)

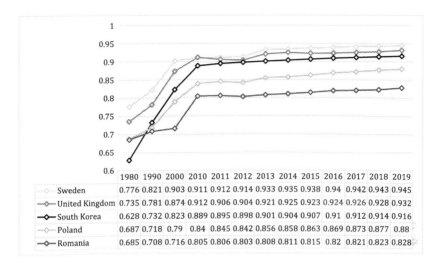

	1980	1990	2000	2010	2011	2012	2013	2014	2015	2016	2017	2018	2019
Sweden	0.776	0.821	0.903	0.911	0.912	0.914	0.933	0.935	0.938	0.94	0.942	0.943	0.945
United Kingdom	0.735	0.781	0.874	0.912	0.906	0.904	0.921	0.925	0.923	0.924	0.926	0.928	0.932
South Korea	0.628	0.732	0.823	0.889	0.895	0.898	0.901	0.904	0.907	0.91	0.912	0.914	0.916
Poland	0.687	0.718	0.79	0.84	0.845	0.842	0.856	0.858	0.863	0.869	0.873	0.877	0.88
Romania	0.685	0.708	0.716	0.805	0.806	0.803	0.808	0.811	0.815	0.82	0.821	0.823	0.828

Fig. 9.22 The trend of the Human Development Index between 1980 and 2020. (Source: Author's contribution based on the *Human Development Report* (2020), *The Next Frontier: Human Development and the Anthropocene* published by UNDP)

Kingdom was larger than that recorded in 2012, with the same trend between 2015 and 2019 (difference of 0.016 in 2019). Between 1980 and 1990, Korea recovered the gap with other countries. Sweden, after 2000, is growing moderately, with the index growing roughly constant, with slight increases. Since 2010, and until 2019, both Sweden and the United Kingdom have been recording approximately the same values, the differences being insignificant (0.013 in the favor of Sweden, in 2019).

In general, the overall strategic objective can be achieved because in the period 2000–2019, the HDI value for Romania increased from 0.716 to 0.828, marked by a relative period of stagnation between 2010 and 2012, and again in the period 2016–2018.

The implementation of the health reform, with well-defined objectives for the transition to positive natural growth of the population (-3.6% in 2012), as well as the significant decrease in infant mortality and the completion of the education reform, with a maximum focus on increasing the quality of the process and on the stability of long-term solutions, are essential for Romania to contribute to the improvement of the Human Development Index by 2025.

The implementation of the requirements of the two directions—the improvement of the education and health indicators—requires the allocation for health, education, and research, adding up to the level of 2025 of expenditures, with shares of *gross domestic product* at least equal to the average of the values of the EU countries.

REFERENCES

ARACIS (*Romanian Agency for Quality Assurance in Higher Education*). (2009). *Primary and Secondary Indicators for Quality Evaluation* (no. 1, p. 6).
CHEMS (Commonwealth Higher Education Management Service). (1998). *Benchmarking in Higher Education: An International Review*. CHEMS.
Global Knowledge Index. (2020), UNDP and MBRF 2020, p. 11.
Human Development Report. (2020). *The Next Frontier, Human Development and the Anthropocene* (p. 2). UNDP.
Jahan, S. (2015, December 15). *Human Development Report 2015, Work for Human Development*. Published for UNDP
Klaus Schwab, World Economic Forum, (WEF, 2014)—The Global Competitiveness Report 2014–2015.
Kraay, A. (2018). *Methodology for a World Bank Human Capital Index*. Policy Research Working Paper 8593, World Bank.
Mărginean, I. (2012). Romania's Performance in the Field of Human Development. *Quality of Life Review, XXIII*(4), 285–286.
MBRF, UNDP/RBAS (2019). Global Knowledge Index 2019: Executive Report.
MBRF, UNDP/RBAS (2021). Global Knowledge Index 2021: Executive Report.
Mereuţă, C. (2014). *Strategic Priorities of Romania's Development on the Horizon 2025*. Retrieved August 2, 2015, from Economiaonline.ro
Stiftung, B. (2010). *European Lifelong Learning Indicators, Making Lifelong Learning Tangible!*
The Global Competitiveness Report. (2019). WEF, p. 478
The Global Competitiveness Report, Special Edition. (2020). WEF, p. 5
The Human Capital Report. (2020a). *Human Capital in the time of Covid-19* (p. 15). World Bank Group.
The Human Capital Report. (2020b). *Update. Human Capital in the time of Covid-19* (p. 5). World Bank Group.
World Economic Forum. (2015). *The Human Capital Report. Employment, Skills and Human Capital Global Challenge Insight Report* (p. 8).

CHAPTER 10

The Relationships GCI-ELLI-HCI

Through this research, we have aimed to analyze the link between the European Human Capital Index (HCI) and the Global Competitiveness Index (GCI), as well as the link between the European Lifelong Learning Index (ELLI) and the Global Competitiveness Index (GCI). The established hypotheses were as follows:

- There is a direct link between the qualitative and quantitative characteristics of human capital stocks, synthesized by the *Human Capital Index* and the level of competitiveness expressed by the *Global Competitiveness Index*;
- There is a direct link between the lifelong learning process, expressed by the *European Lifelong Learning Index* (ELLI), and the competitiveness expressed by the *Global Competitiveness Index* (GCI).

The analysis of the link between the two variables was made on the basis of the data available for 2019 for the countries of the EU and South Korea, according to Table 10.1.[1]

---

[1] **Even if the Human Capital Report was issued in 2020 (the last edition before that was issued for 2018), data are for March 2020 and can be therefore considered as a good comparative measure with the CGI 4.0. 2019.

Table 10.1 Human Capital European Index (HCI) and the Global Competitiveness Index (GCI), 2019–2020

Countries	HUMAN CAPITAL INDEX (HCI) 2020	GLOBAL COMPETITIVENESS INDEX (GCI) 2019
Belgium	0.760	76.38
Bulgaria	0.614	64.90
Czech Republic	0.752	70.85
Denmark	0.755	81.17
Germany	0.751	81.80
Estonia	0.777	70.91
Ireland	0.793	75.12
Greece	0.690	62.58
Spain	0.728	75.28
France	0.763	78.81
Croatia	0.710	61.94
Italy	0.728	71.53
Cyprus	0.756	66.39
Latvia	0.707	66.98
Lithuania	0.706	68.35
Luxembourg	0.686	77.03
Hungary	0.683	65.08
Malta	0.709	68.55
Netherlands	0.790	82.39
Austria	0.747	76.61
Poland	0.753	68.89
Portugal	0.769	70.45
Romania	0.584	64.36
Slovenia	0.775	70.20
Finland	0.796	80.25
Sweden	0.795	81.25
United Kingdom	0.783	81.20
South Korea	0.799	79.62
Slovakia	0.665	66.77

Source: author contributions based on *The Human Capital Report* 2020 and *Global Competitiveness Report* data, 2019

To highlight the link, a correlation graph was built by representing the pairs of values of the indicators in a system of coordinated axes.

From the preliminary graphical analysis, Fig. 10.1, we can appreciate that there is a direct link between the two indicators. The measurement of

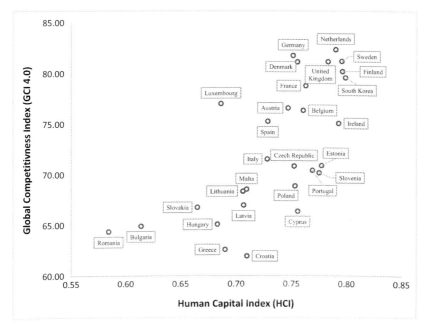

Fig. 10.1 The relationship between the European Index of Human Capital and the Global Competitiveness Index in 2019–2020. Source: author's contribution based on SPSS 22 analysis

the intensity of the link between the considered variables was made using the Spearman coefficient. The Spearman coefficient is an extension of the Pearson correlation coefficient in which the empirical values of the correlated variables are replaced by their corresponding ranks (Jaba, 2002).

The Spearman coefficient is calculated based on the relationship Hapenciuc (2004):

$$r_s = 1 - \frac{6 \sum d_i^2}{n\left(n^2 - 1\right)} \tag{10.1}$$

in which:
d_i - represents the difference in the ranks of the correlated variables;
n - number of units studied.

Table 10.2   The relationship between the Human Capital Index (HCI) and the Global Competitiveness Index in 2021

			HCI2021	GCI2021
Spearman Coefficient	HCI 2021	Correlation coefficient	1.000	0.935[a]
		Sig. (2-tailed)		0,000
		N	28	28
	GCI 2021	Correlation coefficient	0.935[a]	1.000
		Sig. (2-tailed)	0,000	
		N	28	29

Source: author's contribution based on SPSS 22 analysis
[a]The correlation is significant at the level of 0.01 (2-tailed)

The calculations were made using the program SPSS 22, and the values obtained for this coefficient are centralized in Table 10.2.

The value of the Spearman correlation coefficient shows that at the level of the European Union and South Korean countries, there is a positive and very strong correlation. The corresponding Sig. value is less than 0.01, which allows us to state that the value of the Spearman coefficient is statistically significant.

The Correlation Between the European Lifelong Learning Index (ELLI) and the Global Competitiveness Index (GCI) in the Countries of the European Union

The analysis was based on the data available for 23 countries within the European Union, published in the reports: *ELLI Index –Europe, 2010* and *Global Competitiveness Report, 2010-2011*, Table 10.3.

The link between the European Lifelong Learning Index (ELLI) and the Global Competitiveness Index (GCI) in the European Union countries is graphically shown in Fig. 10.2.

The correlogram from Fig. 10.2 shows that there is a direct link between the Lifelong Learning Index (ELLI) and the Global Competitiveness Index (GCI).

To measure the intensity of the link between the Lifelong Learning Index (ELLI) and the Global Competitiveness Index (GCI), the Spearman

Table 10.3 The European Lifelong Index (ELLI), the Global Competitiveness Index and the Global Competitiveness Index (GCI) in the countries of the European Union in 2010

	ELLI 2010	GCI 2010
Belgium	57.32	5.07
Bulgaria	20.07	4.13
Czech Republic	42.2	4.57
Denmark	75.65	5.32
Germany	47.77	5.39
Estonia	40.86	4.61
Greece	20.07	3.99
Spain	46.09	4.49
France	53.45	5.13
Italy	36.76	4.37
Lithuania	29.71	4.14
Luxembourg	58.48	5.05
Hungary	27.11	4.33
Netherlands	66.13	5.33
Austria	53.91	5.09
Poland	29.35	4.51
Portugal	33.24	4.38
Romania	17.31	4.16
Slovenia	47.62	4.42
Finland	64.96	5.37
Sweden	71.23	5.56
United Kingdom	56.92	5.25
Slovakia	31.17	4.25

Source: author's contribution based on *ELLI Index –Europe data, 2010* and *Global Competitiveness Report, 2010-2011*

coefficient was calculated, and the values obtained are centralized in Table 10.4.

Analyzing the data in Table 10.4, we note that there is a direct and very strong link between the *European Lifelong Learning Index* (ELLI) and the *Global Competitiveness Index* (GCI). The value of the Spearman coefficient is significant, and the corresponding Sig. value being less than 0.01.

The obtained results confirm the established hypotheses. Thus, we can say that there is a direct link between the qualitative and quantitative characteristics of human capital stocks, synthesized by the *Human Capital Index* (HCI), and the level of competitiveness expressed by the *Global Competitiveness Index* (GCI) at the level of the countries analyzed. The

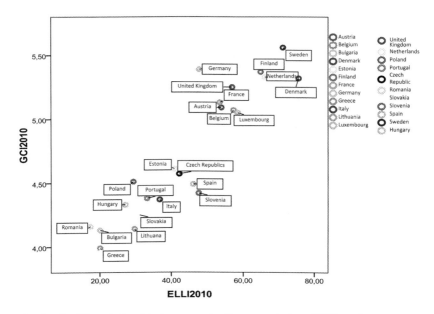

Fig. 10.2   The relationship between the European index of lifelong learning and the global competitiveness index in 2010. Source: author's contribution based on SPSS 22 analysis

Table 10.4   The relationship between the Lifelong Learning Index (ELLI) and the Global Competitiveness Index (GCI) in 2010

			ELLI 2010	GCI 2010
Spearman Coefficient	ELLI 2010	Correlation coefficient	1.000	0.891[a]
		Sig. (2-tailed)	.	0,000
		N	23	23
	GCI 2010	Correlation coefficient	0.891[a]	1.000
		Sig. (2-tailed)	0.000	.
		N	23	23

Source: author's contribution based on SPSS 22 analysis

[a]The correlation is significant at the level of 0.01 (2-tailed)

value obtained for the Spearman correlation coefficient shows us that at the level of the European Union countries and South Korea, there is a positive and very strong correlation. The corresponding Sig. value is less than 0.01, which allows us to state that the value of the Spearman coefficient is statistically significant.

The link between lifelong learning, expressed by the *European Lifelong Learning Index* (ELLI), and competitiveness expressed by the *Global Competitiveness Index* (GCI) is direct. The Spearman coefficient value indicates a very strong, statistically significant link, and the corresponding Sig. value being less than 0.01.

REFERENCES

Hapenciuc, C. V. (2004). *Practical Statistics Handbook – Formulas, Questions, Tests, Dictionary.* Didactic and Pedagogical Publishing House, Bucharest.
Jaba, E. (2002). *Statistics* (3rd ed.). Economic Publishing – house.

CHAPTER 11

The 2020 Strategy

"Europe 2020" is the European Commission's economic growth strategy for the period 2010–2020. The strategy aims to create favorable conditions for smart, sustainable, and inclusive growth. The aim of the three priorities is to help the EU and the member states achieve a high level of employment, productivity, and social cohesion.

THE GOALS AND OBJECTIVES OF THE EUROPE 2020 STRATEGY FOR THE FIELD OF EDUCATION

The European Union has also set five headline targets to be achieved by 2020.

Given that educational progress contributes to improving job prospects and reducing poverty, that more research and innovation offers more favorable conditions for the creation of new jobs, and that investment in green technologies creates new business opportunities and jobs, we can say that the above objectives are interdependent and mutually reinforcing.

Moreover, the five European targets for 2020 are transposed into national targets so that each member state can follow its progress. In the case of Romania, the national objectives regarding the 2020 Strategy and to be achieved by 2020 are listed in Table 11.1.

The objectives outlined have a direct connection with the level of training and the level of education due to their influence on economic growth.

© The Author(s), under exclusive license to Springer Nature
Switzerland AG 2023
D.-M. Neamțu, *Education and Economic Development*,
https://DOI.org/10.1007/978-3-031-20382-4_11

Table 11.1   The goals related to the Europe 2020 Strategy

Europe 2020 strategy objectives	UE	The goals % Romania	Romania 2014
Employment rate (in %)	75%	70%	65.4%
R&D as % of GDP	3%	2%	0.39
Participation in lifelong learning	15%	10%	1.5%
Early school leaving (in %)	10%	11.3%	18.5%
Tertiary education	40%	26.7%	23.8%

Source: Adaptation after the European Commission (2015), *Let Us Understand the Policies of the European Union—Europe 2020: Europe's Growth Strategy*, p. 3

This influence is materialized in increased employment, productivity, participation, and skills training. Some of these variables are analyzed in detail below.

All member states are committed to contributing to the achievement of the Europe 2020 strategy objectives. However, given that each country has a particular economic situation, member states translate the EU's overall objectives into national objectives. The latter are included in the National Reform Programme (NRP), which is a document of a member state's policies and measures to support growth and job growth, with the aim of achieving the objectives of the strategy. The NRPs shall be presented in parallel with stability or convergence programs, which shall set out the budgetary plans of the member state, that is, for the next three- or four-year period. Unsurprisingly, the importance of improving competitiveness through innovation and rapid growth in labor productivity is at the heart of the Europe 2020 strategy (European Commission, 2010). The strategy explicitly states that such improvements depend to a large extent on improving the qualification of the workforce. In fact, two of the strategy's six objectives depend on improving vocational education and training, the workforce, and four of the European Commission's seven "flagship initiatives" aimed at supporting the implementation of the EU 2020 strategy are directly or indirectly linked to improving the level of qualification. Six priority objectives have been formulated (in fact, only five as the one directly targeting education consists of two distinct objectives: one on participation in higher education and one on early school leaving).

The objectives for improving the education level of the population are as follows: (1) If 75% of the population aged 20–64 should have a job, each country will have to ensure that its citizens have the capacity to take up a job and will keep it for the rest of their lives; (2) if a country invests 3% of its gross domestic product (GDP) in R&D (R&D), it will need capable researchers, highly qualified scientists and engineers to make a judicious use of these resources; (3) if a country aims to reduce the ESL rate to below 10%, it is necessary to ensure that no one is left behind in the first grades; (4) if 40% of a country's younger generation should complete a form of university education, it should ensure that those young people acquire useful skills with their diploma. The four "flagship initiatives" of the EU 2020, which substantially include elements of vocational education and training, are *Youth on the Move, An Innovation Union, An Agenda for New Skills and Jobs*, and *A European Platform to Combat Poverty*.

BENCHMARKS AND TRENDS OF THE ROMANIAN UNIVERSITY SYSTEM DURING 2000–2020

Unlike in the past, higher education institutions have taken on the responsibility of preparing a much wider range of professions as a result of the expansion of university education in both developing and industrialized countries. Substantial reforms are being implemented in the higher education system, aimed at raising awareness of institutions and stimulating responsiveness to the needs of society and the economy. Previous debates on global issues of improving the effectiveness and efficiency of education show that higher education has acquired vital importance for economic development, and the expansion of higher education, as well as the improvement of its relevance and quality, has become a priority.

Considering the importance of higher education in the process of European integration, EU officials have developed political signals appropriate to the definition of a *European Knowledge Area*, having as basic pillars the *European Higher Education Area* and the *European Research Area*. The need for a positive perspective of the contribution of higher education to economic development is given by its ability to transplant it to the changes of the economic and social environment: curricular harmonization, educational offerings, institutional culture, and managerial practices.

In the context of the creation, accumulation, and increasing dissemination of knowledge at the global level and especially at the level of the developed economies and societies of the world, attention is focused on higher education and its potential to generate economic and social development. In this context, universities contribute to the formation of intellectual elites and put the basis of the future productive workforce. However, the intangible assets gained territory nowadays when the work productivity is based on knowledge. In the late 1980s, Romania inherited an educational system designed to meet the needs of the workforce of the socialist and political industry of communist cadres. A total of 164,507 students attended the courses of the technological institutes in the field, occupying a fairly large share of the *46 public universities.* In one of his works, *Paradigms of University Management*, in the year 2002, Professor Brătianu highlighted an incipient but safe competition not only between private and public universities but also between them and new authorized training providers such as renowned companies or other institutions. Additionally, two strategic groups are identified on the educational market, namely, *the strategic group of state* and *private universities*, the latter suffering for a long period in the 1990s from the lack of institutional accreditation. The period between 1990 and 1992 was one of the radical changes in the system to meet, first of all, the internal requirements for education. During the years 1993–1994, a series of major decisions were adopted, and a series of negotiations were initiated with external funders to support education in Romania, an important element for the higher education system to support the requirements determined by the transition process to a market economy and a democratic society.

Political and Legislative Benchmarks

Political, legal, and legislative aspects can considerably influence the decisions made by higher education institutions. Political-legal or politico-institutional factors refer to the action of relations of dependence, dominance, and power that manifest themselves in a society. In this respect, various authors have developed more or less complete theories. According to Professor Someșan, they are specific to each country and represent mainly the political forces, the structures of the society, the social classes, the legal regulations, the degree of state involvement through some institutions in the economy, and the degree of stability of the political climate Someșan and Cosma (2001).

The currently tumultuous political life makes us think more and more of the state, and we often tend to attribute to it all the failures of our society. It is often forgotten that the state is a worldly reality and not a transcendent one, being a social reality in which traditions and various institutions subjected to the transformations of time have unfolded throughout the ages. From this point of view, in Romania, there is a certain stability, but not a sufficient stability, to provide the necessary comfort. The influence of the political factor is yet another destabilizing element for this country. This leads to disorder, recklessness, lack of calculated and grounded measures, negatively and equally influencing both the economy and society, which is stuck, lacking mobility and will. Romania has entered a difficult constructive path, which needs to maintain and develop an essential ingredient to achieve success: political stability.

The ideas for reforming higher education, analyzed for the first time in history from a global perspective, appeared with the 900th anniversary of the establishment in 1088 of the fourth university in the world, in Bologna; the first places in the world, being occupied by the *University of Medical Sciences, Ahvaz Jundishapur-Khozettan—Iran*, founded by Shapur I., in 200 BC; *Al-Karaouine-Fes University*, Morocco, founded in 859, is recognized by the *Guinness Book of Records* as the oldest university with a continuous flow of operation; and *Al-Azhar University—Cairo*, Egypt opened its doors in 975.

On the 18th of September 1988, the University Chancellors from EU member states, at that time, met in Bologna to lay the foundations for a long-term process of compatibility of national higher education systems by adopting common principles and rules. The result was the elaboration of a document called *Magna Charta Universitatum*. The title of this document refers to an essential act of humanity—a symbol of sustainability and civilization in the spirit of democracy—*Magna Charta Libertatum* of 1215 (Pachef 2008). The fundamental principles proclaimed by the document are university autonomy, the development of universities as centers for the propagation of sustainable development, special attention to education and research, the mobility of students and academics, and the recognition of titles and diplomas obtained at the end of the training.

By the *Sorbonne Declaration*, the ministers of education of Germany, France, Italy, and the United Kingdom sign, on May 25, 1998, a declaration reiterating the desire to build a unique European university space. The four signatories "are committed to encouraging the creation of a common frame of reference, which will improve the recognition of university diplomas, facilitate the mobility of students but also the finding of a job." This ends with the launch of a call to join this process, both to the other member states of the European Union and to other European states, to strengthen the "place of Europe" in the world.

Romania is among the first countries to sign the *Bologna Process*. Thus, Romania has been participating in the *Bologna Process* from the very beginning of this process, that of signing the *Bologna Declaration* in 1999. To date, Romania has voluntarily taken on policy alignment in the field of higher education in line with the objectives and policies that were stipulated by the Bologna Trial. As a result, the higher education system in Romania has undergone a series of fundamental changes through the compatibility of legislation, the promotion of national public policies, the creation of new institutional structures, new regulations and policies at the university level. To achieve the intended goal, the following general objectives have been set:

- recognition of diplomas: adaptation of a system of diplomas easily recognizable and compatible;
- adopting a system of organizing studies based on two cycles;
- implementation of the credit system (ECTS);
- promoting the mobility of students, academic and administrative staff;
- promoting European cooperation in quality evaluation; and
- promoting the European dimension of higher education, especially with regard to the development of study programs, cooperation between institutions, and mobility programs.

The meeting in Prague in 2001 brought as novelty elements the desire to involve the whole of Europe in the process of enlargement of the European Union. The delegated ministers also agreed that education is a public good and responsibility, and the students are full members of this community. The conclusions of this important meeting also found the establishment of the necessity of permanent education as an essential condition of modern man.

On the 19th of September 2003, in Berlin, in the German capital, 33 ministers met again to review the achievements of the two years that had passed since the previous meeting (2001, Prague). In this event, the common will to transform Europe into "the most competitive and dynamic knowledge-based economy in the world, capable of producing sustained economic growth—with more jobs and great social cohesion—is emerging." Additionally, it was desired to include doctoral studies as a third cycle of education so that the first cycle (the bachelor's degree) would ensure a multidisciplinary character and to model the student to make flexibility and accommodation without difficulty to the different social requirements. Analyzing the abovementioned documents, the following trends can be recorded at both the European and national levels regarding the "future of higher education":

- achieving the interaction between higher education and economics;
- the adequacy of study programs to economics;
- establishing specific indicators to achieve quality in education;
- supporting students' and university teachers' mobilities;
- higher education accessible at any age by promoting lifelong learning;
- organizing the higher education system on distinct cycles;
- improvement of credit systems for the recognition of the results of studies carried out in other countries; and
- the compatibility of higher education qualifications in different countries.

After 1989, given the profound political, economic, and social transformations, the higher education system had to make special efforts for adaptation and reconsidered its role in society. In this respect, legislative changes were necessary. A comprehensive analysis of the period 1990–2011 from a legislative point of view highlights the period 1990–1993 as the period characterized by a *fuzzy legislation* Brătianu (2002). Education has gone through a spontaneous transition during this period (Miroiu, 1998). Overall, this period was characterized by much confusion, fear, chaos, and institutional developments on the basis of local initiatives. The dimensions and extent of university autonomy were established for the first time in Education Law no. 84/1995 and then revised and detailed in the amendments made in 1999.

The new education reform was started as early as 1990 but had amplified effects since 1997 and had the following key objectives for higher education institutions:

- interdisciplinary and multidisciplinary study programs, diversified, continuously elaborated;
- institutional curriculum and services, strongly oriented toward the market;

- decentralization of additional budgetary funds;
- introduction of quality management systems and information technology;
- scientific research much more promoted in universities;
- increasing the types and forms of education and diversifying the financial support granted to higher education (these aimed to increase the schooling capacity in higher education);
- opening a new perspective for the financing of social services for students;
- developing additional options for postgraduate studies while creating new institutions for in-depth studies;
- transferability and accreditation through the transfer of credits between programs and institutions; and
- preparation for European integration.

The educational reforms in the period after 1990 were numerous and brought about significant changes to the higher education system. The period 1990–1995 was characterized by general reparative changes in the educational system as a result of Romania's transition from the communist to the democratic system. The period 1999–2010 was dominated by a new series of reforms aimed at aligning the higher education system with the principles and objectives of the *Bologna Process.*

In 2008, the *National Pact for Education* was signed, a document assumed by all political parties represented in the Parliament and actors from civil society, which includes eight general objectives for the educational system, which were to be achieved in the next five years. The beginning of 2011 meant the adoption of a new law, the National Education Law no. 1/2011, which brought a series of essential changes regarding the vision of the higher education system. The major changes with direct impact, which resulted from the implementation of the new legislative framework, were the classification of universities into three categories—universities of education, universities of education and research and universities of advanced research, the change of the financing system, influenced by this classification of universities, a new model of governance and institutional management (by reconfiguring the internal structures).

Over the past decade, Romania has witnessed important reforms both in terms of policies and in terms of the development of the higher education sector. Recent changes in the field of policies include changes in the structure of most study programs as a result of Romania's participation in the Bologna process; a reform of higher education funding (in 1999) involving the transition from the financing of *inputs* to funding based on a registered student; a substantial increase in global funding in recent years; and, starting with 2000, the introduction of provisions allowing state universities to register fee-based students, which is a new major source of income for expanding universities and improving the quality of services offered by them. Moreover, if applied successfully, the National Education Law of 2011 may lead to better management of higher education institutions and to better results.

In Romania, improving the education and training system is essential not only for the achievement of the two EU 2020 objectives, directly related to the field of education (i.e., increasing the enrollment rate in higher education and reducing the ESL rate) but also for transforming the country into a driving force of economic growth in Europe (Manea et al., 2021).

Economic Benchmarks and Developments

The current progress of technology has been largely enhanced by education, with an increasing number of activities and jobs developing that require more knowledge and more training. The services in the contemporary world are based on quality educational systems capable of responding to these challenges while developing the need for human emancipation by acquiring the knowledge and skills essential for building a modern society. Education allows society to interpret the world around it correctly, innovating new ways and means to conform to their environment and generating opinions on economic and social life. Macroeconomic indicators, determined by the economic factor, can influence the change in the supply and demand for educational services.

One of the best indicators of responsibility, with which they operate in the case of education, is its funding, as it directly influences all educational processes, quality, and equity. Education must not be seen as a cost that a state must bear to guarantee a right but as a long-term investment that generates future income and contributes to the development of society. In our opinion, the myth that all education issues are linked to funding should not be created. Funding is a problem, often a serious one, but it should be noted that until the system works as a well-functioning system, funding will continue to remain a problem.

For the analysis of the changes experienced by the higher education system in Romania, a series of data provided by the National Institute of Statistics and Economic Studies, the Statistical Commission of the European Union—EUROSTAT and the United Nations Organization for Education, Science and Culture—UNESCO were used. The evolution of data on the indicators that characterize the higher education system was analyzed: the evolution of the number of state and private universities, the number of students enrolled in higher cycles, the number of teachers in state higher education, the evolution of fields of study, school population, and the number of graduates by education levels. According to an OECD study OECD (2011), a state earns on the one hand tens of thousands of dollars from each graduate of higher education, on average the amount of $91,036, and on the other hand, the states are distinguished by a general development of the economy through the innovations brought by them to the labor market. By means of Fig. 11.1, we tried to highlight the evolution of the number of people enrolled in state and private higher education for the period related to 1990–2020, during which the educational reforms were numerous and produced significant changes to the education system, as we also mentioned in the previous paragraphs. What can be

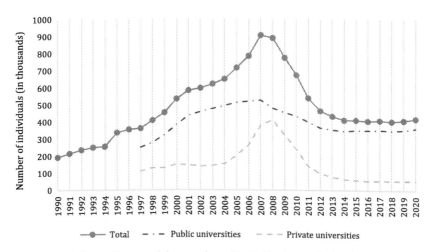

Fig. 11.1   The evolution of the number of individuals enrolled in higher education (1990–2020). (Source: National Institute of Statistics and Economic Studies, 2020, http://statistici.insse.ro:8077/tempo-online/#/pages/tables/insse-table)

easily seen is related to the fact that the way in which the number of private universities has oscillated is much different from that of the state universities and that there is no link between registrations, in the sense of decreasing the number of enrollees at state universities with the increase in the number of applications for registrations at private universities.

After the 1990s, Romanian higher education experienced an important quantitative explosion, an effect also favored by the absence of an adequate legislative framework, the system being subjected to countless restructurings and reforms. The number of higher education institutions, both private and public, has significantly increased the number of students and consequently the number of teaching positions, in parallel with the expansion of the number of study programs. If in 1991 there were 56 higher education units, their number reached a maximum of 126 universities in 2000, after which it began to decrease, reaching 108 in the academic year 2009–2010, then steadily decreasing to a total of 89 higher education units in the academic year 2020–2021 (*Report on the Status of Higher Education in Romania* 2020–2021). Compared to the dynamics of universities/higher education institutions, those of faculties are even more accelerated. If in 1991, the number of faculty members was 257, in 2005 it reached the maximum of 770, and steadily decreased again until it reached a number of 541 faculty members in the 2020–2021 academic year, according to data from the National Institute of Statistics, included in the *Report on the Status of Higher Education in Romania* (2020–2021), published by the Ministry of Education. In 2012, according to the *Report on the Status of Higher Education in Romania* (2020–2021), according to the data published by the ESS, there were 57 public (state) universities and 51 private universities accredited or authorized to operate provisionally in Romania,[1] whereas for the 2020–2021 academic year, the data show that there are 54 public universities and only 35 private universities (only approximately two-thirds of the number registered ten years before). Within them, also for the 2020–2021 academic year, 541 faculty members functioned (out of which 404 are in universities financed by the state budget), of whom 418,346 students were enrolled (23% fewer than in 2012), and 361,734 were registered in the records of faculty members within

[1] We consider here those organizations that administer study programs at university level, which are institutionally accredited according to the law and have implicitly obtained the right to use the title of university or another similar name.

state universities, with the number of students registered in private faculty members dropping by almost 40% compared to 2012.

In 2021, according to the data published on the website of the Ministry of Education The Government Rule (2021), there were 34 accredited private higher education institutions, 53 state higher education institutions (7 military and 46 civil universities), 5 private higher education institutions authorized to operate provisionally, and 1 higher education institute authorized to operate provisionally, which offered master's degree programs/postgraduate studies, aspects captured through Fig. 11.2. The main factor that gave an increase in the number of private universities, especially in the period 2003–2008, was the demand from the population in this segment; however, the economic crisis and the decrease in the rate of passing the baccalaureate exam were among the factors that determined the steep decrease of the school population on this educational segment until 2012 and a continuously decreasing trend until now and led to the decrease in the number of private higher institutions in 2021 almost down to the number of faculties first recorded in 1997. This trend has led, as expected, to a decrease in the revenues recorded by private universities.

The number of accredited universities decreased from 37 in 2014, with that year seeing four universities with all study programs entered in

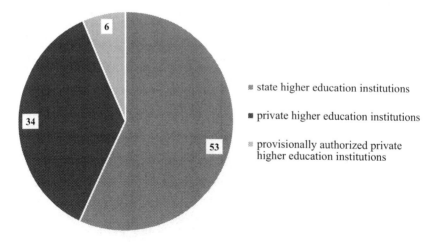

Fig. 11.2 Distribution of universities in 2021 based on form of property. (Source: Author contributions based on https://www.edu.ro/institutii-invatamant-superior data, 2022)

liquidation starting with the academic year 2014–2015 and without having the right to organize the entrance exam, while three other universities were monitored by the Romanian Agency for Quality Assurance in Higher Education (ARACIS).

Private universities have felt the effects of the accelerated decline in the number of students. The academic year 2008–2009 was a peak one, in the context in which at private universities, over 410,000 students studied with tuition fees because at the level of the 2014/2015 academic year, their number was decreasing, well below 80,000, and further decreasing to 56,612 students in the 2020–2021 academic year. The types of specializations from private universities in 2014 can be seen in Fig. 11.3.

Many private universities are pendulating between "to be" and "not to be," and some are already closed or are in the process of being closed or merged because they are no longer economically sustainable. Similarly, in the case of state universities, things have taken it in a less favorable direction. The effects of the decrease in the number of students (especially those with tuition fees) have led to a decrease in their own incomes and problems in terms of self-financing.

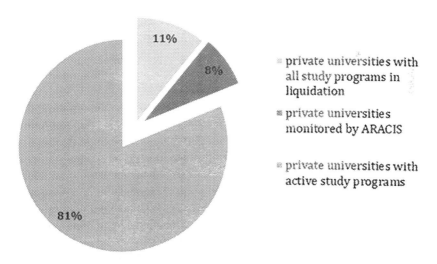

Fig. 11.3 The types of specializations from private universities in 2014. (Source: Author's contribution based on www.edu.ro data, 2014)

A difficulty encountered in recent years by state higher education institutions is reflected in the decrease in the number of people employed in the system according to the data in Table 11.2, especially in the period 2011/2012 due to the application of certain legal provisions and at the same time the suspension, for a while of the competitions for filling the teaching positions. The total number of full-time teachers increased again beginning with the 2018–2019 academic year, as shown in the table.

From Table 11.3, a very large decrease in the number of students enrolled in university study programs with tuition fees at the level of all three study cycles can be observed (in the case of state universities). In the context in which we compare the number of bachelor's or master's students in 2020 compared to 2007, a halving of their number can be observed.

In the case of students enrolled in the first year of study in the fee-based regime, there was a significant decrease. If, in 2009, more than 144,000 fee-based students were enrolled, in 2013 their number decreased by over 57%, to a numerical value of 61,596, and further declined to 60,961 in 2020 (CNFIS, 2020). This decline is observed in all study cycles, in

Table 11.2 The number of full-time teachers based on educational positions in state universities

Academic year	Professor	Associate Professor	Lector/ Lecturer	Assistant Professor	Tutor	Total
2020/2021	4.043	5.942	9.050	4.571	0	23.606
2019/2020	4.088	5.844	9.021	4.609	0	23.562
2018/2019	4.184	5.773	8.975	4.841	0	23.774
2017/2018	4.308	5.660	8.524	3.654	1	22.147
2016/2017	4.228	5.518	8.477	3.980	4	22.207
2015/2016	4.240	5.380	8.317	4.314	72	22.323
2014/2015	4.071	5.299	8.258	4.923	396	22.947
2013/2014	3.855	5.065	8.278	5.274	573	23.045
2012/2013	3.734	4.748	8.086	5.742	814	23.124
2011/2012	4.232	4.596	7.445	6.214	1.106	23.593
2010/2011	4.733	4.647	6.755	6.523	1.633	24.291
2009/2010	5.023	4.846	7.024	6.733	1.748	25.374
2008/2009	5.113	4.717	6.725	6.839	1.795	25.189
2007/2008	5.046	4.503	6.596	6.794	1.849	24.788
2006/2007	4.917	4.315	6.547	6.824	1.940	24.543

Source: Author's processing based on CNFIS 2015 and CNFIS 2020

Table 11.3 The number of enrolled students in the state universities

Academic Years	Physical students Total (LMD)	Of which Budget	Tuition	Bachelor Total (L)	Of which Budget	Tuition	Master Total (M)	Of which Budget	Tuition	PhD Total (D)	Of which Budget	Tuition
2020	457.230	300.337	156.893	340.195	217.592	122.603	96.385	70.195	26.190	20.650	12.550	8.100
2019	448.964	297.994	150.970	336.295	216.779	119.516	92.826	68.886	23.940	19.843	12.329	7.514
2018	449.139	292.912	156.227	339.619	212.968	126.651	90.723	68.324	22.399	18.797	11.620	7.177
2017	445.064	291.142	153.922	337.669	212.107	125.562	89.716	67.788	21.928	17.679	11.247	6.432
2016	449.152	289.982	159.170	341.720	211.898	129.822	90.642	67.212	23.430	16.790	10.872	5.918
2015	448.939	287.927	161.012	338.214	209.517	128.697	94.123	67.777	26.346	16.602	10.633	5.969
2014	461.582	287.300	174.282	346.493	208.777	137.716	98.124	68.076	30.048	16.965	10.447	6.518
2013	472.739	285.652	187.087	354.945	208.475	146.470	99.770	66.605	33.165	18.024	10.572	7.452
2012	520.853	289.087	231.766	391.170	211.078	180.092	107.828	66.444	41.384	21.855	11.565	10.290
2011	576.290	288.580	287.710	426.435	209.101	217.334	123.973	66.307	57.666	25.882	13.172	12.710
2010	616.506	282.237	334.269	447.660	204.369	243.291	139.211	62.792	76.419	29.635	15.076	14.559
2009	624.654	284.616	340.038	473.393	220.872	252.521	120.673	46.550	74.123	30.588	17.194	13.394
2008	650.247	289.132	361.115	525.880	240.919	284.961	91.825	27.195	64.630	32.542	21.018	11.524
2007	644.807	290.855	353.952	521.633	245.495	276.138	89.488	20.263	69.225	33.686	25.097	8.589

Source: Author's processing based on CNFIS, 2020

comparable proportions. Following the analysis, it can be noticed that the decrease in the number of students in the fee-based regime can be correlated both with the decrease in the number of high school graduates who pass the baccalaureate exam, reflected especially in the situation in the first year of bachelor's degree studies, and with the financial difficulties caused by the economic crisis, which determines school dropout, as seen from the global decline, evident for all years of study.

In Romania's case, employment remains a priority in programs for developing measures and strategies aimed at economic growth. The educational level of young people is one of the important factors that influence access to the labor market and that concerns the entire society, so the largest unemployment rates are registered in the case of young people with a low level of education (secondary education—5.1%, primary or without graduated school—8.1%) but also in the case of those with high school education (as high as 4.1% for people with higher education leaving in rural areas). The number of young people who leave school early is high (15.3% in 2020, for the age group 18–24 years), which implicitly leads to an increase in the risk of becoming unemployed or inactive.

The evolution of the number of students from the tax programs for all three undergraduate cycles is shown in Fig. 11.4. The high costs of the education system were mentioned by 55% of young people as an obstacle to continuing the schooling process. The mismatches between the qualifications of young people and their competences, required by employers, determine the increase in unemployment among young people, an aspect evident in a study aimed at improving the professional skills among graduates and young people in the future:

- Forty-nine percent consider that there is a mismatch between the knowledge acquired within a higher education institution and the needs of the labor market.
- Sixty-nine percent believe that practical activities should come first.
- Eighty-five percent of employers believe that there are discrepancies between the theoretical training of young people and the practical training.

Why is there a high level of youth unemployment? Among the answers given, we highlight a few aspects:

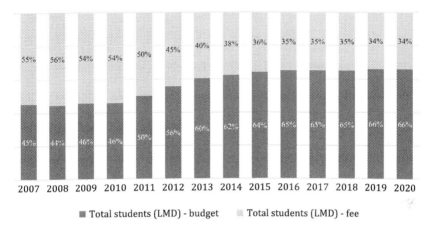

Fig. 11.4   The evolution of the number of students from the tax programs for all three undergraduate cycles. (Source: CNFIS, data available according to the reports made by state universities)

- Only 18% of the respondents participated in a qualification, initiation, or improvement course; young people do not have confidence in the effectiveness of short-term vocational training courses or retraining programs and in the fact that it would be possible to get out of unemployment when they attend these courses.
- From the perspective of employers, the lack of work experience makes young people vulnerable to competition with other employees. Professional experience is the main criterion for separating the job, regardless of the position or position occupied.
- Other obstacles, from the recruiter's perspective, may be represented by too little openness to work—73%; the salary requirements are not directly proportional to the 71% efficiency in the labor market; categorical refusal to work something different from their basic training—65%.

Considering the dynamics of economic life, in all its complexity, starting from the distortions existing at the global level, a forecast of Romanian higher education in a certain time horizon involves a certain risk. This is precisely why the increase in the long-term adaptability of the labor force to the requirements of the market must be achieved mainly through investment in the development of human resources, based on a lifelong learning strategy, as well as through the flexibility of the labor market.

The way in which the Romanian economy works and evolves requires the presence of economists specialized in solving fundamental economic problems who are able to rationally understand, anticipate, and predict the dominant trends of the economy in crisis situations and to identify solutions to overcome the difficulties that arise. The financial factor is, in our view, an effect and not a cause. When you do not truly care about anything, then nothing is a priority. When there is political will, concentration and determination, all other elements begin to unfold by themselves. In other words, when we manage to focus our attention and political will on the project, resources will be easily attracted.

As for the financing of state higher education, the budget allocated to this sector for 2014 was 2.382 billion lei (a percentage of 0.36% of GDP), a value that increased up to approximately 6.06 billion lei (0.58% of GDP). Of this, 987 million went to student support, and 4.96 billion went to institutional funding for higher education (0.47% of GDP). In Romania, the maximum level of institutional funding of higher education was registered in 2008–2009, with significant reductions being recorded during the economic crisis. In 2013, compared to 2008, the financing of state higher education institutions decreased by approximately 30% in real values (taking inflation into account). These data place Romania in the majority group of countries in Europe (countries that are part of the EUA study), where the financing of higher education institutions recorded significant decreases, higher than 10%, in real values between countries such as the Czech Republic, Spain, Greece, Hungary, Italy, Lithuania, and the United Kingdom. The data between 2015 and 2020 from the CNFIS 2020 report show, however, an improvement in terms of financing state higher education, with the percentage of GDP allocated to higher education state funding increasing from 0.37% in 2015 to 0.58% in 2020.

In terms of the latest developments in the higher education funding process, it should be pointed out that 2019–2020 looks better than the 2013–2014 period (during the economic crisis). For the 2013–2014 period, 13 of the 27 countries included in the EU analysis, for which data were available at the time, recorded increases or stagnations in the level of funding in nominal terms, with Bulgaria recording a higher increase (over 12% and 10.8% increase of the percentage from GDP allocated to education in 2013 and 2014, respectively, compared to the previous year). Romania fell into this group of countries with a nominal increase in the level of financing, from 2.8% to 3%, and an annual inflation of 1.1% in 2014, compared to 4% in 2013. The EUA back-analysis covered 27 European countries (based on available data, with the United Kingdom no longer available in most of the Eurostat data), of which almost half (11 countries) recorded a lower share of expenditure on financing higher education in gross domestic product (GDP) in 2014 than in 2008. Romania fell into this category of countries, with a decrease from 4.3% in 2008 to 3% in 2014.

For the period 2019–2020, according to the latest Eurostat available data (europa.eu), all countries increased their share of GDP allocated to education in 2020 compared to 2019. It is worth mentioning that for nine countries, including Romania, the share of GDP allocated to education has nevertheless been smaller than in 2008, with larger decreases (of over 10%) recorded for Ireland (-34%), Portugal (-16.7%), Romania (-14%), and Hungary (-11.3%). Overall, considering the increase that most of the countries recorded for 2020 compared to 2019, at the level of EU27, higher education funding has increased by 6.4% from 2008 to 2020.

Most of the member states of the European Union, together with the global economic crisis, have reduced by themselves the average allocated to education, thus the value of education funding as a percentage of GDP entering a downward trend, from 5.1% in 2009 to 4.9% in 2011, and further down to 4.7% in 2019, only recovering in 2020 (with 5%), and in at the level of all EU states, according to the data provided by Eurostat (europa.eu). The analysis of the share of GDP of public expenditures on education reveals the general aspects of financing, representing an important indicator of substantiation of macroeconomic policies for any country. Moreover, in 2008, in Romania, the representatives of the parliamentary political parties assumed the same allocation of at least 6% of GDP for education within the National Pact for Education, a document that defines eight priority objectives for Education in Romania for a period of five years (2008–2013)—"Ensuring in the period 2008–2013, from the annual budget allocation, of at least 6% of GDP for education and at least 1% for research." The percentage of the GDP for higher education and the scholarship per student during 2008–2020 in Romania can be seen in Table 11.4.

The paradox is that with the economic crisis, at which time the investment in education became even more important due to the recognized

Table 11.4   The percentage of the GDP for higher education and the scholarship per student during 2008–2020 in Romania

Year	GDP (million lei, in current prices)	Percentage of GDP allocated to higher education	Average allowance per student (LEI)
2008	534,785	1.3	6004
2009	528,457	1.0	5930
2010	527,704	0.9	5828
2011	558,668	0.9	5090
2012	590,385	0.8	5107
2013	632,654	0.7	5461
2014	668,128	0.6	5503
2015	710,349	0.8	5823
2016	761,448	0.7	7149
2017	854,677	0.6	8272
2018	947,780	0.7	10,187
2019	1,055,279	0.8	12,482
2020*	1,057,112	0.7	14,558

Source: CNFIS, national data for GDP 2008–2020 (insse.ro)

*2020 annual GDP—not definitive data

role it can play for exiting the crisis, the trend of allocating GDP to educa-tion became a downward one, given that there was an upward trend from 2001 to 2008. This discrepancy between the assumptions made by the decision-makers and reality has led to critical situations in the higher edu-cation system, the lack of adequate funding generating a series of negative effects for both universities and students.

Social Analysis

The social environment is made up of all the factors, conditions, relation-ships, and institutions that follow the system of values, traditions, customs, beliefs and norms that form society and govern human behavior. These elements influence the activity of higher education through the specific ways of correlating the individual and social interests, with a direct impact on the conscious activity of the individuals and groups that activate in society. The basis for substantiating the analyses on vocational education and training, the quality of life and cultural developments, and the social dimension is represented by the social factor, along with the economic factors, with important influences on the strategic orientation of the development of society.

Social Factors

Education is a key social activity for the individual and society, which makes it a fundamental institution in any society. The social factors as are part of the social life aspects can act as a binder in the maintenance and functioning of society, facilitating its members to effectively pursue common goals, but also complementary individual ones:

- High unemployment
- Low standard of living
- Education is not seen as a means of social and economic promotion
- The opportunity of an extensive offer on the labor market in the context of European development
- Reducing the school population

Taking into account the ratio between the working population and the inactive population, as well as the employment rate, the Romanian labor market has experienced great instability. The industrial sector was the most affected due to the decrease in the number of employed people in the economy, and agriculture still has a high share of 38% of the total employed population. The major changes that have occurred in the evolution of the labor market are the result of job losses, especially in state-owned units, which had collective redundancies and restructuring or liquidation processes.

Demographic Factors

Education is generally directly influenced by demographic aspects: population number, population dynamics, structure, density, mobility, and so on. The emergence of the global problem regarding population dynamics also marks the demographic forecast. In 2020, according to the United Nations International Children's Emergency Fund (UNICEF) *Social Trends* Report, developed together with the National Institute of Statistics, the population of Romania will decrease by 2020 to a numerical value below 18 million inhabitants, with approximately 3 million inhabitants less than in 2000. Romania's demographic prospects are pessimistic, and this trend is within the European demographic conjuncture. The factors that explain the shrinking and aging of the population in Romania after the 1990s are negative external migration, increased global mortality and a low birth rate corroborated with the forced "pronatalist" policy of the communist regime until the 1990s.

Analyzing the data presented above, the most important conclusions regarding the current situation in this area can be summarized as follows:

- In Romania, the share of the population aged between 30–34 years with tertiary education, corresponding to 2011, was 20.3%, of 26.4% in 2020, and of 24.8% in 2021 (albeit with a break in the series for 2021) (europa.eu), in the context of an assumed European target of 40% and of a national target of 26.7% assumed through the National Reform Plan. At the same time, the evolution of the number of students has decreased in the last four years.
- The degree of inclusion in higher education decreases as young people get older.
- The distribution of the population by development regions of Romania does not always correlate with the distribution of the number of students by region, as there are regions with a deficit in terms of the number of students and regions with a much higher proportion in relation to the population.

Romanian migration managed to have a very large influence on current Romanian society in the form in which we know it today. Approximately 10–12% of all legal emigrants are represented by graduates of higher education, while graduates of high school and postsecondary education represent approximately 26% of all official emigrants. Romanian migration has begun to be characterized, recently, by the following aspects: the migration of the young population, especially able to work, which leads to the crisis of the labor market but also of the social services and insurance services, because the population employed on the Romanian labor market must resist under a much more pronounced pressure; in parallel, the aging of the population persists and is getting worse due to the mixing of decreasing fertility rates and structural changes by sex and age group.

In these circumstances, Romania can and should learn from the experience of other states and best practices; without adopting a unitary package of measures aimed at both the demographic aspects and the problems of the labor market and its connection with the education system, it will be very difficult to overcome the current economic crisis and the future demographic crisis.

The National-Cultural Factor

One of the missions of higher education institutions is to facilitate cultural expansion, understood as a source of broadening knowledge, of acquiring respect for other cultures and groups of people, of educating a normal receptivity of cultural differentiation. When we define the *role of higher education as the main vector of economic development* and as a solution to the most urgent problems of society, we risk losing sight of broader problems, such as those that build the human perspective, which favor agitated skepticism and unlimited curiosity, from which our deep understanding comes to the surface so quickly.

How can we develop minds capable of innovation if we are not able to imagine a world different from the one we are living in now? In Brătianu's opinion, cultural values are shaped by "our attempt to understand the reality in which we live and to give it an existential meaning" (Brătianu 2015a, b). History shows us that the world has been characterized by diversity and it can be and it will be diverse. Anthropology can demonstrate that societies are and have been different in other parts of the world throughout time and space. Literature can provide for us a lot of things—how to regard the world differently, a thing which is enabled by the study of arts in general. "The cultural values are acquired throughout the entire educational process. The process of forming values develops simultaneously with the process of defining the identity of each of us. We seek to identify our own meaning in life, what is good what is bad, what we like and what we do not like, what are the criteria according to which we make decisions, what is important or not for us" (Bodea 2011).

In science, universities have a different obligation to nurture and fulfill the deep human desire to understand ourselves and the world we inhabit and inherit, from small, elementary particles to traversing galaxies—even when there is no practical application, and even when we would correctly accelerate our efforts to "harvest" new technologies from knowledge—in their basic form. Economic and scientific growth are necessary but not enough for a university. It is worth remembering that most of the useful scientific discoveries have their origins in research activities, born out of curiosity about who we are and how we can perceive the most intriguing mysteries of the natural world.

Technological Analysis

Technology plays an important role in the economic development of nations in the context of a constantly changing world. UNDP (2001) demonstrated that the degree of technology of an economy depends on the level of higher education. Most countries that have an increased level of registration in higher education later become leaders in technology, performing in this area. The reciprocity of this statement being valid, many of the countries with a low enmity rate in higher education (especially those below 10%) have great difficulties in terms of technology. However, those in the middle of the ranking (e.g., Singapore and Hong Kong, for whom the level of this index is approximately 20%) have also managed to perform, becoming leaders in technology. Following the trend of the largest economic powers in the world, it can be said that technological evolution distinguishes between competitors, representing one of the most important resources of competitive advantage.

Romania had an overall score[2] of 0.31 in 2015, according to the DESI,[3] and ranked 28th among the 28 EU member states, while in 2020, Romania ranked 26th, with an overall score of 40, and in 2021, Romania scored less (32.9) and lost its position in the DESI ranking. The components of the Digital Economy and Society Index (DESI) in 2021 are presented in Fig. 11.5. Due to the low level of e-skills, only 31% of Romanians have basic e-skills, with one of the lowest percentages of ICT specialists—2.4% of the total workforce in all EU countries (albeit significantly higher than in 2015), with only 6% learning companies out of the total number of enterprises (20% in the EU), as well as the very low level of e-government users (16% compared to the EU average of 64%), seems to be holding back the development of the digital economy and the use of new technologies. According to Fig. 11.5, Romania falls into the group of

---

[2] Digital Economy and Society Index (DESI) is a composite index, prepared by the European Commission (DGCNECT), to assess the progress of EU countries toward a digital economy and society. This index integrates a set of relevant indicators, structured around five dimensions: connectivity, human capital, internet use, digital technology integration, and digital public services.

[3] DESI 2021 is made up of indicators relating mainly to the calendar year 2020 (unless no data were available for the calendar year and the most recent available data were used instead). DESI scores for the latest editions are from 0 to 100 (0 to 1 in the 2015 edition), with a higher score reflecting the better performance of the country concerned.

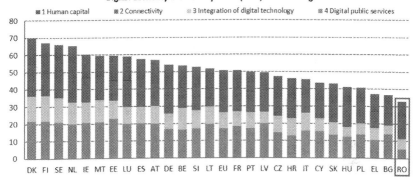

| | Romania | | EU |
	rank	score	score
DESI 2021	27	32.9	50.7

Digital Economy and Society Index (DESI) 2021 ranking

▓ 1 Human capital   ▓ 2 Connectivity   ▒ 3 Integration of digital technology   ▓ 4 Digital public services

DK FI SE NL IE MT EE LU ES AT DE BE SI LT EU FR PT LV CZ HR IT CY SK HU PL EL BG RO

Fig. 11.5 The level of digital skills in Romania, DESI 2021. (Source: European Commission (2021), *Country Profile, Romania—Index of the Digital Economy and Society*)

low-performing countries, ranking last among the analyzed countries,[4] below the EU average of 50.7.

The functioning of the education system, as a promoter of scientific knowledge, at all educational levels, through the implementation of information technologies and through rapid access to information, has a favorable impact on the development of the activity. In the economic and technological evolution, it is necessary to permanently develop new economic solutions to adapt to the evolution of society. Romania performs significantly better than the EU average in terms of the indicator on the percentage of ICT graduates, with 6.3% in 2019 (data accounted for in DESI 2021), compared to the 3.9% EU average. Even if this is positive, it is still not enough to make up for Romania's e-skills shortage, considering that, according to the same report, less than one-third (31%) of people aged 16–74 years have at least basic digital skills, compared to the average 56% at the level of the European Union.

[4] In DESI 2021, the group of low-performing countries consists of Bulgaria, Cyprus, Greece, Croatia, Hungary, Italy, Poland, Romania, Slovenia, and Slovakia.

Why Do We Need Research—Innovation for?

Innovation has always been an engine of economic and social development. A World Bank report (2007) exemplifies how competitiveness and productivity at work are positively influenced by research and technological development, which leads to well-being. A very telling example is of the two countries South Korea and Ghana, which, although they have departed from the same level of development, after 40 years have reached significant discrepancies, and two-thirds of them are due to the way in which they have accumulated knowledge.

In Romania, a small part of the population is concerned about science, and it should be pointed out that this aspect systematically and directly affects our daily lives. Investment in scientific research remains vital because science is indispensable for the well-being and prosperity of a nation.

The situation in Romania represents a real challenge and responsibility for economic development, as stated in the Europe 2020 strategy. This is achievable to the extent that high levels of correlation between innovation and development capacity are confirmed. The phenomenon is exactly the opposite for Romania, having the following plausible causes:

- insufficient financial support from the state and weak contribution from the private sector in terms of research and development;
- the failure of public funds to create a multiplier effect in the private sector through inefficient use;
- little investment in research, which has led to a lack of interest in innovation;
- the increase of public debt, which has also had an impact on innovation in the short and medium term, by increasing the volume of public expenditures;
- lack of connections between academic research and industrial applications; and
- the disinterest in this area and the lack of motivation of the human factor, which led to a shortage of human capital, in the R&I sector.

The answer to the question from which we started is twofold. Innovation can ensure competitiveness and economic progress, but the lack of it can also mean limited public and private resources due to the lack of acquisition of modern technology from other countries. Only increasing national competitiveness and regional economies can support investment in one's own research and innovation.

On the other hand, research and innovation are in the same way as local specific needs. They have an importance that goes beyond the borders of the country, of society, the investment in research and innovation being justified by the need to find the solution of the different problems of the society in which we live. In this context, they must be customized or adapted by the need to solve the specific problems of Romanian society, regardless of their nature; therefore, investment in their own research and innovation is justified by the Research and Innovation Strategy (2014–2020). Accepting this reality, increasing the competitiveness of the national economy is supported by investment in research and innovation, which can be the key to regional economic development.

Completing the series of exemplifications and summarizing, we note for the justification of our scientific approach that the PEST analysis, which we have implicitly carried out, has been an effective tool for understanding and measuring the development of higher education, correctly indicating the rise or decline, as well as the proposal of strategies for the recovery of the educational system. In the short term, the PEST matrix reflects the existing situation, highlighting the positive, negative, and neutral impact of external factors on the education sector. In the medium and long term, it allows the forecasting of the situation under various development scenarios. The fact is that education itself is an element of major importance, not only when we talk about the past of society but especially when we think about its future. It is noticed that, in general, the educational system around the world and, implicitly, the local one faces a series of obstacles that are quite difficult to overcome, such as the following:

- lack of innovation in the education system;
- poor infrastructure (hard and soft), for the training and improvement of teachers;
- lack of innovative and effective mechanisms for financing the system;
- major deficiencies in the collaboration and development of some systems of efficiency of the education system;
- the complexity of the results of the educational process and the long time required to obtain them;
- the rigidity, size, and complexity of education systems;
- lack of good management and a global vision of education.

- the level of wages is still far from being correlated with the social importance of work and responsibility for the formation of new generations;
- the gap between the number of students registered in the system and the number of graduates, which increases annually;
- the nonexistence of protectionist policies of the banking systems, for study credits, reimbursable after graduation/employment;
- unimplemented online teaching/examination system that is not implemented homogeneously and coherently;
- cognitive vocational training at the expense of formative training (the difficult integration of university graduates into the labor market and a relatively high unemployment rate among them); and
- national education policies without continuity (destabilization of the national educational strategy, salary, university curricula, etc.).

The strengths of the Romanian educational system should not be neglected when trying to remove the existing problems. Thus, the research of the strengths reflects the following: the existence of partnerships between national universities, such as a better exchange of knowledge and *know-how*; a larger number of accredited higher education programs (bachelor, master, doctorate, postgraduate studies); the exchange of relevant and new knowledge through the access of students to prestigious databases; a better absorption rate of European funds at the university level compared to the rest of the economy that contributes to the increase of the indicators of the national economy at the parameters of knowledge, research, and academic innovation; encouraging student mobility and multiculturalism through their constant participation in programs such as ERASMUS; and a high percentage of students funded from the national budget compared to other EU countries.

Authors such as John Kenneth Galbraith have tried to show that such an evolution *as individuals and as a society is inextricably linked to education*: "The essential factor of evolution, whether of the individual or of his children on the social scale, is education. Ignorance only leads to hard, awkward, boring work and often not to work at all. Improvement comes with education and only with it; without education there is nothing and the only plausible recourse is to murder and violence. Perhaps they should, as the best education, benefit those who are lowest on the social ladder, because they most need the means, which will allow them that ancestry, that escape from ignorance" Galbraith (1997).

We agree that education plays an active role in the design of society and that the way it is targeted influences the future of today's generations. Many of the contemporary problems could also be solved by improving access to quality education. According to representatives of some international bodies, the education system could be improved if more attention was given to achieving a correspondence between the two markets, the educational and the labor markets.

Another aspect, highlighted both by the developments in recent years and by international comparisons, concerns the aggravation of the chronic underfunding of the higher education system in Romania. If a minimum of US$16.5 billion were spent annually in the world on education, then developing countries could actually make a difference. While this figure may seem quite high, it should be borne in mind that it is the equivalent of what consumers in the United States spend in a single season shopping WEF (2010).

Among Romania's commitments in the Bologna Process is that of the social dimension of education, which primarily concerns issues such as widening access to higher education and improving the participation of underrepresented groups. In this respect, to achieve these objectives, Romania needs national strategies, as well as concrete instruments. At the level of national policies, Romania does not have a strategy on the social dimension of education, which would include the definition of underrepresented groups, clear objectives, in relation to their inclusion, and indicators to be able to assess progress toward these targets. In this regard, Romania has developed a set of tools designed to facilitate the access of different categories of disadvantaged young people to higher education, but these are not pursued to analyze their impact (examples: student scholarships, scholarships for students from rural areas, etc.); there is no clear definition of the categories of disadvantaged young people in terms of access, participation and graduation in higher education.

Investment in research and development as a research implementation is the key to long-term economic development by constantly increasing labor productivity. Sustainable economic growth depends on the ability of nations to understand, select, adapt, transmit, and use scientific information and technological knowledge in accordance with development goals and national culture. The main factors on which this impact depends are the state and level of education, an efficient management in all sectors of economic and social activity, the quality and state of development of investments in research and development, rural development and the development of administrative capacity. At the same time, the difficult situation in which higher education finds itself not only a challenge but also an obligation to respond to some major requirements, which must be placed at the top of the priorities on the national agenda: to reach a quality level, to increase funding by diversifying funding sources, to improve leadership and responsibility, and to adopt efficient strategic management.

The reasons for emigration are both economic and socio-professional in nature; most emigrants want a better future for themselves and their families, a social integration that is appropriate to their lifestyle, high wages and a better education for their children. Since the free movement of people is one of the four liberties of the union, according to statistics, the highly skilled workforce leaving the country is 15,000 Romanian researchers. Creating wage conditions and improved infrastructure are factors designed to avoid *brain drain*[5] and waste of research qualifications in other better sectors/countries.

REFERENCES

Bodea, L. (2011). University—Active Factor in Increasing the Quality of Life? In *Theoretical and Applied Economics* (p. 115). Supplement. *Cited in* Galbraith, J. K. (1997, p. 67).

Brătianu, C. (2002). *Paradigms of University Management* (p. 122). Economic Publishing House. *Cited in* Miroiu, A. (1998).

Brătianu, C. (2015a). *Strategic Thinking* (p. 65). ProUniversitaria Publishing House. *Cited in* Bodea, D. (2013, p. 38).

Brătianu, C. (2015b). *Strategic Thinking* (p. 65). ProUniversitaria Publishing House.

CNFIS. (2020). *Raport Public Anual 2020*. The State of Higher Education Funding.

European Commission. (2010). *Europe 2020. A Strategy for Smart, Sustainable and Inclusive growth*.

European Commission. (2015). Let Us Understand the Policies of the European Union—Europe 2020: Europe's Growth Strategy, p. 3.

European Commission. Shaping Digital Future. http://ec.europa.eu/digital-agenda/en/digital-agenda-scoreboard

Eurostat. General Governmental Expenditure by Function. https://ec.europa.eu/eurostat/databrowser/product/page/GOV_10A_EXP__custom_2783726

[5] *Brain drain* is the phenomenon of emigration of educated or talented people. Initially, the *brain-drain* phenomenon was examined exclusively from an economic perspective taking into account the differentiations between *muscle-power*, muscle power and *brain drain*, brain power.

Galbraith, J. K. (1997). The Good Society: The Humane Agenda. *Utopian Studies,* *8*(2), 140–141.

Manea, A., Hoinaru, R., & Păcuraru-Ionescu, C. P. (2021, December). Ethics Education in Romanian Economics Faculties, Members of AFER. In *Proceedings of the International Conference on Business Excellence* (Vol. 15 (1), pp. 705–714).

Miroiu, M. (1998). Inequality of Opportunity in Education. În Adrian Miroiu (coord). *Romanian Education Today: Diagnostic Study,* Polirom Publishing House, Iasi.

OECD. (2011). Education at Glance 2011: OECD Indicators. *OECD Publishing, Indicator, A9,* 166.

Pachef, R. C. (2008). *Evaluation in Higher Education* (p. 72). Didactic and Pedagogical Publishing House.

Report on the Status of Higher Education in Romania. (2020–2021). Ministry of Education, p. 6.

Romanian Research and Innovation Strategy. (2014–2020). www.cdi2020.ro

Someșan, C., & Cosma, S. (2001). *The Basics of Marketing* (p. 52). Efes Publishing House.

UNDP. (2001). *Human Development Report.* Oxford University Press.

WEF. (2010). *World Economic Forum Global Education Initiative Report.* Davos-Klosters. www.weforum.org

World Bank. (2007). *Building Knowledge Economies: Advanced Development Strategies.*

CHAPTER 12

Quantification of the Impact Level of Education on the Economic Development of Nations

The causes of geographical differences have been analyzed in most theories of regional sciences, which have tried to provide answers to the question of why some regions are distinguished by faster development than others. The explanations are numerous and have been consistent with the reference period. Treiman and Yip (1989), in a comparative study conducted in 21 countries, found that education was a strong determinant of occupational status in many industrialized countries. In particular, in the last two decades, the analysis of regional disparities has become truly important, especially as there has been an increase in the number of empirical studies on convergence (Rey & Janikas, 2005). Analysts, theorists, and practitioners have also used the concept of disparity (discrepancy, inequality, imbalance) to express the differences identified using appropriate mathematical techniques and specific indicators. Education and labor sports are key factors that are changing very quickly and have a major impact on socioeconomic development.

In Romania, *development regions* represent "areas corresponding to groups of counties, constituted by their voluntary association on the basis of convention ... the regions constitute the framework for the design, implementation and evaluation of regional development policies, as well as for the collection of specific statistical data, in accordance with European regulations issued by Eurostat for the second level of territorial classification, NUTS 2, existing in the European Union" (Eurostat).

D.-M. Neamțu, *Education and Economic Development*, https://doi.org/10.1007/978-3-031-20382-4_12

The context of the analysis of economic disparities for Romania is given by the presence of the eight development regions (statistical regions), as can be seen in Table 12.1, created after integration into the European Union. When establishing the eight regions created under *the Law of Regional Development*, the criterion of complementarity of resources, economic, social activity, and functional links was considered. The eight development regions are as follows:

The analysis of regional differences was carried out using direct indicators and specific derivatives of certain areas of economic activity: the level of education of the population, the participation of the adult population in lifelong learning, unemployment and employment, and gross domestic product per inhabitant.

GENERAL ASPECTS OF THE LEVEL OF EDUCATION OF ROMANIA'S REGIONS

The Northeast region represents a part of the historical province of Moldova and benefits from a rich historical, cultural, and spiritual tradition, which complements the particularly attractive natural environment. It is the largest development region of Romania in terms of the area owned, 36,850 km², as well as the number of inhabitants 3,734,546. In this area, the essential factor in the development of the regional economy is, to a very large extent, human capital. The Northeast region comprises

Table 12.1 Development regions in Romania

	NUT 2 region	NUT 3 regions—counties
RO11	Northwest	Bihor, Bistrița-Năsăud, Cluj, Maramureș, Sălaj, Satu-Mare
RO12	Center	Alba, Sibiu, Brașov, Covasna, Harghita, Mureș
RO21	Northeast	Bacău, Botoșani, Iași, Neamț, Suceava, Vaslui
RO22	Southeast	Brăila, Buzău, Constanța, Galați, Tulcea, Vrancea
RO31	South-Muntenia	Argeș, Călărași, Dâmbovița, Giurgiu, Ialomița, Prahova, Teleorman
RO32	Bucharest-Ilfov	Municipiul București, județul Ilfov
RO41	Southwest Oltenia	Dolj, Gorj, Mehedinți, Olt, Vâlcea
RO42	West	Arad, Caraș-Severin, Hunedoara, Timiș

Source: Eurostat data, 2022, accessed on 28.05.2022

https://ec.europa.eu/eurostat/web/nuts/history

all forms of education registering at the level of 2020, with 601,062 young people included in the process of formal training and education (decrease from 664,538—in 2014).

On the higher education component, at the level of 2020, a total of 73,684 students (a 5.5% increase compared to the 2014 data) were enrolled in university centers of the region on various university programs (license/master/doctorate/postdoctoral). In particular, this region faces a major problem, with the migration of young graduates to more developed regions, as the supply of jobs in the region is extremely low in some areas compared to other regions.

At the level of 2020, within the Northeast region, there were ten universities, seven of which were state universities: "Vasile Alecsandri" Bacău University, Technical University "Gh. Asachi" Iasi, University of Agricultural Sciences and Veterinary Medicine, "Ion Ionescu de la Brad" Iasi, "Al. I. Cuza" University of Iasi, "Gr. T. Popa" University of Medicine and Pharmacy (UMF) Iasi, "Stefan cel Mare" University of Suceava, "G. Enescu" University of Arts of Iasi, and three private universities: "Petre Andrei" University, "Apollonia" University of Iasi, and "George Bacovia" University of Bacău. From this point of view, the northeastern region benefits from a high number of graduates, representing 14% of all graduates at the national level.

The Southeast region is the second largest of the eight regions of Romania, covering 35,762 km² or 15% of the total area of the country and comprising six counties (Braila, Buzau, Constanta, Tulcea, Galati and Vrancea). With regard to education at the regional level, we note the presence of educational institutions in which 406,482 persons (447,976 in 2014) are included in formal education, at the level of 2020, out of which 39,621 students (40,516 in 2014) enrolled in various academic programs. Notable here is the lack of educational infrastructure in some remote rural areas, so children's participation in education is limited or even nonexistent due to inaccessibility. For these reasons, there are very large differences in the degrees of coverage in different forms of education. This decline in educational services indicates inequalities in the opportunities of children from different social backgrounds to education. The programs offered by higher education institutions tend to access only those with higher income.

In the region, the state-owned higher education makes its presence felt through numerous faculties, the main university centers being in Constanta and Galati: the "Maritim" University, "Mircea cel Bătrân" Academy,

"Ovidius" University, and "Dunarea de Jos" University operate within the center of the University of Galati and two private universities such as "Danubius" University of Galati and "Andrei Saguna" of Constanta.

The South-Muntenia region is located in the southern part of Romania, with an area of 34,453 km², representing 14.5% of the country's area and occupying the third largest of the eight development regions. The poverty rate in the South-Muntenia region is among the highest in Romania, with a significant value both in rural areas, fourth place at the national level after the Northeast, Southeast and Southwest regions and in urban areas, the second place at the national level, after the Southwest region and on par with the Southeast region.

The South-Muntenia region is characterized by an average level of training and qualification of the population; here, school dropout is increasing. The school population is constantly declining at almost all levels of training. The largest decrease was among the university population. Of the 430,858 people attending formal education courses in 2020 (a decrease of 11.5% from 2014), 20,871 people (an even steeper decrease – by almost 15% compared to the 2014 data) were enrolled in higher education in various state institutions, such as "Petrol-Gaze" Ploiesti University, "Valahia" University of Targoviste, University of Pitesti, and private institutions such as "Constantin Brâncoveanu" University of Pitești.

The southwest Oltenia region comprises five counties (Dolj, Olt, Vâlcea, Mehedinti, and Gorj) with an area of 29,212 km² and a population of 2,306,450 inhabitants. There is a low level of development in the region due to the unattractiveness of the area for foreign investment, which places it in seventh place among the regions of the country. The extractive sector is still an important component in the region's economy. The economic situation of the region has also taken its toll on the education system.

The educational infrastructure at the regional level is in a fairly advanced state of degradation, witnessing a major decrease in the number of school populations, with 312,016 people enrolled in different forms of formal education in 2020, out of which 30,991 were enrolled in higher education in the same year (a very small increase compared to the 2014 data – 29,345). Currently, the university education system comprises six institutions of higher education; thus, in the Oltenia region, there are three state universities (two in Craiova - University of Craiova, University of Medicine and Pharmacy Craiova, and one in Targu Jiu – State University "Constantin Brâncuși") and three private universities (two in Craiova and one in Râmnicu Vâlcea).

The Western region consists of four counties (Arad, Caraş-Severin, Hunedoara and Timis). Historically characterized by its relative modernity and multiculturalism, the region has an important cultural identity that continues to shape it today.

The Western region is recognized as having a considerable number of state universities, hosting a larger population of students, in particular, in Timisoara, Western University, Polytechnics University, "Victor Babes" University of Medicine and Pharmacy, University of Agricultural Sciences and Veterinary Medicine of Banat in Timisoara, "Aurel Vlaicu" University of Arad, "Eftimie Murgu" University in Reşita, University of Petrosani, and private universities: "Tibiscus" University of Timisoara, "Vasile Golgis" University of Arad, and "Dragan" European University in Lugoj. At the level of 2020, the school population at all levels of education, regardless of the forms of education, amounted to 306,667 (a decrease of 8% compared to 2014), out of which 58,989 (800 students more than in 2014) represented the number of those attending higher education courses. The Western region, although it has a rather high rate of enrollment in higher education, is outclassed by the capital, as Bucharest is by far the main university center in the country.

The Northwest region of Romania territorially folds to the administrative units of the northwest of the country, belonging to the counties of Cluj, Bihor, Sălaj, Satu-Mare, Maramures and Bistrita-Năsăud, with an area of 34,159 km², covering 14.32% of the area of the national territory, with a population of 2,774,914 inhabitants.

The most important cities are Cluj-Napoca, Baia-Mare, Oradea, Zalău, Satu-Mare, and Bistrita, which are both regional poles of economic development and cities with a special cultural and historical heritage. After Bucharest-Ilfov, it is the most economically attractive region among Romania's development regions. This classification is based on the following aspects: massive foreign investment, the labor market and wages more than satisfactory, the services sector occupies a share of 50% of the total economy, and the development of the business environment.

It is worth noting that in this region, the university environment had 98,713 students enrolled in various university programs at the level of the reference year 2020, representing the largest increase (by 9.2%) from 2014 compared to all other regions out of a smaller school population of 494,445—compared 514,067 in 2014—enrolled in a form of formal training and education. Fifteen universities, including eight major state universities, are active in the Northwest region, which function as centers of excellence in higher education: "Babeș-Bolyai" University, Technical University of Cluj, "Iuliu Hatieganu" University of Agricultural Sciences and Veterinary Medicine, University of Medicine and Pharmacy—being among the oldest in the country polarizing a large part of the educational resources—the region accumulating valuable human and research capital. As far as private universities are concerned, there are seven institutions, four being in Cluj, "Bogdan Voda" University, "Avram-Iancu" University, "Sapienția" University, Protestant Theological Institute, and three universities in Oradea such as "Emanuel" University, "Partium" Christian University, and "Agora" University.

The region's economy is booming, with dynamic growth in recent years in sectors such as construction, textiles, machinery, and equipment, with low youth unemployment.

The Center region, through its strategic geographical position in the center of the country, makes connections with six of the eight development regions. It consists of six counties (Alba, Brasov, Covasna, Harghita, Mureș, and Sibiu) that total an area of 34,100 km^2 on the upper and middle courses of Mureș and Olt, representing 14.3% of the country's territory.

At the level of the Center region, the educational infrastructure is well developed, especially in the counties of Brasov, Mureș, and Sibiu, with the opposite pole being Covasna and Harghita. Due to the multilingual nature of the Central region, education is mainly in the Romanian language but also in Hungarian in the Harghita and Covasna counties and in German in the Sibiu and Mureș areas. The total school population, at the level of 2020, registered 425,476 (decrease of 4.03% from 2014) attending a form of education, the largest share being registered in the counties of Brasov, Mureș, and Sibiu, which are also the most important in terms of demographics. The number of students enrolled in higher education was 59,737 in the region. Due to the existence of Transylvania University, a university center with tradition, 37% of the number of students at the regional level was registered in Brasov. The lack of higher education institutions at the level of Covasna and Harghita counties (with the exception of some extensions of some universities and faculties) has led to the share of students being less than 3% in both 2014 and 2020.

In the Center region, there are 13 institutions of higher education, 8 of which are public institutions: Transylvania University of Brasov, "Lucian Blaga" University of Sibiu, University of Medicine and Pharmacy of Târgu

Mureş, "1 December" University of Alba-Iulia, "Petru Maior" University of Targu Mures, University of Arts of Targu Mures, and a significant number of university branches located in these centers and other cities of the region. Private universities Romanian-German University, Sibiu and "Dimitrie Cantemir" University of Târgu Mureş, together with the medical and dramatic art university education of Târgu Mureş as well as forestry and car construction in Brasov, have a long and valuable tradition, representing important landmarks of Romanian higher education.

The Bucharest-Ilfov region is the only metropolitan area with more than two million inhabitants, which represents 10.28% of the country's population. Bucharest is the most important university center in Romania, with 16 state universities and 9 private universities. The 2020 data show that the Bucharest-Ilfov region hosts 27.3% of Romanian universities and 31.74% of the total number of Romanian students. Due to the presence of the capital, the Bucharest-Ilfov region is absolutely the most important attraction for young people from all over the country who intend to go through university internships. Among the strengths of this region, we list the following: an upward trend in GDP; the increasing occupancy rate; high potential for highly qualified human resources with a high level of multilingualism; an expansion of innovative companies; the largest concentration of university and research centers in Romania; and the growing presence of large, powerful companies and multinationals, both in the traditional and emerging sectors of the regional economy.

At the level of 2020, the region registered 517,598 young people included in a form of education within formal education (i.e., an increase of 6.4% from 2014), out of which more than 34.3% (177,884 people) attend university courses at different levels (bachelor/master/doctorate/postdoctoral), according to the available data of the National Statistical Institute, who updated the indicator in August 2021.

There are significant regional differences in the actual number of enrollments in higher education, at the level of both 2014 and 2020 (Table 12.2).

Disparities are recorded between Southern Romania and the rest of the country in terms of access to higher education. A fairly good participation rate was achieved much faster in the developed regions, which cover the central and northern parts of Romania. The South-Muntenia, Southwest Oltenia, and Southeast regions were marked by massive declines, well ahead of the other development regions. This is particularly noticeable in the case of the Northeast region. With the largest population in the age

Table 12.2 Number of persons enrolled in higher education by development region (2000–2020)

	2000	2007	2012	2013	2014	2016	2018	2020
Northwest region	81,312	99,788	69,410	70,436	90,418	91,370	93,552	98,713
Center region	53,045	96,589	52,221	47,262	57,619	55,777	56,284	59,737
Northeast region	64,496	83,518	59,471	56,175	69,802	66,930	67,427	73,684
Southeast region	39,296	62,739	38,640	34,962	40,516	38,755	38,722	39,621
South-Muntenia region	31,709	37,232	22,361	20,532	24,540	22,372	20,650	20,871
Bucharest-Ilfov region	172,876	389,769	139,396	129,043	171,224	172,209	172,709	177,884
Southwest Oltenia region	35,397	52,450	28,226	25,375	29,345	28,383	28,627	30,991
West region	61,463	85,268	54,867	49,449	58,189	55,790	55,778	58,989

Source: author's contribution based on INS data, Tempo-online, accessed on 20.05.2022

group 20–24 years, according to statistical data published by the INS, the number of students enrolled in this region for the entire 2014–2020 period is only in third place, as a share, after that of students enrolled in the Bucharest-Ilfov region and the Northwest region, both with a much smaller population number. It is obvious that the Bucharest-Ilfov region leads the ranking secondment in terms of the number of people enrolled in higher education.

We also notice disparities in terms of the number of faculties, which according to Table 12.3 folds the ranking of regions according to the level of economic development. At the level of the Bucharest-Ilfov region, in 1990–2020, the largest number of faculty members was registered because this area is the largest university center at the national level, with a large number of prestigious universities. In the second place is the Northwest region, which—at the level of 2020—registered 89 faculty members (decreasing from 95 in 2014), while third place is occupied by the Central region, with 65 faculty members in 2020 (decreasing from 73 faculty members in 2014). Although the Northeast region is experiencing a low level of economic development in the regions, it registers 61 faculties

Table 12.3 Number of faculties by development regions

Development regions	1990	2000	2005	2010	2014	2015	2016	2017	2018	2019	2020
Northwest region	32	110	123	97	95	91	91	91	90	90	89
Center region	18	78	102	78	73	69	66	66	63	65	65
Northeast region	36	92	92	74	69	65	66	64	63	61	61
Southeast region	11	50	66	54	52	50	50	50	48	50	51
South-Muntenia region	5	38	51	36	38	38	31	30	30	30	30
Bucharest-Ilfov region	53	193	184	171	159	158	160	158	159	157	155
Southwest Oltenia region	9	46	58	42	35	34	34	33	31	32	32
West region	22	89	94	77	62	62	62	62	61	61	58

Source: author's contribution based on INS data, Tempo-online, accessed on 20.05.2022

(69 in 2014, respectively) at the 2020 level, a rather small difference from the Center region. At the other pole of the hierarchy are the Southwest Oltenia region (32 faculties in 2020) and South-Muntenia region (30 faculties in 2020)—they have switched places at the bottom of the hierarchy beginning with 2015.

The trend in the number of enrollments for each development region is influenced by the number of existing universities in Romania.

In the 2019–2020 academic year, 54 public (state) universities and 35 accredited private universities were operating in Romania, with a total number of 541 faculty members and 560,490 students, according to a public report published by CNFIS in 2020. If we look at the distribution by development regions, according to Fig. 12.1, we note that private universities predominate in the Bucharest-Ilfov region, as do state universities (17 state universities and 15 private universities). At the level of the Central, Northwest, and Northeast regions, there were seven state universities each, whereas the top regions in terms of the number of private universities are led by far by the Bucharest-Ilfov region, with Northwest coming in the second place.

Another interesting development is that of the share of students' enrollment in universities, depending on their ownership form.

From Fig. 12.2, we note that in the 2019–2020 school year, the number of students enrolled in private and state universities has various distributions according to the development region. Inside the Bucharest-Ilfov

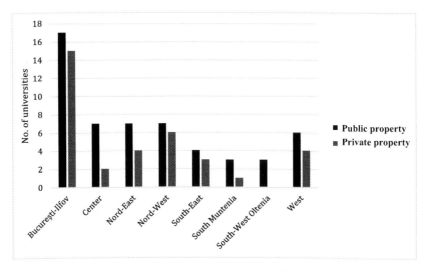

Fig. 12.1 Classification of universities by region by form of ownership (2020). Source: author's contribution based on data extracted from TEMPO Online, accessed on May 28,2022. http://statistici.insse.ro:8077/tempo-online/#/pages/tables/insse-table

region, 77.9% of the total students were enrolled in private universities, and 22.1% of the total number of students were enrolled in state universities. Out of the total number of students enrolled, the Bucharest-Ilfov region share represented 57.39% of their total number of students enrolled in private universities and 28.16% in state universities.

The second largest enrollment in private universities was registered for the 2019–2020 school year by the Southeast region, followed by the Northwest region (8.79 and 8.36%, respectively). On the other hand, the Northwest, Northeast and Center regions recorded high shares of students enrolled in state universities (18.9%, 14.45%, and 11.18%, respectively). The Southeast, Southwest, and South-Muntenia regions recorded the lowest shares of students enrolled in state universities (6.83%, 5.58%, and 4.02%, respectively).

The diagnosis carried out highlights a first distortion factor: the concentration of university infrastructure in nine university centers, which hold more than three-fourth of the total number of students and teachers. The capital has three times as many students as its share, given that it holds

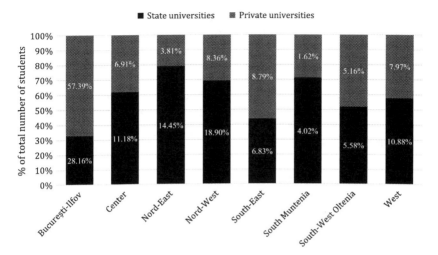

Fig. 12.2 Share of persons enrolled in universities by form of ownership and by development regions in the 2019–2020 school year. Source: author's contribution based on data from TEMPO Online (accessed on May 25, 2022)

less than 10% of the country's total population. Given that there is a very high potential for training in the capital and that, as a rule, capitals have representational functions in the field of research or academia that go beyond national limits, this weight does not seem to be extremely exaggerated.

Outside the capital, a strong university infrastructure is concentrated in three other university centers, Cluj-Napoca, Iasi, and Timisoara, which total more than one-fourth of the whole number of students. In these centers, the university infrastructure is complex, serving several fundamental fields of science: university, technical, medical, agricultural, and artistic. If we look at the theoretical spaces that would go to these university centers, we would see the extremely high expenditure on the accessibility of potential students to these centers. To alleviate such a concentration of university institutions, other centers have emerged, which tend to become regional centers, in distinct historical regions (Craiova in Oltenia, Constanta in Dobrogea, Oradea in Crisana) or at the interference of regional influences of other centers in the first category (Brașov, Sibiu, or Galati).

The trend of decreasing the share of traditional centers is maintained and accentuated due to the emergence of new university centers with a regional role located in spaces with high human potential. These are historical regions such as Dobrogea and Crisana but also other spaces located at the interference of historical regions (Arad area, southern Moldova, Maramures). This explains the fulminant increase in the number of students in the case of Constanta and Oradea regional centers. For traditional centers, although in absolute value, there is a significant increase, relative value marks a decrease due to the share of new university centers. Since, for the time, the poorest historical areas (primarily Moldova) were disadvantaged, a coherent state policy is required in this regard for balanced territorial equipment in the field of higher education.

Comparative Analysis of the Dispersion of University Centers and the Number of Students in Countries: United Kingdom, Sweden, South Korea, Poland, and Romania

In the same context, we note that the conduct of a comparative analysis of the dispersion of the number of students by university centers in countries such as the United Kingdom, Sweden, Poland, South Korea, and Romania highlights both the particular and general aspects of the proposed topic, according to the table in *Annex No. 22.*

Detailing the above, we find that the statistical data recorded in the United Kingdom, according to Table 12.4, put England in the first place, with 81.3% of the number of students registered, at the level of the 2019–2020 academic reference year, in the United Kingdom (2,435,825 students). In the second place comes Scotland, with 10.7% (increasing from 9.37% in 2014), in the third place is Wales with a value of 5.6%, and in the fourth is Northern Ireland with 2.4% students.

By processing the data in the table, we see that the student trend at the level of the regions of England presents a *sinusoidal line*. Therefore, in the UK capital, in London, there is 12.7% of the total population of the United Kingdom and 435,085 students, or 17.9% of the total number of students and 48 universities out of 163 in total in the United Kingdom. England's Southeast region ranks second with 11.23%, while England's Northwest region is in the third place, with approximately 9.91% being assessed at the 2019–2020 academic year levels.

We also note that London is outclassed by the Southeast region of England in terms of the number of students enrolled in 2013–2014 but

Table 12.4   Student dispersion by region in the United Kingdom, 2020 and 2021

Region	2013/2014	2019/2020	2020/2021
Total England	**1,902,370**	**1,979,905**	**2,146,640**
Northeast	101,250	111,025	120,180
Northwest	226,595	241,440	263,445
Yorkshire and the Humber	192,835	198,655	213,800
East Midlands	157,735	185,095	192,670
West Midlands	188,950	218,285	235,210
East of England	126,495	143,035	163,650
London	366,605	435,085	485,020
Southeast	389,310	273,475	286,805
Southwest	152,595	173,810	185,860
Wales	129,130	136,355	145,170
Scotland	215,600	260,490	282,875
Northern Ireland	52,260	59,075	66,245
Total number of students from United Kingdom	**2,299,355**	**2,435,825**	**2,640,930**

Source: https://www.hesa.ac.uk/data-and-analysis/students/where-study (Higher Education Statistics Agency), accessed on 28/05/2022

not in the next two periods of analysis. This is explained by the fact that English students preferred during the economic crisis the areas that required lower costs for attending university studies and were more accessible in terms of the entrance exam in these institutions. It should be noted that 33.26% of the students who choose London as their university center are international students who have a very good financial situation. The information in Table 12.4 points out that Scotland is also among the preferences of young people to continue university studies (both for young Europeans and young English) because there are no tuition fees in this region.

Another country of major interest, in our opinion, given the rankings of international reports with *benchmarking* value is South Korea. In 2020, 70.4% (statista.com) of high school graduates continued their university studies. *The country of quiet mornings* enjoys a high-performance education system in which 3,201,561 students are enrolled (go.kr). Thirty percent of students are in Seoul, that is, a total of 979,599 (go.kr) students attended the courses of 88 private and public universities. We note that there are 426 higher education institutions in the country.

Statistics show that Poland has made remarkable and continuous progress both economically and educationally. At the level of 2020, Polish university education registered 1,215,137 (gov.pl) students out of a population of 37,899,070 (worldbank.org). A total of 18.7% of the total number of students are found in the 68 universities in the Warsaw subregion, including the capital city of Warsaw, and the total number of university institutions operating in Poland is 349 (decreased from the 2014 date, which accounted for 438 higher education institutions).

According to Fig. 12.3, it is noted that most universities are concentrated in the Central and Southern regions of Poland in four major university centers: Warsaw, with more than 40 universities, and Poznan (24 universities), Wroclaw (23 universities), and Krakow (21 universities),

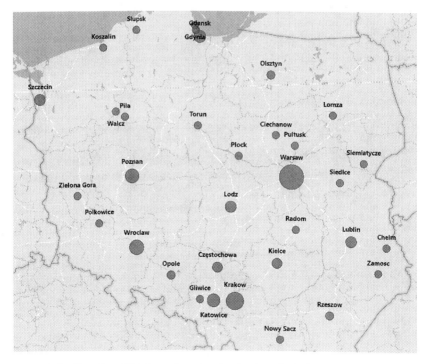

Fig. 12.3 Density of higher education institutions in Poland. Source: author's own elaboration based on data from https://www.universityguru.com/universities%2D%2Dpoland

where more than 100,000 students are studying. Universities (go.kr) with between 20,000 students and up to 100,000 students are located in 13 counties of Poland, which are also major centers of academic institutions, with a total share of 60.9% of all students in Poland. A difference of 39.1% of students attend university courses in counties whose higher education institutions hold between 2000 and 20,000 students, spread evenly on Polish territory.

Sweden, a promoter of a new model in developments between education and the labor market, according to available data, has 428,770 (studeravidare.se) students attending university courses. Of these, 20.54% are in the country's capital, of the 27 existing universities, whereas Stockholm accounts for approximately 10% of Sweden's population. There are 48 (studeravidare.se) colleges, polytechnics, and universities nationwide, including 32 universities. According to Fig. 12.4, we note that the university infrastructure is concentrated in the south of Sweden, specifically around the largest and most developed cities, and is quite diversified: in addition to universities (marked with orange), there are noted polytechnics (marked in blue) that predominate at the country level. Colleges are marked with green and university campuses in red and are equally numerous but much more territorially dispersed.

At the level of the countries analyzed, that is, at the level of the capitals, which are the largest university centers because there is a very high potential for training, the distribution of students is as follows for the 2020 data: London with a percentage of 13.1% (12.7% in 2014) of the population holds 17.9% (15.9% in 2014) of the number of students in the United Kingdom; Seoul with 19.1% (21.07% in 2014) of the country's population holds 30.6% of the number of students in South Korea, Warsaw with 4.6% of the country's population holds 18.7% (15.2% in 2014) of the number of students, Stockholm with 9.5% of Sweden's population holds 18.9% (20.54% in 2014) students, and Bucharest with approximately 11.2% of the country's population holds 31.7% of the Romanian student population (insignificant change from the 2014 data—10.77% with 31.85%, respectively). It is noted, at the level of proportions, that distortion is produced visibly in the Bucharest-Ilfov region, due to regional disparities, the regions having an unequal level of development at the level of Romania. We note that at the level of Poland, in Warsaw, the number of students is more than three times the share of the inhabitants of the capital. This demonstrates the interest of young people in studying in Warsaw's renowned universities. The distribution of students at the university level

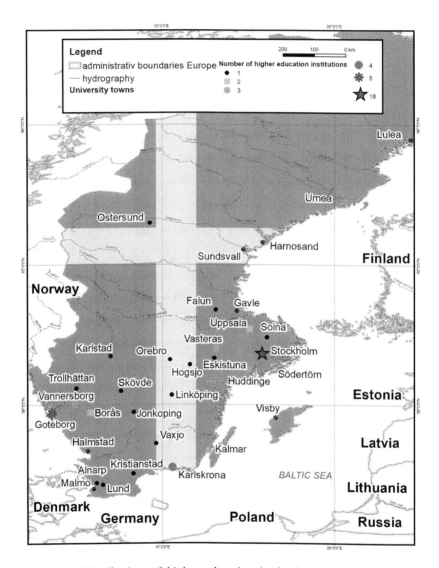

Fig. 12.4 Distribution of higher education institutions in Sweden. Source: author's own elaboration, based on data from https://english.uka.se/about-us/publications/reports%2D%2Dguidelines/reports%2D%2Dguidelines/2021-09-10-an-overview-of-swedish-higher-education-and-research-2021.html

is also balanced in the four countries of the United Kingdom, Poland, Sweden, and South Korea, with the exception of Romania. If we look at the situation at the level of the capitals, we see the exceptions: London, which ranks first in the region and number of students, and Bucharest, which holds one-third of the number of students at the level of Romania. Employment opportunities can be the attraction effects that lead to a higher proportion of highly skilled young people or who want to study in university centers in the capitals.

If we were to make a ranking of the countries, according to Annex No. 22, in terms of the number of students in the countries analyzed, we note that the first place in the ranking is occupied by South Korea, followed by the United Kingdom, Poland, Romania, and Sweden. Different from this ranking, in terms of the number of students at the capital level, we note that the first place is London, followed by Seoul, Warsaw, Bucharest, and Stockholm. On the other hand, the ratio between the number of students at the level of capitals and the number of the population of the capital as a share highlights the fact that the first place is occupied by Bucharest, the second place by Seoul, with subsequent places occupied in order by Stockholm, Warsaw, and London, but only by minor differences in percentages.

In conclusion, it is necessary that the higher education network be optimized in relation to the size of the population and the need for equitable access of the population to university services.

REGIONAL DISPARITIES IN THE LEVEL OF EDUCATION OF THE POPULATION

The European Commission's report entitled *Attention to differences—the inequality of EU regions in education* highlights the existence of important differences between the regions of the European Union in the level of education achieved.

The report is based on Eurostat data and contains more than 100 maps that allow you to view regional disparities. The most important findings of the report are (europa.eu):

- regional disparities in education hinder economic growth and balanced regional development;
- regional disparities in education give rise to inequalities between EU regions;

- the nature, scale, and effects of educational inequalities vary considerably between EU regions;
- the efficient use of the European Structural Funds can help to reduce regional disparities in education and their effects;
- more systematic data collection at the subregional level is needed to improve the knowledge base and to inform policy makers on this subject.

Share of the Population with a Low Level of Education

According to the data available on the European Commission's website for the period 2000–2014, there is a trend at the European Union level to decrease the share of people who have passed at most one form of pre-school, primary, and secondary education in the total population aged 25–64. In Romania, the share of the population with a low level of training decreased from 30.7% in 2000 to 19.6% in 2020, as shown by the data in Annex 21.

In 2014, there was a certain increase in the share held by the population with a low level of training in the total population of 25–64 years. The increase is quite significant, according to definitive data recorded in the European statistics as shown in Fig. 12.5.

There is an obvious trend to reduce the gap between Romania and the European Union beginning with 2016 (i.e., the European economies began to recover after the global economic crisis) in terms of the share of the population with a low level of training. The largest gap between Romania and the EU of 5.7% was recorded in 2001, and the smallest difference in 2019 was 0.3%. The economic crisis triggered in 2008 is visible on the graph by the increase in the share of the population with a low level of education in Romania. The decrease in the level of the population's income has led, on the one hand, to the postponement of studies and, on the other hand, to an increase in school dropouts. This attitude has led to an increase in the share of the population with a low level of education in the total population aged 25–64 years, according to Fig. 12.6.

An analysis of the gender distribution of the share of the population that has promoted at most one form of preschool, primary, and secondary education in Romania highlights an existing gap between the two sexes, rather than the female one.

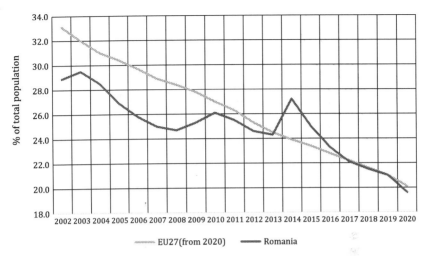

Fig. 12.5 Share of the population aged 25–64 years with a low level of training in Romania and the European Union between 2002 and 2020. Source: author's contribution according to data available on Eurostat, accessed on 28.05.2022. *2020 data provisory*

Between 2000 and 2020, there was a reduction in the gap between the two sexes in Romania, from 12.8 in 2000 to 5.5 in 2014 and 3.0 in 2019 and 2020. The female population continued to prepare through a higher form of education, which led to a reduction in the share of the population with a low level of training. In the period 2000–2008, the reduction in the share of the female population with a low level of training is revealed by the reduction of 7.7%, from 37%, in 2000 to 29.30 in 2008. The more difficult economic situation that followed after 2008 caused certain fluctuations in the population structure after the level of preparedness. The share of the male population with a low level of training has experienced similar developments to that of the female population.

According to the European Commission Report entitled *Attention to differences—inequality of EU regions in education*, the regions with the highest share of people who have promoted at most one form of preschool, primary, and secondary education (levels 0–2, ISCED 2011) as a percentage of the population over the age of 15 are generally found in Portugal, Italy, and Spain as shown in Table 12.5. The Extremadura region in Spain has the highest shares of people with low qualifications,

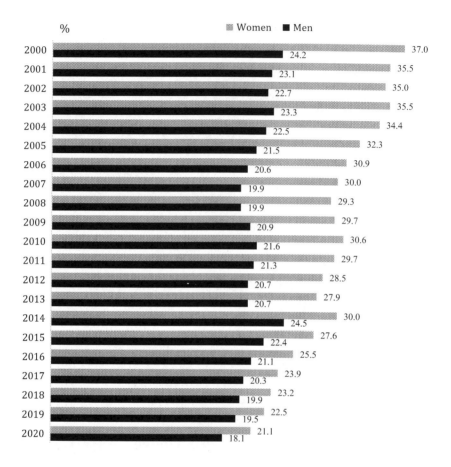

Fig. 12.6 Share of population aged 25–64 years, with a low level of education in Romania, by sex, between 2000 and 2020. Source: personal elaboration

with the Alentejo region from Portugal moving from the top to the bottom of this statistics in the last decade.

The distribution by development regions at the Romanian level of the population with a low level of training highlights that in 2020, the lowest share (9%) was located in the most developed region of the country, namely, Bucharest-Ilfov. If in 2014, the region with the highest share of people with a low level of training was in the Southeast region, in 2020

Table 12.5 Share of persons who have passed at most one form of preschool, primary, and secondary education

Region	Share
Extremadura (ES)	51.4
Ciudad de Ceuta (ES)	51.3
Norte (PT)	49.4
Puglia (IT)	48.4
Sicilia (IT)	48.0
Isole (IT)	47.7
Castilla-La Mancha (ES)	47.3
Andalucia (ES)	47.2
Sardegna (IT)	46.7
Alentejo (PT)	46.6

Source: Author's elaboration based on Eurostat data, 2020 (https://ec.europa.eu/eurostat/databrowser/view/EDAT_LFS_9918/default/table?lang=en&category=educ.educ_outc.edat.edat1.edat1_)

the region that ranks first on this indicator is the Northeast with 27.8%. The position of the Northeast region in terms of the share of the population with a low level of training can also be attributed to the fact that this area has the lowest employment rate of working resources.

Lack of jobs and unattractive pay demotivate the population to raise the level of training. In addition, a lack of infrastructure limits young people's participation in education due to inaccessibility. Industrial restructuring, discontinuity in the territory of industrial activities, and lack of correlation with tertiary and agricultural activities are probably other factors that have led to a decrease in interest in further studies.

The comparison by development regions for 2020 compared to 2014 reveals, according to Fig. 12.7, a clear trend of declining population share with a low level of preparedness for all regions of the country, a maintaining trend from 2000. Following the analysis, we can say that higher shares in the population with a low level of training are found in less developed regions, while low weights are found in regions with a higher level of development.

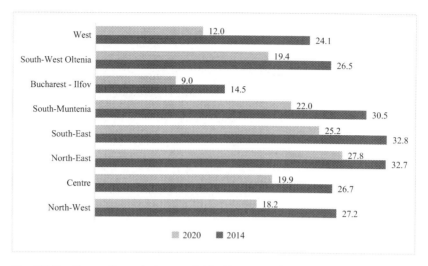

Fig. 12.7 Share of population aged 25–64 years with a low level of training by development regions in 2020 compared to 2014. Source: personal elaboration based on Eurostat data, accessed on 28.05.2022

Share of the Population with a High Level of Education

Changes in population structure by the level of education are also evident by analyzing the share of the population with a high level of training (ISCED levels 5, 6, 7, 8). In this respect, the comparative analysis of the evolution of the share of the population with a high level of preparedness in Romania and the European Union in the period 2000–2020 shows that the share of the population with a high level of training experienced an upward trend throughout the period covered by the analysis, as shown in Fig. 12.8.

In Romania, the share of the population with a high level of training increased from 9.3% in 2000 to 15.9% in 2014 and to 18.7% in 2020. The evolution in Romania is similar to that found at the European Union level, from 19.5% in 2000 to 29.3% (27.7%—EU27) in 2014 and up to 32.8% in 2020. However, the gaps between Romania and the European Union in terms of the share of the population with a high level of training continued to increase. If the difference was 9.9% in 2001 and 13.4% in 2014, the gap reached 15.9% to the detriment of Romania in 2020. This widening gap between Romania and the European Union can be attributed to

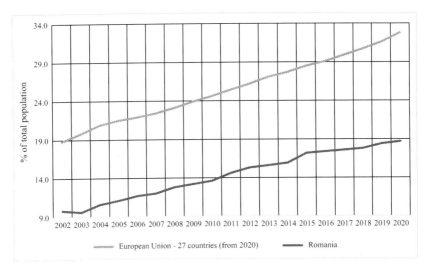

Fig. 12.8 Share of the population aged 25–64 years with a high level of training in Romania and the European Union in the period 2000–2020. Source: personal elaboration based on http://ec.europa.eu/eurostat/data/database data, accessed on 28.05.2022

the lower level of income of the population that can be allocated to increasing the level of preparedness, as well as the difficulties in terms of access for the rural population to education.

Another motivation is that many young people fail to pass national assessments and the baccalaureate exam. The increasing number of high school graduates, the serious competition made by the faculties outside the country, and the financial difficulties that students have contributed to this gap between the European Union and Romania.

The evolution of the gender distribution of the share of the population with a higher level of education at the level of Romania in the period 2000–2014 is presented in Fig. 12.9.

The graphic representation of the share of the population with a high level of preparedness for the two genres shows profound structural changes. Thus, we can see that between 2000 and 2020, relations were reversed between genders, moving from a gap of 2.2% in favor of the male population in 2000 to a gap of 1.1% in 2014 and 2.6% in 2020 in favor of the female population. Over the period as a whole, the share of the female

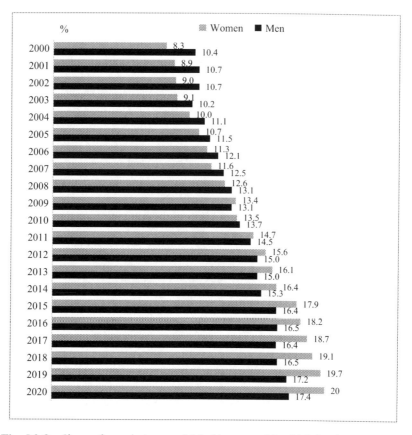

Fig. 12.9 Share of population aged 25–64 years, with a high level of education in Romania, by sex, in the period 2000–2020. Source: personal elaboration based on http://ec.europa.eu/eurostat/data/database data, accessed on 28.05.2022

population increased from 8.3% in 2000 to 16.4% in 2014 and further up to 20% in 2020. The 25- to 64-year-old male population, which has a high level of training, increased by 4.9% from 10.4% in 2000 to 15.3% in 2014 and by only 2.1% in 2020 compared to 2014. One possible explanation for the higher share of women, 20% who have higher education compared to men (17.43%), is their greater difficulty in entering the labor market. In this context, it is considered that holding a higher education diploma makes it easier to find a job. The increase of less than 2.1% of the share of the male population with a high level of training (although the absolute increase is 13.7%) is justified by the existence of a higher employment rate in management positions requiring a higher level of training.

The regions with the highest share of people with university education were mostly in the United Kingdom, Belgium, France, and Denmark in 2014, whereas the 2020 data (which no longer include the United Kingdom) show the Warsaw region in Poland as the European region with the highest share of population having Levels 5–8 (tertiary education). The top also includes regions from Sweden, Spain, France, and Norway, as can be seen in Table 12.6.

The graphic representation by regions of Romania in 2020 compared to 2014 shows that the highest share of graduates with a high level of training is in the Bucharest-Ilfov region (40.5%), and the lowest share is found in the Northeast region (11.8%). The largest increase in the share of the population with a high level of training, between 2014 and 2020, was recorded in the Northwest region (from 14.2% to 20.1%), as seen in Fig. 12.10, whereas for 2014 compared to 2000, the largest increase was in the Bucharest-Ilfov region.

The Bucharest-Ilfov region is also distinguished by a demand for a higher skilled workforce, which motivates the population to raise the level

Table 12.6 Share of persons with a qualification in university education

Region	Share
Warszawski stoleczny	50.9
Sostines regionas	51.9
Prov. Brabant wallon	50.8
Zürich	49.1
Oslo og Akershus	47.7
País Vasco	48.7
Stockholm	46.4
Utrecht	48.1
Helsinki-Uusimaa	46.5
Île de France	47.6

Source: Author's elaboration based on Eurostat data, 2020 (https://ec.europa.eu/eurostat/databrowser/view/EDAT_LFS_9918/default/table?lang=en&category=educ.educ_outc.edat.edat1.edat1_)

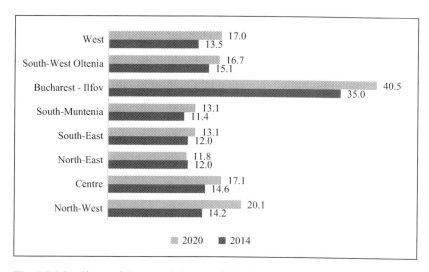

Fig. 12.10 Share of the population aged 25–64 years with a high level of training by development region in 2020 compared to 2014. Source: author's contribution based on http://ec.europa.eu/eurostat/data/database data, accessed on 28.05.2022

of training. The opportunities offered by the capital are numerous: the standard of urban living, prestige, existence of universities, and social and professional structure give the Bucharest-Ilfov region a strength and economic dynamics superior to those of the other regions. The region is distinguished by a very high GDP/resident compared to the other regions. The foreign direct investment attracted accounts for 75% of the total foreign investment at the national level. The Bucharest-Ilfov region is detached from the other regions of the country by the high density of SMEs and is also a national leader in innovation capacity and IT.

There are very large discrepancies between the Bucharest-Ilfov region and the other regions. At the level of 2014, only 12% of the population aged 25–64 in the Northeast and Southeast regions had higher education, whereas in 2020, data show a slight improvement for the Southeast and South-Muntenia regions and a further decline in the Northeast region (with 11.8%). Within the Southeast region, higher shares in the population with a high level of training are found more in the counties of Constanta and Galati, where there are a number of economic agents who carry out activities in the field of tourism or related to this field and who require staff to hire a certain professional training.

In the Northeast region, the migratory movement of the population has been quite strong in recent years, with the workforce having to become more mobile amid financial difficulties. Within this region, Botoşani and Vaslui counties occupy the last positions in the national hierarchy of GDP per capita. More than 80% of the expenditure on research and development activities in the region is concentrated in Iasi County.

The Northeast region has become more attractive to potential investors because in most of the region, skilled labor is cheaper compared to other regions of the country. The main employer, in most localities in the region, is the public and not the private environment.

DIFFERENCES IN ADULT PARTICIPATION IN LIFELONG LEARNING

One indicator highlighting the increase in the population's preparedness to adapt to changes in the labor market is the participation of adults in lifelong learning. In Romania, only 1.5% of the population aged 25–64 participated in education and training activities in 2014 and only 1% in 2020. Although increasing since 2000, the share of the population participating in training and training activities is very small compared to that recorded at the European Union level (9.1% in 2020). The gaps between Romania and the European Union are increasing, from 4.3% in 2002 to 8.1% in 2020, with as high as a 9.7% gap recorded in 2018, as seen in Fig. 12.11.

The gender distribution of the share of the population aged 25–64 years who participated in education and training activities between 2002 and 2020 is shown in Fig. 12.12.

The differences between the two categories of population after participation in education and training activities ranged, during the period under review, from differences in favor of the male population in 2000, equalization in 2002, to differences in favor of the female population in 2009. By the regions of the European Union, we note that the regions with the highest participation of adults aged 25–64 in education and training activities (as a percentage of the total population) in 2020 are found, according to Table 12.7, in Sweden and Switzerland.

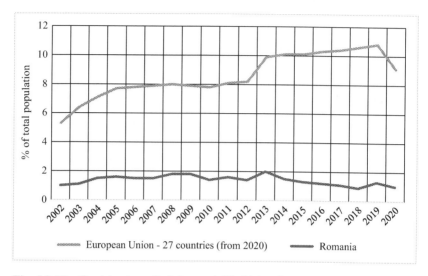

■■■■ European Union - 27 countries (from 2020)   ■■■■ Romania

Fig. 12.11 Participation of adults aged 25–64 in education and training activities between 2002 and 2020. Source: personal contribution based on data from https://ec.europa.eu/eurostat/databrowser/view/TRNG_LFSE_04__custom_2815485/default/table?lang=en, accessed on 29.05.2022

This is justified by the fact that these countries have successfully implemented the idea of lifelong learning. Taking the top spot in *benchmarking* reports, these countries demonstrate that investment in education and professional development increases performance and competitiveness in the global economy. The acquisition of high standards of education and quality training in all sectors contributes to increasing the chance of employment and mobility in a constantly changing society.

For the regions with the lowest participation of adults aged 25–64 in education and training activities (as a percentage of the total population), it is noted that most are from Romania and Greece, with one each for Bulgaria and Poland, as shown in Table 12.8.

Low rates of adult participation in education and training activities in regions of Romania, Bulgaria, or Greece are determined by the difficult situation these countries have found themselves in recent years, and all have recorded sharp decreases from 2014 to 2020 in the rates of participation of adults (25–64 years) in education and training, particularly explicable by the pandemic effects and the fact that they were poorly prepared

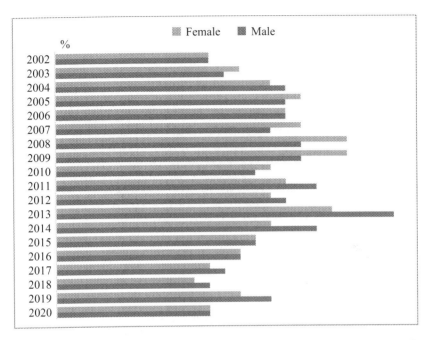

Fig. 12.12 Participation of adults aged 25–64 in education and training activities between 2002 and 2020 in Romania by sex, Source: personal contribution based on data from https://ec.europa.eu/eurostat/databrowser/view/TRNG_LFSE_04__custom_2815485/default/table?lang=en, accessed on 29.05.2022

to switch to online training classes. Furthermore, these countries also have the lowest percentages of GDP allocated to education, being in the last third of EU countries, according to statistics of global reports at the level of 2019–2020.

If in 2014, the southwestern Oltenia region of Romania had the lowest share of adults aged 25–64 who participated in education and training activities (0.7%), in 2020, data show that the lowest share is recorded in the northeastern and southeastern regions, while the South-Muntenia region recorded the highest share of adults participating in education and training activities (2.2%), followed by the Western region, with a share of

Table 12.7 Participation of adults aged 25–64 in education and training activities in 2020

Region	2020
Zürich (Switzerland)	32.9
Helsinki-Uusimaa (Finland)	30.8
Stockholm (Sweden)	30.1
Östra Sverige (Sweden)	29.8
Nordwestschweiz (Switzerland)	29.3
Sydsverige (Sweden)	29.3
Östra Mellansverige (Sweden)	29.3
Västsverige (Sweden)	28.5
Zentralschweiz (Switzerland)	28.2
Södra Sverige (Sweden)	28.2
Manner-Suomi (Finland)	27.3
Norra Mellansverige (Sweden)	26.6
Norra Sverige (Sweden)	26.4

Source: personal contribution based on data from https://ec.europa.eu/eurostat/databrowser/view/ TRNG_LFSE_04__custom_2815485/default/ table?lang=en, accessed on 29.05.2022

Table 12.8 Participation of adults aged 25–64 in education and training activities in 2020

Region	2020
Peloponnisos (Greece)	0.5
Northeast (Romania)	0.6
Southeast (Romania)	0.6
Northwest (Romania)	0.7
Bucharest-Ilfov (Romania)	0.8
Southwest Oltenia (Romania)	0.8
Centre (Romania)	1.0
Sterea Ellada (Greece)	1.3
Severoiztochen (Bulgaria)	1.4
Mazowiecki regionalny (Poland)	1.5

Source: personal contribution based on data from https://ec.europa.eu/eurostat/databrowser/view/ TRNG_LFSE_04__custom_2815485/default/ table?lang=en, accessed on 29.05.2022

1.5%. We note that in the Bucharest-Ilfov region, only 0.8% (decreasing from 1.2% in 2014) of the adult population aged 25–64 years participated in education and training activities in 2020, a sharply downward trend in

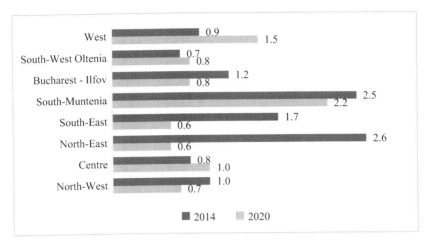

Fig. 12.13 Participation of adults aged 25–64 in education and training activities by development region. Source: personal contribution based on data from https://ec.europa.eu/eurostat/databrowser/view/TRNG_LFSE_04__custom_2815485/default/table?lang=en, accessed on 29.05.2022

the Northeast region (from 2.6% in 2014 to merely 0.6% in 2020) as can be seen in Fig. 12.13.

There are possible explanations for these differences between development regions. Thus, regions with a low level of development have included the unemployed population in education and training activities through projects carried out through European funds. The participation rate in continuous training has the highest score in the Northeast region, as approximately half of the companies in the region had at least three employees who took part in a minimum refresher course. By county, the highest share was recorded in Bacau, Botoşani and Neamţ. At the regional level, the lack of people specializing in technical fields was an additional reason for increasing adult participation in education and training activities.

INEQUALITIES IN POPULATION EMPLOYMENT, UNEMPLOYMENT, AND ECONOMIC DEVELOPMENT BY DEVELOPMENT REGION

Differences in Population Occupancy by Level of Training

In the period 2000–2020, changes in the employment of the population with a higher level of training in Romania compared to the European Union are visible on the graph in Fig. 12.14.

In 2014, the employment rate of the population aged 25–64 years with a higher level of training was 86%, larger than that at the European Union level (83.3%). The analysis of the data for the period 2000–2020 shows, in Romania, a minimum value of 82% in 2003 and a maximum value of 90.5% in 2019. Romania, although it started in 2000 with a value of 84.5%, close to that recorded at the European Union level (84.1%), the developments in employment rates among the population aged 25–64 years with a higher level of training were not similar.

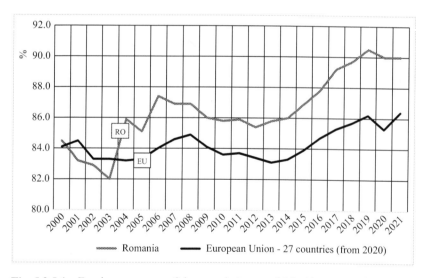

Fig. 12.14 Employment rate of the population aged 25–64 years, with a higher level of training (ISCED 5–8). Source: author's contribution based on data http://ec.europa.eu/eurostat/data/database, accessed on 24.06.2022

By education levels for Romania, between 2006 and 2009, there was a sharper decrease in the employment rate among the population with a medium level of education. The employment rate among this population category decreased from 71% in 2006 to 68.5% in 2009, as shown in Fig. 12.15.

Between 2008 and 2012, the employment rate of 25–64 years of age, with a higher level of training, steadily decreased from 86.9% to 85.5%, roughly corresponding to the global economic crisis. Overall, the view of the situation for the period 2000–2020 allows us to state that a low level of education is associated with a low employment rate, which shows the implications of raising the level of education of the population.

A comparison by sex and average employment rate of the population aged 15–64 years by the level of education is shown in Table 12.9.

Data presented by the National Statistical Institute in the publication "Labor force in Romania. Employment and unemployment—2020" highlight very large gaps by sex and average for the 2014 data, with even more acute differences in 2020, as shown in Tables 12.5–12.9 above. In

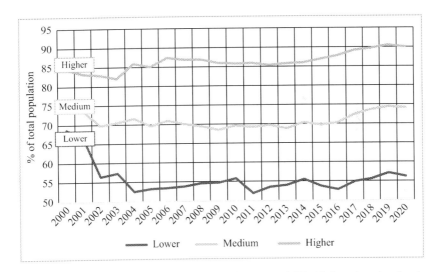

Fig. 12.15 Employment rate of the population aged 25–64, by education levels in Romania, in the period 2000–2020. Source: author's contribution based on http://ec.europa.eu/eurostat/data/database data, accessed on 24.06.2022

Table 12.9   Employment rate (15–64 years) by sex and average in Romania in 2020

	Total	Level of education		
		High	Medium	Low
Male	74.4	90.9	77.1	55.9
Female	56.5	87.0	57.9	31.9
Urban	67.1	89.5	66.8	27.3
Rural	63.8	85.2	69.7	50.9

Source: Author's contribution based *on statistical annexes from publication "Labor force in Romania. Employment and unemployment – 2020", INS, Bucharest, 2020*

this context, we have a much higher employment rate among the male population overall, and these gaps are significantly large as the level of training decreases. The differences between the employment rate recorded among the male and female populations increase from 3.9% (4.5% in 2014) in the higher-trained population to 24% (significant gap increase from 2004's 16%) among the low-trained population. Low-level men find it easier to find a job than the female population for whom available jobs are often paid the minimum on the economy.

By average, the unemployment rate is higher among the rural population, which on the whole is characterized by an older, feminized population with a lower level of training. Nevertheless, we see a significantly higher level of employment among the rural population with a low level of training compared to that of urban areas. In rural areas, a significant proportion of the population aged 15–65 years is included in agriculture, a branch where available jobs do not necessarily require a higher level of training.

By development regions, the highest employment rate in 2020 is found in the Northeast region (72.5%, compared to 66.8% in 2014), whereas the lowest employment rate in 2020 is found in the Center and West regions (60.3%), closely followed, with 60.5% by the Southeast region (60.5%), who recorded the lowest employment rate in 2014 (54.5%). By education level, in the Bucharest-Ilfov development region, the population aged 15–64 years, with a higher level of education, has the highest employment chance, with an employment rate of 90.6%. At the same time, the West region and the Center region have the lowest employment rates of medium and higher education, respectively, as seen *in* Table 12.10. In the Southeast

Table 12.10 Employment rate (15–64 years) by development regions in 2020

Development regions	Total	Level of education		
		High	Medium	Low
Northwest region	66.5	89.9	69.6	40.5
Center region	60.3	89.1	66.0	29.0
Northeast region	72.5	88.3	75.8	61.7
Southeast region	60.5	86.2	65.6	40.0
South-Muntenia region	64.4	89.3	69.4	40.7
Bucharest-Ilfov region	72.1	90.6	67.6	36.2
Southwest Oltenia region	64.4	87.7	65.0	47.5
West region	60.3	84.6	61.7	30.7

Source: author's contribution based *on statistical annexes from publication "Labor force in Romania. Employment and unemployment – 2020"*, INS, Bucharest, 2020

region, 62% of the population of Vrancea County lives in rural areas, with 49% of them working in agriculture. In this region, there is also the highest rate of migration of young people of the activities to economic growth areas from the country. Another factor contributing to the outrunning of this region was industrial restructuring, a fairly high dropout rate among high school students, and a declining rate of the school population.

In the Northeast development region, the population with a low level of training has the highest occupancy rate compared to the other regions of Romania. The comparison of employment rates by education levels shows that a higher level of education corresponds to a higher employment rate for all regions of the country.

Changes in Terms of Unemployment in Romania

The evolution of the unemployment rate among the population aged 25–64 years in Romania was similar to that at the European Union level for the period 2000–2020. The unemployment rate in Romania increased from 3.4% in 2000 to 4.7% in 2014. In the period 2000–2008, the employment rate among the population with a higher level of education experienced a downward trend, reaching a minimum of 1.9% in 2008, after which a process of growth began. The economic crisis triggered in 2008 also affected the higher-educated population by losing their jobs, as seen in Figs. 12.5 and 12.16. The post-economic crisis growth (2014–2019) reflected in the unemployment rate for the higher education

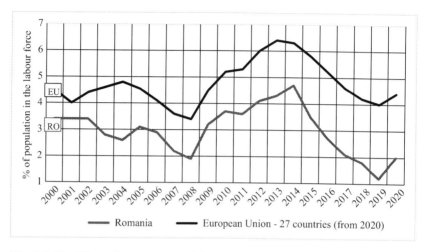

Fig. 12.16 Unemployment rate of the population with higher education aged between 20 and 64 years in the period 2000–2020. Source: author's contribution based on http://ec.europa.eu/eurostat/data/database data, accessed on 19.05.2022

population aged 25–64, with a sharp decrease down to 1.2% in 2019, after which the pandemic negatively influenced employment status, with a 2% unemployment rate in 2020 (while the EU average for the same year and for the same group was 4.4%) as shown in Fig. 12.16.

In Romania, unemployment is due either to the structural characteristics of the labor market or to qualifications that are inadequate to the requirements of this market. Another explanation lies in the fact that the structure of the economy has changed with the advent of new technologies that require people with a higher level of training. This change also has an effect on reducing the numbers of employed people by giving up the existing, inadequately qualified one. A higher unemployment rate is recorded in regions where investment is low, the population is less proficient, and the level of development is very low.

If we examine the evolution of the unemployment rate among the population aged 25–64 by education level, we will see that the highest unemployment rate is found in the case of the population with a low level of education. In 2014, the unemployment rate among the population with a low level of education was 6.4%, compared to a rate of 4.7% for the population with a higher level and 5.8% for the population with an average level of education. The same happened in 2020, with the pandemic weighting even more on the lower education group—unemployment rate increased from 5.7% up to 7.9%, compared to the increase by 0.8 percentage points (from 1.2% to 2%) for the population aged 25–64 with a higher education level.

It seems that in Romania, the labor market seems to be more attractive to those who have a university degree. According to labor market statistics in 2015, 65% of the number of active jobs were for graduates of higher education and only 25% for those who graduated only from high school, with employing companies focusing less on middle-school graduates. Additionally, in a fairly small percentage, 12% of all jobs were for elementary school and vocational school graduates. In summary, even though Romania has one of the lowest rates of higher education graduates in Europe, approximately 70% of job ads are addressed to those with a university degree, which explains the data on the evolution of unemployment, the chances for those with middle education being lower.

From the graph shown in Fig. 12.17, we can argue that the unemployment rate was higher among the population with a lower level of education, while the population with a higher level of education had a lower unemployment rate. The comparison for 2020, by sex and average of the employment rate among the population aged 15–64 years, shows a higher unemployment rate among the male population and the urban population, respectively. The weighted average of unemployment based on gender and background in Romania in 2020 can be seen in Table 12.11.

Higher unemployment among men than among women is due to seasonal *job* types, where women, such as in the tourist service area, hotels, restaurants, or cuisine, have priority. Until the onset of the economic and financial crisis in 2008, there were many places available in construction, with men taking priority. The massive layoffs in 2014, caused by restructurings in the mining industry, led to a decrease in predilection for men. In recent years, there have been many vacancies for women in areas such as sales and the textile industry, where men are not usually employed. A comparison between data from 2020 and 2014 shows that unemployment rates have been higher for both men and women with low levels of education, as well as for rural populations (total and low education).

By development region, the highest unemployment rate (7.4%) was in the Southeast region, with an improved rate compared to 2014 (10.4%), while the lowest unemployment rate in 2020 is somewhat surprisingly

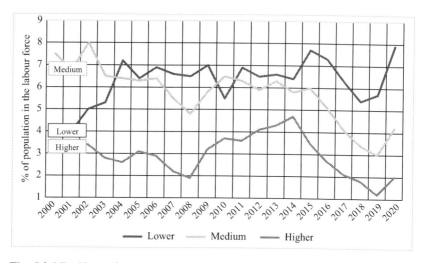

Fig. 12.17 Unemployment rate among the population aged 20–64 by education level in Romania in the period 2000–2020. Source: author's contribution based on http://ec.europa.eu/eurostat/data/database data, accessed on 19.05.2022

Table 12.11 The weighted average of unemployment based on gender and background in Romania in 2020

	Total	Level of education		
		High	Medium	Low
Male	5.3	2.0	5.1	8.9
Female	4.7	2.4	5.0	7.0
Urban	4.4	1.9	4.7	14.1
Rural	5.8	4.1	5.5	6.7

Source: author's contribution based *on statistical annexes from publication "Labor force in Romania. Employment and unemployment – 2020", INS, Bucharest, 2020*

recorded in the Northeast region (3.0%)—top performer in 2014 was the Northwest region, with 3.8%. By education level, the population aged 15–64 years, with a higher level of education, in the Bucharest-Ilfov region had the lowest unemployment rate, while the same population in the Southeast region had the highest unemployment rate. In the Bucharest-Ilfov region, only 1.8% of the population with a higher level of training did not have a job, a significant change from 2014 (5.1%). In the Central region, there was the highest unemployment rate (21.6%) among the population with a low level of education, almost two times as much as in 2014 (12.9%). In regions with a higher level of development, there was a lower unemployment rate among the population with a higher level of training. The unemployment rate based on regions of development in Romania in 2020 can be seen in Table 12.12.

More developed regions offer more opportunities to find a job for the population with higher education. The Bucharest-Ilfov region has the lowest unemployment rate among the population with a higher level of education, followed by the Northwest and Northeast regions, each with a 2.2% unemployment rate for the mentioned target group. The Western region, which previously (3.5% in 2014) held the record for the lowest unemployment rate among highly educated people, falls only to third place in 2020. It is the leader in the Romanian market in terms of the number of employment thanks to the automotive industry, which is by far the largest employer in the region, of the major volume of investments, so that at the level of 2014–2015, employers called for the resettlement of 2000 people from other areas with low levels of development. In this region, there are requests for investment projects that still require a high-level workforce. The Northwest region is the most attractive of Romania's development regions due to the labor and wage markets, foreign investment, the private environment, and the development of modern

Table 12.12 The unemployment rate based on regions of development in Romania in 2020

Development regions	Total	Level of education		
		High	Medium	Low
Northwest region	3.8	2.2	3.7	6.8
Center region	7.1	2.6	5.3	21.6
Northeast region	3.0	2.2	3.6	2.0
Southeast region	7.4	3.3	7.1	11.2
South-Muntenia region	5.9	2.4	5.4	10.2
Bucharest-Ilfov region	4.7	1.8	6.2	13.8
Southwest Oltenia region	5.0	2.0	6.0	4.4
West region	4.6	2.4	4.4	11.3

Source: author's contribution based *on statistical annexes from publication "Labor force in Romania. Employment and unemployment – 2020", INS, Bucharest, 2020*

technologies. In this area, almost all industries and a considerable number of companies with foreign capital are represented. The lowest unemployment rates, in terms of the population with a low level of training, are found in less economically developed regions, such as the Northeast region or the southwest Oltenia region, because the majority of the employed population here has a medium/low level of training. A higher unemployment rate is recorded in the regions shown where investment is low and the population is underqualified.

Unemployment is caused in Romania by functional illiteracy. In Romania, more than three quarters of the unemployed in rural areas are almost illiterate: more than 15% of them are illiterate, 20% of them have primary classes, and 40% have managed to attend primary school. Rural unemployed account for 60% of all those on the record, and their low level of training makes it difficult to retrain in the jobs required in the labor market.

The GDP per Capita on a Regional Basis

The GDP[1] per capita registered an upward trend in Romania in the period 2000–2020, and the economic crisis triggered in 2008 was visible on the graph by the decrease in the value of this indicator in 2009. The evolution of GDP/resident is the basis for assessing the level of development of the regions. In Romania, the GDP per capita—calculated in current prices—increased from 1800 euros per capita in 2000 to 11,360 euros per capita in 2020, compared to an increase from 18,370 euros per capita in 2000 to 29,910 euros in 2020 at the European Union level, as shown in Fig. 12.18. The data using the purchasing power standard (PPS) show that purchasing power has significantly increased in Romania since 2000, with a gap between the European Union average GDP per inhabitant and Romania decreasing from 13,500 euro in 2000 to 8400 euro in 2020.

The difference in GDP/resident in Romania and in the European Union (EU-28 until 2020) increased from 18,000 euros in 2000 to only 18,550 euros in 2020. However, the ratio of GDP/dweller in Romania to GDP/resident in the European Union decreased from 10.89 in 2000 to

---

[1] According to the INS, gross domestic product (GDP) is equal to the sum of the final uses of goods and services of resident institutional units (actual final consumption, gross fixed capital formation) plus exports minus imports of goods and services. Regional GDP is the regional correspondent of GDP.

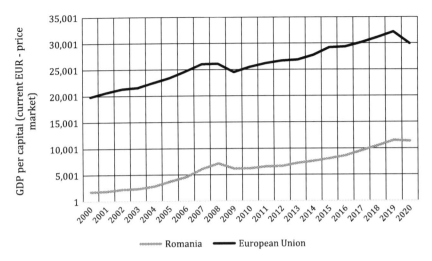

Fig. 12.18 Evolution of GDP per capita in Romania and the European Union in the period 2000–2020. Source: author contributions based on https://data. worldbank.org/indicator/NY.GDP.PCAP. CD, accessed on 29.05.2022

3.70 in 2013. In other words, GDP/dweller in Romania was approximately four times lower in 2013 than in the European Union, compared to 2000, when it was almost 11 times lower. This gap is because European industry has made a major contribution to job creation, innovation, and exports, and is interdependent with service activities. Romania's economy has seen a slight rebound from 2010 to 2012, which contributed to representative GDP/resident growth in 2013. The possible factors that positively influenced GDP growth were investments as the main component, improvement of lending activity, and growth of private consumption.

The evolution of GDP per inhabitant is the basis for assessing the level of development of the regions and was assessed using data expressed in the purchasing power standard (PPS). By development region, the highest GDP per capita in 2020 was in the Bucharest-Ilfov region, and the lowest GDP per capita was in the Northeast region, with a value of 13,600 euro/ inhabitant (PPS value).

The calculated differences between GDP per inhabitant in the most developed region of the country, Bucharest-Ilfov, and the least developed region, Northeast, increased from 7300 euro/inhabitant in 2000 to 35,600 euros in 2020, with a maximum in 2019 of 36,500 euro/

inhabitant. As seen in Fig. 12.19, the Northeast region does not exactly occupy a leading position in terms of regional development compared to the other eight regions of the country, the industry being underrepresented and the agriculture that is taking place is one of subsistence. Since this sector contributes the most to GDP creation, it can also be inferred that there is no economic diversification, with the rural population focusing mainly on agriculture and hence the dependence of the regional economy on this sector. A distribution of the population by sector is presented as follows: more than 40% work in agriculture, almost a quarter in industry, and the rest, approximately a third, in services. We can appreciate that, for the most part, from year to year, the situation has changed favorably in terms of GDP growth in the total region, with an upward trend.

At the same time, discrepancies were reported at the interregional and intraregional levels, toward which the overall *objective of the National Regional Development Strategy* has emerged, an objective aimed at stimulating economic growth and reducing differences at the regional level in terms of business and infrastructure.

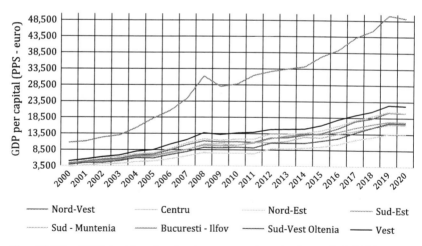

Fig. 12.19 GDP/resident by development regions in the period 2000–2020. Source: author's contribution based on https://ec.europa.eu/eurostat/data-browser/view/NAMA_10R_2GDP__custom_2816051/default/table?lang=en, accessed on 29.05.2022

THE LINK BETWEEN THE LEVEL OF EDUCATION
AND THE DEGREE OF REGIONAL ECONOMIC DEVELOPMENT

An area with a low level of education is a hindrance to the economic development of that area, just as a low level of development cannot provide the necessary resources to raise the level of preparedness. The correlation by development regions, in the period 2000–2013, between *the GDP* per capita and *the share of the population with a higher level of education* is shown in the graph in Fig. 12.20.

The correlation in Fig. 12.20 shows the gap between the Bucharest-Ilfov region and the country's other development regions. Throughout the period under review, the Bucharest-Ilfov region presents both the highest *share* of *the population with higher education* and the highest *gross domestic product* per capita. Given the elimination of the values corresponding to the Bucharest-Ilfov region, which have extremely high

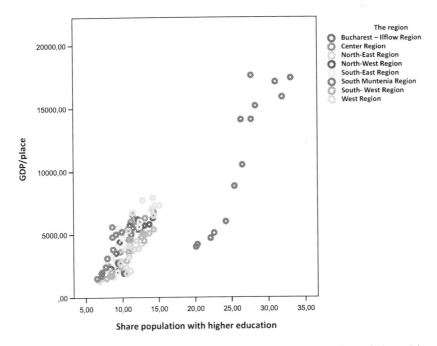

Fig. 12.20 Graphic representation of GDP/place and share of population with higher education by development regions in the period 2000–2013. Source: author's contribution based on analysis in the SPSS22 programme

values compared to the other development regions of the country, we notice the correlation of the pairs of values corresponding to the two variables represented by the correlation in Fig. 12.21.

We note, therefore, that a high *share* of the *population with higher education* correlates with a higher *gross domestic product* per capita, while a low *share* of the *higher-educated population* is found in a region with a low *gross domestic product* per capita. There is a direct link between the variables analyzed. To determine the intensity of the link between the *share* of the *population with higher education* and the *GDP* per inhabitant, we applied the Pearson correlation coefficient, and the results can be seen in Table 12.13.

Following the application of the Pearson correlation coefficient, a statistically significant value of 0.808 was obtained. The coefficient shows us that there is a direct and very strong correlation between *gross domestic product* per capita and *the share of the population with higher education*.

The graphic representation of *gross domestic product* per inhabitant and the *share of the population with a low level of education* by development regions in the period 2000–2013 is shown in the graph in Fig. 12.22.

The representation in the same axis system of the pairs of numbers corresponding to the *share of the population with a low level of education* and the *gross domestic product per inhabitant* in the eight development regions of the country highlights the gaps between the Bucharest-Ilfov region and the other development regions of the country. We can see that in the Bucharest-Ilfov region, the lowest weights held by the population with a *low level of education* correlate with the highest values of *gross domestic product* per capita. Among the variables analyzed at the level of the eight development regions, for the period 2000–2013, there is an indirect link.

Given the elimination of the values corresponding to the Bucharest-Ilfov region, which have extremely high values compared to the other development regions of the country, the correlation of the pairs of values corresponding to the two variables represented in Fig. 12.23 *is observed*.

We find that the highest *weights* held by the *population with a low level of training* are associated with a *lower gross domestic product* per capita, while in regions where the *population with a low level of training holds a lower share*, there is a higher *gross domestic product* per capita.

The intensity of the link between the *share* of the *population with a low level* of education and the *gross domestic product per inhabitant* was studied using the Pearson correlation coefficient. Following the application of the Pearson correlation coefficient, a negative value of 0.769, statistically significant, was obtained according to Table 12.14. The coefficient shows

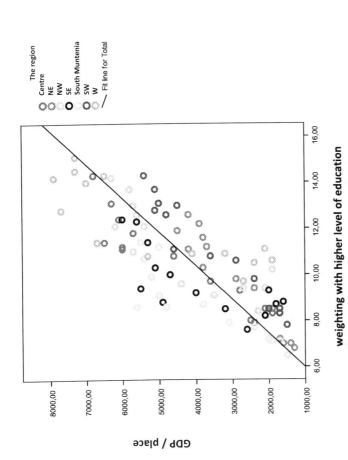

Fig. 12.21 Graphic representation of GDP/place and population weighting with higher level of education, by development regions, without Bucharest-Ilfov region, in the period 2000–2013. Source: author's contribution based on analysis in the SPSS programme, v.22

Table 12.13   The relationship between the GDP per capita and the weighted average of the higher-educated population

		GDP/ place	Share of the population with higher education
GDP/place	Pearson correlation	1	0.808**
	Sig. (2-tailed)		0.000
	N	98	98
Share of the population with higher education	Pearson correlation	0.808**	1
	Sig. (2-tailed)	0.000	
	N	98	98

**Correlation is significant at the 0.01 level (2-tailed).
Source: author's contribution based on analysis in SPSS programme, v.22

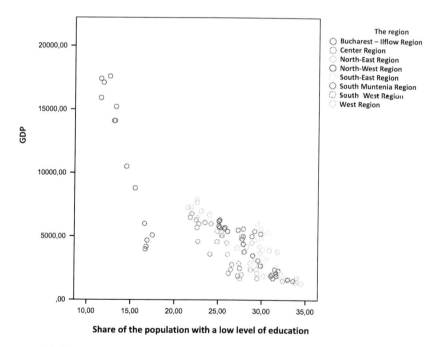

Share of the population with a low level of education

Fig. 12.22   Graphic representation of the share of the population with a low level of education and of GDP/place by development regions in the period 2000–2013. Source: author's contribution based on analysis in the SPSS programme, v. 22

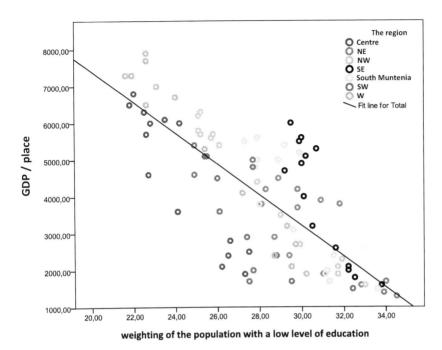

Fig. 12.23 Graphic representation of the weighting of the population with a low level of education and GDP/place by development regions, without the Bucharest-Ilfov region, in the period 2000–2013. Source: author's contribution based on analysis in the SPSS programme, v. 22

that there is a negative, very strong correlation between *gross domestic product* per capita and the *share of the population with a low level of education*. We can say that as there is a higher level of economic development, the *share of the population with a lower level of education* decreases. In regions with a high *share of the population with a low level of education*, *gross domestic product* per capita is low.

294   D.-M. NEAMȚU

Table 12.14 Correlation between GDP/place and the weighting of the population with a low level of education

		GDP/place	Share of the population with lower education
GDP/place	Pearson correlation	1	-0.769**
	Sig. (2-tailed)		0.000
	N	98	98
Share of the population with lower education	Pearson correlation	-0.769**	1
	Sig. (2-tailed)	0.000	
	N	98	98

**Correlation is significant at the 0.01 level (2-tailed)
Source: author's contribution based on analysis in SPSS programme, v.22

Given that we consider that the *variable gross domestic product per inhabitant* depends on the *share of the population with a higher level of education* and the *share of the population with a low level of education*, we apply a model of *multiple linear regression*[2] in the form:

$$Y = a + b_1^* x_1 + b_2^* x_2 \qquad (12.1)$$

The coefficients of the *multiple linear regression* model have been determined using the SPSS program and are centralized in Table 12.15.

Based on the determination of coefficients, the *multiple linear regression* model can be written as follows:

---

[2] For the correct, representative choice of the multiple linear regression model in our analysis, we considered the following hypotheses that allowed the use of this model: visual analysis of the organization and shape of the point cloud obtained in Figure 12.21 and Figure 12.23, which gave us indications of the appreciation of a linear trend and a direct link between the variables used; the estimated standard error (estimate residue inspection) revealed that the regression right achieves the minimum value of the error squares. This hypothesis decides the normality of distribution and diagnosis of outliers, the method of the smallest squares which involved checking all individual errors, and the coefficient of determination shall have a high value close to 1. This result suggests our confidence that the estimated equation of the regression model provides a good approximation of the scatter chart points and the Anova test that statistically confirms the significance of the correlation ratio.

Table 12.15 Coefficients of the linear regression model

Model	Unstandardized coefficients		Standardized coefficients	T	Sig.
	B	Std. error	Beta		
1 (Constant)	5382,265	1708,459		3150	0,002
Share of the population with higher education	445,202	64,095	0,529	6946	0,000
Share of low-education population	-213,658	41,472	-0,392	-5152	0,000

[a]Dependent variable: GDP

Source: author's contribution based on analysis in the SPSS program. v.22:

Table 12.16 Summary model

Model	R	R square	Adjusted R square	Std. error of the estimate
1	0,854[a]	0,729	0,723	945,49,329

[a]Predictors: (Constant) share of population with low education, share of population with higher education

Source: author's contribution based on analysis in SPSS programme, v.22

$$GDP / place = 5382,265 + 0,529 * Pond_{PSS} - 0,392 * Pond_{pes} \quad (12.2)$$

The Pearson correlation ratio for the *multiple linear regression* model is 0.854. The coefficient of determination is 0.729, and the adjusted coefficient is 0.723 (Table 12.16).

The regression model used explains in a proportion of 72.9% the variation of the variable *gross domestic product per inhabitant* according to the variation of variables the *share of the population with a low level of education* and the *share of the population with a higher level of education* (Table 12.17).

The Pearson correlation ratio is statistically significant, with F test values of 127,523, Sig. value less than 0.01.

Table 12.17 ANOVA[b]

Model		Sum of squares	df	Mean square	F	Sig.
1	Regression	228,001,072,039	2	114,000,536,020	127,523	,000[a]
	Residual	84,925,968,777	95	893,957,566		
	Total	312,927,040,816	97			

a. Predictors: (Constant) share of population with low education, share of population with higher education

b. Dependent variable: GDP

Source: author's contribution based on analysis in SPSS programme, v.22

REFERENCES

Rey, S. J., & Janikas, M. V. (2005). Regional Convergence, Inequality and Space. *Journal of Economic Geography, 5*, 155–176.

Treiman, D. J., & Yip, K. B. (1989). Educational and Occupational Attainment in 21 Countries. In M. L. Kohn (Ed.), *Cross-National Research in Sociology* (pp. 373–394). Sage Publications.

PART IV

Detached From Contemporary Reality

Empirical Research on the Gap between Level of Education and Employability Based on Work Satisfaction

Our research has as its starting point the principle of triangulation (triangulation strategy) in the context of a dynamic and complex reality in the sociohuman field, which requires the corroboration of several theoretical and methodological perspectives and the study of several data sources, with the aim of obtaining a more complete and valid image of the reality proposed for analysis. In this context, two complementary studies were carried out, one qualitative and one quantitative, each with objectives derived from the purpose of the research.

The first research program is a quantitative analysis based on a statistical survey that provided a detailed perspective on the perception of graduates of higher education and those who decided to continue their studies through another form of training at the Ştefan cel Mare University in Suceava—regarding the interconnection between the level of education, the degree of employability, and professional and personal development in the context of the satisfaction with the work performed. The planned research method for empirical data collection used self-administration and an online questionnaire as a research tool. The functioning of this relationship constitutes an explanatory argument that is significant for any of the societies of the present world because it involves a complex of established relationships between the structural elements of these nations.

The second study was a qualitative one, pursuing the same objectives, and as a working methodology used, it included semi-structured

D.-M. Neamţu, *Education and Economic Development*,
https://doi.org/10.1007/978-3-031-20382-4_13

interviews. This was achieved through two parallel studies and aimed at detecting the views of employers in the reference fields, as well as human resources recruiters on how higher education graduates meet their expectations in terms of university training, in the idea of comparing them, to build an overview of how the link between higher education and the labor market is achieved. As a method of qualitative research for both categories of stakeholders, the semi-structured, deep, unrehearsed, intensive, and personal interview was chosen as the method with the greatest potential for data extraction.

Methodological triangulation involves the use of several data collection techniques (interviews, document analysis) to obtain various forms of expression and discourse, thus excluding the deviations and shortcomings inherent in each of them.

A historical debate continues as a dispute between qualitative and quantitative researchers, each adhering to his/her own paradigms, stating that the two cannot be mixed (Howe, 1988). According to the researchers (Onwuegbuzie and Johnson, 2004), these two paradigms of research have given rise to two research cultures: on the one hand, they support superiority, "deep and rich observational data," and on the other hand, they support the virtues of "concrete and generalizable data."

In this context, Alpert (2010) argues that the method of the mixed approach was considered to be the most appropriate methodology, thus allowing researchers to use a diversified area in the use of tools and observation points, developing new points of view and foundation scans of qualitative research interpretation, which make possible a multidimensional investigation. Thus, the mixed approach method was the most appropriate methodology for this study, which aimed to analyze a robust corpus of data. Through the method of triangulating data obtained with the help of research tools, we have contributed to supporting the conclusions and the evolution of the generalization trend. The mixed methods used include qualitative research, quantitative research, and case studies of international and national projects carried out up to the time of the research.

DEFINING THE DECISION-MAKING ISSUE

The inconsistencies between the needs of employing companies and the workforce prepared by higher education institutions are increasingly highlighted in numerous studies and statistical data, becoming a topic of general interest. The relationship between the labor market and the national education system is decisive for any of the societies of the present world, as it involves a complex of established relationships between the structural elements of those societies. Much of the attention given to the development of higher education in recent years focuses on the issue of the employability of graduates in the labor market.

The relationship between graduates of higher education and the labor market is presented in a holistic framework that integrates different problems concerning job-specific requirements, the segmentation of the labor market or determinants of the career of graduates in general, and the function of educational systems that provide the necessary skills for the labor market.

Professional skills are a key factor in determining to what extent a graduate has or does not have employment potential. They are, according to Bradley and Nguyen (2004), a condition for completing the academic curriculum vitae and are essential for the selection process for employment. Authors such as Garcia-Araciland and Van der Velden (2008) and Rychen and Salganik (2003) have concluded that these key skills can be achieved through experience, training, or more informal means. Many studies point out that some generic social skills, such as communication skills, *leadership*, customer orientation, understanding, and emotional intelligence, are directly related to success in the labor market (Kiong-Hock 1986).

There is a whole branch of literature that focuses on identifying the most important skills for increasing the absorption capacity of graduates of higher education in the labor market. Cotton (2001) shows that employers need generic skills, such as teamwork, communication skills, or problem-solving skills, in combination with specific skills acquired through experience or formal education.

Two important analyses, the CHEERS (uni-kassel.de) project (Careers after Higher Education: a European research study, 1998) and the REFLEX project (Research into Employment and Professional Flexibility: New requirements for higher education in Europe, 2004) and its extension HEGESCO (Higher Education as a Generator of Strategic Competences, 2009) (Hegesco, 2009), both funded by the European Commission, aimed to study the conditions of employment of graduates, the links between universities and the labor market, and the role that skills play in this relationship (Schomburg, 2007). Their results confirm that labor markets have unified criteria well ahead of education systems (reflexproject.co.uk).

A growing number of papers are addressing these issues, but there is no agreement on the best combination of skills to strengthen success in the labor market (Ashton and Green 1996; Barth al. 2007; Biesma et al. 2007). One of the possible reasons which underlies the lack of consensus is the difficulty of measuring the competences and the variety of approaches available to do so, which generates divergent results (Ashton and Green 1996; Biesma et al. 2007).

Another study, DEHEMS, aimed to analyze the empirical links between schooling history and entering the labor market or initial career models. Understanding the professional success of graduates by higher education managers is important in curriculum training to make them fit for the current challenges and facilitate the transition of graduates to the labor market. The DEHEMS project aims to identify the activities of higher education institutions aimed at strengthening the employability of graduates (Melink & Pavlin, 2009).

The transition of higher education graduates from education to the labor market is characterized by several processes. One of the most attractive is the transfer of knowledge, as a result of the information process inclined toward the adaptation of these skills for certain work situations. In this way, the early career of higher education graduates is often accompanied by the so-called matching problem, which relates to the compatibility between the individual, education, and professional destination.

This relationship can be defined horizontally in the wrong way if a person works in a position that suits him or her in terms of level but does not suit him or her in terms of the educational field. Vertical, inappropriate refers to the situation where a person works in a function that suits him in terms of the field but does not suit him in terms of educational level. Inherently, the matching issue concerns several theoretical concerns, such as labor market segmentation, mobility, professionalization, and professionalism or seniority.

Verhaest and Van der Velden, in *Cross-country differences in graduate overeducation and its persistence*, provide a highly relevant overview of the interconnection between graduates and employers. Underuse of qualification not only has negative economic consequences but also has a negative impact on people's mental abilities. Thus, it is stressed that in addition to the characteristics of the job offer (age, education, work experience, gender, job search intensity), in determining the position on the labor market, an important role in this equation is also the demand for labor (specific sector of activity, fields, specifics of the company).

In the specialized literature, there are various studies that analyze the effectiveness of educational systems, focusing in particular on the results of the professional path of graduates on the labor market. The main motivation for linking schooling plans with the needs of the labor market lies in economic and social development as a source of improving the standard of living throughout society.

The French Ministry of Higher Education and Research conducts an annual study on the employment rates of undergraduate graduates. There are six indicators: employment rate, type of employment according to the national framework or intermediate professions, stable employment rate, full-time employment rate, average annual net salary of full-time employees, and estimated annual gross salary on the basis of the median salary. The results are presented each year by the Ministry and are taken into account in the elaboration of national strategies and public policies in the field of professional orientation.

The International Center for Higher Education Research (INCHER), at the University of Kassel, has been carrying out some of its reference activities since 2007 and the Cooperation Project for the Study of Graduates (KOAB). The methodology used in this study is based on the questionnaire, which was first administered 18 months after graduation and then 54 months after graduation. This method has the advantage of analyzing the professional situation of graduates at two different times, leading to a longitudinal investigation.

The European Association of Universities (EUA) has carried out the Trackit study, which is a meta-analysis of the methods used by universities or ministries to track the professional trajectory of university graduates in EU Member States. Among the most important conclusions of this study are the following:

- In most of the states analyzed, the main resource used is administrative information, which is useful in tracking the educational path of students, and in the case of graduates, the survey is usually used due to the absence of an administrative system for recording data on graduates.
- Some states use a centralized approach to track students' career paths using administrative data at their disposal.

- Additionally, student career tracking is supplemented by the use of qualitative and quantitative research aimed at revealing students' perceptions.
- Some countries use cooperative approaches, in which individual universities are included in a process coordinated at the national level by an organization.
- Certain universities choose to carry out complementary research activities compared to those of administrative career tracking of graduates and use focus groups or interviews to capture a qualitative facet.

The findings of the Trackit study show that the results of these studies are used to improve curricula, particularly in terms of their content. The conclusions also include the fact that only in a few cases are these results taken into account at the national level for the development of public policies or strategies, leading to the facilitation of the transition from education to career and being more used internally at the university level.

At the Romania level, several studies have been carried out. University Graduates and Labor Market (APM) study, co-financed by the POSDRU 2007–2013 program by the European Union and implemented by the Executive Union for the Financing of Higher Education, Development and Innovation Research, in partnership with the International Center for Higher Education Research (INCHER), followed the detailed analysis of the academic and professional trajectories of the period immediately following the completion of a university education course in Romania. Among the conclusions obtained, we believe that the following are worth remembering:

- The job search process begins after graduating for the majority of graduates.
- A large proportion of subjects who have studied in private education have been working since the beginning of their studies, and they retain this job during the years of study but also after completion.
- Among the factors that increase success in the labor market are graduation from a public educational institution and the occupation of a place funded by the state, as well as educational history.
- Gender is another indicator that influences the chances in the labor market, regardless of the time of career; male subjects have greater access to adequate employment.

The study Active adaptation of university education to the requirements of the labor market, carried out between December 2008 and November 2009, the beneficiary of which was the Romanian Agency for Quality Assurance in Higher Education, aimed to establish the degree of correlation of university offerings and learning outcomes with employment requirements according to employers' representatives. The majority of graduates surveyed stated that during their studies they obtained all the necessary skills and competencies in the workplace; the percentages ranged from 52% for the law field, to 55% for communication sciences, to 63% for mechanical engineering, to 61% for IT. The results of the study show that, for the most part, the graduates of the undergraduate studies of the four fields concerned positively assessed the quality of the studies followed. Another important aspect is that 46% of respondents reported that no practical problems were addressed during the years of study, which graduates subsequently faced in the workplace.

The Romanian Quality Barometer of Higher Education Quality (2010–2011) tracked the state of quality in the Romanian higher education system in the European context. Although the study does not confer representativeness and cannot be generalized, studies carried out by Romanian Agency for Quality Assurance in Higher Education (ARACIS) in 2010 and 2011 may be classified among the *tracer studies or graduate studies*. It can also be stated that one of the differences from other such studies concerned the quality of higher education in the perception of students, teachers, and employers, so that a single questionnaire was distributed to all subjects in the sample. The results of the research revealed an optimistic trend, as almost two-thirds of the graduate respondents in the 2009 class already had a job in 2010: half had a *full-time job*; half had a *part-time job*; one-third said they work in the field of studies; 20% claimed to work in related fields; and a third claimed that they work in different fields. The same outlook was maintained in 2010, when 48% responded that they were working full-time, 13% part-time, and 7% were employed in part-time projects, and 31% replied that they did not work.

The sociology on the labor market study – 2011 followed the trajectory of University of Bucharest sociology graduates after 1990. This study provided data on the profession of sociologists, and the necessary professional and cross-cutting skills, possibilities, and methods of professional insertion, which can be used for more complex scientific studies that can be used both scientifically and with practical purposes for the development of public policies. It was also intended to obtain objective data on the professional trajectory of graduates: the number of jobs, the period of time until the first employment, the methods by which the employment was carried out, the field in which the graduate was employed, the type of company in which the employment was carried out, the size of the company, the level of income, and another aspect, such as geographical mobility.

Research on recent graduates of higher education and their integration into the labor market DOCIS-ACPART 2010 was carried out by the National Agency for Qualifications in Higher Education and Partnership with the Economic and Social Environment (ACPART) between November 2008 and October 2011 and aimed at "modernising the qualification system in the higher education system, compatible with the European space and correlation with the requirements of the labor market." The main objective was to follow the graduates' trajectory on the labor market, the type of work performed, and the link between the completed field and that of professional activity.

The Project Observatory for the Employment of Graduates of University Studies of the National School of Political and Administrative Studies, carried out in 2008–2009, aimed to identify the professional trajectory and employment integration of graduates of higher education within The National University of Political Studies and Public Administration (SNSPA).

The Career Counseling and Guidance Center of the Ștefan cel Mare University of Suceava began, as early as 2006, a study starting from the question *What happens to the graduates of Ștefan cel Mare University of Suceava?* The purpose of this study was to track and capture the professional trajectory of university graduates. The results showed that among the reasons that graduates do not yet have a job are the following: the lack of correlation of the available job with the training obtained, the actual lack of jobs, the intention to start a business, passivity toward finding a job, or intention to emigrate (Annex 20).

The research presented above confirms that the problem of employability is a current problem that concerns an increasing number of institutional actors in the field of higher education in Europe due to the high rates of youth unemployment in most European countries.

Our research aims to provide information to help underpin the choice of an action variant, according to certain decision-making criteria in the field of education. It is important that education decision-makers identify situations that can constitute real problems but also favorable opportunities that should be exploited.

The underlying causes of decision-making problems in the field of Romanian education are as follows:

- *The changes in the microenvironment and external macroenvironment of Romanian universities.* The accessibility of the educational offerings of internationally renowned foreign universities represents strong competition for Romanian universities.
- *Clear ignorance of the external environment.* Lack of information on dimensions, structure and trends of supply and demand, amount of taxes, changes in the lifestyle of the population, in the purchasing behavior of educational services, medium- and long-term trends in demographic, economic, political, social, cultural, technological environment.
- *Dysfunctions in the work of universities.* The downward evolution of the number of students, graduates with a bachelor's degree, master's students, the unfavorable image of Romanian education, and the inefficiency of some legislative measures adopted are other causes that can lead to serious decision-making problems.
- *Planned changes in the objectives and policies of Romanian universities.* The orientation toward other educational markets and better correlation between the components of educational policies (services, taxes, distribution and promotion of educational offerings) could be solved on the basis of information obtained by carrying out applied research.
- *Launching new service ideas.* The emergence and testing of new concepts of educational services and their distribution and promotion can be solved by the final consumer of educational services.

On the basis of the above, we can define the decision-making issue underlying this research as finding the answer to the question: *How can the provision of educational services be improved to meet the requirements of the labor market?*

QUANTITATIVE RESEARCH ON UNIVERSITY GRADUATES'
OPINIONS IN TERMS OF INTERCONNECTIONS BETWEEN
THE LEVEL OF EDUCATION AND EMPLOYABILITY BASED
ON WORK SATISFACTION

The quantitative study has a varied nature, covering a vast area of university institutions where some of the respondents have completed one of their higher education programs and then are determined to continue their university studies at the Ştefan cel Mare University of Suceava. Among the reasons that led them to go through other forms of higher education were lack of a job corresponding to training, desire for professional and personal development, professional mobility, quality of university training, and desire for change toward full satisfaction.

This analysis is aimed at people who currently (university year 2014–2015) have completed their bachelor's studies and are pursuing master/doctorate/postdoctoral studies at the Ştefan cel Mare University of Suceava.

Ştefan cel Mare University of Suceava, established in 1963, is one of the most dynamic institutions of higher education in Eastern Europe, offering a quality university and post-university education. "Young, but by the good results thus far, prestigious, in the process of affirmation in the gallery of older and newer university centers, gaining and having already, after half a century, the foundations, joints, valences of its own individuality and its present and future peculiarity – the University Ştefan cel Mare represents the salutary and necessary quintessence of these places, loaded with history and glory" (Purici et al. 2013).

Ştefan cel Mare University of Suceava defines itself as a public institution of higher education that aims to develop the educational and continuous training offer of the institution according to the needs and requirements of the local community and the Northeast region, and to correlate these with the directions of development and progress established at the national and international level. To achieve this goal, it has the following aims:

- organization of teaching and appropriation of professional-scientific knowledge, with a view of forming highly trained specialists for education, science, culture, art, social activities, economic, administrative, legal and sports activities;
- continuous training of university graduates through programs of specialization and improvement, conversion and reconversion, organized in the spirit of progress, knowledge and permanent education (USV Strategic Plan 2013–2017.

Through the dynamism and diversity characteristic of this open university for development and cooperation, trying to meet the social demands of the time, it provides its approximately 8500 students with an appropriate curriculum with over 130 programs of studies at bachelor's degree, master's degree, doctoral degree, and postdoctoral level from five direction natural sciences, engineering sciences, human sciences, social sciences, economic science and administrative sciences. This structure determines and encourages inter, trans, and multidisciplinary approaches on the didactic line, but especially on the research line.

An important role in the Suceava University Centre is the evolution and development of the material base through the existence of a university library remarkable in its encyclopedic character, which contributes to the increase in prestige and the degree of preparation of students. 'The geographical advantage enjoyed by the institution of higher education from Suceava, by its location in an area of cultural interference, had to be exploited by offering programmes of study in various fields, leading both to the promotion of the peculiarities of Bukovina, multiculturalism, its plurilingual and interfaiths, as well as to the support of European fundamental principles and the affirmation of Romanian culture and science in the world circuit of values' (USV 2012).

Complexly integrated into the System of European Values, Ştefan cel Mare University promotes numerous research projects and programs through close cooperation at the national and international level, achieving notable results in the fields of research and innovation. The importance that this higher education institution attaches to the development of university offerings in line with the needs of the labor market is apparent from the mission and objectives set out in the 2014 University State Report, which states: 'Defined according to the requirements of the labor market and the evolution of knowledge and centered on the needs of students, which involve obtaining expertise in the fields in which they specialize, the USV pays particular attention to the formation of a culture of learning. It invests students with the power to be responsible, to actively engage in their own training, to evaluate their evolution and to develop their ability to specialize and their desire to progress in knowledge. The specific needs of the students, the level of the education and training, the requirements of the labor market and, by implication, the way in which we award graduation diplomas at the end of our studies are identified on the basis of a continuous dialog with our graduates and their employers, students and their families, with our students and colleagues in the preuniversity environment, to understand their demands and expectations as best as possible' (USV 2014).

Establishing the Target, Objectives, and Assumptions of the Research

Defining the purpose involves indicating the information needed by the decision-makers in the field to choose a particular variant of the action.

The purpose of this research is to determine the opinions of consumers of higher education services on the degree of correlation of the vocational training of university graduates with the requirements of the real economy to employ. The need to carry out this research arose from the identification, at the national level, of important dysfunctions in the mechanisms of correlation of the higher education system with integration into the labor market. The empirical relevance of this research lies in the usefulness of the results obtained for several interested categories and *stakeholders*[1]: students, graduates, management of higher education institutions, and management of employing companies.

Research Objectives

Studying the opinions of consumers of higher education services involves the formulation of the following objectives:

- assessment of the level of competence acquired during higher education
- identification of the period necessary to find a *job* after completing higher education
- highlighting aspects of the labor market status of higher education consumers
- measuring the fulfilment of consumers' expectations of higher education services with regard to the occupied job
- highlighting perceptions of a favorable or unfavorable nature and the intensity of the views of consumers of higher education services on the correspondence between the provision of educational services and labor market requirements

---

[1] The *stakeholder* represents a person, group, or organization with interests and involvement in a particular area or situation. The word brings together people with the same characteristics. Not all *stakeholders* have the same involvement and influence, while not all *stakeholders* are equally influenced by the results of actions in the sector concerned.

- highlighting the differences between the views of higher education consumers, depending on the level of education
- underlining the issues that education consumers take into account when assessing a job

Research Hypotheses

Establishing hypotheses has significant practical value in designing our research. These assumptions will help us clarify expectations regarding the results and establish the information that will be required in the analysis process.

In this respect, the assumptions corresponding to the objectives of the research are as follows:

1. Graduates of higher education believe that the level of skill acquired during their studies is high;
2. The period required to find a job after completing higher education is between three and six months;
3. Most graduates with higher education have the status of employee with an employment contract;
4. The expectations of graduates of higher education regarding job occupation are met to a satisfactory degree;
5. There will be significant differences between the opinions of undergraduate graduates and those with doctoral degrees in terms of the level of competence acquired during their studies;
6. There will be significant differences between the opinions of graduates, depending on the graduate program, in terms of the extent to which the job meets their expectations;
7. There will be significant differences between the opinions of graduates, grouped according to different criteria in terms of the extent to which the job meets their expectations;
8. There will be significant differences between the opinions of graduates, grouped according to different criteria, in terms of the degree of satisfaction with certain aspects related to the job (the activity they perform, the management style, the possibilities of professional development, the level of pay, the requirements of the job).

Presenting the Research Methodology

- *Selecting the data gathering and systematization*

The analysis was based on the completion of selective research among university graduates who continued with another form of higher training at the University Ștefan cel Mare. This study analyzed their perception of the interconnection between the level of education—the level of employability, professional and personal development—and satisfaction with the work performed. The planned research method for empirical data collection used the questionnaire as a research tool, self-administered and online on the www.isondaje.ro platform.

The data collection was carried out in two stages: May–June 2015, the questionnaire being distributed when the students were in the exam session, as well as through the faculty secretariats; and the second phase of July–August, during the student holidays, by e-mail, by accessing the easy-to-use http://www.isondaje.ro/sondaj/390553391/ link, through which all the information was collected in a personal database at the same time. In total, 400 questionnaires were distributed and collected, of which only 258 were kept following verification of the accuracy of the data.

The research was complemented by two qualitative, parallel studies, by organizing in-depth interviews among employers, directly, personally, and unrehearsed, on the one hand, and the second study among companies specializing in the recruitment of qualified higher labor, at the national level, on the other.

The study aimed to detect the opinions of employers in the reference fields, as well as human resources recruiters, on how university vocational training corresponds favorably to employability, in the idea of comparing them, to build an overview of how the link between higher education and the labor market is achieved.

- *Designing the questionnaire*

The questionnaire[2] used in the research contained 20 questions, mostly closed questions and open questions referring to issues that can be coded without further difficulty. Following the logic of the graduate's career path, to collect empirical data, the questionnaire was used, the questions

---

[2] An adaptation after the questionnaire conducted by Babeș-Bolyai University of Cluj and the Department of the Center for Counseling and Career Guidance, within Ștefan cel Mare University of Suceava.

of which were structured on four themes: the completed curriculum; first job; status on the labor market; and sociodemographic data. To this end, we ensured a good validity of construction in drawing up the questionnaire. Thus, for the operationalization of the main themes measured by the questionnaire, a wide variety of dimensions that can be included within them were covered.

The first category comprises five questions concerning the completed program, other programs of study followed, and the level of competence acquired following the completion of university studies.

The second category comprises a set of three questions aimed at getting the first job after completing studies, the necessary period, and the type of *job*.

The third category of questions concerns the current status of the labor market, the degree of satisfaction, the type of organization, the title of the *job*, and the level of pay.

The last category of questions relates to the sociodemographic information of the respondents.

Testing the Questionnaire

The testing of the questionnaire aimed to verify the understanding, interpretation, and acceptability of the questions.

The questionnaire was tested on a small number of people belonging to the population studied, that is, 20 people. The sample consisted of as many different people as possible from the perspective of the completed studies.

During this stage, the following aspects were verified:

- if the terms used were easy to understand and do not lead to confusion
- if the order of questions did not lead to negative reactions
- if the form of the questions allowed the necessary information to be collected
- if the questions were not too long and did not cause disinterest or irritation for those under investigation
- if certain questions were not useful
- if the introduction and linking texts were sufficient and effective
- if the answers to the closed questions were sufficient
- if the number of open questions was not too high to tire the person under investigation

Following the analysis carried out, a number of changes were made, and the final form of the questionnaire is given in Annex 19.

Establishing the Size of the Sample

The sample size shall be determined on the basis of the statistical formula as follows:

$$n = t^{2*}p^* (1-p)/e^2 \qquad (13.1)$$

where:

n = the size of the sample

t = the theoretical value of accepted probability (we used a t=1.61 for a 90% confidence level)

p = the percentage in which the population has the sampling feature (usually = 0.50)

e = permissible representativeness limit error (values between 1% and maximum 5% are accepted)

Thus, in the case of this research, for a maximum permissible error of 5% and 95% confidence level, the calculations are as follows:

$$n = \left(1.606^{2*} 0.5^* (1-0.5)\right)/0.05^2 = 258 \qquad (13.2)$$

To determine the opinions of graduates of higher education who continue with another form of training, we investigated the opinions of 258 people.

- *Establishing the sample of university graduates based on the faculty variable*

The total community consists of 1910 master's students, 210 doctoral students, 55 postdoctoral fellows, and a total of 2175 people from Ștefan cel Mare University of Suceava. We have noted that 1910 masters out of a total of 2175 people represent 87.81% master's students; 210 PhD students out of a total of 2175 persons represent 9.65% of PhD students, and 55 postdoctoral fellows out of 2175 represent 2.52% postdoctoral fellows in the total community.

For the determination of the sample, the quota sampling method was used, determining the weight of the subjects according to the faculty variable; thus, Table 13.1 shows the number of respondents and the percentage for each faculty member:

- *The structure of the sample based on level of education*

We calculate the sample structure according to the level of studies: 87.81% × 258 = 227 master's students; 9.65% × 258 = 25 PhD students; 2.52% × 285 = 7 postdoctoral fellows. Based on the determined weights, we determine the structure of the master's sample according to the variable faculty, as follows:

1. Faculty of Economic Sciences and Public Administration – 37.32% × 227 = 85 people
2. Faculty of Food Engineering – 9.26% × 227=21 people
3. Faculty of Electrical Engineering and Computer Science – 11.3% × 227 = 26 people
4. Faculty of Mechanical Engineering, Mechatronics, and Management – 4.8% × 227 = 11 people
5. Faculty of History and Geography – 11.26% × 227 = 26 people
6. Faculty of Forestry – 7.1% × 227 = 16 people
7. Faculty of Education Sciences – 6.8% × 227=15 people

Table 13.1   Studied sample

Nr. crt.	Faculty name	Number of subjects	Percentage
1.	Faculty of Economic Sciences and Public Administration	713	37.32%
2.	Faculty of Physical Education and Sport	60	3.14%
3.	Faculty of Food Engineering	177	9.26%
4.	Faculty of Electrical Engineering and Computer Science	216	11.3%
5.	Faculty of Mechanical Engineering, mechatronics and management	93	4.8%
6.	Faculty of History and Geography	215	11.25%
7.	Faculty of Letters and Communication Sciences	170	8.9%
8.	Faculty of Forestry	136	7.1%
9.	Faculty of Education Sciences	130	6.8%
Total		1910	

Source: author's contribution

8. Faculty of Letters and Communication Sciences – 8.9% × 227 = 20 people
9. Faculty of Physical Education and Sport – 3.14% × 227 = 7 people

The sample consisted of 227 master's students: 85-Faculty of Economic Sciences and Public Administration; 21-Faculty of Food Engineering; 26-Faculty of Electrical Engineering and Computer Science; 11-Faculty of Mechanical Engineering, Mechatronics, and Management; 26-History geography; 16-Silviculture; 15-Sciences of Education; 20-Faculty of Letters and Communication Sciences; 7-Physical Education and Sport. Along with the master's students, 25 doctoral students and seven postdoctoral fellows were interviewed.

Data Processing, Analysis, and Interpretation

The results obtained from the centralization of the questionnaires applied among graduates are presented below on the topics addressed.

Theme a: Program of Completed Studies and the Level of Skill Acquired after the Completion of Higher Education
The centralization of the questionnaires applied allowed the determination of the structure of the sample contained in the analysis. Thus, of the 258 respondents, 87.2% completed a form of training at Ştefan cel Mare University, and the rest at other universities in the country, such as Alexandru Ioan Cuza University of Iasi, the Academy of Economic Studies Bucharest, Gh. Asachi Technical University in Iasi, Vasile Alecsandri University in Bacau, University of Oradea, University of Bucharest, University of Medicine and Pharmacy Iasi, and University of Pitesti or Spiru Haret University (Fig. 13.1). This diversity allowed us to learn the opinions of graduates of higher education from various famous university centers in the country who decided to continue their education through another form of higher training, masters or doctorate, at the University Ştefan cel Mare in Suceava.

A total of 258 respondents took part in the research, of which 76.4% completed bachelor's studies, 20.9% completed master's studies, and only 2.7% completed doctoral studies, as can be seen in Table 13.2.

The distribution of respondents, according to the level of the program they were enrolled in at the time of the research, shows that almost 50% of the 54 respondents who completed a master's degree continued their

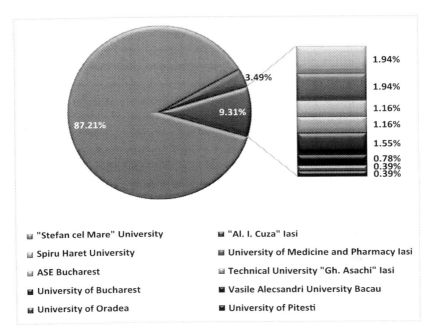

Fig. 13.1 Sample structure by graduate university. (Source: author's contribution)

Table 13.2 The structure of the sample based on the level of the graduated program

Graduated program level	No. of people	Weight	Cumulative weight
License	197	76.4	76.4
Master's	54	20.9	97.3
Doctorate	7	2.7	100.0
Total	258	100.0	

Source: author's contribution

training with their doctoral studies. We can see that 29 of the respondents who already have a master's degree have signed up for another, which will increase their employment opportunities in the labor market.

Thus, the research included 227 master's degree students. A total of 87.8% of the total respondents, 25 PhD students (9.7%), and seven respondents (2.5%) were included in a postdoctoral research program, as can be seen in Table 13.3.

Our research aimed at the achievement by respondents of a self-assessment of the level of competence acquired during the university program already completed at the time of the research. As an output of the results centralization, there was a high and very high degree in terms of self-assessment of the skills level acquired during university studies.

The average[3] of the assessments calculated for the 20 aspects (Fig. 13.2) considered to assess the level of skill acquired during completed university studies is between the *average score*[4] of 3.58 (knowledge of other fields or disciplines) and the average score of 4.23 (team work ability), as can be seen in Table 13.4.

The average score of the competence acquired by the graduates of higher education is 3.98, which is equivalent to a self-assessment of the knowledge acquired by them at a high level. Depending on the average score of the items proposed in the questionnaire, the graduates considered that they have high competence regarding the ability to work in a team, the ability to identify new opportunities, the ability to quickly accumulate new knowledge, the ability to work on a computer, the ability to provide solutions in various situations, the ability to convey clear information, the ability to effectively manage working time, and the ability to work in

Table 13.3 The structure of the sample based on the level of the currently attending program

Level of the program being graduated	No. of people	Weight	Cumulative weight
Master's	227	87.8	87.8
Doctorate	25	9.7	97.5
Postdoctoral	7	2.5	100.0
Total	258	100.0	

Source: author's contribution

[3] The average is an indicator that characterizes a sample from the point of view of a studied feature. The average is calculated simply by adding all the values in a data string, dividing the total by the amount of data.

[4] The average score consists of measuring a statistical characteristic, which shows to what degree it possesses a property that is co-responsible to the studied characteristic by using a scale of measurement that exhibits isomorphic properties with those of the studied characteristic, according to Hapenciuc, C.V. (2016).

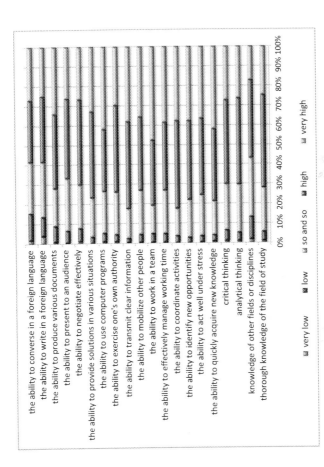

Fig. 13.2 Assessment of competence at the time of graduation from a form of university training. (Source: author's contribution)

Table 13.4 Averages and standard errors

Nr.	Aspects	Average	Standard errors
1	Thorough knowledge of the field of study	3.89	0.869
2	Knowledge of other fields or disciplines	3.58	0.967
3	Analytical thinking	3.90	0.880
4	Critical thinking	3.89	0.909
5	The ability to quickly acquire new knowledge	4.15	0.884
6	The ability to act well under stress	4.08	0.863
7	The ability to identify new opportunities	4.12	0.824
8	The ability to coordinate activities	4.16	0.806
9	The ability to effectively manage working time	4.06	0.909
10	The ability to work in a team	4.23	0.891
11	The ability to mobilize other people	4.04	0.888
12	The ability to transmit clear information	4.17	0.796
13	The ability to exercise one's own authority	3.98	0.861
14	The ability to use computer programs	4.09	0.941
15	The ability to provide solutions in various situations	4.06	0.817
16	The ability to negotiate effectively	3.87	0.921
17	The ability to present to an audience	3.86	0.893
18	The ability to produce various documents	3.96	0.967
19	The ability to write in a foreign language	3.66	1.078
20	The ability to converse in a foreign language	3.68	1.075
	Average level of competence	**3.98**	**0.039**

Source: author's contribution

stressful conditions. At the opposite pole, with lower average scores, they appreciated the ability to know other disciplines or areas of interest other than those studied; the ability to converse/write in a foreign language is a general problem, as well as the ability to present in front of an audience, and the thorough knowledge of the field of study.

Theme B: Obtaining the First Job after Completing Studies, the Necessary Period, and the Type of Job

After completing studies, we noticed that the most appropriate description of the situation in the first six months was the continuation through another form of training, with a percentage of 33.60%; employment in the field of completed studies, 22.92%; or opening one's own business, with a percentage of 6.72%. As shown in Fig. 13.3, 12.65% were employed in another field, while 4.3% of respondents worked as volunteers. Only 4.35%

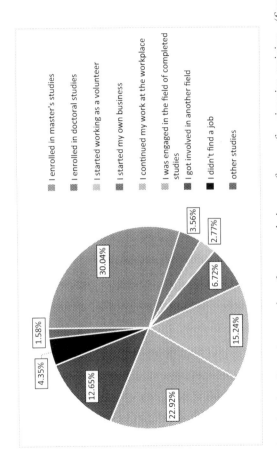

Fig. 13.3 Situation in the first six months after completing a form of university training. (Source: author's contribution)

of respondents said that, even if they had been looking for a job, they had not been able to get one.

In general, we can say that the time required to get the first job after completing studies varies between a period of less than three months and a period of more than 12 months. However, over 75% of the respondents said that they found a *job* in the first six months after completing their university studies. The duration of getting the first job after graduating can be seen in Table 13.5.

Approximately 7% of respondents said they kept their jobs after completing their studies. Participation in a form of university training is sometimes based on the motivation of keeping the job. Over 15% of the respondents replied that the period required to obtain their first *job*, after completing their university studies, was more than six months.

Theme C: Current Status on the Labor Market, Degree of Satisfaction, Type of Organization, Job Title, and Salary Level

At the time of the research, approximately half (49.22%) of the respondents said they had a fixed-term employment contract, while 12.40% had an employment contract for an indefinite period. A fairly large share (14.73%) of respondents said they did not have a job, although they were looking for one. Almost 2% of respondents said they had no intention of getting a job in the next six months (Fig. 13.4).

The assessment of the extent to which the workplace corresponds to vocational training revealed that for 24.81% of respondents, the workplace corresponds to a fairly large extent to their expectations, while 24.03% consider that it fully corresponds to their professional training and expectations. A fairly large number (13.57%) of respondents did not want to make any assessment, as shown in Fig. 13.5.

Table 13.5 The duration of getting the first job after graduating

The duration of getting a job	No respondents	Share	Cumulative share
Have the same job	17	6.6	6.6
Less than 3 months	110	42.6	49.2
Between 3 and 6 months	89	34.5	83.7
Between 6 and 12 months	20	7.8	91.5
Over 12 months	22	8.5	100.0
Total	258	100.0	

Source: author's contribution

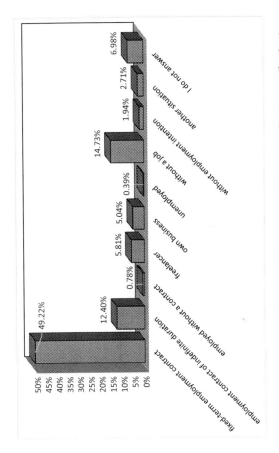

Fig. 13.4 Statute on the labor market at the time of the research. (Source: author's contribution)

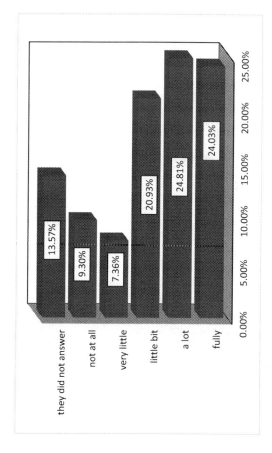

Fig. 13.5 Extent to which the workplace meets expectations. (Source: author's contribution)

Depending on the type of organization in which they work (Table 13.6), our research included a share of 30.2% of respondents who have a job in a public organization, while 31.4% work in a private organization. We note that more than 6% of the respondents have opened their own business, while 26.4% have not declared their membership in a particular type of organization. Of the respondents, 3.1% work in a joint venture and only 2.7% in an NGO.

The analysis of the degree of satisfaction of the respondents regarding the job through the prism of some aspects related to the activity carried out, the management style, the level of salary depending on the level of education, the possibilities of advancement, and the precise requirements of the *job* can be found in Fig. 13.6.

There is a certain degree of dissatisfaction concerning the salary level, and the average score of the responses is 2.95. The other aspects considered have average scores above 13.6, which reflects a state of satisfaction with the work performed, the management style within the company, the existence of professional development possibilities, and the requirements of the *job* corresponding to the level of education.

Grouping of respondents by profession (Table 13.7) shows that most of them are economists (44.6%), followed by engineers (35.3%), philologists (5.8%), and athletes (5.4%). Educators (3.5%), lawyers (1.2%), physiotherapists (1.9%), bachelors in Administrative sciences (1.2%), political scientists, psychologists, and sociologists also took part in the research.

Regarding declared occupation, we note the following, shown in Table 13.8.

Table 13.6 Type of organization the respondents are part of

Type of organization	No. of respondents	Share	Cumulative shares
Public organization	78	30.2	30.2
Private organization	81	31.4	61.6
Joint venture organization	8	3.1	64.7
NGO	7	2.7	67.4
Own company	16	6.2	73.6
Other situation	68	26.4	100.0
Total	258	100.0	

Source: personal contribution

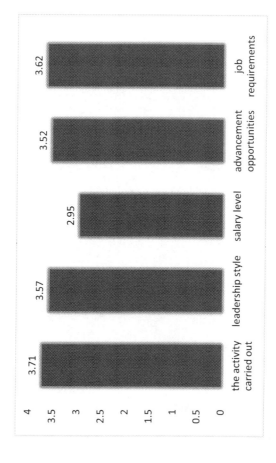

Fig. 13.6 Average degree of satisfaction with aspects related to the workplace. (Source: author's contribution)

Table 13.7 Respondents' occupations

Profession	No. of respondents	Share	Cumulative shares
Economist	115	44.6	44.6
Educator	9	3.5	48.1
Philologist	15	5.8	53.9
Engineer	91	35.3	89.1
Jurist	3	1.2	90.3
Physical therapist	5	1.9	92.2
Bachelor in Administrative Sciences	3	1.2	93.4
Political scientist	1	0.4	93.8
Psychologist	1	0.4	94.2
Sociologist	1	0.4	94.6
Sportsman	14	5.4	100.0
Total	258	100.0	

Source: author's contribution

Table 13.8 Respondents' jobs

Occupation	No. of respondents	Shares	Cumulative shares
Public officials	39	15.2	15.2
Accountants and experts	9	3.6	18.8
Experts in IT	21	8.3	27.1
Economists	50	20.0	47.1
Hotel and restaurant service	5	2.0	49.1
Teachers	43	16.7	65.8
Medical staff	1	0.4	66.2
Sellers/traders	11	4.2	70.4
Volunteers	2	0.8	71.2
Unemployed	2	0.8	72.0
Translators	2	0.8	72.8
They did not specify	73	27.2	100.0
Total	258	100.0	

Source: author's contribution

The occupations of the respondents who participated in the research were diverse. Out of the 258 respondents, 73 subjects did not want to specify their occupation, the main reason being the lack of an occupation. We note that there are also respondents whose jobs do not correspond to superior training, namely, sellers/traders, in a fairly small number of 11 people, with a share of 4.2%. The distribution of respondents by the level of salary for the activity carried out is shown in Fig. 13.7.

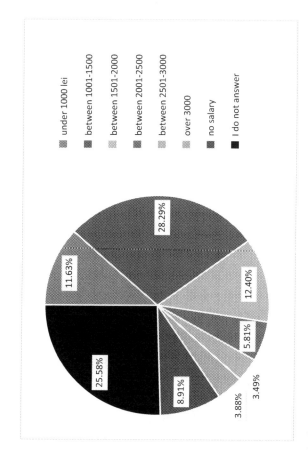

Fig. 13.7 Level of gross salary of respondents. (Source: author's contribution)

The degree of dissatisfaction of respondents with the salary level, which does not reflect the level of training, is justified by the fact that over 40% of the respondents said they have a salary below 1500 RON, 12.40% have a salary between 1501 and 2000 RON, 5.81% have a salary between 2001 and 2500 RON, and 3.49% between 2501 and 3000 RON. A quarter of the respondents did not want to specify their gross salary, while 8.9% said they did not had a salary/income. Only 3.88% of respondents have an income of over 3000 RON.

Theme D: Sociodemographic Information of Respondents
The research evaluated the opinions of respondents aged between 22 and 50 years. Of the 258 respondents, approximately half (49.2%) were under 25 years old, 22.9% were between 25 and 30 years old, 11.2% were between 30 and 35 years old, and 16.7% were over 35 years old, as can be seen in Table 13.9.

The research involved 142 women, who represent 55% of the total, and 116 men (45%), as can be seen in Table 13.10.

Most of those who participated in the research have their permanent residence in Suceava County. From Botoşani County, 6.6% of the

Table 13.9 Respondents' classification based on age

Age	No. of respondents	Percentage	Cumulative percentages
Under 25 years old	127	49.2	49.2
Between 25 and 30 years old	59	22.9	72.1
Between 30 and 35 years old	29	11.2	83.3
Over 35 years old	43	16.7	100.0
Total	258	100.0	

Source: author's contribution

Table 13.10 Respondents' classification based on gender

Gender	No. of respondents	Percentage	Cumulative percentages
Female	142	55.0	55.0
Male	116	45.0	100.0
Total	258	100.0	

Source: author's contribution

Table 13.11   Respondents' classification based on residence

No.	County	No. of respondents	Percentage	Cumulative percentages
1	Bacău	2	0.8	0.8
2	Botoşani	17	6.6	7.4
3	Bucharest	4	1.6	8.9
4	Harghita	1	0.4	9.3
5	Iaşi	2	0.8	10.1
6	Maramureş	1	0.4	10.5
7	Neamţ	10	3.9	14.3
8	Roman	3	1.2	15.5
9	Suceava	218	84.5	100.0
	Total	258	100.0	

Source: author's contribution

respondents were from Neamţ County. The rest of the respondents were from Bucharest, Harghita, Iaşi, Bacău, Roman, and Maramureş, as can be seen in Table 13.11.

Analysis of Differences of Opinion between Respondents, Grouped According to Different Criteria

There are significant differences between the opinions of bachelor's degree graduates and those with doctoral degrees regarding the level of competence acquired during their studies.

Using the *semantic differential*,[5] all respondents had to give each item a grade from 1 to 5, corresponding to the rating that, in his/her opinion, is the most representative of the statement in question.

The comparison made based on the average score of competences by groups of respondents, according to the level of the completed university study program, reveals the existence of a significant difference between the level of competence acquired during the studies by those who have completed bachelor's degree studies and those who have completed doctoral studies (Fig. 13.8).

The differences between the average score of the competences acquired after completing a bachelor's degree (3.96) and master's studies (3.98) are

[5] The semantic differential is the type of scale used in a survey, in which the question formulated is included in the range of a pair of bipolar attributes. Between them, a numerical scale with three, five, or seven levels shall be inserted, the respondent having to express his/her opinion by marking the position corresponding to his/her choice.

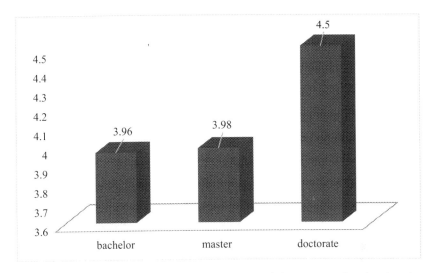

Fig. 13.8 Average level of competence acquired during completed university studies. (Source: author's contribution)

not significant; mainly, there is a balance between the general competences acquired during the studies.

There are significant differences between the opinions of graduates according to the completed higher education program regarding the extent to which the workplace meets expectations

The comparison of the extent to which the workplace meets the respondents' expectations due to the level of their last completed study program is shown in Table 13.12.

Graduates of undergraduate studies considered that the extent to which the job meets expectations has an average score of 2.85, with the lowest of the average scores recorded by the three groups of graduates. The respondents with doctoral studies appreciated that the workplace corresponds to a very large extent with their expectations, with an average score of 4.14, and there was also the lowest standard deviation within this group. Depending on the level of the completed study program, there are important differences between the expectations of the groups of respondents.

The research examined whether the differences were significant between the opinions of respondents grouped by the level of the completed study program. To observe where exactly these differences are and if they are

Table 13.12   The extent to which the job meets the expectations based on the level of education of the last graduated program

Graduated program level	No. of respondents	Average	Standard deviation	Standard mean error
Bachelor's	197	2.85	1.780	0.127
Master's	54	3.69	1.226	0.167
Doctorate	7	4.14	0.690	0.261
Total	258	3.06	0.106	1.698

Source: author's contribution

statistically significant, it was necessary to make comparisons using the independent samples t-test for independent samples in SPSS, with the option of Levene's test[6] (Table 13.13) between the series of respondents, taken two by two. In conclusion, we analyzed a number of combinations of three series taken by two and three comparisons.

To avoid our results being false positives, we were more severe about the Sig. value using the Bonferroni correction that set the materiality threshold to Sig.=0.05/no. of comparisons ≈ 0.01.

The differences of opinion, from the perspective of the *expectations of bachelor's and master's degree graduates* regarding the workplace, differ significantly from a statistical point of view. The Sig. value corresponding to the *t-test* is less than 0.01, which means that the expectations of the graduates regarding the job differ depending on the level of education completed. In this context, we could say that the workplace for those who have graduated from master's studies corresponds to a much greater extent to the expectations of graduates with bachelor's degrees. In other words, the level of completed education significantly influences the expectations of respondents in the context of the satisfaction with the work performed.

The differences are also obvious when we analyze the responses of respondents who have only graduated with a *bachelor's degree* compared to those who have obtained a *PhD* degree on the extent to which the *job* meets the expectations of respondents. To check if there are differences of

---

[6] Levene's test is an inferential statistic used to assess the equality of variances for a variable calculated for two or more groups of variables. It can be used as a main test to answer a stand-alone question, given that two subsamples from a given population have equal or different variations.

Table 13.13 Independent samples t-test

	Levene's test for equality of variances		t-test for equality of means					95% confidence interval of the difference	
	F	Sig.	T	Df	Sig. (2-tailed)	Mean difference	Std. error difference	Lower	Upper
Equal variances assumed	18.600	0.000	-3.231	249	0.001	-0.832	0.258	-1.340	-0.325
Equal variances not assumed			-3.973	121.000	0.000	-0.832	0.210	-1.247	-0.418

Source: author's contribution based on the analysis in SPSS 22

opinion between respondents who have only the level of *bachelor's degree* and those who have obtained a *PhD* title, we applied an *independent samples t-test* in SPSS (Table 13.14).

The workplace is considered almost entirely in accordance with the expectations of those who already have the title of *Doctor.* The Sig. value corresponding to the *t-test* being very close to 0.01 confirms that the differences are statistically significant between the two groups of respondents. This indicates that university tuition can be a determining factor in job satisfaction in the field of completed studies.

There are significant differences between the opinions of graduates, depending on the type of organization in which they work, regarding the extent to which the workplace meets expectations.

If we analyze the extent to which the *workplace* meets the expectations of the respondents, grouped by the *type of organization* in which they work, as shown in Table 13.15, we find that the differences are quite large between the groups. Thus, the workplace, with an average score of 4.75, almost entirely meets the expectations of those working in a *joint venture organization.*

Employees working in a public organization said that the workplace almost fully meets expectations, with an average score of 4.09, as shown in Fig. 13.9. Next are the employees who work in a private organization, with an average score of 3.40, those who opened their own company, with an average score of 3.31, and those who work in an NGO, with an average score of 2.86. The average score calculated for the 68 people who have not declared their membership in a particular organization is justified by the fact that most of them have not actually found a job as of the time of this research, some of them carrying out various and temporary activities, in fact waiting for the desired *job.*

There are significant differences between the opinions of the graduates, depending on the type of organization in which they work, regarding the degree of satisfaction with certain aspects related to the job (the activity they perform, the management style, the possibilities of professional development, the level of salary, the requirements of the job in the field of completed studies), as shown in Fig. 13.9.

The analysis of the degree of satisfaction regarding certain aspects related to the workplace highlighted the existence of differences of opinion between the respondents, grouped according to the *type of organization* they belong to, as shown in Fig. 13.10. Thus, we can see that respondents who work in a public organization tend to be more satisfied

Table 13.14 Independent samples t-test

	Levene's test for equality of variances		t-test for equality of means					95% confidence interval of the difference	
	F	Sig.	T	Df	Sig. (2-tailed)	Mean difference	Std. error difference	Lower	Upper
Equal variances assumed	8.957	0.003	-1.909	202	0.058	-1.290	0.676	-2.623	0.042
Equal variances not assumed			-4.448	9.15	0.002	-1.290	0.290	-1.944	-0.636

Source: author's contribution based on the analysis in SPSS 22

Table 13.15 The extent to which the job meets the respondents' expectations based on the type of organization they work for

Type of organization	No. of respondents	Average	Standard deviation	Standard mean error
Public organization	78	4.09	1.034	0.117
Private organization	81	3.40	1.092	0.121
NGO	7	2.86	1.574	0.595
Own company	16	3.31	1.302	0.326
Joint venture organization	8	4.75	0.463	0.164
Other situation	68	1.25	1.652	0.200

Source: author's contribution

than those who work in a private organization with the activity they perform, the management style, the possibilities of professional development, and the requirements of the *job*. At the same time, we see a higher degree of satisfaction with the level of pay for those who work in a private organization.

Thus, we can say that the employees in *public organizations* are more satisfied than those in *private organizations*. When they refer to the activity carried out, the average scores recorded are 4.10 (in public organizations) and 3.63 (in private organizations), *the job requirements* are 4.0 (in public organizations) and 3.59 (in private organizations), and the *salary level* is 2.76 (in public organizations) and 3.21 (in private organizations). We find that there is a higher degree of satisfaction for those who perform in private companies than in public ones with regard to the level of wages. The differences of opinion between the employees within the *public organizations* and those of the *private organizations* are not significant from the point of view of the average score when expressing their degree of satisfaction with the *management style*, the average scores registering values of 3.78 (in public organizations) and 3.58 (in private organizations) and the *possibilities of professional development* within each organization, with average scores of 3.69 (in public organizations) and 3.53 (in private organizations).

To compare and check the significant differences in the opinions of respondents grouped according to the type of organization in which they work, *public organizations* versus *private organizations*, we applied the *independent samples t-test*, as can be seen in Table 13.16.

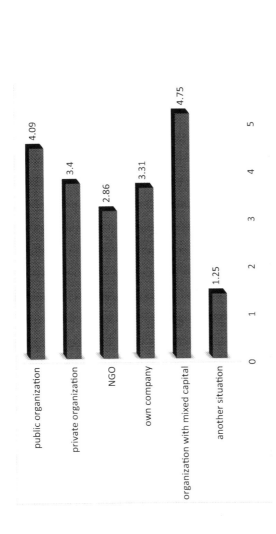

Fig. 13.9 The extent to which the workplace meets the expectations of respondents according to the type of organization in which they work. (Source: author's contribution)

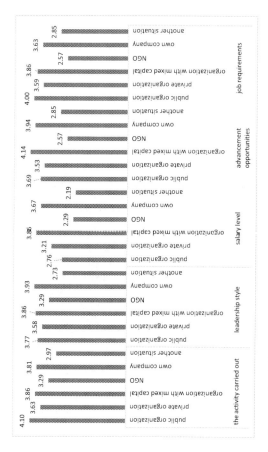

Fig. 13.10 The degree of satisfaction of the respondents according to the type of organization in which they work. (Source: author's contribution)

Table 13.16 Independent samples t-test

		Levene's test for equality of variances		t-test for equality of means					95% confidence interval of the difference	
		F	Sig.	T	Df	Sig. (2-tailed)	Mean difference	Std. error difference	Lower	Upper
Carried out activity	Equal variances assumed	11.856	0.001	2.800	155	0.006	0.479	0.171	0.141	0.817
	Equal variances not assumed			2.812	149.646	0.006	0.479	0.170	0.142	0.815
Leadership style	Equal variances assumed	2.086	0.151	0.988	153	0.325	0.198	0.201	-0.198	0.595
	Equal variances not assumed			0.992	152.524	0.323	0.198	0.200	-0.197	0.593
Salary level	Equal variances assumed	0.343	0.559	-2.007	153	0.047	-0.453	0.225	-0.898	-0.007
	Equal variances not assumed			-2.011	153.000	0.046	-0.453	0.225	-0.897	-0.008

(continued)

Table 13.16 (continued)

		Levene's test for equality of variances		t-test for equality of means					95% confidence interval of the difference	
		F	Sig.	T	Df	Sig. (2-tailed)	Mean difference	Std. error difference	Lower	Upper
Opportunities for professional development	Equal variances assumed	0.811	0.369	0.840	153	0.402	0.168	0.200	-0.228	0.564
	Equal variances not assumed			0.841	152.927	0.402	0.168	0.200	-0.227	0.564
Job requirements	Equal variances assumed	4.849	0.029	2.078	153	0.039	0.413	0.199	0.020	0.805
	Equal variances not assumed			2.088	151.999	0.038	0.413	0.198	0.022	0.803

Source: author's contribution based on the analysis in SPSS 22

The use of the *t-test* revealed that the differences in respondents' opinions are significant in terms of the work performed, the salary level, and the requirements of the job, the value of Sig. registering values of less than 0.05. The differences between the opinions of the respondents grouped by *type of organization* are significant in terms of the activity performed, the salary level, and the requirements of the *job* that *correspond to the level of training*. The other differences, *the possibility of professional development and the leadership style*, are not confirmed from a statistical point of view; the value of Sig. corresponding to the *t-test* has a value of more than 0.05, which suggests that the test result is not representative. Therefore, there are no significant differences with regard to the options expressed by the respondents. Employees believe that neither the possibility of professional development nor the management style depends on the type of employing organization.

There are significant differences between the opinions of graduates, depending on the level of salary, regarding the extent to which the job meets the expectations.

The level of pay has a decisive role to the extent that the job meets the expectations of the respondents. Thus, we find that those who have a salary level below 1000 lei have a low level of satisfaction, while in the case of obtaining a salary over 2000 lei, the job tends to correspond to expectations almost entirely.

As the level of wages increases, the degree of fulfilment of expectations at work also increases, as shown in Table 13.17, from an average score of 2.73, in the case of employees who have less than 1000 lei, to a maximum value of 4.30, in the case of employees who receive between 2501 and 3000 lei.

To check if there are differences of opinion between respondents, we applied an independent samples t-test. Bonferroni correction sets the materiality threshold to Sig. = $0.05/C26 \approx 0.003$ (Table 13.18).

Following the application of *the independent samples t-test*, we found that the differences between the opinions of the respondents who have less than 1000 lei and the others who obtain over this amount are not statistically significant; the Sig. value corresponding to the t-test is more than 0.003.

Additionally, insignificant differences are obtained for the other comparisons from one salary step to another. However, the differences are significant in terms of the opinions of those who are separated by two pay increments. To confirm or disprove these differences, we applied the

Table 13.17 The extent to which the job meets expectations based on the gross salary level

Gross salary level	N	Average	Standard deviation	Standard mean
Under 1000 lei	30	2.73	1.461	0.267
Between 1001 and 1501	73	3.60	1.077	0.126
Between 1501 and 2000	32	3.84	1.139	0.201
Between 2001 and 2500	15	4.40	0.910	0.235
Between 2501 and 3000	9	4.67	0.500	0.167
Over 3000	10	4.30	0.675	0.213

Source: author's contribution

independent samples t-test, with the Bonferroni correction setting the materiality threshold to Sig.= $0.05/C26 \approx 0.003$.

Following the test, we found that the Sig. value corresponding to the t-test is less than 0.003, which gives representativeness to the test and confirms from a statistical point of view that the differences between the opinions of the respondents who are separated by two salary steps, between 1501 and 2000 lei and those who have between 2501 and 3000 lei, are significant (as can be seen in Table 13.19).

There are significant differences between the opinions of the graduates, depending on the level of salary, regarding the degree of satisfaction with certain aspects related to the job (the activity performed, the management style, the salary level, the possibilities of advancement, the requirements of the job).

The analysis of the differences of opinion between the respondents grouped by the *gross salary*, regarding the satisfaction regarding certain aspects related to the *job* (*the activity performed, the management style, the salary level, the possibilities of advancement, the requirements of the job*), reveals large gaps between different groups of employees. The degree of satisfaction is higher given that the salary has a value of over 2000 lei (Fig. 13.11).

The differences are obvious if we analyze the degree of satisfaction of the respondents, grouped by *salary level*, regarding certain aspects related to the job, as shown in Fig. 13.10.

Table 13.18 Independent samples t-test for the comparison of the averages regarding the degree of meeting the job expectations of the employees earning a salary less than 1000 lei, as well as of those earning a salary ranging between 1001 and 1500 lei

	Levene's test for equality of variances		t-test for equality of means					95% confidence interval of the difference	
	F	Sig.	T	df	Sig. (2-tailed)	Mean difference	Std. error difference	Lower	Upper
Equal variances assumed	5.874	0.017	-3.342	101	0.001	-0.869	0.260	-1.385	-0.353
Equal variances not assumed			-2.948	42.546	0.005	-0.869	0.295	-1.464	-0.274

Source: author's contribution based on the analysis in SPSS 22

Table 13.19 Independent samples t-test for the comparison of the averages regarding the degree of meeting the job expectations of the employees earning a salary ranging between 1501 and 2000 lei, as well as of those earning a salary ranging between 2501 and 3000 lei

| | Levene's test for equality of variances | | t-test for equality of means | | | | | 95% confidence interval of the difference | |
	F	Sig.	t	Df	Sig. (2-tailed)	Mean difference	Std. error difference	Lower	Upper
Equal variances assumed	2.593	0.115	-2.096	39	0.043	-0.823	0.393	-1.617	-0.029
Equal variances not assumed			-3.148	31.228	0.002	-0.823	0.261	-1.356	-0.290

Source: author's contribution based on the analysis in SPSS 22

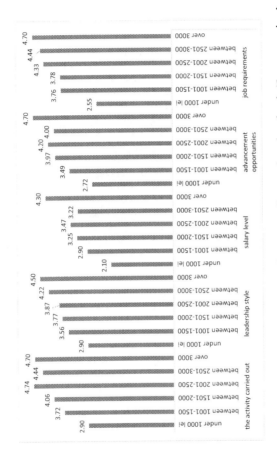

Fig. 13.11 The degree of satisfaction of the respondents according to the salary level. (Source: author's contribution)

The differences are significant for the respondents who are on the first two payroll steps. Thus, we can see that those who have a gross salary below 1000 lei have a low degree of satisfaction, the average score having a value of 2.9, regarding the activity carried out, compared to those who have over 1000 lei, the average score being 3.72.

To confirm or disprove these differences from a statistical point of view, we applied the *independent samples t-test* (Table 13.20).

The test results indicate that the Sig. value corresponds to a t-test less than 0.05, which suggests that the differences in the variables analyzed according to the salary level are statistically significant for respondents who are not on consecutive salary steps.

The differences become statistically insignificant between those who have a salary level between 1001 and 1500 lei and those who have a salary level between 1501 and 2000 lei.

Following the application of the independent samples t-test (as shown in Table 13.21), the results indicate a Sig. value corresponding to the t-test higher than 0.05, which suggests that the differences in the analyzed variables depending on the salary level are statistically insignificant in the case of the respondents who are on consecutive salary steps. In conclusion, we can say that there are significant differences between the opinions of the respondents, grouped according to certain criteria, regarding the correspondence between the level of training and the place of work currently held.

The results indicated that, in general, the respondents' opinions are different, as evidenced by the analysis of the 24 average comparisons for the topic "Graduated study program" and the 16 comparisons of averages for the theme "Status on the labor market." This allows us to state that the level of training, in the respondents' opinions, visibly influences the degree of satisfaction with certain aspects related to the workplace (the activity they perform, the management style, the possibilities of professional development, the level of salary, the requirements of the *job* in the field of completed studies) and the extent to which it meets expectations, so the assumptions are confirmed.

Table 13.20 Independent samples t-test

		Levene's test for equality of variances		t-test for equality of means					95% confidence interval of the difference	
		F	Sig.	t	df	Sig. (2-tailed)	Mean difference	Std. error difference	Lower	Upper
The activity carried out	Equal variances assumed	1.112	0.294	-3.255	100	0.002	-0.822	0.253	-1.323	-0.321
	Equal variances not assumed			-3.046	47.401	0.004	-0.822	0.270	-1.365	-0.279
Leadership style	Equal variances assumed	0.530	0.468	-2.324	98	0.022	-0.667	0.287	-1.236	-0.097
	Equal variances not assumed			-2.365	54.120	0.022	-0.667	0.282	-1.232	-0.102
Salary level reflects the level of training	Equal variances assumed	0.799	0.373	-2.936	98	0.004	-0.798	0.272	-1.337	-0.259
	Equal variances not assumed			-3.215	64.192	0.002	-0.798	0.248	-1.294	-0.302

(continued)

Table 13.20 (continued)

		Levene's test for equality of variances		t-test for equality of means					95% confidence interval of the difference	
		F	Sig.	t	df	Sig. (2-tailed)	Mean difference	Std. error difference	Lower	Upper
Opportunities for professional development	Equal variances assumed	0.113	0.738	-2.752	98	0.007	-0.769	0.279	-1.323	-0.214
	Equal variances not assumed			-2.774	52.989	0.008	-0.769	0.277	-1.325	-0.213
Job requirements correspond to professional training	Equal variances assumed	0.014	0.907	-4.432	98	0.000	-1.209	0.273	-1.750	-0.668
	Equal variances not assumed			-4.551	55.178	0.000	-1.209	0.266	-1.741	-0.677

Source: author's contribution based on the analysis in SPSS 22

Table 13.21 Independent samples t-test

		Levene's test for equality of variances		t-test for equality of means					95% confidence interval of the difference	
		F	Sig.	t	df	Sig. (2-tailed)	Mean difference	Std. error difference	Lower	Upper
The carried out activity	Equal variances assumed	1.044	0.309	-1.475	102	0.143	-0.340	0.231	-0.798	0.117
	Equal variances not assumed			-1.506	62.601	0.137	-0.340	0.226	-0.792	0.111
Leadership style	Equal variances assumed	1.012	0.317	-0.767	100	0.445	-0.211	0.275	-0.756	0.334
	Equal variances not assumed			-0.803	63.734	0.425	-0.211	0.263	-0.736	0.314
Salary level reflects the level of training	Equal variances assumed	0.596	0.442	-1.232	101	0.221	-0.349	0.283	-0.910	0.213
	Equal variances not assumed			-1.201	56.339	0.235	-0.349	0.290	-0.930	0.233

(continued)

Table 13.21 (continued)

		Levene's test for equality of variances		t-test for equality of means					95% confidence interval of the difference	
		F	Sig.	t	df	Sig. (2-tailed)	Mean difference	Std. error difference	Lower	Upper
Possibilities of personal development	Equal variances assumed	0.854	0.358	-1.771	101	0.079	-0.476	0.269	-1.009	0.057
	Equal variances not assumed			-1.795	61.816	0.077	-0.476	0.265	-1.006	0.054
Job requirements correspond to professional training	Equal variances assumed	0.003	0.958	-0.077	101	0.939	-0.021	0.268	-0.553	0.512
	Equal variances not assumed			-0.077	59.667	0.939	-0.021	0.269	-0.558	0.517

Source: author's contribution based on the analysis in SPSS 22

QUALITATIVE RESEARCH FROM THE POINT OF VIEW
OF EMPLOYERS REGARDING THE COMPATIBILITY BETWEEN
THE LEVEL OF EDUCATION AND EMPLOYABILITY

This stage of the qualitative research had as its general purpose the completion of the quantitative research picture to identify some aspects, conditionings, and factors of the relationship level of training—employability—which were not noted in the quantitative phase of the research. This desideratum was realized on two parallel qualitative studies, which included as a universe of investigation two categories of *stakeholders*, namely, employers-companies from Suceava and experts in the recruitment of a highly qualified labor force, at the national level.

To determine the opinions of employers and recruiters to identify qualitative aspects of the relationship level of studies—employability, were organized individual semi-directed depth interviews. The interviews were conducted with the support of the Employers' Federation of SMEs Suceava, within the twentieth edition of the jubilee edition regarding the top private companies in Suceava County, an event that brought together over 300 SME companies from Suceava County, on October 2, 2015, together with organizations and bodies at the national level and public and local authorities. Another opportunity for dialogue occurred on the occasion of the 2015 edition of the Gala of Excellence in Business, organized on October 23, 2015. The aim of this event was to award the business performance in Suceava County by the Chamber of Commerce and Industry. The companies on the top represented a barometer of the county's economic reality and a recognition of the achievements obtained by the management of the local companies in 2014. The interviews were aimed at conducting a dialogue with the managers of companies with experience in the field of employment and the business environment, becoming the calling card of success and economic performance, an activity that was carried out between September 15 and October 30, 2015.

The recruitment firms of the highly qualified workforce on which we conducted the interview are the companies specialized in the recruitment and selection activities of personnel, which provide employers with quality human capital, according to development needs. They also track the compatibility of future employees with the requirements of the positions and evaluate the professional ability to determine compatibility with the requested *job*. These considerations were the basis for the selection, at the national level, of the recruitment firms of the highly qualified workforce for the conduct of interviews. At the same time, we aimed for the interviews to be conducted with the experts/recruiters from these companies, with managers or representatives who hold the certificate of human resources inspector and have superior capacities to evaluate the qualification of the candidates due to experience and the large number of interviews conducted. I noted that according to the opinions of the experts, they solve staff crises in the companies and help people find *jobs* corresponding to their training,, and typologies. 'Man must be there, where he can be of use' (Euripides).

A point of view was obtained through the representative of the recruitment agency for the highly qualified workforce, founded in July 2010, being one of the largest leaders on the human resources services market. This company is part of the Confederation of European private employment services through an agent. Of the 18 agencies, one representative offered us the point of view on the proposed topic, being a world leader in the provision of specialized services in human resources, offering a full range of services including mass recruitment, recruitment and selection of a highly specialized workforce, and *training*. This company also supports the actions of the National Alliance of Student Organizations in Romania (ANOSR), especially those aimed at integrating young people into the labor market.

Another company that met our questions was AMS-HR, which offers advanced personnel recruitment, diagnosis, and organizational consultancy services to find people who are as efficient and as well trained as possible. In addition to the companies presented above, the representatives of (AJOFM), MWG Romania, a recruitment company (*headhunting*), which since the beginning of 1962 has been carrying out predictive studies on the employment prospects of labor with over 59,000 employers in 42 countries and territories, have also responded to our requests. The company specializes in permanent recruitment, evaluation and selection, outsourcing, and consultancy in the field of human resources.

The Research Objectives, Methodology, and Benchmarks

Knowing the opinions of employers and recruiters requires the establishment of the following common objectives:

- formulating the main strengths and weaknesses of the training obtained after completing higher education

- identifying the aspects that employers take into account when deciding to employ highly educated people
- highlighting the favorable or unfavorable opinions of employers regarding the graduates of a higher education program

A specific objective was to collect suggestions regarding the improvement of the absorption of higher education graduates on the labor market, the implementation of reforms and changes at the university and system level to facilitate the efficiency and empowerment of students, and the correlation of graduates' skills with the needs of employers.

Given the exploratory nature of this qualitative stage, we used rationally conducted theoretical sampling (*judgment sample/purposive sample*). One of the most important criteria in the selection of companies was their experience in hiring graduates of higher education. The interviews were conducted based on a sample of 30 employers on the Suceava market and five experts/recruiters[7] in the field of specialized recruitment firms at the national level with experience and expertise in the area of human resources. The estimated time for each interview was approximately 20 minutes, which was recorded using a tape recorder.

As a method of qualitative research for both categories of *stakeholders*, the semi-structured, in-depth, unrepeatable, intensive, and personal interview was chosen as the method with the greatest potential for data extraction, through the possibility of granting interaction to the situation, being a technique that allows the deep and nuanced understanding of the human being and his/her relations with the world or of the specific points of view of certain groups (McCracken 2005). It should be emphasized that conducting interviews implies the assimilation and elaboration of a complex process, which is the premise of research success. In other words, we summarize Oakley's words: "The interview is like marriage: everyone knows what it is. Many people practice it, yet many secrets hide behind closed doors" (Oakley, 1999). Thus, the methodology was an inductive one, dependent on the context (the objectives of the research, the researched community), subjectivity, dependence on values, and a high degree of interaction between the researcher and the subject.

---

[7] The recruiters, in our approach, are the specialists who work in the specialized recruitment companies and act as a binder between the candidate and the employing company. The recruiter's role in the company is to minimize the amount of time a manager would seek, meet, and hire highly qualified candidates.

The interview guide was common for both local employers and recruiters, representatives of recruitment firms nationwide, and included a set of eight questions so that the interviewee could provide answers with complete information about the topic of discussion.

The investigation was directed to three main, parallel themes, established according to the objectives of the research previously identified:

- identifying the main strengths and weaknesses of the preparation of graduates following the completion of higher education
- the aspects that employers take into account when deciding to employ highly educated persons
- the opinions of the employers regarding the graduates who have completed a certain form of higher education, and the causes of the malfunction in the mechanisms of correlation of the higher education system with the insertion on the labor market

Conducting Interviews

The objectives of the research were presented to those interviewed from the very beginning of the discussion, using the interview guide as a basis. This clarification of the approach facilitated the focus of the opinions of those interviewed on the topic of research, and then the focus of the discussion generated narratives that combined the common professional expertise and experience of employers with the deepening guidelines required by the interview guide, generating relevant results for a better understanding of current approaches in the field of higher education in conjunction with the labor market. Thus, in the same context, an attempt was made to obtain a point of view from the recruitment experts on the relationship between the professional training of employees and their absorption on the labor market.

Conducting this type of qualitative research was time consuming and I think it would be helpful to underline certain barriers I have faced using this research method. Therefore, the dependence on the state of the participants (interviewed population); the difficulties in standardization (uniqueness of the interview situation); the respect for anonymity or the difficulty in reaching the participants were just a few of the encountered impediments.

Data Processing and Analysis from the Point of View of both Employers and Experts/Recruiters

To capture the opinions of employers and experts in the field of the labor market, companies from various fields of activity were selected, such as advertising, cadaster, research-design, trade, production, and education. Their distribution, according to the field of activity, is shown in Table 13.22:

From the companies included in the research, the people who responded to our initiative to discuss the expectations and the degree of satisfaction with the level of training and the competences acquired by the graduates with higher education had the position of company administrator, human resources manager, or company manager (as can be seen in Table 13.23).

The presentation of the companies included in the research, according to the number of employees, highlights the fact that there are eight companies that have fewer than 10 employees, an equal number of companies have between 10 and 49 employees, nine companies have between 50 and 249 employees, and only five companies have more than 250 employees. The structure of the 30 companies, by the number of employees, is shown in the structure diagram in Fig. 13.12.

Theme 1: Identifying the Main Strengths and Weaknesses of Graduate Training Following the Completion of Higher Education
In response to the question *To what extent do you declare yourself satisfied with the general training of your highly educated employees?* those interviewed stated that they are generally satisfied with the level of training of

Table 13.22 The distribution of companies based on their field of activity

Field of activity	No. of companies	Share (%)
Research-design	3	10.0
Trade	3	10.0
Accounting and accounting expertise	3	10.0
Education	6	20.0
Industry	3	10.0
Advertising	1	3.3
Financial intermediation	4	13.3
Public administration	2	6.7
Tourism	5	16.7
Total	**30**	**100.0**

Source: author's contribution

Table 13.23   The distribution of the positions of the interviewed individuals

Function	No. of companies	Share (%)
Company administrator	4	13.3
Human resources manager	4	13.3
Manager	22	73.3
Total	**30**	**100.0**

Source: author's contribution

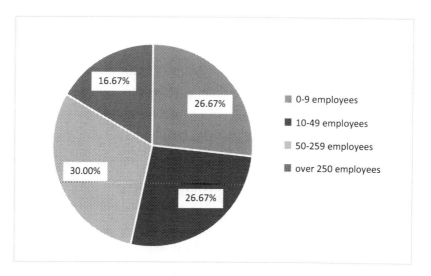

Fig. 13.12   The distribution of the studied companies based on their number of employees. (Source: author's contribution)

employees with higher education. Following the processing of the answers, the results obtained are centralized in Table 13.24.

From the centralization of the answers, it can be seen that over 53% of those interviewed said that they are satisfied to a large extent with the level of training of the university graduates. Only two employers said at the interview that they were satisfied to a small extent with the specialized training of the graduates.

The evaluation carried out by the 30 employers included in the research regarding the level of competence, the degree of satisfaction related to the

Table 13.24 Employer's degree of satisfaction regarding the overall training of employees with higher education

Degree of satisfaction	No. of employers	Share (%)
To a small extent	2	6.7
Somewhat	12	40.0
Largely	14	46.7
Very much	2	6.7
Total	30	100.0

Source: author's contribution

Table 13.25 The average and standard error

	No. of employers	Minimum	Maximum	Average	Standard error
Level of competence	30	2	5	3,67	0.802
Degree of satisfaction	30	2	5	3.53	0.730
The relationship between theoretical and practical training	30	1	5	2.80	0.961

Source: author's contribution based on the analysis in the SPSS 22 program

theoretical training, and the relationship between the theoretical and the practical training is presented in Table 13.25.

According to the answers provided by the 30 employers, the skills of the employees with higher education were evaluated at an average score of 3.67, with a standard deviation of 0.73, which indicates a medium to high level. Regarding the appreciation of the ratio between the theoretical and practical training of the graduates of higher education, the answers provided outlined a low to satisfactory level, with an average score of 2.80 and a standard deviation of 0.961.

The theoretical and practical knowledge acquired after graduating from a form of higher training is considered sufficient by the employees with higher education, at least for the period of initiation within the company and probation period. For an employee to be able to perform within the company, the position for which he was recruited often requires a period of internship/training between three and six months. Employers have realized the importance of training courses having employees who contribute to the performance of the company. The rapid changes in the technological environment of the companies represent a reality that also requires the continuous training of the employees to capitalize on the opportunities offered by the introduction of new technologies to increase efficiency. The selection of employees also takes into account their ability to adapt to the changes that occur in the internal and external environment of the company.

In general, employers of graduates of higher education consider that they leave the university system equipped with theoretical information in the field that is more or less appropriate, but with a lack of practical experience.

In their view, academic performance is considered a necessary condition but not sufficient to form the image of a desirable candidate. Recruiters aim to ensure that the human resource they select corresponds in terms of general skills: the ability to communicate, to relate to other people, to work in a team, to use a computer, to speak a foreign language, and to utilize skills specific to the workplace.

The results of the analysis indicated that, in general, the perceptions of the two types of interviewees are similar. It is worth noting that the opinions regarding the three topics under analysis are unanimous: Both categories of *stakeholders*, employers and recruiters, are of the opinion that what graduates lack is the practical aspect because they do not have the ability to put into practice the theoretical knowledge acquired. Here, there are some profound perspectives of analysis: The quality and level of training of graduates leave room for interpretation, generally dissatisfaction, regarding the lack of specific skills and abilities, and a failure to adapt the curriculum to the requirements of the labor market.

The main criticisms addressed in higher education are directed toward the impossibility of achieving the interconnection between the business environment and the university environment by correlating the theoretical knowledge gained with practical experiences.

Among the shortcomings noted by employers, regarding the employees with higher education, most of them (21.2%) considered that the lack of practice in the specialized field is the main disadvantage. Other minuses found in graduates from the university environment refer to non-assumption of responsibilities (20%), poor communication with clients (18.8%), lack of knowledge specific to the field of activity (16.5%), lack of discipline in work (12.9%), and superficial treatment of certain activities within the company (10.6%).

The comparison made between employers and graduates of higher education, regarding the degree of satisfaction with the work performed and the level of competence acquired by graduates of higher education, highlights that there are significant differences between these two categories. Thus, employers have considered as average the level of competence of employees with higher education, while the interviewed graduates tend to declare that the level of competence acquired after completing a form of university education is high. The differences are insignificant in terms of the degree of satisfaction/satisfaction with the work performed. The graph in Fig. 13.13 shows the existing differences from the two analyzed perspectives.

The obtained results require the search for and discovery of the causes that lead to the existence of significant differences between the ways of assessing the competences obtained from higher education from the two perspectives: those of employees and those of employers. The analysis of how to assess the competences of candidates with higher education in the employment process allowed the identification of aspects that the education system must insist on in the preparation of students.

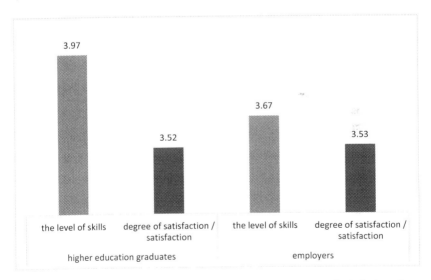

Fig. 13.13 The level of skill and the degree of contentment/satisfaction from the point of view of employers and graduates of higher education. (Source: author's contribution)

From the employers' perspective, the higher professional qualification interrelates with a series of processes, such as the need for technological progress and labor productivity, emigration-immigration, the demographic and educational-cultural dynamics of the active population, and the available capital of the company. These factors, in the opinion of employers, act more or less on the demand for labor in the market, either upward or downward.

Diplomas, in the opinion of experts/recruiters, are essential, first because any work has its specificity but also because the law requires, depending on the activity performed, having a certified person. Experts believe that in theory things are ideal, that each employee should be placed on the place that suits him better. However, the reality points out the other face of the things, according to which the work test and the experience make the difference. Therefore, the expectations of those who want to get hired have great chances to be deceived.

Theme 2: What Employers Take into Account when Deciding to Hire People with Higher Education

The processing of employers' responses, as a result of the discussion on the issues pursued at employment, gave us a complex picture of how the evaluation of each person is carried out at the job interview. In this approach, we found that 24.4% of employers considered experience/practice in the field to be a priority. This aspect is difficult to offer from the perspective of the university graduate, who often had neither the time nor the opportunity to obtain the practical experience requested by the employer.

Other selection criteria used for recruitment were the qualifications of the candidate (23.3%), the level of education (20.9%), the recommendations brought by the graduate certifying his/her value (16.3%), and the prestige of the graduated faculty, which also confirms the candidate's level of training. Differences of opinion relate to how to conduct *job* interviews between a recruiter and a company manager/employer. While the manager of the company, as a rule, focuses more on the functions of the job, the recruiter focuses on the employee in his complexity (personality, professional ability, knowledge, compatibility, and achievements throughout his career).

The reasons invoked by the two categories of interviewees for the rejection of some candidates with higher education at the job interviews refer to the following: lack of competences related to the studied field, requests related to a certain level of salary, failure to sum up an employment contract for a certain period of time, lack of motivation in obtaining the *job* concerned, absence of desire to assume responsibilities at work, and deficiencies in communication and collaboration within a possible team or work department.

Theme 3: Employers' Recommendations on Improving the Educational Offer to Better Meet the Demands of the Labor Market
The recommendations directed to the management system in the university field to increase the degree of adaptation of the university training to the requirements of the labor market were oriented in several directions. Lack of motivation and the assumption of responsibilities at work are often associated with deficient conduct or poor presence in the university environment of counseling and career guidance activities. Although they realize the importance of counseling activities to choose a successful career, future graduates do not become effectively involved in the actions carried out in the university environment, actions that benefit from the participation of opinion leaders from the organizational environment.

The allocation of time for the development of the skills of future graduates in terms of teamwork, formal and informal communication, the focus on the formation of complementary skills such as fluent communication in at least two languages of international circulation, and the high-level use of computer programs in the field of activity are other relevant recommendations communicated by employers to optimize the relationship between theoretical knowledge and practice acquired by graduates of higher education and the requirements of the labor market.

Employers have expressed interest in establishing partnerships with the academic environment so that there is a better correlation of university specializations with the places available on the labor market. The involvement of practitioners in the teams of the projects carried out within the universities will contribute to a better adaptation of the curriculum to the requirements of the labor market.

Increasing the number of practice partnerships with economic agents and public institutions, as well as monitoring with maximum responsibility the practical activities that students carry out, will lead to better knowledge of the field studied and obtaining the required experience in employment.

More active involvement in providing information for career guidance, by organizing *workshops* on career management or *job* fairs, will provide the necessary support to connect to the changes that occur in the require-ments of the labor market. The analysis of the changes in the labor market and the estimation of the trends, which will be registered over a period of at least five years, will be able to ensure a better correlation from a quanti-tative and qualitative point of view between the demand and the labor supply. Raising the level of education must be accompanied by an increase in the capacity to take responsibility for the work done.

As a result, both employers and recruiters interviewed made several proposals for the implementation of higher education curricula and often said they should be (formally) more involved in the planning and delivery of the higher education curriculum. They also support the idea of using the data collected, following the conduct of research (surveys) that cen-tralizes clear, precise information on the relationship between higher edu-cation and graduates. More specifically, they tend to see the usefulness of such information from a dynamic perspective and to identify some inter-dependent beneficiaries of the feedback provided by the data collection mechanisms (such as surveys on graduates and the labor market), namely, *students* who will be better informed about the choice of a certain field of study and how well they fit a certain profile; *higher education institutions* that could inform themselves about actions to improve the curriculum; and *employers* who could use the data for recruitment as well as for provid-ing feedback to HEIs.

At the level of a forecast, as a conclusion of the recruiters, they high-lighted the fact that at the level of the sectors of activity, the employment plans remain optimistic in the finance, insurance, real estate services, busi-ness services, and hotel and restaurant sectors, with an extra 4.5% at the level of 2016. According to the opinions of highly skilled workforce recruiters, future employment plans are positive, regardless of the size of the employing organization. "We expect that at the level of 2016, the number of new hires will increase more alertly compared to 2015. In 2015, there were over 160,000 new hires by the end of the year. At the level of 2016, we expect at least 180,000 new jobs because there are appli-cations for financing and investment projects, not only for expansion but also for new investments, *greenfield*,[8] which require manpower. There will also be an upward trend, especially in the IT industry, which continues to

[8] The term *greenfield* is used in this context as an investment in which an investor starts from scratch, on a land without infrastructure with a project, and in the end obtains a per-fectly functional industrial unit.

expand, but software experts are increasingly difficult to find, even on higher wages. We believe that the tuition figures should increase in the IT area because there are potential candidates and teachers who could be stimulated by partnerships with private companies" (D. M.).

Development of a conceptual model based on the relationship between higher education and employability in the context of well-being

To highlight our analysis, being both a difficult and a complex approach, we have proposed and developed a conceptual framework that will correlate the level of higher education with employability in the context of the satisfaction with the work performed by highlighting, at the same time, the factors that positively influence this relationship for socioeconomic development based on performance.

Human capital, well-being, and socioeconomic development are three important vectors essential for economic development based on knowledge for a modern society in the twenty-first century (Fig. 13.14).

The intercorrelation between the three factors shows that they cannot act independently of each other and that there is a synergistic effect for economic performance.

The center of the model underlines the bilateral link between a higher level of education and employability. In this sense, higher education offers labor market specialists, theories, methods, and scientific tools that economic and social entities can use in their specific activities. A higher social status and a much higher employability rate represent just some of the advantages of university graduates. On the other hand, the co-optation of employers in the teams of the projects carried out within the universities will be able to provide the necessary support and relevant *feedback* for a good connection, both from a qualitative and quantitative point of view, between the demand and the supply of work, in view of institutional performance.

An innovative aspect is that there are bilateral links between all the components of the model. Education can influence human capital in the sense that it provides specialists on the labor market with a high level of initial education and who can continue with vocational training studies throughout their careers, which implies a high degree of work satisfaction, training, and, implicitly, an increase in individual well-being. In our opinion, well-being consists of a perfect and conditioned assembly of skills (which represent the innate talents and valences cultivated by the individual and society through education), of consistent efforts (strong will,

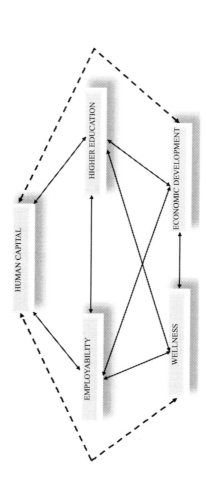

Fig. 13.14 The relationship between higher education and employment based on economic performance. (Source: author's contribution)

intrinsic motivation in achieving ideals complemented by heart aspirations), and of the way of thinking (which essentially edifies the contemporary knowledge system, ethical standards, the set of skills and managerial policies, traditions, and lessons learned through lifelong education). Higher education contributes to economic development by increasing the innovative nature of the economy and acquiring knowledge on the use of technologies that promote employability, well-being, and development.

The link between employability and the three factors of human capital, welfare, and education is much more complex than bilateral influence. They are integral to the matrix of development and function as an engine of the economy. An educated population is a productive population that maximizes the level of knowledge and efficiency, thus contributing to a performing economy. The importance given to human capital, the main source of progress and openness to innovation, and to unprecedented technological progress, leads to a permanent improvement in well-being and society as a whole.

REFERENCES

Melink, M., & Pavlin, S. (2009). *Employability of graduates and higher education management systems (final report of DEHEMS project)*. University of Ljubljana Publishing-house, Faculty of Social Sciences.

Oakley, A. (1999). People's ways of knowing: Gender and methodology. *Open University Press*, 154–170.

Purici, Şt. coord. (2013a). *'Stefan cel Mare' University of Suceava, 50 years (1963–2013), 'Stefan cel Mare' University of Suceava Publishing – House*, p.205.

Purici, Şt. coord. (2013b). *'Stefan cel Mare' University of Suceava, 50 years (1963–2013), 'Stefan cel Mare' University Publishing - House*, p.125 *cited in* The Charter of 'Ştefan cel Mare' University of Suceava (2012, p.7).

Stefan cel Mare' University of Suceava – Report on the activity carried out in 2014., www.usv.ro.

USV, Strategic Plan 2013-2017, pp. 5-6.

REFLEX http://www.reflexproject.co.uk/.

Hegesco (2009). http://www.hegesco.org/.

http://www.uni-kassel.de/wz1/TSEREGS/sum_e.htm.

CHAPTER 14

Conclusions Regarding the Social and Economic Dimension of Education

The centralization of the applied questionnaires allowed the determination of a sample structure included in the analysis: 87.2% of the respondents completed a form of training at the 'Stefan cel Mare' University of Suceava, and the remaining 12.8% decided to continue at the 'Stefan cel Mare' University of Suceava through another form of higher education (i.e., master's or doctorate). Based on the centralization of the results, the following were found:

- high and very high degree, regarding the self-assessment made by the respondents at the time of graduation of a university training program, in relation to the level of competences acquired during the studies;
- the results of the research have shown that after the completion of the studies, the most appropriate description of the situation in the first six months is the continuation through another form of training, employment in the field of completed studies, or opening one's own business. Only 4.35% of respondents said that although they had sought a job, they had not been able to get a job. The study conducted by the *Center for Career Counseling and Guidance* within the 'Stefan cel Mare' University highlighted as main reasons lack of a *job in accordance with the training* (reason invoked by approximately 14.9% of the graduates of the class of 2011, 15.2% of those in the 2012 promotion, and 16.1% of the 2013 promotion), the actual

D.-M. Neamțu, *Education and Economic Development*, https://doi.org/10.1007/978-3-031-20382-4_14

lack of a *job* (the percentages vary from 7.4% in 2011, 7.5% in 2012 to 6.1% in 2013), up to *intentions to start a business* (percentages decrease from older graduates: 4.2% for the 2011 promotion, 4.4% for 2012, and 3.5% for the 2013 promotion).

- 49.22% of respondents have a fixed-term employment contract, while 12.40% have an indefinite employment contract and 14.73% have no job, although they are looking for one.
- For 24.81% of respondents, the workplace corresponds as expected, to a fairly large extent, while 24.03% consider that it fully corresponds, as they are employed in the field of graduated studies.

As a result of the research, we found that there are differences between the respondents' opinions, depending on the form of university training followed or the level of the salary, regarding the degree of satisfaction in relation to the job.

The assessment of the degree of satisfaction, in relation to the aspects related to the job occupied, revealed a certain degree of dissatisfaction with the salary level, the average score of the answers being 2.96 (over 40% of the respondents said that they have a gross salary below 1500 Lei). The other aspects considered have average scores above 3.5, which reflects a state of satisfaction with the work performed, the management style within the company, the existence of professional development possibilities, and the requirements of the *job*.

The analysis of the differences of opinions between the respondents grouped by gross salary regarding satisfaction with certain aspects related to the *job* (the activity performed, the management style, the salary level, the possibilities of advancement, the requirements of the *job* in the field of completed studies) reveals large gaps between different groups of employees. The degree of satisfaction is higher given that the salary has a value of over 2000 Lei. Other differences are obtained if one takes into account the type of organization to which they belong: those who work in a public organization are much more satisfied than those who carry out their activity in a private organization in terms of the activity performed, the management style, the possibility of professional development, and the requirements of the *job*. In this context, the degree of satisfaction of the salary level increases for those who work in a private organization.

The hypotheses initially established have been fully confirmed by the results of the research. In this regard, we have found the following:

- the majority of university graduates believe that the level of competences acquired during their studies is high;
- the majority of graduates, 75%, consider that the period necessary to find a job after completing higher education is between 3 and 6 months;
- over 70% of the graduates with higher education have the status of employee with an employment contract;
- the expectations of graduates of higher education regarding the job occupied are almost entirely met;
- there are significant differences between the opinions of bachelor's degree graduates and those with doctoral studies regarding the level of competences acquired during the studies;
- there are significant differences between the opinions of graduates depending on the completed higher education program with regard to the extent to which the job meets expectations;
- there are significant differences between the opinions of graduates, depending on the type of organization in which they work, regarding the extent to which the workplace meets expectations;
- there are significant differences between the opinions of the graduates, depending on the type of organization in which they work, regarding the degree of satisfaction with certain aspects related to the job (the activity they perform, the management style, the possibilities of professional development, the level of salary, the requirements of the *job*);
- There are significant differences between the opinions of graduates, depending on the level of salary, regarding the extent to which the job meets expectations.

The educational system, starting from the dynamic character of the labor market, has a complex role: on the one hand, the formation of knowledge, general skills, skills, attitudes and behaviors, and, on the other hand, the difficult task of adequately meeting the expectations of the labor market to respond effectively to it through a corresponding social and professional insertion of graduates.

To capture the opinion of employers and recruiters on the labor market, a nonprobabilistic technique was chosen, the characteristics pursued being the size of the company depending on the number of employees, the sector of activity, as well as their experience and expertise in hiring graduates of higher education. From within each company, a management representative or a person from the human resources department answered our questions, the basic condition regarding the experience of the respondent in the selection process. Most of those interviewed (company administrator, human resources representative, managers) have higher education, which is another variable investigated.

The classification of the 30 firms, according to the number of employees, was done as follows: 8 microenterprises, which have fewer than 10 employees; an equal number of firms, that is, 8 small ones have between 10 and 49 employees; 9 medium-sized firms, which have between 50 and 249 employees, and only 5 large firms, which have more than 250 employees.

From the centralization of the answers, we have the following data:

- most of them said they were satisfied to a large and very large extent with the level of training of the graduates of higher education, only a third of the employers said at the interview that they are satisfied to a small extent with the specialized training of the graduates;
- the skills of the employees with higher education were evaluated at an average score of 3.67, with a standard deviation of 0.73, which indicates a medium to high level;
- Regarding the appreciation of the ratio between the theoretical and practical training of the graduates of higher education, the answers provided outlined a low to satisfactory level, with an average score of 2.80 and a standard deviation of 0.961;
- employers of graduates of higher education consider that they leave the university system with a baggage of theoretical information, more or less adequate about the field, but with the lack of practical experience;
- experts aim to ensure that the human resources they recruit correspond in terms of general skills: communication ability, networking with other people, teamwork, using the computer, speaking a foreign language and skills specific to the workplace;
- the impossibility of achieving the interconnection between the business environment and the university environment by correlating the theoretical knowledge accumulated in practical experiences. We found that 24.4% of employers considered experience/practice in the field as a priority;
- The minuses found, regarding the graduates from the university environment, refer to nonassumption of responsibilities (20%), poor

communication with clients (18,8%), lack of knowledge specific to the field of activity (16,5%), lack of discipline in work (12,9%) and superficial treatment of certain activities within the company (10,6%);

- there are significant differences between employers and university graduates; thus, employers have appreciated as average the level of competences of employees with higher education, while the interviewed graduates tend to declare that the level of competences acquired after completing a form of higher education is high;
- the differences are insignificant, as far as the degree of satisfaction/satisfaction in relation to the work performed is concerned.

The opinions, although, seem to be slightly different, depending on employers and recruiters; most employers share similar concerns about the following issues:

- the need to balance scientific and practical skills in higher education curricula;
- the need to address the development of both soft and hard skills through the higher education curriculum;
- the need to acquire more real work experience during higher education.

In general, employers have been satisfied with the level of theoretical knowledge provided by higher education but consider that they are insufficient and that higher education graduates lack practical experience. Therefore, the employers interviewed made several proposals for the implementation of higher education curricula and often said that they should be (formally) involved more in the planning and delivery of the higher education curriculum.

ANNEXES

ANNEX 1: TEMPORAL EVOLUTION OF HUMAN CAPITAL APPROACHES

No.	The issues addressed with regard to human capital	Economists concerned with the study of human capital
1	Educational capital, defined as "the acquired and useful capacities of all inhabitants or members of society," comes from a previous investment that has the behavior of fixed capital. The division of labor has the advantage of increasing the skill of individuals. Investments in education are considered future sources of income	Adam Smith (1723–1790)
2	It emphasizes the role of education in the formation of knowledge and experience	Leon Walras (1834–1910)
3	National wealth is the result of investment in education and training	Friedrich List (1789–1846)
4	Social emancipation could not be achieved without educational emancipation Marshall's vicious circle—people were impoverished because they weren't educated, but they couldn't educate themselves because they were poor—would have turned into a virtuous one if the state had intervened to help those in need and who could not identify their interests	Alfred Marshall (1842–1924)

(*continued*)

D.-M. Neamțu, *Education and Economic Development*, https://doi.org/10.1007/978-3-031-20382-4

(continued)

No.	The issues addressed with regard to human capital	Economists concerned with the study of human capital
5	The production capacities of the individual represent circulating capital The relationship between training and payroll The role of intellectual capital in the formation of ethnic capital	Karl Marx (1818–1883)
6	Education is an investment that has the ability to influence the level of future income and is included in the notion of capital	Irving Fisher (1867–1947)
7	It highlights the role of human capital in economic growth, which is seen as a stock of skills and knowledge Human capital involves investment in health Study the relationship between education, on-the-job training, and income Mincer considered that the only cost of an additional year of school is the anticipated income, thus ignoring direct costs such as tuition fees	Jacob Mincer (1922–2006)
8	It questions the notion of capital, insisting on defining capital as an allocation of time in which human capital also appears. *In addition, at Schultz '... knowledge and skills are a form of capital.'* Knowledge is a very particular economic value, or, in other words, science is a rational activity reserved for those sufficiently trained to understand it Spending on health and education has the potential for increasing the income of the individual	Theodore W. Schultz (1902–1998)
9	Human capital is the monetary and non-monetary activities that influence the future monetary income of the individual These activities include school education, vocational training while working, medical expenses, migration, searching for information about prices and income The investment in human capital is influenced by a series of motivations: the main determinant is the profit/return that is expected from the amounts invested in human capital, and the secondary one is the remuneration, which depends on the amounts invested in human capital, and these are determined, in turn, by the comparison between costs and benefits	Gary S. Becker (n. 1930)
10	Education is the essence of human capital, its importance being superior to the components associated with the state of health	Mark Blaug (1927–2011)

(continued)

(continued)

No.	The issues addressed with regard to human capital	Economists concerned with the study of human capital
11	It builds a model of the employee as an investor in human capital. The number of highly specialized jobs has increased at all levels of education, at the expense of unskilled, low-specialized work, as well as managers at the lower levels, making continuing education a shield against unemployment	Thomas O. Davenport
12	Human capital is "productive resources concentrated in resources of work, skills and knowledge"	OECD (1998)
13	Investments in human capital determine the increase of productivity and, respectively, the economic growth of human capital is 'the engine of economic growth'	R.Lucas, Uzawa, Azaridis, Drazen, P.Barro, P.Romer, Weill, J.Crawfourd

Source: Adaptation after Badea, L., Rogojanu, A. (2012) Controversies Regarding the Relationship of Higher Education—Human Capital-Competitiveness, Theoretical and Applied Economics, Vol. XIX, nr. 12(577), pp. 122–139

ANNEX 2: EVOLUTION OF GDP PER CAPITA, ($) IN THE EUROPEAN UNION, 2000–2020

Country	2000	2005	2010	2012	2013	2014	2018	2019	2020
Austria	24,625.60	38,417.46	46,903.76	48,564.92	50,731.13	51,786.38	51,486.58	50,114.40	48,588.66
Belgium	23,098.89	36,809.70	44,184.95	44,670.56	46,757.95	47,764.07	47,542.77	46,591.49	45,205.34
Bulgaria	1621.24	3899.91	6853.00	7,432.48	7681.93	7901.79	9446.70	9879.27	10,079.20
Croatia	4887.71	10,621.51	14,067.52	13,401.66	13,837.73	13,762.37	15,227.56	15,311.77	14,132.49
Cyprus	14,388.35	24,959.26	31,023.64	28,912.16	27,729.19	27,163.33	29,334.11	29,206.08	27,527.85
Czech Republic	6029.04	13,430.67	19,960.07	19,870.80	20,133.17	19,890.92	23,419.74	23,660.15	22,933.50
Denmark	30,743.55	48,799.83	58,041.40	58,507.51	61,191.19	62,548.98	61,591.93	59,775.74	61,063.32
Estonia	4070.61	10,412.64	14,663.04	17,403.21	19,056.00	20,261.07	23,063.56	23,397.88	23,054.36
Finland	24,345.91	39,054.85	46,505.30	47,708.06	49,892.22	50,327.24	49,988.91	48,628.64	48,755.36
France	22,419.69	34,773.15	40,677.99	40,872.36	42,605.04	43,068.55	41,592.80	40,578.64	39,037.12
Germany	23,694.76	34,520.24	41,572.46	43,855.85	46,298.92	48,023.87	47,973.61	46,794.90	46,252.69
Greece	12,072.93	22,560.15	26,716.65	21,913.00	21,787.79	21,616.71	19,756.99	19,133.76	17,647.23
Hungary	4624.28	11,225.93	13,223.08	12,989.18	13,719.95	14,298.83	16,427.37	16,735.66	15,980.11
Ireland	26,334.57	50,933.02	48,655.37	49,026.02	51,533.03	55,599.85	79,107.60	80,886.62	85,422.54
Italy	20,137.59	32,055.09	36,035.64	35,051.52	35,560.08	35,565.72	34,622.17	33,641.63	31,769.97
Latvia	3361.64	7594.90	11,420.99	13,847.34	15,007.49	15,742.39	17,865.03	17,926.84	17,736.50
Lithuania	3293.23	7854.77	11,987.51	14,367.71	15,729.65	16,551.02	19,186.18	19,575.77	20,232.30
Luxembourg	48,659.60	80,988.14	110,885.99	112,584.68	120,000.14	123,678.70	117,254.74	113,218.71	116,356.16
Malta	10,432.33	15,888.17	21,799.17	22,527.64	24,771.08	26,754.27	30,672.29	30,186.20	28,423.20
Netherlands	26,214.50	41,994.71	50,999.75	50,070.14	52,198.90	52,900.54	53,044.53	52,476.27	52,396.03
Poland	4501.45	8021.51	12,613.01	13,097.27	13,696.47	14,271.31	15,468.48	15,732.20	15,742.45
Portugal	11,526.37	18,780.13	22,520.64	20,563.71	21,653.20	22,103.70	23,562.55	23,330.82	22,194.57
Romania	1659.91	4617.93	8214.08	8507.10	9547.85	10,043.68	12,398.98	12,899.35	12,915.24
Slovakia	5426.62	11,690.11	16,841.77	17,429.83	18,208.42	18,655.79	19,389.98	19,303.55	19,266.51
Slovenia	10,201.30	18,098.91	23,532.48	22,641.81	23,503.28	24,247.17	26,116.86	25,942.95	25,489.50
Spain	14,749.69	26,429.15	30,532.48	28,322.81	29,067.81	29,500.79	30,364.58	29,554.49	27,056.42
Sweden	29,624.91	43,437.06	52,869.04	58,037.82	61,126.94	60,020.36	54,589.06	51,939.43	52,274.41
United Kingdom	28,223.07	42,132.09	39,688.61	42,686.80	43,713.81	47,787.24	43,646.95	43,070.50	41,059.17

Source: https://databank.worldbank.org//reports.aspx?source=2&country=&series=NY.GDP.PCAP.CD%20 &period#, accessed on 15.05.2022

ANNEX 3: EXAMPLES OF VARIABLES USED IN ECONOMETRIC GROWTH MODELS

The author of the model	Dependent variable	Human capital measurement indicator	Data involved in the analysis	Interpreting the impact of education
Barro R. (1991)	The growth rate of real GDP per capita	Enrolment rate in primary and secondary education, by age group	Annual average 1960–1985, for 98 countries	The increase in the enrolment rate in primary and secondary schools by 1%, ensured the increase of GDP per capita by 2.5–3 percentage points
Barro R. (1997)	The growth rate of real GDP per capita	Average level of education of men aged 25 years and over (years of instruction in secondary and tertiary school)	Stock in early 1965, 1975 and 1985, compared to 1990, for 87 countries	The increase in the level of schooling of men in secondary and tertiary education by one percentage point, determines an increase of 1.2 percentage points in GDP per capita
Hanushek, E., Kim D. (1995)	The growth rate of real GDP per capita	• Years of schooling (on average) of the adult male population at the beginning of the period • Results of international tests in mathematics and science	The level of indicators in the early years 1963, 1970, 1981, 1985, 1988, and 1991	• An additional year of male secondary education is associated with an increase of 0.36 percentage points in the growth rate of GDP per capita • The economic growth rate is high in countries where the results of international testing are high
Mankiw, Romer and Weil (1992)	The growth rate of real GDP per person of working age	The average rate of the working-age population possessing secondary level of education, 1960–1985	Period 1960–1985, for 75 countries, including 22 developed countries	An increase of 1%, in the average enrolment rate of the working population in secondary school is associated with an increase of 0.7 percentage points in GDP per person of working age. An increase of 1% in the stock of human capital is associated with a 0.3% increase in GDP

Source: Bucoş, Tatiana (2014) *Education—An Important Factor in Capitalizing on the National Economic Potential*, PhD thesis, ASEM Chişinău, pp.44

ANNEX 3A: BENEFITS OF EDUCATION

No.	Benefits category	Economic nature	Existing research on the extent of the benefits
1.	Individual economic productivity	Private; economic effects; human capital investment	Extensive research on the extent of the economic benefits (Schultz 1961; Mincer 1962; Hansen, 1963; Becker 1964; Conlisk 1971) and changes in time (Allen 2001) Debate on the role of work performed while attending school (Light 2001). Analyses on exploring approaches to eliminating trends in favoring 'skills' and 'publications' (Ashenfelter, Harmon and Oosterbeek 2000)
2.	Non-wage remuneration on the labor market	Private; economic and non-economic effects	Some research on the differences between extra-salary income and working conditions in the context of the level of education (Duncan 1976; Lucas 1977; Freeman 1981; Smeeding 1983) and salary level (Vanness and Wolfe 2002)
3.	Interfamilial productivity	Private; some external effects; economic and non-economic effects	The relationship between the schooling of the wife and the husband's income by excluding selectivity is established (Benham 1974). There are suggestions that this relationship is more compact in entrepreneurial families (Wong 1986) and in families, where the wife carries out a skilled activity (Neuman and Ziderman 1990)
4.	Child quality: Level of education and cognitive development	Private; some external effects; economic and non-economic effects	Substantial evidence that a child's level of education and cognitive development are positively associated with the level of education of parents (Wachtel, 1975; Murnane 1981; This issue was developed by: Sandefur, McLanahan, and Wojtkiewicz 1989; Dawson 1991; Haveman, Wolfe, and Spaulding 1991; Ribar 1993; Haveman and Wolfe, 1994; Duncan, 1994; Angrist and Lavy 1996; Ermisch and Francesconi 1997; Smith, Brooks-Gunn, and Klebanov 1997; Lam and Duryea 1999; Duniform, Duncan, and Brooks-Gunn 2000). Extensive research on a child's self-esteem (Axinn, Duncan, and Thornton 1997)–some evidence that a child's education is positively linked to grandparents' level of schooling (Blau 1999). Some evidence that adult education in the vicinity of a child favors the probability of a child graduating from high school (Clark 1992; Duncan, 1994; Ginther, Haveman, Wolfe and 2000). Some evidence that the high level of training of women, determines a higher level of human capital in children in developing countries (Behrman et al. 1999)

5.	Child quality: Health	Private; some external effects;	Substantial evidence of the positive relationship between a child's health and the education of his parents (Edwards and Grossman 1979; Shakotko, Edwards, and Grossman 1981; Wolfe and Behrman 1982; Behrman and Wolfe 1987; Grossman and Joyce 1989; Strauss 1990; Thomas, Strauss, and Henriques 1991; King and Hill 1993; Glewwe 1999; Lam and Duryea 1999)
6.	Child quality: Fertility	Private; some external effects	Consistent evidence that a mother's education is associated with a diminished probability that (teenage) daughters will give birth to children out of wedlock (Antel 1988; Sandefur and McLanahan 1990; Hayward, Grady, and Billy 1992; and Haveman, and Wolfe 1993; Lam and Duryea 1999; South and Baumer 2000; Haveman, Wolfe and Wilson 2001)
7.	Own health	Private; modest external effects (some of the own health benefits arising from education will be captured in the increased earnings and, consequently, will be included in category 1)	Considerable evidence that the schooling of an individual affects his state of health, (Leigh 1981, 1983; Kemna 1987; Berger and Leigh 1989; Grossman and Joyce 1989; Kenkel 1991; Strauss et al. 1993; Sander 1995); increases life expectancy (Feldman et al. 1989; King and Hill 1993; Crimmins and Saito 2001); diminishes the spread of severe mental illness (Robins 1984), especially depression (Herzog et al. 1998) and perfects the ability to manage stressful events (Thoits 1984) and nervousness (Schieman 2000). High school graduation reduces the mortality rate (Muller 2002). Health-related benefits, deriving from surplus schooling, increase in proportion to age (Ross and Wu 1988, 1995)
8.	The efficiency of consumer choice	Private; some external effects; non-economic effects	Some evidence that schooling leads to more efficient consumer activities. (Michael 1972; Benham and Benham 1975; Pauly 1980; Rizzo and the 1992 Zeckhauser; Morton, Zettelmeyer, Silva and 2001-Risso). Home schooling can have long-term effects (Corman, 1986). College graduates maintain their longer-term computing skills (Pascarella and Terenzini 1991).
9.	Efficiency in the search undertaken by the labor market	Private; non-economic effects	Evidence of reduced costs of job search and increased regional mobility, relative to additional schooling (Metcalf 1973; Greenwood 1975; Da Vanzo 1983). Women who benefit from a surplus of schooling rarely change jobs (Royalty 1998)

(continued)

(continued)

No.	Benefits category	Economic nature	Existing research on the extent of the benefits
10.	Efficiency of the marital option	Private; non-economic effects	Some limited evidence on improving choices in the matrimonial market (Becker, Landes, and Michael 1977).
11.	Achieving the desired family size	Private	Evidence that the effectiveness of contraception is linked to schooling (Easterlin 1968; Ryder and Westoff 1971, Michael and Willis 1976; Rosenzweig and Schultz 1989). Fertility decreases in developing countries, (King and Hill 1993; Lam and Duryea 1999)
12.	Charity	Private and public; non-economic effects	Some evidence that schooling increases the time for charity (volunteering) and cash donations (Mueller 1978; Dye 1980; Hodgkinson and Weitzman 1988; Freeman 1997).
13.	Savings	Private and public; non-economic effects	Control of revenue. Some evidence that a surplus of tuition is associated with increased possibilities to make savings (Solomon 1975)
14.	Technological changes	Public	Some evidence that schooling is positively associated with research, development, and the diffusion of technology (Nelson 1973; Mansfield 1982; Wozniak 1987; Foster and Rosenzweig 1996). Some evidence that technological change is improving the incomes of those with higher education (Bound and Johnson 1992; Author, Katz, and Krueger 1993; Bartel and Sicherman 1999; Allen 2001)
15.	Social cohesion	Public	Descriptive evidence suggesting that schooling is positively associated with voter turnout (Gintis 1971; Campbell et al 1976; Wolfinger and Rosenstone 1980; Hauser 2000); with the reduction of social inequalities and the alleviation of leaving the national territory (Comer 1988); with opposition to government repression and reduced support for the use of violence in protests (Hall, Rodeghier, and Useem 1986). There are suggestions that the education of the individual is associated with trust in others and membership of community-based organisations (Helliwell and Putnam 1999)
16.	Self-confidence or economic autonomy	Private and public	Further education is associated with reduced dependence on transfers during the first years of work (Antel 1988; Kiefer 1985; Rudd, McKenry, and Nah 1990; and Haveman, Wolfe and 1993)

Source: Adapted after Cârstea, L. M. (2013) *Education and Economic Performance*. PhD thesis. 'Al. I. Cuza.' University of Iaşi, pp. 88–90

ANNEX 4: THE INFLUENCING FACTORS
OF ECONOMIC GROWTH

Empirical evidence from the literature suggests the following idea: economic growth is positively linked to:

- The initiated model of the average level of schooling in secondary and higher education Barro (1991–1996, 1998–1999, 2001–2003), Levin and Rench (1992), Benhabib and Spiegel (1994), Sala-i-Martin (2000)
- TFP—Total Factor Productivity—Sarel (1998), Crafts (1999), Levine (2001)
- Technological progress and technological diffusion—Romer (1986, 1987, 1990), Lucas (1988), Grossman and Helpman (1991), Gordon (2002)
- Investing in research and development (R&D)—Grossman and Helpman (1991), Aghion and Howit (1992), Coe and Helpman (1993), Barro and Sala-i-Martin (1995)
- Increasing the capital stock—Romer (1986), Lucas (1988), and Rebelo (1991)
- Labor and capital productivity—Bergocing, Kehoe și Soto (2002)
- Savings rate—Levine and Renelt (1992), Howitt and Aghion (1998), Bernanke and Gurkaynak (2001), Aghion, Comin and Howitt (2006)
- Initial level of life expectancy at birth—Barro (1996, 2003), Doppelhofer, Muller and Sala-i-Martin (2000)
- Investment rates—Barro (1989, 2003), DeLong and Summers (1991), Mankiw, Romer and Weil (1992), Levine and Renelt (1992), Mankiw, Phelps and Romer (1995), Hugo (1999), Bernanke and Gurkaynak (2001)
- Institutional framework—Knack and Keefer (1994). Dhonte, Bhattacharya and Yousef (2000)
- Macroeconomic stability—Fischer (1993), Easterly and Levine (1997)
- A better defence of the rule of law—Barro (1996, 2003)
- Infrastructure investments—Barro (1989), Canning and Fay (1993), Easterly and Levine (1997)
- Defence of Property Rights—Barro (1989)
- Development of financial and banking systems—King and Levine (1993), Levine and Zervos (1996), Rajan and Zingales (1998), Demirguc-Kunt & Maksimovic (1999), Beck, Levine & Loayza (1999)
- Foreign direct investment—Borensztein, De Gregorio and Lee (1995)

ANNEX 5: WEEKLY INCOMES EARNED ACCORDING TO LEVEL OF EDUCATION, 1979–2021

Median usual weakly—in constant (base current year) dollars

Year	Total, 25 years and over	Graduates with secondary education	Graduates with high school education	College graduates	Graduates with a bachelor's degree/ higher degree
Total					
1979	927	734	871	986	1203
1980	897	696	834	953	1179
1981	883	688	819	928	1166
1982	884	670	816	949	1184
1983	891	665	808	943	1197
1984	900	654	803	950	1209
1985	913	651	802	961	1219
1986	924	657	813	967	1241
1987	922	650	815	963	1291
1988	914	636	812	949	1291
1989	903	628	793	956	1288
1990	905	611	778	960	1286
1991	909	597	772	951	1296
1992	909	590	765	918	1321
1993	909	581	769	915	1324
1994	907	557	764	906	1330
1995	903	547	765	899	1322
1996	897	547	764	893	1307
1997	912	542	779	904	1316
1998	953	562	798	930	1368
1999	966	564	799	946	1403
2000	961	571	797	940	1405
2001	966	586	798	946	1413
2002	976	586	808	950	1421
2003	978	585	818	944	1424
2004	983	577	826	951	1419
2005	968	569	811	932	1409
2006	968	565	802	933	1400
2007	967	561	792	923	1405
2008	960	571	779	910	1406
2009	980	575	792	919	1439
2010	974	553	780	914	1425
2011	963	545	771	893	1389
2012	963	557	771	885	1377
2013	964	550	759	872	1392

(*continued*)

(continued)

Year	Total, 25 years and over	Graduates with secondary education	Graduates with high school education	College graduates	Graduates with a bachelor's degree/ higher degree
2014	961	559	765	872	1367
2015	984	564	776	872	1407
2016	999	569	781	879	1421
2017	1002	575	787	882	1413
2018	1005	597	787	891	1428
2019	1026	627	790	907	1448
2020	1077	648	818	946	1488
2021	1057	626	809	925	1452
Women					
1979	682	531	647	738	923
1980	668	514	630	724	909
1981	668	501	622	731	911
1982	689	497	638	741	935
1983	696	506	639	748	958
1984	704	498	644	759	970
1985	713	487	646	764	998
1986	728	492	655	780	1031
1987	735	490	659	794	1066
1988	740	488	658	795	1071
1989	742	488	643	801	1072
1990	744	484	635	796	1079
1991	753	486	638	796	1093
1992	759	486	639	772	1127
1993	769	487	643	781	1131
1994	764	466	637	768	1151
1995	758	464	630	756	1140
1996	766	462	629	762	1133
1997	780	465	639	775	1135
1998	808	472	660	793	1178
1999	811	473	661	796	1207
2000	814	479	662	797	1192
2001	833	485	679	798	1206
2002	858	491	692	820	1222
2003	863	486	700	827	1229
2004	862	481	702	830	1237
2005	851	474	686	816	1228
2006	845	482	674	811	1220
2007	847	484	671	798	1221
2008	845	477	656	792	1204
2009	870	484	686	797	1228

(continued)

(continued)

Year	Total, 25 years and over	Graduates with secondary education	Graduates with high school education	College graduates	Graduates with a bachelor's degree/ higher degree
2010	877	483	676	795	1228
2011	867	477	669	779	1205
2012	859	456	663	779	1183
2013	862	466	668	766	1216
2014	861	468	662	757	1202
2015	871	478	670	760	1217
2016	885	477	676	777	1243
2017	895	494	674	773	1250
2018	895	506	665	773	1235
2019	916	523	671	781	1266
2020	973	550	703	816	1297
2021	954	550	698	803	1272
Men					
1979	1098	881	1077	1150	1385
1980	1063	837	1025	1122	1339
1981	1066	819	1020	1115	1361
1982	1062	792	1011	1111	1359
1983	1057	782	1008	1096	1345
1984	1050	766	993	1109	1398
1985	1067	757	981	1137	1422
1986	1095	759	983	1147	1461
1987	1092	741	968	1137	1494
1988	1075	733	965	1110	1499
1989	1057	732	951	1093	1490
1990	1032	704	925	1093	1494
1991	1018	679	914	1095	1486
1992	1017	666	909	1053	1501
1993	1028	659	902	1059	1493
1994	1045	621	900	1065	1499
1995	1041	614	897	1055	1496
1996	1033	616	890	1041	1507
1997	1039	617	904	1049	1514
1998	1065	638	932	1072	1565
1999	1090	644	946	1085	1594
2000	1093	640	932	1090	1609
2001	1104	643	934	1109	1637
2002	1106	636	932	1104	1647
2003	1099	634	928	1093	1671
2004	1096	642	928	1095	1645
2005	1072	633	907	1065	1623

(continued)

(continued)

Year	Total, 25 years and over	Graduates with secondary education	Graduates with high school education	College graduates	Graduates with a bachelor's degree/ higher degree
2006	1074	632	914	1073	1624
2007	1079	630	903	1062	1629
2008	1081	627	894	1047	1620
2009	1105	633	906	1057	1680
2010	1088	605	884	1052	1656
2011	1070	589	870	1014	1609
2012	1076	600	869	1013	1621
2013	1063	583	853	1000	1626
2014	1056	592	860	999	1586
2015	1084	595	868	1010	1625
2016	1094	622	868	1011	1652
2017	1101	645	881	1013	1636
2018	1107	655	883	1026	1644
2019	1133	682	894	1050	1666
2020	1198	706	923	1075	1721
2021	1160	684	904	1047	1661

Source: Author's contribution, based on primary data from the U.S. Bureau of Labour Statistics https://data.bls.gov/PDQWeb/le, [accessed on 06.06.2022]

ANNEX 6: AVERAGE ANNUAL INCOME ACCORDING TO THE LEVELS OF EDUCATION AND TRAINING COURSES (2012–2022)

Education, work experience, and specialization in the workplace	Employment				Change 2012–2022		Average annual salary (US$)
	Number		Percentage		Number	Percentage	
	2012	2022	2012	2022			
Education levels							
Total, occupation	145,355.8	160,983.7	100.0	100.0	15,628.0	10.8	34,750
Doctorate	4002.4	4640.8	2.8	2.9	638.4	16.0	96,420
Master	2432.2	2880.7	1.7	1.8	448.5	18.4	63,400
Bachelor's degree	26,033.0	29,176.7	17.9	18.1	3143.6	12.1	67,140
Associate Professor	5954.9	7000.9	4.1	4.3	1046.0	17.6	57,590
Vocational education—unrecognized diplomas	8554.2	9891.2	5.9	6.1	1337.1	15.6	34,760
High school—with unrecognized diplomas	1987.2	2212.2	1.4	1.4	225.0	11.3	28,730
High school with a baccalaureate diploma	58,264.4	62,895.2	40.1	39.1	4630.8	7.9	35,170
Secondary education	38,127.6	42,286.0	26.2	26.3	4158.4	10.9	20,110

Previous work experience in different occupations

Total, occupation	145,355.8	160,983.7	100.0	100.0	15,628.0	10.8	34,750
5 years or more	4831.9	5091.8	3.3	3.2	259.9	5.4	90,760
Less than 5 years	16,167.7	17,6635	11.1	11.0	1495.9	9.3	52,270
None	124,356.2	138,228.4	85.6	85.9	13,872.2	11.2	32,260

Typical specialization by profession for the formation of competences

Total, occupation	145,355.8	160,983.7	100.0	100.0	15,628.0	10.8	34,750
Internship	5989.1	6658.9	4.1	4.1	669.8	11.2	53,570
Apprenticeship	2336.9	2855.2	1.6	1.8	518.3	22.2	45,440
Long-term training courses	6876.5	7448.7	4.7	4.6	572.2	8.3	41,810
Medium-term training courses	23,057.8	24,968.5	15.9	15.5	1910.8	8.3	36,950
Short-term training courses	58,928.4	64,673.7	40.5	40.2	5745.3	9.7	22,960

Source: OECD (2021), Education at a Glance 2021: OECD Indicators https://www.oecd-ilibrary.org/education/education-at-a-glance-2021_b35a14e5-en

ANNEX 7: CORRELATION OF PISA TESTS WITH SOME ECONOMIC VARIABLES

Programme for International Student Assessement (PISA) international test results, GDP per capita and R&D investments, 2009–2018

| Country | Results of the international test (PISA) | | | | | | GDP per capita (US$, current prices) | | R&D investments (% of GDP) | |
| | Mathematics | | Sciences | | Reading | | | | | |
	2009	2018	2009	2018	2009	2018	2009	2018	2009	2018
OECD countries										
Finland	541	507	554	522	536	520	47,481	49,988	3.73	2.76
Australia	514	491	527	503	515	503	42,783	57,180	2.35	
Germany	513	500	520	503	497	498	41,650	47,973	2.74	3.11
United Kingdom	492	502	514	505	494	504	38,952	43,646	1.87	
United States	487	478	502	502	500	505	47,099	63,064	2.80	
Italy	483	487	489	468	486	476	37,226	34,622	1.22	1.42
Ex-socialist countries, EU members currently										
Slovenia	501	509	490	507	483	495	24,792	26,116	1.81	1.95
Hungary	490	481	503	481	494	476	13,081	16,427	1.12	1.51
Poland	495	516	508	511	500	512	11,526	15,468	0.66	1.21
Lithuania	477	481	491	482	468	476	11,820	19,186	0.82	0.94
Bulgaria	428	436	439	424	429	420	6988	9446	0.49	0.75
Romania	427	430	428	426	424	428	8548	12,398	0.44	0.50

a. Correlation of PISA test results with labor productivity

Country	PISA test results			National labor productivity (in 2000 dollars)		
	1964–2000	*2000–2009*	*2018*	*2000*	*2009*	*2018*
Japan	531	536	520	39169	41309	39808
Finland	512	541.5	516.3	24346	47481	49989
United Kingdom	495	514	503.7	28223	38952	43647
United States	490	497	495	36335	47100	63064
Germany	487	498.5	500.3	23695	41650	47974
Spain	482	485	481[a]	14750	32170	30365
Italy	475	480	477	20138	37227	34622
Greece	460	467	453.3	12073	29829	19757
Portugal	456	475	492	11526	23151	23563

[a]average score for Mathematics; Reading results for Spain were not published after the OECD detected "anomalies" that indicated the students responded unnaturally quickly to the questions—"in less than 25 seconds." (El País)

b. Correlation of PISA test results with the number of patent applications, 2000–2009

Country	PISA test results			Researchers per million people			Resident patent applications per million people (count by applicant's origin)			EPO Patent Applications (per million people), 2018	
	1964–2000	2000–2009	2018	2000	2009	2018	2000	2009	2018	Total	HT[b]
Japan	531	536	520	5078	5099	5331	3054	2307	2005	179.2	—
Finland	512	541.5	516.3	6736	7546	6861	735	609	564	312.1	—
United Kingdom	495	514	503.7	2895	4077	4603	448	334	280	88.1	—
United States	490	497	495	3497	4090	4412[b]	584	733	872	132.5	—
Germany	487	498.5	500.3	3168	3922	5212	874	891	884	332.3	—
Spain	482	485	481[a]	1878	2772	3001	80	105	71	36	—
Italy	475	480	477	1166	1723	2307	195	215	220	70.7	—
Greece	460	467	453.3	1348	1849	3483	32	72	51	11.2	—
Portugal	456	475	492	1626	3757	4538	10	64	86	21.2	—

Sources: https://databank.worldbank.org/reports.aspx?source=2&series=SP.POP.SCIE.RD.P6&country=;   https://new.epo.org/en/statistics-centre; https://factsmaps.com/pisa-2018-worldwide-ranking; average-score-of-mathematics-science-reading/; https://english.elpais.com/elpais/2019/12/03/inenglish/1575369906_497404.html; https://www3.wipo.int/ipstats/IpsStatsResultvalue; https://www.epo.org/about-us/annual-reports-statistics/annual-report/2018/statistics/patent-applications.html#tab6. Intellectual property right: Patent. Indicator :10—Resident applications per million population (by origin). WIPO statistics database. Last updated: November 2021

[a]Average score for Mathematics; Reading results for Spain were not published after the OECD detected "anomalies" that indicated the students responded unnaturally quickly to the questions—"in less than 25 seconds." (El País)

[b]Data available for 2017

Origin	2000	2001	2002	2003	2004	2005	2006	2007	2008	2009	2010	2011	2012	2013	2014	2015	2016	2017	2018	2019	2020
Finland	735	763	725	662	692	637	664	728	674	609	628	598	665	642	662	601	560	584	564	548	630
Germany	874	866	832	854	866	875	885	888	924	891	910	912	919	917	912	884	893	887	885	884	819
Greece	32	41	38	42	41	48	54	59	65	72	73	72	64	70	68	59	63	56	51	46	50
Italy	195							234	220	215	219	215	205	200	201		215	215	220	229	246
Japan	3054	3042	2899	2804	2884	2880	2715	2605	2578	2306	2265	2250	2249	2132	2090	2036	2049	2053	2005	1943	1807
Portugal	10	15	15	16	17	19	25	30	44	64	55	61	66	71	80	103	85	77	86	95	92
Spain	80	76	81	83	87	92	95	101	108	105	107	104	103	97	95	93	93	83	71	67	68
United Kingdom	448	444	427	424	400	372	365	365	349	334	333	318	316	305	308	306	290	282	280	272	263
United States	584	623	641	651	647	703	743	801	762	733	782	795	856	911	895	899	914	904	872	868	818

Source: Query based on the interactive database https://www3.wipo.int/ipstats/IpsStatsResultval

ANNEX 8: PARTICIPATION RATE IN TERTIARY EDUCATION IN THE PERIOD 1971–2020 (% GROSS)

Years	South Korea	Poland	Romania	Sweden	United Kingdom
1971	6.78	13.32	9.12	21.73	14.58
1972	6.98	12.80	8.59	22.47	15.44
1973	7.15	13.33	8.03	22.06	16.07
1974	7.36	14.51	7.76	22.68	16.72
1975	7.56	15.36	8.07	22.89	18.55
1976	8.30	16.62	8.61	29.52	19.18
1977	8.56	17.46	9.08	31.34	19.33
1978	9.21	17.55	9.51	34.80	19.13
1979	10.35	17.69	10.15	36.21	19.16
1980	12.44	17.52	10.60	36.37	18.85
1981	14.87	17.44	11.12	30.78	18.89
1982	19.07	16.93	11.81	31.42	18.96
1983	23.68	16.34	12.06	32.03	21.06
1984	27.73	16.62	12.20	32.27	21.07
1985	30.94	16.77	11.74	31.14	21.00
1986	33.43	17.35	10.89	30.35	21.52
1987	34.61	17.67	9.91	29.81	22.54
1988	35.15	18.26	9.04	29.97	23.31
1989	35.48	19.75	8.53	30.19	24.40
1990	36.53	20.17	8.41	30.68	26.48
1991	37.60	21.47	9.62	31.98	29.18
1992	39.19	21.19	10.82	34.54	33.23
1993	42.96	23.59	12.07	37.39	37.99
1994	44.56	27.34	13.02	39.79	42.82
1995	48.33	31.18	13.39	42.40	48.26
1996	53.73	35.35	17.66	45.96	50.08
1997	69.24	39.89	18.56	49.64	53.29
1998	66.52	39.20	18.79	51.97	55.54
1999	72.35	44.97	21.29	63.55	60.11
2000	76.66	49.67	23.93	67.07	58.47
2001	79.57	54.76	28.74	70.27	59.27
2002	82.15	57.86	32.82	75.28	62.57
2003	84.36	59.48	38.13	81.42	62.07
2004	87.49	61.06	42.21	83.76	59.35
2005	91.69	63.59	46.38	81.95	58.97
2006	97.05	65.36	52.48	79.32	59.03
2007	101.93	67.21	58.28	74.84	58.49
2008	104.09	70.23	65.79	70.74	56.64
2009	104.28	72.31	68.59	70.74	57.90
2010	102.79	74.76	64.00	73.67	58.92

(continued)

(continued)

Years	South Korea	Poland	Romania	Sweden	United Kingdom
2011	100.75	74.66	58.19	72.83	59.15
2012	97.43	73.96	49.71	68.82	59.40
2013	95.61	71.86	46.85	63.22	57.04
2014	94.85	68.45	47.14	62.18	56.56
2015	94.34	66.95	46.73	62.28	56.46
2016	94.03	67.00	48.24	63.55	58.43
2017	94.35	67.83	49.38	66.99	60.00
2018	95.86	68.62	51.01	72.46	61.38
2019	98.45	69.18	51.35	77.33	65.77

Source: Data-based http://data.worldbank.org/indicator/SE.TER.ENRR, accessed on 07.06.2022

ᵃGross enrolment ratio = ratio of total enrolment, regardless of age, to the population of the age group that officially corresponds to the level of education shown

ᵇData not available for 2021; the last update of the indicator can be found on the World Bank website (see link below) accessed on May 22, 2022

ANNEX 9: GROSS DOMESTIC PRODUCT IN THE PERIOD 1971–2020

(US dollars at current prices per capita)

Years	South Korea	Poland	Romania	Sweden	United Kingdom
1971	301.47	951.89	722.19	5134.31	2648.20
1972	324.18	1044.28	824.39	6023.59	3031.20
1973	406.29	1226.37	949.99	7287.61	3426.86
1974	561.92	1364.85	984.93	8076.01	3663.21
1975	615.75	1441.03	1050.49	10,111.27	4290.77
1976	831.96	1592.70	1169.15	10,867.03	4126.08
1977	1054.04	1750.86	1251.85	11,449.69	4665.18
1978	1404.95	1964.98	1462.71	12,617.81	5955.79
1979	1784.71	2179.45	1565.95	14,865.90	7784.47
1980	1718.95	1663.15	1602.84	17,086.01	10,016.76
1981	1889.36	1561.31	1934.21	15,576.96	9584.95
1982	2000.20	1878.79	2246.58	13,732.08	9125.64
1983	2207.94	2153.41	2066.11	12,603.06	8669.83
1984	2419.85	2138.29	1764.82	13,092.99	8163.63
1985	2482.48	1974.84	2186.12	13,654.94	8642.33
1986	2831.36	2043.38	2369.33	17,948.56	10,603.38
1987	3549.07	1758.40	2636.66	21,732.24	13,104.30
1988	4742.39	1885.88	2713.96	24,452.86	15,962.61

(continued)

(continued)

Years	South Korea	Poland	Romania	Sweden	United Kingdom
1989	5811.29	2244.92	2410.45	25,598.30	16,209.78
1990	6602.43	1739.98	1717.69	30,563.23	19,063.69
1991	7623.31	2249.06	1297.71	31,794.33	19,873.09
1992	8108.08	2473.24	883.64	32,730.31	20,460.06
1993	8856.78	2514.54	1195.86	24,346.43	18,359.20
1994	10,344.02	2889.99	1372.57	26,031.86	19,670.31
1995	12,509.37	3699.92	1629.90	30,250.60	23,156.24
1996	13,336.69	4159.82	1619.00	32,931.46	24,371.48
1997	12,333.41	4134.36	1571.51	30,234.60	26,645.63
1998	8222.35	4529.74	1855.94	30,528.08	28,150.65
1999	10,581.59	4408.61	1612.39	30,887.86	28,603.62
2000	12,161.01	4466.68	1682.84	29,592.97	28,099.52
2001	11,479.77	4954.78	1837.03	27,242.12	27,699.83
2002	13,067.77	5172.19	2107.94	29,913.38	29,956.15
2003	14,560.75	5666.45	2661.39	37,350.09	34,406.64
2004	16,356.35	6643.50	3474.56	42,835.46	40,295.88
2005	19,196.73	7979.00	4596.96	43,393.62	42,049.57
2006	21,546.79	8985.31	5746.54	46,513.05	44,502.47
2007	23,913.91	11,186.01	8300.24	53,613.22	50,352.53
2008	21,294.97	13,911.49	10,289.11	56,050.45	47,111.68
2009	19,128.48	11,465.70	8436.01	46,873.40	38,460.12
2010	23,091.17	12,518.57	8123.80	52,801.31	39,104.22
2011	25,172.12	13,798.29	9014.54	60,643.50	41,621.02
2012	25,537.58	13,040.96	8435.85	57,895.24	41,980.53
2013	27,227.64	13,654.09	9477.10	61,014.85	42,974.81
2014	29,329.77	14,241.38	9980.11	60,044.96	47,009.83
2015	28,840.70	12,562.73	8919.90	51,726.21	44,722.87
2016	29,423.50	12,441.22	9503.28	52,425.23	40,915.51
2017	31,781.13	13,872.47	10,771.15	54,621.35	40,296.02
2018	33,705.26	15,490.10	12,378.50	55,703.57	43,040.85
2019	32,234.50	15,764.57	12,903.99	53,194.37	42,466.45
2020	31,946.98	15,764.11	12,928.59	53,574.53	40,563.53

Source: Data-based   development   http://unctadstat.unctad.org/wds/TableViewer/tableView.aspx?ReportId=96, accessed on 06.06.2022

ANNEX 10: RESULTS OF THE DESCRIPTIVE ANALYSIS
FOR THE DEPENDENT VARIABLE GROSS DOMESTIC PRODUCT
PER INHABITANT AND THE PARTICIPATION RATE
IN TERTIARY EDUCATION IN THE CASE OF THE COUNTRIES
UNDER REVIEW

United Kingdom

The results of the descriptive and graphical analysis, for the dependent variable *Gross domestic product per inhabitant*, indicate a moderately asymmetrical distribution to the right, platykurtic. The independent variable *The participation rate in tertiary education* is moderately asymmetrical to the right and platykurtic. With a coefficient of variation of 0.67, we can say that the distribution of *Gross domestic product* per inhabitant in the period 1971–2013 is very little homogeneous, the arithmetic average not being representative.

The distribution of the *participation rate in tertiary education* is less homogeneous, the value of the coefficient of variation being 0.49.

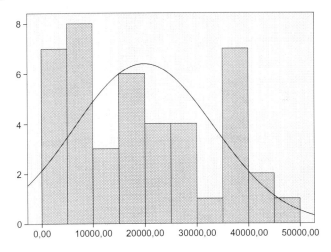

Distribution of *Gross domestic product per inhabitant* in the United Kingdom in the period 1971–2013. (Source: Author's contribution based on the analysis of SPSS 22)

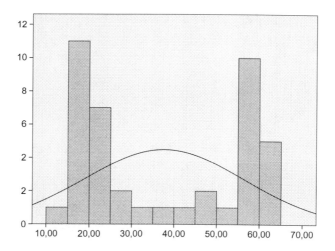

Distribution of the *participation rate in tertiary education* in the United Kingdom in the period 1971–2012. (Source: Author's contribution based on the analysis of SPSS 22)

In order to identify the aberrant values in the distributions of the two analyzed variables, we built the boxplot charts. From these diagrams we can see that no outliers are recorded in any series of statistical data.

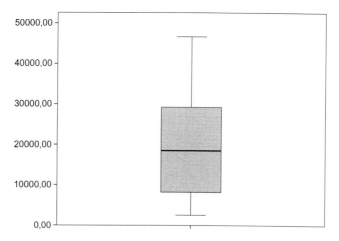

The boxplot diagram for *Gross domestic product per capita* in United Kingdom. (Source: Author's contribution based on SPSS 22 analysis)

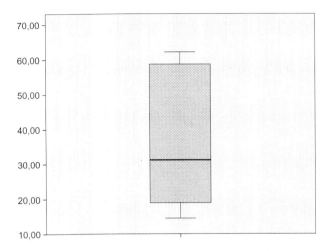

The boxplot chart for *participation rate in tertiary education* in the United Kingdom. (Source: Author's contribution based on the analysis of SPSS 22)

South Korea

The results of the descriptive and graphical analysis, for the dependent variable *Gross domestic product per inhabitant*, indicate a moderately asymmetrical distribution to the right, platykurtic. The independent variable *The participation rate in tertiary education* is moderately asymmetrical to the right and platykurtic. With a coefficient of variation of 0.85, we can say that the distribution of *Gross domestic product per inhabitant* in the period 1971–2013 is very little homogeneous, the arithmetic average not being representative. The distribution of *the participation rate in tertiary education* is very little homogeneous, for this the coefficient of variation being of 0.69.

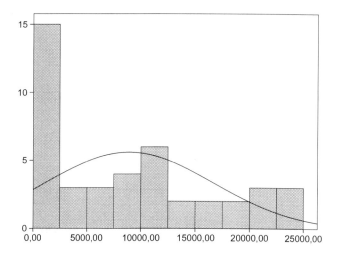

Distribution of *Gross domestic product per inhabitant* in South Korea in the period 1971–2013. (Source: Author's contribution based on the analysis of SPSS 22)

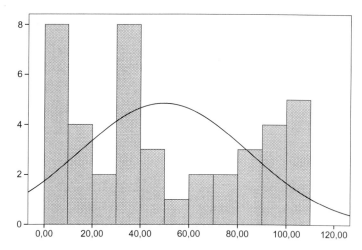

Distribution of the *participation rate in tertiary education* in South Korea in the period 1971–2012. (Source: Author's contribution based on the analysis of SPSS 22)

From the boxplot diagrams made it is noticed that there are no aberrant values in the distributions of the **Gross Domestic Product** per inhabitant and of the **Participation Rate in Tertiary Education** in South Korea during the analyzed period.

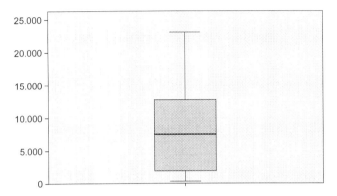

Boxplot diagrams for *Gross domestic product per capita* in South Korea. (Source: Author's contribution based on SPSS 22 analysis)

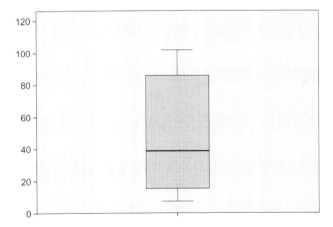

Boxplot diagram for *participation rate in tertiary education* in South Korea. (Source: Author's contribution based on SPSS 22 analysis)

Poland

The results of the descriptive and graphical analysis, for the dependent variable *Gross domestic product per inhabitant*, indicate a moderately asymmetrical distribution to the right, platykurtic. The independent variable *The participation rate in tertiary education* is moderately asymmetrical to the right and platykurtic. With a coefficient of variation of 0.88, it can be said that the distribution of *Gross domestic product per inhabitant* in the period 1971–2013 is very little homogeneous. The distribution of *The participation rate in tertiary education* is very little homogeneous, for this the coefficient of variation being of 0.62.

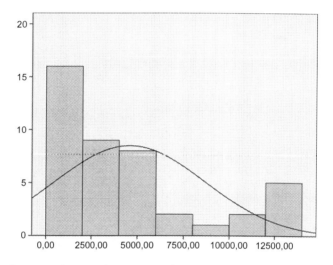

Distribution of *Gross domestic product per inhabitant* in Poland in the period 1971–2013. (Source: Author's contribution based on the analysis of SPSS 22)

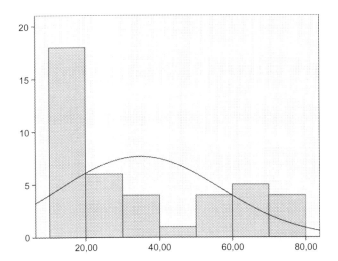

Distribution of the *participation rate in tertiary education* in Poland in the period 1971–2012. (Source: Author's contribution based on the analysis of SPSS)

From the boxplot diagram it can be seen that the values recorded after 2007 in the distribution of **Gross Domestic Product** per inhabitant in Poland are much higher compared to those found in the period 1971–2006. This is due to the process of decentralization that has been the example of a successful state effort. The reform facilitated the proper functioning of Polish democracy and economy and helped the country in the process of European integration. Another strength of Poland was the attraction and management of European funds, which were used as an investment engine for the Polish economy. The results achieved contributed to Poland's economic performance, to be the only country that was not affected by the recession during the crisis.

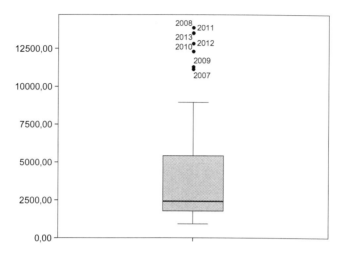

Boxplot diagram for *Gross domestic product* per inhabitant in Poland. (Source: Author's contribution on SPSS 22 analysis)

As regards to the distribution of the *participation rate in tertiary education*, in Poland, during the period under review, it can be said on the basis of the boxplot diagram that there are no aberrant values.

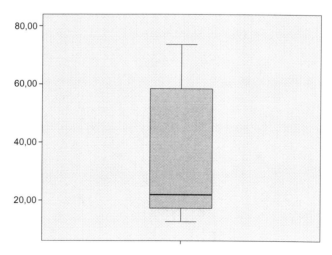

Boxplot diagram for *The participation rate in tertiary education* in Poland. (Source: Author's contribution based on the analysis of SPSS 22_

Romania

The results of the descriptive and graphical analysis, for the dependent variable *Gross domestic product per inhabitant*, indicate a moderately asymmetrical distribution to the right, platykurtic. The independent variable *The participation rate in tertiary education* is moderately asymmetrical to the right and platykurtic. With a coefficient of variation of 0.85, it can be said that the distribution of *Gross domestic product per inhabitant* in the period 1971–2013 is very little homogeneous. The distribution of *The participation rate in tertiary education* is very little homogeneous, for this the coefficient of variation being of 0.78.

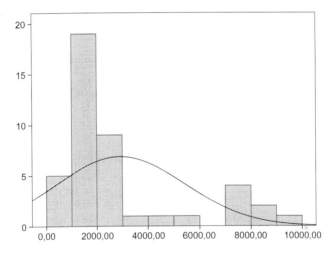

Distribution of *Gross domestic product* per inhabitant in Romania. (Source: Author's contribution based on SPSS 22 analysis)

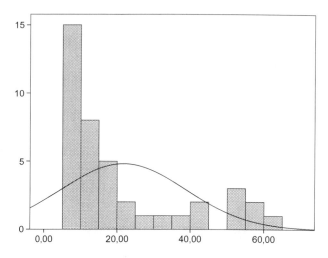

Distribution of *The participation rate in tertiary education* in Romania. (Source: Author's contribution based on the analysis of SPSS 22)

From the boxplot diagram made it can be seen that the values recorded since 2006, in the distribution of the **Gross Domestic Product per inhabitant**, in Romania are much higher compared to those found in the period 1971–2005. Possible arguments for recording these values would be summed up in the following aspects: 2007, Romania's integration into the EU, an important year in the evolution of the Romanian economy, when Romania was facing the greatest opportunity in its recent history; the need to align it with the evolving tendencies of Western society which have enabled it to benefit from the advantages of integration; the absorption of post-accession funds and the functioning of the structural instruments, which has been an important resource for strengthening a performing economy; the main factor of economic growth expressed in GDP, being domestic demand (in particular gross fixed capital formation), the increase in the volume of activity mainly in construction and services.

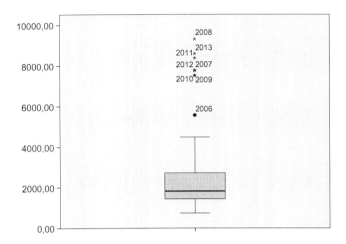

Distribution of *Gross domestic product* per inhabitant in Romania. (Source: Author's contribution based on the analysis of SPSS 22)

Regarding the distribution of the participation rate in tertiary education, in Romania, during the analyzed period, we can see on the basis of the boxing chart that there are extreme values in 2008 and 2009. The explanation for this dynamic is the high pace of GDP growth in this time frame. The economic expansion of that period supported the continuation of studies by enrolling in university study programs. The extreme values of the evolution of the number of students in the reference period can be mainly due to the very rapid establishment of private universities, which allowed them easier access to education, in parallel with the expansion of the number of study programs, an effect also favored by the lack of an adequate legislative framework.

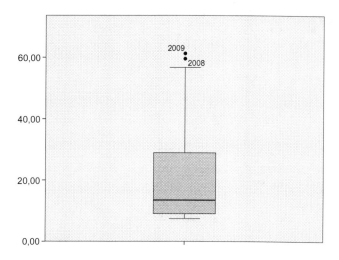

Boxplot diagram for *the participation rate in tertiary education* in Romania. (Source: Author's contribution based on the analysis of SPSS 22)

Sweden
The results of the descriptive and graphical analysis, for the dependent variable *Gross domestic product per inhabitant*, indicate a moderately asymmetrical distribution to the right, platykurtic. The independent variable *The participation rate in tertiary education* is moderately asymmetrical to the right and platykurtic.

The distribution of the *Gross domestic product per inhabitant* in the period 1971–2013 is less homogeneous, the arithmetic mean not being representative, the coefficient of variation being of 0.57. The distribution of *The participation rate in tertiary education* has a low homogeneity, for this the coefficient of variation being of 0.44.

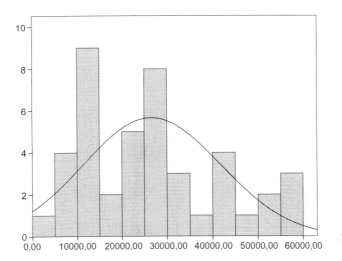

Distribution of *Gross domestic product per inhabitant* in Sweden.
(Source: Author's contribution based on the analysis of SPSS 22)

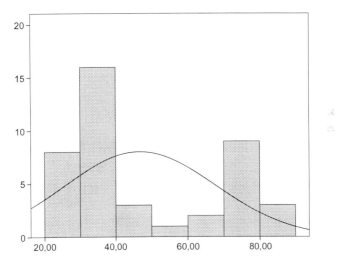

Distribution of *the participation rate in tertiary education* in Sweden.
(Source: Author's contribution based on the analysis of SPSS 22)

In order to identify the aberrant values in the distributions of the two analyzed variables, we built the boxplot charts. From these diagrams we can see that no outliers are recorded in any series of statistical data.

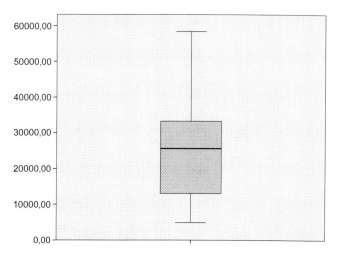

Boxplot diagram for *Gross domestic product per capita* of SPSS 22. (Source: Author's contribution based on the analysis of SPSS 22)

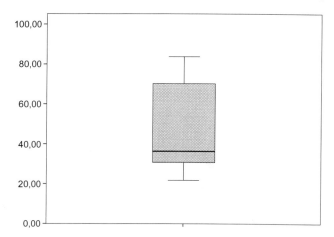

Boxplot diagram for *the participation rate in tertiary education* in Sweden. (Source: Author's contribution based on the analysis of SPSS 22)

Annex 11: Public Expenditure on Higher Education (ISCED 5–8) as a Percentage of GDP

The share of public expenditures for education in the Gross Domestic Product (GDP) of a certain financial year. It highlights the proportion of the annual national financial achievement allocated by the Government to the development of education. Calculation method: divide the amount of total public expenditure for education by the Gross Domestic Product of a certain financial year and multiply by 100.

Country	2000	2001	2002	2003	2004	2005	2006	2007	2008	2009
1. Poland	0.72	0.83	1.05	1.02	1.14	1.18	0.95	0.93	1.04	1.05
2. Hungary	1.02	1.04	1.10	1.20	1.00	1.01	1.01	1.01	1.00	1.09
3. Czechia	0.69	0.72	0.79	0.85	0.86	0.81	1.12	0.98	0.88	0.96
4. Slovakia	0.71	0.81	0.86	0.83	0.96	0.79	0.88	0.77	0.76	0.79
5. Slovenia	...	1.25	1.25	1.27	1.28	1.23	1.22	1.19	1.19	1.35
6. Estonia	...	1.02	1.07	1.02	0.85	0.91	...	1.02	1.09	1.31
7. Latvia	0.86	0.85	0.86	0.70	0.65	...	0.84	0.86	0.93	0.77
8. Lithuania	...	1.33	1.39	0.99	1.06	1.02	0.99	1.00	1.03	1.13
9. Cyprus	0.85	0.66	0.81	1.42	1.35	1.44	1.49	1.46	1.68	1.86
10. Malta	...	...	0.85	...	0.49	...	...	0.90	0.97	1.11
11. Romania	...	0.78	0.70	0.70	0.70	0.81	0.90	1.09	1.13	1.13
12. Bulgaria	...	0.54	0.51	0.79	0.49	0.69	0.67	0.61	0.82	0.88
13. Croatia	0.92	...	0.73	0.72	0.69	...	...	0.79	0.94	0.83
14. Austria	1.40	1.32	1.25	1.26	1.39	1.43	1.42	1.43	1.43	1.50
15. Finland	1.94	1.92	1.95	1.98	1.98	1.92	1.88	1.78	1.81	2.05
16. Sweden	1.83	1.85	1.96	1.96	1.90	1.79	1.71	1.63	1.71	1.90
17. Spain	0.91	0.94	0.94	0.97	0.95	0.93	0.93	0.97	1.05	1.12
18. Portugal	0.94	0.98	0.91	0.95	0.83	0.92	0.93	1.12	0.91	1.03
19. Greece	0.78	1.03	1.11	1.06	1.27	1.43	...	...	...	...
20. Denmark	2.43	2.64	2.63	2.44	2.45	2.32	2.19	2.22	2.12	2.34
21. Ireland	1.25	1.17	1.13	1.05	1.05	1.05	1.09	1.10	1.27	1.46
22. United Kingdom	0.71	0.71	0.96	0.95	0.92	1.10	1.00	0.86	0.77	0.73
23. Netherlands	...	...	...	...	...	...	...	...	...	...
24. Belgium	...	...	...	...	...	1.26	...	...	1.35	1.45
25. Germany	...	...	...	...	...	...	1.08	1.11	1.18	1.30
26. France	...	...	...	...	...	...	...	...	...	...
27. Italy	0.79	0.76	0.82	0.75	0.74	0.73	0.77	0.73	0.80	0.83
28. Luxembourg	...	...	...	...	...	...	...	...	...	...

ᵃ Continued on the next page

Country	2010	2011	2012	2013	2014	2015	2016	2017	2018
1. Poland	1.15	1.10	0.72	1.22	1.19	1.22	1.06	1.08	1.06
2. Hungary	0.95	1.07	1.02	0.90	0.76	0.64	0.74	0.79	0.81
3. Czechia	0.91	1.09	0.69	0.87	0.79	0.77	0.70	0.70	0.92
4. Slovakia	0.80	0.92	0.71	0.96	0.97	1.38	0.83	0.79	0.76
5. Slovenia	1.33	1.34	...	1.11	1.05	0.98	0.95	0.95	1.01
6. Estonia	1.19	1.25	...	1.36	1.48	1.38	1.39	1.13	1.18
7. Latvia	0.80	1.01	0.86	1.35	1.13	1.17	0.75	0.69	0.74
8. Lithuania	1.25	1.46	...	1.32	1.33	1.18	0.82	0.75	0.79
9. Cyprus	1.34	1.34	0.85	1.45	1.34	1.31	1.28	1.16	...
10. Malta	1.43	1.07	...	1.46	1.35	1.27	1.37	1.21	...
11. Romania	0.99	0.85	...	0.72	0.68	0.66	0.71	0.72	0.75
12. Bulgaria	0.57	0.61	...	0.65	...	...	...	0.81	...
13. Croatia	0.78	0.92	0.92	1.00	...	...	...	0.86	...
14. Austria	1.58	1.50	1.40	1.79	1.77	1.78	1.78	1.71	1.70
15. Finland	2.07	2.06	1.94	2.00	1.98	1.88	1.82	1.65	1.54
16. Sweden	1.89	1.85	1.83	1.93	1.91	1.85	1.84	1.79	1.79
17. Spain	1.14	1.15	0.91	0.98	0.97	0.96	0.92	0.93	0.92
18. Portugal	1.09	1.01	0.94	0.90	0.91	0.89	...	0.80	0.78
19. Greece	...	...	0.78	...	...	0.73	...	0.63	0.67
20. Denmark	2.34	2.37	2.43	2.28	2.34	...	...	2.43	2.20
21. Ireland	1.34	1.27	1.25	1.15	1.02	0.88	0.73	0.96	0.91
22. United Kingdom	0.93	1.23	0.71	1.33	1.36	1.27	1.39	1.45	1.45
23. Netherlands	...	...	...	...	...	1.61	1.75	1.59	1.71
24. Belgium	1.43	1.41	...	1.45	1.48	1.43	1.44	1.45	1.49
25. Germany	1.34	1.36	...	1.27	1.28	1.26	1.26	1.25	1.27
26. France	...	...	...	...	...	...	...	1.23	1.23
27. Italy	0.81	0.80	0.79	0.81	0.80	0.76	0.73	0.75	0.77
28. Luxembourg	...	...	...	0.55	0.51	0.51	...	0.46	0.40

Source http://data.uis.unesco.org/?queryid=181, accessed on 31.05.2022

ANNEX 12: (A) EU-WIDE UNIVERSITY GRADUATES (2000–2012)

GEO/TIME	2000	2005	2007	2008	2009	2010	2011	2012
Belgium	100	100	100	100	100	100	100	100
Agricultural Sciences and Veterinary Medicine	2.25	2.52	27.50	2.52	2.74	2.62	2.39	2.37
Engineering, production, and construction	11.77	10.38	9.45	9.40	10.04	10.67	10.44	10.53
Health and well-being	19.20	16.68	19.36	19.75	19.68	21.39	22.35	23.28
Humanities and arts	10.97	10.39	10.87	10.51	10.40	10.03	10.44	9.96
Science, Mathematics, and IT	9.17	6.17	6.52	6.63	5.91	5.78	5.19	5.22
Services	1.80	1.11	1.91	1.61	1.46	1.55	1.82	1.84
Social Sciences, Business Administration, and Law	33.48	31.67	29.54	29.75	29.67	29.40	29.43	29.00
Education Sciences and Continuing Education	11.28	12.86	12.34	11.37	11.00	11.32	11.44	11.43
Others	0.06	8.23	7.52	8.46	9.10	7.24	6.51	6.37
Bulgaria								
Agricultural Sciences and Veterinary Medicine	2.2	2.3	2.5	2.4	2.3	2.4	2.4	2.3
Engineering, production, and construction	20.1	21.2	19.7	19.5	19.6	18.7	18.8	19.2
Health and well-being	6.4	6.0	6.2	6.5	6.7	6.9	7.3	7.6
Humanities and arts	9.0	8.4	7.9	7.8	7.7	7.7	7.9	7.6
Science, Mathematics, and IT	4.6	5.4	5.1	5.0	4.9	5.1	5.2	5.3
Services	6.7	6.9	8.0	7.9	8.0	8.3	8.5	8.5
Social Sciences, Business Administration, and Law	40.3	42.3	44.0	45.0	44.1	42.8	41.3	40.5

(continued)

(continued)

GEO/TIME	2000	2005	2007	2008	2009	2010	2011	2012
Education Sciences and Continuing Education	10.6	7.3	6.4	5.7	5.5	5.5	5.9	6.6
Others	0.1	0.2	0.2	0.2	1.1	2.7	2.7	2.3
Czech Republic								
Agricultural Sciences and Veterinary Medicine	4.0	3.8	3.7	3.6	3.7	3.7	3.7	3.8
Engineering, production, and construction	16.1	19.7	14.2	15.7	14.7	14.2	13.8	13.5
Health and well-being	12.5	9.8	11.9	10.3	10.2	10.4	10.7	11.1
Humanities and arts	8.2	9.5	8.7	8.7	8.8	8.9	8.9	9.3
Science, Mathematics, and IT	13.3	9.5	8.7	10.8	10.8	11.0	11.2	11.4
Services	3.2	4.5	4.1	4.9	5.1	5.2	5.3	5.2
Social Sciences, Business Administration, and Law	23.6	28.1	28.6	31.2	32.7	33.4	32.3	31.9
Education Sciences and Continuing Education	12.0	14.7	12.7	13.3	12.7	12.4	12.1	12.0
Others	7.2	0.5	7.4	1.5	1.2	0.9	1.9	1.7
Denmark								
Agricultural Sciences and Veterinary Medicine	1.9	1.4	1.5	1.5	1.4	1.5	1.5	1.5
Engineering, production, and construction	10.0	10.3	10.1	9.8	9.6	10.0	10.6	10.8
Health and well-being	24.0	22.0	22.0	21.5	21.6	21.1	20.8	20.8
Humanities and arts	17.5	15.0	15.3	15.3	14.6	14.1	12.8	12.7
Science, Mathematics, and IT	10.2	8.2	8.7	8.2	8.7	8.6	8.5	8.3
Services	2.0	2.0	2.2	2.2	2.1	2.3	2.5	2.4
Social Sciences, Business Administration, and Law	23.4	29.8	29.0	30.4	31.2	31.9	33.6	33.9

Education Sciences and Continuing Education	11.0	11.2	11.3	11.2	10.7	10.4	9.8	9.6
Others	a	a	a	a	a	a	a	a
Germany								
Agricultural Sciences and Veterinary Medicine	1.5	1.4	1.5	1.5	1.4	1.4	1.5	1.5
Engineering, production, and construction	15.8	15.7	15.5	15.8	15.4	16.4	17.8	18.3
Health and well-being	16.3	14.7	14.5	14.4	18.3	17.9	17.2	16.4
Humanities and arts	16.5	15.7	15.5	15.2	14.0	13.7	13.3	12.9
Science, Mathematics, and IT	12.7	15.0	15.3	15.2	14.3	14.2	14.3	14.5
Services	2.3	2.5	3.1	3.0	2.8	2.8	2.7	2.6
Social Sciences, Business Administration, and Law	26.9	27.5	27.4	27.5	26.3	26.2	25.7	25.9
Education Sciences and Continuing Education	7.8	7.3	7.1	7.2	7.4	7.1	7.4	7.7
Others	0.2	0.0	0.1	0.2	0.2	0.2	0.2	0.2
Estonia								
Agricultural Sciences and Veterinary Medicine	2.5	2.6	2.4	2.3	2.2	2.2	2.3	2.2
Engineering, production, and construction	13.8	12.2	13.1	13.0	13.3	13.4	14.4	14.8
Health and well-being	8.9	8.8	8.3	8.2	8.3	9.1	9.3	9.7
Humanities and arts	11.7	11.3	11.4	12.1	12.3	13.6	13.7	13.6
Science, Mathematics, and IT	7.5	10.4	9.9	9.6	9.5	10.4	11.2	11.5
Services	5.9	8.6	8.1	7.9	7.8	8.0	8.0	7.9
Social Sciences, Business Administration, and Law	40.8	38.1	39.8	40.2	39.6	36.4	33.8	32.8
Education Sciences and Continuing Education	9.0	8.1	6.9	6.7	7.0	6.8	7.4	7.5

(continued)

(continued)

GEO/TIME	2000	2005	2007	2008	2009	2010	2011	2012
Others	a	a	a	a	a	a	a	a
Ireland								
Agricultural Sciences and Veterinary Medicine	1.2	1.3	1.2	1.3	1.4	1.5	1.6	1.7
Engineering, production, and construction	11.4	10.3	10.3	12.8	12.6	12.5	11.8	11.7
Health and well-being	7.7	11.5	13.1	15.6	15.6	15.3	15.9	17.2
Humanities and arts	15.1	16.9	14.7	15.7	16.0	16.3	13.1	17.1
Science, Mathematics, and IT	16.9	12.3	11.0	12.5	12.9	14.0	14.4	16.4
Services	3.3	4.2	4.9	5.2	5.0	3.9	4.3	4.2
Social Sciences, Business Administration, and Law	20.4	21.8	22.0	29.8	27.4	26.4	24.8	25.4
Education Sciences and Continuing Education	4.1	5.0	5.6	6.4	6.7	6.1	5.5	5.4
Others	20.0	16.6	17.2	0.6	2.5	4.1	8.7	0.8
Greece								
Agricultural Sciences and Veterinary Medicine	a	5.9	5.8	5.8	a	4.8	4.7	4.5
Engineering, production, and construction	a	16.5	17.0	17.0	a	17.9	18.0	17.6
Health and well-being	a	6.9	9.6	9.2	a	7.8	7.8	7.9
Humanities and arts	a	11.6	13.5	14.0	a	12.4	13.6	14.3
Science, Mathematics, and IT	a	15.7	13.6	13.6	a	13.4	14.4	15.0
Services	a	5.0	3.1	3.6	a	2.6	2.8	2.8
Social Sciences, Business Administration, and Law	a	31.9	31.8	31.4	a	32.2	31.7	31.5
Education Sciences and Continuing Education	a	6.5	5.7	5.3	a	5.7	6.3	6.3

Others	[a]	[a]	[a]	[a]	[a]	3.1	0.7	0.1
Spain								
Agricultural Sciences and Veterinary Medicine	3.3	2.3	2.0	1.9	1.8	1.7	1.6	1.5
Engineering, production, and construction	16.1	17.6	17.6	17.7	17.5	17.3	17.7	16.9
Health and well-being	8.6	10.9	11.7	12.3	12.5	12.6	12.7	12.8
Humanities and arts	10.7	10.5	10.3	10.4	10.4	10.6	11.0	11.0
Science, Mathematics, and IT	12.6	12.2	10.5	9.9	10.4	9.1	9.8	9.5
Services	3.4	5.4	5.6	5.8	4.9	5.8	5.3	5.5
Social Sciences, Business Administration, and Law	36.8	32.2	31.6	31.7	31.8	31.4	31.2	31.6
Education Sciences and Continuing Education	8.3	8.6	9.2	9.8	9.9	10.9	10.7	11.1
Others	0.2	0.3	1.4	0.5	0.8	0.5	0.0	[a]
France								
Agricultural Sciences and Veterinary Medicine	[a]	[a]	1.05	1.17	1.11	1.19	1.19	1.11
Engineering, production, and construction	[a]	[a]	12.82	13.04	12.94	13.20	13.24	13.39
Health and well-being	[a]	[a]	15.10	15.59	15.92	15.95	16.03	15.98
Humanities and arts	[a]	[a]	16.04	15.43	14.73	14.17	13.55	13.43
Science, Mathematics, and IT	[a]	[a]	12.38	12.27	12.52	12.31	12.21	11.58
Services	[a]	[a]	3.35	3.31	3.36	3.39	3.36	3.41
Social Sciences, Business Administration, and Law	[a]	[a]	35.59	36.14	36.50	37.22	36.65	38.13
Education Sciences and Continuing Education	[a]	[a]	2.82	2.68	2.57	2.40	2.48	2.54
Others	[a]	[a]	0.84	0.36	0.34	0.17	1.29	0.43

(continued)

(continued)

GEO/TIME	2000	2005	2007	2008	2009	2010	2011	2012
Croatia								
Agricultural Sciences and Veterinary Medicine	a	3.61	3.80	3.84	3.82	4.23	3.75	3.86
Engineering, production, and construction	a	16.26	15.73	15.43	15.87	15.32	15.27	15.76
Health and well-being	a	7.45	6.99	7.15	7.29	8.42	9.00	9.35
Humanities and arts	a	9.33	9.74	9.52	9.02	9.54	9.58	9.54
Science, Mathematics, and IT Services	a	7.64	7.75	7.92	7.98	6.80	8.21	8.52
	a	13.47	10.16	9.87	8.82	8.82	7.69	8.68
Social Sciences, Business Administration, and Law	a	37.42	41.73	41.85	42.95	42.21	42.20	40.27
Education Sciences and Continuing Education	a	4.82	4.09	4.42	4.23	4.68	4.31	4.02
Others	a	a	a	a	a	a	a	a
Italy								
Agricultural Sciences and Veterinary Medicine	2.1	2.3	2.3	2.1	2.2	2.1	2.2	2.3
Engineering, production, and construction	16.8	15.9	15.6	15.3	15.4	15.7	17.7	16.3
Health and well-being	10.9	12.5	12.9	13.1	13.2	11.6	13.1	15.0
Humanities and arts	15.9	15.7	15.3	13.4	15.0	14.5	12.9	14.6
Science, Mathematics, and IT Services	7.6	7.7	7.9	7.6	7.7	7.7	8.1	8.0
	0.8	2.5	2.7	2.8	2.8	2.8	3.4	2.8
Social Sciences, Business Administration, and Law	40.3	36.7	35.6	35.1	34.8	33.8	34.8	34.0
Education Sciences and Continuing Education	5.5	6.5	7.3	6.7	6.5	4.7	7.0	5.5
Others	0.2	0.3	0.4	3.9	2.4	7.2	0.9	1.3

Cyprus								
Agricultural Sciences and Veterinary Medicine	0.2	0.1	0.1	0.1	0.2	0.3	0.5	0.5
Engineering, production, and construction	6.4	5.0	6.8	7.7	8.8	9.8	10.8	12.0
Health and well-being	6.1	4.7	6.1	6.5	6.7	7.1	7.6	7.9
Humanities and arts	8.9	8.7	9.5	10.4	10.3	10.1	10.4	10.9
Science, Mathematics, and IT	11.1	12.8	11.9	9.8	8.8	8.5	8.7	8.8
Services	17.6	13.8	6.1	7.1	5.9	4.3	4.5	4.7
Social Sciences, Business Administration, and Law	35.3	43.9	49.9	49.5	51.5	51.7	48.6	45.6
Education Sciences and Continuing Education	13.5	10.3	9.7	8.9	7.7	8.2	9.0	9.5
Others	0.90	0.61	a	a	a	a	a	a
Latvia								
Agricultural Sciences and Veterinary Medicine	1.8	1.5	1.1	1.0	1.0	1.1	1.2	1.3
Engineering, production, and construction	10.2	9.5	10.4	11.0	11.3	12.6	13.8	14.5
Health and well-being	4.2	4.7	6.3	6.9	7.2	8.1	10.2	10.4
Humanities and arts	7.7	6.6	7.2	7.5	7.5	8.4	8.9	9.3
Science, Mathematics, and IT	6.3	5.2	5.1	4.8	4.9	5.5	6.1	6.6
Services	3.3	4.4	5.6	5.9	6.1	6.1	7.0	7.9
Social Sciences, Business Administration, and Law	46.9	54.5	53.7	53.7	52.9	49.9	46.0	43.3
Education Sciences and Continuing Education	19.5	13.6	10.5	9.2	9.0	8.2	6.8	6.7
Others	a	a	0.08	0.08	0.06	0.03	0.03	a

(continued)

(continued)

GEO/TIME	2000	2005	2007	2008	2009	2010	2011	2012
Lithuania								
Agricultural Sciences and Veterinary Medicine	4.33	2.33	2.19	2.11	2.03	1.91	1.94	2.17
Engineering, production, and construction	22.37	18.62	18.20	17.96	17.99	17.05	16.70	16.66
Health and well-being	8.39	8.86	8.43	8.57	8.52	8.84	9.65	10.42
Humanities and arts	8.31	7.00	7.13	7.12	7.14	7.29	7.43	7.62
Science, Mathematics, and IT	5.03	6.24	5.88	5.50	5.21	5.07	5.25	5.47
Services	4.93	2.90	3.12	3.13	2.96	2.89	2.96	3.05
Social Sciences, Business Administration, and Law	30.73	41.23	42.82	44.64	45.95	46.46	46.43	45.53
Education Sciences and Continuing Education	15.92	12.82	12.23	10.97	10.20	10.48	9.63	9.07
Others	a	a	a	a	a	a	a	a
Luxembourg								
Agricultural Sciences and Veterinary Medicine	a	a	a	a	a	a	a	0.41
Engineering, production, and construction	8.12	a	a	a	a	a	8.05	7.21
Health and well-being	6.57	a	a	a	a	a	4.54	7.35
Humanities and arts	11.33	a	a	a	a	a	12.03	11.18
Science, Mathematics, and IT	9.31	a	a	a	a	a	11.22	11.01
Services	a	a	a	a	a	a	a	a
Social Sciences, Business Administration, and Law	44.89	a	a	a	a	a	47.25	46.34
Education Sciences and Continuing Education	19.78	a	a	a	a	a	16.72	16.50
Others	a	a	a	a	a	a	0.19	a

Hungary								
Agricultural Sciences and Veterinary Medicine	3.94	3.08	2.69	2.54	2.40	2.38	2.39	2.45
Engineering, production, and construction	17.79	12.38	11.46	12.45	13.24	14.02	14.90	15.19
Health and well-being	8.06	7.64	8.82	8.94	9.09	9.30	9.44	9.69
Humanities and arts	8.93	7.82	8.63	9.12	9.71	9.62	9.34	9.08
Science, Mathematics, and IT	3.71	5.45	6.88	6.88	6.99	7.07	7.21	7.35
Services	3.49	7.94	9.14	9.15	9.93	10.54	10.36	10.02
Social Sciences, Business Administration, and Law	37.54	42.68	40.60	40.90	41.04	40.44	39.83	39.44
Education Sciences and Continuing Education	16.54	13.02	11.78	10.02	7.61	6.62	6.53	6.78
Others	a	a	a	a	a	a	a	a
Malta								
Agricultural Sciences and Veterinary Medicine	0.25	0.76	0.09	0.46	0.28	0.23	0.22	0.27
Engineering, production, and construction	6.51	7.81	7.88	7.79	8.88	9.44	8.95	8.19
Health and well-being	19.32	14.51	17.62	17.50	20.92	11.60	18.14	20.37
Humanities and arts	10.20	13.45	16.21	17.91	17.49	18.07	17.59	13.23
Science, Mathematics, and IT	5.02	5.94	10.28	9.42	7.42	16.37	11.08	12.67
Services	0.24	0.22	1.89	1.39	1.28	1.19	1.27	1.98
Social Sciences, Business Administration, and Law	34.55	41.60	35.41	34.98	33.16	33.15	32.71	33.16
Education Sciences and Continuing Education	23.91	15.71	10.62	10.55	10.56	9.95	10.03	10.11
Others	a	a	a	a	a	a	a	a

(*continued*)

(continued)

GEO/TIME	2000	2005	2007	2008	2009	2010	2011	2012
The Netherlands								
Agricultural Sciences and Veterinary Medicine	2.00	1.58	1.16	1.09	1.06	1.05	1.10	1.06
Engineering, production, and construction	10.71	7.87	8.10	8.11	8.37	8.03	7.66	7.87
Health and well-being	16.53	15.80	16.86	16.94	17.14	16.93	17.76	17.43
Humanities and arts	7.82	7.88	8.53	8.45	8.33	8.32	8.57	8.00
Science, Mathematics, and IT	5.85	7.58	6.52	6.23	6.08	6.16	6.23	6.49
Services	2.40	3.02	6.19	6.24	6.28	6.35	6.51	6.67
Social Sciences, Business Administration, and Law	40.18	39.85	37.50	37.30	37.70	38.19	39.30	38.82
Education Sciences and Continuing Education	13.10	14.82	14.64	13.88	13.22	13.04	11.76	11.25
Others	1.41	0.28	0.51	1.76	1.84	1.94	1.10	2.40
Austria								
Agricultural Sciences and Veterinary Medicine	1.95	1.53	1.14	1.29	1.25	1.32	1.34	1.30
Engineering, production, and construction	13.96	12.14	12.71	13.90	14.67	14.70	14.48	14.56
Health and well-being	8.30	9.44	7.89	9.60	8.87	7.89	7.57	7.57
Humanities and arts	11.83	13.74	15.44	14.37	13.67	13.42	12.89	12.51
Science, Mathematics, and IT	11.56	11.99	11.98	11.65	11.19	10.99	10.96	10.93
Services	1.18	2.00	1.82	2.06	2.45	2.41	2.37	2.37
Social Sciences, Business Administration, and Law	39.97	35.88	36.45	36.24	36.65	37.15	36.54	35.56
Education Sciences and Continuing Education	11.07	13.24	12.37	10.67	11.07	11.91	13.63	14.96
Others	0.18	0.04	0.20	0.23	0.18	0.20	0.22	0.24

Poland

Agricultural Sciences and Veterinary Medicine	2.34	2.08	2.19	2.09	2.02	1.90	1.76	1.69
Engineering, production, and construction	13.79	11.73	12.57	12.39	12.99	13.18	13.97	14.75
Health and well-being	2.36	3.88	6.06	6.60	7.18	7.72	8.11	8.53
Humanities and arts	9.52	8.53	10.16	10.11	9.50	9.15	9.13	9.03
Science, Mathematics, and IT	4.26	8.25	9.46	8.94	8.45	8.05	7.95	8.00
Services	4.86	6.50	5.64	5.92	6.26	6.73	7.35	8.13
Social Sciences, Business Administration, and Law	43.41	39.85	40.31	40.33	40.75	39.69	38.28	36.88
Education Sciences and Continuing Education	12.65	12.74	13.60	13.62	12.85	13.58	13.46	12.99
Others	6.80	6.44	a	a	a	a	a	a

Portugal

Agricultural Sciences and Veterinary Medicine	3.09	2.04	1.89	2.06	1.90	1.83	1.83	1.85
Engineering, production, and construction	17.93	21.81	22.31	22.30	22.16	22.07	21.64	21.95
Health and well-being	7.56	14.49	16.52	16.55	16.73	16.30	16.15	15.88
Humanities and arts	8.00	8.57	8.48	8.71	8.62	8.91	9.28	9.55
Science, Mathematics, and IT	9.42	7.61	7.29	7.52	7.35	7.32	7.23	7.25
Services	4.06	5.47	5.72	5.78	6.28	6.38	6.42	6.43
Social Sciences, Business Administration, and Law	35.59	31.36	31.96	31.94	31.98	31.78	31.82	31.26
Education Sciences and Continuing Education	14.36	8.64	5.83	5.14	4.97	5.41	5.62	5.73
Others	a	a	a	a	a	a	a	0.10

(*continued*)

(continued)

GEO/TIME	2000	2005	2007	2008	2009	2010	2011	2012
Romania								
Agricultural Sciences and Veterinary Medicine	3.94	2.95	2.73	2.18	2.01	2.14	2.21	2.62
Engineering, production, and construction	21.86	20.33	17.15	16.46	16.97	17.86	20.11	22.78
Health and well-being	7.28	6.28	5.56	6.38	6.39	7.51	9.18	10.79
Humanities and arts	10.84	10.60	9.92	8.46	7.84	7.81	8.11	8.52
Science, Mathematics, and IT	5.58	4.70	6.23	5.59	4.90	4.85	5.18	5.84
Services	3.20	3.11	4.26	3.18	3.18	3.26	4.19	4.49
Social Sciences, Business Administration, and Law	41.92	47.08	51.02	56.04	57.26	54.96	49.00	42.95
Education Sciences and Continuing Education	1.19	2.22	2.47	1.71	1.45	1.60	2.01	2.02
Others	4.17	2.73	0.65	a	a	a	a	a
Slovenia								
Agricultural Sciences and Veterinary Medicine	3.12	3.18	3.20	3.31	3.31	3.21	3.21	3.12
Engineering, production, and construction	18.43	15.82	16.71	18.15	19.05	18.92	19.52	19.26
Health and well-being	7.28	7.16	7.23	7.55	8.12	8.71	9.95	10.71
Humanities and arts	6.89	7.63	7.78	8.11	8.17	8.33	8.47	8.67
Science, Mathematics, and IT	5.04	5.37	5.56	5.91	6.18	6.69	7.03	7.48
Services	6.50	7.93	9.49	9.61	9.50	9.29	9.47	9.21
Social Sciences, Business Administration, and Law	41.98	43.85	41.67	39.30	37.97	37.45	34.66	33.62
Education Sciences and Continuing Education	10.75	9.07	8.37	8.05	7.71	7.40	7.69	7.94
Others	a	a	a	a	a	a	a	a

Slovakia

Agricultural Sciences and Veterinary Medicine	4.41	3.18	2.59	2.56	2.29	2.13	2.21	2.21
Engineering, production, and construction	20.76	17.37	15.66	14.98	14.67	14.97	15.20	14.78
Health and well-being	10.66	13.95	16.20	17.58	17.95	18.18	17.24	17.78
Humanities and arts	6.15	5.72	6.21	6.50	6.57	6.91	7.31	7.52
Science, Mathematics, and IT	7.30	9.05	8.95	8.45	8.57	8.37	8.51	8.42
Services	8.00	6.76	5.55	5.59	6.02	6.17	6.25	6.24
Social Sciences, Business Administration, and Law	25.55	27.53	29.39	29.31	30.12	30.74	30.96	30.56
Education Sciences and Continuing Education	17.19	16.44	15.46	15.03	13.80	12.52	12.32	12.50
Others	a	a	a	a	a	a	a	a

Finland

Agricultural Sciences and Veterinary Medicine	2.35	2.26	2.23	2.25	2.24	2.21	2.21	2.20
Engineering, production, and construction	25.62	26.41	25.44	24.94	25.21	24.89	23.92	24.07
Health and well-being	14.17	12.93	13.71	14.25	15.25	15.58	16.19	16.49
Humanities and arts	14.59	14.48	14.61	14.63	14.46	14.27	14.14	13.78
Science, Mathematics, and IT	10.59	11.59	11.20	10.92	10.39	10.21	10.14	9.86
Services	3.97	4.70	4.91	4.95	5.11	5.06	5.36	5.42
Social Sciences, Business Administration, and Law	23.22	22.34	22.73	22.90	22.49	22.79	23.02	23.17
Education Sciences and Continuing Education	5.48	5.29	5.16	5.16	4.86	4.98	5.02	5.02
Others	0.006291985	a	a	a	a	a	a	8

(continued)

(continued)

GEO/TIME	2000	2005	2007	2008	2009	2010	2011	2012
Sweden								
Agricultural Sciences and Veterinary Medicine	0.91	0.80	0.94	0.99	0.96	0.98	0.99	1.01
Engineering, production, and construction	19.11	16.42	16.09	15.81	16.24	16.67	16.71	16.56
Health and well-being	15.88	16.86	17.67	18.22	17.93	17.22	17.28	17.74
Humanities and arts	12.86	12.94	12.49	13.10	13.72	13.58	13.45	13.45
Science, Mathematics, and IT	11.45	9.50	9.40	8.90	8.86	8.63	9.17	9.34
Services	1.61	1.72	1.96	2.08	2.26	2.48	2.52	2.40
Social Sciences, Business Administration, and Law	25.46	26.46	26.25	26.11	26.39	27.18	27.00	27.11
Education Sciences and Continuing Education	12.54	15.12	15.00	14.61	13.41	13.21	12.84	12.32
Others	0.19	0.18	0.20	0.18	0.22	0.06	0.05	0.07
The United Kingdom								
Agricultural Sciences and Veterinary Medicine	1.04	0.85	0.91	0.97	0.97	0.98	1.06	1.07
Engineering, production, and construction	8.81	8.10	8.42	8.18	8.32	8.49	8.50	8.43
Health and well-being	13.25	18.50	16.03	18.19	17.97	17.75	17.58	17.57
Humanities and arts	13.87	16.71	17.08	16.81	16.10	16.14	16.11	16.49
Science, Mathematics, and IT	14.77	14.19	13.39	12.91	12.94	13.33	13.48	13.71
Services	a	0.63	3.13	1.63	1.68	1.69	1.74	1.72
Social Sciences, Business Administration, and Law	23.48	26.86	26.93	26.55	26.90	27.56	27.76	28.36
Education Sciences and Continuing Education	6.61	8.78	9.16	8.68	8.99	8.98	8.87	8.02
Others	18.17	5.38	4.96	6.09	6.12	5.09	4.91	4.63

European Union 28

Agricultural Sciences and Veterinary Medicine	2.09	1.91	1.88	1.83	1.78	1.77	1.76
Engineering, production, and construction [a]	14.44	14.03	14.09	14.17	14.44	14.99	15.01
Health and well-being [a]	11.84	12.52	13.00	13.64	13.59	13.98	14.35
Humanities and arts [a]	12.42	13.03	12.60	12.36	12.20	11.99	12.23
Science, Mathematics, and IT [a]	10.47	10.53	10.23	10.12	10.03	10.29	10.43
Services [a]	3.76	4.16	4.01	3.95	4.07	4.20	4.22
Social Sciences, Business Administration, and Law [a]	33.54	33.91	34.46	34.47	34.06	33.31	32.85
Education Sciences and Continuing Education [a]	9.22	8.48	8.19	7.99	7.96	8.22	8.04
Others [a]	2.18	1.43	1.54	1.47	1.87	1.25	1.11

Source: http://ec.europa.eu/eurostat/web/education-and-training/statistics-illustrated

ANNEX 12: (B) EU-WIDE UNIVERSITY GRADUATES (2013–2020)—ISCED 2011 FIELDS OF STUDY

Country	2013	2014	2015	2016	2017	2018	2019	2020
Austria	100.00	100.00	100.00	100.00	100.00	100.00	100.00	100.00
Education	10.90	11.46	12.71	12.24	12.92	11.58	11.30	11.92
Arts and humanities	10.65	8.67	9.01	7.49	7.84	8.08	7.65	7.21
Social sciences, journalism, and information	8.49	8.20	10.15	11.34	9.40	7.25	7.52	7.58
Business, administration, and law	24.57	23.59	21.62	21.73	22.88	24.35	24.04	24.29
Natural sciences, mathematics, and statistics	5.11	5.29	5.58	5.75	5.79	6.08	5.92	5.56
Information and Communication Technologies	4.22	4.45	4.02	4.05	3.94	4.39	4.48	4.36
Engineering, manufacturing, and construction	19.12	21.15	19.68	20.49	20.10	20.57	21.00	20.66
Agriculture, forestry, fisheries, and veterinary	1.51	1.64	1.62	1.65	1.66	1.60	1.59	1.46
Health and welfare	–	–	6.65	7.35	7.47	8.42	8.71	8.83
Services	8.73	8.95	8.88	7.84	7.88	7.56	7.68	8.06
Generic programs and qualifications/ other	0.06	0.08	0.09	0.08	0.14	0.12	0.10	0.07
Belgium	100.00	100.00	100.00	100.00	100.00	100.00	100.00	100.00
Education	9.47	9.02	9.05	8.58	8.39	7.88	7.72	8.11
Arts and humanities	11.14	10.74	10.57	10.03	9.71	9.31	9.46	9.22
Social sciences, journalism, and information	11.74	11.66	10.83	10.28	9.60	10.20	10.34	11.20
Business, administration, and law	19.55	18.21	20.20	21.14	21.33	20.32	20.60	22.77

(continued)

(continued)

Country	2013	2014	2015	2016	2017	2018	2019	2020
Natural sciences, mathematics, and statistics	3.51	3.76	4.29	3.92	3.65	3.72	3.89	3.87
Information and Communication Technologies	1.75	1.76	1.09	1.55	1.85	2.10	2.14	2.16
Engineering, manufacturing, and construction	12.01	12.42	11.36	11.58	11.20	11.17	11.52	11.55
Agriculture, forestry, fisheries and veterinary	2.27	2.31	1.80	1.95	2.12	1.97	1.98	1.92
Health and welfare	23.90	25.28	25.59	26.52	27.14	28.79	26.57	24.95
Services	1.72	1.54	1.32	1.59	1.32	1.34	1.33	1.32
Generic programs and qualifications/other	2.94	–	3.89	2.85	3.69	3.19	4.44	2.92
Bulgaria	100.00	100.00	100.00	100.00	100.00	100.00	100.00	100.00
Education	6.99	7.60	8.01	8.83	8.91	9.42	10.42	12.75
Arts and humanities	6.66	6.68	6.67	7.08	6.75	6.53	6.88	6.72
Social sciences, journalism, and information	16.68	16.46	15.84	14.90	13.18	13.11	12.77	12.14
Business, administration, and law	36.24	34.87	33.93	34.10	32.94	31.85	30.85	28.10
Natural sciences, mathematics, and statistics	3.68	3.59	3.66	3.44	3.31	3.10	3.14	2.93
Information and Communication Technologies	2.80	2.69	3.12	2.87	3.74	3.77	4.05	4.63
Engineering, manufacturing, and construction	14.26	14.32	14.01	13.36	13.46	12.41	12.63	11.95
Agriculture, forestry, fisheries, and veterinary	1.50	1.55	1.68	1.69	1.83	1.93	1.81	1.91

(continued)

(continued)

Country	2013	2014	2015	2016	2017	2018	2019	2020
Health and welfare	5.30	5.89	6.59	7.28	8.37	9.40	9.50	10.78
Services	5.79	6.25	6.40	6.46	7.50	8.48	7.96	8.09
Generic programs and qualifications/other	0.09	0.09	0.08	–	–	–	–	–
Croatia	100.00	100.00	100.00	100.00	100.00	100.00	100.00	100.00
Education	4.29	3.99	3.87	6.02	5.65	6.85	7.12	7.53
Arts and humanities	10.10	9.62	9.85	8.85	9.10	8.74	8.90	9.23
Social sciences, journalism, and information	9.68	8.13	8.24	7.31	7.20	7.58	7.89	7.84
Business, administration, and law	32.25	33.11	31.40	31.46	29.67	25.21	22.93	21.78
Natural sciences, mathematics, and statistics	4.08	4.85	5.00	4.53	5.13	5.10	5.02	5.35
Information and Communication Technologies	3.88	3.26	4.06	4.71	5.52	4.02	4.37	4.65
Engineering, manufacturing, and construction	14.49	15.25	14.81	16.05	16.36	17.21	17.87	18.50
Agriculture, forestry, fisheries, and veterinary	4.15	4.17	4.46	4.05	4.25	3.60	3.92	3.50
Health and welfare	8.68	9.83	10.18	9.79	10.38	11.82	12.27	12.28
Services	9.25	8.00	8.13	7.21	6.73	9.85	9.71	9.34
Generic programs and qualifications/other	–	–	–	–	–	–	0.00	–
Cyprus	100.00	100.00	100.00	100.00	100.00	100.00	100.00	100.00
Education	13.16	19.10	17.62	16.75	23.44	19.61	24.39	20.93
Arts and humanities	8.47	7.25	9.18	8.66	7.55	6.97	7.13	8.03

(continued)

(continued)

Country	2013	2014	2015	2016	2017	2018	2019	2020
Social sciences, journalism, and information	6.99	7.36	6.52	7.92	7.06	7.25	6.94	8.30
Business, administration, and law	38.78	36.22	35.35	35.48	35.87	38.97	36.99	38.59
Natural sciences, mathematics, and statistics	3.60	2.78	3.01	3.65	2.54	2.52	2.61	2.69
Information and Communication Technologies	3.92	3.52	3.02	2.43	2.72	2.57	2.91	2.70
Engineering, manufacturing, and construction	11.49	10.72	11.35	10.19	9.72	10.06	8.06	7.72
Agriculture, forestry, fisheries, and veterinary	0.54	0.88	0.74	0.56	0.94	0.82	0.66	0.44
Health and welfare	8.03	7.73	8.03	7.61	5.47	6.15	6.33	7.01
Services	5.04	4.44	5.18	6.74	4.71	5.08	3.98	3.60
Generic programs and qualifications/other	–	–	–	–	–	–	–	–
Czechia	100.00	100.00	100.00	100.00	100.00	100.00	100.00	100.00
Education	11.60	10.28	10.07	9.81	9.55	11.39	13.24	–
Arts and humanities	8.37	7.64	7.69	8.00	7.69	8.71	8.63	–
Social sciences, journalism, and information	9.47	8.20	10.38	10.72	9.69	10.95	10.49	–
Business, administration, and law	26.48	24.45	20.71	20.13	18.67	19.88	18.87	–
Natural sciences, mathematics, and statistics	5.77	5.17	4.76	5.13	4.88	5.72	5.75	–
Information and Communication Technologies	4.73	4.24	3.92	4.02	4.55	4.93	5.04	–

(continued)

(continued)

Country	2013	2014	2015	2016	2017	2018	2019	2020
Engineering, manufacturing, and construction	13.46	13.04	14.49	14.86	14.43	15.47	15.08	–
Agriculture, forestry, fisheries, and veterinary	3.84	3.13	3.02	3.18	3.00	3.44	3.49	–
Health and welfare	10.32	9.93	9.96	10.79	11.16	12.17	12.23	–
Services	4.65	4.50	6.69	6.93	6.93	7.26	7.17	–
Generic programs and qualifications/ other	1.32	9.41	8.31	6.42	9.44	0.07	0.03	–
Denmark	100.00	100.00	100.00	100.00	100.00	100.00	100.00	100.00
Education	6.87	7.38	8.80	5.78	6.03	5.23	5.22	5.16
Arts and humanities	12.25	11.74	12.86	13.17	12.27	11.54	11.44	10.56
Social sciences, journalism, and information	8.55	8.47	10.42	11.07	10.23	10.01	10.12	10.02
Business, administration, and law	26.54	26.45	20.42	24.86	24.72	25.65	25.40	26.12
Natural sciences, mathematics, and statistics	3.98	3.85	4.62	5.60	5.26	5.44	5.54	5.31
Information and Communication Technologies	4.29	4.38	4.36	4.53	4.76	4.76	4.92	5.36
Engineering, manufacturing, and construction	12.18	12.55	10.65	10.33	10.96	12.01	12.08	12.34
Agriculture, forestry, fisheries, and veterinary	1.35	1.34	2.03	1.24	1.20	1.24	1.22	1.20
Health and welfare	–	–	21.61	20.33	20.86	20.88	20.47	20.56
Services	3.00	2.62	4.16	3.04	3.62	3.08	3.55	3.32
Generic programs and qualifications/ other	–	–	0.08	0.04	0.08	0.16	0.04	0.05

(continued)

(continued)

Country	2013	2014	2015	2016	2017	2018	2019	2020
Estonia	100.00	100.00	100.00	100.00	100.00	100.00	100.00	100.00
Education	8.13	7.78	7.97	7.61	6.83	7.29	8.15	7.06
Arts and humanities	13.17	13.04	12.28	12.46	12.50	13.11	12.38	12.98
Social sciences, journalism, and information	7.10	8.04	8.52	8.80	7.62	8.00	7.85	7.17
Business, administration, and law	23.73	23.11	24.68	24.04	23.21	22.79	23.79	24.80
Natural sciences, mathematics, and statistics	7.80	6.42	7.09	6.91	6.44	6.32	6.41	6.12
Information and Communication Technologies	4.46	5.20	4.92	6.35	7.45	6.66	7.96	8.40
Engineering, manufacturing, and construction	14.82	14.79	14.46	14.20	14.95	14.76	13.54	12.95
Agriculture, forestry, fisheries, and veterinary	2.27	1.95	1.88	1.78	1.98	1.73	1.91	1.49
Health and welfare	12.50	13.07	12.04	11.73	13.00	12.52	12.20	13.45
Services	6.02	6.59	6.17	6.12	6.00	6.84	5.82	5.58
Generic programs and qualifications/ other	–	–	–	–	–	–	–	–
Finland	100.00	100.00	100.00	100.00	100.00	100.00	100.00	100.00
Education	6.20	6.21	6.51	6.42	6.71	6.76	6.62	6.98
Arts and humanities	13.21	13.16	12.88	12.32	11.19	10.48	11.01	11.26
Social sciences, journalism, and information	6.93	7.25	7.28	7.21	7.42	7.12	7.01	7.34
Business, administration, and law	17.56	17.91	18.01	18.27	18.89	18.85	18.79	19.86
Natural sciences, mathematics, and statistics	4.61	4.43	4.87	4.77	4.79	4.61	4.46	5.25

(continued)

(continued)

Country	2013	2014	2015	2016	2017	2018	2019	2020
Information and Communication Technologies	6.68	6.57	6.66	7.06	6.30	7.03	7.35	7.49
Engineering, manufacturing, and construction	17.07	17.17	16.95	17.70	16.16	16.48	16.56	15.21
Agriculture, forestry, fisheries, and veterinary	2.05	1.95	2.25	2.23	2.25	2.11	2.18	2.38
Health and welfare	20.76	20.59	19.47	19.71	21.43	21.93	21.32	19.55
Services	4.92	4.77	5.11	4.32	4.85	4.62	4.70	4.68
Generic programs and qualifications/other	–	–	–	–	–	–	–	–
France	100.00	100.00	100.00	100.00	100.00	100.00	100.00	100.00
Education	2.69	2.61	3.31	3.99	4.17	4.12	4.10	4.04
Arts and humanities	9.42	9.37	9.28	9.36	9.35	8.61	8.52	8.29
Social sciences, journalism, and information	8.00	7.87	7.79	7.55	6.82	7.38	7.47	7.54
Business, administration, and law	34.57	33.68	33.85	33.25	34.49	34.26	34.45	35.35
Natural sciences, mathematics, and statistics	6.37	6.28	7.29	7.63	7.92	7.96	8.19	8.18
Information and Communication Technologies	3.12	3.00	3.03	3.03	2.97	3.50	3.59	3.61
Engineering, manufacturing, and construction	16.04	16.34	14.92	14.90	14.79	13.94	14.00	14.10
Agriculture, forestry, fisheries, and veterinary	1.44	1.59	1.55	1.47	1.37	1.56	1.56	1.67
Health and welfare	15.46	15.80	15.67	15.43	14.19	14.53	14.10	13.07
Services	–	–	3.26	3.35	3.46	3.95	3.75	3.99

(continued)

(continued)

Country	2013	2014	2015	2016	2017	2018	2019	2020
Generic programs and qualifications/other	–	–	0.04	0.04	0.46	0.20	0.28	0.14
Germany	100.00	100.00	100.00	100.00	100.00	100.00	100.00	100.00
Education	9.36	9.67	9.61	9.89	11.43	11.23	9.69	9.51
Arts and humanities	13.14	12.91	12.17	11.71	11.30	11.39	10.03	9.46
Social sciences, journalism, and information	6.78	6.93	6.86	7.07	7.42	7.51	6.88	6.94
Business, administration, and law	22.21	22.38	22.81	23.36	22.56	22.68	24.51	25.48
Natural sciences, mathematics, and statistics	10.27	10.22	9.85	9.46	9.24	9.05	8.04	7.84
Information and Communication Technologies	4.32	4.37	4.54	4.55	4.70	4.86	4.54	4.87
Engineering, manufacturing, and construction	21.14	21.41	22.34	22.03	21.62	21.40	24.20	23.11
Agriculture, forestry, fisheries, and veterinary	1.98	1.92	1.90	1.84	1.85	1.83	1.86	1.86
Health and welfare	7.84	7.38	7.17	7.33	7.24	7.43	7.11	7.39
Services	2.84	2.80	2.60	2.56	2.39	2.46	3.02	3.20
Generic programs and qualifications/other	–	–	0.14	0.20	0.25	0.16	0.12	0.35
Greece	100.00	100.00	100.00	100.00	100.00	100.00	100.00	100.00
Education	10.35	9.85	6.93	7.40	7.30	7.93	8.56	7.11
Arts and humanities	11.59	11.35	13.83	12.95	12.16	11.20	11.78	10.65
Social sciences, journalism, and information	12.92	12.72	11.39	12.22	13.41	13.91	14.85	15.83
Business, administration, and law	18.03	19.72	20.75	21.23	20.25	21.85	19.75	20.89

(continued)

(continued)

Country	2013	2014	2015	2016	2017	2018	2019	2020
Natural sciences, mathematics, and statistics	7.28	7.40	9.08	8.43	9.60	9.08	8.89	9.38
Information and Communication Technologies	4.89	4.37	2.90	3.16	2.89	3.09	3.38	3.52
Engineering, manufacturing, and construction	18.85	18.08	17.61	16.57	16.91	16.09	15.06	14.52
Agriculture, forestry, fisheries, and veterinary	5.17	4.02	2.91	2.34	2.46	2.67	2.60	2.65
Health and welfare	8.47	10.90	11.51	12.18	11.74	11.14	11.48	11.92
Services	2.30	1.60	3.08	3.53	3.28	3.01	3.63	3.53
Generic programs and qualifications/other	0.14	–	–	–	–	–	–	–
Hungary	100.00	100.00	100.00	100.00	100.00	100.00	100.00	100.00
Education	13.52	13.54	16.21	16.64	15.97	14.15	14.56	9.43
Arts and humanities	8.99	9.27	9.50	9.70	8.78	9.03	8.91	6.44
Social sciences, journalism, and information	9.65	9.81	10.25	9.81	10.12	10.23	10.27	9.03
Business, administration, and law	32.97	29.09	24.90	23.41	24.42	25.42	25.34	20.57
Natural sciences, mathematics, and statistics	3.69	3.79	4.16	4.21	4.44	3.89	3.72	2.64
Information and Communication Technologies	2.93	3.06	2.37	4.32	4.31	4.59	4.91	3.14
Engineering, manufacturing, and construction	12.25	13.93	15.55	14.28	14.52	14.04	14.73	9.72
Agriculture, forestry, fisheries, and veterinary	2.06	2.33	2.57	3.16	3.90	3.95	3.78	2.83
Health and welfare	–	–	7.92	8.35	7.84	8.60	8.42	5.13

(continued)

(continued)

Country	2013	2014	2015	2016	2017	2018	2019	2020
Services	6.39	6.78	5.13	4.82	4.78	4.83	4.78	8.03
Generic programs and qualifications/other	–	–	1.46	1.30	0.93	1.27	0.60	23.04
Ireland	100.00	100.00	100.00	100.00	100.00	100.00	100.00	100.00
Education	7.97	6.60	6.51	8.16	9.46	8.59	9.10	8.92
Arts and humanities	11.87	11.52	13.30	13.27	12.06	11.63	11.00	10.21
Social sciences, journalism, and information	6.36	6.24	6.46	5.54	6.00	5.85	6.24	6.12
Business, administration, and law	21.63	22.84	25.88	24.67	24.84	26.73	25.85	26.59
Natural sciences, mathematics, and statistics	5.07	5.86	7.85	7.81	7.37	7.57	7.88	7.71
Information and Communication Technologies	4.87	5.45	6.96	7.22	7.26	7.94	7.77	8.63
Engineering, manufacturing, and construction	11.09	10.27	9.58	8.96	9.25	8.59	9.66	10.07
Agriculture, forestry, fisheries, and veterinary	1.18	1.15	1.51	1.53	1.39	1.48	1.43	1.28
Health and welfare	14.11	15.10	16.44	16.94	16.82	16.76	16.53	15.67
Services	5.65	5.28	4.80	5.60	5.20	4.08	3.71	4.02
Generic programs and qualifications/other	10.21	9.70	0.71	0.30	0.36	0.79	0.83	0.78
Italy	100.00	100.00	100.00	100.00	100.00	100.00	100.00	100.00
Education	4.50	6.81	–	3.30	4.06	6.94	6.92	12.59
Arts and humanities	16.01	15.84	–	16.02	16.31	16.82	16.87	15.84
Social sciences, journalism, and information	13.42	13.16	–	12.42	12.10	14.25	14.41	13.92
Business, administration, and law	18.80	18.91	–	19.33	19.25	17.65	17.74	17.23

(continued)

(continued)

Country	2013	2014	2015	2016	2017	2018	2019	2020
Natural sciences, mathematics, and statistics	7.10	6.93	–	7.42	7.27	7.56	7.89	7.44
Information and Communication Technologies	0.98	0.92	–	1.01	0.99	1.27	1.33	1.40
Engineering, manufacturing, and construction	16.05	16.00	–	14.84	15.07	15.36	15.25	13.84
Agriculture, forestry, fisheries, and veterinary	2.05	2.07	–	2.32	2.46	2.52	2.50	2.27
Health and welfare	15.60	16.22	–	13.73	13.34	14.49	13.65	12.28
Services	2.26	2.23	–	0.14	0.19	2.64	2.90	3.00
Generic programs and qualifications/other	–	–	9.83	9.47	8.96	0.47	0.54	0.20
Latvia	100.00	100.00	100.00	100.00	100.00	100.00	100.00	100.00
Education	7.49	6.27	6.75	7.36	4.14	7.72	8.74	8.54
Arts and humanities	8.24	9.62	7.91	7.76	7.74	7.08	6.99	6.13
Social sciences, journalism, and information	7.65	8.25	9.30	9.65	9.12	8.85	7.69	7.60
Business, administration, and law	32.21	33.29	31.99	30.65	30.52	28.47	28.41	29.42
Natural sciences, mathematics, and statistics	2.35	2.77	3.53	3.15	3.13	2.73	3.03	2.69
Information and Communication Technologies	3.61	3.96	4.42	4.81	4.96	4.69	4.38	4.62
Engineering, manufacturing, and construction	13.09	14.59	12.51	12.56	12.79	12.74	12.52	12.03
Agriculture, forestry, fisheries, and veterinary	1.07	1.41	1.69	1.85	1.67	2.20	1.51	1.43
Health and welfare	–	–	13.99	14.26	17.07	17.48	18.45	19.11

(continued)

(continued)

Country	2013	2014	2015	2016	2017	2018	2019	2020
Services	6.05	7.07	7.91	7.95	8.87	8.02	8.28	8.45
Generic programs and qualifications/other	–	–	–	–	–	–	–	–
Lithuania	100.00	100.00	100.00	100.00	100.00	100.00	100.00	100.00
Education	10.82	8.79	7.07	6.54	6.17	5.95	5.89	6.11
Arts and humanities	7.72	7.97	8.03	8.63	8.58	8.51	8.75	8.20
Social sciences, journalism, and information	10.85	11.96	12.15	11.97	10.18	9.01	9.28	8.56
Business, administration, and law	32.09	31.26	31.73	30.18	27.29	25.56	24.43	26.15
Natural sciences, mathematics, and statistics	3.31	3.76	4.00	4.26	4.01	4.27	4.43	4.17
Information and Communication Technologies	2.15	2.11	1.82	2.02	2.75	3.11	3.68	3.99
Engineering, manufacturing, and construction	18.02	17.82	17.28	17.53	18.91	19.44	19.16	17.87
Agriculture, forestry, fisheries, and veterinary	1.79	2.04	2.09	2.24	2.47	3.26	3.05	3.08
Health and welfare	11.34	12.41	13.78	14.21	16.97	18.05	18.67	19.45
Services	1.74	1.89	2.03	2.39	2.61	2.81	2.62	2.39
Generic programs and qualifications/other	–	–	0.02	0.04	0.04	0.03	0.05	0.02
Luxembourg	100.00	100.00	100.00	100.00	100.00	100.00	100.00	100.00
Education	23.13	25.93	20.65	8.80	7.49	10.10	10.84	13.38
Arts and humanities	8.06	7.80	8.48	11.41	9.61	9.98	10.43	10.45
Social sciences, journalism, and information	7.63	7.15	8.86	11.59	11.73	10.72	9.57	11.41

(continued)

(continued)

Country	2013	2014	2015	2016	2017	2018	2019	2020
Business, administration, and law	41.25	39.04	38.68	40.07	43.82	42.50	42.20	37.47
Natural sciences, mathematics, and statistics	5.44	4.71	4.74	5.53	4.98	5.82	5.16	5.01
Information and Communication Technologies	4.25	3.63	5.86	5.77	4.58	5.82	4.99	6.40
Engineering, manufacturing, and construction	6.25	5.58	5.30	6.60	7.67	7.19	8.81	7.84
Agriculture, forestry, fisheries, and veterinary	–	–	0.25	2.08	0.11	0.23	0.35	0.21
Health and welfare	4.00	6.12	7.17	6.42	7.32	6.79	6.03	7.36
Services	–	–	–	1.72	2.69	0.86	1.62	0.48
Generic programs and qualifications/other	–	0.05	–	–	–	–	–	–
Malta	100.00	100.00	100.00	100.00	100.00	100.00	100.00	100.00
Education	8.20	7.87	10.93	8.46	6.44	5.16	8.79	6.65
Arts and humanities	13.41	13.79	12.98	12.74	11.70	9.75	8.97	9.03
Social sciences, journalism, and information	10.31	10.04	8.32	10.97	9.50	10.44	9.61	10.20
Business, administration, and law	29.71	26.10	26.66	28.91	31.70	31.65	34.07	35.17
Natural sciences, mathematics, and statistics	6.23	5.66	8.50	4.72	3.62	4.66	3.88	3.97
Information and Communication Technologies	9.02	9.56	8.47	7.90	7.93	6.94	6.04	6.48
Engineering, manufacturing, and construction	10.04	9.68	7.82	9.31	8.76	8.82	7.19	6.78

(continued)

(continued)

Country	2013	2014	2015	2016	2017	2018	2019	2020
Agriculture, forestry, fisheries, and veterinary	0.34	0.48	0.23	0.66	0.66	0.33	0.35	0.32
Health and welfare	10.70	14.35	12.98	14.22	16.94	19.88	18.23	17.74
Services	1.89	2.22	1.57	2.12	2.73	2.35	2.83	2.85
Generic programs and qualifications/other	0.13	0.25	1.54	–	0.02	–	0.02	0.82
Netherlands	100.00	100.00	100.00	100.00	100.00	100.00	100.00	100.00
Education	11.62	11.27	–	–	9.82	9.67	8.82	8.64
Arts and humanities	8.88	8.62	–	–	8.75	8.68	8.55	8.32
Social sciences, journalism, and information	–	–	–	–	13.97	13.43	13.86	14.26
Business, administration, and law	–	–	–	–	27.47	27.23	27.31	27.90
Natural sciences, mathematics, and statistics	2.92	2.98	–	–	6.05	6.38	6.78	6.85
Information and Communication Technologies	–	–	–	–	2.51	2.83	3.13	3.42
Engineering, manufacturing, and construction	8.75	8.70	–	–	8.06	8.25	8.67	8.57
Agriculture, forestry, fisheries, and veterinary	1.36	1.45	–	–	1.30	1.29	1.29	1.27
Health and welfare	18.72	18.61	–	–	17.12	17.10	16.52	15.40
Services	4.50	4.57	–	–	4.89	5.06	5.01	5.31
Generic programs and qualifications/other	–	–	3.18	–	0.06	0.07	0.06	0.07
Poland	100.00	100.00	100.00	100.00	100.00	100.00	100.00	100.00
Education	–	–	13.52	13.58	13.33	14.66	13.16	12.46
Arts and humanities	–	7.27	7.41	7.17	6.91	7.02	6.83	6.95

(continued)

(continued)

Country	2013	2014	2015	2016	2017	2018	2019	2020
Social sciences, journalism, and information	–	10.06	10.60	10.49	9.84	8.95	8.71	9.06
Business, administration, and law	–	26.50	23.65	24.29	24.33	23.47	23.68	25.52
Natural sciences, mathematics, and statistics	–	3.76	4.13	4.12	3.60	3.30	3.22	3.22
Information and Communication Technologies	–	2.91	3.05	3.12	3.53	3.81	3.82	3.74
Engineering, manufacturing, and construction	–	13.74	15.09	15.62	15.81	14.55	13.77	12.49
Agriculture, forestry, fisheries, and veterinary	–	1.40	1.52	1.48	1.71	1.78	1.69	1.70
Health and welfare	–	12.34	13.19	12.85	13.28	14.83	17.38	15.58
Services	–	7.15	7.84	7.26	7.55	7.40	7.15	7.48
Generic programs and qualifications/other	0.62	–	0.01	0.01	0.12	0.25	0.59	1.79
Portugal	100.00	100.00	100.00	100.00	100.00	100.00	100.00	100.00
Education	7.77	7.06	6.90	5.28	4.81	4.42	4.23	4.12
Arts and humanities	9.38	9.58	9.02	9.41	9.99	10.08	10.03	9.51
Social sciences, journalism, and information	11.31	11.25	11.34	11.28	10.94	11.15	11.01	11.41
Business, administration, and law	18.50	18.37	18.66	19.08	19.36	20.26	20.50	21.34
Natural sciences, mathematics, and statistics	5.80	6.03	6.23	6.58	6.27	6.13	6.09	6.20
Information and Communication Technologies	1.34	1.24	1.15	1.17	1.92	2.19	2.27	2.56
Engineering, manufacturing, and construction	20.69	20.35	20.52	21.27	20.91	19.58	19.63	19.06

(continued)

(continued)

Country	2013	2014	2015	2016	2017	2018	2019	2020
Agriculture, forestry, fisheries and veterinary	1.59	1.76	1.88	1.94	2.22	2.35	2.41	2.55
Health and welfare	18.28	18.61	18.57	18.20	17.41	17.50	17.33	16.75
Services	5.34	5.75	5.69	5.75	6.15	6.30	6.46	6.45
Generic programs and qualifications/other	–	–	0.03	0.03	0.04	0.05	0.05	0.03
Romania	100.00	100.00	100.00	100.00	100.00	100.00	100.00	100.00
Education	2.61	1.94	3.54	4.15	4.96	4.47	4.66	5.29
Arts and humanities	8.14	8.60	9.18	9.77	9.05	9.13	8.98	9.48
Social sciences, journalism, and information	14.88	14.57	9.10	9.10	8.64	9.23	9.17	9.62
Business, administration, and law	27.75	26.94	29.69	28.39	27.67	26.73	26.72	26.43
Natural sciences, mathematics, and statistics	4.39	4.84	5.82	5.71	5.33	5.16	5.05	5.06
Information and Communication Technologies	0.90	0.95	5.35	4.92	5.57	5.82	6.32	6.68
Engineering, manufacturing, and construction	21.50	22.20	17.18	18.14	18.23	17.12	18.65	17.35
Agriculture, forestry, fisheries, and veterinary	2.11	2.05	4.10	4.02	4.40	4.18	4.30	3.87
Health and welfare	14.57	14.86	11.03	10.30	11.60	13.39	11.24	11.31
Services	3.16	3.05	5.02	5.50	4.54	4.77	4.92	4.90
Generic programs and qualifications/other	–	–	–	–	–	–	–	–
Slovakia	100.00	100.00	100.00	100.00	100.00	100.00	100.00	100.00
Education	13.16	12.70	13.06	13.13	12.78	13.66	13.33	14.24
Arts and humanities	7.02	7.17	7.37	7.49	7.71	7.63	7.82	7.75

(continued)

(continued)

Country	2013	2014	2015	2016	2017	2018	2019	2020
Social sciences, journalism, and information	8.64	9.17	11.50	11.90	11.56	11.78	10.88	10.01
Business, administration, and law	23.31	24.17	21.37	20.33	20.38	20.07	20.85	20.21
Natural sciences, mathematics, and statistics	4.92	4.67	5.57	5.53	5.71	5.69	5.66	5.26
Information and Communication Technologies	2.61	2.94	2.87	3.19	3.34	3.95	3.87	4.36
Engineering, manufacturing, and construction	13.46	13.23	12.70	12.43	12.13	12.43	12.29	12.56
Agriculture, forestry, fisheries, and veterinary	1.76	1.79	1.98	2.26	2.19	2.33	2.49	2.33
Health and welfare	–	–	17.52	17.76	18.18	16.51	16.56	16.77
Services	6.22	6.05	6.07	5.96	6.03	5.95	6.24	6.51
Generic programs and qualifications/other	–	–	–	–	–	–	–	–
Slovenia	100.00	100.00	100.00	100.00	100.00	100.00	100.00	100.00
Education	9.20	9.66	10.05	11.15	11.22	11.13	10.99	11.17
Arts and humanities	9.71	9.71	9.46	10.54	9.05	8.96	8.88	7.72
Social sciences, journalism, and information	12.16	11.69	12.00	11.45	10.40	9.27	9.25	9.77
Business, administration, and law	22.87	22.76	22.33	23.25	20.34	20.48	18.22	19.08
Natural sciences, mathematics, and statistics	5.91	6.05	6.03	4.59	6.39	6.56	6.39	6.94
Information and Communication Technologies	3.68	4.12	3.47	3.47	3.67	3.51	4.06	4.15
Engineering, manufacturing, and construction	16.87	16.02	16.15	16.96	16.56	17.16	17.53	17.56

(*continued*)

(continued)

Country	2013	2014	2015	2016	2017	2018	2019	2020
Agriculture, forestry, fisheries, and veterinary	2.94	2.99	2.91	2.80	2.47	2.98	3.27	2.28
Health and welfare	10.06	9.87	10.11	8.36	12.50	12.11	12.50	12.42
Services	6.61	7.13	7.49	7.43	7.42	7.84	8.92	8.92
Generic programs and qualifications/other	–	–	–	–	–	–	–	–
Spain	100.00	100.00	100.00	100.00	100.00	100.00	100.00	100.00
Education	13.78	16.25	16.25	16.51	16.37	17.01	16.21	17.43
Arts and humanities	9.06	8.58	8.84	9.13	9.07	8.91	8.94	8.89
Social sciences, journalism, and information	7.69	7.35	6.96	7.09	7.06	6.97	7.18	7.53
Business, administration, and law	20.07	19.39	19.22	18.60	18.89	19.33	19.26	19.18
Natural sciences, mathematics, and statistics	4.86	4.61	5.07	5.16	5.28	5.20	4.76	4.75
Information and Communication Technologies	4.12	3.96	3.95	3.88	3.97	3.92	4.18	3.97
Engineering, manufacturing, and construction	16.46	15.78	16.35	14.84	14.20	13.15	13.01	12.09
Agriculture, forestry, fisheries, and veterinary	1.47	1.26	1.14	1.19	1.27	1.07	1.13	1.11
Health and welfare	14.71	15.17	14.54	15.96	16.36	16.80	17.42	17.35
Services	7.79	7.65	7.07	7.43	7.34	7.55	7.90	7.70
Generic programs and qualifications/other	–	–	0.61	0.21	0.19	0.09	–	–
Sweden	100.00	100.00	100.00	100.00	100.00	100.00	100.00	100.00
Education	13.18	13.77	12.07	12.20	12.22	12.98	12.97	13.75
Arts and humanities	6.05	5.93	6.18	6.02	5.99	5.62	6.30	6.28

(continued)

(continued)

Country	2013	2014	2015	2016	2017	2018	2019	2020
Social sciences, journalism, and information	12.29	12.37	12.72	12.97	11.87	11.80	12.04	12.13
Business, administration, and law	16.30	16.54	17.89	17.10	16.18	16.40	16.13	15.74
Natural sciences, mathematics, and statistics	4.28	4.17	4.33	4.56	4.43	4.11	4.08	4.02
Information and Communication Technologies	3.41	3.63	3.52	3.73	4.28	4.27	4.30	4.71
Engineering, manufacturing, and construction	18.21	17.87	18.13	18.30	18.80	18.26	18.94	18.27
Agriculture, forestry, fisheries, and veterinary	0.96	0.85	0.87	0.78	0.91	0.82	0.79	0.90
Health and welfare	22.77	22.71	21.83	22.16	23.05	23.22	22.08	21.91
Services	2.54	2.13	2.37	2.08	2.24	2.44	2.29	2.22
Generic programs and qualifications/other	–	–	0.08	0.09	0.04	0.08	0.08	0.06
United Kingdom	100.00	100.00	100.00	100.00	100.00	100.00	100.00	100.00
Education	9.87	9.72	9.59	9.09	8.74	8.26	7.85	–
Arts and humanities	16.11	16.26	15.49	15.36	15.15	14.68	14.76	–
Social sciences, journalism, and information	9.32	9.87	11.82	11.75	11.64	11.57	11.81	–
Business, administration, and law	20.57	19.97	21.96	22.22	22.07	22.25	24.09	–
Natural sciences, mathematics, and statistics	12.60	13.28	13.38	13.39	13.58	13.84	13.40	–
Information and Communication Technologies	3.59	3.49	3.61	3.69	3.76	4.01	3.98	–
Engineering, manufacturing, and construction	8.99	8.83	9.15	9.13	9.08	9.06	8.86	–

(continued)

(continued)

Country	2013	2014	2015	2016	2017	2018	2019	2020
Agriculture, forestry, fisheries, and veterinary	0.94	0.93	0.99	0.96	0.97	0.91	0.96	–
Health and welfare	15.70	15.39	13.26	13.66	14.25	14.69	13.61	–
Services	1.52	1.47	–	0.10	0.13	0.14	0.14	–
Generic programs and qualifications/other	–	–	0.73	0.64	0.62	0.58	0.52	–
European Union–28 countries (2013–2020)	100.00	100.00	100.00	100.00	100.00	100.00	100.00	100.00
Education	–	9.34	9.02	8.96	9.19	9.45	8.94	–
Arts and humanities	–	11.03	10.94	11.03	10.79	10.72	10.57	–
Social sciences, journalism, and information	–	9.19	9.90	9.61	9.42	9.57	9.59	–
Business, administration, and law	–	23.47	24.01	24.19	24.32	24.16	24.66	–
Natural sciences, mathematics, and statistics	–	6.98	7.45	7.60	7.56	7.75	7.59	–
Information and Communication Technologies	–	3.12	3.51	3.48	3.58	3.80	3.90	–
Engineering, manufacturing, and construction	–	15.02	14.69	14.97	14.63	14.16	14.58	–
Agriculture, forestry, fisheries, and veterinary	–	1.63	1.68	1.68	1.71	1.72	1.73	–
Health and welfare	–	14.23	13.57	13.66	13.83	14.43	14.12	–
Services	–	–	3.75	3.66	3.71	3.90	3.95	–
Generic programs and qualifications/other	0.73	0.65	1.38	1.17	1.25	0.35	0.39	–

Source: Author's elaboration based on primary data from Eurostat, http://appsso.eurostat.ec.europa.eu/nui/submitViewTableAction.do, accessed on 06.06.2022

Number of people who graduated from an education programme by field. https://stats.oecd.org/Index.aspx?DataSetCode=EDU_GRAD_FIELD

Annex 13: Global Competitiveness Index (GCI) 2014–2015

Country/Economy	GCI 2014–2015 Rank (Out of 144)	GCI 2014–2015 Score (1–7)	Rank among GCI2013– 2013–2014 Economies[a]	Rank among GCI2013– 2014 rank (Out of 148)[b]
Switzerland	1	5.70	1	1
Singapore	2	5.65	2	2
United States	3	5.54	3	5
Finland	4	5.50	4	3
Germany	5	5.49	5	4
Japan	6	5.47	6	9
Hong Kong SAR	7	5.46	7	7
Netherlands	8	5.45	8	8
United Kingdom	9	5.41	9	10
Sweden	10	5.41	10	6
Norway	11	5.35	11	11
United Arab Emirates	12	5.33	12	19
Denmark	13	5.29	13	15
Taiwan, China	14	5.25	14	12
Canada	15	5.24	15	14
Qatar	16	5.24	16	13
New Zealand	17	5.20	17	18

Country/Economy	GCI 2014–2015 Rank (Out of 144)	GCI 2014–2015 Score (1–7)	Rank among 2013–2014 Economies[a]	GCI 2013–2014 rank (Out of 148)[b]
Sri Lanka	73	4.19	73	65
Botswana	74	4.15	74	74
Slovak Republic	75	4.15	75	78
Ukraine	76	4.14	76	84
Croatia	77	4.13	77	75
Guatemala	78	4.10	78	86
Algeria	79	4.08	79	100
Uruguay	80	4.04	80	85
Greece	81	4.04	81	91
Moldova	82	4.03	82	89
Iran, Islamic Rep.	83	4.03	83	82
El Salvador	84	4.01	84	97
Armenia	85	4.01	85	79
Jamaica	86	3.98	86	94
Tunisia	87	3.96	87	83
Namibia	88	3.96	88	90
Trinidad and Tobago	89	3.95	89	92

Country				
Belgium	18	5.18	18	17
Luxembourg	19	5.17	19	22
Malaysia	20	5.16	20	24
Austria	21	5.16	21	16
Australia	22	5.08	22	21
France	23	5.08	23	23
Saudi Arabia	24	5.06	24	20
Ireland	25	4.98	25	28
Korea, Rep.	26	4.96	26	25
Israel	27	4.95	27	27
China	28	4.89	28	29
Estonia	29	4.71	29	32
Iceland	30	4.71	30	31
Thailand	31	4.66	31	37
Puerto Rico	32	4.64	32	30
Chile	33	4.60	33	34
Indonesia	34	4.57	34	38
Spain	35	4.55	35	35
Portugal	36	4.54	36	51
Czech Republic	37	4.53	37	46
Azerbaijan	38	4.53	38	39
Mauritius	39	4.52	39	45
Kuwait	40	4.51	40	36
Lithuania	41	4.51	41	48
Latvia	42	4.50	42	52
Poland	43	4.48	43	42

Country				
Kenya	90	3.93	90	96
Tajikistan	91	3.93	n/a	n/a
Seychelles	92	3.91	91	80
Lao PDR	93	3.91	92	81
Serbia	94	3.90	93	101
Cambodia	95	3.89	94	88
Zambia	96	3.86	95	93
Albania	97	3.84	96	95
Mongolia	98	3.83	97	107
Nicaragua	99	3.82	98	99
Honduras	100	3.82	99	111
Dominican Republic	101	3.82	100	105
Nepal	102	3.81	101	117
Bhutan	103	3.80	102	109
Argentina	104	3.79	103	104
Bolivia	105	3.77	104	98
Gabon	106	3.74	105	112
Lesotho	107	3.73	106	123
Kyrgyz Republic	108	3.73	107	121
Bangladesh	109	3.72	108	110
Suriname	110	3.71	109	106
Ghana	111	3.71	110	114
Senegal	112	3.70	111	113
Lebanon	113	3.68	112	103
Cape Verde	114	3.68	113	122
Côte d'Ivoire	115	3.67	114	126

(continued)

(continued)

Country/Economy	GCI 2014–2015		Rank among 2013–2014 Economies[a]	GCI 2013–2014 rank (Out of 148)[b]
	Rank (Out of 144)	Score (1–7)		
Bahrain	44	4.48	44	43
Turkey	45	4.46	45	44
Oman	46	4.46	46	33
Malta	47	4.45	47	41
Panama	48	4.43	48	40
Italy	49	4.42	49	49
Kazakhstan	50	4.42	50	50
Costa Rica	51	4.42	51	54
Philippines	52	4.40	52	59
Russian Federation	53	4.37	53	64
Bulgaria	54	4.37	54	57
Barbados	55	4.36	55	47
South Africa	56	4.35	56	53
Brazil	57	4.34	57	56
Cyprus	58	4.31	58	58
Romania	59	4.30	59	76
Hungary	60	4.28	60	63
Mexico	61	4.27	61	55

Country/Economy	GCI 2014–2015		Rank among 2013–2014 Economies[a]	GCI 2013–2014 rank (Out of 148)[b]
	Rank (Out of 144)	Score (1–7)		
Cameroon	116	3.66	115	115
Guyana	117	3.65	116	102
Ethiopia	118	3.60	117	127
Egypt	119	3.60	118	118
Paraguay	120	3.59	119	119
Tanzania	121	3.57	120	125
Uganda	122	3.56	121	129
Swaziland	123	3.55	122	124
Zimbabwe	124	3.54	123	131
Gambia, The	125	3.53	124	116
Libya	126	3.48	125	108
Nigeria	127	3.44	126	120
Mali	128	3.43	127	135
Pakistan	129	3.42	128	133
Madagascar	130	3.41	129	132
Venezuela	131	3.32	130	134
Malawi	132	3.25	131	136
Mozambique	133	3.24	132	137

Rwanda	62	4.27	62	66
Macedonia, FYR	63	4.26	63	73
Jordan	64	4.25	64	68
Peru	65	4.24	65	61
Colombia	66	4.23	66	69
Montenegro	67	4.23	67	67
Vietnam	68	4.23	68	70
Georgia	69	4.22	69	72
Slovenia	70	4.22	70	62
India	71	4.21	71	60
Morocco	72	4.21	72	77

Myanmar	134	3.24	133	139	
Burkina Faso	135	3.21	134	140	
Timor-Leste	136	3.17	135	138	
Haiti	137	3.14	136	143	
Sierra Leone	138	3.10	137	144	
Burundi	139	3.09	138	146	
Angola	140	3.04	139	142	
Mauritania	141	3.00	140	141	
Yemen	142	2.96	141	145	
Chad	143	2.85	142	148	
Guinea	144	2.79	143	147	

Source: World Economic Forum, WEF, 2014

The Global Competitiveness Index (GCI), is a comprehensive tool that measures the microeconomic and macroeconomic foundations of national competitiveness. Please use the citations: https://www3.weforum.org/docs/WEF_GlobalCompetitivenessReport_2014-15.pdf

ANNEX 14: HUMAN CAPITAL INDEX, 2020, 2018 BACK-CALCULATED AND 2010

Economy	Components of HCI 2020							HCI	
	Probability of survival to age 5	Expected years of school	Harmonized test scores	Learning adjusted years of schooling	Adult survival rate	Fraction of children under 5 not stunted	HCI 2020	HCI 2018 back-calculated	HCI 2010
Afghanistan	0.94	8.9	355	5.1	0.79	0.62	0.4	0.39	–
Albania	0.99	12.9	434	9	0.93	0.89	0.63	0.63	0.54
Algeria	0.98	11.8	374	7.1	0.91	0.88	0.53	0.53	0.53
Angola	0.92	8.1	326	4.2	0.73	0.62	0.36	0.36	–
Antigua and Barbuda	0.99	13	407	8.4	0.9	–	0.6	0.58	–
Argentina	0.99	12.9	408	8.4	0.89	0.92	0.6	0.62	0.59
Armenia	0.99	11.3	443	8	0.89	0.91	0.58	0.58	–
Australia	1	13.6	516	11.2	0.95	–	0.77	0.78	0.75
Austria	1	13.4	508	10.9	0.94	–	0.75	0.77	0.74
Azerbaijan	0.98	12.4	416	8.3	0.88	0.82	0.58	0.63	0.5
Bahrain	0.99	12.8	452	9.3	0.93	–	0.65	0.66	0.6
Bangladesh	0.97	10.2	368	6	0.87	0.69	0.46	0.46	–
Belarus	1	13.8	488	10.8	0.85	–	0.7	–	–
Belgium	1	13.5	517	11.2	0.93	–	0.76	0.76	0.75
Benin	0.91	9.2	384	5.7	0.77	–	0.4	0.4	0.37
Bhutan	0.97	10.2	387	6.3	0.81	0.79	0.48	–	–
Bosnia and Herzegovina	0.99	11.7	416	7.8	0.91	0.91	0.58	0.62	–
Botswana	0.96	8.1	391	5.1	0.8	–	0.41	0.41	0.37
Brazil	0.99	11.9	413	7.9	0.86	–	0.55	0.55	0.53

Brunei Darussalam	0.99	13.2	438	9.2	0.88	0.8	0.63	—	—
Bulgaria	0.99	12.3	441	8.7	0.87	0.93	0.61	0.67	0.64
Burkina Faso	0.92	7	404	4.5	0.76	0.75	0.38	0.38	0.32
Burundi	0.94	7.6	423	5.2	0.72	0.46	0.39	0.39	0.34
Cambodia	0.97	9.5	452	6.8	0.84	0.68	0.49	0.49	—
Cameroon	0.92	8.7	379	5.3	0.7	0.71	0.4	0.39	0.38
Canada	1	13.7	534	11.7	0.94	—	0.8	0.8	0.77
Central African Republic	0.88	4.6	369	2.7	0.59	0.59	0.29	—	—
Chad	0.88	5.3	333	2.8	0.65	0.6	0.3	0.3	0.29
Chile	0.99	13	452	9.4	0.92	—	0.65	0.67	0.63
China	0.99	13.1	441	9.3	0.92	0.92	0.65	0.65	—
Colombia	0.99	12.9	419	8.6	0.89	0.87	0.6	0.6	0.58
Comoros	0.93	8.2	392	5.1	0.78	0.69	0.4	0.4	—
Congo Dem. Rep.	0.91	9.1	310	4.5	0.75	0.57	0.37	0.36	—
Congo, Rep.	0.95	8.9	371	5.3	0.74	0.79	0.42	0.42	0.41
Costa Rica	0.99	13.1	429	9	0.92	—	0.63	0.6	0.6
Côte d'Ivoire	0.92	8.1	373	4.8	0.66	0.78	0.38	0.37	0.3
Croatia	1	13.4	488	10.4	0.92	—	0.71	0.73	0.69
Cyprus	1	13.6	502	10.9	0.95	—	0.76	0.75	0.69
Czechia	1	13.6	512	11.1	0.92	—	0.75	0.76	0.73
Denmark	1	13.4	518	11.1	0.93	—	0.76	0.77	0.75
Dominica	0.96	12.4	404	8	0.86	—	0.54	0.55	—
Dominican Republic	0.97	11.9	345	6.6	0.84	0.93	0.5	0.51	—
Ecuador	0.99	12.9	420	8.7	0.88	0.76	0.59	0.6	0.53
Egypt, Arab Rep.	0.98	11.5	356	6.5	0.86	0.78	0.49	0.49	0.48

(continued)

(continued)

Economy	Components of HCI 2020						HCI		
	Probability of survival to age 5	Expected years of school	Harmonized test scores	Learning adjusted years of schooling	Adult survival rate	Fraction of children under 5 not stunted	HCI 2020	HCI 2018 back-calculated	HCI 2010
El Salvador	0.99	10.9	436	7.6	0.82	0.86	0.55	0.54	–
Estonia	1	13.5	543	11.7	0.9	–	0.78	0.77	0.73
Eswatini	0.95	6.4	440	4.5	0.6	0.74	0.37	0.37	0.31
Ethiopia	0.94	7.8	348	4.3	0.79	0.63	0.38	0.38	–
Fiji	0.97	11.3	383	7	0.78	0.91	0.51	–	–
Finland	1	13.7	534	11.7	0.93	–	0.8	0.81	0.82
France	1	13.8	510	11.3	0.93	–	0.76	0.76	0.76
Gabon	0.96	8.3	456	6	0.79	0.83	0.46	0.46	–
Gambia	0.94	9.5	353	5.4	0.75	0.81	0.42	0.4	0.37
Georgia	0.99	12.9	400	8.3	0.85	–	0.57	0.61	0.54
Germany	1	13.3	517	11	0.93	–	0.75	0.76	0.76
Ghana	0.95	12.1	307	6	0.77	0.82	0.45	0.44	–
Greece	1	13.3	469	10	0.93	–	0.69	0.69	0.71
Grenada	0.98	13.1	395	8.3	0.85	–	0.57	0.54	–
Guatemala	0.97	9.7	405	6.3	0.85	0.53	0.46	0.46	0.44
Guinea	0.9	7	408	4.6	0.76	0.7	0.37	0.37	–
Guyana	0.97	12.2	346	6.8	0.77	0.89	0.5	0.49	–
Haiti	0.94	11.4	338	6.1	0.78	0.78	0.45	0.44	–
Honduras	0.98	9.6	400	6.1	0.86	0.77	0.48	0.48	–
Hong Kong SAR, China	0.99	13.5	549	11.9	0.95	–	0.81	0.82	0.78
Hungary	1	13	495	10.3	0.88	–	0.68	0.71	0.69
Iceland	1	13.5	498	10.7	0.95	–	0.75	0.74	0.76
India	0.96	11.1	399	7.1	0.83	0.65	0.49	0.48	–

Indonesia	0.98	12.4	395	7.8	0.85	0.72	0.54	0.54	0.5
Iran, Islamic Rep.	0.99	11.8	432	8.2	0.93	–	0.59	0.59	0.56
Iraq	0.97	6.9	363	4	0.84	0.87	0.41	0.4	–
Ireland	1	13.9	521	11.6	0.94	–	0.79	0.81	0.77
Israel	1	13.8	481	10.6	0.95	–	0.73	0.76	0.72
Italy	1	13.3	493	10.5	0.95	–	0.73	0.75	0.75
Jamaica	0.99	11.4	387	7.1	0.86	0.94	0.53	0.54	–
Japan	1	13.6	538	11.7	0.95	–	0.8	0.84	0.82
Jordan	0.98	11.1	430	7.7	0.89	–	0.55	0.55	0.56
Kazakhstan	0.99	13.7	416	9.1	0.84	0.92	0.63	0.78	0.59
Kenya	0.96	11.6	455	8.5	0.77	0.74	0.55	0.54	–
Kiribati	0.95	11.2	411	7.4	0.81	–	0.49	0.47	–
Kosovo	0.99	13.2	374	7.9	0.91	–	0.57	0.57	–
Kuwait	0.99	12	383	7.4	0.94	–	0.56	0.56	0.57
Kyrgyz Republic	0.98	12.9	420	8.7	0.85	0.88	0.6	0.59	–
Lao PDR	0.95	10.6	368	6.3	0.82	0.67	0.46	0.46	–
Latvia	1	13.6	504	11	0.84	–	0.71	0.74	0.68
Lebanon	0.99	10.2	390	6.3	0.93	–	0.52	0.52	–
Lesotho	0.92	10	393	6.3	0.52	0.65	0.4	0.4	0.34
Liberia	0.93	4.2	332	2.2	0.78	0.7	0.32	0.32	–
Lithuania	1	13.8	496	11	0.84	–	0.71	0.73	0.69
Luxembourg	1	12.4	493	9.8	0.94	–	0.69	0.69	0.7
Macao SAR, China	0.99	12.9	561	11.6	0.96	–	0.8	0.76	0.65
Madagascar	0.95	8.4	351	4.7	0.8	0.58	0.39	0.39	0.39
Malawi	0.95	9.6	359	5.5	0.74	0.61	0.41	0.41	0.36
Malaysia	0.99	12.5	446	8.9	0.88	0.79	0.61	0.63	0.58

(continued)

(continued)

Economy	Components of HCI 2020						HCI		
	Probability of survival to age 5	Expected years of school	Harmonized test scores	Learning adjusted years of schooling	Adult survival rate	Fraction of children under 5 not stunted	HCI 2020	HCI 2018 back-calculated	HCI 2010
Mali	0.9	5.2	307	2.6	0.75	0.73	0.32	0.32	–
Malta	0.99	13.4	474	10.2	0.95	–	0.71	0.71	0.68
Marshall Islands	0.97	9.4	375	5.7	0.7	0.65	0.42	0.4	–
Mauritania	0.92	7.7	342	4.2	0.8	0.77	0.38	0.37	–
Mauritius	0.98	12.4	473	9.4	0.86	–	0.62	0.62	0.6
Mexico	0.99	12.8	430	8.8	0.86	0.9	0.61	0.61	0.59
Micronesia, Fed. Sts.	0.97	11.8	380	7.2	0.84	–	0.51	0.47	–
Moldova	0.98	11.8	439	8.3	0.84	0.94	0.58	0.58	0.56
Mongolia	0.98	13.2	435	9.2	0.8	0.91	0.61	0.62	–
Montenegro	1	12.8	436	8.9	0.91	0.91	0.63	0.62	0.59
Morocco	0.98	10.4	380	6.3	0.93	0.85	0.5	0.49	0.47
Mozambique	0.93	7.6	368	4.5	0.68	0.58	0.36	0.36	–
Myanmar	0.95	10	425	6.8	0.8	0.71	0.48	0.47	–
Namibia	0.96	9.4	407	6.1	0.71	0.77	0.45	0.45	0.39
Nauru	0.97	11.7	347	6.5	0.93	–	0.51	–	–
Nepal	0.97	12.3	369	7.2	0.86	0.64	0.5	0.5	–
Netherlands	1	13.9	520	11.5	0.95	–	0.79	0.8	0.8
New Zeeland	0.99	13.7	520	11.4	0.94	–	0.78	0.77	0.78
Nicaragua	0.98	10.8	392	6.7	0.85	0.83	0.51	0.51	–
Niger	0.92	5.5	305	2.7	0.77	0.52	0.32	0.32	–
Nigeria	0.88	10.2	309	5	0.66	0.63	0.36	0.35	–

North Macedonia	0.99	11	414	7.3	0.91	0.95	0.56	0.54	0.54
Norway	1	13.7	514	11.2	0.94	–	0.77	0.77	0.77
Oman	0.99	12.8	424	8.6	0.91	–	0.61	0.61	0.55
Pakistan	0.93	9.4	339	5.1	0.85	0.62	0.41	0.4	–
Palau	0.98	11.7	463	8.7	0.87	–	0.59	0.57	–
Panama	0.98	10.7	377	6.5	0.89	–	0.5	0.51	0.51
Papua New Guinea	0.95	10.3	363	6	0.78	0.51	0.43	0.42	–
Paraguay	0.98	11.3	386	7	0.86	0.94	0.53	0.53	0.51
Peru	0.99	13	415	8.6	0.89	0.88	0.61	0.59	0.55
Philippines	0.97	12.9	362	7.5	0.82	0.7	0.52	0.55	0.7
Poland	1	13.4	530	11.4	0.89	–	0.75	0.76	0.74
Portugal	1	13.9	509	11.3	0.93	–	0.77	0.78	0.59
Qatar	0.99	12.8	427	8.8	0.96	–	0.64	0.63	0.6
Romania	0.99	11.8	442	8.4	0.88	–	0.58	0.59	0.6
Russian Federation	0.99	13.7	498	10.9	0.8	–	0.68	0.73	–
Rwanda	0.96	6.9	358	3.9	0.81	0.62	0.38	0.38	–
Samoa	0.98	12.2	370	7.2	0.89	0.95	0.55	0.52	–
Saudi Arabia	0.99	12.4	399	7.9	0.92	0.81	0.58	0.58	0.55
Senegal	0.96	7.3	412	4.8	0.83	0.94	0.42	0.42	0.39
Serbia	0.99	13.3	457	9.8	0.89	–	0.68	0.76	0.65
Seychelles	0.99	13.1	463	9.7	0.85	0.71	0.63	0.63	0.57
Sierra Leone	0.89	9.6	316	4.9	0.63	–	0.36	0.35	–
Singapore	1	13.9	575	12.8	0.95	–	0.88	0.89	0.85
Slovakia	0.99	12.6	485	9.8	0.9	–	0.66	0.68	0.68
Slovenia	1	13.6	521	11.4	0.93	–	0.77	0.79	0.75

(continued)

(continued)

Economy	Components of HCI 2020						HCI		
	Probability of survival to age 5	Expected years of school	Harmonized test scores	Learning adjusted years of schooling	Adult survival rate	Fraction of children under 5 not stunted	HCI 2020	HCI 2018 back-calculated	HCI 2010
Solomon Islands	0.98	8.3	351	4.7	0.86	0.68	0.42	0.43	–
South Africa	0.97	10.2	343	5.6	0.69	0.73	0.43	0.42	0.43
South Korea	1	13.6	537	11.7	0.94	–	0.8	0.83	0.82
South Sudan	0.9	4.7	336	2.5	0.68	0.69	0.31	0.31	–
Spain	1	13	507	10.5	0.95	–	0.73	0.74	0.71
Sri Lanka	0.99	13.2	400	8.5	0.9	0.83	0.6	0.59	–
St. Kitts and Nevis	0.99	13	409	8.5	0.88	–	0.59	0.57	–
St. Lucia	0.98	12.7	418	8.5	0.87	0.98	0.6	0.59	–
St. Vincent and the Grenadines	0.98	12.3	391	7.7	0.83	–	0.53	0.54	–
Sudan	0.94	7.1	380	4.3	0.79	0.62	0.38	0.38	–
Sweden	1	13.9	519	11.6	0.95	–	0.8	0.8	0.76
Switzerland	1	13.3	515	10.9	0.95	–	0.76	0.77	0.77
Tajikistan	0.97	10.9	391	6.8	0.87	0.82	0.5	0.54	–
Tanzania	0.95	7.2	388	4.5	0.78	0.68	0.39	0.39	–
Thailand	0.99	12.7	427	8.7	0.87	0.89	0.61	0.62	0.58
Timor—Leste	0.95	10.6	371	6.3	0.86	0.54	0.45	0.45	0.41
Togo	0.93	9.7	384	6	0.74	0.76	0.43	0.42	0.37

Tonga	0.98	11.6	386	7.1	0.83	0.92	0.53	0.52	–
Trinidad and Tobago	0.98	12.4	458	9.1	0.85	–	0.6	0.6	0.55
Tunisia	0.98	10.6	384	6.5	0.91	0.92	0.52	0.51	0.53
Turkey	0.99	12.1	478	9.2	0.91	0.94	0.65	0.63	0.63
Tuvalu	0.98	10.8	346	6	0.79	–	0.45	0.44	–
Uganda	0.95	6.8	397	4.3	0.74	0.71	0.38	0.38	0.34
Ukraine	0.99	12.9	478	9.9	0.81	–	0.63	0.64	0.63
United Arab Emirates	0.99	13.5	448	9.6	0.94	–	0.67	0.68	0.62
United Kingdom	1	13.9	520	11.5	0.93	–	0.78	0.78	0.77
United States	0.99	12.9	512	10.6	0.89	–	0.7	0.71	0.69
Uruguay	0.99	12.2	438	8.6	0.89	–	0.6	0.6	0.59
Uzbekistan	0.98	12	474	9.1	0.87	0.89	0.62	–	–
Vanuatu	0.97	10.1	348	5.6	0.87	0.71	0.45	0.44	–
Vietnam	0.98	12.9	519	10.7	0.87	0.76	0.69	0.69	0.66
West Bank and Gaza	0.98	12.2	412	8	0.89	0.93	0.58	0.57	–
Yemen	0.95	8.1	321	4.2	0.8	0.54	0.37	0.37	–
Zambia	0.94	8.8	358	5	0.73	0.65	0.4	0.39	–
Zimbabwe	0.95	11.1	396	7	0.65	0.77	0.47	0.46	0.41

Source: *Human Capital Index 2020 Update: Human Capital in the time of Covid-19*, World Bank Group 2021

Rank	Country	Score
Under 15 Age Group		
1	Finland	97.67
2	Ireland	96.05
3	Singapore	95.47
4	New Zealand	95.07
5	Japan	94.76
6	Barbados	93.88
7	Belgium	93.86
8	Cyprus	93.57
9	Netherlands	93.41
10	Estonia	93.20
11	Slovenia	93.20
12	Norway	93.16
13	Qatar	93.12
14	France	93.05
15	Canada	93.00
16	Switzerland	92.78
17	Lithuania	92.58
18	Austria	92.24
19	Iceland	92.23
20	Korea, Rep.	91.91
21	Sweden	91.88
22	Croatia	91.87
23	United Kingdom	91.70
24	Italy	91.68
25	Denmark	91.61
26	Luxembourg	90.83
27	Ukraine	90.48
28	Poland	90.10
29	Australia	89.98
30	Greece	89.81
31	Latvia	89.39
32	Israel	89.16
33	Kazakhstan	88.80
34	Jordan	88.65
35	Malta	88.59
36	Czech Republic	88.52
37	United Arab Emirates	88.41
38	Serbia	88.19
39	Portugal	88.17
40	United States	88.09
41	Slovak Republic	87.81
42	Spain	87.76
43	Sri Lanka	87.32

(*continued*)

(continued)

Rank	Country	Score
44	Russian Federation	86.81
45	Mauritius	86.77
46	Armenia	86.75
47	Indonesia	86.04
48	Trinidad and Tobago	86.03
49	Mongolia	85.54
50	Hungary	85.24
51	Kuwait	85.20
52	Iran, Islamic Rep.	84.82
53	Chile	84.74
54	Malaysia	84.71
55	China	84.44
56	Macedonia, FYR	84.09
57	Kyrgyz Republic	83.83
58	Argentina	83.75
59	Albania	83.56
60	Guyana	83.41
61	Turkey	83.26
62	Azerbaijan	83.22
63	Tajikistan	83.05
64	Romania	82.98
65	Jamaica	82.71
66	Saudi Arabia	82.38
67	India	82.03
68	Thailand	81.91
69	Moldova	81.79
70	Uruguay	81.18
71	Tunisia	81.05
72	Mexico	79.93
73	Philippines	79.66
74	Bhutan	79.59
75	Germany	79.56
76	Botswana	79.47
77	Venezuela	79.13
78	Vietnam	78.98
79	Panama	78.73
80	Costa Rica	78.49
81	El Salvador	77.97
82	Egypt	77.73
83	Nepal	76.56
84	Morocco	76.37
85	Bulgaria	76.15
86	Bolivia	76.06

(continued)

(continued)

Rank	Country	Score
87	Peru	75.62
88	South Africa	75.32
89	Bangladesh	74.98
90	Algeria	74.64
91	Dominican Republic	74.64
92	Lao PDR	74.47
93	Colombia	73.92
94	Zambia	72.10
95	Brazil	71.86
96	Kenya	71.58
97	Namibia	70.99
98	Paraguay	70.25
99	Ghana	69.49
100	Rwanda	69.48
101	Nicaragua	69.26
102	Cameroon	69.23
103	Honduras	68.39
104	Lesotho	67.82
105	Guatemala	67.73
106	Cambodia	67.21
107	Côte d'Ivoire	65.05
108	Burundi	64.10
109	Uganda	63.84
110	Senegal	63.78
111	Madagascar	62.89
112	Yemen	62.70
113	Mozambique	61.70
114	Tanzania	61.44
115	Pakistan	60.52
116	Mali	59.27
117	Malawi	59.24
118	Myanmar	59.12
119	Mauritania	57.85
120	Burkina Faso	57.05
121	Guinea	56.86
122	Nigeria	53.01
123	Ethiopia	52.37
124	Chad	50.50
15–24 Age Group		
1	Canada	88.70
2	Finland	85.04
3	Norway	83.87

(continued)

(continued)

Rank	Country	Score
4	Netherlands	83.81
5	Switzerland	83.08
6	Australia	82.87
7	United States	82.86
8	Austria	82.70
9	Denmark	82.31
10	New Zealand	81.83
11	Sweden	81.23
12	Germany	79.87
13	Russian Federation	79.13
14	Iceland	78.97
15	Slovenia	78.66
16	Belgium	78.62
17	Ukraine	77.51
18	Estonia	77.09
19	Czech Republic	76.69
20	Philippines	76.48
21	Japan	76.26
22	Singapore	75.96
23	France	75.89
24	Latvia	75.89
25	Israel	75.88
26	Korea, Rep.	75.81
27	Ireland	75.68
28	Lithuania	75.65
29	Vietnam	74.99
30	Malaysia	74.85
31	United Kingdom	74.77
32	Poland	74.57
33	Uruguay	74.27
34	Kazakhstan	74.27
35	Peru	73.90
36	Malta	73.52
37	Kyrgyz Republic	73.46
38	Hungary	73.38
39	Chile	72.74
40	Panama	72.73
41	Thailand	72.70
42	Luxembourg	72.68
43	Bulgaria	72.57
44	Colombia	72.35
45	Romania	72.28

(continued)

(continued)

Rank	Country	Score
46	Portugal	72.17
47	Italy	72.07
48	Slovak Republic	71.89
49	Croatia	71.80
50	Turkey	71.75
51	Costa Rica	71.61
52	Argentina	70.63
53	Cyprus	70.59
54	Greece	70.40
55	El Salvador	70.35
56	Spain	69.70
57	Sri Lanka	69.63
58	China	69.60
59	Guatemala	69.32
60	Mongolia	68.76
61	Armenia	68.74
62	Paraguay	68.73
63	Mexico	68.61
64	Moldova	68.54
65	Indonesia	67.35
66	Brazil	67.01
67	Macedonia, FYR	66.98
68	United Arab Emirates	66.53
69	Jordan	66.36
70	Saudi Arabia	66.10
71	Qatar	65.97
72	Serbia	65.20
73	Iran, Islamic Rep.	65.17
74	Venezuela	65.05
75	Myanmar	63.91
76	Bolivia	63.87
77	Tajikistan	63.52
78	Mauritius	63.43
79	Zambia	63.40
80	Dominican Republic	62.72
81	Jamaica	62.08
82	Egypt	61.66
83	Albania	61.62
84	Nepal	61.62
85	Azerbaijan	61.54
86	Honduras	61.22
87	Guyana	61.04
88	Cameroon	60.36

(*continued*)

(continued)

Rank	Country	Score
89	Uganda	60.36
90	Tanzania	60.05
91	Bangladesh	59.28
92	Lao PDR	59.06
93	Tunisia	59.05
94	Rwanda	58.66
95	Ghana	58.64
96	Trinidad and Tobago	58.38
97	Ethiopia	58.37
98	India	57.50
99	Barbados	57.25
100	Bhutan	56.54
101	Nicaragua	56.22
102	Botswana	56.20
103	Morocco	56.07
104	Cambodia	56.02
105	Madagascar	55.69
106	Malawi	54.72
107	Algeria	54.67
108	South Africa	54.44
109	Namibia	52.81
110	Mozambique	52.21
111	Kenya	51.54
112	Lesotho	51.31
113	Pakistan	50.85
114	Nigeria	50.16
115	Mali	49.50
116	Kuwait	47.83
117	Côte d'Ivoire	47.43
118	Senegal	47.32
119	Burundi	47.28
120	Burkina Faso	46.34
121	Mauritania	42.57
122	Yemen	42.00
123	Guinea	41.00
124	Chad	40.41
25–54 Age Group		
1	Finland	81.49
2	Switzerland	80.03
3	Sweden	79.62
4	Norway	79.48
5	Japan	78.61
6	Denmark	78.15

(*continued*)

(continued)

Rank	Country	Score
7	Netherlands	77.55
8	Germany	77.55
9	Belgium	77.24
10	France	76.98
11	Luxembourg	76.69
12	United Kingdom	76.42
13	Ireland	75.94
14	Canada	75.84
15	Austria	75.42
16	Iceland	75.06
17	United States	74.64
18	Slovenia	74.43
19	Australia	74.26
20	Lithuania	74.24
21	New Zealand	74.15
22	Singapore	74.12
23	Estonia	73.59
24	Latvia	73.30
25	Cyprus	72.92
26	Czech Republic	72.85
27	Poland	72.38
28	Hungary	71.86
29	Russian Federation	71.77
30	Malta	71.65
31	Israel	71.40
32	Portugal	71.12
33	Slovak Republic	70.86
34	Korea, Rep.	70.36
35	Bulgaria	70.09
36	Romania	69.26
37	Croatia	69.18
38	Spain	69.11
39	Italy	68.99
40	Greece	67.79
41	Ukraine	66.75
42	Malaysia	66.33
43	Kazakhstan	66.23
44	Panama	65.94
45	Serbia	65.61
46	Costa Rica	65.49
47	Chile	64.72
48	Argentina	64.51
49	Uruguay	64.49

(*continued*)

(continued)

Rank	Country	Score
50	Armenia	64.40
51	Philippines	64.27
52	Kyrgyz Republic	63.72
53	United Arab Emirates	63.70
54	Mongolia	63.48
55	Mexico	63.12
56	Colombia	62.96
57	Thailand	62.91
58	Trinidad and Tobago	62.84
59	Bolivia	62.79
60	Macedonia, FYR	62.23
61	China	61.85
62	Paraguay	61.47
63	Ghana	61.41
64	El Salvador	61.28
65	Peru	61.21
66	Brazil	61.17
67	Albania	61.03
68	Vietnam	60.63
69	Azerbaijan	60.47
70	Indonesia	60.00
71	Tajikistan	59.85
72	Mauritius	59.57
73	Sri Lanka	59.21
74	Jamaica	59.16
75	Qatar	59.07
76	Cameroon	58.40
77	Turkey	58.37
78	South Africa	58.24
79	Zambia	57.76
80	Moldova	56.72
81	Guyana	56.59
82	Barbados	56.47
83	Botswana	56.09
84	Dominican Republic	56.01
85	Jordan	55.91
86	Bhutan	55.90
87	Egypt	55.66
88	Nicaragua	55.60
89	Cambodia	55.48
90	Uganda	55.17
91	Guatemala	55.17
92	Kenya	54.55

(continued)

(continued)

Rank	Country	Score
93	Namibia	54.55
94	Madagascar	54.51
95	Iran, Islamic Rep.	53.73
96	Tanzania	53.72
97	Saudi Arabia	53.69
98	Honduras	53.55
99	Lesotho	53.07
100	Venezuela	53.04
101	Morocco	52.97
102	Mozambique	52.08
103	Pakistan	51.37
104	Malawi	51.33
105	Kuwait	51.15
106	Senegal	49.82
107	Tunisia	49.81
108	Lao PDR	49.78
109	India	49.34
110	Burkina Faso	48.54
111	Bangladesh	48.35
112	Rwanda	48.15
113	Guinea	47.59
114	Nepal	47.55
115	Ethiopia	47.37
116	Myanmar	47.00
117	Nigeria	46.25
118	Côte d'Ivoire	45.18
119	Algeria	44.93
120	Mali	44.52
121	Chad	38.83
122	Burundi	37.54
123	Mauritania	37.46
124	Yemen	34.06
55–64 Age Group		
1	New Zealand	85.72
2	Japan	85.24
3	Norway	85.14
4	Sweden	84.40
5	Canada	84.15
6	Finland	83.72
7	Denmark	83.66
8	Switzerland	83.45
9	Germany	82.67
10	Australia	82.64

(*continued*)

(continued)

Rank	Country	Score
11	Estonia	82.59
12	Kazakhstan	81.21
13	Lithuania	80.89
14	Netherlands	80.63
15	United States	80.61
16	Latvia	80.52
17	Russian Federation	80.45
18	Bulgaria	79.43
19	Ukraine	79.19
20	Israel	79.10
21	Austria	79.01
22	United Kingdom	78.73
23	Armenia	78.54
24	Korea, Rep.	78.42
25	Belgium	77.87
26	Azerbaijan	77.73
27	Czech Republic	77.69
28	Ireland	77.65
29	Romania	77.31
30	France	77.24
31	Hungary	77.13
32	Slovenia	76.75
33	Kyrgyz Republic	76.72
34	Slovak Republic	76.26
35	Poland	75.46
36	Panama	75.39
37	Luxembourg	75.36
38	Italy	75.23
39	Cyprus	74.86
40	Philippines	74.50
41	Uruguay	74.48
42	Tajikistan	74.40
43	Chile	74.22
44	Mongolia	74.21
45	Iceland	74.15
46	Moldova	73.88
47	Croatia	72.95
48	Peru	72.94
49	Malta	72.88
50	Argentina	72.88
51	Colombia	72.70
52	Greece	71.73
53	Singapore	71.35

(continued)

(continued)

Rank	Country	Score
54	Spain	70.95
55	Costa Rica	70.87
56	Macedonia, FYR	70.38
57	Serbia	70.37
58	Vietnam	70.32
59	Paraguay	70.15
60	Nicaragua	69.27
61	Mexico	69.24
62	Bolivia	69.22
63	Albania	68.27
64	Sri Lanka	68.26
65	Portugal	67.96
66	Qatar	66.94
67	Dominican Republic	66.63
68	Ghana	66.05
69	El Salvador	65.94
70	Brazil	65.72
71	Thailand	65.71
72	United Arab Emirates	65.34
73	Jamaica	64.42
74	Indonesia	63.87
75	Malaysia	63.80
76	Zambia	63.51
77	Mauritius	63.50
78	Turkey	63.41
79	Trinidad and Tobago	63.25
80	Guyana	62.51
81	Guatemala	62.42
82	South Africa	61.96
83	China	61.74
84	Namibia	61.19
85	Cambodia	60.78
86	Cameroon	60.72
87	Honduras	60.68
88	Uganda	59.65
89	Morocco	58.56
90	Tanzania	57.74
91	Kuwait	57.40
92	Bangladesh	57.22
93	Jordan	57.21
94	Barbados	56.76
95	Kenya	56.76

(continued)

(continued)

Rank	Country	Score
96	Iran, Islamic Rep.	56.72
97	Madagascar	56.65
98	Egypt	56.12
99	Burundi	56.07
100	Malawi	55.41
101	Myanmar	54.74
102	Venezuela	53.95
103	Botswana	53.65
104	Bhutan	53.44
105	Senegal	52.87
106	Mozambique	52.48
107	Saudi Arabia	52.23
108	Pakistan	50.96
109	Lesotho	49.67
110	Guinea	49.07
111	Lao PDR	49.02
112	Ethiopia	48.90
113	Tunisia	48.72
114	Rwanda	47.71
115	India	46.42
116	Burkina Faso	45.93
117	Nigeria	45.43
118	Mali	44.80
119	Nepal	44.62
120	Algeria	43.93
121	Côte d'Ivoire	41.37
122	Chad	37.31
123	Mauritania	34.73
124	Yemen	25.54

Source: WEF_Human_Capital_Report_2015

ANNEX 15: HUMAN CAPITAL INDEX (HCI), 2012

Country	Rank	Score	Rank	Score	Rank	Score	Rank	Score	Rank	Score
Switzerland	1	1.455	4	1.313	1	0.977	1	1.736	2	1.793
Finland	2	1.406	1	1.601	9	0.844	3	1.250	1	1.926
Singapore	3	1.232	3	1.348	13	0.762	2	1.345	5	1.471
Netherlands	4	1.161	7	1.106	4	0.901	8	1.150	4	1.484
Sweden	5	1.111	14	0.977	2	0.960	6	1.154	10	1.351
Germany	6	1.109	19	0.888	8	0.877	9	1.149	3	1.522
Norway	7	1.104	15	0.970	6	0.890	5	1.182	8	1.373
United Kingdom	8	1.042	10	1.031	17	0.682	10	1.072	7	1.384
Denmark	9	1.024	18	0.891	3	0.943	12	0.932	11	1.330
Canada	10	0.987	2	1.355	20	0.548	15	0.875	17	1.168
Belgium	11	0.985	6	1.191	11	0.780	21	0.673	14	1.296
New Zealand	12	0.978	5	1.204	15	0.743	17	0.804	18	1.163
Austria	13	0.977	25	0.713	7	0.886	14	0.886	6	1.424
Iceland	14	0.957	8	1.075	5	0.900	16	0.826	20	1.026
Japan	15	0.948	28	0.628	10	0.836	11	1.027	13	1.302
United States	16	0.920	11	1.027	43	0.239	4	1.235	16	1.181
Luxembourg	17	0.881	35	0.522	16	0.704	13	0.928	9	1.372
Qatar	18	0.834	26	0.684	44	0.206	7	1.154	15	1.294
Australia	19	0.831	13	0.988	18	0.663	19	0.675	23	0.999
Ireland	20	0.824	9	1.033	25	0.516	22	0.645	19	1.103
France	21	0.746	22	0.776	14	0.744	25	0.520	24	0.943
Malaysia	22	0.644	34	0.526	39	0.301	18	0.736	22	1.014
Korea, Rep.	23	0.640	17	0.899	27	0.481	23	0.596	30	0.582

Country										
United Arab Emirates	24	0.610	29	0.626	70	-0.032	24	0.527	12	1.320
Israel	25	0.587	27	0.651	29	0.457	20	0.674	32	0.568
Barbados	26	0.581	12	1.007	42	0.245	29	0.340	27	0.730
Estonia	27	0.571	20	0.862	22	0.536	39	0.142	26	0.745
Malta	28	0.473	24	0.716	28	0.473	30	0.330	37	0.371
Spain	29	0.465	31	0.590	12	0.778	70	-0.185	28	0.679
Portugal	30	0.453	37	0.411	23	0.532	34	0.243	29	0.624
Cyprus	31	0.452	16	0.938	32	0.352	33	0.252	41	0.268
Slovenia	32	0.445	21	0.825	26	0.516	41	0.106	38	0.332
Czech Republic	33	0.387	36	0.452	36	0.310	36	0.210	31	0.576
Lithuania	34	0.360	23	0.745	41	0.252	56	-0.018	36	0.462
Costa Rica	35	0.320	39	0.382	30	0.445	28	0.378	50	0.077
Chile	36	0.305	49	0.250	38	0.306	37	0.194	35	0.471
Italy	37	0.266	40	0.378	19	0.601	75	-0.243	39	0.329
Latvia	38	0.248	30	0.615	48	0.151	54	-0.011	43	0.237
Saudi Arabia	39	0.245	55	0.098	72	-0.041	61	-0.099	21	1.023
Bahrain	40	0.232	48	0.274	64	0.011	43	0.099	33	0.544
Oman	41	0.220	62	0.032	37	0.307	78	-0.280	25	0.822
Panama	42	0.207	66	-0.006	60	0.055	31	0.301	34	0.477
China	43	0.186	58	0.069	65	0.010	26	0.516	47	0.147
Thailand	44	0.158	79	-0.242	40	0.281	27	0.482	48	0.112
Kazakhstan	45	0.124	43	0.359	69	-0.031	40	0.107	51	0.061
Croatia	46	0.099	38	0.394	24	0.526	88	-0.378	60	-0.146
Mauritius	47	0.099	50	0.234	45	0.202	64	-0.143	49	0.102
Uruguay	48	0.096	67	-0.037	21	0.543	84	-0.340	44	0.219
Poland	49	0.087	42	0.376	47	0.173	63	-0.139	57	-0.064
Sri Lanka	50	0.020	51	0.172	35	0.323	62	-0.127	70	-0.288

(continued)

(continued)

Country	Rank	Score	Rank	Score	Rank	Score	Rank	Score	Rank	Score
Russian Federation	51	0.010	41	0.377	62	0.027	66	-0.163	63	-0.201
Jordan	52	0.005	44	0.350	68	-0.015	97	-0.481	46	0.167
Indonesia	53	0.001	61	0.040	84	-0.215	32	0.262	58	-0.082
Hungary	54	0.000	33	0.530	73	-0.064	77	-0.275	62	-0.190
Greece	55	-0.011	47	0.280	34	0.331	86	-0.365	71	-0.291
Bulgaria	56	-0.048	46	0.282	33	0.333	100	-0.496	74	-0.311
Brazil	57	-0.054	88	-0.497	49	0.150	45	0.078	52	0.054
Mexico	58	-0.057	82	-0.291	56	0.074	48	0.011	53	-0.022
Kuwait	59	-0.059	80	-0.285	58	0.065	80	-0.297	40	0.281
Turkey	60	-0.065	77	-0.220	51	0.117	83	-0.337	45	0.181
Ecuador	61	-0.099	69	-0.090	76	-0.094	47	0.034	68	-0.244

Country	Overall index		Education		Health and wellness		Workforce and employment		Enabling environment	
	Rank	Score	Rank	Score	Rank	Score	Rank	Score	Rank	Score
Argentina	62	-0.120	56	0.091	31	0.362	92	-0.408	84	-0.527
Ukraine	63	-0.124	45	0.316	55	0.078	67	-0.166	96	-0.725
Azerbaijan	64	-0.157	71	-0.153	94	-0.414	55	-0.016	55	-0.044
Macedonia, FYR	65	-0.160	52	0.165	63	0.013	115	-0.784	54	-0.033
Philippines	66	-0.161	65	0.011	96	-0.473	38	0.164	78	-0.344
Tunisia	67	-0.165	70	-0.099	46	0.173	101	-0.499	66	-0.236
Jamaica	68	-0.171	81	-0.285	50	0.126	76	-0.246	69	-0.279
Romania	69	-0.176	57	0.077	61	0.048	85	-0.364	83	-0.463
Vietnam	70	-0.202	73	-0.176	88	-0.291	57	-0.040	73	-0.302
Colombia	71	-0.202	72	-0.169	79	-0.116	73	-0.229	72	-0.296
Albania	72	-0.216	54	0.136	54	0.083	71	-0.207	105	-0.874
Armenia	73	-0.218	60	0.042	71	-0.035	113	-0.678	64	-0.201
Lebanon	74	-0.220	32	0.548	77	-0.099	96	-0.458	104	-0.870
Peru	75	-0.227	84	-0.323	82	-0.204	50	-0.003	81	-0.377
Trinidad and Tobago	76	-0.233	53	0.164	121	-1.043	53	-0.008	56	-0.047
Georgia	77	-0.258	74	-0.191	66	-0.005	102	-0.514	76	-0.321
India	78	-0.270	63	0.020	112	-0.868	49	0.005	67	-0.239
Botswana	79	-0.291	85	-0.386	86	-0.270	93	-0.416	59	-0.090
Lao PDR	80	-0.297	83	-0.320	91	-0.407	59	-0.097	80	-0.364
Kenya	81	-0.306	90	-0.503	103	-0.603	35	0.226	79	-0.347
Morocco	82	-0.328	93	-0.590	59	0.061	99	-0.485	77	-0.328
Moldova	83	-0.337	64	0.014	53	0.092	110	-0.654	102	-0.801
Guatemala	84	-0.341	105	-0.968	81	-0.196	46	0.035	65	-0.234
Serbia	85	-0.343	59	0.053	52	0.115	118	-0.945	89	-0.596

(continued)

(continued)

Country	Overall index		Education		Health and wellness		Workforce and employment		Enabling environment	
	Rank	Score	Rank	Score	Rank	Score	Rank	Score	Rank	Score
South Africa	86	-0.361	92	-0.589	98	-0.533	105	-0.588	42	0.265
Ghana	87	-0.363	91	-0.505	99	-0.533	60	-0.099	75	-0.317
Bhutan	88	-0.370	89	-0.498	83	-0.208	74	-0.231	85	-0.545
Mongolia	89	-0.400	76	-0.198	80	-0.139	106	-0.610	92	-0.651
El Salvador	90	-0.405	95	-0.612	92	-0.409	68	-0.175	82	-0.425
Suriname	91	-0.420	87	-0.423	67	-0.010	109	-0.640	90	-0.607
Kyrgyz Republic	92	-0.440	78	-0.233	75	-0.073	112	-0.673	100	-0.781
Nicaragua	93	-0.446	94	-0.594	78	-0.100	89	-0.386	94	-0.704
Iran, Islamic Rep.	94	-0.487	68	-0.051	87	-0.274	119	-1.059	88	-0.564
Dominican Republic	95	-0.499	97	-0.732	85	-0.223	91	-0.401	91	-0.641
Cambodia	96	-0.505	99	-0.839	102	-0.596	42	0.104	93	-0.688
Namibia	97	-0.539	98	-0.817	100	-0.560	108	-0.620	61	-0.160
Paraguay	98	-0.546	102	-0.906	57	0.072	94	-0.433	108	-0.916
Bolivia	99	-0.552	86	-0.409	113	-0.878	69	-0.185	97	-0.736
Honduras	100	-0.560	103	-0.947	89	-0.335	90	-0.397	87	-0.561
Venezuela	101	-0.564	75	-0.194	74	-0.068	114	-0.746	120	-1.250
Senegal	102	-0.602	112	-1.202	90	-0.404	51	-0.006	101	-0.794
Malawi	103	-0.629	101	-0.897	107	-0.723	52	-0.007	106	-0.890
Tanzania	104	-0.680	100	-0.870	117	-0.957	58	-0.087	103	-0.805
Madagascar	105	-0.725	107	-0.997	109	-0.749	44	0.084	118	-1.238
Uganda	106	-0.727	108	-1.036	118	-0.959	65	-0.147	99	-0.767
Cameroon	107	-0.728	96	-0.687	111	-0.850	79	-0.295	113	-1.082
Lesotho	108	-0.751	110	-1.084	101	-0.588	95	-0.438	107	-0.894
Côte d'Ivoire	109	-0.759	114	-1.302	95	-0.418	72	-0.208	114	-1.107
Bangladesh	110	-0.782	104	-0.959	104	-0.606	103	-0.543	110	-1.019

Egypt	111	−0.790	113	−1.206	97	−0.521	116	−0.878	86	−0.555
Pakistan	112	−0.837	111	−1.166	115	−0.920	104	−0.545	95	−0.718
Benin	113	−0.865	109	−1.044	106	−0.689	98	−0.481	119	−1.244
Nigeria	114	−0.878	116	−1.411	120	−1.034	81	−0.328	98	−0.740
Algeria	115	−0.954	106	−0.991	93	−0.413	121	−1.345	112	−1.066
Ethiopia	116	−0.961	115	−1.380	108	−0.749	111	−0.660	111	−1.056
Mozambique	117	−0.966	117	−1.474	114	−0.916	82	−0.337	115	−1.135
Mali	118	−1.034	120	−1.747	110	−0.826	107	−0.614	109	−0.949
Burkina Faso	119	−1.077	121	−1.817	116	−0.943	87	−0.374	117	−1.173
Guinea	120	−1.272	118	−1.482	119	−1.026	117	−0.911	122	−1.667
Mauritania	121	−1.297	119	−1.744	105	−0.666	122	−1.404	121	−1.373
Yemen	122	−1.395	122	−1.972	122	−1.134	120	−1.320	116	−1.153

Source: World Economic Forum (2013) The Human Capital Report, www.weforum.org

Ranking by pillar

Education

Rank	Country	Score	Rank	Country	Score
1	Finland	1.601	62	Oman	0.032
2	Canada	1.355	63	India	0.020
3	Singapore	1.348	64	Moldova	0.014
4	Switzerland	1.313	65	Philippines	0.011
5	New Zealand	1.204	66	Panama	-0.006
6	Belgium	1.191	67	Uruguay	-0.037
7	Netherlands	1.106	68	Iran, Islamic Rep.	-0.051
8	Iceland	1.075	69	Ecuador	-0.090
9	Ireland	1.033	70	Tunisia	-0.099
10	United Kingdom	1.031	71	Azerbaijan	-0.153
11	United States	1.027	72	Colombia	-0.169
12	Barbados	1.007	73	Vietnam	-0.176
13	Australia	0.988	74	Georgia	-0.191
14	Sweden	0.977	75	Venezuela	-0.194
15	Norway	0.970	76	Mongolia	-0.198
16	Cyprus	0.938	77	Turkey	-0.220
17	Korea, Rep.	0.899	78	Kyrgyz Republic	-0.233

Health and wellness

Rank	Country	Score	Rank	Country	Score
1	Switzerland	0.977	62	Russian Federation	0.027
2	Sweden	0.960	63	Macedonia, FYR	0.013
3	Denmark	0.943	64	Bahrain	0.011
4	Netherlands	0.901	65	China	0.010
5	Iceland	0.900	66	Georgia	-0.005
6	Norway	0.890	67	Suriname	-0.010
7	Austria	0.886	68	Jordan	-0.015
8	Germany	0.877	69	Kazakhstan	-0.031
9	Finland	0.844	70	United Arab Emirates	-0.032
10	Japan	0.836	71	Armenia	-0.035
11	Belgium	0.780	72	Saudi Arabia	-0.041
12	Spain	0.778	73	Hungary	-0.064
13	Singapore	0.762	74	Venezuela	-0.068
14	France	0.744	75	Kyrgyz Republic	-0.073
15	New Zealand	0.743	76	Ecuador	-0.094
16	Luxembourg	0.704	77	Lebanon	-0.099
17	United Kingdom	0.682	78	Nicaragua	-0.100

Rank	Country	Value	Rank	Country	Value
18	Denmark	0.891	18	Australia	0.663
19	Germany	0.888	19	Italy	0.601
20	Estonia	0.862	20	Canada	0.548
21	Slovenia	0.825	21	Uruguay	0.543
22	France	0.776	22	Estonia	0.536
23	Lithuania	0.745	23	Portugal	0.532
24	Malta	0.716	24	Croatia	0.526
25	Austria	0.713	25	Ireland	0.516
26	Qatar	0.684	26	Slovenia	0.516
27	Israel	0.651	27	Korea, Rep.	0.481
28	Japan	0.628	28	Malta	0.473
29	United Arab Emirates	0.626	29	Israel	0.457
30	Latvia	0.615	30	Costa Rica	0.445
31	Spain	0.590	31	Argentina	0.362
32	Lebanon	0.548	32	Cyprus	0.352
33	Hungary	0.530	33	Bulgaria	0.333
34	Malaysia	0.526	34	Greece	0.331
35	Luxembourg	0.522	35	Sri Lanka	0.323
36	Czech Republic	0.452	36	Czech Republic	0.310
37	Portugal	0.411	37	Oman	0.307
38	Croatia	0.394	38	Chile	0.306
39	Costa Rica	0.382	39	Malaysia	0.301
40	Italy	0.378	40	Thailand	0.281
41	Russian Federation	0.377	41	Lithuania	0.252

Rank	Country	Value	Rank	Country	Value
79	Thailand	−0.242	79	Colombia	−0.116
80	Kuwait	−0.285	80	Mongolia	−0.139
81	Jamaica	−0.285	81	Guatemala	−0.196
82	Mexico	−0.291	82	Peru	−0.204
83	Lao PDR	−0.320	83	Bhutan	−0.208
84	Peru	−0.323	84	Indonesia	−0.215
85	Botswana	−0.386	85	Dominican Republic	−0.223
86	Bolivia	−0.409	86	Botswana	−0.270
87	Suriname	−0.423	87	Iran, Islamic Rep.	−0.274
88	Brazil	−0.497	88	Vietnam	−0.291
89	Bhutan	−0.498	89	Honduras	−0.335
90	Kenya	−0.503	90	Senegal	−0.404
91	Ghana	−0.505	91	Lao PDR	−0.407
92	South Africa	−0.589	92	El Salvador	−0.409
93	Morocco	−0.590	93	Algeria	−0.413
94	Nicaragua	−0.594	94	Azerbaijan	−0.414
95	El Salvador	−0.612	95	Côte d'Ivoire	−0.418
96	Cameroon	−0.687	96	Philippines	−0.473
97	Dominican Republic	−0.732	97	Egypt	−0.521
98	Namibia	−0.817	98	South Africa	−0.533
99	Cambodia	−0.839	99	Ghana	−0.533
100	Tanzania	−0.870	100	Namibia	−0.560
101	Malawi	−0.897	101	Lesotho	−0.588
102	Paraguay	−0.906	102	Cambodia	−0.596

(continued)

(continued)

Ranking by pillar

Education						Health and wellness					
Rank	Country	Score	Rank	Country	Score	Rank	Country	Score	Rank	Country	Score
42	Poland	0.376	103	Honduras	−0.947	42	Barbados	0.245	103	Kenya	−0.603
43	Kazakhstan	0.359	104	Bangladesh	−0.959	43	United States	0.239	104	Bangladesh	−0.606
44	Jordan	0.350	105	Guatemala	−0.968	44	Qatar	0.206	105	Mauritania	−0.666
45	Ukraine	0.316	106	Algeria	−0.991	45	Mauritius	0.202	106	Benin	−0.689
46	Bulgaria	0.282	107	Madagascar	−0.997	46	Tunisia	0.173	107	Malawi	−0.723
47	Greece	0.280	108	Uganda	−1.036	47	Poland	0.173	108	Ethiopia	−0.749
48	Bahrain	0.274	109	Benin	−1.044	48	Latvia	0.151	109	Madagascar	−0.749
49	Chile	0.250	110	Lesotho	−1.084	49	Brazil	0.150	110	Mali	−0.826
50	Mauritius	0.234	111	Pakistan	−1.166	50	Jamaica	0.126	111	Cameroon	−0.850
51	Sri Lanka	0.172	112	Senegal	−1.202	51	Turkey	0.117	112	India	−0.868
52	Macedonia, FYR	0.165	113	Egypt	−1.206	52	Serbia	0.115	113	Bolivia	−0.878
53	Trinidad and Tobago	0.164	114	Côte d'Ivoire	−1.302	53	Moldova	0.092	114	Mozambique	−0.916
54	Albania	0.136	115	Ethiopia	−1.380	54	Albania	0.083	115	Pakistan	−0.920
55	Saudi Arabia	0.098	116	Nigeria	−1.411	55	Ukraine	0.078	116	Burkina Faso	−0.943
56	Argentina	0.091	117	Mozambique	−1.474	56	Mexico	0.074	117	Tanzania	−0.957
57	Romania	0.077	118	Guinea	−1.482	57	Paraguay	0.072	118	Uganda	−0.959
58	China	0.069	119	Mauritania	−1.744	58	Kuwait	0.065	119	Guinea	−1.026
59	Serbia	0.053	120	Mali	−1.747	59	Morocco	0.061	120	Nigeria	−1.034
60	Armenia	0.042	121	Burkina Faso	−1.817	60	Panama	0.055	121	Trinidad and Tobago	−1.043
61	Indonesia	0.040	122	Yemen	−1.972	61	Romania	0.048	122	Yemen	−1.134

Ranking by pillar

	Workforce and employment				Enabling environment			
Rank	Country	Score	Rank	Country	Score	Country	Rank	Score
1	Switzerland	1.736	62	Sri Lanka	-0.127	Finland	1	1.926	Hungary	62	-0.190
2	Singapore	1.345	63	Poland	-0.139	Switzerland	2	1.793	Russian Federation	63	-0.201
3	Finland	1.250	64	Mauritius	-0.143	Germany	3	1.522	Armenia	64	-0.201
4	United States	1.235	65	Uganda	-0.147	Netherlands	4	1.484	Guatemala	65	-0.234
5	Norway	1.182	66	Russian Federation	-0.163	Singapore	5	1.471	Tunisia	66	-0.236
6	Sweden	1.154	67	Ukraine	-0.166	Austria	6	1.424	India	67	-0.239
7	Qatar	1.154	68	El Salvador	-0.175	United Kingdom	7	1.384	Ecuador	68	-0.244
8	Netherlands	1.150	69	Bolivia	-0.185	Norway	8	1.373	Jamaica	69	-0.279
9	Germany	1.149	70	Spain	-0.185	Luxembourg	9	1.372	Sri Lanka	70	-0.288
10	United Kingdom	1.072	71	Albania	-0.207	Sweden	10	1.351	Greece	71	-0.291
11	Japan	1.027	72	Côte d'Ivoire	-0.208	Denmark	11	1.330	Colombia	72	-0.296
12	Denmark	0.932	73	Colombia	-0.229	United Arab Emirates	12	1.320	Vietnam	73	-0.302
13	Luxembourg	0.928	74	Bhutan	-0.231	Japan	13	1.302	Bulgaria	74	-0.311
14	Austria	0.886	75	Italy	-0.243	Belgium	14	1.296	Ghana	75	-0.317
15	Canada	0.875	76	Jamaica	-0.246	Qatar	15	1.294	Georgia	76	-0.321

(continued)

(continued)

Ranking by pillar

Workforce and employment

Rank	Country	Score	Rank	Country	Score
16	Iceland	0.826	77	Hungary	−0.275
17	New Zealand	0.804	78	Oman	−0.280
18	Malaysia	0.736	79	Cameroon	−0.295
19	Australia	0.675	80	Kuwait	−0.297
20	Israel	0.674	81	Nigeria	−0.328
21	Belgium	0.673	82	Mozambique	−0.337
22	Ireland	0.645	83	Turkey	−0.337
23	Korea, Rep.	0.596	84	Uruguay	−0.340
24	United Arab Emirates	0.527	85	Romania	−0.364
25	France	0.520	86	Greece	−0.365
26	China	0.516	87	Burkina Faso	−0.374
27	Thailand	0.482	88	Croatia	−0.378
28	Costa Rica	0.378	89	Nicaragua	−0.386
29	Barbados	0.340	90	Honduras	−0.397
30	Malta	0.330	91	Dominican Republic	−0.401
31	Panama	0.301	92	Argentina	−0.408
32	Indonesia	0.262	93	Botswana	−0.416

Enabling environment

Rank	Country	Score	Rank	Country	Score
16	United States	1.181	77	Morocco	−0.328
17	Canada	1.168	78	Philippines	−0.344
18	New Zealand	1.163	79	Kenya	−0.347
19	Ireland	1.103	80	Lao PDR	−0.364
20	Iceland	1.026	81	Peru	−0.377
21	Saudi Arabia	1.023	82	El Salvador	−0.425
22	Malaysia	1.014	83	Romania	−0.463
23	Australia	0.999	84	Argentina	−0.527
24	France	0.943	85	Bhutan	−0.545
25	Oman	0.822	86	Egypt	−0.555
26	Estonia	0.745	87	Honduras	−0.561
27	Barbados	0.730	88	Iran, Islamic Rep.	−0.564
28	Spain	0.679	89	Serbia	−0.596
29	Portugal	0.624	90	Suriname	−0.607
30	Korea, Rep.	0.582	91	Dominican Republic	−0.641
31	Czech Republic	0.576	92	Mongolia	−0.651
32	Israel	0.568	93	Cambodia	−0.688

Rank	Country	Value		Rank	Country	Value
33	Cyprus	0.252		94	Paraguay	-0.433
34	Portugal	0.243		95	Lesotho	-0.438
35	Kenya	0.226		96	Lebanon	-0.458
36	Czech Republic	0.210		97	Jordan	-0.481
37	Chile	0.194		98	Benin	-0.481
38	Philippines	0.164		99	Morocco	-0.485
39	Estonia	0.142		100	Bulgaria	-0.496
40	Kazakhstan	0.107		101	Tunisia	-0.499
41	Slovenia	0.106		102	Georgia	-0.514
42	Cambodia	0.104		103	Bangladesh	-0.543
43	Bahrain	0.099		104	Pakistan	-0.545
44	Madagascar	0.084		105	South Africa	-0.588
45	Brazil	0.078		106	Mongolia	-0.610
46	Guatemala	0.035		107	Mali	-0.614
47	Ecuador	0.034		108	Namibia	-0.620
48	Mexico	0.011		109	Suriname	-0.640
49	India	0.005		110	Moldova	-0.654
50	Peru	-0.003		111	Ethiopia	-0.660
51	Senegal	-0.006		112	Kyrgyz Republic	-0.673
52	Malawi	-0.007		113	Armenia	-0.678

Rank	Country	Value		Rank	Country	Value
33	Bahrain	0.544		94	Nicaragua	-0.704
34	Panama	0.477		95	Pakistan	-0.718
35	Chile	0.471		96	Ukraine	-0.725
36	Lithuania	0.462		97	Bolivia	-0.736
37	Malta	0.371		98	Nigeria	-0.740
38	Slovenia	0.332		99	Uganda	-0.767
39	Italy	0.329		100	Kyrgyz Republic	-0.781
40	Kuwait	0.281		101	Senegal	-0.794
41	Cyprus	0.268		102	Moldova	-0.801
42	South Africa	0.265		103	Tanzania	-0.805
43	Latvia	0.237		104	Lebanon	-0.870
44	Uruguay	0.219		105	Albania	-0.874
45	Turkey	0.181		106	Malawi	-0.890
46	Jordan	0.167		107	Lesotho	-0.894
47	China	0.147		108	Paraguay	-0.916
48	Thailand	0.112		109	Mali	-0.949
49	Mauritius	0.102		110	Bangladesh	-1.019
50	Costa Rica	0.077		111	Ethiopia	-1.056
51	Kazakhstan	0.061		112	Algeria	-1.066
52	Brazil	0.054		113	Cameroon	-1.082

(continued)

Ranking by pillar

Workforce and employment

Rank	Country	Score	Rank	Country	Score
53	Trinidad and Tobago	-0.008	114	Venezuela	-0.746
54	Latvia	-0.011	115	Macedonia, FYR	-0.784
55	Azerbaijan	-0.016	116	Egypt	-0.878
56	Lithuania	-0.018	117	Guinea	-0.911
57	Vietnam	-0.040	118	Serbia	-0.945
58	Tanzania	-0.087	119	Iran, Islamic Rep.	-1.059
59	Lao PDR	-0.097	120	Yemen	-1.320
60	Ghana	-0.099	121	Algeria	-1.345
61	Saudi Arabia	-0.099	122	Mauritania	-1.404

Enabling environment

Rank	Country	Score	Rank	Country	Score
53	Mexico	-0.022	114	Côte d'Ivoire	-1.107
54	Macedonia, FYR	-0.033	115	Mozambique	-1.135
55	Azerbaijan	-0.044	116	Yemen	-1.153
56	Trinidad and Tobago	-0.047	117	Burkina Faso	-1.173
57	Poland	-0.064	118	Madagascar	-1.238
58	Indonesia	-0.082	119	Benin	-1.244
59	Botswana	-0.090	120	Venezuela	-1.250
60	Croatia	-0.146	121	Mauritania	-1.373
61	Namibia	-0.160	122	Guinea	-1.667

Annex 16: Global Competitiveness Index (GCI 4.0) 2018–2019

Rank	Economy	Score	Diff. from 2018 Rank	Diff. from 2018 Score
	Singapore	84.8	+1	+1.3
	United States	83.7	–1	–2.0
	Hong Kong SAR	83.1	+5	+0.9
	Netherlands	82.4	+2	...
	Switzerland	82.3	–1	–0.3
	Japan	82.3	–1	–0.2
	Germany	81.8	–4	–1.0
	Sweden	81.2	+1	–0.4
	United Kingdom	81.2	–1	–0.8
	Denmark	81.2	—	+0.5
	Finland	80.2	...	...
	Taiwan, China	80.2	+1	+1.0
	Korea, Rep.	79.6	+2	+0.8
	Canada	79.6	–2	–0.3
	France	78.8	+2	+0.8
	Australia	78.7	–2	–0.1
	Norway	78.1	+1	–0.1
	Luxembourg	77.0	+1	+0.4
	New Zealand	76.7	–1	–0.8
	Israel	76.7	—	+0.2
	Austria	76.6	+1	+0.3
	Belgium	76.4	–1	–0.3
	Spain	75.3	+3	+1.1
	Ireland	75.1	–1	–0.6
	United Arab Emirates	75.0	+2	+1.6
	Iceland	74.7	–2	+0.2
	Malaysia	74.6	–2	+0.3
	China	73.9	—	+1.3
	Qatar	72.9	+1	+1.9
	Italy	71.5	–1	+0.8
	Estonia	70.9	+1	+0.2
	Czech Republic	70.9	–3	–0.3
	Chile	70.5	—	+0.3
	Portugal	70.4	—	+0.2
	Slovenia	70.2	—	+0.6
	Saudi Arabia	70.0	+3	+2.5
	Poland	68.9	—	+0.7
	Malta	68.5	–2	+0.2
	Lithuania	68.4	+1	+1.2
	Thailand	68.1	–2	+0.8
	Latvia	67.8	+1	+0.7
	Slovak Republic	66.8	–1	–0.1
	Russian Federation	66.7	—	+1.1
	Cyprus	66.4	—	+0.8
	Bahrain	65.4	+5	+1.7
	Kuwait	65.1	+8	+2.0
	Hungary	65.1	+1	+0.8

Rank	Economy	Score	Diff. from 2018 Rank	Diff. from 2018 Score
	Mexico	64.9	–2	+0.3
	Bulgaria	64.9	+2	+1.3
	Indonesia	64.9	–5	–0.2
	Romania	64.4	+1	+0.8
	Mauritius	64.3	–3	–0.5
	Oman	63.6	–6	–0.8
	Uruguay	63.5	–1	–0.8
	Kazakhstan	62.9	+4	+1.1
	Brunei Darussalam	62.8	+6	+1.3
	Colombia	62.7	+3	+1.1
	Azerbaijan	62.7	+11	+2.1
	Greece	62.6	–2	+0.9
	South Africa	62.4	+7	+1.7
	Turkey	62.1	—	+1.6
	Costa Rica	62.0	–7	–0.1
	Croatia	61.9	+5	–1.9
	Philippines	61.9	–12	–0.5
	Peru	61.7	–2	+0.5
	Panama	61.6	–2	+0.6
	Viet Nam	61.5	+10	+3.5
	India	61.4	–10	–0.7
	Armenia	61.3	+1	+1.6
	Jordan	60.9	+3	+1.6
	Brazil	60.9	+5	+1.4
	Serbia	60.9	–2	...
	Montenegro	60.8	–2	+1.2
	Georgia	60.6	–8	–0.3
	Morocco	60.0	—	+1.5
	Seychelles	59.5	–2	+1.9
	Barbados	58.9	n/a	n/a
	Dominican Republic	58.3	+4	+0.9
	Trinidad and Tobago	58.3	–1	+0.1
	Jamaica	58.3	–1	+0.4
	Albania	57.5	–5	–2.9
	North Macedonia	57.3	+2	+0.7
	Argentina	57.2	–2	+0.9
	Sri Lanka	57.1	+1	+1.1
	Ukraine	57.0	–2	...
	Moldova	56.7	+2	+1.1
	Tunisia	56.4	—	–0.8
	Lebanon	56.3	–8	–1.3
	Algeria	56.3	+3	+2.5
	Ecuador	55.7	–4	–0.1
	Botswana	55.5	—	+1.3
	Bosnia and Herzegovina	54.7	–1	+0.6
	Egypt	54.5	+1	+1.3
	Namibia	54.5	+5	+1.8

Rank	Economy	Score	Diff. from 2018 Rank	Diff. from 2018 Score
	Kenya	54.1	–2	+0.5
	Kyrgyz Republic	54.0	+1	+3.0
	Paraguay	53.6	–2	+0.3
	Guatemala	53.5	–2	+0.2
	Iran, Islamic Rep.	53.0	–10	–1.3
	Rwanda	52.8	+8	+1.9
	Honduras	52.7	—	+0.2
	Mongolia	52.6	–3	–0.1
	El Salvador	52.6	–5	–0.2
	Tajikistan	52.4	–2	+0.2
	Bangladesh	52.1	–2	...
	Cambodia	52.1	+4	+1.9
	Bolivia	51.8	–2	+0.4
	Nepal	51.6	+1	+0.8
	Nicaragua	51.5	–5	...
	Pakistan	51.4	–3	+0.3
	Ghana	51.2	–5	–0.1
	Cape Verde	50.8	–1	+0.6
	Lao PDR	50.1	–1	+0.8
	Senegal	49.7	+3	+0.7
	Uganda	48.9	+2	+2.1
	Nigeria	48.3	–1	+0.8
	Tanzania	48.2	–5	+1.0
	Côte d'Ivoire	48.1	–4	+0.6
	Gabon	47.5	n/a	n/a
	Zambia	46.8	–2	+0.2
	Eswatini	46.4	–1	+1.1
	Guinea	46.1	–4	+2.8
	Cameroon	46.0	–2	+0.8
	Gambia, The	45.9	–5	+0.5
	Benin	45.8	–2	+1.4
	Ethiopia	44.4	–4	–0.1
	Zimbabwe	44.2	–1	+1.5
	Malawi	42.7	+1	+1.3
	Mali	43.6	–4	...
	Burkina Faso	43.4	–6	–0.6
	Lesotho	42.9	–1	+0.5
	Madagascar	42.9	n/a	n/a
	Venezuela	41.8	–6	–1.3
	Mauritania	40.9	–3	+0.1
	Burundi	40.3	+1	+2.7
	Angola	38.1	+1	+3.1
	Mozambique	38.1	—	–1.7
	Haiti	36.3	—	–0.1
	Congo, Dem. Rep.	36.1	–4	–2.1
	Yemen	35.5	–1	–0.9
	Chad	35.1	–1	–6.4

East Asia and the Pacific | Eurasia | Europe and North America | Latin America and the Caribbean | Middle East and North Africa | South Asia | Sub-Saharan Africa

this figure will be printed in b/w

Source: World Economic Forum (http://www.weforum.org/)—The Global Competitiveness Report, 2019

Annex 17: (a) Human Development Index and Its Components, 2019

HDI rank	Country	Human Development Index (HDI) Value 2019	SDG3 Life expectancy at birth (years) 2019	SDG4.3 Expected years of schooling (years) 2019^e	SDG4.4 Mean years of schooling (years) 2019	SDG8.5 Gross national income (GNI) per capita (2017 PPP $) 2019	GNI per capita rank minus HDI rank 2019	HDI rank 2018
VERY HIGH HUMAN DEVELOPMENT								
1	Norway	0.957	82.4	18.1^b	12.9	66,494	7	1
2	Ireland	0.955	82.3	18.7^b	12.7	68,371	4	3
2	Switzerland	0.955	83.8	16.3	13.4	69,394	3	2
4	Hong Kong, China (SAR)	0.949	84.9	16.9	12.3	62,985	7	4
4	Iceland	0.949	83.0	19.1^b	12.8^e	54,682	14	4
6	Germany	0.947	81.3	17.0	14.2	55,314	11	4
7	Sweden	0.945	82.8	19.5^b	12.5	54,508	12	7
8	Australia	0.944	83.4	22.0^b	12.7^e	48,085	15	7
8	Netherlands	0.944	82.3	18.5^b	12.4	57,707	6	9
10	Denmark	0.940	80.9	18.9^b	12.6^e	58,662	2	10
11	Finland	0.938	81.9	19.4^b	12.8	48,511	11	11
11	Singapore	0.938	83.6	16.4	11.6	88,155^d	-8	12
13	United Kingdom	0.932	81.3	17.5	13.2	46,071	13	14
14	Belgium	0.931	81.6	19.8^b	12.1^e	52,085	6	13
14	New Zealand	0.931	82.3	18.8^b	12.8^e	40,799	18	14
16	Canada	0.929	82.4	16.2	13.4^e	48,527	5	14
17	United States	0.926	78.9	16.3	13.4	63,826	-7	17
18	Austria	0.922	81.5	16.1	12.5^e	56,197	-3	18
19	Israel	0.919	83.0	16.2	13.0	40,187	14	21
19	Japan	0.919	84.6	15.2	12.9^f	42,932	9	20
19	Liechtenstein	0.919	80.7^g	14.9	12.5^h	131,032^d,j	-18	19
22	Slovenia	0.917	81.3	17.6	12.7	38,080	15	24
23	Korea (Republic of)	0.916	83.0	16.5	12.2	43,044	4	22
23	Luxembourg	0.916	82.3	14.3	12.3^*	72,712	-19	23
25	Spain	0.904	83.6	17.6	10.3	40,975	6	25
26	France	0.901	82.7	15.6	11.5	47,173	-1	26
27	Czechia	0.900	79.4	16.8	12.7^c	38,109	9	26
28	Malta	0.895	82.5	16.1	11.3	39,555	6	28
29	Estonia	0.892	78.8	16.0	13.1^c	36,019	9	30
29	Italy	0.892	83.5	16.1	10.4^j	42,776	0	29
31	United Arab Emirates	0.890	78.0	14.3	12.1	67,462	-24	30
32	Greece	0.888	82.2	17.9	10.6	30,155	14	33
33	Cyprus	0.887	81.0	15.2	12.2	38,207	2	32
34	Lithuania	0.882	75.9	16.6	13.1	35,799	5	35
35	Poland	0.880	78.7	16.3	12.5^e	31,623	8	34
36	Andorra	0.868	81.9^g	13.3^k	10.5	56,000^i	-20	36
37	Latvia	0.866	75.3	16.2	13.0^c	30,282	8	37
38	Portugal	0.864	82.1	16.5	9.3	33,967	2	38
39	Slovakia	0.860	77.5	14.5	12.7^e	32,113	3	39
40	Hungary	0.854	76.9	15.2	12.0	31,329	4	42
40	Saudi Arabia	0.854	75.1	16.1	10.2	47,495	-16	40
42	Bahrain	0.852	77.3	16.3	9.5	42,522	-12	41
43	Chile	0.851	80.2	16.4	10.6	23,261	16	43
43	Croatia	0.851	78.5	15.2	11.4^*	28,070	6	44
45	Qatar	0.848	80.2	12.0	9.7	92,418^d	-43	45
46	Argentina	0.845	76.7	17.7	10.9^c	21,190	16	46
47	Brunei Darussalam	0.838	75.9	14.3	9.1^f	63,965	-38	47
48	Montenegro	0.829	76.9	15.0	11.6^m	21,399	13	48
49	Romania	0.828	76.1	14.3	11.1	29,497	-1	49
50	Palau	0.826	73.9^g	15.8^j	12.5^j	19,317	15	52
51	Kazakhstan	0.825	73.6	15.6	11.9^j	22,857	9	53
52	Russian Federation	0.824	72.6	15.0	12.2^j	26,157	2	49
53	Belarus	0.823	74.8	15.4	12.3^m	18,546	14	49
54	Turkey	0.820	77.7	16.6^c	8.1	27,701	-4	54
55	Uruguay	0.817	77.9	16.8	8.9	20,064	9	56
56	Bulgaria	0.816	75.1	14.4	11.4	23,325	2	55
57	Panama	0.815	78.5	12.9	10.2^f	29,558	-10	58
58	Bahamas	0.814	73.9	12.9^k	11.4^j	33,747	-17	58
58	Barbados	0.814	79.2	15.4	10.6^n	14,936	20	60
60	Oman	0.813	77.9	14.2	9.7^j	25,944	-5	56
61	Georgia	0.812	73.8	15.3	13.1	14,429	22	63
62	Costa Rica	0.810	80.3	15.7	8.7	18,486	6	61
62	Malaysia	0.810	76.2	13.7	10.4	27,534	-11	63
64	Kuwait	0.806	75.5	14.2	7.3	58,590	-51	62
64	Serbia	0.806	76.0	14.7	11.2	17,192	8	65
66	Mauritius	0.804	75.0	15.1	9.5^f	25,266	-10	66

HDI rank	Country	Human Development Index (HDI) Value 2019	SDG3 Life expectancy at birth (years) 2019	SDG4.3 Expected years of schooling (years) 2019	SDG4.3 Mean years of schooling (years) 2019	SDG8.5 Gross national income (GNI) per capita (2017 PPP $) 2019	GNI per capita rank minus HDI rank 2019	HDI rank 2018
HIGH HUMAN DEVELOPMENT								
67	Seychelles	0.796	73.4	14.1	10.6 [k]	26,903	-15	69
67	Trinidad and Tobago	0.796	73.5	13.0 [i]	11.0 [f]	26,231	-14	67
69	Albania	0.795	78.6	14.7	10.1 [e]	13,998	18	68
70	Cuba	0.783	78.8	14.3	11.8 [i]	8,621 [q]	45	71
70	Iran (Islamic Republic of)	0.783	76.7	14.8	10.3	12,447	26	70
72	Sri Lanka	0.782	77.0	14.1	10.6	12,707	23	73
73	Bosnia and Herzegovina	0.780	77.4	13.8 [k]	9.8	14,872	7	76
74	Grenada	0.779	72.4	16.9	9.0 [o]	15,641	3	74
74	Mexico	0.779	75.1	14.8	8.8	19,160	-8	76
74	Saint Kitts and Nevis	0.779	74.8 [k]	13.8 [i]	8.7 [n]	25,038	-17	75
74	Ukraine	0.779	72.1	15.1 [i]	11.4 [o]	13,216	19	78
78	Antigua and Barbuda	0.778	77.0	12.8 [i]	9.3 [k]	20,895	-15	80
79	Peru	0.777	76.7	15.0	9.7	12,252	19	78
79	Thailand	0.777	77.2	15.0 [i]	7.9	17,781	-10	80
81	Armenia	0.776	75.1	13.1	11.3	13,894	9	72
82	North Macedonia	0.774	75.8	13.6	9.8 [m]	15,865	-7	82
83	Colombia	0.767	77.3	14.4	8.5	14,257	3	83
84	Brazil	0.765	75.9	15.4	8.0	14,263	1	84
85	China	0.761	76.9	14.0 [i]	8.1 [f]	16,057	-11	87
86	Ecuador	0.759	77.0	14.6 [i]	8.9	11,044	19	84
86	Saint Lucia	0.759	76.2	14.0 [i]	8.5 [i]	14,616	-4	86
88	Azerbaijan	0.756	73.0	12.9 [i]	10.6	13,784	3	88
88	Dominican Republic	0.756	74.1	14.2	8.1 [i]	17,591	-18	89
90	Moldova (Republic of)	0.750	71.9	11.5	11.7	13,664	2	91
91	Algeria	0.748	76.9	14.6	8.0 [o]	11,174	13	91
92	Lebanon	0.744	78.9	11.3	8.7 [n]	14,655	-11	90
93	Fiji	0.743	67.4	14.4 [n]	10.9	13,009	1	93
94	Dominica	0.742	78.2 [g]	13.0 [p]	8.1 [k]	11,884	7	94
95	Maldives	0.740	78.9	12.2 [p]	7.0 [p]	17,417	-24	98
95	Tunisia	0.740	76.7	15.1	7.2	10,414	14	94
97	Saint Vincent and the Grenadines	0.738	72.5	14.1 [i]	8.8 [i]	12,378	0	96
97	Suriname	0.738	71.7	13.2	9.3 [m]	14,324	-13	98
99	Mongolia	0.737	69.9	14.2 [i]	10.3 [m]	10,839	7	97
100	Botswana	0.735	69.6	12.8 [i]	9.6 [o]	16,437	-27	102
101	Jamaica	0.734	74.5	13.1 [i]	9.7 [i]	9,319	13	98
102	Jordan	0.729	74.5	11.4 [p]	10.5 [f]	9,858	8	103
103	Paraguay	0.728	74.3	12.7 [m]	8.5	12,224	-4	104
104	Tonga	0.725	70.9	14.4 [i]	11.2 [f]	6,365	25	105
105	Libya	0.724	72.9	12.9 [n]	7.6 [o]	15,688	-29	106
106	Uzbekistan	0.720	71.7	12.1	11.8	7,142	17	107
107	Bolivia (Plurinational State of)	0.718	71.5	14.2 [i]	9.0	8,554	9	108
107	Indonesia	0.718	71.7	13.6	8.2	11,459	-4	110
107	Philippines	0.718	71.2	13.1	9.4	9,778	4	111
110	Belize	0.716	74.6	13.1	9.9 [m]	6,382	18	108
111	Samoa	0.715	73.3	12.7 [i]	10.8	6,309	19	113
111	Turkmenistan	0.715	68.2	11.2 [i]	10.3 [m]	14,909	-32	112
113	Venezuela (Bolivarian Republic of)	0.711	72.1	12.8 [i]	10.3	7,045 [x]	11	101
114	South Africa	0.709	64.1	13.8	10.2	12,129	-14	115
115	Palestine, State of	0.708	74.1	13.4	9.2	6,417	12	114
116	Egypt	0.707	72.0	13.3	7.4 [f]	11,466	-14	117
117	Marshall Islands	0.704	74.1 [g]	12.4 [o]	10.9 [i]	5,039	21	116
117	Viet Nam	0.704	75.4	12.7 [i]	8.3 [f]	7,433	3	118
119	Gabon	0.703	66.5	13.0 [o]	8.7 [f]	13,930	-30	119
MEDIUM HUMAN DEVELOPMENT								
120	Kyrgyzstan	0.697	71.5	13.0	11.1 [m]	4,864	23	120
121	Morocco	0.686	76.7	13.7	5.6 [f]	7,368	1	121
122	Guyana	0.682	69.9	11.4 [i]	8.5 [m]	9,455	-10	121
123	Iraq	0.674	70.6	11.3 [m]	7.3 [i]	10,801	-16	123
124	El Salvador	0.673	73.3	11.7	6.9	8,359	-6	124
125	Tajikistan	0.668	71.1	11.7 [i]	10.7 [f]	3,954	25	126
126	Cabo Verde	0.665	73.0	12.7	6.3 [i]	7,019	-1	125
127	Guatemala	0.663	74.3	10.8	6.6	8,494	-10	128
128	Nicaragua	0.660	74.5	12.3 [i]	6.9 [f]	5,284	6	127
129	Bhutan	0.654	71.8	13.0	4.1	10,746	-21	131
130	Namibia	0.646	63.7	12.6 [i]	7.0 [f]	9,357	-17	129
131	India	0.645	69.7	12.2	6.5 [i]	6,681	-5	130
132	Honduras	0.634	75.3	10.1	6.6	5,308	1	132
133	Bangladesh	0.632	72.6	11.6	6.2	4,976	7	134
134	Kiribati	0.630	68.4	11.8 [m]	8.0 [m]	4,260	12	133

HDI rank	Country	Human Development Index (HDI) Value 2019	SDG3 Life expectancy at birth (years) 2019	SDG4.3 Expected years of schooling (years) 2019	SDG4.4 Mean years of schooling (years) 2019	SDG8.5 Gross national income (GNI) per capita (2017 PPP $) 2019	GNI per capita rank minus HDI rank 2019	HDI rank 2018
135	Sao Tome and Principe	0.625	70.4	12.7 j	6.4 j	3,952	16	135
136	Micronesia (Federated States of)	0.620	67.9	11.5 k	7.8 n	3,983	13	136
137	Lao People's Democratic Republic	0.613	67.9	11.0	5.3 f	7,413	-16	137
138	Eswatini (Kingdom of)	0.611	60.2	11.8 j	6.9 m	7,919	-19	139
138	Ghana	0.611	64.1	11.5	7.3 f	5,269	-3	138
140	Vanuatu	0.609	70.5	11.7 n	7.1	3,105	20	140
141	Timor-Leste	0.606	69.5	12.6 j	4.8 p	4,440	3	141
142	Nepal	0.602	70.8	12.8	5.0 f	3,457	13	143
143	Kenya	0.601	66.7	11.3 p	6.6 f	4,244	5	141
144	Cambodia	0.594	69.8	11.5 p	5.0 f	4,246	3	144
145	Equatorial Guinea	0.592	58.7	9.7 n	5.9 k	13,944	-57	145
146	Zambia	0.584	63.9	11.5	7.2 p	3,326	10	145
147	Myanmar	0.583	67.1	10.7	5.0 p	4,961	-6	148
148	Angola	0.581	61.2	11.8 p	5.2 p	6,104	-17	145
149	Congo	0.574	64.6	11.7 n	6.5 o	2,879	13	149
150	Zimbabwe	0.571	61.5	11.0 m	8.5	2,666	14	150
151	Solomon Islands	0.567	73.0	10.2 j	5.7 m	2,253	17	151
151	Syrian Arab Republic	0.567	72.7	8.9 j	5.1 n	3,613 i	2	152
153	Cameroon	0.563	59.3	12.1	6.3 m	3,581	1	153
154	Pakistan	0.557	67.3	8.3	5.2	5,005	-15	154
155	Papua New Guinea	0.555	64.5	10.2 p	4.7 f	4,301	-10	156
156	Comoros	0.554	64.3	11.2	5.1 n	3,099	5	154
LOW HUMAN DEVELOPMENT								
157	Mauritania	0.546	64.9	8.6	4.7 f	5,135	-21	157
158	Benin	0.545	61.8	12.6	3.8 p	3,254	0	158
159	Uganda	0.544	63.4	11.4 p	6.2 p	2,123	15	160
160	Rwanda	0.543	69.0	11.2	4.4 j	2,155	12	159
161	Nigeria	0.539	54.7	10.0 p	6.7 p	4,910	-19	161
162	Côte d'Ivoire	0.538	57.8	10.0	5.3 f	5,069	-25	161
163	Tanzania (United Republic of)	0.529	65.5	8.1	6.1 f	2,600	2	164
164	Madagascar	0.528	67.0	10.2	6.1 n	1,596	16	163
165	Lesotho	0.527	54.3	11.3 j	6.5 m	3,151	-6	165
166	Djibouti	0.524	67.1	6.8 j	4.1 n	5,689	-34	166
167	Togo	0.515	61.0	12.7	4.9 m	1,602	12	168
168	Senegal	0.512	67.9	8.6	3.2 j	3,309	-11	167
169	Afghanistan	0.511	64.8	10.2	3.9 f	2,229	0	169
170	Haiti	0.510	64.0	9.7 j	5.6 p	1,709	7	170
170	Sudan	0.510	65.3	7.9 j	3.8 f	3,829	-18	171
172	Gambia	0.496	62.1	9.9 p	3.9 m	2,168	-1	172
173	Ethiopia	0.485	66.6	8.8 j	2.9 p	2,207	-3	174
174	Malawi	0.483	64.3	11.2 j	4.7 f	1,035	13	174
175	Congo (Democratic Republic of the)	0.480	60.7	9.7 j	6.8	1,063	11	174
175	Guinea-Bissau	0.480	58.3	10.6 m	3.6 m	1,996	1	178
175	Liberia	0.480	64.1	9.6 n	4.8 f	1,258	8	173
178	Guinea	0.477	61.6	9.4 m p	2.8 p	2,405	-12	177
179	Yemen	0.470	66.1	8.8 j	3.2 f	1,594 i	2	179
180	Eritrea	0.459	66.3	5.0 j	3.9 n	2,793 n	-17	180
181	Mozambique	0.456	60.9	10.0	3.5 j	1,250	3	181
182	Burkina Faso	0.452	61.6	9.3	1.6 p	2,133	-9	183
182	Sierra Leone	0.452	54.7	10.2 j	3.7 f	1,668	-4	182
184	Mali	0.434	59.3	7.5	2.4 m	2,269	-17	184
185	Burundi	0.433	61.6	11.1	3.3 p	754	4	184
185	South Sudan	0.433	57.9	5.3 n	4.8 n	2,003 n	-10	186
187	Chad	0.398	54.2	7.3	2.5 p	1,555	-5	187
188	Central African Republic	0.397	53.3	7.6 j	4.3 f	993	0	188
189	Niger	0.394	62.4	6.5	2.1 j	1,201	-4	189

HDI rank	Country	Human Development Index (HDI) Value 2019	SDG3 Life expectancy at birth (years) 2019	SDG4.3 Expected years of schooling (years) 2019[a]	SDG4.4 Mean years of schooling (years) 2019	SDG8.5 Gross national income (GNI) per capita (2017 PPP $) 2019	GNI per capita rank minus HDI rank 2019	HDI rank 2018
OTHER COUNTRIES OR TERRITORIES								
	Korea (Democratic People's Rep. of)	..	72.3	10.8[j]	..			
	Monaco	..	..	..	..			
	Nauru	..	..	11.2[j]	..	16,237		
	San Marino	..	..	13.0	..	..		
	Somalia	..	57.4	..	..	..		
	Tuvalu	..	..	12.3[j]	..	6,132		

Notes
a. Data refer to 2019 or the most recent year available.
b. In calculating the HDI value, expected years of schooling is capped at 18 years.
c. Based on data from OECD (2019b).
d. In calculating the HDI value, GNI per capita is capped at $75,000.
e. Updated by HDRO based on data from Eurostat (2019).
f. Based on projections from Barro and Lee (2018).
g. Value from UNDESA (2011).
h. Imputed mean years of schooling for Austria.
i. Estimated using the purchasing power parity (PPP) rate and projected growth rate of Switzerland.
j. Updated by HDRO based on data from UNESCO Institute for Statistics (2020)
k. Based on data from the national statistical office.
l. Estimated using the PPP rate and projected growth rate of Spain.
m. Updated by HDRO based on data from United Nations Children's Fund (UNICEF) Multiple Indicator Cluster Surveys for 2006–2019.
n. Based on cross-country regression.
o. Updated by HDRO using projections from Barro and Lee (2018).
p. Updated by HDRO based on data from ICF Macro Demographic and Health Surveys for 2006-2019.
q. Based on cross-country regression and the projected growth rate from UN ECLAC (2020).
r. Updated by HDRO based on data from CEDLAS and World Bank (2020).
s. HDRO estimate based on data from World Bank (2020a), United Nations Statistics Division (2020b) and UN ECLAC (2020)
t. HDRO estimate based on data from World Bank (2020a) and United Nations Statistics Division (2020b), and the projected growth rate from UNESCWA (2020).
u. HDRO estimate based on data from World Bank (2020a), United Nations Statistics Division (2020b) and IMF (2020).

Source: author's adaptation of tables in the *Human Development Report 2020: The next frontier, Human development and the Anthropocene (UNDP)*

this figure will be printed in b/w

ANNEX 18: (A) INEQUALITY-ADJUSTED HUMAN DEVELOPMENT INDEX, 2019

HDI rank	Country	HDI	IHDI			Coefficient of human inequality	Inequality in life expectancy	Inequality-adjusted life expectancy index
		Value	Value	Overall loss (%)	Diff. from HDI rank[b]		(%)	Value
		2019	2019	2019	2019	2019	2015–2020	2019
	Very high human development							
1	Norway	0.957	0.899	6.1	0	6.0	3.0	0.931
2	Ireland	0.955	0.885	7.3	-3	7.2	3.4	0.926
2	Switzerland	0.955	0.889	6.9	-1	6.8	3.5	0.947
4	Hong Kong, China (SAR)	0.949	0.824	13.2	-17	12.6	2.5	0.973
4	Iceland	0.949	0.894	5.8	2	5.6	2.4	0.946
6	Germany	0.947	0.869	8.2	-4	7.9	3.8	0.908
7	Sweden	0.945	0.882	6.7	0	6.5	2.9	0.938
8	Australia	0.944	0.867	8.2	-3	7.9	3.7	0.940
8	Netherlands	0.944	0.878	7.0	0	6.9	3.1	0.928
10	Denmark	0.940	0.883	6.1	4	6.0	3.6	0.903
11	Finland	0.938	0.888	5.3	7	5.3	3.0	0.924
11	Singapore	0.938	0.813	13.3	-15	12.8	2.5	0.954
13	United Kingdom	0.932	0.856	8.2	-3	7.9	4.1	0.905
14	Belgium	0.931	0.859	7.7	1	7.7	3.6	0.914
14	New Zealand	0.931	0.859	7.7	1	7.5	4.3	0.917
16	Canada	0.929	0.848	8.7	-1	8.4	4.6	0.916
17	United States	0.926	0.808	12.7	-11	12.1	6.3	0.848
18	Austria	0.922	0.857	7.0	3	6.9	3.7	0.912
19	Israel	0.919	0.814	11.4	-6	10.9	3.3	0.937
19	Japan	0.919	0.843	8.3	1	8.1	2.9	0.965
19	Liechtenstein	0.919	...	...	...	...	...	...
22	Slovenia	0.917	0.875	4.6	12	4.6	2.9	0.916
23	Korea (Republic of)	0.916	0.815	11.0	-2	10.7	3.0	0.941
23	Luxembourg	0.916	0.826	9.8	2	9.6	3.4	0.925
25	Spain	0.904	0.783	13.4	-10	13.1	3.0	0.949
26	France	0.901	0.820	9.0	2	8.9	3.8	0.927
27	Czechia	0.900	0.860	4.4	14	4.4	3.0	0.886
28	Malta	0.895	0.823	8.0	5	7.9	4.6	0.918
29	Estonia	0.892	0.829	7.1	9	6.9	3.6	0.871
29	Italy	0.892	0.783	12.2	-6	11.8	3.1	0.947
31	United Arab Emirates	0.890	...	...	...	...	5.2	0.845

Inequality in education[a] (%)	Inequality-adjusted education index Value	Inequality in income[a] (%)	Inequality-adjusted income index Value	Income shares held by (%)			Gini coefficient
				Poorest 40 percent	Richest 10 percent	Richest 1 percent	
2019[d]	2019	2019[d]	2019	2010–2018[e]	2010–2018[e]	2010–2017[e]	2010–2018[e]
2.3	0.908	12.6	0.858	23.2	21.6	9.4	27.0
3.3	0.892	15.0	0.838	20.5	25.9	11.3	32.8
1.8	0.883	14.9	0.841	20.2	25.5	10.6	32.7
9.8	0.793	25.6	0.724	…	…	…	…
2.8	0.900	11.7	0.841	23.7	22.5	7.6	26.8
2.3	0.922	17.7	0.786	20.4	24.6	12.5	31.9
3.7	0.884	13.0	0.828	22.2	22.3	9.0	28.8
2.7	0.899	17.3	0.771	19.6	27.0	9.1	34.4
5.4	0.865	12.2	0.843	22.6	23.3	6.2	28.5
2.9	0.894	11.4	0.853	22.8	24.0	10.7	28.7
2.2	0.907	10.6	0.835	23.4	22.6	10.1	27.4
11.0	0.751	25.0	0.750	…	…	14.0	…
2.7	0.902	17.0	0.769	19.0	26.8	12.6	34.8
8.2	0.828	11.4	0.837	22.9	21.9	7.8	27.4
1.8	0.909	16.4	0.759	…	…	8.7	…
2.7	0.870	18.1	0.766	19.1	25.1	13.6	33.8
2.8	0.875	27.1	0.711	15.4	30.5	20.5	41.4
2.9	0.840	14.1	0.821	21.3	23.0	9.3	29.7
5.7	0.833	23.7	0.691	15.7	27.7	…	39.0
4.7	0.812	16.7	0.763	20.5	26.4	10.4	32.9
…	…	…	…	…	…	…	…
2.1	0.891	8.7	0.820	24.8	20.4	7.7	24.2
8.8	0.789	20.2	0.731	20.3	23.8	12.2	31.6
6.3	0.756	19.0	0.806	18.4	25.8	11.9	34.9
16.9	0.691	19.5	0.732	18.4	25.4	11.9	34.7
9.5	0.740	13.5	0.804	21.1	25.8	11.2	31.6
1.4	0.878	8.9	0.818	24.9	21.5	10.1	24.9
6.2	0.774	13.0	0.786	21.9	23.3	11.4	29.2
2.3	0.862	14.8	0.758	20.9	22.5	11.1	30.4
10.6	0.709	21.8	0.716	18.0	26.7	8.7	35.9
18.2	0.656	…	…	18.2	21.4	22.8	32.5

(continued)

(continued)

HDI rank	Country	HDI Value	IHDI Value	Overall loss (%)	Diff. from HDI rank[b]	Coefficient of human inequality	Inequality in life expectancy (%)	Inequality-adjusted life expectancy index Value
		2019	2019	2019	2019	2019	2015–2020[c]	2019
32	Greece	0.888	0.791	10.9	-1	10.8	3.5	0.924
33	Cyprus	0.887	0.805	9.2	1	9.1	3.6	0.904
34	Lithuania	0.882	0.791	10.3	1	10.0	5.5	0.813
35	Poland	0.880	0.813	7.6	7	7.6	4.3	0.865
36	Andorra	0.868	...	...	...	...	...	...
37	Latvia	0.866	0.783	9.6	0	9.2	5.4	0.805
38	Portugal	0.864	0.761	11.9	-5	11.8	3.5	0.921
39	Slovakia	0.860	0.807	6.2	7	6.1	5.0	0.841
40	Hungary	0.854	0.791	7.4	6	7.3	4.2	0.838
40	Saudi Arabia	0.854	...	...	...	...	6.4	0.794
42	Bahrain	0.852	...	...	...	...	5.5	0.833
43	Chile	0.851	0.709	16.7	-11	15.9	6.3	0.868
43	Croatia	0.851	0.783	8.0	4	7.9	4.3	0.861
45	Qatar	0.848	...	...	...	...	5.7	0.874
46	Argentina	0.845	0.729	13.7	-4	13.2	8.6	0.797
47	Brunei Darussalam	0.838	...	...	...	...	7.6	0.794
48	Montenegro	0.829	0.749	9.7	0	9.4	3.6	0.844
49	Romania	0.828	0.730	11.8	-1	11.4	6.3	0.808
50	Palau	0.826	...	...	...	...	...	...
51	Kazakhstan	0.825	0.766	7.2	4	7.1	7.7	0.761
52	Russian Federation	0.824	0.740	10.2	2	10.0	7.1	0.751
53	Belarus	0.823	0.771	6.3	7	6.3	4.4	0.806
54	Turkey	0.820	0.683	16.7	-11	16.5	9.0	0.808
55	Uruguay	0.817	0.712	12.9	-1	12.6	7.9	0.821
56	Bulgaria	0.816	0.721	11.6	2	11.3	6.1	0.795
57	Panama	0.815	0.643	21.1	-17	20.1	12.0	0.792
58	Bahamas	0.814	...	...	...	...	6.8	0.773
58	Barbados	0.814	0.676	17.0	-9	15.9	8.7	0.831
60	Oman	0.813	0.706	13.2	0	12.9	6.7	0.831
61	Georgia	0.812	0.716	11.8	5	11.5	7.9	0.762
62	Costa Rica	0.810	0.661	18.4	-11	17.5	7.1	0.862
62	Malaysia	0.810	...	...	...	...	6.1	0.811
64	Kuwait	0.806	...	...	...	...	5.9	0.803
64	Serbia	0.806	0.705	12.5	2	12.1	4.9	0.819
66	Mauritius	0.804	0.694	13.7	1	13.6	9.4	0.766
	High human development							
67	Seychelles	0.796	0.670	15.8	-6	15.2	9.6	0.743

Inequality in education[a] (%)	Inequality-adjusted education index Value	Inequality in income[a] (%)	Inequality-adjusted income index Value	Income shares held by (%)			Gini coefficient
				Poorest 40 percent	Richest 10 percent	Richest 1 percent	
2019[d]	2019	2019[d]	2019	2010–2018[e]	2010–2018[e]	2010–2017[e]	2010–2018[e]
11.1	0.755	17.8	0.709	18.9	25.9	13.4	34.4
10.5	0.740	13.2	0.779	21.3	25.5	11.6	31.4
3.9	0.863	20.6	0.706	17.9	28.4	10.4	37.3
4.9	0.826	13.5	0.752	21.7	23.5	14.0	29.7
10.0	0.648	...	...	...	...	...	...
2.5	0.861	19.6	0.694	18.4	26.9	10.9	35.6
15.0	0.653	16.9	0.731	19.8	26.7	10.6	33.8
1.6	0.813	11.7	0.770	23.8	19.9	5.3	25.2
3.1	0.796	14.5	0.743	21.1	23.9	12.1	30.6
18.0	0.647	...	...	...	...	19.7	...
22.7	0.594	...	...	...	...	18.0	...
10.4	0.726	31.1	0.567	15.5	36.3	23.7	44.4
4.7	0.767	14.7	0.727	20.7	22.9	8.2	30.4
11.8	0.581	...	...	...	...	29.0	...
6.0	0.804	25.2	0.606	14.9	29.9	...	41.4
...	...	...	...	...	...	...	...
7.8	0.740	16.9	0.673	15.9	27.7	8.5	39.0
5.3	0.724	22.7	0.664	17.0	24.9	15.2	36.0
1.9	0.839	...	...	...	...	...	...
3.2	0.804	10.3	0.736	23.4	23.0	...	27.5
4.2	0.789	18.8	0.683	18.3	29.9	20.2	37.5
3.7	0.807	10.8	0.704	24.5	21.4	...	25.2
16.5	0.611	24.1	0.645	15.9	32.6	23.4	41.9
6.5	0.715	23.4	0.614	16.3	29.7	14.0	39.7
6.1	0.732	21.8	0.644	16.7	31.9	12.6	40.4
11.4	0.620	36.9	0.542	11.9	37.1	...	49.2
6.3	0.693	...	...	...	...	...	...
5.5	0.739	33.6	0.502	...	...	...	...
11.9	0.633	20.1	0.671	...	...	19.5	...
4.1	0.826	22.5	0.582	18.0	27.5	...	36.4
11.6	0.642	33.9	0.521	12.8	36.3	...	48.0
12.1	0.638	...	...	15.9	31.3	14.6	41.0
22.1	0.497	...	...	...	...	19.9	...
7.5	0.724	24.0	0.591	17.3	25.6	12.8	36.2
13.2	0.639	18.2	0.684	18.8	29.9	13.8	36.8
6.7	0.678	29.3	0.598	15.2	39.9	20.4	46.8

(continued)

(continued)

HDI rank	Country	HDI	IHDI			Coefficient of human inequality	Inequality in life expectancy	Inequality-adjusted life expectancy index
		Value	Value	Overall loss (%)	Diff. from HDI rank[b]		(%)	Value
		2019	2019	2019	2019	2019	2015–2020[c]	2019
67	Trinidad and Tobago	0.796	…	…	…	…	14.9	0.701
69	Albania	0.795	0.708	10.9	7	10.9	7.2	0.836
70	Cuba	0.783	…	…	…	…	5.1	0.858
70	Iran (Islamic Republic of)	0.783	0.693	11.5	3	11.3	9.2	0.792
72	Sri Lanka	0.782	0.673	13.9	-1	13.8	7.0	0.815
73	Bosnia and Herzegovina	0.780	0.667	14.5	-3	14.2	5.4	0.835
74	Grenada	0.779	…	…	…	…	11.2	0.716
74	Mexico	0.779	0.613	21.3	-13	20.8	10.5	0.758
74	Saint Kitts and Nevis	0.779	…	…	…	…	…	…
74	Ukraine	0.779	0.728	6.5	16	6.5	7.4	0.742
78	Antigua and Barbuda	0.778	…	…	…	…	5.8	0.826
79	Peru	0.777	0.628	19.2	-8	18.8	10.8	0.779
79	Thailand	0.777	0.646	16.9	-2	16.7	7.9	0.810
81	Armenia	0.776	0.699	9.9	12	9.7	8.7	0.774
82	North Macedonia	0.774	0.681	12.0	8	11.8	7.9	0.791
83	Colombia	0.767	0.595	22.4	-12	21.6	10.7	0.787
84	Brazil	0.765	0.570	25.5	-20	24.4	10.9	0.766
85	China	0.761	0.639	16.0	2	15.7	7.9	0.806
86	Ecuador	0.759	0.616	18.8	-3	18.4	11.5	0.776
86	Saint Lucia	0.759	0.629	17.1	0	16.9	10.6	0.773
88	Azerbaijan	0.756	0.684	9.5	16	9.4	13.9	0.702
88	Dominican Republic	0.756	0.595	21.3	-7	21.1	17.0	0.691
90	Moldova (Republic of)	0.750	0.672	10.4	13	10.3	9.6	0.722
91	Algeria	0.748	0.596	20.3	-2	19.7	14.1	0.752
92	Lebanon	0.744	…	…	…	…	7.4	0.840
93	Fiji	0.743	…	…	…	…	14.9	0.621
94	Dominica	0.742	…	…	…	…	…	…
95	Maldives	0.740	0.584	21.1	-10	20.4	6.0	0.852
95	Tunisia	0.740	0.596	19.5	-1	18.9	9.0	0.794
97	Saint Vincent and the Grenadines	0.738	…	…	…	…	11.3	0.717

Inequality in education[a]	Inequality-adjusted education index	Inequality in income[a]	Inequality-adjusted income index	Income shares held by (%)			Gini coefficient
				Poorest 40 percent	Richest 10 percent	Richest 1 percent	
(%)	Value	(%)	Value				
2019[d]	2019	2019[d]	2019	2010–2018[g]	2010–2018[g]	2010–2017[g]	2010–2018[g]
...	...	...	...	...	...	...	...
12.3	0.655	13.2	0.648	19.5	24.8	8.2	33.2
7.8	0.728	...	...	...	...	...	...
5.0	0.719	19.7	0.585	16.2	31.3	16.3	40.8
12.0	0.657	22.4	0.568	17.7	32.9	...	39.8
17.0	0.590	20.2	0.603	19.8	25.1	9.0	33.0
...	...	...	...	...	...	...	...
18.4	0.574	33.4	0.529	14.9	36.4	...	45.4
...	...	...	...	...	...	...	...
3.6	0.770	8.5	0.675	24.0	22.0	...	26.1
...	...	...	...	...	...	...	...
17.0	0.614	28.6	0.519	14.8	32.1	...	42.8
18.3	0.557	23.8	0.596	18.3	28.1	20.2	36.4
2.9	0.718	17.4	0.616	20.3	29.2	...	34.4
8.4	0.646	19.2	0.619	17.9	23.8	7.7	34.2
18.6	0.555	35.5	0.483	12.1	39.7	20.5	50.4
21.2	0.547	41.0	0.442	10.4	42.5	28.3	53.9
11.7	0.580	27.4	0.557	17.2	29.3	13.9	38.5
13.9	0.605	29.9	0.498	13.8	34.4	...	45.4
12.6	0.588	27.4	0.547	11.0	38.6	...	51.2
5.3	0.673	8.9	0.678	...	...	...	...
15.8	0.560	30.4	0.544	15.6	35.2	...	43.7
7.3	0.659	14.0	0.639	24.4	22.0	9.9	25.7
33.7	0.445	11.4	0.631	23.1	22.9	9.7	27.6
6.2	0.567	...	...	20.6	24.8	23.4	31.8
...	...	...	...	18.8	29.7	...	36.7
...	...	...	...	...	...	...	...
29.3	0.405	25.8	0.578	21.2	25.2	...	31.3
30.7	0.458	16.9	0.583	20.1	25.6	10.7	32.8
...	...	...	...	...	...	...	...

(continued)

(continued)

HDI rank	Country	HDI	IHDI			Coefficient of human inequality	Inequality in life expectancy	Inequality-adjusted life expectancy index
		Value	Value	Overall loss (%)	Diff. from HDI rank[b]		(%)	Value
		2019	2019	2019	2019	2019	2015–2020[c]	2019
97	Suriname	0.738	0.535	27.5	-17	26.0	12.8	0.693
99	Mongolia	0.737	0.634	14.0	11	14.0	13.1	0.667
100	Botswana	0.735	...	...	...	...	19.4	0.615
101	Jamaica	0.734	0.612	16.6	4	15.9	10.0	0.754
102	Jordan	0.729	0.622	14.7	9	14.6	10.6	0.750
103	Paraguay	0.728	0.557	23.5	-7	22.8	13.8	0.719
104	Tonga	0.725	...	...	...	...	10.4	0.702
105	Libya	0.724	...	...	...	...	9.1	0.740
106	Uzbekistan	0.720	...	...	...	...	13.9	0.685
107	Bolivia (Plurinational State of)	0.718	0.546	24.0	-9	23.7	22.5	0.614
107	Indonesia	0.718	0.590	17.8	2	17.7	13.9	0.685
107	Philippines	0.718	0.587	18.2	-1	17.8	15.3	0.668
110	Belize	0.716	0.554	22.6	-5	21.6	11.1	0.747
111	Samoa	0.715	...	...	...	...	10.0	0.738
111	Turkmenistan	0.715	0.586	18.0	2	17.5	23.4	0.568
113	Venezuela (Bolivarian Republic of)	0.711	0.588	17.3	6	17.0	17.1	0.664
114	South Africa	0.709	0.468	34.0	-18	31.2	19.2	0.549
115	Palestine, State of	0.708	0.613	13.4	16	13.4	12.0	0.732
116	Egypt	0.707	0.497	29.7	-9	28.7	11.6	0.707
117	Marshall Islands	0.704	...	...	...	...	...	...
117	Viet Nam	0.704	0.588	16.5	10	16.5	12.9	0.742
119	Gabon	0.703	0.544	22.6	0	22.5	22.8	0.552
	Medium human development							
120	Kyrgyzstan	0.697	0.630	9.6	25	9.5	11.3	0.702
121	Morocco	0.686	...	...	...	...	13.0	0.759
122	Guyana	0.682	0.556	18.5	5	18.3	19.0	0.622
123	Iraq	0.674	0.541	19.7	2	19.4	15.9	0.655
124	El Salvador	0.673	0.529	21.4	1	21.1	12.5	0.718
125	Tajikistan	0.668	0.584	12.6	12	12.4	16.7	0.655
126	Cabo Verde	0.665	...	...	...	...	12.2	0.716
127	Guatemala	0.663	0.481	27.5	-2	26.9	14.6	0.713
128	Nicaragua	0.660	0.505	23.5	1	23.2	13.1	0.728
129	Bhutan	0.654	0.476	27.2	-2	26.3	17.1	0.660
130	Namibia	0.646	0.418	35.3	-14	33.6	22.1	0.524

Inequality in education^a (%)	Inequality-adjusted education index (Value)	Inequality in income^a (%)	Inequality-adjusted income index (Value)	Income shares held by (%)			Gini coefficient
				Poorest 40 percent	Richest 10 percent	Richest 1 percent	
2019^f	2019	2019^f	2019	2010–2018^g	2010–2018^g	2010–2017^g	2010–2018^g
18.4	0.551	46.7	0.400	...	...	...	...
11.9	0.649	16.9	0.588	20.2	25.7	...	32.7
23.3	0.518	...	...	10.9	41.5	22.6	53.3
5.6	0.651	32.0	0.466	...	...	...	...
15.4	0.564	17.9	0.569	20.3	27.5	16.1	33.7
16.7	0.531	37.8	0.452	13.9	35.9	...	46.2
4.5	0.740	...	...	18.2	29.7	...	37.6
...	...	...	...	...	...	13.5	...
0.7	0.723	...	...	...	...	...	...
17.6	0.573	31.2	0.463	14.7	30.4	...	42.2
16.2	0.545	23.1	0.551	17.2	30.4	...	39.0
10.1	0.610	28.1	0.498	15.0	34.8	...	44.4
15.9	0.584	37.9	0.390	...	...	...	...
4.9	0.678	...	...	17.9	31.3	...	38.7
2.9	0.634	26.2	0.558	...	...	...	...
8.8	0.638	25.2	0.481	...	...	...	...
17.3	0.599	57.0	0.312	7.2	50.5	19.2	63.0
11.6	0.599	16.6	0.524	19.2	25.2	15.8	33.7
38.1	0.383	36.5	0.455	21.8	26.9	15.8	31.5
4.3	0.677	...	...	...	...	...	...
17.6	0.519	19.1	0.526	18.6	27.5	...	35.7
23.5	0.498	21.2	0.588	16.8	27.7	10.9	38.0
3.4	0.706	13.8	0.506	23.4	23.6	...	27.7
...	...	...	...	17.4	31.9	15.0	39.5
10.7	0.536	25.1	0.515	...	...	...	...
29.7	0.392	12.7	0.618	21.9	23.7	22.0	29.5
29.1	0.393	21.8	0.523	17.1	29.4	...	38.6
6.0	0.641	14.5	0.475	19.4	26.4	...	34.0
23.7	0.429	...	...	15.4	32.3	...	42.4
30.8	0.359	35.4	0.433	13.1	38.1	...	48.3
25.7	0.425	30.7	0.415	14.3	37.2	...	46.2
41.7	0.289	20.0	0.565	17.5	27.9	...	37.4
25.0	0.438	53.6	0.318	8.6	47.3	21.5	59.1

(*continued*)

(continued)

HDI rank	Country	HDI	IHDI			Coefficient of human inequality	Inequality in life expectancy	Inequality-adjusted life expectancy index
		Value	Value	Overall loss (%)	Diff. from HDI rank[b]		(%)	Value
		2019	2019	2019	2019	2019	2015–2020	2019
131	India	0.645	0.475	26.4	-1	25.7	19.7	0.613
132	Honduras	0.634	0.472	25.6	-2	24.8	13.3	0.737
133	Bangladesh	0.632	0.478	24.4	3	23.7	17.3	0.669
134	Kiribati	0.630	0.516	18.1	8	17.9	24.7	0.560
135	Sao Tome and Principe	0.625	0.520	16.8	10	16.7	17.0	0.643
136	Micronesia (Federated States of)	0.620	...	...	...	...	16.1	0.618
137	Lao People's Democratic Republic	0.613	0.461	24.8	0	24.7	22.6	0.571
138	Eswatini (Kingdom of)	0.611	0.432	29.3	-5	29.0	25.1	0.463
138	Ghana	0.611	0.440	28.0	-3	27.8	24.2	0.514
140	Vanuatu	0.609	...	...	...	...	14.4	0.665
141	Timor-Leste	0.606	0.436	28.1	-2	26.7	21.7	0.596
142	Nepal	0.602	0.446	25.9	3	24.9	17.5	0.645
143	Kenya	0.601	0.443	26.3	3	26.2	22.5	0.557
144	Cambodia	0.594	0.475	20.0	10	19.9	18.1	0.628
145	Equatorial Guinea	0.592	...	...	...	...	34.6	0.390
146	Zambia	0.584	0.401	31.3	-2	30.6	26.5	0.496
147	Myanmar	0.583	...	...	...	...	22.8	0.560
148	Angola	0.581	0.397	31.7	-3	31.7	32.0	0.430
149	Congo	0.574	0.430	25.1	2	24.9	22.8	0.529
150	Zimbabwe	0.571	0.441	22.8	7	22.5	24.2	0.484
151	Solomon Islands	0.567	...	...	...	...	12.1	0.717
151	Syrian Arab Republic	0.567	...	...	...	...	13.0	0.705
153	Cameroon	0.563	0.375	33.4	-7	33.4	33.5	0.402
154	Pakistan	0.557	0.384	31.1	-4	30.2	29.9	0.510
155	Papua New Guinea	0.555	0.390	29.7	0	29.6	24.1	0.520
156	Comoros	0.554	0.303	45.3	-21	44.2	28.9	0.485
	Low human development							
157	Mauritania	0.546	0.371	32.1	-4	31.8	30.0	0.484
158	Benin	0.545	0.343	37.1	-10	36.9	34.9	0.418
159	Uganda	0.544	0.399	26.7	7	26.7	27.2	0.486

Inequality in education[a]	Inequality-adjusted education index	Inequality in income[a]	Inequality-adjusted income index	Income shares held by (%)			Gini coefficient
				Poorest 40 percent	Richest 10 percent	Richest 1 percent	
(%)	Value	(%)	Value				
2019[f]	2019	2019[f]	2019	2010–2018[e]	2010–2018[e]	2010–2017[e]	2010–2018[e]
38.7	0.340	18.8	0.515	18.8	31.7	21.3	37.8
23.3	0.382	37.8	0.373	10.4	39.1	...	52.1
37.3	0.332	16.6	0.492	21.0	26.8	...	32.4
9.6	0.537	19.4	0.457	...	...	...	...
18.3	0.463	14.9	0.473	11.5	49.2	8.8	56.3
...	...	26.4	0.410	16.2	29.7	...	40.1
31.3	0.331	20.3	0.518	19.1	29.8	...	36.4
24.1	0.423	37.9	0.410	10.5	42.7	18.2	54.6
35.1	0.365	24.1	0.454	14.3	32.2	15.1	43.5
...	...	19.7	0.417	17.8	29.4	...	37.6
44.9	0.281	13.6	0.495	22.8	24.0	...	28.7
40.9	0.308	16.3	0.448	20.4	26.4	...	32.8
22.9	0.412	33.1	0.379	16.5	31.6	15.0	40.8
27.3	0.352	14.3	0.485	...	...	...	...
...	...	...	...	...	...	17.3	...
20.4	0.443	44.8	0.292	8.9	44.4	23.1	57.1
26.9	0.339	...	...	21.9	25.5	...	30.7
34.3	0.328	28.9	0.442	11.5	39.6	15.2	51.3
20.9	0.429	31.0	0.350	12.4	37.9	20.4	48.9
14.6	0.501	28.8	0.353	15.1	34.8	17.2	44.3
...	...	19.4	0.379	18.4	29.2	...	37.1
...	...	...	...	...	...	14.7	...
31.7	0.373	35.0	0.351	13.0	35.0	15.7	46.6
43.5	0.227	17.2	0.489	21.1	28.9	...	33.5
35.7	0.282	28.9	0.404	15.1[f]	31[f]	...	41.9[f]
47.6	0.252	56.0	0.228	13.6	33.7	14.1	45.3
40.8	0.234	24.6	0.449	19.9	24.9	10.6	32.6
43.7	0.269	32.0	0.358	12.8	37.6	17.5	47.8
27.9	0.377	24.9	0.346	15.9	34.2	16.9	42.8

(continued)

(continued)

HDI rank	Country	HDI Value	IHDI Value	Overall loss (%)	Diff. from HDI rank[b]	Coefficient of human inequality	Inequality in life expectancy (%)	Inequality-adjusted life expectancy index Value
		2019	2019	2019	2019	2019	2015–2020[c]	2019
160	Rwanda	0.543	0.387	28.7	3	28.4	19.5	0.607
161	Nigeria	0.539	0.348	35.4	-2	35.2	37.1	0.336
162	Côte d'Ivoire	0.538	0.346	35.7	-4	35.3	33.3	0.388
163	Tanzania (United Republic of)	0.529	0.397	25.0	10	24.9	25.3	0.522
164	Madagascar	0.528	0.390	26.1	9	26.0	21.1	0.571
165	Lesotho	0.527	0.382	27.5	6	27.4	33.1	0.353
166	Djibouti	0.524	...	...	...	...	23.4	0.555
167	Togo	0.515	0.351	31.8	4	31.7	30.5	0.439
168	Senegal	0.512	0.348	32.0	4	31.2	21.2	0.581
169	Afghanistan	0.511	...	...	...	...	28.3	0.495
170	Haiti	0.510	0.303	40.6	-9	40.0	32.2	0.459
170	Sudan	0.510	0.333	34.7	-3	34.3	27.4	0.506
172	Gambia	0.496	0.335	32.5	1	31.2	28.5	0.463
173	Ethiopia	0.485	0.348	28.2	8	27.3	24.9	0.538
174	Malawi	0.483	0.345	28.6	5	28.6	25.1	0.510
175	Congo (Democratic Republic of the)	0.480	0.335	30.2	4	30.2	36.1	0.400
175	Guinea-Bissau	0.480	0.300	37.5	-7	37.4	32.3	0.399
175	Liberia	0.480	0.325	32.3	1	31.8	29.8	0.476
178	Guinea	0.477	0.313	34.4	0	33.1	31.3	0.440
179	Yemen	0.470	0.321	31.7	4	30.9	24.7	0.534
180	Eritrea	0.459	...	...	...	...	21.4	0.560
181	Mozambique	0.456	0.316	30.7	4	30.7	29.8	0.441
182	Burkina Faso	0.452	0.316	30.1	5	29.5	32.0	0.435
182	Sierra Leone	0.452	0.291	35.6	-2	34.5	39.0	0.326
184	Mali	0.434	0.289	33.4	-1	32.4	36.7	0.383
185	Burundi	0.433	0.303	30.0	5	29.6	28.5	0.457
185	South Sudan	0.433	0.276	36.3	-2	36.0	36.2	0.372
187	Chad	0.398	0.248	37.7	-1	37.4	40.9	0.311
188	Central African Republic	0.397	0.232	41.6	-1	41.3	40.1	0.307
189	Niger	0.394	0.284	27.9	3	27.4	30.9	0.451
	Other countries or territories							
	Korea (Democratic People's Rep. of)	...	...	...	...	...	11.5	0.712
	Monaco	...	...	...	...	...	...	...

Inequality in education[a] (%)	Inequality-adjusted education index Value	Inequality in income[d] (%)	Inequality-adjusted income index Value	Income shares held by (%)			Gini coefficient
				Poorest 40 percent	Richest 10 percent	Richest 1 percent	
2019[f]	2019	2019[f]	2019	2010–2018[g]	2010–2018[g]	2010–2017[g]	2010–2018[g]
29.3	0.324	36.4	0.295	15.8	35.6	...	43.7
40.4	0.297	28.1	0.423	15.1[f]	32.7	15.3	43.0[f]
45.6	0.246	27.0	0.433	15.9	31.9	17.1	41.5
27.0	0.313	22.4	0.382	17.4	33.1	16.2	40.5
29.3	0.343	27.6	0.303	15.7	33.5	15.0	42.6
19.6	0.428	29.6	0.367	13.5	32.9	19.0	44.9
...	...	27.7	0.441	15.8	32.3	15.7	41.6
37.7	0.322	26.9	0.307	14.5	31.6	13.7	43.1
46.4	0.185	25.9	0.392	16.4	31.0	13.0	40.3
45.4	0.226	...	...	...	...	...	...
37.3	0.286	50.4	0.212	15.8	31.2	...	41.1
42.5	0.198	33.0	0.369	19.9	27.8	11.2	34.2
47.7	0.213	17.5	0.384	19.0	28.7	13.4	35.9
43.5	0.193	13.4	0.405	19.4	28.5	14.3	35.0
28.4	0.336	32.4	0.239	16.2	38.1	31.1	44.7
26.8	0.363	27.6	0.258	15.5	32.0	18.1	42.1
41.9	0.240	37.9	0.281	12.8	42.0	19.3	50.7
42.9	0.243	22.7	0.296	18.8	27.1	12.0	35.3
50.1	0.176	17.8	0.395	19.8	26.4	12.4	33.7
46.1	0.189	21.8	0.327	18.8	29.4	15.7	36.7
...	...	...	...	...	...	14.3	...
33.8	0.262	28.4	0.273	11.8	45.5	30.9	54.0
39.2	0.190	17.3	0.382	20.0	29.6	14.3	35.3
46.9	0.216	17.7	0.350	19.6	29.4	10.5	35.7
43.9	0.160	16.6	0.393	20.1[f]	25.7[f]	9.5	33.0[f]
39.5	0.252	20.9	0.241	17.9	31.0	14.6	38.6
39.6	0.185	32.3	0.307	12.5[f]	33.2[f]	14.1	46.3[f]
43.0	0.164	28.4	0.297	14.6	32.4	15.6	43.3
34.5	0.231	49.2	0.176	10.3[g]	46.2	30.9	56.2[g]
35.0	0.162	16.4	0.314	19.6	27.0	11.4	34.3
...	...	...	...	...	...	...	...
...	...	...	...	...	...	...	...

(continued)

(continued)

HDI rank	Country	HDI	IHDI			Coefficient of human inequality	Inequality in life expectancy	Inequality-adjusted life expectancy index
		Value	Value	Overall loss (%)	Diff. from HDI rank[b]		(%)	Value
		2019	2019	2019	2019	2019	2015–2020[c]	2019
	Nauru	...	...	...	...	...	...	...
	San Marino	...	...	...	...	...	...	...
	Somalia	...	...	...	...	...	38.9	0.352
	Tuvalu	...	...	...	...	...	...	...
	Human development groups							
	Very high human development	0.898	0.800	10.9	–	10.7	5.2	0.869
	High human development	0.753	0.618	17.9	–	17.6	10.1	0.765
	Medium human development	0.631	0.465	26.3	–	25.9	20.8	0.601
	Low human development	0.513	0.352	31.4	–	31.3	30.8	0.441
	Developing countries	0.689	0.535	22.4	–	22.3	16.7	0.657
	Least developed countries	0.538	0.384	28.6	–	28.4	26.4	0.514
	Small island developing states	0.728	0.549	24.6	–	24.2	16.7	0.667
	World	0.737	0.587	20.4	–	20.2	14.7	0.692

SDG10.1

Source: Author's adaptation based on the *Human Development Report 2020: The next frontier, Human development and the Anthropocene (UNDP)*

HDI Human Development Index, *IHDI* Inequality-adjusted HDI

[a]See http://hdr.undp.org/en/composite/IHDI for the list of surveys used to estimate inequalities

[b]Based on countries for which an Inequality-adjusted Human Development Index value is calculated

[c]Calculated by HDRO from the 2015–2020 period life tables from UNDESA (2019a)

[d]Data refer to 2019 or the most recent year available

[e]Data refer to the most recent year available during the period specified

[f]Refers to 2009

[g] Refers to 2008

Inequality in education[a]	Inequality-adjusted education index	Inequality in income[a]	Inequality-adjusted income index	Income shares held by (%)			Gini coefficient
(%)	Value	(%)	Value	Poorest 40 percent	Richest 10 percent	Richest 1 percent	
2019[d]	2019	2019[d]	2019	2010–2018[e]	2010–2018[e]	2010–2017[e]	2010–2018[e]
...	...	...	...	...	...	...	...
...	...	...	...	...	...	...	...
...	...	...	...	...	...	16.9	...
10.5	...	...	...	17.4	30.7	...	39.1
6.4	0.803	20.4	0.733	18.3	27.7	15.6	–
14.5	0.572	28.0	0.539	16.6	31.3	...	–
37.1	0.334	19.7	0.499	18.8	31.0	...	–
37.9	0.263	25.1	0.375	16.7	31.9	16.0	–
25.5	0.439	24.6	0.531	17.4	31.3	17.7	–
36.0	0.280	22.9	0.394	17.9	30.8	16.3	–
22.0	0.493	34.0	0.504	...	...	...	–
22.1	0.497	23.8	0.589	17.6	30.6	17.1	–

ANNEX 18: (B) HUMAN INDEX TRENDS, 1990–2019

HDI rank	Country	Human Development Index (HDI) value					
		1990	2000	2010	2014	2015	2017
Very high human development							
1	Norway	0.849	0.915	0.940	0.944	0.947	0.954
2	Ireland	0.773	0.867	0.901	0.928	0.935	0.947
2	Switzerland	0.840	0.898	0.941	0.942	0.947	0.949
4	Hong Kong, China (SAR)	0.784	0.830	0.904	0.926	0.930	0.941
4	Iceland	0.807	0.867	0.898	0.931	0.934	0.943
6	Germany	0.808	0.876	0.927	0.937	0.938	0.943
7	Sweden	0.821	0.903	0.911	0.935	0.938	0.942
8	Australia	0.871	0.903	0.930	0.933	0.938	0.941
8	Netherlands	0.836	0.882	0.917	0.932	0.934	0.939
10	Denmark	0.806	0.870	0.917	0.935	0.933	0.936
11	Finland	0.790	0.864	0.916	0.928	0.930	0.935
11	Singapore	0.721	0.821	0.909	0.926	0.931	0.933
13	United Kingdom	0.781	0.874	0.912	0.925	0.923	0.926
14	Belgium	0.813	0.880	0.910	0.918	0.922	0.929
14	New Zealand	0.826	0.876	0.906	0.916	0.921	0.926
16	Canada	0.850	0.867	0.901	0.918	0.921	0.926
17	United States	0.865	0.886	0.916	0.920	0.921	0.924
18	Austria	0.803	0.847	0.904	0.913	0.915	0.919
19	Israel	0.801	0.861	0.895	0.909	0.910	0.913
19	Japan	0.818	0.858	0.887	0.906	0.908	0.915
19	Liechtenstein	...	0.862	0.904	0.911	0.911	0.916
22	Slovenia	0.774	0.832	0.889	0.894	0.894	0.907
23	Korea (Republic of)	0.732	0.823	0.889	0.904	0.907	0.912
23	Luxembourg	0.797	0.860	0.898	0.903	0.906	0.913
25	Spain	0.761	0.832	0.872	0.888	0.895	0.903
26	France	0.786	0.849	0.879	0.893	0.895	0.897
27	Czechia	0.738	0.804	0.870	0.888	0.891	0.896
28	Malta	0.752	0.795	0.853	0.874	0.880	0.888
29	Estonia	0.735	0.787	0.852	0.871	0.877	0.885
29	Italy	0.776	0.838	0.879	0.882	0.882	0.886
31	United Arab Emirates	0.723	0.782	0.820	0.847	0.859	0.881
32	Greece	0.761	0.804	0.865	0.875	0.877	0.879
33	Cyprus	0.735	0.804	0.856	0.862	0.865	0.878
34	Lithuania	0.738	0.762	0.831	0.859	0.862	0.873
35	Poland	0.718	0.790	0.840	0.858	0.863	0.873

		Change in HDI rank	Average annual HDI growth (%)			
2018	2019	2014–2019[a]	1990–2000	2000–2010	2010–2019	1990–2019
0.956	0.957	0	0.75	0.27	0.20	0.41
0.951	0.955	7	1.15	0.39	0.65	0.73
0.955	0.955	0	0.67	0.47	0.16	0.44
0.946	0.949	7	0.57	0.86	0.54	0.66
0.946	0.949	4	0.72	0.35	0.62	0.56
0.946	0.947	–3	0.81	0.57	0.24	0.55
0.943	0.945	–3	0.96	0.09	0.41	0.49
0.943	0.944	–2	0.36	0.30	0.17	0.28
0.942	0.944	–1	0.54	0.39	0.32	0.42
0.939	0.940	–6	0.77	0.53	0.28	0.53
0.937	0.938	–2	0.90	0.59	0.26	0.59
0.936	0.938	0	1.31	1.02	0.35	0.91
0.928	0.932	0	1.13	0.43	0.24	0.61
0.930	0.931	1	0.80	0.34	0.25	0.47
0.928	0.931	3	0.59	0.34	0.30	0.41
0.928	0.929	–1	0.20	0.39	0.34	0.31
0.925	0.926	–3	0.24	0.33	0.12	0.24
0.921	0.922	0	0.53	0.65	0.22	0.48
0.916	0.919	1	0.72	0.39	0.29	0.48
0.917	0.919	2	0.48	0.33	0.39	0.40
0.919	0.919	0	…	0.48	0.18	…
0.912	0.917	2	0.73	0.66	0.35	0.59
0.914	0.916	–1	1.18	0.77	0.33	0.78
0.913	0.916	0	0.76	0.43	0.22	0.48
0.905	0.904	1	0.90	0.47	0.40	0.60
0.898	0.901	–1	0.77	0.35	0.28	0.47
0.898	0.900	–1	0.86	0.79	0.38	0.69
0.894	0.895	2	0.56	0.71	0.54	0.60
0.889	0.892	2	0.69	0.80	0.51	0.67
0.890	0.892	–1	0.77	0.48	0.16	0.48
0.889	0.890	6	0.79	0.48	0.91	0.72
0.881	0.888	–3	0.55	0.73	0.29	0.53
0.885	0.887	0	0.90	0.63	0.40	0.65
0.876	0.882	0	0.32	0.87	0.66	0.62
0.877	0.880	0	0.96	0.62	0.52	0.70

(continued)

(continued)

HDI rank	Country	Human Development Index (HDI) value					
		1990	2000	2010	2014	2015	2017
36	Andorra	...	0.813	0.837	0.863	0.862	0.863
37	Latvia	0.711	0.735	0.824	0.845	0.849	0.859
38	Portugal	0.718	0.792	0.829	0.847	0.854	0.858
39	Slovakia	0.741	0.765	0.831	0.847	0.850	0.855
40	Hungary	0.708	0.772	0.831	0.838	0.842	0.846
40	Saudi Arabia	0.697	0.743	0.809	0.852	0.859	0.852
42	Bahrain	0.749	0.795	0.800	0.820	0.848	0.854
43	Chile	0.706	0.756	0.803	0.837	0.842	0.847
43	Croatia	0.677	0.757	0.815	0.835	0.840	0.845
45	Qatar	0.750	0.816	0.834	0.835	0.839	0.848
46	Argentina	0.718	0.781	0.829	0.836	0.840	0.843
47	Brunei Darussalam	0.767	0.802	0.827	0.838	0.838	0.838
48	Montenegro	...	...	0.802	0.813	0.816	0.822
49	Romania	0.708	0.716	0.805	0.811	0.815	0.821
50	Palau	...	0.744	0.786	0.825	0.820	0.822
51	Kazakhstan	0.690	0.685	0.764	0.798	0.806	0.815
52	Russian Federation	0.735	0.722	0.781	0.807	0.809	0.820
53	Belarus	...	0.686	0.795	0.814	0.814	0.819
54	Turkey	0.583	0.660	0.739	0.796	0.801	0.814
55	Uruguay	0.694	0.743	0.782	0.803	0.806	0.814
56	Bulgaria	0.708	0.720	0.788	0.806	0.809	0.811
57	Panama	0.675	0.735	0.774	0.795	0.799	0.811
58	Bahamas	...	0.797	0.805	0.805	0.808	0.812
58	Barbados	0.732	0.771	0.797	0.808	0.809	0.810
60	Oman	...	0.693	0.782	0.802	0.814	0.819
61	Georgia	...	0.690	0.751	0.783	0.790	0.799
62	Costa Rica	0.665	0.721	0.765	0.796	0.797	0.804
62	Malaysia	0.643	0.723	0.772	0.791	0.796	0.805
64	Kuwait	0.705	0.781	0.788	0.796	0.801	0.805
64	Serbia	0.722	0.716	0.766	0.784	0.789	0.798
66	Mauritius	0.624	0.678	0.751	0.789	0.789	0.797
High human development							
67	Seychelles	...	0.714	0.764	0.775	0.786	0.789
67	Trinidad and Tobago	0.668	0.717	0.784	0.785	0.792	0.795
69	Albania	0.650	0.671	0.745	0.787	0.788	0.790
70	Cuba	0.680	0.691	0.781	0.767	0.772	0.777

2018	2019	Change in HDI rank 2014–2019	Average annual HDI growth (%) 1990–2000	2000–2010	2010–2019	1990–2019
0.867	0.868	−4	...	0.29	0.40	...
0.863	0.866	3	0.33	1.15	0.55	0.68
0.860	0.864	−1	0.99	0.46	0.46	0.64
0.858	0.860	−2	0.32	0.83	0.38	0.51
0.850	0.854	1	0.87	0.74	0.30	0.65
0.854	0.854	−4	0.64	0.85	0.60	0.70
0.852	0.852	6	0.60	0.06	0.70	0.45
0.849	0.851	0	0.69	0.60	0.65	0.65
0.848	0.851	2	1.12	0.74	0.48	0.79
0.845	0.848	0	0.85	0.22	0.19	0.42
0.842	0.845	−2	0.84	0.60	0.21	0.56
0.836	0.838	−6	0.45	0.31	0.15	0.31
0.826	0.829	2	...	...	0.37	...
0.823	0.828	2	0.11	1.18	0.31	0.54
0.822	0.826	−3	...	0.55	0.55	...
0.819	0.825	7	−0.07	1.10	0.86	0.62
0.823	0.824	1	−0.18	0.79	0.60	0.39
0.823	0.823	−4	...	1.49	0.39	...
0.817	0.820	5	1.25	1.14	1.16	1.18
0.816	0.817	1	0.68	0.51	0.49	0.56
0.813	0.816	−2	0.17	0.91	0.39	0.49
0.812	0.815	5	0.86	0.52	0.58	0.65
0.812	0.814	−3	...	0.10	0.12	...
0.810	0.814	−6	0.52	0.33	0.23	0.37
0.813	0.813	−3	...	1.22	0.43	...
0.805	0.812	7	...	0.85	0.87	...
0.808	0.810	−3	0.81	0.59	0.64	0.68
0.805	0.810	1	1.18	0.66	0.54	0.80
0.807	0.806	−5	1.03	0.09	0.25	0.46
0.803	0.806	3	−0.08	0.68	0.57	0.38
0.801	0.804	−2	0.83	1.03	0.76	0.88
0.790	0.796	2	...	0.68	0.46	...
0.795	0.796	−1	0.71	0.90	0.17	0.61
0.792	0.795	−4	0.32	1.05	0.72	0.70
0.781	0.783	5	0.16	1.23	0.03	0.49

(continued)

(continued)

HDI rank	Country	Human Development Index (HDI) value					
		1990	2000	2010	2014	2015	2017
70	Iran (Islamic Republic of)	0.565	0.658	0.742	0.774	0.774	0.787
72	Sri Lanka	0.629	0.691	0.754	0.773	0.776	0.775
73	Bosnia and Herzegovina	...	0.679	0.721	0.758	0.761	0.774
74	Grenada	...	...	0.754	0.766	0.770	0.770
74	Mexico	0.656	0.708	0.748	0.761	0.766	0.771
74	Saint Kitts and Nevis	...	...	0.746	0.768	0.768	0.770
74	Ukraine	0.725	0.694	0.755	0.771	0.765	0.771
78	Antigua and Barbuda	...	...	0.763	0.760	0.762	0.768
79	Peru	0.613	0.679	0.721	0.760	0.759	0.767
79	Thailand	0.577	0.652	0.724	0.742	0.749	0.765
81	Armenia	0.654	0.669	0.747	0.764	0.768	0.769
82	North Macedonia	...	0.677	0.743	0.755	0.761	0.767
83	Colombia	0.603	0.666	0.729	0.753	0.756	0.763
84	Brazil	0.613	0.685	0.727	0.756	0.756	0.761
85	China	0.499	0.588	0.699	0.731	0.739	0.750
86	Ecuador	0.648	0.675	0.726	0.756	0.764	0.760
86	Saint Lucia	...	0.695	0.730	0.735	0.747	0.759
88	Azerbaijan	...	0.635	0.726	0.740	0.744	0.754
88	Dominican Republic	0.599	0.659	0.706	0.730	0.738	0.746
90	Moldova (Republic of)	0.690	0.643	0.713	0.737	0.736	0.743
91	Algeria	0.572	0.637	0.721	0.736	0.740	0.745
92	Lebanon	...	...	0.766	0.748	0.744	0.748
93	Fiji	0.662	0.695	0.715	0.733	0.737	0.740
94	Dominica	...	0.703	0.740	0.741	0.739	0.736
95	Maldives	...	0.622	0.685	0.718	0.724	0.731
95	Tunisia	0.567	0.651	0.716	0.726	0.729	0.734
97	Saint Vincent and the Grenadines	...	0.681	0.718	0.733	0.733	0.734
97	Suriname	...	...	0.710	0.735	0.740	0.732
99	Mongolia	0.578	0.588	0.696	0.732	0.735	0.728
100	Botswana	0.573	0.581	0.663	0.711	0.717	0.726

		Change in HDI rank	Average annual HDI growth (%)			
2018	2019	2014–2019[a]	1990–2000	2000–2010	2010–2019	1990–2019
0.785	0.783	1	1.54	1.21	0.60	1.13
0.779	0.782	0	0.94	0.88	0.41	0.75
0.777	0.780	8	...	0.60	0.88	...
0.773	0.779	2	...	...	0.36	...
0.776	0.779	4	0.77	0.55	0.45	0.59
0.773	0.779	0	...	...	0.48	...
0.774	0.779	-1	-0.44	0.85	0.35	0.25
0.772	0.778	1	...	...	0.22	...
0.771	0.777	0	1.03	0.60	0.83	0.82
0.772	0.777	8	1.23	1.05	0.79	1.03
0.771	0.776	-4	0.23	1.11	0.42	0.59
0.770	0.774	2	...	0.93	0.46	...
0.764	0.767	2	1.00	0.91	0.57	0.83
0.762	0.765	-2	1.12	0.60	0.57	0.77
0.755	0.761	12	1.65	1.74	0.95	1.47
0.762	0.759	-4	0.41	0.73	0.50	0.55
0.758	0.759	6	...	0.49	0.43	...
0.754	0.756	1	...	1.35	0.45	...
0.751	0.756	10	0.96	0.69	0.76	0.81
0.746	0.750	0	-0.70	1.04	0.56	0.29
0.746	0.748	0	1.08	1.25	0.41	0.93
0.747	0.744	-6	...	...	-0.32	...
0.742	0.743	1	0.49	0.28	0.43	0.40
0.738	0.742	-6	...	0.51	0.03	...
0.734	0.740	8	...	0.97	0.86	...
0.738	0.740	7	1.39	0.96	0.37	0.92
0.736	0.738	-3	...	0.53	0.31	...
0.734	0.738	-5	...	...	0.43	...
0.735	0.737	-3	0.17	1.70	0.64	0.84
0.730	0.735	5	0.14	1.33	1.15	0.86

(*continued*)

(continued)

HDI rank	Country	Human Development Index (HDI) value					
		1990	2000	2010	2014	2015	2017
101	Jamaica	0.645	0.678	0.732	0.729	0.731	0.734
102	Jordan	0.625	0.711	0.737	0.729	0.730	0.726
103	Paraguay	0.598	0.643	0.696	0.715	0.721	0.726
104	Tonga	0.654	0.675	0.699	0.707	0.720	0.723
105	Libya	0.724	0.780	0.798	0.728	0.697	0.714
106	Uzbekistan	...	0.599	0.669	0.696	0.701	0.713
107	Bolivia (Plurinational State of)	0.551	0.627	0.667	0.690	0.697	0.710
107	Indonesia	0.523	0.603	0.665	0.690	0.695	0.707
107	Philippines	0.593	0.632	0.671	0.696	0.701	0.708
110	Belize	0.610	0.640	0.695	0.705	0.710	0.714
111	Samoa	0.633	0.651	0.698	0.703	0.707	0.710
111	Turkmenistan	...	...	0.666	0.689	0.694	0.701
113	Venezuela (Bolivarian Republic of)	0.644	0.676	0.757	0.775	0.769	0.743
114	South Africa	0.627	0.631	0.664	0.693	0.701	0.705
115	Palestine, State of	...	...	0.684	0.697	0.701	0.706
116	Egypt	0.548	0.613	0.668	0.685	0.691	0.698
117	Marshall Islands	...	...	...	...	...	0.699
117	Viet Nam	0.483	0.586	0.661	0.683	0.688	0.696
119	Gabon	0.613	0.621	0.652	0.682	0.685	0.694
Medium human development							
120	Kyrgyzstan	0.640	0.620	0.662	0.686	0.690	0.694
121	Morocco	0.457	0.529	0.616	0.652	0.658	0.673
122	Guyana	0.548	0.616	0.649	0.671	0.674	0.677
123	Iraq	0.560	0.595	0.636	0.645	0.649	0.667
124	El Salvador	0.536	0.615	0.668	0.668	0.668	0.671
125	Tajikistan	0.617	0.555	0.638	0.652	0.652	0.657
126	Cabo Verde	...	0.569	0.632	0.654	0.656	0.660
127	Guatemala	0.481	0.549	0.606	0.648	0.652	0.655
128	Nicaragua	0.497	0.577	0.622	0.649	0.652	0.661
129	Bhutan	...	...	0.574	0.618	0.628	0.646
130	Namibia	0.581	0.544	0.589	0.631	0.638	0.644
131	India	0.429	0.495	0.579	0.616	0.624	0.640
132	Honduras	0.519	0.566	0.610	0.616	0.618	0.630

		Change in HDI rank	Average annual HDI growth (%)			
2018	2019	2014–2019ᵃ	1990–2000	2000–2010	2010–2019	1990–2019
0.734	0.734	-2	0.50	0.77	0.03	0.45
0.728	0.729	-3	1.30	0.36	-0.12	0.53
0.727	0.728	1	0.73	0.80	0.50	0.68
0.723	0.725	2	0.32	0.35	0.41	0.36
0.721	0.724	-4	0.75	0.23	-1.08	0.00
0.717	0.720	4	...	1.11	0.82	...
0.714	0.718	6	1.30	0.62	0.82	0.92
0.712	0.718	6	1.43	0.98	0.86	1.10
0.711	0.718	3	0.64	0.60	0.76	0.66
0.714	0.716	-3	0.48	0.83	0.33	0.55
0.709	0.715	-3	0.28	0.70	0.27	0.42
0.710	0.715	4	...	...	0.79	...
0.733	0.711	-44	0.49	1.14	-0.69	0.34
0.707	0.709	-2	0.06	0.51	0.73	0.42
0.708	0.708	-6	...	...	0.38	...
0.701	0.707	1	1.13	0.86	0.63	0.88
0.702	0.704	...	...	...	...	...
0.700	0.704	1	1.95	1.21	0.70	1.31
0.697	0.703	0	0.13	0.49	0.84	0.47
0.696	0.697	-4	-0.32	0.66	0.57	0.29
0.680	0.686	2	1.47	1.53	1.20	1.41
0.680	0.682	-2	1.18	0.52	0.55	0.76
0.671	0.674	4	0.61	0.67	0.65	0.64
0.670	0.673	-3	1.38	0.83	0.08	0.79
0.661	0.668	-2	-1.05	1.40	0.51	0.27
0.663	0.665	-4	...	1.06	0.57	...
0.657	0.663	-1	1.33	0.99	1.00	1.11
0.659	0.660	-3	1.50	0.75	0.66	0.98
0.649	0.654	1	...	...	1.46	...
0.645	0.646	-2	-0.66	0.80	1.03	0.37
0.642	0.645	1	1.44	1.58	1.21	1.42
0.633	0.634	0	0.87	0.75	0.43	0.69

(continued)

(continued)

HDI rank	Country	Human Development Index (HDI) value					
		1990	2000	2010	2014	2015	2017
133	Bangladesh	0.394	0.478	0.557	0.579	0.595	0.616
134	Kiribati	...	0.553	0.593	0.617	0.625	0.627
135	Sao Tome and Principe	0.452	0.498	0.561	0.591	0.604	0.619
136	Micronesia (Federated States of)	...	0.546	0.601	0.604	0.612	0.616
137	Lao People's Democratic Republic	0.405	0.471	0.552	0.589	0.598	0.608
138	Eswatini (Kingdom of)	0.541	0.465	0.510	0.568	0.581	0.597
138	Ghana	0.465	0.494	0.565	0.590	0.590	0.602
140	Vanuatu	...	...	0.590	0.594	0.598	0.601
141	Timor—Leste	...	0.484	0.628	0.620	0.610	0.599
142	Nepal	0.387	0.453	0.537	0.576	0.583	0.588
143	Kenya	0.482	0.461	0.551	0.580	0.587	0.595
144	Cambodia	0.368	0.424	0.539	0.565	0.570	0.582
145	Equatorial Guinea	...	0.525	0.576	0.586	0.589	0.584
146	Zambia	0.421	0.425	0.527	0.561	0.569	0.578
147	Myanmar	0.342	0.414	0.515	0.550	0.557	0.572
148	Angola	...	0.400	0.517	0.565	0.572	0.582
149	Congo	0.500	0.461	0.520	0.560	0.580	0.574
150	Zimbabwe	0.478	0.430	0.482	0.547	0.553	0.563
151	Solomon Islands	...	0.475	0.537	0.559	0.563	0.562
151	Syrian Arab Republic	0.550	0.600	0.672	0.556	0.537	0.564
153	Cameroon	0.448	0.440	0.505	0.540	0.549	0.557
154	Pakistan	0.402	0.447	0.512	0.530	0.536	0.550
155	Papua New Guinea	0.380	0.450	0.522	0.542	0.548	0.549
156	Comoros	...	0.465	0.521	0.543	0.545	0.550
Low human development							
157	Mauritania	0.397	0.464	0.505	0.531	0.536	0.540
158	Benin	0.364	0.416	0.494	0.527	0.532	0.536
159	Uganda	0.320	0.404	0.498	0.519	0.525	0.532

		Change in HDI rank	Average annual HDI growth (%)			
2018	2019	2014–2019[a]	1990–2000	2000–2010	2010–2019	1990–2019
0.625	0.632	8	1.95	1.54	1.41	1.64
0.628	0.630	–3	...	0.70	0.67	...
0.624	0.625	1	0.97	1.20	1.21	1.12
0.618	0.620	–2	...	0.96	0.35	...
0.609	0.613	1	1.52	1.60	1.17	1.44
0.605	0.611	5	–1.50	0.93	2.03	0.42
0.606	0.611	–1	0.61	1.35	0.87	0.95
0.603	0.609	–5	...	...	0.35	...
0.599	0.606	–12	...	2.64	–0.40	...
0.596	0.602	0	1.59	1.72	1.28	1.54
0.599	0.601	–3	–0.44	1.80	0.97	0.76
0.585	0.594	0	1.43	2.43	1.09	1.66
0.582	0.592	–6	...	0.93	0.30	...
0.582	0.584	0	0.09	2.17	1.15	1.13
0.579	0.583	3	1.93	2.21	1.39	1.86
0.582	0.581	–4	...	2.60	1.31	...
0.573	0.574	–2	–0.81	1.21	1.10	0.48
0.569	0.571	1	–1.05	1.15	1.90	0.61
0.564	0.567	–3	...	1.23	0.61	...
0.563	0.567	–2	0.87	1.14	–1.87	0.11
0.560	0.563	1	–0.18	1.39	1.22	0.79
0.552	0.557	2	1.07	1.37	0.94	1.13
0.549	0.555	–2	1.71	1.50	0.68	1.31
0.552	0.554	–4	...	1.14	0.68	...
0.542	0.546	–2	1.57	0.85	0.87	1.10
0.541	0.545	–1	1.34	1.73	1.10	1.40
0.538	0.544	2	2.36	2.11	0.99	1.85

(*continued*)

(continued)

HDI rank	Country	Human Development Index (HDI) value					
		1990	2000	2010	2014	2015	2017
160	Rwanda	0.248	0.341	0.492	0.521	0.526	0.535
161	Nigeria	...	...	0.482	0.523	0.526	0.531
162	Côte d'Ivoire	0.404	0.421	0.468	0.492	0.503	0.525
163	Tanzania (United Republic of)	0.368	0.390	0.481	0.504	0.514	0.523
164	Madagascar	...	0.462	0.511	0.520	0.522	0.526
165	Lesotho	0.498	0.459	0.460	0.498	0.503	0.517
166	Djibouti	...	0.360	0.454	0.492	0.499	0.510
167	Togo	0.406	0.427	0.466	0.493	0.499	0.506
168	Senegal	0.376	0.390	0.468	0.499	0.506	0.512
169	Afghanistan	0.302	0.350	0.472	0.500	0.500	0.506
170	Haiti	0.414	0.442	0.471	0.492	0.496	0.505
170	Sudan	0.331	0.403	0.469	0.499	0.504	0.509
172	Gambia	0.349	0.403	0.459	0.468	0.471	0.480
173	Ethiopia	...	0.292	0.421	0.455	0.462	0.474
174	Malawi	0.333	0.388	0.431	0.465	0.468	0.473
175	Congo (Democratic Republic of the)	0.369	0.349	0.435	0.460	0.464	0.475
175	Guinea-Bissau	...	...	0.436	0.459	0.464	0.470
175	Liberia	...	0.435	0.455	0.478	0.477	0.481
178	Guinea	0.282	0.340	0.416	0.452	0.457	0.471
179	Yemen	0.401	0.444	0.506	0.502	0.483	0.467
180	Eritrea	...	...	0.436	0.457	0.454	0.454
181	Mozambique	0.227	0.307	0.401	0.425	0.433	0.446
182	Burkina Faso	...	0.293	0.384	0.413	0.422	0.439
182	Sierra Leone	0.287	0.295	0.399	0.438	0.431	0.443
184	Mali	0.234	0.312	0.408	0.419	0.417	0.427
185	Burundi	0.299	0.300	0.411	0.438	0.437	0.434
185	South Sudan	...	...	0.410	0.428	0.425	0.426
187	Chad	...	0.293	0.369	0.401	0.398	0.396
188	Central African Republic	0.334	0.325	0.365	0.368	0.375	0.391
189	Niger	0.220	0.262	0.331	0.365	0.372	0.386

		Change in HDI rank	Average annual HDI growth (%)			
2018	2019	2014–2019[a]	1990–2000	2000–2010	2010–2019	1990–2019
0.540	0.543	-1	3.24	3.73	1.10	2.74
0.534	0.539	-3	…	…	1.25	…
0.534	0.538	7	0.41	1.06	1.56	0.99
0.524	0.529	-1	0.58	2.12	1.06	1.26
0.527	0.528	-4	…	1.01	0.36	…
0.522	0.527	2	-0.81	0.02	1.52	0.20
0.518	0.524	3	…	2.35	1.61	…
0.510	0.515	1	0.51	0.88	1.12	0.82
0.516	0.512	-3	0.37	1.84	1.00	1.07
0.509	0.511	-5	1.49	3.04	0.89	1.83
0.508	0.510	-1	0.66	0.64	0.89	0.72
0.506	0.510	-5	1.99	1.53	0.94	1.50
0.487	0.496	1	1.45	1.31	0.87	1.22
0.478	0.485	5	…	3.73	1.58	…
0.478	0.483	0	1.54	1.06	1.27	1.29
0.478	0.480	0	-0.56	2.23	1.10	0.91
0.472	0.480	1	…	…	1.07	…
0.480	0.480	-3	…	0.45	0.60	…
0.473	0.477	1	1.89	2.04	1.53	1.83
0.468	0.470	-16	1.02	1.32	-0.82	0.55
0.456	0.459	-3	…	…	0.57	…
0.452	0.456	2	3.07	2.71	1.44	2.43
0.443	0.452	3	…	2.74	1.83	…
0.447	0.452	-2	0.28	3.07	1.40	1.58
0.431	0.434	0	2.92	2.72	0.69	2.15
0.431	0.433	-5	0.03	3.20	0.58	1.29
0.429	0.433	-3	…	…	0.61	…
0.397	0.398	-1	…	2.33	0.84	…
0.395	0.397	-1	-0.27	1.17	0.94	0.60
0.391	0.394	-1	1.76	2.37	1.95	2.03

(continued)

(continued)

HDI rank	Country	Human Development Index (HDI) value					
		1990	2000	2010	2014	2015	2017
	Human development groups						
	Very high human development	0.782	0.826	0.870	0.885	0.889	0.894
	High human development	0.567	0.629	0.705	0.730	0.735	0.744
	Medium human development	0.433	0.492	0.571	0.601	0.609	0.624
	Low human development	0.345	0.381	0.468	0.497	0.500	0.507
	Developing countries	0.517	0.571	0.642	0.668	0.673	0.683
	Least developed countries	0.353	0.403	0.489	0.513	0.520	0.531
	Small island developing states	0.599	0.646	0.706	0.715	0.720	0.724
	World	0.601	0.644	0.699	0.720	0.724	0.732

Source: Author's adaptation based on the *Human Development Report 2020: The next frontier, Human development and the Anthropocene (UNDP)*

[a]A positive value indicates an improvement in rank

2018	2019	Change in HDI rank 2014–2019[a]	Average annual HDI growth (%) 1990–2000	2000–2010	2010–2019	1990–2019
0.896	0.898	–	0.55	0.52	0.35	0.48
0.748	0.753	–	1.04	1.15	0.73	0.98
0.627	0.631	–	1.29	1.50	1.12	1.31
0.509	0.513	–	1.00	2.08	1.03	1.38
0.685	0.689	–	1.00	1.18	0.79	1.00
0.534	0.538	–	1.33	1.95	1.07	1.46
0.726	0.728	–	0.76	0.89	0.34	0.67
0.734	0.737	–	0.69	0.82	0.59	0.71

ANNEX 19: QUESTIONNAIRE

'STEFAN CEL MARE' UNIVERSITY OF SUCEAVA

Questionnaire

regarding the analysis of the perception of the bachelor/master/doctorate graduates concerning the relationship between the level of education – employability – professional and personal development in the context of the satisfaction of the work

---

Your answers are used exclusively for statistical analysis and are not associated with the names of the respondents.

A. GRADUATED UNIVERSITY STUDY PROGRAM

A$_1$. What's the last study program you graduated from?

(mention the name of the university, faculty, specialization and year of graduation)

☐

University...

....

☐

Faculty...

....

☐ Study

program...

☐ Graduation

year...

....

A$_2$. What university training program have you graduated from finishing high school until now?

(mention all the university training programs graduated so far)

You graduated	University	Faculty/Specialization	Year
B. ☐ bachelor level program 1	....	....	
C. ☐ bachelor level program 2		....	....
D. ☐in-depth studies		....	....
E. ☐ master`s degree 1............		....	....
F. ☐ master`s degree 2............		....	....
G. ☐ doctorate		....	....
H. ☐other programs, specify			

A$_3$.   You have attended your studies............................

1.   ☐ full-time   1.2. ☐ with fee   1.3. ☐ no fee
2.   ☐ no frequency   2.2. ☐ with fee   2.3. ☐ no fee
3.   ☐ I'm not responding.

A4. What undergraduate programs or other forms of study are you pursuing at the moment? (multiple variants of answer can be chosen)

Attending now	University	Faculty/ Specialization	From the year
1. ☐bachelor	....	......	....
2. ☐master` degree	....	......	....
3. ☐doctorate	....	......	....
4. ☐other courses, specify.........		......	....
5. ☐NO.	....	....	....

A5. How do you assess, at the time of graduation of the bachelor / master / doctorate, the level of competences acquired during the studies followed within the USV? (please mark with x your answer for all 20 points mentioned)

	Very low 1	2	3	4	Very high 5
1. thorough knowledge of the field of study	☐	☐	☐	☐	☐
2. knowledge of other fields or disciplines	☐	☐	☐	☐	☐
3. analytical thinking	☐	☐	☐	☐	☐
4. critical thinking	☐	☐	☐	☐	☐
5. the ability to quickly accumulate new knowledge	☐	☐	☐	☐	☐
6. the ability to act well under stress	☐	☐	☐	☐	☐
7. the ability to identify new opportunities	☐	☐	☐	☐	☐
8. the ability to coordinate activities	☐	☐	☐	☐	☐
9. the ability to efficiently manage working time	☐	☐	☐	☐	☐
10. the ability to work in a team	☐	☐	☐	☐	☐
11. the ability to mobilize other people	☐	☐	☐	☐	☐
12. the ability to convey clear information	☐	☐	☐	☐	☐
13. the ability to exercise one's own authority	☐	☐	☐	☐	☐
14. the ability to use computer programs	☐	☐	☐	☐	☐
15. the ability to provide solutions in various situations	☐	☐	☐	☐	☐
16. the ability to negotiate effectively	☐	☐	☐	☐	☐
17. the ability to make a presentation in front of an audience	☐	☐	☐	☐	☐
18. the ability to draw up various documents	☐	☐	☐	☐	☐
19. the ability to write in a foreign language	☐	☐	☐	☐	☐
20. the ability to converse in a foreign language	☐	☐	☐	☐	☐

AFTER COMPLETING THE BACHELOR`S/ MASTER'S. FIRST JOB.

B₁. What is the most appropriate description of your situation in the first 6 months after obtaining your bachelor/master/doctorate?

(several variants can be chosen)

1.   ☐ I enrolled in master's studies
2.   ☐ I enrolled in doctoral studies;
3.   ☐ I started working as a volunteer;
4.   ☐ I opened my own business;
5.   ☐ I continued my work at the workplace I already had;
6.   ☐ I am engaged in the field of completed studies;
7.   ☐ I was employed in a field other than that of specialization;
8.   ☐ I was looking for a job, but I was unable to get a job;
9.   ☐ other situations, specify;
10. ☐NO.

B₂. During your bachelor's/master's/doctoral studies did you have a job?

(choose a most appropriate answer)

1. ☐permanent   ☐ full time   ☐ part time
2. ☐most of the time   ☐ full time   ☐ part time
3. ☐during certain periods/occasionally   ☐ full time   ☐ part time
4. ☐rarely   ☐ full time   ☐ part time
5. ☐ not at all
6. ☐ NO.

B₃. How long did it take to get your first job after completing your bachelor's/master's/PhD degree?

☐ at........ months after graduation;

☐ that's not the case, I have the same job as before graduation;

☐ I'm not responding.

THE STATUS ON THE LABOUR MARKET AT PRESENT. CURRENT JOB.

C₁. Currently you are:

1.   ☐ employee with an indefinite employment contract;
2.   ☐ employee with a fixed-term employment contract;
3.   ☐ employee without an employment contract;
4.   ☐ freelancer;
5.   ☐ I have my own business;
6.   ☐ unemployed with the related rights;
7.   ☐ I don't have a job, but I'm looking for one;
8.   ☐ I have no job and I do not intend to get a job in the next 6 months;
9.   ☐other situation, specify...
10. ☐ NO.

C₂. How long have you been working at your current job?

☐ under 3 months;
☐ between 3-6 months;
☐ between 6-12 months;
☐ over 12 months;
☐ I'm not responding.

C₃. To what extent does your current job meet your expectations?

Not at all   In its entirety

1	2	3	4	5
☐	☐	☐	☐	☐

C₄. The organization you work for is:

1. ☐ public organization
2. ☐ private organization
3. ☐ joint venture organization
4. ☐ NGO
5. ☐ own company
6. ☐ other, specify...

C₅. What is the name of your profession?
(e.g.: computer scientist, engineer, lawyer, mathematician)

....

C₆. What is the name of the job you are occupying now?
(e.g.: legal adviser, expert, director, clerk, inspector, accountant)

....

C₇. Your gross salary level is:

☐ under 1000 lei;
☐ between 1001 - 1501 lei;
☐ between 1501 - 2,000 lei;
☐ between 2,001 and 2,500 lei;
☐ between 2,501 and 3000 lei;
☐ Over 3000 lei
☐ I have no salary;
☐ I'm not responding.

C₈. How pleased you are with:

Please mark your reply with x. for all the above matters:

	Very dissatisfied			Very satisfied	
	1	2	3	4	5
1. the activity you currently perform:	☐	☐	☐	☐	☐
2. the management style of the hierarchical superior:	☐	☐	☐	☐	☐

3. the salary level reflects the level of training: ☐   ☐   ☐   ☐   ☐
4. the existence of the possibility of professional
   development: ☐   ☐   ☐   ☐   ☐
5. the requirements of the job correspond
   to the professional training: ☐   ☐   ☐   ☐   ☐

SOCIO-DEMOGRAPHIC DATA
D_1. What is your age?
☐ Under 25 years old
☐ Between 25-30 years
☐ Between 30-35 years
☐ Over 35 years

D_2. Gender?
☐ F
☐ M

D_3. Place of provenance:
1.   City..
2.   County..

D_4.   The city where you now live:

1.   City..
2.   County..
Date of completion DD/MM/YYY............/................./..................

THANK YOU FOR YOUR COOPERATION!

Annex 20: What Happens to the Graduates of the "Stefan cel Maré" University in Suceava?

It is a question that has become the subject of a permanent study conducted by the **Centre for Career Counselling** and Guidance since 2006.

Research Methodology:
The goal: capturing the professional route of the graduates of the "Stefan cel Mare" University of Suceava
   The tool used: graduate questionnaire
   The elaboration and processing of the questionnaires was carried out by:

- Associate Prof. PhD. Carmen Cornelia Balan
- Psychologist PhD. Liliana Bujor
- Psychologist PhD. Diana Teodorescu

The application of the questionnaires was carried out by the staff of the *Department of Studies Acts*, coordinator Maria Musca, USV Chief Secretary.

The Investigated Batch:

- Graduates who received their diploma between July 2006 and December 2014 from the *Department of Study Documents*
- Lot size: 14,967 graduates Type of diploma:
  - bachelor's, 11,531
  - master's, 3158
  - DPPD certificate, 75
  - in-depth studies, 26
  - college diploma, 4
  - doctorate, 30
  - did not specify the type of diploma, 143
- Year of graduation from the faculty
  - by 2000, 76 graduates
  - 2001–2005, 406 graduates
  - 2006, 330 graduates
  - 2007, 873 graduates
  - 2008, 2662 graduates
  - 2009, 2066 graduates
  - 2010, 1514 graduates
  - 2011, 1508 graduates
  - 2012, 1342 graduates
  - 2013, 490 graduates
  - did not specify, 264

Results
In order to capture the dynamics aspects, the results were processed starting from the answers of the **bachelor's graduates** and according to the **membership promotion.**

- In this report, the promotions of **2011** (1508 graduates), **2012** (1342 graduates), and **2013** (490 graduates) were considered.

1. Current Status of the USV Graduate

Promotion	Status						
	Employee with indefinite work card	Fixed-term part-time employee	Employee without work card	Unemployed	Neither unemployed nor employee	Attendant of a form of education	No
2011	728 (48.3%)	164 (10.9%)	37 (2.5%)	36 (2.4%)	257 (17%)	240 (15.9%)	46 (3.1 %)
2012	594 (44.3%)	163 (12.1%)	30 (2.2%)	31 (2.3%)	232 (17.3%)	257 (19.2%)	35 (2.6%)
2013	234 (47.8%)	51 (10.4%)	12 (2.4%)	11 (2.2%)	64 (13.1%)	107 (21.8%)	11 (2.2%)

The graduates of the 2011 promotion are 48.3% of the employees with an *indefinite work card*. The next promotion, 2012 (44.3%), registers a decrease in the percentage of those employed with a *work card*, but in 2013 the percentage is in a slight increase (47.8%), which proves that most graduates are among those employed with indefinite work cards.

The percentage of *unemployed* decreases from one promotion to another, and that of graduates *without a work card* does not exceed 3% in any of the three promotions analyzed.

Graduates without any status remain around 17% percent in the 2011, 2012 promotions and we see a percentage decrease for 2013 (13.1%).

The number of graduates who attend a form of education after graduating from bachelor's degree studies presents, as is natural, a significant increase from older to new promotions (15.9%, 19.2%, and 21.8%).

The reasons why our graduates are not employed range from *we did not find a job according to the training* (reason invoked by about 14.9% of the graduates of the class of 2011 and 15.2% of those in 2012 and 16.1% class of 2013), *we did not actually find a job* (the percentages vary between 7.4%—2011, 7.5%—2012, and 6.1% in 2013), *up to intentions to start a business* (percentages decrease from older graduates–4.2% for 2011, 4.4% for 2012, and 3.5% for 2013).

Quite high percentages also register graduates with a passive attitude toward finding a job; they do not have a job because they did not look for 5% of the 2011 graduates, 7.8% from 2012, and 7.6% from 2013.

Emigration intentions register the highest percentage for the 2011 class—5.6%.

2. Professional Category

We must mention that the response rate to this item is very low and even registers a trend in the analysis of the dynamics of the three promotions: the graduates in 2011 have a lower availability of response (44.2%) compared to those in 2012 (45.5%) and those in 2013 (46.7%). Given that the analysis of this item for all USV graduates does not reveal important aspects, given the multitude of trades, we decided to perform this analysis for each faculty.

3. Satisfaction Degree

It is measured directly by an item that requires to indicate on a five-step scale *the degree of satisfaction with the training acquired within the faculty.*

We see some interesting aspects. The percentage of graduates who are *very satisfied* increases from 2011 to 2013. Most graduates are *largely satisfied* (for all three promotions analyzed) with the training acquired within the faculty, but the percentage decreases from 2011 progressively to 2013.

Promotion	Degree of satisfaction					
	To a very large extent	To a large extent	So and so	To a small extent	To a very small extent	No
2011	382 (25.3%)	713 (47.3%)	215 (14.3%)	60 (4%)	30 (2%)	108 (7.2%)
2012	366 (27.3%)	533 (39.7%)	195 (14.5%)	83 (6.2%)	41 (3.1%)	124 (9.2%)
2013	188 (38.4%)	173 (35.3%)	58 (11.8%)	18 (3.7%)	7 (1.4%)	46 (9.4%)

ANNEX 21: POPULATION AGED 25–64 YEARS WITH A LOW LEVEL OF EDUCATION BY REGION

GEO/ TIME	Northwest	Center	Northeast	Southeast	South-Muntenia	Bucharest-Ilfov	Southwest Oltenia	West
2000	33.0	27.3	34.5	33.8	33.6	16.7	32.4	30.2
2001	31.7	26.2	33.9	32.5	31.3	16.8	29.5	29.5
2002	31.7	26.5	32.8	32.2	31.1	16.9	27.5	28.7
2003	31.9	27.5	34.0	32.2	31.2	17.5	27.7	29.7
2004	29.9	26.6	31.0	31.6	31.5	16.6	28.8	29.3
2005	29.0	24.1	29.4	30.5	29.6	15.5	27.4	27.2
2006	27.9	22.7	28.7	30.1	28.0	14.5	26.1	25.4
2007	25.8	22.8	28.1	30.0	27.8	13.2	24.9	24.0
2008	25.1	21.8	28.3	29.9	27.9	12.6	25.5	22.6
2009	26.1	22.6	29.8	29.2	28.9	13.1	26.0	22.6
2010	25.7	24.2	31.8	30.2	29.9	13.3	27.7	23.1
2011	25.2	23.5	30.9	30.7	29.2	11.9	27.7	21.9
2012	25.1	22.5	29.8	30.0	27.9	11.6	25.4	21.6
2013	25.2	22.0	28.9	29.5	27.3	11.6	24.9	22.6
2014	27.2	26.7	32.7	32.8	30.5	14.5	26.5	24.1
2015	24.4	25.4	31.8	30.4	26.5	14.5	23.9	20.0
2016	24.5	23.2	30.7	28.2	23.8	13.0	20.8	18.8
2017	24.4	20.4	30.0	27.6	22.1	10.9	20.2	18.1
2018	22.1	20.6	29.2	26.6	22.3	11.0	20.2	17.5
2019	20.0	20.9	29.3	25.6	22.7	10.5	20.2	16.0
2020	18.2	19.9	27.8	25.2	22.0	9.0	19.4	12.0

Source: Eurostat, 2020, https://ec.europa.eu/eurostat/databrowser/view/EDAT_LFS_9903__custom_2749583/default/table

Population Aged 25–64 Years with a Higher Level of Education by Region

GEO/ TIME	Northwest	Center	Northeast	Southeast	South-Muntenia	Bucharest-Ilfov	Southwest Oltenia	West
2000	8.8	8.3	6.8	8.8	6.5	20.1	7.8	10.6
2001	10.2	8.5	7.0	8.7	7.1	20.3	8.3	11.1
2002	9.4	7.9	7.0	9.3	7.1	22.1	8.5	10.5
2003	8.4	8.0	7.2	8.2	7.2	22.6	8.5	9.7
2004	9.4	9.3	8.5	7.6	7.7	24.2	9.8	10.9
2005	9.1	9.7	9.4	8.5	7.9	25.4	10.6	10.9
2006	9.6	10.8	9.8	9.2	8.7	26.5	10.8	10.8
2007	11.0	11.1	10.3	8.8	8.6	26.3	11.1	11.4
2008	12.1	11.4	11.1	9.4	8.6	27.7	12.8	12.8
2009	12.1	11.8	11.2	10.0	9.1	27.7	13.0	14.3
2010	12.6	11.2	11.6	10.3	9.9	28.3	12.6	14.0
2011	13.0	12.4	12.2	11.4	10.7	31.0	13.1	14.5
2012	13.7	13.1	12.6	12.3	11.2	31.9	13.7	15.1
2013	14.2	14.3	11.9	12.4	11.4	33.1	14.3	14.2
2014	14.2	14.6	12.0	12.0	11.4	35.0	15.1	13.5
2015	17.4	17.8	11.6	12.9	12.8	33.6	16.7	16.1
2016	17.4	17.5	11.5	12.9	13.3	35.1	16.8	15.5
2017	17.1	17.9	12.1	12.7	13.1	36.1	16.1	16.0
2018	17.7	18.1	12.7	13.1	12.7	37.5	14.7	15.7
2019	18.9	18.3	11.7	13.8	12.9	40.3	15.4	16.3
2020	20.1	17.1	11.8	13.1	13.1	40.5	16.7	17.0

Source: Eurostat, 2020, https://ec.europa.eu/eurostat/databrowser/view/EDAT_LFS_9903__custom_2749583/default/table

Population Aged 25–64 Years by Education Levels and by Gender—Romania

GEO/TIME	Low level			High level		
	Total	Men	Women	Total	Men	Women
2000	30.7	24.2	37.0	9.3	10.4	8.3
2001	29.4	23.1	35.5	9.8	10.7	8.9
2002	28.9	22.7	35.0	9.8	10.7	9.0
2003	29.5	23.3	35.5	9.6	10.2	9.1
2004	28.5	22.5	34.4	10.6	11.1	10.0
2005	26.9	21.5	32.3	11.1	11.5	10.7
2006	25.8	20.6	30.9	11.7	12.1	11.3
2007	25.0	19.9	30.0	12.0	12.5	11.6
2008	24.7	19.9	29.3	12.8	13.1	12.6
2009	25.3	20.9	29.7	13.2	13.1	13.4
2010	26.1	21.6	30.6	13.6	13.7	13.5
2011	25.5	21.3	29.7	14.6	14.5	14.7
2012	24.6	20.7	28.5	15.3	15.0	15.6
2013	24.3	20.7	27.9	15.6	15.0	16.1
2014	27.2	24.5	30.0	15.9	15.3	16.4
2015	25.0	22.4	27.6	17.2	16.4	17.9
2016	23.3	21.1	25.5	17.4	16.5	18.2
2017	22.1	20.3	23.9	17.6	16.4	18.7
2018	21.5	19.9	23.2	17.8	16.5	19.1
2019	21.0	19.5	22.5	18.4	17.2	19.7
2020	19.6	18.1	21.1	18.7	17.4	20

Source: Eurostat, 2020, https://ec.europa.eu/eurostat/databrowser/view/EDAT_LFS_9903__custom_2749583/default/table

Employment Rate of the Population Aged 25–64 Years Depending on the Level of Education

GEO/TIME	Total	Low level	Medium level	High level
2000	73.3	68.7	74	84.5
2001	72.4	66.5	73.6	83.2
2002	67.3	56.4	69.8	82.9
2003	67.7	57.3	70.5	82
2004	67.5	52.5	71.6	85.9
2005	66.9	53.2	69.6	85.1
2006	68.4	53.4	71	87.4
2007	68.1	53.8	70.1	86.9
2008	68.1	54.6	69.5	86.9
2009	67.3	54.7	68.5	86
2010	68.2	55.8	69.6	85.8
2011	67.2	51.9	69.2	85.9
2012	68.1	53.5	69.7	85.4
2013	67.8	54	68.8	85.8
2014	68.8	55.5	70.4	86
2015	68.6	53.7	69.7	86.9
2016	69.2	52.8	70.3	87.8
2017	71.5	54.9	72.5	89.2
2018	72.6	55.6	73.7	89.7
2019	73.8	57.1	74.4	90.5
2020	73.5	56.2	74.1	90

Source: Eurostat, 2020, https://ec.europa.eu/eurostat/databrowser/view/UNE_EDUC_A_H__custom_2814951/default/table?lang=en

ANNEX 22: REGIONAL DISPARITIES IN THE NUMBER OF STUDENTS AND UNIVERSITY CENTERS IN SOUTH KOREA, GREAT BRITAIN, SWEDEN, POLAND, AND ROMANIA

Country/ Population—2020	Capital/ Number of students in 2020	Population— 2020	Number of universities—2020	Number of students—2020	Percentage (%) the population of the capital from the total population (%)	the students of the capital from total no. (%)
Country/Sweden Population—2020	**Capital/ Stockholm** Number of students in 2020				**Percentage (%)** the population of the capital from the total population (%)	the students of the capital from total no. (%)
10,353,440	520,075	978,770	18	98,135.0	9.5%	18.9%
Country/United Kingdom	**Capital/London**				**Percentage (%)**	
68,560,862	2,435,825	8,982,000	48	435,085	13.1%	17.9%
Country/Polonia	**Capital/Warsaw**				**Percentage (%)**	
37,899,070	1,215,137	1,702,139	68	227,627	4.5%	18.7%
Country/South Korea	**Capital/Seoul**				**Percentage (%)**	
51,836,240	3,201,561	9,911,088	46 (9 are state and 37 private)	979,599	19.1%	30.6%
Country/Romania	**Capital/Bucharest**				**Percentage (%)**	
19,257,520	560,490	2,161,842	31	177,718	11.2%	31.7%

Sources: authors elaboration according to available data, http://europa.eu/about-eu/countries/member-countries/index_ro.htm; http://www.uka.se/download/18.6e65a548l4e9d64344d17c3c/144007151431 4/arsrappor-2015.pdf; http://www.stockholm.se/OmStockholm/stockholmare/; http://www.masterstudies.com/universities/Sweden/Stockholm/; http://www.phdstudies.ro/universit%C4%83%C8%9Bi/Suedia/Stockholm/; http://europa.eu/about-eu/countries/member-countries/index_ro.htm; https://www.hesa.ac.uk/stats; http://www.studylondon.ac.uk/universities?gclid=CLW Liqr2I8oCFRThGwodZ_gDKA; https://www.ucl.ac.uk/srs/statistics/tables/3/total; https://en.wikipedia.org/wiki/List_of_universities_in_the_United_ Kingdom_by_enrollment; https://www.cia.gov/library/publications/the-world-factbook/geos/pl.html; http://warszawa.stat.gov.pl/en/; http://www.studenckamarka.pl/serwis.php?pok=1909&s=73; https://www.cia.gov/library/publications/resources/the-world-factbook/geos/ks.html; http://world-populationreview.com/world-cities/seoul-population/; http://www.topuniversities.com/where-to-study/asia/south-korea/guide#tab=1; http://english. scoul.go.kr/seoul-views/meaning-of-seoul/4-population/; https://data.worldbank.org/indicator/SP.POP.TOTL; http://statistici.insse.ro:8077/tempo-online/#/pages/ podgrup/tablica; https://www.worldometers.info/world-population/poland-population/; http://kostat.go.kr/portal/eng/pressReleases/8/1/index.board tables/insse-table; https://bucuresti.insse.ro/populatia/; http://bucuresti.insse.ro/populatia/; http://kostat.go.kr/portal/eng/pressReleases/8/1/index.board

REFERENCES

BOOKS

Aristotle. (2009). *Politics*. Antet XX Press Publishing-house.

Ashenfelter, O., & Layard, R. (1986). *Handbook of Labour Economics* (Vol. 2). Elsevier.

Avram, E. (2012). *University Marketing—Approach from the Perspective of the Consumer of Higher Education*. PhD thesis, The Academy of Economics Studies.

Avram, R. (2011). *Investing in Education and Socio-economic Development in the New Economy and Knowledge-based Society*. PhD thesis, ASE.

Bandow, D., & Vasquez, I. (2001). *Perpetuating Poverty*. Cato Institute.

Bastiat, F. (2011). *The State*. In *What is Seen and What is Not Seen, and Other Essays*. European Institute Publishing House.

Bârzea, C. coord. (2005). *National System of Indicators for Education—User Manual*.

Becker, G. S. (1964). *Human Capital: A Theoretical and Empirical Analysis with Special Reference to Education*, First Edition.

Becker, G. S. (1998). *Human Behaviour: An Economic Approach*. ALL Publishing-house.

Becker, G. (1994). *Human Capital—A Theoretical and Empirical Analysis with Special Reference to Education*. ALL Publishing-house.

Becker, G., & Lewis, H. G. (1992). *On the Interaction between the Quantity and Quality of Children*. University of Chicago.

Benhabib, J., & Spiegel, M. (2005). *Human Capital and Technology Diffusion*. Handbook of Economic Growth.

Berg, I. (1970). *Education for Jobs; The Great Training Robbery*. ERIC.

Blaug, M. (1970). *Economics of Education*. Middlesex.

Bloom, D., Canning, D., & Chan, K. (2005). *Higher Education and Economic Development in Africa*. Harvard University.

Boozer, A. M., Ranis, G., Stewart, F., & Suri, T. (2003). *Paths to Success: The Relationship Between Human Development and Economic Growth*. Economic Growth Center, Yale University.

Brăilean, T. (2001). *The New Economy*. In *The End of Certainties*. European Institute Publishing—house.

Brătianu, C. (2002a). *Strategic Management* (2nd ed.). University of Craiova Publishing House.

Brătianu, C. (2002b). *Paradigms of University Management*. Economic Publishing—house.

Brătianu, C., & Atanasiu, M. G. (2002). *Quality Assurance in Higher Education in the UK*. Economic Publishing-house.

Brătianu, C. (2014). *Critical Thinking*. Pro Universitaria Publishing—house.

Bucoș, T. (2014). *Education—An Important Factor in Valuing the National Economic Potential*. PhD thesis.

Bulat, G. (2012). *Educational Marketing from the Perspective of Quality and Labour Market, Institute of Education Sciences*. PhD thesis.

Cârstea, L. M. (2012). *Economic Education and Performance*. PhD thesis, "Al. I. Cuza" University of Iasi.

Center for Higher Education Policy Studies. (2011). *Quality—Related Funding, Performance Agreements and Profiling in Higher Education, An International Comparative Study*.

CHEMS (Commonwealth Higher Education Management Service). (1998). *Benchmarking in Higher Education: An International Review*. CHEMS.

Chen, D. H. C., & Dahlman, C. J. (2005). *The Knowledge Economy, the KAM Methodology and World Bank Operations*. The World Bank.

Collins, R. (1979). *The Credential Society: An Historical Sociology of Education and Stratification*. New York: Academic Press.

Cojocaru, V., & Făuraș, C. (2006). *Education in Economic Approach*. Academy of Economic Studies of Moldova Publishing—house.

Costache, L., coord. UNICEF. (2014). *The Cost of Insufficient Investment in Education in Romania*. Alpha MDN Publishing-house.

Coteanu, I. (1998). *The Explanatory Dictionary of the Romanian Language*. The Encyclopedic Universe, Publishing House.

Cucoș, C. (2006). *Introduction to Pedagogy and Curriculum Theory*. "A.I.Cuza" University Publishing House.

De Soto, H. (2000). *The Mystery of Capital. Why Capitalism Triumphs in the West and Fails Everywhere else?* Pub Basic Book.

Dima, A. M. coord. (2013). *Multivariate Critical Analysis of Convergence in European Higher Education.* Research Project, ASE/

Ding, Z., & Min Z. Y. (1999). *Comparative Education Society of Hong Kong.* IJCED, Emerald Publishing.

Dinu, M. (2004). *Globalization and Its Approximations.* Economic Publishing-house.

Dore, R. (1976). *The Diploma Disease: Education, Qualification and Development.* George Allen & Unwin, London.

Douglas, M. (2002). *How Institutions Think.* Polirom Publishing—house.

Drâmba, O. (1987). *History of Culture and Civilization* (Vol. 1–4) Bucharest.

Dunca, I. (2009). *Politics and Metapolitics at Platon.* Lumen Publishing-house.

Durkheim, E. (1984). *The Division of Labour in Society.* Free Press.

Durkeim, E. (1980). *Education and Sociology.* Didactic and Pedagogical Publishing—house.

Durkheim, E. (1956). *Education and Sociology.* New York: Free Press.

Edvinsson, L., & Malone, M. (1997). *Intellectual Capital.* Harper Business, New York.

Faure, E. (1974). *Learning to Be.* Didactic and Pedagogical Publishing House.

Friedman, M., & Friedman, R. (1998). *Freedom of Choice: A Personal Point of View.* All Publishing-house.

Friedman, M. (1955). *The Role of Government in Education. From Economics and the Public Interest,* ed. Robert A. Solo. By the Trustees of Rutgers College in New Jersey. Reprinted by permission of Rutgers University Press.

Gazier, B. (1992). *Economie du travail et de l'emploi.* Paris, Dalloz.

George, St. E. (2006). *Positioning Higher Education for the Knowledge Based Economy, Higher Education.*

Gheorghiu, D. M., & Saint Martin, M. (2011). *Education and Social Borders, France, Romania, Brazil, Sweden.* Polirom Publishing—house.

Goody, J. R., & Watt, I. (1968). *The Consequences of Literacy.* Cambridge University Press.

Gyorghyi, A. S. (1981). *Plea for Life.* Politică Publishing-house.

Hanson, M. (2008). *Economic Development, Education and Transnational Corporation.* Publishing Routledge Studies in Development Economics.

Hapenciuc, C. V. (2004). *Practical Textbook of Statistics—Formulas, Questions, Tests, Dictionary.* Didactic and Pedagogical Publishing—house.

Hapenciuc, C. V., Condratov, I., Stanciu, P., & Cioban, G. (2008). *Selective Research—Case studies, Projects.* Didactic and Pedagogical Publishing-house.

Hanusek, E. A., & Kim, D. (1995). *Schooling, Labour Force Quality and Economic Growth.* National Bureau of Economic Research, Massachusetts Avenue Cambridge.

Harmon, C., Oosterbeek, H., & Walker, I. (2003). *The Returns to Education: A Review of Evidence, Issues and Deficiencies in the Literature*.

Hayek, F. A. (1945). *The Use of Knowledge in Society*. Reprinted in Individualism and Economic Order, (1948). University of Chicago Press.

Hayek, F. A. (1985). *La route de la servitude*.

Huntington, S. P. (1997). *Clash of Civilizations and Restoration of the World Order*. Antet Publishing House, Political Sciences Collection.

Inkeles, A., & Holsinger, D. B. (1974). *Education and Individual Modernity in Developing Countries*. Leiden.

Jaba, E. (2002). *Statistics* (3rd ed.). Economic Publishing—house.

Jevons, W. S. (1871). The Theory of Political Economy, History of Economic Thought Books from McMaster University Archive for the History of Economic Thought.

Kaili, E., Psarrakis, D., & Van Hoinaru, R. (Eds.). (2019). *New Models of Financing and Financial Reporting for European SMEs: A Practitioner's View*. Springer International.

Kant, I. (1996). *Treatise on School Pedagogy*. P. R. A. Publishing—house.

Kasper, W. S., & Manfred, E. (1998). *Institutional Economics: Social Order and Public Policy*. The Locke Institute, Edward Elgar Publishing House.

Korka, M. (2008). *Implementing the Modern Approach of Quality Assurance in Romanian Higher Education*. The Academy of Economic Studies Publishing—house.

Korka, M. (2009). *Quality Education for the Labour Market*. Bucharest University Publishing—house.

Kuznets, S. (1963). *Notes on the Take-Off, The Economics of Take-Off into Sustained Growth*. Macmillan.

List, F. (1973). *The National System of Political Economy*. The Academy of the Socialist Republic of Romania Publishing—house.

Lynn, R., & Vanhanen, T. (2002). *IQ and the Wealth of Nation*.

Macavei, E. (2001). *Pedagogy—Theory of Education*. Aramis Publishing—house.

Mahbub ul Haq. (1996). *Reflections on Human Development* (1st ed.). Oxford University Press.

Marinescu, C. (2001). *Education: Economic Perspective*. Economic Publishing—house.

Marinescu, M. (2010). *The Place and Role of the Romanian University in the European Context*. Publishing-house of the University of Oradea.

Marshall, A. (1907). *Principles of Economics* (5 ed.). Macmillan.

Marx, K., & Friedrich, E. (1966). *Capital—Critique of Political Economy, Opere* (Vol. 23) Editura Polirom.

McClelland, D. C., & Winter, D. G. (1969). *Motivating Economic Achievement*. Free Press.

Mehedinți, S. (2008). *Ethnos. An Introduction to the Study of Mankind.* Terra Publishing—house.

Meier, G. M., & Rauch, J. E. (2005). *Leading Issues in Economic Development.* New York, Oxford: Oxford University Press.

Mereuță, C. (2014). *Strategic Priorities of Romania's Development on the Horizon 2025.* Published by Economiaonline.ro/.

Mihuț, I. S. (2013). *Economic Growth and Convergence Criteria Within the Emerging Economies of Central and Eastern Europe.* PhD thesis, Cluj-Napoca.

Mill, J. S. (1915). *Principles of Political Economy.* Ashley Edition. http://www.econlib.org/library/Mill/mlP.htm

Miroiu, M. (1998). Inequality of Opportunity in Education. În Adrian Miroiu (coord). *Romanian Education Today: Diagnostic Study,* Polirom Publishing House, Iasi.

Mokir, J. (1999). *Knowledge, Technology and Economic Growth During the Industrial Revolution.* Kluwert.

Molas-Gallart, J., et al. (2002). *Measuring and Mapping Third Stream Activities. Final Report to the Russell Group of Universities.* SPRU, University of Sussex.

Moldovan, I. (2013). *Education for the Fulfilment of Life: Economic and Social Perspectives.* PhD thesis, The Academy of Economic Studies of Bucharest.

Moussis, N. (2013). *Guide to European Policies* (9th revised ed.). European Study Service.

Murray, N. R. (1999). *Education: Free & Compulsory.* Ludwig von Mises Institute Auburn.

Myrdal, G. (1958). *Economic Theory and Underdeveloped Regions.* Vora and Co..

Neagu, C., & Simion, M. (2004). *Pedagogue of Vocation.* Terra Publishing-house.

North, D. C. (2003). *Institutions.* Știința Publishing House.

Pachef, R. C. (2008). *Evaluation in Higher Education.* Didactic and Pedagogical Publishing—house.

Pană, M. (2009). *Education and Economic—Development.* PhD thesis, The Academy of Economics Studies Publishing—house.

Pană, M. C. (2011a). *Education and Freedom.* In *Institutional Landmarks of Development.* ASE Publishing—house.

Pană, M. C. (2011b). *Education From Family Institutions to Etatization.* The Academy of Economics Studies Publishing—house.

Palicica, M., & Albert, F. (2002). *Sociology and Education.* EUROBIT Publishing—house.

Patel, I. G. (2003). *Higher Education and Economic Development.* Corporation New Delhi Publishing: National Institute of Educational Planning and Administration.

Pohoață, I., & Popescu, C. (2007). *Human Capital, Social Capital and Economic Growth.* "Al.I.Cuza" University Publishing—house.

Pohoață, I. (1996). *Universal Economic Doctrines*. Publishing House of the Academic Foundation "Gh. Zane".

Pohoață, I. (2002). *European Strategies and Policies for Sustainable Development*. Course support, "Alexandru Ioan Cuza" University of Iasi. Centre for European Studies.

Popescu, S., & Brătianu, C. (2004). *Quality Guide in Higher Education*. University of Bucharest Publishing—house.

Portes, A. (1995). *The Economic Sociology and the Sociology of Immigration: Essays on Networks, Ethnicity, and Entrepreneurship*. Russell Sage Foundation.

Purici, Ș. coord. (2013). *"Ștefan cel Mare" University of Suceava, 50 years old (1963–2013)*. 'Ștefan cel Mare' Publishing-house.

Putnam, R. (1995). *Turning in, Turning out: The Strange Disappearance of Social Capital in America*. Political Science and Politics.

Ricci, F., & Zachariadis, M. (2008). *Longevity and Education Externalities: A Macroeconomic Perspective*. Working papers 09.02.278, University of Toulouse.

Richard, J. C. (2006). *Communicative Language Teaching Today*. Cambridge University Press.

Rousseau, J. J. (1958). *Discourse on Inequality Between People*. Scientific Publishing—house.

Rousseau, J. J. (1957). *The Social Contract*. Scientific Publishing House.

Rychen, D. S., & Salganik, L. H. (2003). *Key Competencies for a Successful Life and a Well—Functioning Society*. Hogrefe & Huber Publishers.

Schleicher, A. (2006). *The Economics of Knowledge: Why Education is Key for Europe's Success* (Vol. 1). Lisbon Council Policy.

Schultz, T. P. (2002). *Discussion: Social and Nonmarket Benefits from Education in an Advanced Economy*.

Schumpeter, J. (1993a). *Business Cycles. A Theoretical, Historical and Statistical Analysis of the Capitalist Process*. Company.

Schumpeter, J. (1993b). *The theory of Economic Development, 3-rd Edition*. Transaction Publishers.

Scott, R. W. (2004). *Institutions and Organizations*. Polirom Publishing—house.

Selejean-Suță, S. (1996). *Economic Doctrines. A Panoramic Look*. Efficient Publishing—house.

Sen, A. (2004). *Development as Freedom*. Economic Publishing—house.

Smith, A. (2005). *An Inquiry into the Nature and Causes of The Wealth of Nations* (p. 621). A Penn State Electronic Classics Series Publication, Pennsylvania State University. Retrieved September 25, 2015, from www2.hn.psu.edu

Smith, A. (2011). *The Wealth of Nations*. In *The 5th Book*. Publica Publishing-house.

Someșan, C., & Cosma, S. (2001). *Basics of Marketing*. Efes Publishing-house.

Stănciulescu, E. (2002). *Sociological Theories of Education*. Polirom Publishing—house.

Stiglitz, J., & Boadway, R. (1994). *Economics and the Canadian Economy*. W. W. Norton & Company.

Stoican, M. (2012). *Human Capital Development in the Conditions of Innovation Economy Formation*. PhD thesis, Academy of Economic Studies of Moldova.

Suciu, M. C. (2000). *Investing in Education*. Economic Publishing—house.

Șerbu, M. V. (2012). *The Interdependence Between Higher Education and Economic Development by Reference to the Requirements of the Labour Market*. PhD thesis, The Academy of Economics Sciences.

Toffler, A. (1993). *The Third Wave*. Politică Publishing-house.

Topel, R. (1999). *Labour Markets and Economic Growth*. http://citeseerx.ist.psu.edu/viewdoc/download?doi=10.1.1.200.3817&rep=rep1&type=pdf

Țăranu, A. M. (2009). *The School Between the Local Community and the Challenges of Globalization*. European Institute Publishing—house.

Veblen, T. (2005). *The Vested Interests and The Common Man*. www.onlinebooks.library.upenn.edu

Vedder, R. K. (2004). *Going Broke by Degree: Why College Costs too Much*. AEI.

Vlăsceanu, L. (coord). (2002). *School at a Crossroads—Change and Continuity in the Curriculum of Compulsory Education*. Impact study. Polirom Publishing—house.

Vlăsceanu, M. (1996). *The Non-profit Sector. Contexts, Organization, Management*. Paideia Publishing—house.

Vlăsceanu, M. (2005). *Organization: Design and Organizational Change. Introduction to Organizational Behaviour*. Comunicare.ro Publishing—house.

Weber, M. (1947). *The Theory of Social and Economic Organizations*. New York: Free Press.

Weil, D. N. (2004). *Economic Growth.*, Addison Wesley

West, E. G. (1965). *Liberty and Education: John Stuart Mill's Dilemma*. Philosophy.

Zgreabăn, I. E. (2011). *Education in Economic Perspective*. Case Studies Romania, PhD thesis, The Academy of Economics Studies.

ARTICLES

Abramovitz, M. (1986). Catching-up, Forging Ahead and Falling Behind. *Journal Economic History*, nr. 46.

Acemoglu, D., & Robinson, J. (2008). *The Role of Institutions in Growth and Development*. Commission on Growth and Development, Working Paper no. 10, World Bank.

Aghion, P., & Durlauf, S. (2005). *Handbook of Economic Growth*. Elsevier North—Holland

Aghion, P., & Howitt, P. (1992). A Model of Growth Through Creative Destruction. *Econometrica*, 60(2), 322–351.

Andersson, A. E. (2009). *Returns to Higher Education*. CESIS Electronic Working Paper Series, Paper No. 163, The Royal Institute of Technology Centre of Excellence for Science and Innovation Studies.

Andrén, D., Earle, J., & Sapatoru, D. (2005). The Wage Effects of Schooling under Socialism and in Transition: Evidence from Romania, 1950–2000. *Journal of Comparative Economics, 33*(2), 300–323.

Appiah, E., Mahon, M., & W. (2002). The Social Outcomes of Education and Feedbacks on Growth in Africa. *Journal of Development Studies, vol., 38*(4), 27–68.

Archer, B. (1979). *Design Studies*, 1(1), 17–20.

Arionesei G., Burac, D., Neamțu, D., & Vranciu, L. (2013). Knowledge Economy and the Two New Resources: Education and Research. In *Proceedings of the International Conference on Information* (pp. 272–275). Business and Education Technology (ICIBET 2013).

Arionesei, G., & Neamțu, D. (2012). Quality in Education in a Knowledge-based Economy. In *Proceedings of the 6th International Management Conference Approaches in Organizational Management* (pp. 562–569). The Academy of Economic Studies Publishing of Bucharest.

Ashton, D., & Green, F. (1996). *Education, Training and the Global Economy*. Edward Elgar.

Badea, L. (2011). *University—Is It An Active Factor in Increasing the Quality of Life? in Theoretical and Applied Economics*. Supplement.

Badea, L., & Rogojanu, A. (2012). Controversies Regarding the Relationship of Higher Education—Human Capital—Competitiveness. *Theoretical and Applied Economics, XIX*(12(577)), 122–139.

Barro, R. (1990). Government Spending in a Simple Model of Endogenous Growth *Journal of Political Economy 98*, October, 103–125.

Barro, R. (1991). Economic Growth in a Cross-section of Countries. *Quarterly Journal of Economics, 106*(2), 407–443.

Barro, R. J. (2001). Human Capital and Growth. *American Economic Review, 91*(2).

Barro, R., & Sala-i-Martin, X. (1992). Convergence. *Journal of Political Economy, 100*(2), 223–251.

Barth, M., Godeman, J., Rieckmann, M., & Stoltenberg, U. (2007). Developing Key Competencies for Sustainable Development in Higher Education. *International Journal of Sustainability in Higher Education, 8*(4), 416–430.

Bashir, S., Herath, J., & Gebremedhin, T. (2012, August 12–14). *An Empirical Analysis of Higher Education and Economic Growth in West Virginia*. Selected Paper for Presentation at Agricultural & Applied Economics Association Annual Meeting.

Bedrule-Grigoruță, M. V. (2006). Human Capital and Investment in Education. *Annals of the "A.I. Cuza" University, 1*(52–53), 136–144.

Bejinaru, R. (2017). Dynamic Capabilities of Universities in the Knowledge Economy. *Journal of Management Dynamics in the Knowledge Economy*, 5(4), 577–595. https://doi.org/10.25019/MDKE/5.4.07

Bejinaru, R., Hapenciuc, C. V., Condratov, I., & Stanciu, P. (2018). The University Role in Developing the Human Capital for a Sustainable Bioeconomy. *Amfiteatru Economic*, 20(49), 583–598. https://doi.org/10.24818/EA/2018/49/583

Bejinaru, R., & Prelipcean, G. (2017, March 30–31). Successful Strategies to be Learnt from World-Class Universities. *The 11th International Conference on Business Excellence Strategy, Complexity and Energy in Changing Times* (pp. 350–358). University of Economic Studies, DeGruyter Open, Vol 11(1) July 2017. https://www.degruyter.com/view/j/picbe.2017.11.issue-1/picbe-2017-0037/picbe-2017-0037.xml

Biesma, R. G., Pavlova, M., Van Merode, G., & Groot, W. (2007). Using Conjoint Analysis to Estimate Employers Preferences for Key Competences of Master Dutch Graduates Entering the Public Health Field. *Economics of Education Review*, 26, 375–386.

Bils, M., & Klenow, J. (2000). Does Schooling Cause Growth? *The American Economic Review*, 90, Nr.5.

Blaug, M. (1985). *Where are we now in the economics of education?* 4(1), 17–28.

Bradley, S., & Nguyen, A. N. (2004). *International Handbook on the Economics of Education—The school—to Work Transition* (pp. 484–521). Edward Elgar Publisher.

Burghelea, C., Ene, C. M., & Uzlău, C. (2013). The Impact of Economic Models on the Development of the European Union's Economies. *Theoretical and Applied Economics*, XX(4 (581)).

Burke, J. R., & Onwuegbuzie, A. J. (2004). Mixed Methods Research: A Research Paradigm Whose Time Has Come. *Educational Researcher*, 33(7), 14–26.

Caraiani, P., Dutescu, A., Hoinaru, R., & Stănilă, G. O. (2020). Production network structure and the impact of the monetary policy shocks: Evidence from the OECD. *Economics Letters*, 193, 109271.

Card, D. (2001). Estimating the Return to Schooling: Progress on Some Persistent Econometric Issues. *Econometrica*, 69(5), 1127–1160.

Chakraborty, D., & Mukherjee, S. (2010). The Relationship Between Trade, Investment and Environment: Same Empirical Findings. *SAGE Journals*, 45(2).

Chatterji, B. (1998). On Education. *JSTOR*, 50(34), Published By: Economic and Political Weekly, pp. 39–43.

Cioban, G., & Neamțu, D. (2014). The Role of Education in Occupying the Workforce. *Educational Research International (ERInt)*, 3(4), 73–80.

Cohen, D., & Soto, M. (2007). Growth and Human Capital Good Data, Good Results. *Journal of Economic Growth*, 12(1), 51–76.

Coleman, J. S. (1988). Social Capital in the Creation of Human Capital. *American Journal of Sociology*, *94*, Published By: The University of Chicago Press.

Colombo, M. G., & Grilli, L. (2005). Founders' human capital and the growth of new technology-based firms: A competence-based view. *Research Policy*, *34*(6), 795–816.

Conti, G., & Giaccaria, P. (2001). *Local Development and Competitiveness*. The Geo Journal Library—Kluwer Academic Publishers.

Davenport, T. H., & Grover, V. (2001). General Perspectives on Knowledge Management: Fostering a Research Agenda. *Journal of Management Information Systems*, *18*, 5–23.

Deaconu, A., Osoian, C., Zaharie, M., & Achim, S. A. (2014). Skills in the Higher Education System: An Empirical Investment From the Employers' Perspective. *Economic Amphitheater Contemporary Priorities of Business Education*, *XVII*(37), 692–708.

Derek, H. C., & Hiau, L. K. (2005). *A Model on Knowledge and Endogenous Growth*. The World Bank Washington DC.

Duflo, E. (2001). Schooling and Labor Market Consequences of School Construction in Indonesia: Evidence from an Unusual Policy Experiment. *The American Economic Review*, *91*(4), Published By: American Economic Associatio.

Dziewulak, D. (2013). Szkolnictwo wyzsze w swietle raportow edukacyjnych. *Studia BAS*, *3*(35), 149–174.

Galbraith, J. K. (1997). The Good Society: The Humane Agenda. *Utopian Studies*, *8*(2), 140–141.

Garben, S. (2012). *The Future of Higher Education in Europa: The Case for a Stronger Base in Eu Law*. The London School and Economics and Political Science, Paper No. 50/2012.

García-Aracil, A., & Van der Velden, R. (2008). Competencies for Young European Higher Education Graduates: Labour Market Mismatches and their Payoffs. *Journal of Higher Education*, 219–239.

Glewwe, P. (2002). Schools and Skills in Developing Countries: Education Policies and Socioeconomic Outcomes. *Journal of Economic Literature*, *40*(2), 436–482.

Grossman, G. M., & Helpman, E. (1991). Trade, Innovation, and Growth. *The American Economic Review*, *80*(2), 86–91.

Hanushek, E. A., & Kim, D. (1995). *Schooling, Labour Force Quality and Economic Growth*. NBER Working Paper No. W5399.

Hanushek, E. A., & Kim, D. (2000). Labour Force Quality, and the Growth of Nation. *American Economic Review*, *90*(5), 1184–1208.

Hapenciuc, C. V. (2002). *Statistical Study of the Quality of Higher Education*. University of Suceava Publishing House.

Hapenciuc, C. V. (2008). The Implications of Computerization in the Changes Occurring in the Romanian Higher Education Variation and Structure. *The Annals of University of Oradea*, 854–859. Economy, Business Administration and Statistics.

Hapenciuc, C. V., Burciu, A., & Cioban, G. (2006). *Implementation of The System of The Management of Education Quality, Basic Requirement for UE Integration.* http://papers.ssrn.com/sol3/papers.cfm?abstract_id=1071866-

Hartog, J. (2000). Over-Education and Earnings: Where Are We, Where Should We Go? *Economics of Education Review*, *19*, 131–147. https://doi.org/10.1016/S0272-7757(99)00050-3

Haveman, R., & Wolfe, B. (1984). Schooling and Economic Well-Being: The Role of Nonmarket Effects. *Journal of Human Resources, 19*(3), 377–407.

Heckman, J. J., & Carneiro, P. (2003). *Human Capital Policy* (p. 50). Discussion Paper No. 821, Iulie, Germania. publicație online www.iza.org/publications/dps/

HEFCE. (Higher Education Funding Council for England). (2003). *Benchmarking Methods and Experiences.* Consortium for Excellence in Higher Education. http://www.acu.ac.uk/chems/onlinepublications/961780238.pdf

Hoinaru, R. (2018). What Are the Objectives of Corporate Reporting? Sustainable Value for Who?. In *Proceedings of the International .Conference on Business Excellence* (Vol. 12 (1), pp. 436–445). Sciendo.

Hoinaru, R., Robe, A. D., Manea, S. A., Damasaru, C., & Niță, S. (2021). Human Resources Accounting and Accountability: Medical Aspects, Regulation and Economics of Burn Out in Non-financial Reporting. In *Proceedings of the International Conference on Business Excellence* (Vol. 15 (1), pp. 695–704). Sciendo.

Holland, D., Liadze, I., Rienzo, C., & Wilkinson, D. (2013). *The Relationship Between Graduates and Economic Growth Across Countries.* Department of Business Innovations & Skills (BIS) Research Paper No.110.

Hove, K. R. (1988). Against the Quantitative-Qualitative Incompatibility Thesis or Dogmas Die Hard. *Educational Researcher, 17*(8), 10–16.

Huw, L. E., & Roberts, J. (2002). Twin Engines of Growth: Skills and Technology as Equal Partners in Balanced Growth. *Journal of Economic Growth, 7*, 87–115.

Ilie, A. G., Maftei, M., & Colibășanu, O. A. (2013). Sustainable Success in Higher Education Through the Exchange of Best Practices As a Result of a Benchmarking Process. Published in the Journal of the Economic Amphitheater. *Economic Interferences: Quality—Information Technologies—Consumer, XIII* (5), pp. 570–578.

Ion, I. (2013). Education in Romania—How Much is it Worth? *Romanian Journal of Economic Forecasting, 1*, 149–163.

Jane, J. (1986). *Cities and the Wealth of Nation: Principles of Economic Life.* Penguin.

Jones, G., & Schneider, W. J. (2006). Intelligence, Human Capital, and Economic Growth: A Bayesian Averaging of Classical Estimates. *Journal of Economic Growth, Springer, 11*(1).

Jørn, R., & Hildegunn, S. (2013). *Regional Convergence of Income and Education: Investigation of Distribution Dynamics.* Published Urban Studies, Impact Factor 1,493.

Jorgenson, D. W., & Fraumeni, B. M. (1992). Investment in Education and U.S. Economic Growth. *The Scandinavian Journal of Economics, 94.* Harvard University and Cambridge, MA, USA.

Jurajda, S. (2003). Gender Wage Gap and Segregation in Enterprises and the Public Sector in Late Transition Countries. *Journal of Comparative Economics, 31*(2), 199–222.

Kichenham, A. D. (2010). Mixed Methods in Case Study Research. In A. Mills, G. Durepos, & E. Wiebe (Eds.), *Encyclopaedia of Case Study Research* (pp. 562–565).

Kiker, B. F. (1996). The Historical Roots of The Concept of Human Capital. *J.P.E., LXXIV* (5), pp. 481–499. University South Karolina. http://www.jstore.org//pss/1829595

King, R. G., & Rebelo, S. (1990). Public Policy and Economic Growth: Developing Neoclassical Implication. *Journal of Political Economy, 98*(5), 126–150.

Kiong-Hock, L. (1986). Affective, Cognitive and Vocational Skills: The Employers Perspective. *Economics of Education Review, 5*(4), 395–401.

Knight, J., Ed. (2014). International Education Hubs: Student, Talent, Knowledge—Innovation Models. DOI https://doi.org/10.1007/978-94-007-7025-6

Krueger, A. B., & Lindahl, M. (2001). *Education for Growth: Why and For Whom?*, Working Paper no. 7591, Journal for Economic Literature.

Krugman, P. (1991). History and Industry Location: The Case of the Manufacturing Belt. *The American Economic Review, 81*(2), 80–83.

Kwabena, G. B., Padisson, O., & Mitiku, W. (2006). Higher Education and Economic Growth in Africa. *Journal of Development Studies, 42*(3), 509–529.

Lester, R. K. (2006). *A Framework for Understanding How Higher Education Influences Regional Economic Growth.* http://www.chicagofed.org/news_and_conferences_and_events/files/2006_higher_education_lester.pdf

Lipset, S. M. (1959). Some Social Requisites of Democracy: Economic Development and Political Legitimacy. *The American Political Science Review, 53*(1), 69–105.

Lixandrioaia, M. (2013). *General Theoretical Framework: the Concept of Human Capital.* Economic Tribune No. 8/2012. http://tribunaeconomica.ro/blog/?p=602

Lucas, R. (1998). On the Mechanics of Economic Development. *Journal of Monetary Economics, 22*(1), 13–42.

Manea, A., Hoinaru, R., & Păcuraru-Ionescu, C. P. (2021). Ethics education in Romanian economics faculties, members of AFER. In *Proceedings of the International Conference on Business Excellence* (Vol. 15 (1), pp. 705–714).

Mankiw, N. G., Romer, D., & Weil, D. A. (1992). Contribution to the Empirics of Economic Growth. *The Quarterly Journal of Economics, 107*(2), 433.

Mărginean, I. (2012). Romania's Performance in the Field of Human Development. *Quality of Life Review, XXIII*(4), 285–286.

Marginson, S. (2010). Higher Education in the Global Knowledge Economy. *Procedia Social and Behavioural Science.*

Marinescu, C. *The Institutional Foundations of Economic Performance. Synthesis Study* (p. 17). ideas.repec.org/p/ror/seince/111208.htm

McCracken, G. (2005). *Culture and Consumption II: Markets, Meaning, and Brand Management.*

Melink, M., & Pavlin, S. (2009). *Employability of Graduates and Higher Education Management Systems.* Final report of DEHEMS project, Publisher University of Ljubljana, Faculty of Social Sciences

Meulemeester, J. L., & Rochat, D. (1995). A Causality Analysis of the Link Between Higher Education and Economic Development. *Economics of Education Review, 14*(4), 351–361.

Michael, R. T. (1975). Education and Consuption. *National Bureau of Economic Research,* 233–252.

Mincer, J. (1958). Investment in Human Capital and Personal Income Distribution. *Journal of Political Economy, 66*(4), 281–302.

Mincer, J. (1970). The Distribution of Labour Incomes: A Survey With Special Reference to The Human Capital Approach. *Journal of Economics, 8*(1), 8.

Morly, L. (2001). Producing new Workers: Quality, Equality and Employability in Higher Education. *Quality in Higher Education, 7*(2), 131–138.

Murphy, K. M., Shleifer, A., & Vishny R. V. (1991). The Allocation of Talent: Implications for Growth. *Quarterly Journal of Economics, 106*(2), 503–530.

Neamțu, D. (2012). Education, an Investment in Human Capital. *Journal of Economics and Business Research, XVIII*(2), 150–160.

Neamtu, D. (2014). Analysis of the Economic Growth Trends in Romania Between 2010–2012. *The USV Annals of Economics and Public Administration, 14,* ISSUE(1(19)).

Neamțu, D. (2014). Education, the Economic Development Pilar. *The 6th International Conference Edu World 2014 'Education Facing Contemporary World Issues', 180*(2015), 413–430.

Neamțu, D., & Burac, D. (2015). Higher Education, Factor of Economic and Social Progress. In *INTED2015 Proceedings, 9th International Technology, Education and Development Conference* (pp. 4328–4337).

Neamțu, D., Burac, D., & Vranciu, L. (2013a). Education and Challenges of the Contemporary World. In *Proceedings of 3rd International Conference on Social*

Sciences and Society (ICSSS 2013), Published in Advances in Education Research (Vol. 32, pp. 297–302). IERI Publishing-house.

Neamțu, D., & Scurtu, L. (2013). Education, Welfare and Economic Growth. In *Post Crisis Economy: Challenges and Opportunities* (pp. 161–168).'Lucian Blaga' University Publishing-house.

Neamțu, D., Vranciu, L., & Arionesei, G. (2013b). The Role of the Social Capital in the Economic Development. In *ICBE International Conference, Journal of Management & Marketing—Challenges for the Knowledge Society* (Vol. 8). Special Issue.

Nelson, R. R., & Phelps, E. S. (1966). Investment in Humans, Technological Diffusion and Economic Growth. *The American Economic Review, 56*(1/2), 69–75.

Nicolesco, I. (2014). *Polish Reform—The Recipe for Success in PISA Tests.* http://adevarul.ro/educatie/scoala/reforma-poloneza-reteta-succesului-testele-pisa-1_52ece9e5c7b855ff56fc1968/index.html

Norton, J. K. (1958). *Education Pays Compound Interest.* in National Education Association Journal, No. 47, p. 57

Oakley, A. (1999). *People's ways of Knowing: Gender and Methodology* (pp. 154–170). Open University Press.

Olaniyan, D. A., & Okemakinde, T. (2008). Human Capital Theory: Implications for Educational Development. *European Journal of Scientific Research, 24*(2), 157–162.

Olson, M., Jr. (1996). Big Bills Left on the Sidewalk: Why Some Nations are Rich, and Other Poor. *Journal of Economic Perspective, 10*(2), 3–24.

Pânzaru, S., & Ştefan, A. (2008). *Economic Growth and Development in European and Mondial Context.* http://managementgeneral.ro/pdf/2_2008_7.pdf

Paternostro, S., & Sahn, D. E. (1999). *Wage Determination and Gender Discrimination in a Transition Economy: The Case of Romania.* Policy Research Working Paper no. 2113, The World Bank.

Petrakis, P. E., & Stamatakis, D. (2002). Growth and Educational Levels: a Comparative Analysis. *Economics of Education Review, 21*, 513–521.

Pillay, P. (2011). *Higher Education and Economic Development* (pp. 43–46). Published by the Centre for Higher Education Transformation (CHET).

Pirtea, M., & Miloş, L. (2009). Foreign Direct Investments –Are They the Main Determinants of Sustainable Growth in Romania? *Annals of 'Constantin Brâncuşi' University of Târgu Jiu, Economics Series, 3.*

Prelipcean, G., & Bejinaru, R. (2018, October 11–12). University agenda for Developing Students' Skills in the Knowledge Economy. In *Strategica – International Conference—Sixth Edition,"Challenging the Status Quo in Management and Economics"* (pp. 600–610).

Psacharopoulos, G. (1992). Rates of Return to Investment in Education Around the World. *Comparative Education Review, 16*, 31–53.

Psacharopoulos, G., & Patrinos, H. A. (2004). Returns to Investment in Education: A Further Update. *Education Economics, 12*(2).

Pupăzan-Mungiu, M. C., & Vasilescu, M. (2011). *Productivity—A Way of Expressing Performance and Economic Efficiency.* Annals of 'Constantin Brâncuşi' University, No. 3, Economics Series.

Ramirez, A., Ranis, G., & Stewart, F. (1998). *Economic Growth and Human Development.* Working Paper No. 18. Yale University.

Ranis, G. (2004). *Human Development and Economic Growth.* Yale University, Center Discussion Paper No. 887.

Ranis, G., & Stewart, F. (2005). *Dynamic Links Between the Economy and Human Development.* United Nations, Department of Economics and Social Affairs, Working Papers, No. 8.

Ranis, G., Stewart, F., & Ramirez, A. (2000). Economic Growth and Human Development. *World Development, 28*(2), 197–219.

Rebelo, S., & King, R. (1990). Public Policy and Economic Growth: Developing Neoclassical Implications. *Journal of Political Economy, 98*(5).

Rey, S. J., & Janikas, M. V. (2005). Regional Convergence, Inequality and Space. *Journal of Economic Geography, 5,* 155–176.

Rindermann, H. (2008). Relevance of Education and Intelligence at the National Level for the Economic Welfare of People. *Intelligence, 36,* 306–322.

Risikat, O., & Dauda, S. (2010). Investment in Education and Economic Growth in Nigeria: An Empirical Evidence. *International Research Journal of Finance and Economics,* pp. 158 –169. http://www.sciencedirect.com/

Romer, P. (1990). Endogenous Technological Change. *Journal of Political Economics, 98* (Part 2). The Problem of Development: A Conference of the Institute for the Study of Free Enterprise Systems.

Romer, P. M. (1986). Increasing Returns and Long-Run Growth. *Journal of Political Economy, 94*(5).

Romer, P. M. (1989). *Human Capital and Growth: Theory and Evidence.* National Bureau of Economic Research, Working Paper No. 3173.

Roşca, I. G., Păunescu, C., & Pârvan, C. (2010). Shaping the Future of Higher Education in Romania: Challenges and Driving Factors. *Management & Marketing, 5*(1), 57–70.

Rothbard, M. *Liberal Manifesto: Against Educational Socialism.* Ludwing von Mises Institute Romania. w.w.w.misesromania.org *The Private Internal Rates of Return to Tertiary Education.* New Estimates for 21 OECD Working Papers no. 591.

Schejbal, D., & Wilson, D. (2008). *The Value of Continuing Education. The Journal of the University Continuing Education Association: Continuing Higher Education Review, 72.*

Schomburg, H. (2007). The Professional Success of Higher Education Graduates. *European Journal of Education, 42* (1), pp. 35–37. http://ssrn.com/abstract=1978290

Schultz, T. (1962, October). *Reflection on Investment in Man the Journal of Political Economy, 70* (5, part. 2), Investment in Human Beings, p. 18 http:///www.jstor.org/stable/pdfplus/1818907.pdf

Schultz, T. W. (1961). Investment in Human Capital. *The American Economic Review, 51* (l).

Skoufias, E. (2003). The Structure of Wages During the Economic Transition in Romania. *Economic Systems, 27*(4), 345–366.

Solow, R. (2000). *Growth Theory, An Exposition.* Oxford University Press, New York, Technical Change and the Aggregate Production Function in Review of Economic and Estadistics.

Spence, M. (1973). Job Market Signaling. *The Quarterly Journal of Economics, 87,* No. 3, Published By: Oxford University Press, 355–374.

Stephan, P. E. (1997). Educational Implications of University–Industry Technology Transfer. *The Journal of Technology Transfer, 26,* 199–205.

Stewart, G., & Ramirez, F. (2000). A Economic Growth and Human Development. *World Development, 2,* 197–219.

Stiglitz, J. (1975). The Theory of Screening. Education and Distribution of Income. *The American Economic Review, 25,* 498–509.

Symanski, D. M., & Henard, D. H. (2001). Customer Satisfaction: A Meta—Analysis of the Empirical Evidence. *Journal of Academy of Marketing Science, 29*(1), pp. 16–35   http://davidhenard.com/Landing_Page/CV_Bio_Research_files/Szymanski%20%26%20Henard%202001.pdf

Teles, V. K., & Andrade, J. (2008). Public Investment in Basic Education and Economic Growth. *Journal of Economic Studies, 35*(4), 352–364.

Temple, J. (1999). *The New Growth Evidence. Journal of Economic Literature, 37*(1), 112–156, Published by American Economic Association.

Tiago, N. S. (2007). Human Capital Composition, Growth and Development: An R&D Growth Model Versus Data. *Empirical Economics, 32,* 41–65.

Tilak, J. B. T. (2003). *Higher Education and Development.* International Seminar, University XXI.

Trani, E. P., & Holsworth, R. D. (2010). *The Indispensable University, Higher Education, Economic Development and the Knowledge Economy.* Published in partnership with the American Council on Education.

Trasca, D. L., Stefan, G. M., Aceleanu, M. I., Sahlian, D. N., Stanila, G. O., & Hoinaru, R. (2019). Unique Unemployment Insurance Scheme in Euro Zone. Terms and Conditions, Impact. *Economic Computation and Economic Cybernetics Studies and Research, 53*(2), 241–256.

Treiman, D. J., & Yip, K. B. (1989). *Educational and Occupational Attainment in 21 Countries.* In M. L. Kohn (Ed.), *Cross-National Research in Sociology* (pp. 373–394). Sage Publications.

Tsai, Y., & Wu Wang, S. (2010). The Relationships Between Organisational Citizenship Behaviour. *Job Satisfaction and Turnover Intention, JCN, 19*(23–24).

Tsai, C.-L., Hung, M.-C., & Harriott, K. (2010). Human Capital Composition and Economic Growth. *Social Indicators Research, 99*(1), 41–59.

Vandenbussche, J., Aghion, P., & Meghir, C. (2006). *Growth, Distance to Frontier and Composition of Human Capital.* Harvard University.

Vasile, V., Prelipcean, G., & Sandru, M. D. (2010). *Improving Professional Skills Among Graduates and Young People: A Chance for the Future.* European Institute Publishing—house.

Verhaest, D., & Van der Velden, R. (2010). *Cross-Country Differences in Graduate Overeducation and Its Persistence.* http://econpapers.repec.org/paper/unmu-maror/2010007.htm

Voicu, B. (2004). Human Capital: Components, Levels, Structures. Romania in the European Context. *Quality of Life, XV*(1–2), 137–157.

Voicu, B., Tufiş, C., & Voicu, M. (2010). *Recent Graduates of Higher Education and Their Integration Into the Labour Market. Development of an Operational System of Higher Education Qualifications in Romania—DOCIS.* UECNCFPA editor.

Voinea, L., & Mihăescu, F. (2011). *A Contribution to the Public-Private Wage Inequality Debate: The Iconic Case of Romania* (pp. 1–31). The wiiw Balkan Observatory—Working Papers

Weiss, A. (1995). Human Capital vs. Signalling Explanation of Wages. *Journal of Economic Perspective, 9*(4), 133–154.

Wobmann, L. (2003). Specifying Human Capital. *Journal of Economic Surveys, 17*(3), 239–270.

Zak, P., & Park, K. W. (2002). Population Genetics and Economic Growth. *Journal of Bioeconomics.*

REPORTS

Berlin Declaration. (2003).

Bologna Declaration. (1999, June 19).

CNFIS. (2020). *Raport Public Anual 2020.* The State of Higher Education Funding.

Prague Declaration. (2001).

Sorbonne Declaration. (1998, May 25).

Magna Charta Universitatum. (1998). Bologna.

RAEQHE (2009) *Primary and Secondary Indicators for Quality Evaluation, No. 1.*

The National Bank of Romania. (2014). *Inflation Report.* http://www.bnro.ro/PublicationDocuments.aspx?icid=3922

Barometer of public opinion—youth. (2012). *Improving Professional Skills Among Graduates and Young People: A Chance for the Future—Report.*

Cheers. http://www.uni-kassel.de/wz1/TSEREGS/sum_e.htm

European Commission Eurostat—Database. (2013, July 20). *Expenditure on Education As % of GDP or Public Expenditure.*

European Commission (2015). *Country Profile, Romania—Digital Economy and Society Index (DESI)*

European Commission. (2010). *Europe 2020. A Strategy for Smart, Sustainable and Inclusive growth.*

European Commission, Eurostat—Statistics in focus. (2013, December).

Communiqué of the Conference of Ministers for Higher Education. (2003). *The Formation of the European Higher Education Area.*

Communiqué of the meeting of European ministers responsible for higher education. (2001). *Towards a European Higher Education Area.*

Communiqué of the Ministers responsible for Higher Education. (2007). *Towards a European Higher Education Area: Responses to the Challenges of a Globalised World.*

Communiqué of the Ministers responsible for Higher Education. (2009). *Bologna Process 2020–European Higher Education Area in the New Decade.*

Communiqué of the Ministers responsible for Higher Education. (2012). *Strengthening the European Higher Education Area.*

National Council for Financing Higher Education. (2013). *Annual Public Report 2012–The Status of Higher Education Funding and the Necessary Optimization Measures.*

National Council for Financing Higher Education. (2014). *The Status of Higher Education Funding and the Necessary Optimization Measures.*

Joint Declaration on Harmonising the Structure of the European Higher Education System of the Four Ministers in Office for Higher Education in Germany, France, Italy and the United Kingdom. (1998).

European Commission (2010). *Europe 2020, A European Strategy for Smart, Sustainable and Inclusive Growth.*

European Commission. (2015). Let Us Understand the Policies of the European Union—Europe 2020: Europe's Growth Strategy, p. 3.

European Commission, Education and Culture. (2013). *Sustainable Growth in the European Union—The Role of Education and Training,* doi: 102766/42398.

Eurydice. (2011). *The Upgrade of Higher Education in Europe: Financing and the Social Aspect.*

Government of Romania. (2011). *National Reform Programme 2011–2013.*

Klugman, J. lead author (2010). *Human Development Report 2010—The Real Health of Nations: Pathways to Human Development.* Published for the UNDP.

Hegesco.(2009). http://www.hegesco.org/

Hotnews.ro. (2014). *Results and Conclusions of the Evaluation PISA-2012.*

National Institute of Statistics and Economic Sciences. (2003–2013).

National Institute of Statistics. (2014). *Romania's International Migration.*

Institutions and organizations / promep.softwin.ro/promep/news/show/1244

Jahan, S. (2015). *Human Development Report 2015, Work for Human Development.* Published for UNDP at 15 December 2015.

Learning a Living. First Results of the Adult Literacy and Life Skills Survey. (2005). http://www.oecd.org/dataoecd/44/7/34867438.pdf

Mind the Gap—Education Inequality Across EU Regions. http://europa.eu/rapid/press-release_IP-12-960_ro.htm

Ministry of National Education. (2011). *Report on the Status of Higher Education in Romania.*

Ministry of Public Finance. (2013). *Budget Report* 2013.

Official Gazette of Romania. (2011). *National Education Law* no.1/2011.

OECD (2014). *Education at a Glance 2014: OECD Indicators* (pp.134–136). OECD Publishing. https://doi.org/10.1787/eag-2014-en

OECD. (2007). *Higher Education and Regions: Globally Competitive, Locally Engaged.* Organization for Economic Cooperation and Development.

OECD. (2010). *Education at a Glance, OECD Indicators.* OECD Publications. http://www.oecd.org

OECD. (2013). *Education at a Glance: OECD Indicators.* OECD Publishing.

OECD (2000). *Analysis of the National Policy in the Field of Education: Romania.*

OECD. (2008). *Tertiary Education for the Knowledge Society: OECD Thematic Review.* Organisation for Economic Co-operation and Development.

OECD. (2011). *Education at Glance 2011: OECD Indicators. OECD Publishing, Indicator A9,* 166.

OECD (2012). *Highlights from Education at a Glance* (pp. 38–40). OECD Publishing-house. http://www.oecd.org/edu/highlights.pdf

NCFHE. (2013). *Annual Public Report—2012. The Status of Higher Education and the Necessary Optimization Measures.*

Report. (2013). *Elements for a Research Methodology Regarding the Professional Path of Graduates in Romania, Within Policies Based on Evidence and the Impact on the Labour Market Project.*

REFLEX. http://www.reflexproject.co.uk/

Santiago, P., Tremblay, K., Basri, E., & Arnal, E. (2008). *Tertiary Education for the Knowledge Society: OECD Thematic Review of Tertiary Education: Synthesis Report.*

Schwab, K., & Sala-i-Martin, X. (2014). *The Global Competitiveness Report 2014–2015.,* World Economic Forum

Stiftung Bertelsmann. (2010). *European Lifelong Learning Indicators, Making Lifelong Learning Tangible!*

Research and Innovation Strategy. (2014–2020). www.cdi2020.ro

Study on Improving Professional Competences Among Graduates and Young People: A Chance For the Future, Research Barometer of Public Opinion—Youth. (2012).

UNDP. (2001). *Human Development Report*. Oxford University Press.

Veblen, T. (1918). *The Higher Learning In America: A Memorandum On the Conduct of Universities By Business Men*, http://www.ditext.com/veblen/veblen.html

Waller, W. (1932). *The sociology of teaching*. John Wiley & Sons, Inc. https://doi.org/10.1037/11443-000

WEF. (2010). *World Economic Forum Global Education Initiative Report*, Davos-Klosters. www.weforum.org

World Bank. (2007). *Building Knowledge Economies: Advanced Strategies for Development*.

World Bank. (2008). *MENA Development Report*, op. cit. p. 40.

World Economic Forum. (2013a). *The Global Competitiveness Report 2010–2011, 2012–2013*.

World Economic Forum (2013b, 2014). *The Human Capital Report*.

World Economic Situation Prospects. (2014). United Nations.

WEB SOURCES

http://www.mises.org

http://www.21stcenturyskills.org. p.13.

http://blog.econacademia.net/2015/04/investitiile-dezvoltarea-resurselor-umane-romania-nivelul-universitar/

http://www.aramt.ro/

http://www.actrus.ro/buletin/2_2000/articol15.html

http://www.adecco.ro/responsabilitate-sociala/educatie/

http://ovidiuioandumitru.ro/romania-pe-un-loc-codas-la-dezvoltarea-umana/

http://ro.scribd.com/doc/184822037/indicele-dezvoltarii-umane-idu#scribd

http://www.analizeeconomice.ro/2015/04/harta-polilor-de-dezvoltare-economica

http://www.anc.edu.ro/uploads/images/legislatie/isced_2011_unesco_ro_final.pdf

http://www.businesswoman.ro/ro/index.php?p=articol&a=1169

https://beyondreamz.files.wordpress.com/2010/01/doctrine_pedagogice.pdf

http://www.cicadit.ro/ro/projects_n2_2_1.html

http://www.contributors.ro/economie/prioritati-strategice-ale-dezvoltarii-romaniei-la-orizont-2025/

http://www.zf.ro/eveniment/romania-trebuie-sa-treaca-in-liga-i-a-statelor-din-ue-in-urmatorul-deceniu-obiectivul-este-posibil-doar-prin-educatie-si-sanatate-13707047

http://articole.famouswhy.ro/formarea_convingerilor__sentimentelor_si_a_atitudinilor_prin_educatia_morala/

http://www.cse.uaic.ro/_fisiere/documentare/suporturi_curs/ii_strategii_si_politici_europene_de_dezvoltare_durabila.pdf

http://geopolitics.ro/coreea-de-sud-pendulul-dintre-democratie-si-plutocratie/

http://adevarul.ro/educatie/scoala/reforma-poloneza-reteta-succesului-testele-pisa-1_52ece9e5c7b855ff56fc1968/index.html

http://buget.gov.ro/

http://data.worldbank.org/indicator/ny.gdp.pcap.cd

http://discutii.mfinante.ro/static/10/mfp/buget2013/Ministerul_Educatiei_Nationale.pdf

http://ec.europa.eu/eurostat/data/database

http://economiaonline.ro/tag/prioritati-strategice-ale-dezvoltarii-romaniei/

http://econpapers.repec.org/article/eeeecoedu/v_3a14_3ay_3a1995_3ai_3a4_3ap_3a351-361.htm Meulemeester.

http://www.ecol.ro/content/liberalismulintraditiaordiniispontane

http://www.scritube.com/management/managementuldezvoltarii-umane34132.php

http://bpsoroca.md/pdf/diviziunea%20internationala%20a%20muncii.pdf

http://unctadstat.unctad.org/wds/tableviewer/tableview.aspx?reportid=96

http://www.ubbcluj.ro/ro/studenti/files/acte_studii/chestionar%20licenta%20 16.06.2014.pdf

http://www.weforum.org/

http://www.ziare.com/scoala/educatie/topul-surprinzator-al-celor-mai-bune-sistemede-educatie-tari-din-asia-pe-primele-locuri-1297731

http://www.insse.ro

Printed in the United States
by Baker & Taylor Publisher Services